EVERYMAN DICTIONARY OF FIRST NAMES

Leslie Dunkling & William Gosling

FOURTH EDITION

Everyman, I will go with thee
and be thy guide

EVERYMAN
J. M. DENT • LONDON

First published 1983
First published in paperback, with revisions, 1984
Second edition 1987
Third edition 1991
Fourth edition 1993
Reprinted 1993

Made and printed in Great Britain by
The Guernsey Press Co. Ltd, Guernsey, C.I.

J. M. Dent
Orion Publishing Group
Orion House,
5 Upper St Martin's Lane, London WC2H 9EA

A catalogue record for this book is available from the British Library

ISBN 0 460 861859

Contents

Introduction

The English-speaking countries share not only their language, but their basic stock of first names. In this dictionary an attempt is made to explain where those names came from, when they have been most used, and if possible, why they were most used at that particular time. The comments about usage are based on authoritative and wide-ranging name-counts, the latest ones having been made in the early 1990s.

It is in the latter area, especially, that *Everyman's Dictionary of First Names* differs so much from previous dictionaries of a similar kind. Writers on names have always concerned themselves with their original meanings, and many authors have made passing remarks about whether a particular name was popular or not, but the names dealt with in previous works have mostly been gathered in a rather haphazard way, and remarks about their use have been based on subjective impression rather than statistical fact. That statement is not wholly true of E. G. Withycombe's *Oxford Dictionary of English Christian Names*, since the author made careful counts of names occurring in medieval records. Her remarks about that period ought therefore to be reliable. Unfortunately she was clearly less interested in, and therefore less thorough in researching, more recent name usage, especially that of non-aristocratic families. In some ways her marked interest in the naming habits of the nobility at the expense of ordinary people recalls the founding father of first-name studies, William Camden (1551–1623), the historian and antiquary.

Camden's list of names, together with his etymological and other comments on them, was published in 1623 as an appendix to his monumental guide-book to Britain, *Britannia*. In a single volume, which he modestly entitled *Remains*, he dealt with first names, surnames, proverbs, anagrams, heraldry, epitaphs, numismatics and other equally entertaining subjects, bringing to each a scholarly training coupled with a journalistic eye for the good anecdote. He was a kind of seventeenth-century H. L. Mencken, and his work (reprinted in 1974 as *Remains Concerning Britain*), still has many delights to offer the modern reader.

Camden described his list of first names as 'those most usual to the English nation'. A study of seventeenth-century parish registers shows that he did indeed mention most of the frequently used male names of the period, though he did not distinguish between them and the names that had survived in use only in certain noble families. His list of girls' names had many important omissions, such as Martha, Ellen and Esther. Only on rare occasions did he offer a hint as to the relative popularity at the time of the individual names. We can deduce from his remarks, for instance, that Joan was decidedly out of fashion, Jane being preferred.

Camden's *Remains*, then, is of very great interest, as of course is Miss Withy-combe's dictionary, but both have rather more to offer the student of history than modern parents, say, who are trying to find a name for their baby.

In the nineteenth century the popular novelist Charlotte Yonge brought out her discursive work *History of Christian Names*. This was first published in 1863 and was considerably revised in 1884. The scope of the work was ambitious, to say the least, dealing with the names of the ancient Hebrews, Greeks and Romans before launching into Teutonic and Norse mythology. It ended with chapters on the names used in countries such as Russia, Italy, Spain, France, Germany and Britain, but by this time Miss Yonge was clearly running out of steam. She devoted only two paragraphs, for instance, to American first-name usage, her main conclusion being that Americans name their children as the British name theirs, only 'our habits are exaggerated'. She devotes half a sentence to black American names, commenting on the occurrence of such classical names as Cato, Scipio and Leonidas, only to say that their use by black American families discouraged their use 'among the other classes'. She forgets to add that such names had usually been bestowed by plantation owners who wanted distinctive names for their slaves which were not part of the normal first-name stock. There was probably also a wish to display their own learning, a factor which continues to influence some parents in their choice of names. One thinks of the character in William Faulkner's story *The Town*, the man 'with a capacity for using people to serve his own appetites, all clouded over with a veneer of culture and religion; the very names of his two sons, Byron and Virgil, were not only instances but warnings.'

Once again the emphasis in *History of Christian Names* was on the original meanings of the names, with Miss Yonge demonstrating that there was a wealth of material awaiting the attention of comparative philologists. Modern scholars have not really taken up the challenge in a serious way, though another amateur philologist was independently covering much the same ground as Miss Yonge while she was working on the *History*.

Sophy Moody had the misfortune to publish her *What Is Your Name?* a few months after *History of Christian Names* had appeared. In many ways hers is the more entertaining book, but apart from being 'pipped at the post' she was over-shadowed by her 'formidable rival', as she herself described Charlotte Yonge. Her book faded into obscurity, though it was reprinted in 1976 by the Gale Research Company. It contains a great deal of historic name lore which is of permanent interest. Like Miss Yonge, Sophy Moody was not afraid to range over a wide field. She deals with the ancient Hebrews, Greeks and Romans, but also makes much of both Arabic and American Indian names. Her etymological comments are not always trustworthy, and she frequently forgets that she is not writing for her usual audience of young children, but her comments on naming habits in various cultures remain interesting.

In the present century a large number of books about first names have been published in Britain and America, the most useful of which are listed in the Bibliography. 'Useful' books are those in which the author has not merely listed names with a word or two of etymological explanation, usually 'borrowed' from Miss Withycombe. Professor Weekley's various books on names, especially his *Jack and Jill*, provide a reasonable source in English for a second opinion on etymologies. Professor George Stewart's *American Given Names,* though a great disappointment when compared with his distinguished works on American place names, is of occasional use. *What to Name Your Baby*, by Nurnberg and Rosenblum, has for many years been one of the more attractive works in this field. It perhaps over-emphasizes the influence of literature on naming habits, but it rightly reminds readers of the famous people with whom a name is associated. It also clearly shows that the authors did some original thinking about their subject and did not simply rephrase other people's words.

It would have been foolish for the authors of the present dictionary to ignore what previous writers have said about first names, and we have accordingly consulted a wide range of works. Three points must be emphasized, however:

(1) the decision about which names to deal with in our Dictionary was made on the basis of the statistical evidence we had before us, and was not influenced by whether another writer happened to have dealt with them. Whenever we were able to find evidence that a name came into general use in America or Britain at some period since the seventeenth century, and that usage was not confined to one or two families, we included it.

The entries in this dictionary therefore reflect with considerable accuracy the names which have been generally used at one time or another in the English-speaking world in the last few centuries. It would, of course, have been impossible to deal with *every* name that has been used as a first name. In Britain and America parents have the legal right to bestow any name they like on their child, and some might argue that they occasionally abuse that freedom. (Until recently it was not shared by French and German parents, who were likely to find when they tried to insist on bestowing a name which was not on an approved list that the state would not legally acknowledge their child's existence.)

In English-speaking countries the freedom of choice often leads to a surname being used as a first name. A glance at one list of names shows that Flyss, Foden and Follett have all occurred as first names, but our records refer to only one instance of each since the 1830s. Entries for such names would not therefore have been justified, though surnames such as Fletcher, Forster and Franklin are dealt with because they have been used with some frequency. Quite a lot of these surnames-turned-first names find a place in the dictionary, because many were consistently used in the nineteenth century.

(2) our comments about a name's original meaning reflect our own judgment about which of several explanations proposed by different scholars is the more likely. We have not confined ourselves to the views of British or American academics in this respect. When a name is known to be of Scandinavian origin, for example, it is essential to see what Roland Otterbjörk has to say about it in his excellent dictionary of Swedish first names, *Svenska Förnamn*. German names have been thoroughly studied from an etymological point of view, and Drosdowski's *Lexikon der Vornamen* is invaluable. A more modern approach to the subject, combining a discursive survey with a dictionary, is to be found in Wilfried Seibicke's *Vornamen*, where the author shows full awareness of the need for statistical research as well as the traditional etymological approach.

We have made use of these works and similar, reliable, first-name dictionaries in many other languages as the need arose. Details of the books concerned are given in the Bibliography. The etymologies are as accurate as we can get them, though we have little doubt that what might be called a name's usage profile is of more relevance in modern times.

The plain fact is that a name's 'meaning' today has very little to do with its original meaning, unless the latter is immediately obvious, as in names like Faith, Hope and Charity. A name's image depends on how it has been used within living memory, which social groups have used it and with what degree of intensity. Its image can partly depend on the public figure or fictional character the name immediately recalls. Ultimately, of course, every name has a personal meaning for each individual, depending on his or her experience of life.

The compilers of a dictionary such as this cannot be concerned with such personal meanings, and indeed must be careful not to be influenced by their own subjective reactions to a name. All they can do is report when a name is being intensively used or is being generally ignored, and perhaps offer an objective view as to why that situation exists.

(3) the only sure guide to a name's general image at a particular time lies in accurate details of its usage. A hundred families, asked why in recent years they had chosen Michael, say, for their son or Sarah for their daughter, would probably give fifty different reasons. The only common factor would be that they *did* find a reason to use it. In 1900 very few parents anywhere in the English-speaking world could find a reason to use Michael, and Sarah was decidedly unfashionable as recently as the 1930s. It is clear that the general image of both names has changed drastically in recent times.

This precise information about when a name has evoked a favourable impression rather than a generally negative response is not to be found in any previous dictionary of first names. The gathering of such information has been the special concern of the present authors since 1971 and has involved massive name-counts of different kinds. As a result we have been able to refer to mostly unpublished surveys which include the following:

a nationwide examination of British parish registers for the sample years 1600, 1650, 1700, 1725, 1750, 1775 and 1800;

counts based on the Registrar General's Indexes of Births for England and Wales since 1837, at 25-yearly intervals in the nineteenth century, on a yearly basis in more recent times, the sample comprising one birth in every seventy;

similar counts made at the Scottish Registrar General's office in Edinburgh and at the Irish Registrar General's office in Dublin;

an official list of every first name given to a child born in Scotland in 1958;

counts based on lists of graduate students in the years 1900, 1925, 1950 and 1975 at over a hundred American universities;

similar counts based on students at many Canadian and Australian universities;

official computer read-outs of American first-name usage since 1940, indicating whether the parents were white or black, the average yearly sample covering the names given to 25,000 children;

counts based on local and national newspaper announcements of births, from Britain, America, Canada and Australia.

We have also used the lists compiled by Professor Newbell Puckett, edited by Murray Heller and published as *Black Names In America*. Finally, our friend and colleague C. V. Appleton has generously made available to us his unpublished survey of every first name used by the Smiths in England and Wales since 1837. It can be shown that naming habits of the Smiths are completely typical of naming habits in general. Mr Appleton's list is therefore of great value. It shows precisely when a name first came into use, and distinguishes easily between those names used on very rare occasions and those used consistently.

The emphasis in the above-mentioned sources is on America and Britain. We have paid equal attention to both countries, considering it a common fault of previous works in the field that they have concentrated exclusively on either British *or* American names and naming habits. Just as there is a movement of words between the two cultures, so there is a movement of names. It has always been a two-way process, and once again it is accurate figures which make it possible to say whether British parents are taking a name from America or vice-versa.

Some indications have already been given of the criteria we had in mind when deciding whether to deal with a name in the present work. We have also mentioned some of the information we have tried to supply about each name. We are aware that a dictionary such as this is often consulted at that happiest of times – when parents are trying to find a name for their baby – and we have tried to supply parents with the kind of information they need. An ideal entry would indicate the following:

(a) an indication as to whether the name is used for boys, girls or both. This is not something that remains fixed, for traditional male names are likely to be used for girls at any time. The movement is nearly always in that direction: feminine names do not seem to become male names. We have indicated those names which give no real indication of their bearer's sex, since this is usually felt to be an inconvenience by the name-bearer;

(b) language of origin and original meaning, where known;

(c) how the name was introduced to the English-speaking world, e.g. by the Bible, by historical events, from literature;

(d) when the name was first used in English-speaking countries;

(e) examples of surnames which may have derived from the name if it was in use in the Middle Ages;

(f) to what extent the name has been used since its introduction and by which social groups.

General indications of the relative use of different first names are given in the lists of 'top fifties' (pages 301–04). A name which reaches number one position is given to roughly every twenty-fifth child of the same sex born in that particular year. By contrast, only one child of the same sex in every 250 born that year receives the name in fiftieth position.

When a name is used 'regularly but infrequently', as we often phrase it in this dictionary, we mean that an example occurs in our records every few years. It is impossible to say exactly how many people bear such a name at a given moment: the name-bearer may literally be 'one in a million'. Names which we also describe as 'quietly used' fall into this category.

The distribution of names in a particular year is roughly as follows:

one girl in five receives one of the top ten names.

one boy in three receives one of the top ten names,

one girl in two receives a name which is in that year's top fifty,

three boys in every five receive a name which is in that year's top fifty,

125 different names account for at least 80% of all the girls named,

100 different names account for the same proportion of boys.

Since this dictionary has some 4,500 entries, dealing with more than 10,000 names, we feel justified in claiming that the first names borne by at least 95% of the English-speaking population are in this book;

(g) instances of famous name-bearers who may have influenced the name's 'image';

(h) pet forms and diminutives;

(i) variant spelling forms. We have given full details of these, always indicating the most frequent spelling in the head-word. There is little doubt that a name that *can* occur in a variety of forms *will* occur in a variety of forms. The bearer of such a name will constantly see it misspelt, an experience which for many people is rather like having someone consistently tread on their toes;

(j) comments about a name's pronunciation where this is likely to cause problems;

(k) literary occurrences of a name, together with quotations about it;

(l) transferred uses of a first name, e.g. the use of 'Oscar' for the cinema industry's award.

With names that have only been in use a short time, many of these points do not arise. 'New' names are constantly appearing, a few of which become permanent members of our first-name stock. Old names, by contrast, hardly disappear completely, though they may become rarities. The world of first names is a constantly changing one, reflecting the changes in society. Each name in this dictionary has some kind of story to tell about the world in which we live, though we cannot claim to have told the full story in every case.

In that connection it is worth observing that the compilers of a dictionary such as this are required to have a peculiar set of skills. They must have specialized linguistic training, be widely read in American and British literature, be film buffs, have a good knowledge of modern popular songs (which often influence naming), and watch a great deal of television. Since we are only human, we are weaker in some areas than others. There will inevitably be omissions or minor distortions in some of our entries which we hope will be quickly corrected by our readers.

The dictionary is naturally concerned with names rather than naming, but the naming pattern in any particular year, the historical study of how our ancestors named their children in different centuries, how first-naming differs in the various English-speaking countries, the vocative use of names, the motivations of parents when they choose a name, our psychological reactions to our own names and those of others, the common belief – even in our civilized societies – in name magic, all these are topics which deserve an exploration in depth. Most of the subjects mentioned above were fully discussed in the companion to the present work, *First Names First* (1977). Details are also given in the Bibliography of other books which will interest those who have more than a passing interest in names and naming.

First names have probably never been as important as they are today, when everyone claims the right to be recognised as an individual. 'A surname,' said Noah Jacobs in his *Naming Day in Eden*, 'refers to man's natural history, his past legacy and his involvement in an impersonal process; his first name refers to his unique qualities as an individual, and points to the future.' Our first names are like our reflections in a mirror. 'Some names stimulate and encourage the owner, others deject and paralyse him.' That comment of Bulwer Lytton reminds parents of their great responsibility when a name is to be chosen.

But it is to those parents that we dedicate this book. The privilege and pleasant task of choosing a name has become more complex in modern times because of changing attitudes. Victorian parents would probably have been at one with Paul Dombey, in *Dombey and Son* by Charles Dickens. 'He will be christened Paul, of course. His father's name, Mrs Dombey, and his grandfather's.' The more common philosophy of the present day was expressed by John Steinbeck in *East of Eden*:

'I can't think what to name them,' Adam said.

'You have no family name you want – no inviting trap for a rich relative, no proud name to recreate?'

'No, I'd like them to start fresh, insofar as that is possible.'

Fortunately our sensible system of bestowing a first name and a middle name or two allows parents to look to the future while remembering the past. The choice of names today is wider than ever, but by some miracle there is always at least one which is 'just right'. It is probably in the pages that follow: enjoy your hunt for it.

This new edition of *Everyman's Dictionary of First Names* is dedicated to the memory of William F. Gosling, of Market Bosworth, who died in 1984. William was a most kindly man, and a delightful correspondent. His intellectual curiosity and enthusiasm remained as lively as ever, even when he was well into his eighties. He much enjoyed working on this book and would have been delighted at the response to it, especially the letters from those with special knowledge of the subject, or with detailed information about individual names. Amongst such letters, with helpful comments that have been incorporated into this edition, have been those from the following: Ivor Morrish, of Bognor Regis; Cleveland Kent Evans, of Omaha; Peter McClure, of Hull; Amplias Turner, of Kings Lynn; Gordon Wright, of Nottingham; Dudley Diaper, of Wivenhoe; Veronica Brown, of Leicester; Janita Atkin, of Warwick; Dean Burgess VI, of Portsmouth, Virginia; Charles Derry, of Maple Heights, Ohio; E.F.J. Eustace, of Oxford; Merville Hasler, of Oxted. The list of top 50 Australian names which have been added for the second edition were kindly provided by Jodi Cassel, of Brighton, Victoria, Cecily Dynes, of Cremorne, N.S.W. and Helen Vnuk, of Broadview, South Australia.

Many other correspondents have contributed examples of rarely used names, not dealt with in this dictionary. I hope to collect enough of these unusual names to justify one day a supplementary volume to this dictionary. Meanwhile, comment which will help to refine still further the present entries will be much welcomed.

Leslie Dunkling   May, 1993.

If the name you're looking for isn't in this dictionary. . .

(a) it may be a surname which has been converted to first name use. Consult such works as *A Dictionary of Surnames,* by Patrick Hanks and Flavia Hodges; *A Dictionary of British Surnames,* by P. H. Reaney; *New Dictionary of American Family Names,* by Eldson C. Smith; *The Penguin Dictionary of Surnames,* by Basil Cottle; *The Surnames of Scotland,* by George Black; *The Surnames of Ireland,* by Edward MacLysaght; *Welsh Surnames,* by T. J. Morgan and Prys Morgan. Many surnames derive from place-names, so *The Oxford Dictionary of English Place-Names* or the publications of the English Place-Name Society can be useful.

(b) it may be an obscure biblical name. Consult *Dictionary of Proper Names and Places in the Bible,* by O. Odelain and R. Ségineau; *A Concordance to the Old and New Testament,* by Alexander Cruden, or any good dictionary of the Bible.

(c) it may be a foreign name. If you have a clue as to its language of origin, consult the relevant dictionary as suggested by the Bibliography.

(d) it may be a classical Greek or Roman name, well known, little used as a first name in English-speaking countries. Consult a good, modern classical dictionary.

(e) it may be the name of a literary character. See *A Dictionary of Fictional Characters,* by William Freeman.

(f) it may be transferred from another naming system. Trade names, ship names, etc., as well as the better known plant names and jewel names have all been used as first names. Consult a trade name dictionary, *Lloyds' List,* etc.

(g) it may be a deliberate or accidental misspelling of another name. Consider the *sound* of the name, and how that sound could be represented in other spellings.

(h) it may be a word transferred to first-name use. Consult any good dictionary.

(i) it may be an invented name. Normally it is only the people who invented it who can explain how they formed it, but blends (e.g. Sametta from Samuel and Pauletta) and back-spellings (e.g. Senga, Adnil) are relatively common.

Bibliography

The following works have been consulted during the preparation of this dictionary:

Afrikaanse voorname (a dictionary of Afrikaans first names). Die Suid-Afrikaanse Akademie wir Wetenskap en Kuns, 1978.

Ames, Winthrop. *What Shall We Name the Baby?* Hutchinson, 1935.

Antal, Fekete. *Keresztneveink, Védószentjeink* (a dictionary of Hungarian first names). Ecclesia Könyvikiadó, 1974.

Barbé, Jean-Maurice and Nortel, Jean-Pierre. *Dictionnaire des prénoms*. Ouest-France, 1980.

Bardsley, C. W. *Curiosities of Puritan Nomenclature*. Reprint. Gale, 1970.

Benvenuti, Stefano, *Il Nominario*, Mondadori, 1980.

Bernage, Georges. *Prénoms normands et vikings* (a dictionary of Norman first names). Guide Heimdal, 1981.

Black, George F. *The Surnames of Scotland*. New York Public Library, 1971.

Bice, Christopher. *Names for the Cornish*.Lodenek Press, 1970.

Brogger, Waldemar. *Gyldendals navne leksikon* (a dictionary of Norwegian first names). Gyldendal, 1958.

Brookes, Reuben S. and Brookes, Blanche. *A Guide to Jewish Names*. Reuben S. and Blanche Brookes, 1967.

Browder, Sue. *The New Age Baby Name Book*. Warner Books, 1975.

Brown, Ivor. *A Charm of Names*. Bodley Head, 1972.

Burgio, Alfonso. *Dizionario dei nomi propri di persona* (a dictionary of Italian first names). Ceschina, 1970.

Camden, William. *Remains concerning Britain*. Reprint. E. P. Publishing, 1974.

Coghlan, Ronan. *Irish Christian Names*. Johnston and Bacon, 1979.

Collins Gem Dictionary of First Names. Collins, 1968.

Cottle, Basil. *The Penguin Dictionary of Surnames*. Penguin Books, 1967.

Dauzat, Albert. *Dictionnaire des noms de famille et prénoms de France* (mainly a dictionary of French surnames). Larousse, 1951.

Davies, Trefor R. *A Book of Welsh Names*. Shepherd Press, 1952.

Diehl, E. *Inscriptiones Latinae Christianae Veteres*, Berlin, 1931.

Dixon, Piers. *Cornish Names*. Piers Dixon, 1973.

Drosdowski, G. *Lexikon der Vornamen* (a dictionary of German first names). Duden Verlag, 1968.

Dunkling, Leslie. *First Names First*. Dent/Universe/General Publishing, 1977.

——. *The Guinness Book of Names*. Guinness Superlatives, 1974.

——. *Scottish Christian Names*. Johnston and Bacon, 1979.

——. *What's in a Name?* Ventura, 1979.

——. *Our Secret Names*. Sidgwick & Jackson 1981, Prentice Hall 1982.

——. *You Name It!* Faber and Faber, 1987

Foreign Versions of English Names. Grand River Books, 1980.

Freeman, W. *Dictionary of Fictional Characters*. Dent, 1967.

Gencosman, Kemal. *Türk isimleri Sözlügü* (a dictionary of Turkish first names). Hürriyet, 1975.

Grisé-Allard, Jeanne. *1500 Prénoms et leur signification* (a dictionary of French-Canadian first names). Éditions du Jour, 1973.

Heller, M. *Black Names in America*. G. K. Hall, 1975.

Heller, Pierre, *Un prénom pour la vie* (a dictionary of first names). France-impressions, 1972.

Hergemöller, B-U. *Gebräuchliche Vornamen* (a dictionary of German first names). Verlag Regensburg-Munster, 1971.

Janowowa, W. and others. *Slownik imion* (forms of common first names in twenty-three languages). Ossolineum, 1975.

Johnson, C., and Sleigh, L. *The Harrap Book of Boys' and Girls' Names*. Harrap, 1973.

Kaliner, W., and Richter, B. *Namen für unsere Kinder* (a dictionary of German first names). St. Benno-Verlag, 1974.

Kneen, J. J. *The Personal Names of the Isle of Man*. Oxford University Press, 1937.

Köhr, D. *Wie soll es heissen?* (a dictionary of German first names). Falken Bücherei, 1966.

Kupis, B. and others. *Ksiega imion* (a dictionary of Polish first names). Ksiazka i Wiedza, 1975.

Lebel, Paul. *Les noms de personnes* (a discursive work on the origins of French first names and surnames). Presse Universitaire de France, 1968.

Linnartz K. *Unsere Familiennamen* (a dictionary of German surnames). Dummlers Verlag, 1958.

Mackensen, A. *3876 Vornamen* (a dictionary of German first names). Südwest Verlag, 1969.

MacLysaght, E. *The Surnames of Ireland*, Irish University Press, 1969.

Magalhães, R. *Como voce se chama?* (a discursive work, mainly about Portuguese and Brazilian first names). Editora Documentario, 1974.

Mencken, H. L. *The American Language*. Alfred A. Knopf, 1936.

Mercier, Claude, *Les Prénoms,* Marabout, 1979.

Moody, Sophy. *What Is Your Name?* Bentley, 1863, reprinted Gale Research Co., 1976.

Nath, Dwarka. *Naming the Hindu Child*. Dwarka Nath, 1974.

Naumann, H. and others. *Das Kleine Vornamenbuch* (a dictionary of German first names). VEB Bibliographisches Institut, 1978.

——. *Vornamen heute* (a discursive work on first names). VEB Bibliographisches Institut, 1977.

Nurnberg, M., and Rosenblun, MN. *What to Name Your Baby*. Collier, 1962.

Odelain, O., and Séguineau, R. *Dictionary of Proper Names and Places in the Bible,* Robert Hale, 1982.

Otterbjörk, Roland. *Svenska förnamn* (a dictionary of Swedish first names). Esselte Studium, 1964.

Partridge, Eric. *Name This Child*. Hamish Hamilton, 1951.

Pawley White, G. *A Handbook of Cornish Surnames*. G. Pawley White, 1972.

Bibliography

Reaney, P. H. *A Dictionary of British Surnames*. Routledge & Kegan Paul, 1961.
——. *The Origin of English Surnames*. Routledge & Kegan Paul, 1969.
Room, Adrian. *Room's Classical Dictionary*, Routledge & Kegan Paul, 1983.
Rosenfeld, H. *Heimerans Vornamenbuch* (a dictionary of German first names). Bei Heimeran, 1968.
Rule, Lareina. *Name Your Baby*. Benjamin Co., 1963.
Schaar, V. *Woordenboek van voornamen* (a dictionary of Dutch first names), Het Spectrum, 1964.
Seibicke, Wilfried. *Vornamen* (a discursive work and dictionary of German first names). Verlag für Deutsche Sprache, 1977.
Smith, Elsdon C.
——. *Naming Your Baby*. Greenberg, 1943.
——. *New Dictionary of American Family Names*, Harper & Row, 1973.
——. *Personal Names: A Bibliography*, Reprint. Gale, 1965.
Stephens, Ruth. *Welsh Names for Children*. Y. Lolfa, 1970.
Stewart, G. R. *American Given Names*. Oxford University Press, 1979.
Stone, Eugene. *Naming Baby*. Ward Lock, 1954.
Swan, Helena. *Girls' Christian Names*. Swan Sonnenschein, 1900.
Thewes, Roma. *Name Your Daughter*. Corgi Books, 1969.
——. *Name Your Son*. Corgi Books, 1969.
Vilkuna, K. *Etunimet* (a dictionary of Finnish first names). Otava, 1977.
Vinel, A. *Le livre des prénoms* (a dictionary of French first names). Albin Michel, 1972.
Wasserzieher, Ernst. *Hans und Grete* (a dictionary of German first names). Dummlers, 1941.
Weekley, Ernest. *Jack and Jill*. John Murray, 1939.
Weidenham, J. *Baptismal Names*. Reprint. Gale, 1966.
Weitershaus, F. W. *Das Neue Vornamenbuch* (a dictionary of German first names). Mosaik Verlag, 1978.
Withycombe, E. G. *The Oxford Dictionary of English Christian Names*. Oxford University Press, 1977.
Woulfe, P. *Irish Names for Children*, Gill & Macmillan, 1974.
Yonge, C. M. *History of Christian Names*. Reprint. Gale, 1966.

Unpublished

Appleton, C. V. *Christian Names Used by the Smiths in England and Wales, 1837–1978*. 1979.
Gosling, W. *Christian Names of the Eighteenth Century*, 1975.

A

Aaron (m) According to Jerome and Gregory the Great the original meaning of this Hebrew name was 'high mountain'. Biblical, O.T., the brother of Moses. The story of his rod bursting into blossom (Num. 17:8) has always been well known. Little used until the 17th c., then came into regular use until the 1970s. At that point it suddenly became fashionable in all English-speaking countries. In the early 1980s it was still being well used in the U.S., but had faded sharply in Britain. Spelling variants include **Aaran, Aaren, Aarron, Aron, Arran, Arron, Aeron.**

Abagail (f) Fairly common 19th c. variant of **Abigail**.

Abbey (f) Pet form of **Abigail**, formerly used as an independent name. In *Our Mutual Friend*, by Charles Dickens, Miss Abbey Potterson is 'sole proprietor and manager of the Fellowship-Porters'. Some of her customers, Dickens says, 'harboured muddled notions that, because of her dignity and firmness, she was named after, or in some sort related to, the Abbey of Westminster'. **Abbe** and **Abbie** are also found.

Abbot (m) Surname used as a first name, mainly in the 19th c. Original bearer of the name probably worked for an abbot.

Abby (f) Pet form of **Abigail** used as an independent name.

Abdul (m) Arabic 'servant of'. Used increasingly in the early 1980s by black American Muslims. **Abdullah** 'servant of God' was also being used more often.

Abe (m) Pet form of **Abraham, Abel, Abram** etc., occasionally given as an independent name.

Abel (m) Hebrew *Hebhel*, 'breath', or from Assyrian *aplu*, 'son'. Greek *Abel*, Latin *Abel*. Biblical, O.T., Gen. 4. Second son of Adam and Eve, killed in jealousy by his brother Cain. As a Christian name Abel is found on a 6th c. inscription in Ravenna. Common in England in the Middle Ages, as surnames such as *Abel, Abele, Abelson*, etc., show. Revived by the Puritans in

the 16th c. and taken by them to the U.S. Well used in the 17th c. and 18th c., regularly but quietly used since.

Abia(h) (m) Hebrew 'my father is Jehovah'. Biblical, O.T., e.g. 1 Sam. 8:2, 'the name of Samuel's second son was Abiah'. **Abijah** is another form of the name, also used for one or two women in the O.T. Occasionally used.

Abiathar (m) Hebrew 'Father of abundance'. Biblical, O.T., *passim*. In the 19th c. also recorded as **Abiatha** and **Abiather**. Now very rare.

Abiel (m) Hebrew 'My father is God'. Biblical, O.T., 1 Sam. 9:1. Taken to the U.S. by the 17th c. Puritans but rare since 1800.

Abigail (f) Hebrew *Abigal* '(my) father rejoices'. Biblical, O.T. The wife of Nabal, later of King David. Used by the Puritans in the late 16th c. and common in the 17th c. Beaumont and Fletcher made Abigail a 'waiting gentlewoman' in their play *The Scornful Lady* (1616), probably alluding to 1 Samuel 25:24, where Abigail several times calls herself King David's 'handmaid'. In literary use Abigail then became a slang term for a lady's maid. Distinguished in the U.S. during the 18th c. by being name of Abigail Adams (1744–1818), wife of President John Adams (1735–1826) and mother of President John Quincy Adams (1767–1848). Became almost obsolete in all English-speaking countries in the 19th c., but has revived strongly in Britain since the mid-1970s. Pet forms of the name include **Abbie, Abby, Abbey, Abbe, Gail, Gaile, Gale, Gayle, Gaila, Gael,** all also independent names. Variant spellings **Abagail** and **Abigale** occasionally occur. Also found are **Abagil, Abbigale, Abbygail, Abigal, Abigall, Abigel, Abigil.**

Abimelech (m) Hebrew 'my father is king'. The name of three royal personages mentioned in the O.T. Occurs rarely in 19th c. records.

Abishag (f) Hebrew 'father of error'. Biblical, O.T., 1 Kings 1:15, where she looks after King David in his old age. Rarely used.

1

Able (m) Found in the 19th c. Probably a spelling variant of **Abel**.

Abner (m) Hebrew *Abhner* '(my) Father is light'. Biblical, O.T., 1 Sam. 14:50. Saul's cousin (uncle in some readings), later made commander of his army. Introduced to England at the end of the 16th c. and used with reasonable frequency until the end of the 19th c. Now very rarely used, being chiefly associated with Li'l Abner, the hero of Al Capp's cartoon strip. Modern Hebrew form is **Avner**. **Abna, Abnar, Abnor** are spelling variants.

Abraham (m) Hebrew *Abraham* popularly explained as 'father of the multitude'. Biblical, O.T., Gen. 17:5 – 'No longer shall your name be **Abram**, but your name shall be Abraham, for I have made you the father of a multitude of nations.' The first of the patriarchs and father of the Hebrew na tion. Used regularly from the 17th c. and carried to America, along with other O.T. names, by the Pilgrim Fathers. President Abraham Lincoln (1809–65) inspired use of the name, especially after his assassination, but since 1900 it has not appeared in the top fifty names in any English-speaking country. Pet forms **Abe** and **Bram** also occur.

Abram (m) Hebrew *Abram* 'high father'. Original name of the patriarch **Abraham**. Quietly but regularly used.

Absalom (m) Hebrew *Abhshalom* '(my) Father is peace'. Biblical, O.T., 2 Sam. 3:3. Absalom was of royal descent on both sides, was much praised for his personal beauty and was very popular, but behaved undutifully towards his father, King David. Captured and killed when he caught his head (or by popular interpretation, his hair) as he rode beneath a tree. Chaucer writes of a curly-haired **Absolon** (the French form of the name) in his 'Miller's Tale'. In Dryden's famous political satire, *Absalom and Achitophel*, Absalom is used for the illegitimate son of Charles II, the Duke of Monmouth. Surnames such as *Absalom, Absolon, Asplin(g)*,

etc., show that the name was used in the Middle Ages. Also used regularly in the 18th c. and 19th c., but now very rare.

Absolon (m) French form of **Absalom**.

Acquila (m) Also **Acquilla**. Variants of **Aquila**.

Ada (f) Originally a short form of Germanic names beginning with Adal-, such as **Adalheid** (**Adelaide**). Used as an independent name in English-speaking countries from the mid-19th c., and very popular in all of them 1875–1900. Rarely used in modern times.

Adah (f) Hebrew 'ornament'. Biblical, O.T., one of the wives of Lamech, Gen. 4:19. Also one of the wives of Esau, Gen. 36:2. Never commonly used, but made famous in the 19th c. by the American actress Adah Mencken (1835–68).

Adair (m) Early Scottish form of **Edgar** which became a surname and has been revived in modern times, especially in Scotland, as a first name.

Adalaid(e) (f) Mainly 19th c. variants of **Adelaide**.

Adaline (f) Common 19th c. spelling variant of **Adeline**.

Adam (m) From a Hebrew word meaning 'redness', applied to the colour of the earth, also to the colour of the skin. Biblical, O.T., Genesis, name of the first man. The popularity of the name in the Middle Ages is shown by the many surnames which derive from it, such as *Adams, Addams, Atkins,* etc. Continued to be consistently but quietly used through the 18th and 19th c., and only began to be fashionable in the late 1960s. In the early 1980s well used in all English-speaking countries. May have been launched in the 1960s by the British pop singer, and later actor, Adam Faith (Terence Nelhams). It is best known in literature as the name of Adam Bede in George Eliot's novel of that name. Shakespeare used the name in *As You Like It* for a faithful retainer. Thomas Hood punned in typical style in his little poem *A Reflection*:

When Eve upon the first of men
The apple press'd with specious cant,
Oh! what a thousand pities then
That Adam was not adamant.

Sometimes spelt **Addam**, and the pet form **Addy** has been used independently on rare occasions.

Adamina (f) 18th c. feminine form of **Adam**, now little used.

Addie (f) Pet form of **Adeline**, **Adelaide**, etc., used as an independent name since the 1880s.

Addy (m) Pet form of **Adam**, occasionally used as an independent name.

Adeana (f) Spelling variant of **Adina**.

Adela (f) Early short form of **Adelaide**, introduced to Britain at the Norman Conquest (1066) as the name of one of William I's daughters. Little used in modern times. **Adella** is an occasional variant.

Adelaide (f) French form of Old German *Adalheit* 'nobility' (modern German **Adelheid**). Found in a 6th c. Christian inscription as *Adalhildis*, but the name is non-Biblical. In common use in Europe for centuries before being introduced to Britain in the 18th c. Became mildly popular in the latter half of the 19th c., having been made well-known by 'Good Queen Adelaide', wife of King William IV. The Australian city of Adelaide was also named in her honour, Adelaide Bay having been discovered on her birthday. In English-speaking countries has been more widely used in its various pet forms, which include **Ada**, **Adela**, **Adele**, **Adelina**, **Adeline**, **Alice** and **Heidi**.

Adèle (f) French pet form of **Adelaide**. Enjoyed a mild spell of popularity in Britain in the 1970s. Music-lovers associate the name with a character in *Die Fledermaus*, by Johann Strauss. Also found are **Adell** and **Adelle**, especially since the 1960s.

Adelia (f) Form of **Adela**, influenced by the existence of **Delia** as a separate name, used with some regularity in the 19th c.

Adelina (f) Latinized adaptation of **Adèle** ultimately deriving from **Adelaide**. Mostly used while the soprano Adelina Patti (1843–1919) was at the height of her fame in the 19th c.

Adeline (f) Adaptation of **Adèle**, itself a short form of **Adelaide**. Made famous by the barber-shop quartet song 'Sweet Adeline' (1903), but little used as a first name.

Adeliza (f) Popular 19th c. combination of **Adela** and **Liza**.

Adell(e) (f) Modern variants of **Adèle**.

Aden (m) Could be a transferred use of the name of the former British colony, now part of South Yemen. More likely to be a spelling variant of **Aidan**, which is often found as **Aiden**. **Adin** is Hebrew 'ornament' and occurs in 19th c. records.

Adina (f) Hebrew 'desire' (?) Biblical O.T., 1 Chron. 11:42 (where it is mentioned as a male name). In modern use taken to be a female name. Occurs regularly, but infrequently, also in the form **Adine**. A character in Donizetti's opera *L'Elisir d'amore*.

Adlai (m) Hebrew 'my ornament'. Biblical, O.T., 1 Chron. 27:29. Little used, but made well-known in modern times by Adlai Stevenson (1900–65), the politician.

Admiral (m) Naval title used as a first name. Most military and social titles have been so used to varying degrees – **Captain** more often than Admiral.

Adolf (m) Modern German form of **Adolphus**. Rare name in English-speaking countries (and Germany, since Adolf Hitler). In the 19th c. occurs from time to time as **Adolph** (or **Adolphe**, the French form), but **Adolphus** was more usual.

Adolphus (m) Old German *Adalwolf*, Old English *Aethelwulf* 'noble wolf'. Latinized to Adolphus. Modern German **Adolf**. A royal name in Germany during the 17th c. and 18th c. Introduced to Britain mid-19th c., then regularly but infrequently used until the 1930s. Little used at any time in other English-speaking countries. French form **Adolphe** is occasionally found, and **Dolphus** occurs as an independent name.

Adria (f) Feminine form of **Adrian** used to some extent in the U.S. and Britain.

Adrian (m) Latin *Hadrianus* 'of Adria' (city in Northern Italy). Several early popes bore the name, including Nicholas Breakspear (d. 1159) the only English pope, who became Adrian IV. A rare name in all English-speaking countries until *circa* 1950. Then became extremely popular in Britain and Australia, but does not seem to have appealed to American or Canadian parents. Usual feminine forms of the name are **Adriana** and **Adrienne**, but **Adrianne** is also found. **Adria** a rare variant. Sometimes feminine in the U.S.

Adriana (f) Italian (Latin) feminine form of **Adrian**. Character of this name in Shakespeare's *Comedy of Errors*, but never much used.

Adrianne (f) Modern feminine form of **Adrian**. **Adriane** also occurs.

Adrienne (f) French feminine form of **Adrian**, increasingly used in Britain, especially, since the 1950s. **Adriene** and **Adrien** are occasionally used.

Aeneas (m) Greek *Aineias* 'praiseworthy' (from *ainein* 'to praise'). Name of the Trojan hero whose exploits were celebrated by Virgil and others. Used mainly in Scotland as a substitute for the Gaelic *Aonghas* (**Angus**). **Eneas** also occurs, and a feminine **Aenea** has been noted.

Afra (f) Variant of **Aphra**. **Affery** is another form of the name.

Agatha (f) Greek *Agathē* from *'agathos* 'good'. Latin *Agatha*, French *Agathe*. A 3rd c. virgin-martyr whose cult was widespread. Agathe occurs commonly amongst Christian inscriptions of the Roman Empire. Surnames which derive from it, such as *Agas(s)*, *Aggis(s)*, *Aggus(s)*, show that it was well-used in medieval times. Then declined until a partial revival occurred at the end of the 19th c. Best-known bearer of the name in modern times was Agatha Christie (1891–1975), the English writer of detective stories.

Aggie (f) Pet form of **Agatha** or **Agnes**. Occasionally found as an independent name.

Agnes (f) French *Agnès*, Latin *Agnēs*, Greek *(h)agne*, feminine of adjective *(h)agnos* 'pure, chaste'. St Agnes was a Roman maiden martyred in 304. Her cult was widespread from an early date. Common Christian name in early Roman inscriptions in such forms as *Agne*, *Anne*, *Acne*, *Agnes*. Even in Roman times the name tended to be pronounced, and often written, as **Annes**. (French pronunciation of the name approximates to *Anyes*. Pronunciation of the 'g' is a relatively modern restoration.) Surnames such as *Annis*, *Annys*, *Annott*, *Annalt* 'descendant of Agnes', testify to the popularity of the name in the Middle Ages. Remained very popular until the 17th c., when the names of non-scriptural saints began to be avoided. Revived in the 19th c., but only Scottish parents remained faithful to it in the 20th c. Some Scottish parents use it in reversed form, as **Senga**. Even in Scotland, however, use has declined since 1965. **Agness** is a fairly common variant spelling, and pet forms such as **Aggie**, **Nessie**, **Nesta** (Welsh) occur as independent names. Latin diminutive **Agneta**, mostly used in Scandinavia, occasionally found. **Annice** and **Annis** in regular but infrequent use until the 1930s (also as **Anice** and **Anis**, **Anise**), but these may occasionally represent Greek *Anysia*, a christian martyr (see **Annice**). Spanish form of Agnes, **Inez**, also regularly used both in Britain and the U.S. American actress Agnes Moorehead is one of the best-known modern bearers of the name.

Agneta (f) Latin derivative of **Agnes**, mostly used in Scandinavia, occasionally in the English-speaking world. Pet forms **Agna** and **Neta**. **Agnetta** also found.

Agusta (f) Fairly common 19th c. variant of **Augusta**. In a similar way, **Agustus** occurs for **Augustus**.

Ahmad (m) Also **Ahmed**. Arabic 'the

most praised'. One of the many names applied to the Prophet and a favourite Arabic name. Used increasingly in the U.S. by black Muslims.

Aibhlin (f) Irish, normally anglicized as **Eileen** or **Aileen**, but originally a form of **Helen** or **Evelyn**.

Aidan (m) Diminutive of Gaelic *Aed(h)* 'fire'. Famous 7th c. Irish monk. Little used anywhere until the beginning of the 20th c. Popularity has been steadily growing, in Ireland and elsewhere, since the 1960s. Often found as **Aden** and **Aiden**.

Aileen (f) Originally a variant of **Eileen** (Irish *Aibhlin*), now frequently pronounced, and sometimes spelt, as **Ayleen**. Especially common in Scotland, where it was well used in the 1950s.

Ailie (f) Pet form of **Ailis** (Gaelic for **Alice**) and **Ailsa**, occasionally used as an independent name.

Ailsa (f) From the geographical name Ailsa Craig, an island rock at the mouth of the Firth of Clyde in Scotland. Used as a first name by Scottish parents almost exclusively until recent times, but now spreading. The actress Ellen Terry is quoted as saying 'Ailsa Craig! What a magnificent name for an actress!'

Ailwyn (m) Rare variant of **Alvin**.

Aimée (f) French form of **Amy**, 'loved', quietly used in English-speaking countries.

Aina (f) Scandinavian name meaning 'always, until the end'. Especially well-known in Finland, but used occasionally in English-speaking countries. **Ana** may be a variant of this name, or of **Anna**.

Ainslie (m, f) Surname/place name (of uncertain origin) converted to first-name use. The Ainslie spelling is used in Scotland; elsewhere usually **Ainsley**.

Aisha (f) Arabic 'woman'. Most usual spelling in the early 1980s amongst black American Muslim families of a popular Arabic name, borne by the favourite wife of the Prophet Mohammad. Occurs also as **Ayesha**, the form made known by Rider Haggard in his novel *She* (1887). The following variants were used to name American girls (all black) in 1981: **Aesha, Aiesha, Aisia, Ayeisha, Ieasha, Ieashia, Iesha, Ieesha, Ieeshia, Yiesha.**

Aisling (f) Irish 'dream, vision'. Well used in Ireland, especially, since the 1960s. Also found as **Aislinn** and in the phonetic form **Ashling**.

Aithne (f) See **Ethne**.

Alain (m) French form of **Alan**, occasionally used in English-speaking countries.

Alaine (f) Feminine form of **Alain**, the French **Alan**. Not used in France, however. **Alayne** occurs as a spelling variant. **Alaina** and **Alayna** also being used by American parents in the early 1980s.

Alaister (m) See **Alasdair**.

Alan (m) The name of a Welsh and Breton saint, of uncertain meaning. Derivations from 'rock' and 'noble' have been suggested by Gaelic scholars. Camden (1605) writes: 'This (name) came into England with Alan, Earl of Brittany, to whom the Conqueror gave the greatest part of Richmondshire, and hath been most common since that time in the Northern parts.' Popularity during the Middle Ages reflected by the large number of surnames which derive from it: *Allen, Allan, Allain*, etc. Revived in the 19th c., appearing in many forms. Alan is the standard British form, **Allen** is more usual in the U.S. **Allan** is also frequent. Normal Welsh form of the name is **Alun**, in regular use since the 1920s. Also found are **Allin, Allon, Allyn** and **Alyn**. Alyn, especially, has been regularly used in Britain since the 1950s. General upsurge in all forms of the name in the 1950s no doubt influenced by the popularity of the actor Alan Ladd. But it has subsequently suffered a decline in most English-speaking countries, though a 1975 count in Ireland showed that Irish parents were using it well. In modern times many feminine forms have been developed from the name. These include **Alana, Alanna, Alaine, Aleine, Alayne, Alleyne, Alayna, Alena, Allena, Alene, Allene, Aleen, Aline, Alina, Allina**, etc., are possibly pet forms of **Adeline** by origin, though associated with **Alan** by modern parents.

Alana (f) Modern feminine form of **Alan**, spreading slowly. In *Irish Christian Names* Ronan Coghlan derives it from the vocative *a leanbh*, 'O child!' In the 1970s black American parents were beginning to favour the name. Appears also as **Alanna**, **Allana**, **Allena**.

Alaric (m) Old German *Adalrich* 'noble ruler'. Alaric 1, King of the West Goths, sacked Rome in 410. Occasionally used in modern times.

Alasdair (m) Gaelic form of **Alexander**. More often found in a phonetic spelling, especially **Alistair** or **Alastair**. Other variants include **Alaister**, **Alaster**, **Alistar**, **Alister**, **Allistair**, **Allister**, **Allaster**, **Alastor**, **Aleister**, **Alester**, **Alisdair**, **Alistaire**, **Alyster**. Gaelic-speaking Scots will no doubt continue to use Alasdair, while Alistair has a claim to be regarded as the normal English spelling. **Allie** and **Ally** are usual pet forms, and Allie has been used as a name in its own right. In all its forms Alasdair remains basically a Scottish name, though its use has spread to all other English-speaking countries.

Alathea (f) Mainly 19th c. variant of **Alethea**.

Alayna (f) Modern feminine form of **Alan**, found also as **Alayne**.

Alayne (f) Alternative form of **Alaine**.

Alban (m) Latin *Albanus* 'of *Alba*', a town which was on a 'white' hill. Alba was the capital city of the earliest Roman kings and the most ancient city in Latium. As a Christian name Albanus occurs in an early Roman inscription. It was the name of the Romano-Briton (St Alban) who became the first Christian to be martyred on British soil. Alba was also an ancient name for the Highlands of Scotland, deriving from Celtic *alp*, 'rock, mountain'. Alba was extended to *Alban*, *Albany*, and as *Albion* applied to the whole of Britain. Popularly associated with Latin *albus*, 'white'. The Duke of Albany was the Scottish title of the future James II of England. **Albany**

has been used as a christian name, and may be an extension of St Alban's name (cf. *Barbary* for *Barbara*) or an allusion to Scotland. Alban itself was used in the Middle Ages, giving rise to surnames such as *Alban*, *Albon*, *Allbone*, etc. Then became rare, but regularly if quietly used since the beginning of the 19th c. Seems to be confined to Britain.

Albany (m) Variant of **Alban**, or an allusion to Scotland, deriving ultimately from Gaelic *alp*, 'rock, mountain'.

Albert (m) Old German *Adalbert*, Old English *Aethelbeorht* 'noble bright'. Given an enormous boost in 1840 in all English-speaking countries when Queen Victoria married Prince Albert (who was German). Declining rapidly, however, since the 1920s. Of the pet forms, **Bert** and **Bertie** rather than **Al** have been most used as independent names. Usual feminine forms of the name are **Alberta** and **Albertina**. The British actor Albert Finney is one of the best-known modern bearers of the name.

Alberta (f) Usual feminine form of **Albert**, little used in modern times. Canadian usage of the name may relate to the province of Alberta, named in honour of Princess Louise Caroline Alberta, wife of the former Governor General, the Marquis of Lorne.

Albertina (f) Latinized feminine form of **Albert**. Modern American usage leans slightly in favour of the French form **Albertine**.

Albin (m) Latin *Albinus*, from *albus* 'white'. Gaelic **Alpin** probably related to it. Fairly common name amongst Christians in Roman times. Its use in medieval times is reflected by surnames such as *Albin*, *Albinson*, *Aubin*, etc., but it then disappeared until its partial revival in the mid-19th c. **Alban** is a variant, and there is a feminine form **Albina**.

Albina (f) Latin feminine of *Albinus* 'white'. St Albina lived in the 3rd c. Used fairly regularly from the 17th c. until the end of the 19th c., but now rare. **Albinia** was also used.

Albion (m) Celtic *alp* 'rock, mountain'.

Regularly but quietly used as a name in England until the 1930s. See also **Alban**.

Albreda (f) Old German 'elf counsel'. Developed into **Aubrey** when used for men. Very rarely used since the 15th c., but British examples have been noted in the 19th c. and early 20th c.

Alby (m) An English form of Irish **Ailbhe**, rarely used. See **Elvis**.

Alda (f) Old German *ald*, modern German *alt* 'old'. Used by families of Italian descent as the feminine form of **Aldo**. **Alida** is accepted by the Roman Catholic Church as an alternative form of St Alda's name, and is used in English-speaking countries.

Alden (m) Surname of the same meaning as **Alwin**, 'old friend'. In occasional use as a first name.

Aldo (m) Old German *ald*, modern German *alt* 'old'. Popular Italian name, also used in the U.S. Feminine form is **Alda**. Also a pet form of names such as *Baldo*, *Ubaldo* and *Rinaldo*.

Aldous (m) Old German *ald*, modern German *alt*, 'old'. In medieval times gave rise to surnames such as *Aldus*, *Aldis*, *Aldhouse*. Partly revived in the 19th c. and made well-known in the 20th c. by Aldous Huxley (1894–1963). Rarely used. **Aldo** is the Italian form of the name.

Aldred (m) Old English *Ealdraed* 'old counsel'. Its early use led to surnames such as *Aldred*, *Eldred*. Revived to some extent in the 19th c. and continued into the 20th c. Feminine form **Aldreda** is occasionally found.

Aldwyn (m) Old English 'old friend'. **Aldwin** is also found.

Alec (m) Pet form of **Alexander** used independently since the mid-19th c. **Aleck**, **Alic**, **Alick** are variants. **Alex** is preferred form in the U.S. Made famous by the British actor Sir Alec Guinness.

Aled (m) Name of a Welsh river. Made well-known by the boy singer Aled Jones.

Aleen (f) Modern feminine form of **Alan**, or variant of **Aline** (**Adeline**).

Aleine (f) Modern feminine form of **Alan**. **Alaine**, **Alayne**, **Alleyne**, etc., also found.

Alejandro (m) Spanish form of **Alexander**, used mainly in the U.S.

Alena (f) German pet form of **Magdalena**. **Alene** is likewise from **Magdalene**.

Alester (m) Phonetic rendering of **Alasdair**, more commonly found as **Alistair**. **Aleister** has also been used.

Alethea (f) Greek *aletheia* 'truth' from *alethes* 'true'. Used regularly if infrequently in Britain since the 17th c. In the U.S. favoured by black American parents. The forms **Aleta**, **Aletha** are common; **Alethia** and **Alathea** also occur. **Althea** is a separate name.

Alette (f) Latin *ala* 'wing' leads to the French diminutive form Alette. **Aletta** occurs, but neither form is frequently used.

Alex (m) Pet form of **Alexander** used independently. (See **Alec**.)

Alexa (f) Originally a feminine form of **Alexis**, now regarded as a feminine form of **Alexander**. Well used since the 1940s.

Alexander (m) Greek 'defender of men'. Biblical, N.T., Mark 16:21, Acts 4:6, 19:33. Made famous throughout the world *circa* 340 BC by Alexander the Great. Later the name of a number of saints and martyrs including eight popes. Became a royal name in Scotland in the 12th c., since when it has remained an outstanding favourite with Scottish parents. Much used also in its various Gaelic forms, see e.g. **Alasdair**, **Alastair**, **Alistair**. Consistently used for centuries in all English-speaking countries, though especially popular in the U.S. at the end of the 19th c. Diminutive forms such as **Alec**, **Aleck**, **Alex**, **Alick**, **Allie**, **Sandy** and **Sander** have been used frequently as independent names. For the many feminine forms of the name see **Alexandra**. Well-known bearers of the name include the inventor Alexander Graham Bell (1847–1922) the discoverer of penicillin, Sir Alexander Fleming (1881–1955), and General Alexander Haig, recently Secretary of State under President Reagan.

Alexandra (f) Usual feminine form in

modern times of **Alexander**. Use of all forms of **Alexander** in English-speaking countries can be traced back to Scotland, where Alexander I became king in the 12th c. Feminine variants begin with **Alexanderina** and **Alexanderine** and continue with **Alexandrina**, **Alexandrine**, **Alexandrena** (also an **Alexandraeana** in 1905), **Alexandrene**, **Alexanderia**, **Alexandrea**, **Alexandria**, **Alexena**, **Alexina**, **Alexine**, **Alexene**, **Alexis** (not a true member of this group), **Alexia**, **Alexea**. Most recent innovations have been **Alix**, **Alexie** and **Alexi**, and **Alexa** was finding favour in the 1970s. **Sandra** derives from the Italian form of Alexandra, namely *Alessandra*, and this has been by far the most successful of all Alexander's feminine forms. Sandra is also used as a pet name for those whose full name is Alexandra. With the notable exception of Sandra, and to a lesser extent, Alexis, all the above forms remain primarily Scottish in terms of usage. In England, since the marriage of Edward, Prince of Wales, to Princess Alexandra of Denmark at the end of the 19th c., Alexandra has been looked upon as an upper-class name.

Alexandria (f) Alternative form of **Alexandra**, though perhaps used by some parents as a link with the city of Alexandria in Egypt (named after Alexander the Great). Used mainly in Britain, especially in Scotland.

Alexandrina (f) Mainly 19th c. feminine form of **Alexander**. Queen Victoria (1819–1901) was christened Alexandrina Victoria. **Alexandrena** and **Alexandrine** are found, especially in Scotland.

Alexena (f) See **Alexina**.

Alexi(e) (f) 20th c. feminine forms of **Alexander**.

Alexia (f) Occasional feminine form of **Alexander**. **Alexea** also occurs.

Alexina (f) Scottish feminine form of **Alexander** via **Alexandrina**. In use since at least the 1840s. Less common is **Alexena**, but **Alexine** is gaining ground.

Alexine (f) See **Alexina**.

Alexis (m, f) Greek *Alexis* 'helper,

defender'. Originally a male name, now nearly always given to girls.

Aley (f) Variant of **Alley** or **Allie**. Occurs from time to time in early records.

Alf (m) Pet form of **Alfred** used independently from 1880. Now rare. In modern times in Britain, **Alfie** seems to be the preferred form, probably because of a film of that name which appeared in the 1960s.

Alfred (m) Old English *Aelfraed* 'elf counsel'. Latinized as *Aluredus*, leading to French *Alvere*, then *Auveré*, which in turn gave Middle English *Avery*. In spite of the fame of Alfred the Great (849–901) Alfred virtually disappeared after the 14th c., to re-emerge in the late 18th c. Throughout the 19th c. popular in all English-speaking countries, but has declined since the 1920s. Pet forms **Alf** and **Fred** formerly common as independent names. **Alfreda** is the feminine form. One of the best-known bearers of the name in modern times was Alfred Hitchcock (1899–1980).

Alfreda (f) Form of **Elfrida** adapted to make it a feminine form of **Alfred**. Widely used 1880–1930, now mainly favoured by black American families.

Alfredo (m) Spanish/Italian form of **Alfred**, used to some extent in the U.S.

Algar (m) Old English *Aelfgar* 'elf-spear'. In Old Norse there was also *Álfgeirr*, with the same meaning. *Algar* and *Alger* are the names of under-tenants in the Domesday Book. Clearly in use until the 14th c., since it is one of the possible origins of surnames such as *Algar*, *Alger*, *Elgar*, etc. Then disappeared as a Christian name until the mid-19th c., when it returned to regular, if infrequent, use in England and Wales (usually as Algar, less often as Alger). Modern usage may be a transference from the surname. **Alga** and **Alger** also occur.

Algernon (m) Norman French *als gernons* 'with whiskers or moustaches'. Nickname of a common ancestor of the Howards and Percys, aristocratic English families which later adopted Algernon as a first name. In the latter half of the 19th c. use became more general in Britain, but hardly touched this century. History teachers sometimes make use of the name to point out that most Normans (e.g. as shown on the Bayeux Tapestry) were clean-shaven.

Algie (m) Pet form of **Algernon**, occasionally used independently. This spelling usually preferred to **Algy**.

Ali (m) Arabic 'the highest'. Use of the name considerably increased by the early 1980s. Occasional feminine use a pet form of **Alice**.

Alic (m) Common variant of **Alec**. **Alick** also occurs.

Alice (f) Old French *Alis*, *Aalis*, *Adalis*, from Old German *Adalheidis*, *Adalheitis* (= **Adelaide**), 'of noble kind'. Earliest example found is on a 7th c. Christian inscription in France. Used in Britain by the 12th c. as *Alis*, *Alys*, *Adeliz*, *Alicia*, etc. Commonly used in the Middle Ages and consistently used until the 18th c., when it began to wane. No justification for the statement by Withycombe that the name 'fell into general disuse' towards the end of the 17th c. This happened only in the first part of the 19th c., but a revival began with the publication of Lord Lytton's novel *Alice* (1838). Became one of the top names in the English-speaking world again soon after the appearance of Lewis Carroll's *Alice in Wonderland* (1865). By the 1930s had again fallen out of fashion but was now replaced by its diminutive **Alison**. Latinized form **Alicia** (with variant spellings such as **Alycia**, **Alysia**, **Alissa**, **Alyssa**, **Alisha**, etc) steadily but quietly used. See also **Alys**. Pet forms **Alley** and **Allie** were formerly used (infrequently) as independent names.

Alicia (f) Latinized form of **Alice**. More used in the 1970s than Alice itself.

Alick (m) Very common variant of **Alec** or **Aleck**.

Alida (f) See **Alda**.

Alina (f) Pet form of **Adelina**. Returning to favour in modern times, having formerly been popular in the Middle Ages.

Aline (f) Pet form of **Adeline**, steadily but quietly used in modern times, more frequently used in the Middle Ages. **Alina** is the Latinized form.

Alisa (f) Russian form of **Alice** in occasional modern use.

Alisdair (m) See **Alasdair**.

Alisha (f) Phonetic rendering of **Alicia**, the Latinized form of **Alice**. This spelling especially favoured by black American parents.

Alison (f) Originally a French diminutive of **Alice**. Since the 1930s extremely popular in all English-speaking countries, having largely replaced Alice itself. Especially well used in Scotland. **Allison** is a common variant, and the name is also found as **Allyson**, **Alyson**, **Alisoun**, **Alysoun**, **Alisanne**, **Alysanne**. Usual pet form is **Allie**.

Alissa (f) Popular modern variant of **Alicia** (see).

Alistair (m) Phonetic form of **Alasdair**, the Gaelic version of **Alexander**. Alistair is the most frequently-found spelling in modern times. **Alistar**, **Alister** and **Alisdair** are amongst other variants.

Alithea (f) See **Alethea**.

Alix (f) Early form of **Alice**, though used by some parents as a feminine of **Alexander**.

Allan (m) Variant spelling of **Alan**. Has the modern feminine form **Allana**.

Allaster (m) Variant of **Alistair**, itself a form of **Alasdair**.

Allegra (f) Italian 'lively, joyful, merry'. The musical term used as a first name. In occasional use in English-speaking countries. The novelist Elizabeth Taylor commented in *A View of the Harbour* (1968) as follows: ' "What's her name?" "Allegra. Like Lord Byron's daughter." "How funny. I didn't even know he got married," Prudence said. "I should never dare to give a name like that to a child. It is too much of a challenge," Robert said. "She would be almost sure to grow up fat and flat-footed and terribly Andante." ' That this does not necessarily happen is proved by Allegra Kent, the American ballet dancer.

Allen (m) Variant of **Alan**, used more in the U.S. than Britain. Modern feminine forms are **Allena**, **Allene**, **Alleyne**, **Alena**, **Alene**.

Allene (f) Feminine form of **Allen** (see **Alan** or a variant of **Aline** (**Adeline**).

Alles (f) Looks like the German word for 'all, everything', but far more likely to be an accidental variant of **Alice**. Examples noted in the 19th c., with a more recent one in 1940.

Allice (f) This variant of **Alice** occurred regularly in the 19th c., making the girl concerned seem rather cold-hearted.

Allie (f) Pet form of names beginning Al-, especially **Alice**, **Alison**, used mainly in Scotland, occasionally as a name in its own right. **Alley** and **Aley** also occur.

Allin (m) Occasional modern spelling variant of **Alan**, **Allen**.

Allison (f) Common spelling variant of **Alison**. In the U.S. occasionally used for boys, no doubt representing a transferred use of the surname.

Allistair (m) Variant of **Alistair**. **Allister** also occurs.

Allon (m) Hebrew 'an oak'. Biblical, O.T. mentioned 1 Chron.4.37.

Ally (m) Pet form of **Alexander**, **Alasdair**, etc., occasionally used as an independent name, mainly in Scotland.

Allyn (m) Modern spelling variant of **Alan**, found more frequently as **Alyn**.

Allyson (f) Spelling variant of **Alison**.

Alma (f) Latin *alma* 'nurturing, kind'. Alma Mater, 'fostering mother', was a title of several Roman goddesses. Also occurs in the 16th c. poem *Faerie Queene*, by Spenser. The poet seems to have interpreted the name as Italian *alma* 'soul'. Very rare name in Britain until 1854, when the Battle of Alma, a river in the Crimea, was fought. Then slowly became established, and from 1870–1920 was fairly well used in all English-speaking countries. In modern times Alma Mater refers to one's college or university.

Almena (f) Used with some regularity, though never in great numbers, 1870–1910. Occurred also as **Almina**,

Elmena, **Elmina**, **Almeina**. As Almena it also names towns in at least three U.S. States. George R. Stewart thinks the place name is probably a coinage from Indian words, but more likely it arose from the feminine first name. This in turn no doubt a pet form of **Wilhelmina**.

Almira (f) Arabic 'princess'. Used in the U.S. late 19th c. Made known by Almira Sessions (1888–1974), the character actress.

Almond (f) Plant name used as a first name, mainly in the 1890s and early 1900s.

Aloisa (f) Also **Aloisia**. Feminine forms of **Aloysius**, rarely used.

Alonso (m) Italian (and Spanish) short form of **Alfonso**. See **Alphonso**.

Alonzo (m) Spanish form of **Alphonso**. Little used since the 1930s in Britain. Favoured by black American families in the U.S.

Aloysius (m) Latinized form of **Louis** or **Luigi**, St Aloysius Gonzaga having been originally named Luigi. German scholars, however, invariably refer the name to Old High German *Alwisi*, 'the very wise'. Use by Roman Catholics is usually in honour of St Aloysius (16th c.), patron saint of students. Other forms include German **Alois**, Dutch **Aloys**, Spanish **Aloisio**. Usual feminine forms are **Aloysia**, **Aloisa**, **Aloisia**.

Alpha (f) Greek *alpha*, first letter of the alphabet. Used symbolically to mean 'the beginning' especially in the phrase 'alpha and omega' applied to God as 'the beginning and the end'. Other Greek letters are used as first names, perhaps to indicate the order in which children are born into the family. See also **Beta**, **Gamma**, **Delta**, **Zeta**, **Theta**, **Omega**.

Alpheus (m) Semitic 'successor'. Biblical, N.T., *passim*. Regularly used in the second half of the 19th c., but now rare. Variant forms included **Alpheaus** and **Alphoeus**.

Alphonso (m) Usual English form of Spanish **Alfonso** (**Alonso**, **Alonzo**). Probably from Old German *Hildefuns* 'battle ready', the name being taken to

Spain by Gothic tribesmen before the 7th c. Subsequently became a royal name and was much used. Regularly if infrequently used in Britain; favoured in the U.S. by black American families. French and Italian forms of the name are found (**Alphonse** and feminine **Alphonsine**) and **Alfonsus, Alphonzus** and **Alonza** also occur.

Alpin(e) (m) Gaelic *Ailpein*, possibly related to Latin *Albinus* 'white'. Its former use in Scotland led to surnames such as *Macalpine*. Rare in modern times.

Althea (f) Greek *Althaia* 'marsh mallow' (i.e. the bushy shrub which is noted for its healing powers. The Greek word derives from the verb 'to heal'). Althea, or *Althaea*, is mentioned in the *Iliad* as the mother of Meleager. The famous poem by Lovelace, *To Althea From Prison*, includes the lines 'Stone walls do not a prison make/Nor iron bars a cage'. Regularly, but infrequently, used. Alethea may sometimes be intended.

Alun (m) Name of a river in Clwyd, Wales. A first name since the 1920s.

Alured (m) Short form of the Latinized **Alfred**, i.e. *Aluredus* (= *Alvredus*). Occurs in early documents and occasionally revived in modern times.

Alva (m,f) Hebrew 'height'. Minor Biblical name associated with the chiefs of Edom. Correctly a male name (e.g. Thomas Alva Edison, 1847–1931, the inventor, and Professor Alva Lee Davis of the Illinois Institute of Technology) but frequently taken to be the feminine of **Alvin**. **Alvah**, in its Biblical spelling, occurs at Gen. 36:40 amongst a long list of names, most of them unusual in English-speaking countries. Nevertheless, **Elah**, **Kenaz** and **Iram**, mentioned in the same sentence as Alvah, have all been used in modern times as Christian names.

Alvan (m) Hebrew 'height'. Biblical, O.T.

Alvar (m) Old English *aelf-here* 'elf army'. Occurs in the Domesday Book and partially revived in Britain in the 1940s, probably due to the exposure given to the name by the BBC newsreader Alvar Liddell.

Alvena (f) Feminine of **Alven**, variant of **Alvin**.

Alverdine (f) Used from time to time in the 19th c., and has been noted in the 20th c. as **Alvedine**. Appears to be feminine form of **Alfred** via the Latin *Aluredus*.

Alvie (m, f) Pet form of **Alvin** or **Alvina**, occasionally used as an independent name.

Alvin (m) Old English *Aelfwine* 'elf-friend' or *Aethelwine* 'noble-friend', both of which early became *Alwine*. 'Old friend' is another possible derivation. Modern usage is perhaps transferred from the surname. In the U.S. black American parents clearly favour this name. Has a great many variants, including **Ailwyn, Alvan, Alven, Alwyn, Alvyn, Aylwin, Elvin, Elwyn, Elwin**. Feminine forms include **Alvina, Alvine, Alvena, Alwyna, Elvina, Elwina, Alwyne, Alwynne**. Seems likely that American usage of the name *circa* 1918 was influenced by the fame of Sergeant Alvin C. York, whose exploits during the World War One were much publicized.

Alvina (f) Feminine form of **Alvin**. Regularly but quietly used in all English-speaking countries. Usual pet form is **Alvie**. **Alvine** is also found.

Alvis (m) Rarely used modern first name, which has been linked with **Elvis**. First used in Britain in 1939, however, when Elvis Presley was only four years old. (Elvis itself was used the same year in Britain.) Possibly the name was transferred from the Alvis car, on the roads since 1920. The trade name was taken over from the Alvis aluminium piston, and as Adrian Room points out in his *Dictionary of Trade-Name Origins*, it may have blended Al- from 'aluminium' and the Latin word *vis* 'force, power'. See also **Elvis**.

Alvyn (m) Occasional variant of **Alvin**.

Alwin (m) Frequent variant of **Alwyn/Alvin**.

11

Alwyn (m) Common variant of **Alvin**, mostly used in Britain, regularly since the 1880s.

Alwyne (f) Feminine form of **Alwyn**. **Alwyna** and **Alwynne** also occur, but all rare since the late 1930s.

Alycia (f) Variant form of **Alicia**, the Latinized version of **Alice**. Used mainly in the U.S.

Alyn (m) Modern spelling variant of **Alan**, now regularly established. Perhaps influenced by Welsh **Alun**. **Allyn** also occurs.

Alys (f) Medieval form of **Alice**, occasionally found in modern times, perhaps as a fancy spelling, especially in Wales.

Alysia (f) Spelling variant of **Alicia** (see). Used mainly in the U.S.

Alyson (f) Spelling variant of **Alison**.

Alyssa (f) Form of **Alissa**. See **Alicia**. Used mainly in the U.S.

Amabel (f) Latin *amabilis* 'lovable'. Used in the Middle Ages and partially revived in the 19th c. Short form **Mabel** also revived and became far more popular.

Amalia (f) Latin feminine of the clan name *Aemilius* 'industrious'. Italian variant of **Amelia**, rarely used in English-speaking countries.

Amanda (f) Feminine form of Latin *Amandus* 'fit to be loved', the name of several saints. Modern French form of the masculine name is **Amand**. Reaney records an Amanda *filia Johannis* ('daughter of John') in 1221 in Warwickshire, England. Picked up by playwrights such as Colley Cibber (1671–1757) in his *Love's Last Shift* and Sir John Vanbrugh (1664–1726) in his *The Relapse*. Also characters in such famous 18th c. novels as *Peregrine Pickle* and *Tristram Shandy*. Very steadily used in all of the English-speaking countries until the 1940s, when it began to come into fashion, especially in Britain. American usage of the name, predominantly by white American families, still increasing in the early 1980s. Pet forms of the name, **Mandy** (less often **Mandie**, **Mandi**), have been used increasingly as inde-

pendent names since the 1940s. Combinations such as **Amanda-Jane** have also appeared recently.

Amaris (f) Hebrew feminine of **Amariah** 'Jehovah speaks'. In occasional modern use.

Amata (f) Latin (and Italian) form of **Amy**, 'loved'. Occurs regularly in early parish registers, with the variant **Amia**.

Amber (f) French *ambre* from Arabic *anbar* 'ambergris'. Occasionally used with other jewel names when the latter became fashionable in the 19th c., but its use in the 20th c., especially from the 1960s onwards, stems from the novel *Forever Amber* by Kathleen Winsor (later a film). In the book the following passage occurs: 'I think I'll name her Amber – for the colour of her father's eyes.' **Amberetta** is also found.

Ambrose (m) Greek *ambrosios* 'immortal'. Latin *Ambrosius*, French *Ambrose*. Regularly, but never frequently, used in English-speaking countries.

Ambrosine (f) Probably feminine form of **Ambrose**, but also a mineral related to amber and the name may therefore belong to the 'precious stone' group. Used since the mid-19th c. and also found as **Ambrozine, Ambrosina**.

Amelia (f) Probably Latin feminine of *Aemilius* 'industrious'. Could also be formed from Germanic names such as *Amalberga* where *Amal* = 'labour'. Introduced to Britain by Princess Amelia in the 18th c. Used in all English-speaking countries throughout the 19th c. **Emily** has largely replaced it in recent times, though admirers of Henry Fielding (1707–54) may use it with reference to the heroine of his novel *Amelia* (1751).

Amey (f) Mainly 19th c. variant spelling of **Amy**, 'loved'.

Amia (f) Obsolete Latin form of **Amy** 'loved'.

Amias (m, f) See **Amyas**.

Amica (f) Latin feminine form of **Amicus** 'friend beloved', a name used by Roman slaves. French form of the feminine name, **Amice**, brought to Britain at the

Norman Conquest (1066) and probably gave rise to surnames such as *Ames*. Now appears to be obsolete in English-speaking countries, though the Italian *Dizionario dei Nomi Propri di Persona* lists both **Amico** and **Amica**.

Amie (f) Probably a spelling variant of **Amy** 'loved', though in this form appears to be French *amie*, the feminine of *ami* 'friend'. Rarely used.

Amina (f) Short form of **Williamina** in regular, though infrequent, use. In special circumstances may represent the name **Aminah**, mother of the Prophet Mohammad.

Aminta (f) 16th c. Italian adaptation for literary purposes of **Amyntas**, the name of several Macedonian kings in ancient times. **Amintor** used as a male name in their *Maid's Tragedy* (1619) by Beaumont and Fletcher, but neither form has been much used.

Amorous (m) The word used as a name. British parents suddenly and inexplicably began to use it in the 1850s, but it had disappeared by the 1860s. **Amor** also used at this time.

Amos (m) Hebrew 'carrier' or 'strong'. Biblical, O.T., the Book of Amos (the third of the twelve prophets). Regularly used in English-speaking countries from the 17th c. until the end of the 19th c. In modern times it survives, but is rare.

Amplias (f) Miss Withycombe notes a 12th c. example of **Amphelisia**, which survived until the 19th c. mainly as Amplias, also as **Amphillis**, **Amphlis**. All forms possibly derive from Greek *ampelos* 'vine', though Charnock suggested 'speaking two languages'. Only one example of the name noted since the 1880s.

Amy (f) Old French *amée*, feminine past participle of *amer* (modern French *aimer*) 'to love'. The Latin verb is *amare*, with the feminine past participle *amata*. The masculine form *amatus* 'loved' also used as a christian name, e.g. Bishop Amatus, 7th c. In early Roman inscriptions *Amatia* is found, but in the Latin of English parish registers the name became **Amata** or **Amia**. (Modern Italian also has Amata as the feminine form of the name, while **Amato** is used for boys.) Amy quietly used in the 18th c. but became very popular in the latter part of the 19th c. in Britain. Dickens's *Little Dorrit* was published 1855–7, the heroine being an Amy. Louisa M. Alcott's *Little Women* followed in 1868, with an Amy as one of the four main characters. In spite of this, little used in the U.S. until 1950. By the late 1970s had become one of the favourite names throughout North America, though it was predominantly white parents who were using it. Also returning to favour in Britain at this time, having been little used since the 1920s. **Amey** formerly a common variant of the name. **Amie** also found, but not clear whether this is meant to be French *amie*, feminine of *ami* 'friend', or simply a spelling variant of Amy. Some parents use the French form of the name, **Aimée**.

Amyas (m) Latin, from *Amatus* 'loved (of God)' or *Amadeus*, from *amare* 'to love' + *deus* 'God'. By the 17th c. Camden was explaining the name as the male form of **Amy**. Charles Kingsley made Amyas Leigh the hero of his *Westward Ho!* (1855) but this failed to make the name popular. **Amias** is a common variant of Amyas, but the feminine name Amias which appears in Christian inscriptions of the Roman Empire probably derives from Greek *amiantos* 'pure, undefiled'.

Anabel (f) See **Annabel**. Anabele, Anabell, Anabelle also occur.

Anabella (f) See **Annabella**.

Anastasia (f) Greek feminine of *Anastasius*, from *anastasis* 'resurrection'. Name of a 4th c. saint, more recently associated with the daughter of the Russian Czar, Nicholas II. Regularly but infrequently used in English-speaking countries, though pet forms **Stacy** and **Stacey** have recently been extremely popular. **Anastatia** also found.

Anchor (m) The word used as a name, probably with the Biblical reference in mind: '. . . the hope set before us. We have this as a sure and steadfast anchor of the soul . . .' N.T., Heb. 6:19. Rarely used.

Anders (m) Scandinavian, and occasionally Scottish, form of **Andrew**. Infrequently used. The surname which derives from Anders, namely **Anderson**, is more often used as a first name than Anders itself.

Andra (f) Usually considered to be a female form of **Andrew**, but occasionally used for males, when it no doubt derives from a Gaelic male form, **Anndra**.

André (m) French form of **Andrew**. Especially popular amongst black American families.

Andrea (f) Feminine form of **Andreas**, or **Andrew**. Andrea is the most usual form in all English-speaking countries, but others that are found include **Andera, Andra, Andree, Andreana, Andrewina, Andria, Andrienne, Andrietta, Andrina, Andrine, Andrette, Andrene, Andrianna, Andreena, Andrean, Drena, Dreena, Rena**. Such names tend to be especially well used in Scotland, where Andrew has long been a favourite name, and where the habit of forming female names by adding -ena or -ina was formerly common. Occasional male use of Andrea probably derives from a male form of the name Andrew in Gaelic, **Aindrea**.

Andrean(a) (f) See **Andrea**.

Andreas (m) Latin form of **Andrew**, used steadily in all English-speaking countries.

Andrée (f) French feminine form of **André** (**Andrew**) regularly used in English-speaking countries since the 1920s.

Andreena, Andrena, Andrene (f) see **Andrea**.

Andrette (f) Modern feminine form of **Andrew**. See **Andrea**.

Andrew (m) Greek *Andreas* 'manly'. Latin *Andreas*, Old French *Andreu*.

Common name in early Christian inscriptions. Biblical, N.T., the first Apostle, whose relics were allegedly brought to Scotland and kept at St Andrews. St Andrew is patron saint of Scotland and Russia and the name has always been popular in both countries. The commonness of the surnames *Andrews, Anderson*, etc., testifies to the frequent use of Andrew in medieval times. Subsequently well used from the 17th c. until the early 20th c. By 1950 had returned to popularity, and by the 1970s had become one of the most frequently used male names in the English-speaking world. Historically in the U.S. associated with President Andrew Jackson (1765–1845) and with Andrew Carnegie (1835–1919), who came originally from Scotland. In Britain use of the name increased after the naming of Prince Andrew in 1960. Apart from Andrew itself, many other forms of the name are in use. **Andy**, and in recent times, **Drew**, are diminutive forms used independently. The modern French **André** is common, especially amongst black American families. Latin **Andreas** remains in steady use, and the Scandinavian **Anders** is found. Even more common is the transferred use of **Anderson** as a first name. **Andra** and **Andrea**, while normally considered to be female forms of **Andrew**, are also used for men, probably deriving from Gaelic *Anndra*, *Aindrea*. For the many feminine forms of the name see **Andrea**.

Andrewina (f) Also **Andria, Andrietta, Andrianna, Andrienne, Andrina, Andrine**. Feminine forms of **Andrew** in infrequent use. See **Andrea**.

Andy (m) Diminutive of **Andrew**, sometimes used as an independent name.

Aneirin (m) See **Aneurin**.

Anetta (f) See **Annetta**.

Anette (f) See **Annette**.

Aneurin (m) Welsh form of Latin *Honorius* 'honour', though Davies (*A Book of Welsh Names*) suggests a derivation from Welsh *eur* 'gold'. **Aneirin** is the older form of the name, borne by a 6th c. Welsh poet. Made famous in Britain in modern times by the Welsh politician Aneurin Bevan (1897–1960), Minister of Health in the Labour Government. Nye is the pet form.

Angel (m, f) Greek *angelos*, Latin *angelus* 'messenger, angel'. Earliest bearer of the personal name seems to have been St Angelus, who travelled from Jerusalem to preach in Sicily early in the 13th c. He was assassinated, but **Angelo** took hold throughout Italy and remains a favourite name there. In Britain Camden records Angel as a male name in 1605, but the Puritans were not in favour of its use. In *Meditations upon the Creed*, Adams stated that it was 'not fit for Christian humility to call a man Gabriel or Michael, giving the names of angels to the sons of mortality.' A tradition nevertheless arose that Angel was a characteristically Cornish name. In a *Handbook of Cornish Names*, G. Pawley White argues that Angel(l) is a different name there, derived from words meaning 'the light brown, tawny one'. Pronunciation of the name in Cornwall with a hard 'g' lends weight to this interpretation. In modern times Italian/Spanish Angelo is the accepted form in English-speaking countries for males. Angel still in use, more in the U.S. than in Britain, but used now for girls. Also a favourite name for dogs. The many feminine forms of Angel include Angela, the French Angèle, Angelina, Angelia, Angelica (and its German form Angelika), Angeline, Angelique, Angelita (mainly in the U.S.). Pet forms Angie and Angy are occasionally used independently.

Angela (f) Feminine of Greek *angelos*, Latin *angelus* 'messenger, angel'. Began to be used in the 18th c., after rare occurrences earlier. Gained strength slowly throughout the 19th c., eventually establishing itself as a favourite name in all English-speaking countries from the 1920s onwards. Particularly well-used since the 1940s.

Angèle (f) French form of **Angel**, in occasional modern use.

Angelene (f) Form of **Angeline** in use since the 1970s.

Angelia (f) Apparently a spelling variant of **Angela**. Occurs regularly in the U.S. and Britain.

Angelica (f) Italian or Latin feminine form of *angelicus* 'angelic'. German **Angelika** also used occasionally, and French **Angelique** used since the 1960s.

Angelina (f) Italian diminutive of **Angela**, feminine of **Angelo**, Greek *angelos*, Latin *angelus* 'messenger, angel'. Preferred form of the name throughout the 19th c. in English-speaking countries. In modern times Angela has been much preferred.

Angeline (f) French form of **Angelina**, favoured by British parents since the 1930s. Occurs also as **Angelene**.

Angelique (f) See **Angelica**.

Angelita (f) Spanish diminutive of **Angela**, feminine of **Angelo** (see **Angel**). Used to some extent in the U.S., especially in the 1960s.

Angelo (m) Italian/Spanish form of Latin *Angelus*, Greek *Angelos* 'messenger, angel'. The male form of the name which has replaced **Angel** in English-speaking countries. A well-known bearer of the name is Angelo Dundee, Muhammad Ali's boxing mentor.

Angharad (f) Welsh 'much loved'. Occurs in early Welsh history and revived since the 1940s.

Angie (f) Pet form of **Angela**, **Angelina**, **Angelique**, etc., used in its own right since the 1940s. Variant spelling **Angy** is occasionally found.

Angus (m) Gaelic *Aonghas* 'unique choice'. Can also derive from the place name Angus (now Forfarshire) in Scotland. Formerly a common name in Ireland, now predominantly a Scottish name. Its use in the Middle Ages is attested by surnames such as *MacInnes*, *Maguiness*, 'son of Angus'. Since the 1880s has been used in England, and more recently has appeared in Canada and Australia.

Angusina (f) Scottish feminine form of Angus, now little used.

Anice (f) Variant form of **Annice**.

Anika (f) In modern times a form of **Annika**, but as a slave name in the 18th c., an African word which also occurs in the slave lists as **Anaca**, **Anaka**, **Anecky**, **Anikee**, **Annaka**, etc. Heller (*Black Names in America*) suggests a Hausa word meaning 'sweetness of face'.

Anis (f) Variant form of **Annis**.

Anise (f) Form of *Anysia*. See **Annice**.

Anita (f) Spanish diminutive of **Ann**. Given currency from 1930 by the American actress Anita Louise. The Swedish actress Anita Ekberg then helped to publicize it further in the 1950s, when it was most used in English-speaking countries. Pet form **Nita**.

Anja (f) Rare variant of **Anya**.

Ann (f) English form of Hebrew **Hannah**. The Apocryphal Gospels say that Anna and Joachim were the parents of Mary, the mother of Jesus. This caused its popularity in the Western world from the 14th c. onwards. By the 16th c. was one of the most frequently used names in Britain. Remained so (often written in the French way as **Anne**) until the mid-19th c. In Britain then largely displaced by its own diminutive, **Annie**. In the U.S. the Latin form **Anna** preferred 1850–1900, **Ann** returning to favour thereafter. In Britain Ann and Anne were little used 1900–50, but the naming in 1950 of Princess Anne brought both forms back into favour. In all English-speaking countries since the 1960s, however, Ann and Anne have been little used as first names, but very well used as middle names. Early pet forms were **Nan**, **Nanny** and **Nancy**. Other forms in use include Spanish **Anita**, French **Annette**, Russian **Nina**, Swedish **Annika**.

Anna (f) Greek and Latin form of **Hannah**. In Virgil's *Aeneid* Anna is the sister of Queen Dido. Occurs in Christian inscriptions from the 6th c. The Apocryphal Gospels name Anna, wife of Joachim, as the mother of the Virgin Mary. This caused the name to become immensely popular from the 15th c., but in the English form **Ann** or the French form **Anne**. Anna was the written version of the name in Latinized documents, though it eventually became a fashionable spoken as well as written form in the U.S., and to a lesser extent in Britain, in the 19th c. Since 1970 has shown signs of a revival. **Annah** occurred regularly in the 19th c. Dame Anna Neagle is a famous English bearer of the name, while in literature it is most associated with Tolstoy's *Anna Karenina*.

Annabel (f) Probably a mishearing (and misreading) of **Amabel** by origin. In his *Dictionary of British Surnames* Reaney quotes entries in a 13th c. register where Anabel and Amabel clearly refer to the same person. Annabel became well-established in Scotland, made known by such bearers as Annabel Drummond, mother of King James I. The publication of Edgar Allan Poe's *Annabel Lee* (1849) did much to spread the use of the name. Since the 1940s quietly but steadily used in all English-speaking countries. Latinized **Annabella** formerly more popular than **Annabel** itself, but shorter form is now preferred. Lowland Scots pronunciation of Annabel caused it to be spoken and written as **Annaple** in the early 19th c.

Annabella (f) See **Annabel**.

Annabelle (f) Form of **Annabel** in use mainly since the 1940s. This spelling may be intended to give the meaning 'Anna, the beautiful one'. **Annabell** is an occasional variant.

Annalie (f) See **Anneliese**.

Annalisa (f) Usual form in English-speaking countries of **Anneliese**. In use since the 1950s.

Annamarie (f) Popular blend of **Anna** and **Marie**, used since the 1960s. Often written Anna-Marie. **Anna-Mary** occurs rarely.

Annaple (f) Scottish form of **Annabel** used in the early 19th c.

16

Annas (m) Mentioned in N.T. Luke 3.2.

Anne (f) French form of Hebrew **Hannah**, but used freely in Britain since the 14th c. as an alternative spelling of **Ann**. In the 19th c. ten girls spelled their name Ann for every one who spelled it Anne. With the naming of Princess Anne in 1950 the -e spelling became far more usual in most English-speaking countries. Both forms of the name, however, decreasing in use since the 1960s. They remain very popular middle names. Famous Annes include Shakespeare's wife, Anne Hathaway; actress Anne Bancroft; Anne Frank, author of a diary which showed her great courage when being hounded by the Nazis during World War Two. In the famous novel *Anne of Green Gables* (1909), by Lucy Maud Montgomery, Anne insists on the -e spelling. 'A-n-n looks dreadful, but A-n-n-e looks so much more distinguished', says the heroine. The writer G. B. Stern expressed a somewhat similar thought in *A Name to Conjure With*: 'Annie is boisterous, where Anne has style and dignity.'

Anneliese (f) 20th c. German formation from **Anna** and **Liesa** (**Elisabeth**). Now found in English-speaking countries in various guises, such as **Annaleisa**, **Anna-Lisa**, **Annalisa**, **Annelisa**, **Annelise**. Short forms **Annelie**, **Annalie** also occur.

Annemarie (f) Blend of **Anne** and **Marie** much used since the mid-1950s. Often written as **Anne-Marie**.

Anness (f) 19th c. form of **Annis**.

Annet(t) (f) Occasional variants of **Annette**, **Anneth** also occurs.

Annetta (f) Latinized form of French **Annette**, itself a diminutive of **Anne**, for Hebrew **Hannah**. Consistently but quietly used. Pet form **Netta**.

Annette (f) French diminutive form of **Anne**, well used in Britain and Australia 1950–70.

Annice (f) English form of Greek *Anysia* 'fulfilment, completion'. The name of this Christian martyr is also found in its German version, **Anissa**. Early uses are

difficult to separate from phonetic spelling of **Agnes**, usually pronounced *Annis*.

Annie (f) Diminutive of **Ann**, itself an English form of Hebrew **Hannah**. Became immensely popular in Britain and the U.S. in the latter half of the 19th c. Little used since the 1930s. The Annie Laurie of the song was a real person, eldest daughter of Sir Robert Laurie of Maxwelton. Annie Oakley, the sharpshooter who appeared in Buffalo Bill's Wild West show, was actually Phoebe Annie Oakley Mozee (1859–1926). The musical *Annie* may help the name during the 1980s.

Annika (f) Swedish diminutive of **Ann**. In occasional use. **Anneka** also occurs, e.g. Anneka Rice, the TV personality.

Annis (f) In early use nearly always a form of **Agnes**, usually pronounced *Annis*. In modern times (used regularly but infrequently until the 1930s) probably an English form of Greek *Anysia*, a Christian martyr. See **Annice**.

Annita (f) Variant of **Anita** in regular use since the 1950s. **Annitta** also occurs.

Annmarie (f) Blend of **Ann** and **Marie** used since the 1940s. Variants include **Annmaria**, **Annemarie**, **Annamarie**.

Annora (f) Form of **Honora** used in medieval documents, occasionally revived in modern times, when it is possibly thought of as a diminutive of **Ann**.

Annthea (f) Variant of **Anthea** which appeared in the 1940s.

Anntoinette (f) English form of **Antoinette** which came into use in the 1950s.

Anny (f) Variant of **Annie**. Title of a prize-winning French novel by Marc Bernard, published in 1934 in English, and probably responsible for the use of the name.

Anona (f) Appears to be from the Latin *anona* 'pineapple', but has been linked with *Annona*, a Roman goddess of provisions. Used since the 1920s, more in Britain than the U.S. **Nona** is a much older name and may have had some influence, and some parents may think of the name as a diminutive of **Ann**. Much publicized in Britain in the 1950s by the media personality Anona Winn.

Anouska (f) Russian pet form of **Ann**, used in the 1970s to some extent.

Anselm (m) Old German *ansi* 'god, divine' + *helm* 'helmet'. Found in Christian inscriptions of the Roman Empire. St Anselm was archbishop of Canterbury in the 12th c. Often found as **Ansell** until the 15th c., then lost until the end of the 19th c., when it was revived to some extent. Feminine form **Anselma** has been used, together with pet form **Selma, Zelma**.

Ansley (m, f) 19th c. variant of **Ainslie**.

Anstice (f) Rarely used shortened form of **Anastasia**.

Anthea (f) Greek *anthos* 'flower', *antheios* 'flowery'. An 'anthology' is literally a collection of flowers. Anthea was used by pastoral poets such as Robert Herrick in the 17th c., the name being known to them as that of the goddess of spring and one of the titles of Hera. In Britain came into use in the 1920s and was most used 1940–50. Occasional modern spelling variant is **Annthea**. Very rare elsewhere.

Anthony (m) Latin *Antonius*, a Roman clan name of unknown meaning. In the 17th c. interpreted by Camden as deriving from Greek *anthos* 'flower', which accounts for the unnecessary 'h'. The latter has led to a spelling pronunciation in the U.S. which makes Anthony and Antony different names. In Britain both are still pronounced as Antony. St Antony, the 3rd c. recluse, is normally regarded as responsible for the spread of the name into all Christian countries. In fairly common use from the 12th c. in Britain, but had faded by the beginning of the 18th c. Returned to favour in the 1920s and popular in all English-speaking countries since then. Also found are the German **Anton**, French **Antoine**, Italian/Spanish **Antonio**, **Antonino**, **Antonello**. Pet form **Tony** is often used independently. Feminine forms of the name include **Antonia**,

Antoinette, Antonina, Toni, Tonie, Tonia, Tonya. In the U.S. black American families also use Anthony for girls. Some famous modern Anthonys are Sir Anthony Eden (1897–1977), former British Prime Minister; actors Anthony Quinn, Anthony Newley, Anthony Quayle; Anthony Powell, the novelist.

Antione (m) Form of **Antoine** which by the early 1980s was occurring regularly in the U.S. **Antionette** also occurs for **Antoinette**.

Antjuan (m) Also **Antajuan, Anthjuan**. See **Antoine**.

Antoine (m) French form of **Anthony**. In the early 1980s used a great deal by black American families. Appears also as **Antione** and in the curiously half-Spanish form **Antjuan**. The many phonetic spellings include **Antuan, Antuwain, Antwain, Antwaine, Antwan, Antwaun, Antwoin, Antwon, Antwone**.

Antoinette (f) French feminine diminutive of **Antoine** (**Anthony**). Famous in French history because of the ill-fated Marie Antoinette (1755–93), Queen of France. Used in English-speaking countries since the middle of the 19th c. with a minor vogue in the 1940s. In Britain continued into the 1970s; in the U.S. showed signs of fading away by that time. **Antonette** is a common modern variant.

Anton (m) German and Russian form of **Antony/Anthony**, used to some extent in the U.S. Regularly, if quietly, used in Britain since the beginning of the 20th c.

Antoney (m) Occasional modern variant of **Anthony/Antony**. **Antoni** occasionally used for girls.

Antonia (f) Feminine form of **Antony/Anthony**. Signs of increased usage in Britain since 1975. Main use in the U.S. is through its pet forms **Tonia/Tonya**. The writer Antonia Fraser is a well-known bearer of the name.

Antonina (f) Feminine form of **Antonino**, Italian version of **Antony/Anthony**. Used mainly in the U.S.

Antonio (m) Spanish/Italian form of

18

Antony/Anthony. Rare in Britain, but used in the U.S.

Antony (m) Latin *Antonius*, a Roman clan name of unknown origin. See **Anthony**, the more usual modern form in English-speaking countries, though Antony is historically correct.

Anwen (f) Welsh *an* 'very' + *gwyn* 'fair, beautiful'. A 20th c. Welsh name, also occurring as **Anwyn**.

Anya (f) Phonetic rendering of **Anna** as pronounced in Spanish. Has appeared in the 1970s.

Aphra (f) Hebrew *aphrah* 'dust'. **Dust** was actually used as a Christian name by the Puritans in the 17th c. (along with **Ashes**) but Miss Withycombe is probably right to suggest a misreading of O.T., Micah 1:10, where 'the house of Aphra' makes Aphra appear to be a personal name. Best-known bearer of the name was Mrs Aphra Benn (1644–89), novelist and writer of coarse comedies. In modern times more often spelt **Afra**. In Dickens's *Little Dorrit* we have **Affery** Flintwich.

April (f) The name of the month used as a first name. First recorded in 1917 and frequently used in the 1940s. Use of month names probably arose accidentally. **August** was meant to represent **Augustus**, not the time of the year, and **May** was originally a pet form of **Mary, Margaret**, etc. The 7th c. saint *Everildis*, **Everild** in its English form, became **Everil** then **Averil**. By the beginning of the 20th c. that name was being written as **Avril** and equated with French *avril* 'April'. April (**Apryl**) then used as a name followed soon afterwards by **June**, the most popular month name. **July** is recorded in the 19th c. but probably meant for **Julie** or **Julia**. January does not appear to have been used as a first name, though **Janus** occurs. Use of **March** as a first name probably derives from the surname. A **September** Smith was named in Britain in 1884.

Aquila (m) Latin 'eagle'. Common Roman name, mentioned in the Bible, e.g. Acts 18:2. This is probably the source of the mainly 19th c. first-name usage, rather than the friend of Cicero who was one of Caesar's murderers, or the Roman general who was killed by having molten gold poured down his throat. **Acquila** is a frequently found variant; **Acquilla, Aquilla** were other 19th c. variants.

Arabella (f) Latin *orabilis* 'yielding to prayer'. Recorded twice in the 12th c. in Scotland as *Orabilis*. In later medieval records became *Orable, Orabella, Arable*, etc. Surnames such as *Orbell, Arbell* and *Arable* testify to its use at this time. Arabella Stuart, who died a prisoner in the Tower of London in 1615, was known to her contemporaries as Lady Arbell. Infrequently used in England until the end of the 18th c., though Arabella Fermor became well known in 1712 when Pope published his *Rape of the Lock*, based on a real incident in which Lord Petre forcibly cut off a lock of Miss Fermor's hair. Used more towards the middle of the 19th c., by which time Dickens's Arabella Allen, 'a black-eyed young lady, in a very nice little pair of boots', had eloped with Winkle in *The Pickwick Papers*. Suddenly began to be used again in the 1970s by English parents, but the name is seemingly unknown elsewhere.

Araminta (f) Apparently coined by Sir John Vanbrugh (1664–1726) for his Comedy *The Confederacy* (1705). Occasionally used in modern times.

Archbold (m) Variant of **Archibald** used regularly, if infrequently, from the 1870s to the 1920s. **Archabald, Archbald** were also found.

Archelaus (m) Greek 'ruler of the people'. Borne by early kings of Macedonia, but its use in modern times, mainly in the 19th c., probably stems from the Bible. Archelaus is there mentioned frequently as the son of Herod the Great.

Archer (m) Old French *archier*, ultimately from Latin *arcarius* 'bowman'. Occupational surname of the Middle Ages, used quite extensively as a first name in the 19th c. and occasionally in

19

the 20th c. Then became confused with **Archie**. In *Renny's Daughter*, by Mazo de la Roche, it is the name given to the youngest of the three Whiteoaks, because Archer was Alayne Whiteoaks' maiden name.

Archibald (m) Old German *Erkanbald* 'excellent, noble + bold'. Introduced to Britain by Normans in 12th c. and recorded in the Domesday Book as *Erchenbaldus, Arcebaldus, Arcenbaldus*. Scottish Gaelic speakers assumed that the Arch- of Archibald was connected with archbishop, and that the -bald element indicated a bald (tonsured) monk. They therefore used the name as a substitute for **Gilleasbuig** (**Gillespie**), which means'(tonsured) servant of the bishop'. Archibald was at first used by the Campbell chiefs, later it became a general favourite. Throughout the 19th c. and until the 1930s it was among the Scottish top twenty male names. Since then has declined, and now rarely used in any English-speaking country – perhaps because Archibald acquired a stereotyped image of an upper-class ass from the 1920s. Usual pet form of the name, which steers clear of the upper-class image, is **Archie**. This was being mainly used in the U.S. in the 1970s by black American parents.

Archie (m) See **Archibald**.

Areta (f) Greek *arete* 'virtue'. Black American parents, especially, also use the name as **Aretha**, **Arette**, **Aretta**, but it is not in frequent use.

Arfon (m) Welsh place name 'opposite Anglesey' used as a first name in Wales, though infrequently.

Ariane (f) French form of Greek **Ariadne**, in occasional modern use, probably because of the saint (2nd c.) who bore the name. Ariadne itself is sometimes used. The name means 'very holy one'.

Ariel (m) Water-spirit in the demonology of the Cabala, but a spirit of the air in medieval fables. Best known to modern readers as the spirit in Shakespeare's *Tempest* or the sylph in Pope's *Rape of the Lock*. In occasional use as a first name.

Arleen (f) See **Arlene**, **Arline**.

Arlene (f) Variant of **Arline**, and in recent years its more common form. **Arlena** is also found, as are **Arleen** and **Arlyne**.

Arletta (f) Latinized form of **Arlette**, used mainly by black American families in modern times.

Arlette (f) French name which first appeared in English-speaking countries in the mid-19th c., and revived strongly in Britain in the 1940s. Modern American usage appears to favour the Latin form **Arletta**. French authorities explain Arlette as a pet form of **Charlotte** (**Caroletta** in its Latin form). Charlotte itself was often written Charlet in early English documents. Black American families, especially, have turned Caroletta into **Carletta** in modern times, and these various indications all seem to confirm the view that Arlette and Arletta derive from feminine forms of **Charles**.

Arley (m) Surname linked with a place name 'eagle-wood', used from time to time as a first name.

Arline (f) First mention of the name seems to have been in the opera *The Bohemian Girl*, by M. W. Balfe (1808–70). The composer was married to a Hungarian singer called Lina Rosa, the Lina being a pet form of Karolina. By the beginning of the 20th c. Arline had come into regular use. **Arlene** and its variants regularly used by the 1930s, and later given a boost in the U.S. by the actresses Arlene Dahl and Arlene Francis. Many reference works link both names with a Gaelic word for 'pledge', but evidence to support this derivation is hard to come by. Stewart suggests that **Charlene** may have influenced usage, which takes us back to Karolina. For various reasons, then, a derivation from a feminine form of **Charles** is probably most likely.

Arlo (m) Appeared suddenly in the early 1970s but disappeared equally quickly. May be a clipped form of **Carlo**.

Arlyne (f) See **Arlene**, **Arline**.

Armand (m) See **Herman**.

Armando (m) See **Herman**.

Armina (f) Also **Armine**. Feminine forms of **Herman** in occasional use.

Arnaud (m) French form of **Arnold**, occasionally used in English-speaking countries.

Arno (m) Czech form of **Ernest** in occasional use.

Arnold (m) Old German *Arnwalt* 'eagle-power'. Introduced to Britain by the Normans as *Arnaut*, *Ernaut*, it led to surnames such as *Arnold*, *Arnall*, *Arnatt*, *Arnell*, *Arnott*, etc. Became fairly rare as a first name after the 13th c. but began to be used again in the 1870s in Britain, perhaps in compliment to such figures as Thomas Arnold, the headmaster who is celebrated in *Tom Brown's Schooldays* (1857) and Matthew Arnold his son, poet and critic. Not very popular as a first name in any English-speaking country in modern times.

Aron (m) Spelling variant of **Aaron** found since the 1840s. Middle name of Elvis Aron Presley (1935–78). There is an interesting remark about the name in John Steinbeck's famous novel *East of Eden*:

'Are you called Aaron?'

'Yes, sir.'

Lee chuckled. 'He spells it with *a*. The two *a*'s seem a little fancy to his friends.'

Arran (m) In Scotland may be a transferred use of the name of the Scottish island. Elsewhere a common variant of **Aaron**. Also occurs frequently as **Arron**.

Arrow (m) The word used as a name, probably with reference to Zech. 9:14, 'Then the Lord will appear over them, and his arrow go forth like lightning.' Occurs very rarely.

Arthene (f) See **Arthur**.

Artemas (m) The form of the Greek name mentioned in the Bible, N.T., Titus 3:12. Probably means 'devotee of the goddess Artemis', that is, Diana. Used by the American humorous writer Charles Farrar Browne (1834–67) when he became **Artemus** Ward: used with the latter spelling on occasions, indicating that he was the source. **Artemesia**,

Artemise also occur on rare occasions as feminine forms, in that spelling rather than the more correct **Artemisia**.

Arthur (m) Of uncertain origin: possibly Celtic *artos* 'bear' (cognate with Greek *arctos*). Since the first Arthur mentioned in records is Irish, the origin may be Irish *art* 'stone'. Also a Roman clan name *Artorius* and an Old Norse *Arnthor* 'Thor the eagle'. Always associated with King Arthur, who flourished (perhaps) in the 5th c. and 6th c. As Artor, Artur it is mentioned frequently in the Domesday Book, but by the 14th c. it was out of fashion. Began to be used again during the 18th c., then hit a peak of popularity in the 19th c. because of Arthur Wellesley, Duke of Wellington (1769–1852), victor over Napoleon at Waterloo. One of the most-used first names in the English-speaking world until the 1920s, but though still in regular use, now a minor name. In the 19th c. the variant **Arther** was frequently found, and there were attempts to launch feminine forms such as **Arthuretta** and **Arthurina**. Such names as **Artina**, **Artlette**, **Artis** and **Artrice** (all used in the 1970s by black American families) are probably feminine forms based on **Art**, the common pet name for Arthur. Other modern feminine forms include **Arthene**, **Artheia** and **Arthelia**, but these remain rare.

Arthuretta (f) Feminine form of **Arthur** used mainly at the end of the 19th c.

Arthurina (f) Feminine form of **Arthur** used when Arthur itself was popular. **Arthurine** also occurred.

Artina (f) Also **Artis**, **Artlette**, **Artrice**. See **Arthur**.

Asa (m) Hebrew 'physician'. Biblical, O.T., 1 Kings 15:11. Introduced by the Puritans and especially popular in the north of England, according to Bardsley, in the 17th c. and 18th c. In occasional modern use, recently perhaps because of the well-known British soccer player, Asa Hartford.

Ashanti (f) Name of the West African

region and tribe, now used as a first name, mainly by black American families. Occurs also as **Ashanta, Ashante, Ashaunta, Ashuntae**.

Ashby (m) Surname derived from a place name 'farm near ash trees', used from time to time as a first name.

Asher (m) Hebrew 'happy'. Biblical, O.T., Gen. 30:13. One of the sons of Jacob. A Puritan introduction, in regular but infrequent use since the 17th c. Surname Asher derives from a different source, and may occasionally be transferred to first-name status.

Ashlea (m, f) Also **Ashlee, Ashleigh**. See **Ashley**.

Ashley (m, f) Old English *aesclēah* 'ash wood', a common English place name which became a surname, e.g., that of Lord Ashley (later 7th Earl of Shaftesbury) the 19th c. social reformer. His 'Ten Hours Bill' made it illegal for children to work more than ten hours a day in factories. Use of Ashley as a Christian name began in the 1860s. Far more intensely used since 1970 in Australia and Britain, especially, and this may be due to the occurrence of the name (Ashley Wilkes) in Margaret Mitchell's great success, *Gone With The Wind*. In the U.S. increasingly being used for girls and sometimes spelt **Ashlie**. **Ashleigh** also found as an alternative form of both male and female name.

Ashlie (f) Feminine form of **Ashley**.

Ashling (f) Phonetic form of **Aisling**. **Ashlyn** also occurs.

Ashton (m) Common English place name 'ash tree farm' and surname, used frequently as a first name in the 19th c., less so in the 20th c.

Asia (f) The name of the continent occasionally used as a first name. Original meaning was 'sunrise, east'.

Aspasia (f) Greek 'welcome'. Heroine of *The Maid's Tragedy* (1610) by Beaumont and Fletcher. Examples of the name are found in 19th c. records but rarely used in the 20th c.

Asta (f) Short form of such names as **Astrid, Augusta** and **Anastasia**, im-

ported from Scandinavia or Germany. Made known in silent film days by the Danish actress Asta Nielsen.

Aston (m) Place name/surname used as a first name. Originally 'the eastern settlement'.

Astra (f) in use since the 1940s, based on the Latin *astralis* 'of the stars'. The novel *Astra*, by Grace Livingston Hill, may have been the source. **Esther, Stella, Estelle** and **Star** itself are similar names.

Astrid (f) Old Norse *Astrithr*, *Estrithr* 'god-beauty, i.e. divinely beautiful'. **Astri** and **Estrid** are other forms of the name in Scandinavia, and pet forms include **Asta** (also for *Augusta*), **Assa, Assi, Atti**. Long-standing royal name in Norway and more recently, a royal name in Belgium. Used regularly, but infrequently, in Britain since the 1920s. Amongst the students of St Olaf College in Minnesota in the 1930s (Astrid was the wife of St Olaf) only one girl amongst the 702 students, mostly of Norwegian stock, was called Astrid.

Atalanta (f) Greek 'unswaying'. A name from Greek legend in occasional modern use as a first name.

Athelstan (m) Old English 'noble – stone'. Royal name in Anglo-Saxon times, but became obsolete. Sir Walter Scott revived it in his novel *Ivanhoe* (1819) which caused it to be used again occasionally in the 19th c.

Athene (f) Greek *Athene*, the goddess of wisdom. In occasional use.

Athol (m) Scottish place name (of unknown origin) and surname, used intermittently as a first name since the 1870s.

Atlantic (m) The name of the ocean used for a child born at sea. See **Ocean**. **Atlantis**, the legendary island which was swallowed up by the ocean, has also been used as a first name.

Auberon (m) Old German *Adalbero* 'noble bear-like'. Miss Withycombe prefers to explain it as a form of **Aubrey**, but Professor Dauzat (see Bibliog.) is in no doubt about the Adalbero derivation. Well-known in its variant form **Oberon**, the name of the king of the fairies in Shakespeare's *Midsummer Night's Dream*. A well-known bearer in Britain is the writer and journalist Auberon Waugh, son of the novelist Evelyn Waugh. Neither Auberon nor Oberon is frequently used.

Aubert (m) Early French form of **Albert**. The 8th c. saint who bore the name probably inspired its use in Britain in the Middle Ages. Occasionally used in modern times.

Aubrey (m) Old French *Auberi*, *Alberi*, from Old German *Alberich* 'elf counsel'. Introduced to Britain from Normandy by the de Veres, Earls of Oxford, and closely associated with that family for centuries. Its use spread to some extent at the end of the 19th c. Occurs infrequently, sometimes as **Aubary**, **Aubery**, **Aubury**, mainly in Britain.

Auburn (m) The word used as a name. In very rare use.

Audie (m) Probably linked with the Irish form of **Edward** (**Eadbhard**). Made known by Audie Murphy, America's most decorated soldier in World War Two and later an actor in many films. Used occasionally since the late 1940s.

Audley (m) English place name and surname in occasional modern use as a first name. The place name links with an Old English feminine name *Aldgith*.

Audra (f) Variant of **Audrey**, mildly popular in the late 1960s, but quickly disappeared.

Audrey (f) Colloquial form of **Etheldreda** in use by the 16th c. According to Bede, St Audrey died of a tumour in her throat, which she regarded as a punishment for her early love of necklaces. At St Audrey's Fair necklaces were sold, not of good quality apparently, since the word 'tawdry' evolved from them. Revived in English-speaking countries at the turn of the century and very popular everywhere 1920–30. Subsequently faded, in spite of the popularity of Audrey|Hepburn|(1929-93) the actress.

Variants include **Audra**, **Audree**, **Audreen**, **Audria**, **Audrie**, **Audry**.

August (m) German form of **Augustus**. The first syllable is pronounced Ow-, not as in the name of the month. Month names are, of course, used as first names, but usually for girls. See **April**.

Augusta (f) Feminine form of **Augustus** or **Augustin(e)**. Used as a title by the Romans for their womenfolk and found as a Christian name in early inscriptions. Also the Roman name for the City of London. Introduced to Britain by the mother of George III from Germany. Well used in the 18th c. and 19th c. Byron addressed several poems to his sister Augusta, and Bertie Wooster, in P. G. Wodehouse's stories, has a formidable aunt of this name. Has fallen away on all sides in the 20th c.

Augustin (m) Common variant form in the 18th c. of **Augustine**, which has totally replaced it since the 19th c.

Augustina (f) Rarely used feminine form of **Augustin(e)**.

Augustine (m) Latin, diminutive of *augustus* 'venerable'. Found in Christian inscriptions of the Roman Empire. St Augustine of Hippo, bishop and doctor, died 430. In the 6th c. an Augustine became the first Archbishop of Canterbury. Common until the 17th c., when the forms **Augustin** and **Austin** tended to eclipse it. Partially revived in the 19th c. and used irregularly since then.

Augustus (m) Latin *augustus* 'venerable'. Used by the Roman Emperors and borrowed after the Renaissance by German princes. Introduced to Britain by the Hanoverians and much used from the early 18th c. Began to fade in the early 20th c. Other forms include the diminutive **Augustin(e)**, the shortened **Austin** and the Germanic **August**. Feminine variants include **Augusta**, **Augustia**, **Augustina**. Pet forms **Gus** and **Gussie** used on occasions as independent names.

Aulay (m) Form of Gaelic *Amhlaibh* which represents Old Norse *Anleifr* (**Olaf**). Both Aulay and **Macaulay** 'son of

AureliaAxel

Aulay' are occasionally used as first names in Scotland.

Aurelia (f) Latin feminine of *Aurelius*, a Roman clan name derived ultimately from *aurum* 'gold'. One of the commonest names in Christian inscriptions of the Roman Empire. In Britain used in the 19th c. but has since become rare. Thackeray's Peggy O'Dowd in *Vanity Fair* is actually **Auralia** Margaretta O'Dowd.

Auriel (f) Latin *aureola*, feminine diminutive from **aureus** 'golden'. A slave name in the Roman Empire. Camden (1605) lists *Aureola* 'pretty little golden dame'. Revived as Auriel in the 19th c. and used regularly since. **Auriol** is a common variant and **Aureole** occurs. Does not appear to be used outside Britain. See also **Oriel**.

Aurora (f) Latin: the Roman goddess of the dawn. Occurs as a Christian name in inscriptions of the Roman Empire. Its poetical use (e.g. Aurora Raby in Lord Byron's *Don Juan*, 1818, and Elizabeth Barrett Browning's *Aurora Leigh*, 1857) led to some general use. French form **Aurore** is also found, and modern **Aurea** is perhaps a simplified form of the name.

Aurore (f) See **Aurora**.

Austen (m) Variant of **Austin**, but this form probably indicates direct borrowing from the family name. Some usage must undoubtedly honour Jane Austen (1775–1817), one of the most famous women novelists. In Britain Austen was also made well known as a first name by Sir Austen Chamberlain, (1863–1937), winner of the Nobel Peace Prize and half-brother of Prime Minister Neville Chamberlain. Rarely used elsewhere.

Austin (m) Ordinary spoken form of **Augustin(e)** in the Middle Ages. Introduced from France in the 12th c. There it had already become *Aoustin* in the vernacular. Popular use of Austin in the Middle Ages led to the common surnames *Austin*, *Austen*, etc. Modern use may derive directly from the family name. Variants include **Austen, Austyn,**

Ostin and **Osten**. In Scotland often used as a substitute for the Gaelic *Uisdean* (*Huisdean*). Rare elsewhere.

Austyn (m) Variant of **Austin**, used in the 20th c.

Autumn (f) The word used as a name. By the early 1980s becoming more popular in the U.S., especially with black American parents. They were also making use of **Spring** to some extent.

Ava (f) Pet form of **Gustava** or phonetic form of **Eva**, as pronounced in several European countries. Modern usage clearly influenced by the actress Ava Gardner, who appeared on cinema screens from 1940.

Avaril (f) See **Averil**.

Aveen (f) Modern diminutive form of **Ava**.

Averil (f) Old English *eofor* 'boar' + *hild* 'battle'. Late form of the name of St Everild (7th c.). Early uses of **Avril** may represent this name rather than French *avril* 'April'. **Averill, Averilla, Averilda, Averhilda, Avaril, Everil, Everilda** and **Everhilda** are other forms of the name which have been used. See also **April**.

Avery (m) Form of **Alfred** in regular, though infrequent, use.

Avice (f) Latin feminine of *Avitius*, a common ethnic name in the early Roman Empire. Found in a 4th c. Christian inscription as *Avitia*, and by the 12th c. had been brought to Britain as *Avicia*. **Avis** now the commoner spelling.

Avis (f) Originally a form of **Avice**, but some parents no doubt use this form of the name in allusion to Latin *avis* 'bird'. **Avisa** and **Avise** are occasional variants.

Avner (m) Hebrew form of **Abner**.

Avon (f) English river name.

Avril (f) French *avril* 'April'. Used since the beginning of the 20th c. and especially popular in Scotland. **Avrille** and **Avryl** are occasional variants. See **April** for a fuller discussion of month names.

Axel (m) Scandinavian form of **Absalon**, made famous by the Swedish doctor and writer Axel Munthe, author of *Story of*

24

San Michele (1929). Used occasionally in English-speaking countries.

Ayanna (f) In recent use amongst black American families. May have begun as a pet form of **Juliana** or some such name which took on a pronunciation and later, a spelling, of its own. Found also as **Ayana** and **Ayania**.

Ayesha (f) Also **Ayeisha**. See **Aisha**.

Ayleen (f) Spelling variant of **Aileen**, reflecting a modern spelling-pronunciation of what was originally the same name as **Eileen**.

Aylmer (m) Old English *aethel* 'noble' + *maer* 'famous'. This pre-Conquest name survives mainly as a surname, but is occasionally used as a first name. More familiar form is **Elmer**.

Aylwin (m) Rarely used variant of **Alvin**.

Ayshea (f) Modern variant of **Ayesha**.

Azariah (m) Hebrew 'Jehovah has helped'. Biblical, O.T. One of the most popular names in the Bible, in the sense that it is borne by twenty-three different men who are mentioned. Used to some extent in the 19th c., but extremely rare in the 20th c. In 1982 the name occurred in the bizarre context of an Australian murder trial, in which a mother was accused of murdering her daughter **Azaria**.

Azubah (f) Hebrew 'abandoned, forsaken'. Mentioned on four occasions in the Bible, e.g. 1 Kings 22:42. In regular if infrequent use from the 17th c. to the end of the 19th c., but no examples noted after 1890. The form used in the Douai version of the Bible was **Azuba** which is also found. Pet form **Zuba** used on rare occasions as an independent name.

B

Babette (f) French diminutive of **Barbara** or **Elizabeth**, occasionally found in English-speaking countries as an independent name.

Baden (m) From the surname of Lord Baden-Powell, founder of the Boy Scout movement in 1908. Use of Baden as a Christian name dates from 1900, the year in which Baden-Powell became a British national hero for his defence of Mafeking in the Boer War. The name was most used in 1900–1901, but it remains in regular, if infrequent, use. The surname probably derived from a place name, which in turn was based on the Old English personal name *Bada*.

Bailey (m) Occupational surname from the Middle Ages, indicating a 'bailiff', an officer who made arrests and served writs. Used as a first name in the 19th c., though infrequently.

Baker (m) Occupational surname used regularly if infrequently as a first name, mainly in the 19th c.

Baldwin (m) German 'bold friend'. Used occasionally in the 19th c., but is more frequent in its Welsh form **Maldwyn**.

Barbara (f) Latin *Barbara*, from Greek, the feminine of the adjective *barbaros*, 'strange, foreign'. At first used to describe anyone who did not speak Greek. Common Christian name in early Roman inscriptions. Saint Barbara was one of the most popular saints of the Middle Ages, patron of architects and engineers. She was martyred in the 3rd c. Earliest English form was **Barbary**. This survived as a spoken and occasional written form until the end of the 19th c. Surnames such as *Babb*, *Babbs*, *Barbe*, etc., show that the name was much used in the 13th c. and 14th c. Then quietly but regularly used until the beginning of the 20th c., other than in Scotland, where it was already ranked 16th in 1858. From 1900 became more intensively used each year, especially in the U.S. where by 1925 it ranked second to Mary. In the U.S. and Canada it then began to decline. In

Britain continued to be more used until its peak around 1950. Little used since in English-speaking countries. The reason for the name's return to popularity in the 20th c. is not clear. It was already on the ascendant when Shaw published his play *Major Barbara* (1907), and the actress Barbara Stanwyck (born Ruby Stevens) only began to publicize the name in the 1930s. Usual pet forms of the name are **Bab**, **Babs**, **Barbie** and (in Scotland) **Baubie**. **Babe** and **Bobbie** are also found, especially in North America. See **Babette**.

Barbary (f) Earlier form in English of **Barbara**, now obsolete.

Barbie (f) Also **Barby**. Pet forms of **Barbara**.

Barbra (f) Mainly American variant of **Barbara**. The singer Barbra Streisand is probably the best known bearer of this form of the name.

Barclay (m) Scottish form of **Berkeley**.

Barker (m) Surname used as a first name. Regular in the 19th c., infrequent since. Ultimately means either 'shepherd' or 'tanner'.

Barnabas (m) Hebrew 'son of exhortation, encouragement'. Biblical, N.T., Acts *passim*. Now rarely used in this form, **Barnaby** being preferred. Pet form is **Barney**.

Barnaby (m) English form of **Barnabas**, in use since the 1960s. This indicates the influence of television (e.g. the series *Barnaby Jones*) rather than Dickens's *Barnaby Rudge*, with its good-natured but half-witted hero.

Barnard (m) Frequently used variant of **Bernard**.

Barnes (m) Surname originally indicating residence near 'barns'. Sir Barnes Newcome is in *The Newcomes* (1855) by William Thackeray.

Barnet(t) (m) English surname deriving from a place name, occasionally used as a first name. Ultimately it derives from Old English *baernet* 'burning' with reference to land that had been cleared in that way. Some earlier uses of the first name in Britain may have been due to Samuel Augustus Barnett (1844–1913),

social reformer. The name may also in some instances derive from a medieval pronunciation of **Bernard**.

Barney (m) Pet form of **Barnabas** or **Barnaby** used independently.

Baron (m) Surname used as a first name, or a borrowing of the title. Regularly used in Britain and the U.S., though not in great numbers. **Barron** is a common variant.

Barrett (m) Surname of many possible origins, regularly used as a first name throughout the 19th c.; also found on rare occasions in the 20th c. Early 19th c. uses of the name may have been in honour of Elizabeth Barrett, later Mrs Browning, the poet. She was well known from 1826 onwards.

Barrie (f, m) Surname (deriving from place names in Scotland, Wales or Normandy) used as a first name. First appears as such in Britain in 1919, which suggests that the popularity of Sir James Barrie (1860–1937), who wrote *Peter Pan*, had much to do with it. The 1970s introduced the fashionable **Barri**, together with such combinations as **Barrie-Jane**, **Barrie-Anne**. In the U.S. Barrie is sometimes a pet-form of **Bernice** or **Berenice**. Occasionally a variant of **Barry** (m).

Barrington (m) Common English place name (of several different origins) and aristocratic surname, regularly used as a first name, especially in England and Wales. Abbreviates conveniently to **Barry**.

Barron (m) See **Baron**.

Barry (m) Irish *bearach* 'spear, javelin'. There are also places called Barry in Scotland and Wales. First name occurs mainly this century, though a Barry Smith was named in 1846. (Thackeray's novel *Barry Lyndon* was published in 1844.) The name reached a peak of popularity in Britain, Canada and Australia in the 1950s. Well-used in the U.S. at that time, mainly by white families. See **Barrie**.

Barrymore (m) Surname of a celebrated family of American actors, used as a first

name in their honour. Original name of
Lionel Barrymore (1878–1954), Ethel
Barrymore (1879–1959) and John
Barrymore (1882–1942) was Blythe.

Bartha (f) Occasional variant of **Bertha**.
Barta is also found.

Bartholomew (m) Aramaic 'son of
Tolmai (or Talmai)'. Usually said to
be an alternative name of the Apostle
Nathanael. Biblical, N.T. Use of the
name in the Middle Ages led to many
surnames, such as *Bates*, *Batty*, *Bartle*,
Bartlet(t). Of these, **Bartlett**, especially,
is used regularly as a first name, and
Bartle occurs. Bartholomew itself rarely
used since the mid-19th c. in any
English-speaking country.

Bartlett (m) See **Bartholomew**.

Barton (m) Surname deriving from a
common place name, used as a first
name. Originally referred to a place
where 'barley' was grown or threshed.

Barzillai (m) Hebrew 'of iron'. Biblical,
O.T., 2 Sam. 19:31. Occasionally used
from the 17th c. onwards, especially in
the north of England.

Basil (m) Greek *basileios* 'kingly' from
Basileus 'king'. Latin *Basilius*, French
Basile. Common name in early Christian inscriptions. St Basil the Great,
bishop of Caesarea (329–379) was
defender of the Church against the
Arian heresy. Introduced to Britain by
the Crusaders, but not frequently used.
Surnames such as *Bazeley*, *Baseley*,
Bazelle, etc., are usually explained as
being from a feminine form of the name,
Basilia or **Basilie**. In modern times regularly but quietly used in Britain, rare in
the U.S., though publicized to some
extent by the actor Basil Rathbone,
known especially for his interpretation
of Sherlock Holmes in many films. More
commonly found in Eastern European
countries in such forms as Russian
Vassilij, *Vassily*, Hungarian *Bazil*, Polish *Bazyli*. The aromatic herb basil was
formerly supposed to be an antidote to
the venom of the basilisk, a fabulous
reptile. A basilica was originally a royal
palace which was then used as a church.

Basilia (f) Feminine form of **Basil**, much
used in the Middle Ages but long obsolete. The Roman martyrologies refer
to *Basilissa*, *Bassila*, *Bassilia*, *Bassilla*,
but these were not well-known saints,
nor was St Basil himself especially popular in England. E. G. Withycombe may
therefore be right to suggest that a reference to St Veronica in the medieval
Death of Pilate as Basilia was responsible for the name's use. Dr Brewer mentions that Basilia was a mythical island,
famous for its amber, but quotes no
medieval sources for the name. Also the
Latin name for the Swiss town of Basel,
or Basle, but this is hardly likely to have
led to the Christian name. Basilia was in
fact a common medieval Christian
name, but the reason for its popularity
remains something of a mystery.

Basilie (f) Feminine form of **Basil**,
perhaps more directly from the French
Basile. Used in the Middle Ages but has
long been obsolete. More common form
was **Basilia**.

Bassett (m) Surname originally describing a very small person, used regularly
as a first name.

Bathia (f) Variant of **Bethia**.

Bathsheba (f) Hebrew 'daughter of opu-
lence'. Biblical, O.T. (**Bathshua** in
Chronicles). Shrewd and thoroughly
unscrupulous wife of Uriah, who
became the mistress, and later the wife
of King David. Much used by the
Puritans and survived in popular use to
the end of the 19th c. Still occasionally
used in its pet form, **Sheba**.

Baubie (f) Scottish pet form of **Barbara**.

Bazil (m) See **Basil**. **Bazel** and **Bazyl** also
occur.

Beata (f) Latin *beatus* 'blessed' (feminine
beata). Common in several European
countries, but rarely used in the
English-speaking world.

Beatrice (f) Latin *beatricem*, Accusative
case of *beatrix* 'she who makes happy',
ultimately from *beatus* 'happy'. As
Beatrix the name is found amongst
4th c. Christian inscriptions. Used in
Britain in the Middle Ages, then rare

until the mid-19th c. Revived in the 1860s in all English-speaking countries and enjoyed a spell of great popularity until the 1920s. Subsequently little used. In literature made famous by Dante, who makes Beatrice his guide through paradise in his *Divina Commedia*. Beatrix was a common variant of the name in former times. Pet forms Bea, Beattie, Beatty, Trixie and Trissie have all been used as independent names.

Beatrix (f) See Beatrice.

Beattie (f) Transferred use of the surname as first name or a pet form of Beatrice used independently. **Beatty** is sometimes found.

Beau (m) French 'handsome'. Used mainly in the U.S. since 1960.

Beaumont (m) Common French place name which early became an English surname. Original meaning was 'beautiful hill or mountain'. Regularly used as a first name in the 19th c. but rare since the 1920s.

Becky (f) Pet form of Rebecca, regularly used as an independent name, and associated with the unscrupulous but clever Becky Sharp, of Thackeray's *Vanity Fair*.

Bede (m) Old English 'prayer'. Mainly associated with the Venerable Bede (672–735). Occasionally used as a first name in modern times.

Bedelia (f) Also Bidelia. Used in Ireland as a fanciful variant of Bridget probably by extension of Biddy. Delia is the short form, and has an alternative origin.

Bedford (m) English surname/place name regularly used as a first name.

Belinda (f) Of uncertain origin, though probably contains the Germanic element *lindi*, modern German *Lindwurm* 'dragon'. Original meaning was 'serpent', and the reference may have been to that creature's cunning. Used by Pope in *The Rape of the Lock* (1712). Regularly used since, both in Britain and the U.S. The actress Belinda Lee (1935–61) helped to make the name popular in Britain before her tragic death in a car crash. **Belynda** also occurs.

Bell (m, f) Surname, deriving from various sources, used as a first name. Frequent in the 19th c. May also have represented a pet form of names such as Belinda, and Belle may have been intended in some cases.

Bella (f) Usually regarded as an 18th c. abbreviation of Latin forms such as Isabella amd Annabella. At its earliest appearance, however, a Latinization of Old French *bele* 'beautiful', modern French *belle*. Surnames such as *Bella* and *Bele* show that Bella was in use in the 13th c. Then disappeared until the 18th c., when it became fashionable. Subsequently used regularly but infrequently, though Bella Abzug, New York politician, has recently given it publicity in the U.S.

Belle (f) French 'beautiful'. In the 20th c. a direct borrowing of the French word. Formerly a pet form of Isabel or Isobel. Popular in the U.S. and Canada in the 1870s, but used rarely since.

Ben (m) Pet form of Benjamin, Benedict, Bennett, Benson, Bentley, etc., used as a name in its own right. The name Reuben is also likely to be reduced to Ben as a pet form.

Benedetta (f) Italian feminine form of Benedetto, or Benedict, but rarely used in English-speaking countries.

Benedict (m) Latin *Benedictus* 'blessed'. Old French *Beneit*, now *Benoît*, Italian *Benedetto*, Spanish *Benedicto*, *Benito*. Made famous by St Benedict, founder of the Benedictine Order in the 6th c. Usual English form of this name since the 12th c. has been Bennet, based on the medieval French form. Use of the name in the Middle Ages is shown by the common surnames *Bennet*, *Bennett*, *Bennitt*, *Bennison*, etc. The Latinized Benedict has been used mainly by Roman Catholics, though this may change. Little used in the U.S., perhaps because of the associations with Benedict Arnold (1741–1801), the Revolutionary traitor. Shakespeare named a character Benedick in *Much Ado About Nothing*, which leads to

28

occasional literary references to 'a
Benedick (or Benedict) – a married man,
especially one who appeared to be a
confirmed bachelor'. In Scandinavia
Benedict is found as **Bengt** or **Bent**,
forms more commonly used than is
Benedict in English-speaking countries.

Benedicta (f) Feminine of Benedict, very
rarely used. Spanish diminutive **Benita**
preferred in modern times.

Bengt (m) Swedish form of Benedict,
occasionally used by American families
of Swedish descent. Feminine form of
the name is **Bengta**.

Benita (f) Spanish feminine of Benito,
itself a diminutive of **Benedicto**. Regularly used in the U.S. and has appeared
in Britain since the 1930s, without
becoming especially fashionable.

Benito (m) Spanish diminutive of Benedicto, or **Benedict**. Used in the U.S. until
the Italian dictator Benito Mussolini
(1883–1945) sullied its image.

Benjamin (m) Hebrew 'son of my right
hand'. Biblical, O.T., name of the son of
Rachel and Jacob. Rachel, who realized
that she was about to die after giving
birth to him, suggested that he be called
Benoni, 'son of my sorrow'. Jacob
changed it to Benjamin. Used by the
Puritans in the 17th c., then continued
in regular use until the end of the 19th c.
Famous bearers included Benjamin
Franklin (1706–90) and Benjamin
Disraeli (1804–81), but the name had
become almost exclusively Jewish by
the beginning of the 20th c. Suddenly
revived on all sides in the 1960s, and it is
highly likely that Dustin Hoffman's
portrayal of a character called Benjamin
in *The Graduate*, a film released in
1967, reminded parents of the name. At
this time O.T. names were generally in
fashion. Pet forms **Ben**, **Bennie** and
Benny, are often used independently.
Benn is also found, and **Benna** has been
used as a feminine form. Modern spelling variants, accidental or deliberate,
include **Benejaman, Benjamen, Benja-
mon, Benjimon, Benjiman**.

Benn (m) Surname, usually linked with

Benedict, used as a first name from time
to time.

Bennett (m) Often **Bennet**. The usual
English forms of Benedict, introduced
to England as Old French *Beneit*. Bennet
and Bennett were always more frequent
than Benedict itself until the 1970s,
when the latter form showed signs of
becoming fashionable.

Benny (m) Pet form of **Benjamin**,
Benedict, etc., used in its own right. Variant **Bennie** is sometimes used.

Benson (m) Surname, 'son of Ben', regularly used as a first name in the 19th c.
Recently associated with the black
butler in the television series *Soap*, followed by the series based on Benson
himself.

Bent (m) Danish form of Benedict, or
Bennet. Feminine form is **Bente**.

Bentley (m) Place name/surname occasionally used as a first name. The 'bent'
in the name originally referred to 'bent
grass', a kind of coarse, reedy grass. In
the 1920s, especially, associated with
the racing cars developed by W. O.
Bentley, many times winners of the Le
Mans race. Dickens had earlier used the
name for Bentley Drummle, a highly
unpleasant character in *Great Expectations*. Mainly found between the 1880s
and the 1920s, but never used in great
numbers.

Berenice (f) Also **Bernice**. Original pronunciation was *Beren-ikie*; now tends to
be *Beren-eece*. Greek *Pherenice* 'bringing victory', Latin *Berenice, Beronice,
Veronice, Bernice*. Found in Christian
inscriptions in early Rome. Biblical,
N.T., Acts 25:13. Introduced into Britain after the Reformation but scarcely
used until the end of the 19th c., Bernice
being the usual form. Regularly but
infrequently used in the 20th c. Pet
forms include **Barrie, Berry** and **Bunny**.

Beresford (m) English surname derived
from a place name, regularly used as a
first name from the 1880s to the 1930s,
though never in great numbers. Berres-
ford is also found.

Berkeley (m) English place name and

surname, originally indicating a 'birch wood'. Regularly if infrequently used as a first name. Scottish surname **Barclay**, also used on occasion as a first name, derives from it. **Berkley** is a fairly common variant.

Bernadette (f) Feminine form of **Bernard**, made famous by Marie Bernarde Soubirous, the girl who saw visions of the Virgin Mary at Lourdes. Her name began to be used in increasing numbers after her canonization in 1933. A film about her life released in the 1940s also helped the name along, especially amongst Roman Catholic families. By the early 1980s, however, rarely used in any English-speaking country. Bernadette is the usual spelling, but **Bernardette** is a frequent variant. **Bernadett** and **Bernette** are also found.

Bernadina (f) Feminine form of **Bernard** in occasional use since the beginning of the 20th c.

Bernal (m) Old German 'bear – power'. In modern German this name is *Bernald*, *Bernold* or *Bernhold*. Bernal has been used occasionally since the beginning of the 20th c. in English-speaking countries. Occasionally found as **Bernel**.

Bernard (m) Old German 'bear – brave'. Popular name amongst the Normans, who introduced it to Britain in the 11th c. At this time the St Bernard who was later to be patron saint of Alpinists was active. He founded the order after which the famous dogs were later named. Another well-known St Bernard was writing his theological works in the 12th c. Well used in England until the 18th c., when it began to fade. Had almost disappeared by 1850 but revived to reach a minor peak of popularity in the 1920s and '30s, in the U.S. as well as Britain. Subsequently declined again, and in the early 1980s being quietly used. Black American parents were by this time using it far more often than whites. Irish parents were also using it rather more than parents elsewhere in Britain. Some well-known modern bearers of the name are George Bernard Shaw (1856–1950), the playwright, and British actors Bernard Bresslaw and Bernard Cribbins. Often found as **Bernhard**. Feminine forms include **Bernardette** (usually spelt **Bernadette**), **Bernadina**, **Bernardine**, **Bernette**.

Bernardine (f) Occasional feminine form of **Bernard**. **Bernadine** also occurs, with variants **Bernadene** and **Bernadina**.

Bernice (f) Usual modern spelling, especially in the U.S., of **Berenice**.

Berry (m, f) Botanical name introduced in the 1880s. In some cases used as a pet form of **Berenice**, **Bernice**, **Beryl** or **Bertha**. In the U.S. now more often a male name when used independently, perhaps a form of **Bernard**.

Bersaba (f) Cornish form of **Bathsheba**.

Bert (m) Pet form of names which contain this element, such as **Bertram** and **Albert**, but used fairly consistently as an independent name. Variants **Birt** and **Burt** are found.

Berta (f) German form of **Bertha**, or pet form of **Roberta**, occasionally used in English-speaking countries.

Bertha (f) Teutonic: Old German *Berahta*, *Perahta*, name of a female deity from *beraht* 'bright'. Camden listed Bertha as 'a usual Christian name' in 1605. Disappeared, but came into regular use in the mid-19th c. By the 1870s very popular both in Britain and the U.S. Declined in popularity progressively to the 1920s and has since been little used.

Berthold (m) Old German 'bright – power'. Occasionally used in English-speaking countries.

Bertie (m) Pet form of names such as **Albert** and **Bertram**, but used as a name in its own right. Associated in Britain since 1934 with Bertie Wooster, the genial upper-class ass of the P. G. Wodehouse stories.

Bertina (f) Pet form of **Albertina** used independently on rare occasions. **Bertine** from **Albertine** is also found.

Bertram (m) Old German *beraht-hraban* 'bright raven'. Perhaps the same name

30

as **Bertrand**, though the latter may contain the second element *rant* 'shield'. Introduced to Britain by the Normans, and giving rise to many surnames such as *Bartram*, *Bertram*, *Battram*, etc. Became almost obsolete in the 18th c., but strongly revived in the 1860s in England. Well used until 1930, but has since faded. Shakespeare has a Count Bertram in *All's Well That Ends Well*. Usual pet forms of the name are Bert, Bertie and Berty, all also independent names. Always rare in the U.S.

Bertrand (m) Perhaps simply a French form of **Bertram** or an independent name meaning 'bright shield'. Never as frequently used as Bertram, but made well-known by Bertrand Russell (1872–1970), the English mathematician and philosopher.

Berty (m) See Bertie.

Berwyn (m) Old English, possibly 'bear-friend' or 'bright friend'. Anglo-Saxon name, occasionally revived in modern times.

Beryl (f) Sanskrit *veruliya* (*veluliya*) probably deriving from the city of *Velur*, now *Belur*. Greek *berullos*, Latin *beryllus*, Old French *béryl*. Appeared in Britain in the last quarter of the 19th c. when there was something of a vogue for jewel names. Reached its peak in the 1920s, then declined rapidly. Little used in the U.S.

Bessey (f) 19th c. variant of Bessie.

Bessie (f) Pet form of Elizabeth, used independently since the 17th c. Reached a peak in the U.S. in the 1870s. Now rare, though surviving to some extent in Scotland. Bessey and Bessy were frequent variants formerly.

Bessy (f) See Bessie.

Beta (f) Likely to be the pet-form of Elizabeth common to several European languages such as Czech, Slovenian, rather than the Greek letter 'B' which it appears to be. However, **Alpha** and other Greek letters are used as names from time to time. Occurs rarely in English-speaking countries.

Beth (f) Pet form of Elizabeth used independently. Since the 1960s used more frequently than Betty. Also the short form of Bethany.

Bethan (f) Apparently a short form of Bethany. The variant **Bethanne** indicates that it may be thought of as a blend of Beth and Ann(e). First used in the 1940s, intermittently since.

Beth-Ann(e) (f) Combination of Beth and Ann(e) popular since the 1960s in the U.S.

Bethany (f) Biblical place name, of which the first element *beth* means 'house'. The second element is unclear. The village is mentioned in N.T. as the home of Lazarus. Has been enjoying a spell of popularity since the late 1960s. Bethanie is a rare variant.

Bethel (m, f) Surname, or the Biblical place name, used as a first name. The surname is usually Welsh, meaning 'son of Ithel' ('generous lord'); it can also derive from Elizabeth. The Biblical name means 'house of God'; Abraham built an altar there – Gen. 12:8. As a first name, used only occasionally. Found also as Bethell.

Bethia (f) Hebrew *bith yah* 'daughter (worshipper) of Jehovah'. Biblical, O.T., 1 Chron. 4:18. Well used in former times when O.T. names were popular, sometimes in its alternative form Bithiah. In Scotland a substitute for Gaelic Beathag 'life'. Occasionally a Latinized form of Beth.

Bethsheba (f) Variant of **Bathsheba** which occurs in 19th c. records. Obviously influenced by the form of the name in the Douai Version of the Bible, namely Bethsabee.

Betina (f) Variant of Bettina.

Betsy (f) Alternative form of Betty, which it replaced temporarily towards the end of the 19th c. Betsey was formerly a common variant. Both forms now rarely used.

Bette (f) French form of Betty, given much publicity by the actress Bette Davis (1908–), originally Ruth Elizabeth Davies. Used only occasionally in English-speaking countries.

Bettie (f) See **Betty**.

Bettina (f) Spanish/Italian form of **Betty**. Enjoyed a spell of popularity in the 1960s, having been used sporadically earlier this century. Variant **Betina** occurs.

Bettine (f) French diminutive of **Betty**, regularly, if infrequently, used this century in English-speaking countries.

Betty (f) Pet form of **Elizabeth** which has long been used independently. Extremely well used in the 18th c. and early 19th c., then declined. Revived to become one of the most popular names in all English-speaking countries around 1925, but has subsequently faded again. In the 1960s there was a tendency to use it in combination with other names, and **Betty Ann**, **Betty Jo**, **Betty Lou**, **Betty Mae** and **Betty Sue** were used. **Bettie** sometimes occurs as a variant, together with **Betti**. **Bette** is a French version of the name, and the Italians use **Betta** and **Bettina**. Two famous bearers of the name have been Betty Grable – a favourite pin-up of servicemen during World War Two – and Betty Hutton (Betty Jane Thorburg), singer and dancer in many films from 1940 onwards.

Beulah (f) Hebrew: *beulah* 'married (woman)'. Biblical, O.T., Isaiah 62:4. Applied as a place name to Israel. Also in John Bunyan's *Pilgrim's Progress* as the name of the land of heavenly joy. Introduced as a girl's name after the Reformation and in regular but infrequent use since. In the U.S. it is now favoured especially by black American parents. The actress Beulah Bondi appeared very regularly on screen from the 1930s.

Bevan (m) Welsh surname 'son of **Evan**' used this century in Wales, especially, as a first name. **Bevin** also occurs.

Beverley (m, f) Place name (in Yorkshire, England) 'beaver stream', also a surname. T. P. R. Layng reports that Thos. Woods married Beverley Farrar in Huntingdon, England, in 1778. In the U.S. the name is usually **Beverley**. The silent film actress Beverly Baine seems to have taken her stage name from Beverly Hills, the famous suburb of Los Angeles. Beverly was much used in the U.S. as a girl's name 1920-50, subsequently going out of fashion. Reached Britain by 1950 and was amongst the top names of the 1960s. In Britain, as in Australia, Beverley is slightly preferred as the girl's name. This was also the spelling of the male name which came into use in the 18th c., e.g. Beverley Nichols, English novelist. The name in this case was a transferred use of the surname.

Beverly (f) Usual American and Canadian spelling of **Beverley**. The opera singer Beverly Sills, is a well-known name-bearer.

Bevis (m) Place name (from Beauvais, in France) or surname (perhaps Old French *bel fiz* 'dear son') used on rare occasions as a first name. The novel *Bevis* (1882) by Richard Jefferies, seems to have had little effect on usage.

Bianca (f) Italian 'white'. Occasionally used in English-speaking countries. Shakespeare used the name in *The Taming of the Shrew* for Kate's younger sister, who was as mild as her sister was violent. In *Othello* Bianca is a courtesan.

Biddie (f) Irish pet form of **Bridget**, or **Brigid**, occasionally used as an independent name.

Bill (m) Pet form of **William** used as a name in its own right. Use of this form began in the 1840s and has continued regularly but infrequently since. An old joke has it that it is a good name for a baby 'who comes at the end of the month'.

Billie (m, f) Originally a pet form of **William** used independently, now also used as a girl's name.

Billie-Jean (f) Blend of **Billie** and **Jean** made popular in the 1970s by Mrs Billie-Jean King, the tennis player.

Billy (m) Originally a pet form of **William**, now used independently. Variant **Billie** used for both sexes. Combinations such as **Billy Joe** and **Billy Ray** are now popular.

Bina (f) Pet form of **Sabina**, **Robina**, **Albina**, **Columbina**, **Jacobina**, etc., used independently in modern times.

Bing (m) Nickname of the singer, Bing Crosby, born Harry Lillis Crosby. He received the name as a boy because of his admiration of (and possibly resemblance to) a comic-strip character called Bingo. In occasional modern use as a first name.

Binns (m) Surname of several possible origins, regularly used as a first name in the 19th c.

Birch (m) Place name/surname 'birch tree', regularly used as a first name in the 19th c.

Birdie (f) Diminutive of 'bird', occasionally used as a first name.

Birgitta (f) Swedish form of **Bridget**. Has many pet forms, including **Bittan**, **Birgit**, **Britt**, **Britta**, **Brita**, **Berit**. Some argue that it means 'daughter of **Birger** ('protection')' rather than 'the high one' as in the case of Bridget. Forms of this name used by Scandinavian settlers in the U.S.

Birt (m) Common variant of **Bert**.

Birtie (m) Also **Birty**. See **Bertie**.

Birtha (f) See **Bertha**.

Bithiah (f) See **Bethia**.

Bittan (f) Scandinavian pet form of **Birgitta**, or **Bridget**.

Björn (m) Scandinavian name meaning 'bear', made known in modern times by the Swedish tennis champion Björn Borg. Occasionally used in English-speaking countries.

Blackburn (m) English place name and surname, used fairly regularly in the 19th c. as a first name.

Blaine (m) Apparently a use of the surname Blaine, 'servant of St Blaan or Blane', a 7th c. Scottish saint. In regular use as a first name in the U.S. since the 1930s, and in Britain since the 1950s.

Blair (m) Scottish surname, derived from a place name meaning 'a flat piece of land', used regularly if infrequently as a first name. Main use was in the 1950s and '60s. By the early 1980s also being

used as a girl's name in the U.S.

Blaise (m) Latin *blaesus* 'crippled, stuttering'. The Roman family name Blassus (Blasius, Blasio) indicated an ancestor who was a stutterer. St Blaise or Blase was martyred in the 4th c. Still used regularly, if infrequently.

Blake (m) Surname used as a first name in modern times, originally in honour of the English admiral Robert Blake (1598–1657). One well-known bearer of the name is the 'Pink Panther' film director Blake Edwards (1922–). Used rather more in the U.S. than elsewhere, and occasionally for girls.

Blanch (f) Early form of **Blanche**.

Blanche (f) French *blanche* 'white', feminine of *blanc*. Translation of Latin **Candida**, the name of several saints. Blanche or **Blanch** used regularly but infrequently from the 16th c. to the 18th c., then very rare until the end of the 19th c. Became a prime favourite in the U.S. 1870–1900, but little used since in any English-speaking country.

Blodwen (f) Welsh *blodyn* 'flower' and *(g)wen* 'white, fair'. Regularly used by Welsh parents since the 1890s. Apparently a translation of **Blanchefleur** (the heroine of Boccaccio's prose romance *Il Filocopo*). **Blodwyn** is an occasional variant of Blodwen.

Blodyn (f) Welsh *blodyn* 'flower, blossom'. Used as a Christian name in Wales. See also **Flora**.

Blossom (f) Transferred use of the word as first name. Used in the flower name period, at the turn of the century, and occasionally revived in the 1960s.

Bluebell (f) Flower name, used to some extent as a first name when flower names were in vogue at the end of the 19th c. Now rare in Britain, perhaps because it became a favourite name for a cow before numbers and code-names became the norm in farming circles.

Blythe (f) Probably a use of the English river name.

Boadicea (f) Name of an early British queen. She led an army which slew at least 70,000 Romans, but later poisoned herself to avoid capture. Occasionally used by British parents as a first name.

Boaz (m) Hebrew 'in him is strength'. The name of two men mentioned in the Bible, including one of Christ's direct ancestors. Used by the 17th c. Puritans, and carried by them to the U.S. Continued to be used on irregular occasions until the beginning of the 20th c.

Bob (m) Pet form of **Robert** which came after **Rob** and **Dob**. Used as an independent name since the mid-19th c. Occasionally also the pet form of **Roberta**.

Bobbie (m, f) Pet form of **Robert**, **Roberta** and **Barbara**. Used regularly but infrequently.

Bobby (m) Pet form of **Robert** used independently. This spelling is used for males, while **Bobbie** can be used for both sexes. In recent years combinations such as **Bobby Joe**, **Bobby Lee** and **Bobby Ray** have been favoured.

Bolton (m) English place name and surname occasionally used as a first name.

Bonar (m) Old French *bonnaire* 'gentle, courteous'. Shortened form of *debonnaire*. A surname since the 13th c., especially common in Scotland. Andrew Bonar Law (1858–1923) made the name well-known when he was British Prime Minister, but it has never been extensively used.

Boniface (m) Latin *Bonifatius* 'of good fate', i.e. *bonum fatum*, not connected with Latin *facio* 'to do', though 'well-doer' has been the usual interpretation since Camden (1605). Very common name in early Christian inscriptions and the name of several popes, but never much used in English-speaking countries. Change in spelling from *Bonifatius* to *Bonifacius* by the 13th c. presumably due to the pronunciation *-fashjus*. Used by Farquhar in his comedy *The Beaux' Stratagem* (1707) as the surname of the 'bonny-faced' inn-keeper.

Bonita (f) Spanish, feminine of *bonito* 'pretty'. Fashionable name in the early 1940s in the U.S. and introduced to Britain a few years later.

Bonnie (f) A Scottish word, but deriving from French *bonne* 'good'. Bonnie Birdie Twist is a character in *Over Bemerton's* (1908) by E. V. Lucas, but modern use undoubtedly derives from Margaret Mitchell's *Gone With The Wind* (1939). The child of Melanie and Rhett Butler is named Eugene Victoria, but in a discussion about the colour of the child's eyes the mother claims they will be 'as blue as the bonnie blue flag'. ' "Bonnie Blue Butler", laughed Rhett, and Bonnie she became until even her parents did not recall she had been named for two queens'. In the U.S. mainly used by white parents. Variant **Bonny** is occasionally found, but both Bonnie and Bonny sometimes represent a pet form of **Bonita**. Further exposed in the late 1960s by the film *Bonnie and Clyde*.

Booth (m) Surname of William Booth (1829–1929), founder of the Salvation Army, also of his son William Bramwell Booth who continued his work. Used as a first name in their honour mainly in the 19th c.

Boris (m) From a Slavonic word meaning 'battle, fight'. Little used in English-speaking countries, perhaps because of its associations with the well-known horror movie actor Boris Karloff, born William Pratt (1887–1969). Given much publicity when Boris Pasternak won the Nobel Prize for Literature in 1958 with his novel *Dr Zhivago*.

Boy (m) The word used as a name – though only on rare occasions. **Laddie** has also been used as a first name and **Junior** is fairly frequent in both the U.S. and Britain. The only equivalent name for girls appears to be **Colleen**.

Boyce (m) Use of the surname (from French *bois* 'wood') as first name.

Boyd (m) Gaelic *buidhe* 'yellow (hair)'. Well-known Scottish clan name. The surname can also derive from 'isle of Bute'. Long used as a first name in Scotland. Since 1939 the more widespread usage may be due to its occurrence in Margaret Mitchell's *Gone With The*

Wind, where Boyd Tarleton is found.

Brad (m) Pet form of **Bradley** (less often **Bradford**) regularly used as an independent name, especially by white parents in the U.S. and Canada. **Bradd** occurs.

Bradford (m) Common English place name indicating a 'broad ford', and the surname, e.g. of William Bradford, one of the passengers on the *Mayflower*. He became first governor of Plymouth, Mass. Consistently used in the U.S. but rare elsewhere.

Bradley (m) Old English *brād lēah* 'broad clearing', a common English place name leading to a surname. As a Christian name Bradley has mainly been used in the U.S., almost exclusively by white parents. Originally use of the name may have been in honour of General Omar Nelson Bradley, commander of the 12th Army Group in Europe during World War Two. Used intermittently in Britain since the 1850s. The pet form **Brad** occurs regularly as an independent name. In *Our Mutual Friend*, by Charles Dickens, Bradley Headstone is the dangerously passionate man who falls in love with Lizzie Hexam.

Brady (m) Surname used as a first name, especially in the U.S. Derives either from a place name 'broad island', or from a personal nickname 'broad eye'.

Bram (m) Dutch contraction of **Abraham** used to some extent in the U.S. Bram Stoker (1847–1912) wrote *Dracula* (1897).

Bramwell (m) English place name 'broom well' or 'bramble well' which early became a surname. Regularly used as a first name in Britain since the 1880s, probably because of William Bramwell Booth (1856–1929), second General of the Salvation Army. See also **Branwell**.

Branden (m) Frequent modern variant of **Brandon**. **Brandan** also occurs.

Brandi (f) Variant of **Brandy**. Especially well used by black American families in the early 1980s. **Brandee** also occurs.

Brandon (m) Common English place name 'hill covered with broom', or in Ireland 'descendant of **Brendan**', when a surname. In regular use as a first name since the 1930s, especially in the U.S. Since **Brandy** (**Brandi**) became a popular girl's name in the U.S., Brandon has occasionally been used as a feminine name.

Brandy (f) Apparently a transferred use of the word, frequently used as a first name, especially in the U.S. **Brandi** had become the preferred spelling by the early 1980s, especially amongst black American families. **Brandee, Brandie** also occur.

Branwell (m) Variant of **Bramwell**. Occasionally used as a first name, the best-known bearer being (Patrick) Branwell Brontë (1817–48), brother of the Brontë sisters.

Brenda (f) Possibly from Old Norse *brandr* 'sword'. Established early in Scotland and widely used in all English-speaking countries this century, especially in the 1940s. Often taken to be a feminine of **Brendan**.

Brendan (m) Irish 'stinking hair'. Name of a 6th c. Irish saint. Mount Brandon in County Kerry is named for him, which leads to **Brandon** and **Brendon** being used as variants. The popularity of the athlete Brendan Foster helped the name along in Britain in the 1970s. Its use in the U.S. appears to be increasing.

Brent (m) Place name/surname used in modern times as a first name. The place name probably meant 'high place', but some bearers of the surname may have had an ancestor who was 'burnt', i.e. branded as a criminal. There is also a River Brent in England, the origin of which is probably the same as **Bridget**. Earliest use of the first name appears to have been in the U.S. in the 1930s. By 1940 had reached Britain, and usage subsequently increased. Especially popular in Canada in the 1970s. **Brenton** occurs as a variant. The use of the name by Margaret Mitchell in *Gone With the Wind* for one of the Tarleton twins may have helped the name along after 1939.

Brett (m) Latin *Britto* 'Briton, Breton'.

writer Bret Harte (Francis Brett Harte 1836–1902). Especially well used in Australia in recent times, perhaps because of General George Howard Brett, Chief of Allied Air Forces in the South West Pacific during World War Two. **Bret** is occasionally used, and there is a modern extended form of the name, **Bretton**.

Brewster (m) Occupational surname, indicating a (female) 'brewer', used as a first name. American parents sometimes have William Brewster in mind, the Puritan leader.

Brian (m) Of unknown origin, though possibly containing an element which means 'hill'. Long associated with Ireland because of the celebrated King Brian Boroimhe (926–1014). Popular in all English-speaking countries 1925–70, now tending to fade. **Bryan** is a frequent variant, **Bryon** is also found. **Briana** and **Briane** have occasionally been used as feminine forms. By the early 1980s **Briann**, **Brianna**, **Brianne** were also being used in that role, while Brian itself was occasionally given to American girls.

Brice (m) Earlier spelling of **Bryce**.

Bride (f) Obsolete English form of Bridget. The word *bride* 'wife' is not connected.

Bridget (f) From French **Brigitte**, earlier **Brigette**, Latin **Brigitta**, Irish **Brigit**, **Brigid**, **Brighid**. Name of an ancient Irish goddess, probably meaning 'the high one', though Woulfe derives it (*Irish Names for Children*) from Irish *brigh* 'strength'. Made famous by St Bridget (or St **Bride**), patroness of Ireland, who died in the 6th c. The 14th c. Swedish saint **Birgitta**, known also as St Bridget, was the daughter of **Birger**, 'protection', but modern authorities (e.g. Roland Otterbjörk in *Svenska Förnamn*) derive her name from that of the Celtic goddess previously mentioned. In Ireland Bridget (less often Brigid) became a very popular name from the 18th c. Both forms well used until the 1950s, but subsequently fell away. Also

Surname made known as a first name by the American poet and short story popular in Scotland in the 1930s, but never used to any great extent in other English-speaking countries. Irish pet forms **Biddie** and **Bridie** occasionally occur as independent names. **Bedelia** (pet form **Delia**) is a variant of Bridget in Ireland and this also occurs independently. The spelling **Bridgett(e)** occurs fairly frequently. In the U.S., amongst families of Scandinavian descent, pet forms of Birgitta or Brigitta are used as names in their own right. These include **Bittan**, **Birgit**, **Britt**, **Brita**, **Britta**.

Bridie (f) Irish pet form of **Bridget**, or **Bride** (Irish **Brighde**, oblique form of **Brigid**). Found occasionally as an independent name.

Brigette (f) Variant of **Bridget**, influenced by French **Brigitte**. Occurs since the 1950s.

Brigham (m) English place name and surname, originally indicating a 'hamlet near a bridge'. Used as a first name in the mid-19th c., especially, no doubt in honour of Brigham Young (1801–77), the Mormon leader.

Brighton (m) English place name used as a first name, on rare occasions only. The place concerned has a jokey reputation connected with extra-marital weekend activities.

Brigid (f) Irish form of **Bridget**. **Brighid** is a modern variant.

Brigitta (f) Latinized form of **Bridget**, used in Scandinavia as an alternative to **Birgitta**.

Brigitte (f) French form of **Bridget**, used occasionally in English-speaking countries, e.g. Canada. The French actress Brigitte Bardot (Camille Javal) gave the name a particular image of provocative sexiness in the 1950s and '60s.

Brinley (m) Apparently the use of a surname deriving from a place name, used as a Christian name in England and Wales regularly if infrequently since the 1880s. The origin is possibly Old English *brend* 'burnt' *lēah* 'wood' or 'clearing'. Also occurs as **Brynley, Brinly, Brindley, Brynly.**

Briony (f) See **Bryony**.

Brita (f) Pet form of **Birgitta** (Bridget), used occasionally in its own right.

Britannia (f) Latin *Britannia* 'Britain' or 'Brittany'. The feminine personification of Britain on the coins, etc. Occasionally used in Britain as a Christian name since the 18th c., perhaps with special reference to the patriotic song 'Rule, Britannia'. **Britania, Brittania** and **Brittannia** occur as variants.

Britt(a) (f) Pet forms of **Birgitta** (Bridget) used occasionally as independent names.

Brittan (f) Probably a back-formation from **Britannia**, or a phonetic variant of Briton. Used sporadically in Britain.

Brittania (f) See **Britannia**.

Brittany (f) Name of French coastal province used as a first name. Also **Brittney, Britni, Britney**, etc.

Brock (m) Old English 'badger'. Probably the surname used as a first name. Found mainly in the U.S.

Broderick (m) Probably from Norse *Brodhir* 'brother', the name once given to a second son. Became an Irish surname and taken as such to Scotland. Now thought of as a Scottish first name, though it occurs only rarely in that country. Well publicized in the 1930s and '40s by the actor Broderick Crawford (mother's maiden name Helen Broderick).

Bronwen (f) Welsh *bron* 'breast' and *(g)wen* 'fair, white'. **Bronwyn** is a common variant. Both forms steadily used since the end of the 19th c. **Rowena** appears in some ancient manuscripts as **Ronwen**, which has caused some scholars to link the names, but it is unlikely that they are connected. In modern times **Bronya** has also been used – presumably a development from Bronwen, but Welsh name dictionaries give no information about it.

Brook (m, f) Surname used as a first name. As a surname Brook(e) indicates an ancestor who lived near a brook or stream. Brooke also occurs regularly, especially in the U.S., as a first name, with much publicity recently given to the actress Brooke Shields. **Brookes** occurs occasionally, as well as **Brooks**. Since the 1920s **Brookie** has also been in regular, if infrequent, use.

Bruce (m) Surname of Robert Bruce (1274–1329), liberator and king of Scotland. Derives ultimately from a Norman place name. Used as a first name in Scotland, then in other English-speaking countries since the 1930s. **Brucine** has been used as a feminine form.

Bruno (m) Old German *brun* 'of dark complexion, brown' or 'bear-like'. St Bruno (1030–1101) was founder of the Carthusian Order. Used mainly in the U.S. by families of German descent. **Brunetta** occurs as a feminine form.

Bryan (m) Popular variant of **Brian**.

Bryant (m) Surname connected with **Brian**, used as a first name. Especially popular with black American families.

Bryce (m) Celtic personal name of uncertain origin. As a Scottish surname it probably indicated a devotee of St Brice (Bricius, Brixius) of Tours, a 5th c. bishop. Normal spelling of the first name in the 19th c. was **Brice**, but in modern times Bryce is preferred.

Bryden (m) Place name/surname occasionally used as a first name in the 20th c.

Bryn (m) Welsh *bryn* 'hill, mound'. A 20th c. conversion to Christian name status. Fairly well used by Welsh parents. Also serves as a pet form of **Brynley** and **Brynmor**.

Brynley (m) Variant of **Brinley**. **Brynly** also occurs.

Brynmor (m) Welsh *bryn* 'hill' and *mawr* 'great'. Place name used in modern times as a Christian name in Wales. Pet form is **Bryn**.

Bryon (m) Fairly common variant of **Brian** in use since the 1930s.

Bryony (f) Botanical name used as a first

name. Popular since the 1930s. **Briony** is a frequent variant.

Buck (m) See Penny.

Bud (m) Short for **Buddy** 'friend, companion', often used vocatively. The origin is said to be a childish or illiterate pronunciation of 'brother'. Both Bud and Buddy are occasionally used as first names, though Bud Abbott, the straight man of the Abbott and Costello team, was actually William Abbott (1895–1974).

Bunny (f) Pet form of **Bernice** (**Berenice**).

Burnet(t) (m) Surname of several possible origins, regularly used as a first name in the 19th c. **Burnitt** was also used occasionally.

Burt (m) Pet form of **Burton** used as a name in its own right. See Burton. Since the 1940s has been associated with the American actor Burt Lancaster, but never widely used.

Burton (m) From the surname, itself from the common English place name deriving from Old English *burh tun* 'fortified enclosure' or 'farm near a fort'. Came into use in England as a Christian name in the 1850s, possibly as a result of the fame of Sir Richard Francis Burton

(1821–90), the English explorer, writer and linguist. Quietly used this century in all English-speaking countries. **Burt** is the normal pet form, often written as **Bert**.

Buster (m) Nickname, especially in the U.S., for a jovial active boy. Also a term of address to a man whose name is unknown, but one that is not likely to be appreciated by the person so addressed. Nickname of Joseph Francis Keaton, the clown of the silent screen. Use of Buster as a first name may well be in honour of him. Rarely used, but found in Britain as well as the U.S.

Byron (m) From the surname, especially of Lord George Gordon Byron (1784–1824) the English poet. The surname derives from a place name which is based on Old English *byre* 'cow shed or barn'. The meaning could be 'place where there were cow sheds', or by metonymy, 'one who looked after cattle'. First used as a Christian name in the 1850s and regularly in use since. In the U.S. especially favoured by black American parents, but also used by whites.

C

Cadel(l) (m) Welsh 'battle'. Medieval Welsh name rarely used in modern times.

Caesar (m) Latin *Caesarius* 'hairy child' (possibly), though the famous Gaius Julius Caesar was bald. The popular connection with a Caesarian operation arose because Julius Caesar was born in that way, but he was not named to commemorate that fact: the name was already in existence. Well represented as a Christian name in inscriptions of the Roman Empire. A 6th c. bishop who bore the name caused the Roman Catholic Church to sanction its use. Perhaps for ironic reasons it became a

characteristic slave name in the 18th c. Well represented in Puckett's lists (*Black Names in America*), and Mrs Aphra Behn, in her novel *Oroonoko* (1698), says that Oroonoko's owner renamed him Caesar. Still used by black American families, who probably interpret it in the general sense of 'emperor' – cf. *Czar*, *Kaiser* which derive from Caesar. Spelling variants include Caezar, Cesar, Seasar, Sezar.

Cai (m) Welsh form of Caius, itself a form of **Gaius**.

Cain (m) Hebrew 'a spear', Biblical, O.T., the first son of Adam. He murdered his brother Abel in a fit of jealousy. Regularly used throughout the 19th c. Its reappearance in Britain in the 1970s as a girl's name probably points to the use of Welsh *cain* 'beautiful', rather than the biblical character.

Caio (m) Welsh form of **Caius**, a variant of **Gaius**. Also a Welsh place name and its use as a Christian name may occasionally derive from that source.

Caitlin (f) See **Kathleen**.

Caitriona (f) Irish form of **Catriona**. Infrequently used.

Caius (m) Alternative form of **Gaius**.

Caleb (m) Hebrew *Kalebh* either 'a dog' or 'bold, staunch'. Biblical, O.T., Num. 13:6. One of the twelve men sent by Moses to spy out the land of Canaan. With Joshua he entered the promised land. Used by the Puritans in the 16th c. and carried by them to the U.S. Remained in regular use until the 1920s, but now extremely rare in all English-speaking countries.

Callum (m) See **Calum**.

Calum (m) Gaelic form of **Columba**. Also used in Scotland as a pet form of **Malcolm**.

Calvert (m) Old English *calf-hierde* 'calf-herder'. English surname regularly used as a first name, especially during the 19th c.

Calvin (m) Latin *Calvinus*, from *calvus* 'bald'. Name of a Roman clan. First used as a Christian name in honour of John Calvin (1509–64), the Genevan Protestant reformer, who was born Jean Chauvin. *Chauvin* (the name of a literary character which led to 'chauvinist') also means 'bald', from French *chauve*. Later, in the U.S. where the name has always been more used than in Britain, Calvin was associated with President (John) Calvin Coolidge, 1872–1933. Has long been a popular name with black American parents.

Camelia (f) From the flower name Camellia, which commemorated the Jesuit George Joseph Kamel, traveller and botanist. Used as a first name since the 1930s. In some instances may be meant for **Camilla**. **Camellia** also found.

Cameron (m) Transferred use of the Scottish clan name and surname, which derives either from Gaelic *camshron* 'crooked, hook nose' or from a place name where the meaning is 'crooked stream'. Rare as a Christian name until the 1950s, but popular in Scotland, Canada and Australia in the 1970s.

Camilla (f) Latin, feminine of **Camillus**, the origin of which is unknown. Camilla, virgin queen of the Volscians, famous for her swiftness of foot, is mentioned in Virgil's *Aeneid*, Book VII. Lyly used the name for a character in his *Euphues*, and a woman of the name succumbs to temptation in Cervantes' *Don Quixote*. Fanny Burney wrote a novel called *Camilla* in which the heroine is 'light, airy, poor and imprudent, but gentle'. Steadily used in English-speaking countries, especially since the early 19th c. In the U.S. a clear preference for the French form of the name, **Camille**. Pet forms of the name are **Cammie, Cammy, Millie** and **Milly**.

Camille (f) French form of **Camilla**, and the preferred form of the name in the U.S. Camille was the heroine of *The Lady With The Camellias* in an early translation of the story by Dumas (1848), though in the original version she is *Marguerite*. Also a male name in France (for **Camillus**). Usual pet forms are **Cam, Cammie, Cammy, Millie, Milly**.

Camillus (m) Latin name of unknown origin, possibly 'attendant at religious services'. Rare name in English-speaking countries, but found in Europe as French **Camille**, Italian **Camillo**, etc.

Campbell (m) Gaelic *caimbeul* 'crooked mouth'. Famous Scottish surname and clan name, used as a first name since the 1930s.

Candace (f) The modern pronunciation is *Candis*, formerly *Can-day-see*. Dynastic title of unknown meaning used by the queens of Napata (Ethiopia) until the 4th c. of the Roman Empire (Pliny vi:29). Also Biblical, N.T., Acts 8:27. Rarely used in Britain: much stronger in the U.S. and Canada from the 1950s onwards. Candace Stevenson, winner of the 1949 Poetry Society of America award, may have influenced usage. The forms Candice and Candis are found, and pet forms Candy and Candi are used occasionally as independent names.

Candi (f) Pet form of Candace.

Candice (f) See Candace. This form of the name made famous recently by the actress Candice Bergen.

Candida (f) Latin *candida*, feminine of *candidus* 'white'. Regularly found in Christian inscriptions of the Roman Empire, and borne by several saints. Almost unknown in English-speaking countries until the 1950s, in spite of G. B. Shaw's play *Candida*, produced in 1897. Pet forms include Candy and Candie.

Candis (f) See Candace.

Candy (f) Pet form of Candace, Candis, Candida, etc., used independently in modern times. There may occasionally be a direct reference to 'sugar candy', where the origin is ultimately 'cane' sugar.

Captain (m) Military title transferred to first-name use. See also e.g. Admiral, Major.

Cara (f) Latin *cara*, feminine of *carus* 'dear'. The word also occurs in the Italian vocative *cara mia*, which was incorporated into a popular song, much heard in the 1960s. Some confusion with Kara. Both names increasingly used since the 1970s.

Caradoc (m) Alternative form of Caradog.

Caradog (m) Welsh *cariad* 'love'. Latin form of the name is Caractacus. After nine years' resistance of the Romans, Caradog was taken as a prisoner to Rome in AD 51. His manly behaviour much impressed the emperor Claudius, who spared him and sent him home with presents. Occasionally used in modern times, Caradog being the preferred form. In Ireland is also a traditional name, spelt as Carthach. The surname

Craddock derives from Caradog.

Caralyn (f) Form of Carolyn influenced by modern fondness for Cara. Caraline and Caralyne also occur.

Caren (f) Variant of Karen.

Carey (m, f) Regular use of this first name in the 19th c. was probably a transference from the surname, in turn an English form of several Irish family names. Since the 1950s mainly used for girls. As a girl's name it is probably a pet form of Karen, Katharine, etc., or a variant of Kerry, Kerrie.

Carin (f) See Caryn.

Carina (f) Italian diminutive of *cara* 'dear one' in use since the 1960s, though found earlier in the century. Also well used as Karina, and to a lesser extent, Karena. Carine is an occasional variant.

Carissa (f) Variant of Charissa or a diminutive of Italian *cara* 'dear one'. Not frequently used.

Carita (f) Latin, based on *carus*, *cara*, masculine and feminine forms respectively of the word meaning 'dear, beloved'. Latin *caritas* 'charity' is another possible origin. Used as a first name from time to time since the 1890s.

Carl (m) From a word common to several Germanic languages, meaning 'man', especially 'countryman, husbandman'. In English it developed a negative sense as 'churl'. Usual name-form is Charles in English-speaking countries, Karl or Carl being the Germanic equivalent. From the 1850s to the 1950s, Carl and Karl were more used in the U.S. than in Britain. British usage then increased dramatically, Carl being the preferred spelling. American use of the name began to fade sharply in the 1960s.

Carla (f) Feminine form of Carl. Its popularity has been linked with Carl, which means that until the 1950s it was far more commonly used in the U.S. than in Britain. British usage began in the 1940s and was clearly increasing in the 1970s. Variant Karla is found.

Carleen (f) See Carlene.

Carlene (f) Feminine form of Carl. A Carlene Smith was named in Britain as early as 1864, but the name is mainly associated with the 1960s. **Carleen** is now a common variant, and **Carline** is found. Pet forms such as **Carlie**, **Carl(e)y** and **Carli** are now also used as independent names. Variants **Karleen**, **Karlene**, **Karline** all occur, together with **Karli**, **Karlie**.

Carletta (f) Form of **Caroletta** in modern American usage, especially amongst black American families.

Carley (f) Also **Carli(e)**. See **Carlene**.

Carlina (f) Modern shortened form of **Carolina**, influenced by **Carl** and **Carla**.

Carline (f) Form of **Caroline**.

Carlo (m) Italian form of **Charles**, gaining in popularity in English-speaking countries.

Carlos (m) Spanish form of **Charles**, regularly used in English-speaking countries, especially the U.S.

Carlotta (f) Italian feminine of **Carlo** (**Charles**), used mainly in the U.S. and Canada.

Carlton (m) Common English place name ('churls' settlement') and surname, used as a first name regularly since the 1880s. In the U.S., since the 1950s, used almost exclusively by black American families. Featured as a running joke (for a character never seen) in the television series *Rhoda*. In Britain it is often spelt **Carleton**, a variant used rarely in the U.S. though the actor Carleton Carpenter has helped make it known.

Carly (f) See **Carlene**.

Carlyn(n) (f) Forms of **Carlene** in use since the 1960s, though not in great numbers.

Carmel (f) Mountain in Israel, derived from a Hebrew word meaning 'garden'. Often referred to in Scripture as a symbol of beauty, fertility and a happy life. The monastery of the Carmelites, or White Friars, was founded there in the 12th c. The mountain is also associated with the Blessed Virgin. Used as a Christian name, mainly by Roman Catholics, since the 1880s. In Italy there is a male form of the name, **Carmelo**, the Italian feminine being **Carmela**. This some-

times occurs in the U.S. along with **Carmella**, **Carmelle**, **Carmilla** and the diminutive form **Carmelita**. None of these is as popular as the Spanish form of the name, **Carmen**. On rare occasions used as a male name.

Carmela (f) Italian form of **Carmel**, used quietly in the U.S.

Carmelina (f) Diminutive of Italian **Carmela**, occasionally used in the U.S. Pet form **Melina** also occurs as an independent name.

Carmelita (f) Diminutive of **Carmela**, the Italian form of **Carmel**. Quietly but steadily used in the U.S.

Carmella (f) Latinized form of **Carmel** used mainly in the U.S.

Carmelle (f) Form of **Carmel** used in Canada and the U.S.

Carmen (f) Spanish form of **Carmel**, and the preferred form of the name in the U.S. Popularly equated with Latin *carmen* 'song', but one of the titles of the Virgin Mary, Santa Maria del Carmen, is the real source. Made internationally famous by Bizet's opera *Carmen*, first performed in 1875, based on a story by Mérimée.

Carmilla (f) Phonetic version of **Carmila**, the Italian form of **Carmel**.

Carol (f, m) The feminine name was originally a pet form of **Carolina** or **Caroline**, but was quickly associated with (Christmas) carol. Began to appear at the close of the 19th c., reaching its peak in the U.S. 1920–50: the actress Carole Lombard (1908–42), born Jane Alice Peters, who appeared in many films from 1921, probably helped to spread the name during this period. In Britain, Canada and Australia Carol was most used 1950–60. Carol has always been the most usual spelling, but French **Carole**, Latin **Carola** are not infrequent. **Carrol**, **Carroll**, **Caroll**, **Caryl**, etc, are modern alternatives. The male name **Carol** (**Carrol**, **Carroll**), mostly used in the U.S., can be from Dutch **Karel**, Polish **Karol**, Rumanian **Carol**, Slovakian **Karol**, etc., all forms of **Charles**. Carroll is also for Irish

Cearbhall, a common male name often anglicized as Charles.

Carola (f) Latinized form of **Carol**.

Carol-Ann(e) (f) Common modern blend of **Carol** and **Ann(e)**, usually, but by no means always, hyphenated. In the U.S. Carol Ann is the normal form, and by far the most popular of the Carol blends – **Carol Sue** and **Carol Lee** being its only rivals.

Carole (f) French form of **Carol**. In the U.S. Carol has been used about ten times as frequently in modern times; in Britain, during the 1960s especially, Carol was used roughly three times as often as Carole. Both forms now out of fashion in all English-speaking countries. See further at **Carol**.

Caroleen (f) Modern formation influenced by **Carolyn**, **Caroline**, etc. Other variants include **Carolee**, **Carolenia**, **Carolinda**.

Carolin (f) See **Carolyn**.

Carolina (f) Latin form of **Caroline**, regularly but quietly used since the beginning of the 19th c. The U.S. States were named in honour of Charles I and Charles II. At one time **Lina** was used as one of its pet forms, and given as an independent name. In modern times **Carol** and **Carolyn** have largely replaced it.

Caroline (f) Italian feminine form of **Charles**, introduced to Britain by George II's queen. Became a favourite name in the 18th c. and remained so until the end of the 19th c. Then reappeared in the 1940s and by the 1950s was once again one of the leading names, especially in Britain. In modern times often appeared as **Carolyne**, being influenced by the popular American spelling **Carolyn**.

Carolyn (f) Modern form of **Caroline**, first appearing in the U.S. Became very popular there by 1925 and remained so until the 1950s, by which time it had also enjoyed great success in Britain. British usage continued enthusiastically through the 1960s, but the name has subsequently faded on all sides. Variants include the common **Carolynn** and **Carolynne**, while **Carolin** is not uncommon. **Carolyne** is sometimes a variant of Carolyn, but can also be pronounced as Caroline.

Caron (f) Name of a Welsh saint, perhaps based on Welsh *caru* 'to love'. Used only since the mid-1950s, which suggests that some parents see the name as a variant of **Karen**. Carron is also found.

Carren (f) Variant of Caron or Karen. Carran and Carrin are also found. All forms in use since the 1960s.

Carrie (f) Pet form of **Caroline**, extensively used as a name in its own right, especially in the U.S. in the latter half of the 19th c. Revived strongly in the 1970s, especially by white Americans. Usage also spread to Britain at that time. Thackeray had earlier done the name little good by making his character Mr Gann (in *A Shabby Genteel Story*) joke about his daughter: '*Fetch* and Carry I call her, or else Carryvan – she's so useful.' **Carry** was formerly a common form of the name, and modern **Carey** is probably to be associated with it. **Carri** and **Cary** are also found, together with blends such as **Carrie-Ann(e)**.

Carrol(l) (f, m) Alternative forms of **Carol**.

Carron (f) Variant of **Caron** or **Karen** in use since the 1950s.

Carry (f) See **Carrie**. Frequently-used variant in the 19th c., but Carrie always preferred in the 20th c.

Carson (m, f) Surname with several possible origins used occasionally as a first name, especially in the U.S. Carson McCullers (1917–67), the writer, helped to make her name known.

Carter (m). Occupational surname used occasionally as a first name. **Cartwright** 'builder of carts' has also been used.

Carthach (m) Celtic name, based on a word meaning 'love'. Carthach is the Irish equivalent of **Caradog** or **Caradoc**. Woulfe gives the English version of the name as **Cartagh**, **Cartage** and **Carthage**.

Cary (m) Transferred use of the surname,

itself deriving from a place name which probably meant 'pleasant stream'. Used as a first name very occasionally in the 19th c. Accepted in all English-speaking countries as a normal first name in the 1940s, due to the fame of the actor Cary Grant, born in 1904 as Archibald Leach. Since the 1960s has been declining in use.

Caryl (f) Alternative spelling of **Carol**. **Caryle**, **Caryll** and **Carylle** are also found.

Caryn (f) Probably a spelling variant of **Karen**, though Welsh parents may connect it with *caru* 'to love'. Regularly used since the 1950s, and fairly popular in the U.S. in the 1970s. **Carin** also occurs, but the spelling suggests that in that form it may be from **Carina**.

Carys (f) Welsh *caru* 'to love'. Used in Wales since the 1960s.

Casandra (f) Also **Casandera**, **Casandrey**. Variants of **Cassandra**.

Casey (m, f) According to H. L. Mencken, from Polish *Kasimierz* (**Casimir**). Can also be a use of the surname, which derives from Irish *Cathasaigh* 'watchful'. Occasional feminine use of the name may represent a form of **Cassey** or **Cassie**. Mainly famous as the nickname of John Luther Jones (1864–1900), the locomotive engineer who saved the lives of many passengers on the Cannon Ball express. He himself was killed in the accident. The incident has been much celebrated in ballad and song.

Caspar (m). See **Jasper**.

Cass (m, f) Surname which originated as a pet form of **Cassandra**, or a use of that pet name as a first name. Mainly occurs in the 19th c.

Cassandra (f) Greek *Kassandra*, possibly a feminine form of **Alexander**. Name of the prophetic daughter of Priam and Hecuba. Used in Britain in the Middle Ages and relatively common in the 17th c. Remained in regular but infrequent use until the 20th c. Since the 1950s has been something of a favourite with black American parents. Early pet forms of the name were **Cassey** and

Cassy, with **Casson** an occasional variant. In modern times **Cass** and **Cassie** are preferred.

Cassey (f) 19th c. pet form of **Cassandra**. Modern feminine use of **Casey** may derive from this name.

Cassie (f) Preferred modern pet form of **Cassandra**, used in Britain as a name in its own right.

Casson (f) Probably a transferred use of the surname, which derives ultimately from **Cassandra**.

Cassy (f) 19th c. pet form of **Cassandra**.

Castle (m) Use of the surname, originally denoting 'one who worked in the castle', as a first name. Used mainly in the 19th c., never in great numbers.

Catalina (f) Spanish form of **Catherine/Katherine**, used occasionally in the U.S.

Cater (m) Occupational surname, denoting a 'caterer, buyer of provisions for a large household', used as a first name, mainly in the 19th c.

Caterina (f) Italian form of **Catherine**. Occurs in Scotland, which suggests that it might be used as a variant of **Catriona**.

Catharine (f) Frequent variant of **Catherine**.

Catherine (f) French spelling, and normal form in Britain, of a name that began as Greek *Aikaterina*. Original meaning of the Greek name unknown, though it was linked at an early date with Greek *aikia* 'torture', presumably with reference to the sufferings of the legendary St Katherine of Alexandria (cf. the Catherine wheel). This derivation need not be taken seriously. The Romans, who at first used the name as *Katerina*, decided that it must derive from Greek *katharos* 'pure'. Accordingly, they changed the spelling of the name to *Katharina*. Modern Italian **Caterina** preserves the earlier Latin form apart from the initial K-. The initial C/K interchange is one reason for the name's various forms. Then there are the forms which take the central 't' sound as opposed to 'th'. This is followed by either 'a' or 'e' according to the change made by the Romans. There are different ideas about how to represent the final sound of the name in modern times. As a result, the name is found in English-speaking countries in the following forms: **Catarine, Catharin, Catherine, Catheryn, Cathrene, Cathrine, Cathryn, Catrin, Catrine, Katharine, Katharyn, Kathereen, Katherin, Katherine, Katheryn, Katheryne, Kathrene, Kathrine, Kathryn, Kathryne, Kathyrine, Katrine.** Some parents wish to preserve the final -a sound of the original name, and accordingly one finds **Catharina, Catherina, Catrina, Katarina, Katerina, Katherina, Katrina, Katriona, Katryna, Kattrina, Katrena** (leading in turn to **Treena, Trina**). Some of these are phonetic representations of Gaelic **Catriona**, the adaptation in that language of Catherine. Irish version is **Caitriona**, used there in recent years. Another Irish development was **Caitlin**, perhaps influenced by Norman French **Cateline**, in which the original ending of the name was replaced by the popular *-line* ending. Caitlin developed into **Cathleen** and **Kathleen**, plus the inevitable variants such as **Cathaleen, Catherleen, Katheleen, Katheline, Kathileen, Kathlyn, Kathlynn, Katleen.** The earlier pet forms of the name were **Kitty (Kittie)**, which came into independent use. **Kate** is old-established, and has been much used as a name in its own right. Its own diminutives **Katey, Katie, Katy** are also used independently. **Cathie, Cathy, Kathie, Kathy** have all appeared on the scene in modern times, together with the modern Greek equivalent **Katina**. Far more successful this century in terms of usage have been the Danish **Karen** and Swedish **Karin**, short forms of **Katarina**. In English-speaking countries these have taken on forms unknown to the Scandinavians, including **Caren, Carin, Caron, Caronne, Carran, Carren, Carrin, Carron, Caryn, Karan, Karenne, Karon, Karran, Karren, Karyn.** Some parents also use the name **Kerry** in one of its various forms because they associ-

ate it with Catherine. The countless forms mentioned above are testimony to the name's long-standing popularity. Borne by several popular saints, by Queens of England (e.g. three wives of Henry VIII), and by innumerable famous women, the name is likely to be with us for many centuries to come.

Cathleen (f) Irish *Caitlin*, a diminutive of Caitriona or Catherine. Kathleen is the more usual form of the name, but Cathleen is frequent.

Cathrine (f) Frequent variant of Catherine, especially since the 1940s. Cathryn has also been used since 1930.

Cathy (f) Pet form of Catherine, popular since the 1950s as an independent name.

Catrin (f) Welsh form of Catherine. First appears in the 1960s and used regularly, but infrequently, since then.

Catrina (f) Phonetic form of Catriona, or adaptation of Caterina. Ultimately from Catherine. Much used since the 1950s, especially by black American families.

Catriona (f) Gaelic form of Catherine or Katharine, use of which has spread from Scotland since the 1940s. Caitriona is used in Ireland. Pronunciation of the name leads to the phonetic forms Catrina and Katrina, which are usual in the U.S., especially in black American families. Other variants include Katrine, Katryna, Katriona and Katrena. These may be influenced by various foreign forms such as Scandinavian Katarina, Katerina, Italian Caterina, Portuguese Catarina, etc. Robert Louis Stevenson's novel *Catriona* (1893) probably influenced earlier Scottish use of the name.

Caw (m) Welsh form of Caius, a variant of Gaius.

Cearbhall (m) Irish name of unknown origin anglicized as Carroll or Charles.

Cecelia (f) Frequent variant of Cecilia.

Cecil (m) Latin *Caecilius*, the clan name of a Roman family, probably from *caecus* 'blind'. *Cecilius* and the feminine *Caecilia* occur very frequently amongst Christian inscriptions of the Roman

Empire. Little used in Britain until the 1840s. Usage slowly increased, and the name reached a peak of popularity around 1900, helped at that time, no doubt, by the fame of the British statesman Cecil Rhodes (1853–1902), for whom Rhodesia was named in 1894. Other famous bearers of the name include the film producer-director Cecil B. de Mille, English actor Cecil Parker and photographer Cecil Beaton. Has faded steadily since the beginning of the 20th c. In the early 1980s mainly kept alive by black American families.

Cecile (f) French feminine form of Cecil, used regularly but infrequently in English-speaking countries since the 1880s.

Cecilia (f) Latin feminine form of Cecil, mainly used when the male name was at its most popular, 1875–1925. Fanny Burney's novel *Cecilia* (1782) appeared to have no influence on the use of the name. Poetical references to Cecilia often refer to the saint of the name, patroness of musicians. The 19th c. pet form of the name was Sissy, as Dickens made clear in *Hard Times*: ' "Who is that girl?" "Sissy Jupe, sir," explained number twenty, blushing, standing up and curtseying. "Sissy is not a name," said Mr Gradgrind. "Don't call yourself Sissy. Call yourself Cecilia." '

Cecilie (f) Variant of Cecilia influenced by Cecily/Cecile.

Cecily (f) English form of Cecilia used regularly but infrequently from the 1840s onwards. Main period of popularity in the 1920s. See more under Cicely, the earlier form of the name.

Cedric (m) Possibly from Welsh Cedrych or, as Professor Weekley first suggested, a mistake by Sir Walter Scott, who used Cedric to name the Saxon in his *Ivanhoe* (1819), the name Cerdic being intended. Cedric was used again by Frances Hodgson Burnett as hero to *Little Lord Fauntleroy* (1886). Used quietly from that time, with special interest being shown in it from 1920–35. The actor Sir Cedric Hardwicke helped to publicize it

from the 1930s. Now a rare name amongst white families, but well used by black Americans, who sometimes spell it Cedrick.

Cedrych (m) Welsh *ced* 'bounty, boon' and *drych* 'spectacle, pattern'. Trefor Rendall Davies has suggested that this Welsh name was the origin of Cedric.

Ceinwen (f) Welsh 'jewels + beautiful'. Much used in Wales from the 1870s to the 1920s.

Celena (f) Also Celina. Variants of Selena or Selina.

Celeste (f) Male name in France, a short form of Celestin, which in turn represents Latin *Caelestinus*, the name of several early popes. Derives from Latin *caelestis* 'heavenly'. Taken to be a female name in the English-speaking countries (compare the use of Nicola). The actress Celeste Holm has given it considerable publicity since the 1940s.

Celestine (f) French feminine form of Celestin, see Celeste. Celestina is also found, but both Celestine and Celestina are rarely used in English-speaking countries.

Celia (f) Latin *Caelia*, feminine of *Caelius*, name of a Roman gens or clan. Found as a Christian name in Rome in the 4th c. Very rare in English-speaking countries until the 19th c. when it came into regular use, no doubt regarded as a form of Cecilia (actually from *Caecilia*). Reached a minor peak in the 1950s and still quietly used. The Irish form of the name, Sile, gave rise to Sheila.

Celina (f) Variant of Selina.

Céline (f) French authorities explain this as a pet form of Marceline used independently. Others have seen it as a development of Celia, or have derived it from Latin *Caelina* 'heavenly'. The Romans do not seem to have used such a name, however. Used rarely in English-speaking countries.

Cephas (m) Aramaic 'rock'. The name given by Jesus to his Apostle Simon, later known as Peter (the Latin and Greek form of the name). Used regularly until the present century, but now very rare.

Cerdic (m) Probably an Old English adoption of Welsh **Ceredig**, Old Welsh **Ceretic**. Cerdic was the name of a West Saxon king. Thought by some to be the original of **Cedric**.

Ceredig (m) Welsh *caredig* 'kind, beloved'. A Welsh name used since the 6th c. **Caradog**, or **Caradoc**, is connected etymologically.

Ceri (m, f) Welsh *caru* 'to love'. Used mainly in Wales since the 1940s.

Ceridwen (f) Welsh *ceiridd*, oblique form of *cerdd* 'poetry' and *(g)wen* 'fair'. In Welsh legend the goddess of poetic inspiration. Most used in Wales, where the initial C- is pronounced with a k-sound.

Cerise (f) French 'cherry'. In occasional modern use. See further at **Cherry**.

Cerri(e) (f) Forms of **Ceri** in modern use.

Cerys (f) Welsh, a development of *caru* 'to love'. Used mainly in Wales, and found also as **Ceris, Cerris, Ceries**.

Chad (m) Old English *Ceadd(a)*, a personal name of unknown meaning borne by a 7th c. saint. Rarely used until the late 1960s. The Revd. Chad Varah (1911–   ) founded the Samaritans. In some instances it is the pet form of **Chadwick**.

Chaim (m) See **Hyman**.

Chanel (f) Name of a famous French perfume used as a first name in the 1980s. Usage currently confined to black American families. Also found as **Channel, Shanel, Shanell, Shanelle, Shannel**, the *Sh*- spellings reflecting the normal French pronunciation of the name.

Chantal (f) Ultimately a French place name meaning 'stony place', used as a first name in honour of Saint Jeanne of Chantal (1572–1641). Importation of the name from France in modern times has led to a number of variants, including **Chantel, Chantell, Chantelle, Chantele, Shantel, Shantell, Shantelle**. The variants have been especially well used by black American families.

Charis (f) Greek *charis* 'grace', name of one of the Three Graces in Greek mythology. Used in the 20th c. but infrequently.

Charissa (f) Greek *charis* 'grace'. Rarely used.

Charity (f) One of the Puritan 'virtue' names, in use since the 17th c. Formerly **Cherry** was the pet form of the name. Dickens did not help the name's image when he named the elder daughter of Mr Pecksniff, in *Martin Chuzzlewit*, Charity (her sister being **Mercy**). Charity is seen to be a hypocritical shrew.

Charleen (f) See **Charlene**. **Charlaine** also occurs, no doubt influenced by **Charmaine**.

Charlene (f) Modern feminine form of **Charles**, in use since the 1950s. It soon spread, but by the end of the 1970s rapidly disappearing. Charlene is the usual spelling, but **Charleen** and **Charline** are found, together with the occasional **Charlena, Sharlene**.

Charles (m) From a word meaning 'man, farmer'. Made famous by Charles the Great (Charlemagne) who became ruler in the early 9th c. of a vast empire. A royal name in Britain and in several other European countries. In very general use from the 17th c. to the present time, but in Britain it disappeared from the top fifty names in the 1970s. In the U.S. by that time had dropped to 34th place, having been amongst the top five names for the previous 75 years. Feminine forms of the name include **Caroline, Carol, Charlotte**, etc., but individualists have also used **Charlesina, Charlzina, Charletta, Charlinna, Charlisa, Charlita**. Variants of **Charlene** are common. Pet forms of the name such as **Charlie, Charley** and, to a lesser extent, **Charlot**, are regularly used as independent names, but **Chuck** is very rarely given in baptism. See also **Carl, Karl, Carlo, Carlos**. Probably best known in modern times as the name of the Prince of Wales, but has been borne by a host of famous men, including the writers Charles Dickens, Charles Lamb; actors Charles Chaplin, Charles Laughton, Charles Bronson, Charles Coburn,

Charles Boyer, Charles Bickford; singer
Charles Aznavour. General Charles de
Gaulle of France was also an outstand-
ing bearer of the name.

Charlesena (f) Also **Charlesina**. Feminine
forms of **Charles** mainly used at the
beginning of the 20th c.

Charlotta (f) Latinized variant of French
Charlotte, rarely used.

Charlotte (f) French Charlotte, in imitation of Italian **Carlotta**, feminine of
Carlo (**Charles**) from Teutonic **Karl**
'man, husband'. Introduced into England in the 17th c. but popularized by
George III's queen, Charlotte Sophia, in
the latter half of the 18th c. Remained
very popular until the beginning of the
20th c. Well-known bearers of the name
during this period were Charlotte
Brontë, 1816–55, and Charlotte Mary
Yonge, 1823–1901. Subsequently faded
but returned to favour in England in the
1970s. In the U.S. most used in the
1870s. Quietly used in Canada and
Australia. Pet forms of the name
include, **Lottie, Lotty, Totty, Chatty**
and **Charlie**. Variant spellings: Latinized **Charlotta** and (rare) **Charlotty**, the
latter reflecting a dialectal pronunciation.

Charlton (m) English place name 'settlement of free peasants' and surname,
used regularly as a first name since the
1870s. In modern times made famous
by the actor Charlton Heston.

Charmaine (f) Ultimately from Latin
Carminea, feminine form of the Roman
clan name *Carmineus*. Use of the name
in the 1920s was due to the heroine of
the play and film *What Price Glory?* and
a song which was first heard at that
time. Usual spelling at first was **Char-
main**, but with the revival of the song in
the 1950s Charmaine became standard.
Some confusion with **Charmian**. In
recent times mostly used by black
Americans. Also found as **Sharmain,
Sharmaine, Sharman, Sharmane**.

Charmian (f) Greek *charma* 'joy'. In
Shakespeare's *Antony and Cleopatra*
one of the Queen's attendants. Use of

Charmian corresponds with that of
Charmaine, which may indicate some
confusion between the two, though
Charmian should be pronounced
Karmian.

Chavon(ne) (f) Variants of **Siobhan**.

Chay (m) Appeared in 1975 when the
British yachtsman Chay Blyth was
receiving a great deal of publicity.
Further used since then. In the case of
Mr Blyth, the name is a pet form of
Charles.

Chaz (m) Abbreviated form of **Charles**.
Used in the early 1980s by black American parents.

Chelsea (m,f) From the place name in
London, originally meaning 'landing
place (on the river) for chalk or lime-
stone'. Other places, e.g. in Australia,
were later given the name. First-name
usage seems to have begun in Australia
but has now spread to other English-
speaking countries, especially to the
USA. Name of a character played by
Jane Fonda in the film *On Golden
Pond*. Much publicized 1993 onwards
as name of President Clinton's
daughter. **Chelsie** is found, presumably
influenced by **Else, Kelsie**, etc.

Cher (f) French *cher* 'dear one'. Feminine
form **Chère**, which is more correct, is
also found. Used mainly in the late
1960s and early 1970s.

Cheralyn (f) See **Cherilyn**.

Chereen (f) See **Shereen**.

Cherie (f) French 'dear one', properly
written *chèrie* and pronounced with an
initial sh- sound. Occasionally found in
its masculine form **Cheri**, though this is
probably seen as a pet form of names
like **Cherilyn, Cheryl, Sherilyn**. The
phonetic variant **Sherri** is well used in
the U.S. First use of the name no doubt
due to a misunderstanding of the vocative *ma chèrie* 'my darling', often borrowed for popular songs. Other variants
include **Sheree, Sherree, Sheri, Sherie,
Sherry**.

Cherilyn (f) Later development of **Cheryl**.
First used in the 1940s in the U.S. but
did not become as popular as the parent

name. Also found as **Cherilynn**, **Cherri-lyn**, **Cherrylin**, **Cherylene**, **Cheryline**, **Cherylyn**. A change of pronunciation led to forms such as **Sherilyn**.

Cherrie (f) Variant of Cherie or Cherry.

Cherril(l) (f) See Cheryl.

Cherrilyn (f) See Cherilyn.

Cherry (f) In early use a pet form of **Char-ity**, as with the Pecksniff daughter in Dickens's *Martin Chuzzlewit* (1843). In some instances a transferred use of the surname. In modern times a short form of names such as **Cheryl** or a variant of **Cherie**. On rare occasions a direct refer-ence to the fruit, though there has never been a general vogue for fruit names as there has been for flower names. In Whyte-Melville's novel *Cerise*, where the heroine appears to be called 'cherry' in its French form, the name is really a childish corruption of her real name, Thérèse. **Cherrie** is found occasionally, and Cherry itself is mainly used in Britain.

Cherryl(l) (f) See Cheryl.

Cheryl (f) Development from Cherry, first used in the 1920s when **Beryl** was a popular name. Made little impact at the time, but re-surfaced in the early 1940s in both Britain and the U.S. Soon fol-lowed by **Cheryll** and **Cheryle**, then **Cherrill**, **Cherryl**, **Cherril**, **Cherryll**, **Cherryle**, **Cherill**. French **Cherie** had come into use in the meantime, written with the initial *Ch*- but pronounced *Sh*-. By the late 1930s Sherry had therefore come into use as a phonetic form of Cherie. **Sheryl** and **Sherryll** appeared in the 1940s, while later developments were **Sheral**, **Sherell**, **Sheril**, **Sherill**, **Sherrell**. All these forms actually point to two names, Cheryl and Sheryl, as they first appeared. Sheryl and its variants came into use because some bearers of the name Cheryl (and its variants) pro-nounced it as if it were written Sheryl. Cheryl underwent a further develop-ment in the 1940s and gave rise to **Cheri-lyn**, together with its variants **Cheralyn**, **Cherilynn**, **Cherralyn**, **Cherrilyn**, **Cher-rylin**, **Cherrylene**, **Cherryline**, **Cherylyn**.

The inevitable **Sherilyn** (**Sheralyn**, **Sher-ralyn**, **Sherrylyn**, **Sherryllyn**) appeared in the 1950s and later. All these names reached a peak in English-speaking countries in the 1960s, but by the early 1980s had faded drastically.

Cherylyn (f) See Cherilyn.

Chester (m) Common British place name, from Latin *castra* 'camp, Roman site', which became a surname, then first name. In regular if sporadic use in all English-speaking countries, but usually considered an American name, perhaps due to association with Chester A. Arthur, 21st President of the U.S.A. Pet form of the name is **Chet**.

Chet (m) Pet form of **Chester** used inde-pendently, but rarely, and mainly in the U.S.

Chevon(ne) (f) Variants of Siobhan.

Chloe (f) Greek *chloë* 'young green shoot', from *chloos* 'greenish yellow'. Biblical, N.T., mentioned by St Paul (1 Cor 1:11). Mainly literary name of the 17th c., then very rare until the 1970s, when it returned to favour in Britain.

Chris (m, f) Pet form of names such as **Christopher**, **Christian**, **Christine**, etc., used independently since the 1880s. Modern occasional variant is **Kris**.

Chrisanda (f) Appears to be blend of Chris(tine) and (Am)anda or (Mir)anda. First used at the end of the 19th c. and has occurred again in the 20th c.

Chrissie (f) Pet form of **Christina** or **Christine**, used on rare occasions in its own right. Also found as **Chrissy**.

Christa (f) German pet form of Christ-iane, introduced to Britain since the 1960s. Variant **Krista** is usual in the U.S.

Christabel (f) Compound of **Christ** and Latin *bella* 'fair', intended to mean 'fair follower of Christ'. Mainly a literary name, associated especially with a beautiful poem by S. T. Coleridge which appeared in 1816. Regularly if quietly used in Britain, and occasionally found as **Christabella**, **Christabelle** or **Christ-ella**. **Christobel** and **Chrystabel** also occur. Rare elsewhere.

Christal (f) See **Crystal**.

Christella (f) See **Christabel**.

Christen (f) Variant of **Kristen** in modern times, though in the 19th c. was a variant of **Christine**, in occasional use. **Christan** is also found.

Christian (m) Ecclesiastical Latin **Christianus**, from Greek *christos* 'anointed'. A post-biblical name. Usually a female name in the Middle Ages, a male name by the 18th c., perhaps due to the influence of John Bunyan's *Pilgrim's Progress* (1684), in which Christian and his wife **Christiana** are the main protagonists. Regularly used in English-speaking countries since the 18th c., and in the 1970s suddenly very popular in Britain and Australia. Used in the U.S., though not to the same extent. Usual pet forms are **Chris** and **Christy**. Since 1960 **Kristian** has been increasingly used, together with its associated pet forms beginning with K-.

Christiana (f) Earlier feminine form of **Christian**, subsequently replaced by **Christina** and **Christine**. A variant at one time was **Christianna**, and **Christiann** has been used in modern times, pronounced as Christy-Ann.

Christie (m,f) Mainly Scottish diminutive of **Christopher**. See **Christine**, **Crystal**.

Christina (f) Abbreviated form of **Christiana**, ultimately a form of **Christian**. Came into regular use in the 18th c. but reached its mild peak of popularity in the mid-1950s. Until the 1930s used slightly more often than **Christine**, but the latter form then tended to dominate. There was an early Saint Christina of whom little is known. The most famous bearer of the name was probably the English poet Christina Rossetti, though the name has been a royal one in both Sweden and Spain. Considerably revived in the U.S. since the late 1970s, and by the early 1980s Christina had become the preferred form again for the first time in fifty years. **Kristina** was being used as a fairly popular alternative. The revival had not occurred in Britain, where Christine was still being

used to some extent while Christina had all but disappeared. Pet form **Tina** has taken on a life of its own, and the traditional Scottish pet forms **Kirstie** and **Kirsty** have become more widespread in modern times.

Christine (f) French form of **Christina**, first used at the end of the 19th c. in English-speaking countries. During the 1950s and '60s became extremely popular on all sides, but faded sharply in the 1970s. Variants of the name include **Christeen, Christen, Christene, Christien, Kristine, Kristin**. Pet forms **Chris, Chrissie, Christie** (e.g. Christie Brinkley, top U.S. model). The modern run on this name began in the U.S. in the late 1930s and was quickly transferred to Britain, but why?

Christmas (m, f) Old English 'Christ's festival'. Surname since the Middle Ages, originally indicating someone born at Christmas. Used fairly frequently as a first name throughout the 19th c. but now rare. Seasonal births now tend to be marked by such names as **Natalie, Natasha, Noel, Noelle** and (mistakenly) by **Carol(e)**.

Christobel (f) Fairly frequent variant of **Christabel**, in use since the 17th c., also as **Christobell**.

Christopher (m) Greek 'one who carries Christ' i.e. in his heart. The literal interpretation of the name led to the story of St Christopher carrying the Christ child across a river. Not used in Britain until the 15th c. By the 17th c. was fairly popular and remained so for a century. Little used throughout the 19th c. and began the 20th c. very quietly. Usage began to increase rapidly during the early 1940s in both the U.S. and Britain. Became one of the most intensively used names for boys during the 1970s. By the early 1980s there were signs that it might begin to fade. Famous bearers of the name include Christopher Columbus (1451–1506) and the playwright Christopher Marlowe (1564–93), but it is difficult to see why they would have inspired a name-fashion in the 1940s. Possibly, in Britain, the stories for children by A. A. Milne, written for his son Christopher Robin, were ultimately responsible. Written in the 1920s, by the early 1940s they were accepted as classics. By that time everyone had heard the song about Christopher Robin saying his prayers and had an image in their minds of a cherubic infant or a perfect little boy. Those parents who were unable to use Christopher for their sons seem to have turned to **Christine** for their daughters at this time. Others made use of **Robin** for either sex. In modern times, mainly since the 1960s, forms such as **Kristopher**, **Kristofer** have been used. The French **Christophe** occurs, together with its variants **Christof**, **Christoff**, **Christoph**. Pet forms **Chris**, **Kris**, etc. have been used in their own right.

Christy (m) See Crystal.

Chrystal (f) See Crystal.

Chuck (m) See Charles.

Cicelia (f) Variant of Cecelia.

Cicely (f) Latin *Caecilia*, feminine of *Caecilius*, the name of a Roman clan, ultimately from *caecus* 'blind'. Early use of the name is attested by surnames such as *Sisley*, *Sissons*, etc., which derive from it. Used throughout the 19th c. but rare since the 1920s. The Irish form **Sile** was re-formed in English as **Sheila**. Pet form **Cissie** was also used independently. **Cecily** has been a frequently-used variant spelling; others include **Ciceley**, **Cicelie**, **Cicily**, **Cicley**, **Sicely**, **Sicley**.

Cilla (f) See Priscilla.

Cinderella (f) 'Little cinder girl', on the analogy of French *Cendrillon*, from *cendre* 'ashes'. The heroine of an internationally-known fairy tale, who loses her glass slipper in the modern version of the pantomime. This is due to a mistranslation of '*vair*', the French word for 'fur', as if it were French *verre* 'glass'. A variant of the tale was told of Rhodope in 670 BC, by Aelian. Given as a first name from time to time: there have been five Cinderella Smiths named

in England and Wales, for instance, so far this century, the last one in 1966. **Cindy** is the usual pet form.

Cindi (f) See Cindy.

Cindy (f) Pet form of **Cynthia**, **Cinderella**, **Lucinda**, etc. Use of name began around 1956 and was rapidly boosted by the popularity of a song 'Cindy Lou', especially in the U.S. In the 1970s it began to wane, though as **Sindy** it is well-known as a doll's name.

Cissie (f) Pet form of **Cicely**, used as an independent name from the 1880s, but rare since the 1930s. **Cissy** was a common variant, and **Cissy**, **Sissie**, **Sissy**, **Sissey** were also used. The slang term of sissie or cissie, with the meaning 'effeminate or cowardly man', was first used when the name itself began to be common, so the two are presumably linked. Dictionaries usually derive the slang expression from 'sister', however. Whatever its origin, the slang term no doubt helped to kill off the name.

Cissy (f) See Cissie.

Claire (f) French *Claire*, from Latin *clara*, feminine of *clarus*, 'bright, shining, clear'. One of the top names for girls in Britain and Australia in the 1970s, replacing the earlier **Clara**. The British actress Claire Bloom (1931–   ), whose film career began in 1948, probably influenced its use. A popular song 'Claire' by Gilbert O'Sullivan, released in 1972, also contributed to the spread of the name. **Clair** is sometimes found as an alternative spelling, though this is properly the male form, borne by the 7th c. St Clair.

Clancy (m) Irish (*Mac*) *Fhlannchaidh* 'descendant of the red-haired warrior'. An Irish surname in occasional use as a first name.

Clara (f) Latin *clara*, feminine of *clarus* 'bright, shining, clear'. Earlier written and pronounced as **Clare** in English, though recorded as Clara in the Latin of parish registers, etc. In the 19th c. Clara became the normal written and spoken form. Very popular in all English-speaking countries 1850–1900. Clara

Bow, the American actress, was to become the IT girl of the 1920s, but by that time the name was on the wane. Since 1960 replaced in Britain and Australia by the French form **Claire**.

Clare (f) Latin *clara*, feminine of *clarus* 'bright, shining, clear'. St Clare (d. 1253) was founder of the Franciscan nuns, called 'Poor Clares'. Found in England from the 13th c., written as Clare in English, but **Clara** in Latin. The latter form became very popular in the 19th c., but since 1960 **Claire** has been the favoured spelling, with Clare also very much back in fashion. In rare instances is used as a male name, probably deriving from the surname.

Clarence (m) Latin *Clarensis* 'of Clare'. The name of a dukedom created in 1362 for Lionel, son of Edward III, when he married a daughter of the Clare family. The title was revived in 1789 for the future William IV and again in 1890 for Albert Victor, eldest son of Edward VII. The tremendous success of Clarence as a first name in all English-speaking countries during the latter part of the 19th c. is something of a mystery. Miss Withycombe notes that the hero of Maria Edgeworth's novel *Helen* (1834) was Clarence Harvey. By 1840 the name was certainly being used in Britain and twenty years later it was popular everywhere. Mark Twain used Clarence as a character in his *Connecticut Yankee in King Arthur's Court* (1889), making it clear that for him the name now had rather insipid associations. George Stewart believes that use of the name declined because of its connection with 'effete aristocrats'. Ernest Weekley hints that it may have been considered unlucky, since all the royal bearers of the title met unfortunate ends. In Britain now hardly ever used as a first name; in the U.S. black American families remained attached to it until the later 1970s. In the 18th c. Clarence seems to have been used occasionally as a girl's name. **Clarance** was a fairly frequent variant.

Claribel (f) The name of a knight in Spenser's *Faerie Queene* (1596) but interpreted in modern times as a feminine diminutive of **Clare**. Used only occasionally.

Clarice (f) Italian diminutive of **Clare**. Occurs in Tasso's famous 16th c. romance about the adventures of Rinaldo – Clarice being Rinaldo's wife. Most used in English-speaking countries 1875–1925. Still in regular if quiet use, the three-syllable Italian pronunciation having given way to **Claris** (found as an alternative spelling).

Clarinda (f) Diminutive of **Clare**. Popular name in 18th c. drama, and used to some extent in the 19th c.

Claris (f) Variant of **Clarice** or **Clarisse**.

Clarissa (f) Latinized form of **Clarice**, made famous by Samuel Richardson in his novel *Clarissa Harlowe* (1749). Clarissa Harlowe Barton, founder of the American Red Cross Association, presumably had parents who admired the book. Regularly but quietly used in modern times.

Clarisse (f) French diminutive of **Clare**, regularly but quietly used.

Clarita (f) Spanish diminutive of **Clare**. Regularly but quietly used in the U.S.

Clark (m) Transferred use of the surname, which indicated an ancestor who was a cleric, scholar or secretary. Modern use of the first name almost entirely due to the influence of the actor Clark Gable (1901–60), 'king' of Hollywood for nearly thirty years. **Clarke** has also been used.

Clarrie (f) Pet form of **Clara**, **Clarissa**, etc., used as an independent name with some regularity 1870–1930, but now obsolete. **Clari**, **Clarey**, **Clarie**, **Clarry**, etc., were also used.

Claud (m) Latin *Claudius*, name of two famous Roman clans, presumably deriving from *claudus* 'lame'. Used from the 1870s onwards to some extent, but has now acquired an unfortunate reputation as being both effeminate and foolish. This is not so in France and the name has been borne (as **Claude**) by many distinguished men, including Claude Duval, Claude Debussy, Claude Monet.

Claude (m, f) French form of **Claud**, used in France as both a male and female name. Black American families have used it mostly in modern times. See further at **Claud**.

Claudelle (f) Diminutive of French **Claude**. Erskine Caldwell's novel of this name does not seem to have encouraged parents to use it.

Claudette (f) French feminine diminutive of **Claudius**. Modern use of the name in English-speaking countries has been influenced by Claudette Colbert (Lily Claudette Chauchoin), the French-born film actress, since the late 1930s.

Claudia (f) Feminine of **Claudius**. Biblical, 2 Tim. 4:21, the name of a Roman convert. Used regularly but quietly in English-speaking countries. The French **Claude** is sometimes used, but in modern times the diminutive forms **Claudette** and **Claudine** have been preferred. These in turn have occasional variants such as **Claudeen** and **Claudina**. **Gladys** is commonly said to derive from a Welsh form of **Claudia**, though Welsh philologists remain dubious about the connection between the two names.

Claudine (f) French feminine diminutive from **Claudius**, used in English-speaking countries since the 1960s. Especially associated with the heroine of Colette's four novels about adolescence, published in the early 20th c.

Claudius (m) Original form of **Claud**, but little used in English-speaking countries.

Clay (m) Surname used as a first name, or a pet form of **Clayton**, **Clayborne**, etc. Original meaning of the name was to do with working in a clay-pit or living near a clay-bed. Several famous bearers of the surname could have been responsible for the first-name usage, notably Cassius Clay (1810–1903), the American anti-slavery leader, or the modern heavyweight boxer of the same name (later changed to Mohammad Ali).

Clayton (m) British place name and surname, regularly used in all English-speaking countries as a first name since the early 19th c. Original meaning of the name had to do with a settlement on or near a clay-bed.

Cledwyn (m) Name of a Welsh river occasionally used as a first name of Wales.

Clement (m) Latin *clemens* 'mild, merciful'. Fairly common name in early Christian inscriptions. Name of a famous saint, and mentioned briefly in the Bible, N.T., Phil. 4:31. Never widely used in any of the English-speaking countries.

Clementia (f) Latin 'mildness'. The Puritans used **Clemency** (still occasionally found) and **Clemence**. Survived until the 19th c., when it was infrequently used. Girls who bore the name at that time were probably addressed as Clemency.

Clementina (f) Feminine form of **Clement** used regularly but infrequently in the 19th c., but extremely rare since the 1930s. In Richardson's novel *Sir Charles Grandison* (1753) she is in love with the hero, but he marries someone else.

Clementine (f) Feminine form of **Clement** made famous by the song 'My Darling Clementine', but used very rarely in English-speaking countries.

Cleo (m, f) As a male name a pet form of **Cleophas**; as a female name a pet form of **Cleopatra**. Infrequently used, but well known because of the British jazz singer Cleo Laine, born Clementina Campbell.

Cleopatra (f) Greek *Kleopatra* 'fame of her father'. Given to a long line of Graeco-Egyptian princesses, but mainly associated with the queen who fascinated Caesar and Antony. Occasionally used as a first name in English-speaking countries, especially by black Americans.

Cleveland (m) A place name 'hilly district' which became a surname, notably that of President Grover Cleveland (1837–1908). The president's name was then used for several American towns and was also transferred to first-name use. Used regularly if infrequently this century, though only in the U.S. Now favoured by black American families rather more than whites.

Cliff (m) Pet form of **Clifford**, **Clifton** used independently since 1948. In the 1960s given a boost by Cliff Richard, the singer, born in 1940 as Harry Webb.

Clifford (m) Common English place name and aristocratic surname, originally referring to a 'ford near a slope'. Reached its peak in the U.S. in the late 19th c. In Britain most used 1900–30 and is now rare. By the early 1980s mainly being kept alive in the U.S. by black American families.

Clifton (m) Common British place name, originally indicating a 'settlement near a cliff', which became a surname, then first name. Regularly used in Britain, but rather more frequent in the U.S. amongst black American families. The actor Clifton Webb (Webb Parmelee Hollenbeck) made the name known during his long screen career.

Clint (m) Shortened form of **Clinton**, made known by the actors Clint Walker (1927–) and Clint Eastwood (1930–).

Clinton (m) Surname deriving from a common place name ('settlement near a hill') used as a first name. In the U.S. associated especially with De Witt Clinton (1768–1828), governor of New York, after whom many places were named.

Clio (f) Name of the Greek muse of history, used very rarely as a first name.

Clive (m) Surname derived from a place name 'cliff', used as a first name. William Thackeray seems to have launched the name in his novel *The Newcomes* (1855), Clive Newcome being the hero. He may well have had 'Clive of India' in mind, for everyone in Britain at that time knew of the military exploits of Robert Clive (1725–74) in India during the 18th c. Came into general use by the 1870s but very little used until the 1920s. Possible that the actor in silent

films, Clive Brook (Clifford Brook), then made it more widely known. Rose in popularity and was at its peak in Britain in the 1950s and '60s, since when it has declined sharply. American parents do not seem to have taken to the name.

Clodagh (f) Name of a river in Tipperary, Ireland, used very occasionally as a first name.

Clotilda (f) Old German 'loud (famous) battle'. *Clotilde* was a 6th c. French saint and the name is used in France. Rare in English-speaking countries.

Clyde (m) From the name of the River Clyde, in Scotland. Found as a personal name amongst the black slaves of the southern American states. In modern times continues to be associated with black families, though well used by white Americans in the early 1960s.

Cody (m,f) Irish surname, associated with Buffalo Bill Cody (1846–1917) and U.S. place name, rapidly gaining ground as first name in the 1980s. Name of character in TV series *Riptide*. Variants **Kody**, **Codey**, **Codie**, **Kodee**, **Kodie**, etc.

Coleen (f) See **Colleen**.

Colette (f) French pet form of **Nicolette**, mainly used in English-speaking countries since the 1940s, though earlier instances may be found. Reputation of the French novelist Colette (Sidonie Gabrielle Colette, 1873–1954) may have helped to make the name known. **Collette** is a frequent alternative, and **Coletta**, **Colletta** are also found.

Colin (m) Pet form of **Nicholas**, but used since the Middle Ages as a name in its own right. Early popularity is indicated by the frequency of surnames such as *Collins*, *Collings*, *Collinson*, which derive from it. In Scotland and Ireland Colin represents Gaelic *Cailean* 'whelp, youth'. Very popular in Britain and Australia 1940–65. Remains a firm favourite in Scotland and Ireland, but does not seem to have been taken up at any time in the U.S. **Colan** is an occasional variant, while **Collin** is frequent. Surname form **Collins** has also been used as a first name. **Colette, Collette, Colina, Colene, Colena, Coletta,** etc., are used as feminine forms. In some cases **Colleen (Coleen)** is probably used with Colin in mind.

Colina (f) Feminine form of **Colin** used in Britain spasmodically since the 1880s.

Colleen (f) Irish *cailin* 'girl'. Popular name in most English-speaking countries (except Ireland) since the 1940s. Reached a peak in the U.S. in the early 1960s, though only white American parents used it. **Coleen** is frequently found, together with the occasional **Colene, Coline** (which presumably is not meant for French *colline* 'hill'). Some parents have used the name as if it were a feminine form of **Colin.** Colleen McCullough, Australian-born author of *The Thorn Birds*, is a well known bearer of the name.

Collette (f) Frequent variant in English-speaking countries of **Colette. Collet, Collete, Collett** are also found.

Colley (m) British surname, describing someone who was 'black-haired or swarthy', used as a first name. Most famous bearer of the name was Colley Cibber (1671–1757), the English actor and playwright, and hero of Pope's *Dunciad*. **Collis** is a surname of similar meaning also used as a first name from time to time.

Collin (m) See **Colin.**

Collingwood (m) Place name/surname, originally referring to a wood of disputed ownership, regularly used as a first name since the 1840s, though never in great numbers.

Collins (m) Surname, ultimately linked with **Nicholas,** used as a first name. In regular but infrequent use.

Collis (m) See **Colley.**

Colm (m) Irish 'dove'. Irish form of Latin **Columba.** Occurs also in **Malcolm.** Popular since 1970 in Ireland. Sometimes appears as **Colum.**

Colman (m) Short form of Irish *Columbanus* 'dove'. Modern use appears to be restricted to Ireland.

Colonel (m) Military title used as a first name. Occurs from time to time, both in Britain and the U.S. Daniel Defoe has an example in his novel *The Life of Colonel Jack*, where Colonel may however be a nickname. A boy in William Faulkner's story *Barn Burning* has the first name Colonel.

Colston (m) Place name/surname used from time to time as a first name. Originally referred to a settlement belonging to someone who bore an obscure personal name.

Colville (m) Norman place name and surname, used fairly regularly as a first name since the 1840s. **Colvile** and **Colvill** also occur.

Colvin (m) Surname used as a first name, both in the 19th c. and since the 1940s. Original meaning uncertain.

Colwyn (m) River name and place name occasionally used in Wales in modern times as a first name.

Colyn (m) See **Colin.**

Comfort (f) French *conforter* 'to comfort' from Latin *confortare* 'to strengthen' (from *fortis* 'strong'). In Biblical use John 14:26, 'The Comforter which is the Holy Ghost'. A surname since the 13th c. In the 16th c. became a favourite Puritan virtue name. Used in Britain and America until the early 18th c. but infrequent since. On rare occasions used for a man.

Conan (m) Gaelic *Conán*, probably a diminutive of *con* 'high'. This Celtic name seems to have been introduced to Ireland from Brittany after the Norman Conquest. Disappeared from use until made famous by Sir Arthur Conan Doyle (1859–1930), the creator of Sherlock Holmes, who was of Irish extraction. Infrequently used in modern times.

Concetta (f) Italian, with reference to the '(Immaculate) Conception'. Mainly used in the U.S., where the male form Concetto is also found.

Connie (f) Pet form of **Constance,** used since the 1880s but now rare.

Connor (m) Also **Conor** Irish *Concobhar* 'high desire'. Regularly used in Ireland. Also an English river name.

Conrad (m) Germanic 'brave counsel'. Used in Britain since the 1840s but never fashionable. Usage increased slightly in the 1970s, but by 1980 had faded again. In the U.S. reasonably well used in the 1930s and '40s, but has since tended to fade. The hotel executive Conrad Hilton is a well-known bearer of the name.

Conroy (m) English form of several Irish surnames, in occasional use as a first name.

Constance (m, f) Latin *constantia* 'constancy, firmness'. Common name in early Christian inscriptions. Well used in the Middle Ages in Britain, as **Custance** (e.g. in Chaucer's 'Man of Law's Tale'). Taken up by the Puritans of the 17th c., though they came to prefer such forms as **Constant** and **Constancy**. Revived 1900–25 but now faded again.

Constant (m) Latin *Constantius* from *constans* 'steadfast'. Very common name in Christian inscriptions of the Roman Empire. English surname by the 12th c. Much used as a first name by the Puritans 16–17th c. for girls and boys. Revived in the mid-19th c. and used intermittently since. Sometimes represents a short form of **Constantine**.

Constantia (f) Latin 'constancy'. This form of **Constance** used in the Middle Ages, then revived to some extent in the 19th c. Obsolete since the 1870s.

Constantine (m) Latin 'firm, constant'. Common Christian name during the Roman Empire, and the first Christian Roman emperor. Used reasonably well throughout the 19th c. in Britain. Very rarely used in any English-speaking country in modern times.

Conway (m) From the River Conwy 'holy river' in North Wales, which became a place name and surname. Used infrequently as a first name, sometimes in its Welsh form **Conwy**.

Cook (m) Occupational surname used as a first name. In regular use in the 19th c. but 20th c. examples are very rare.

Cooper (m) Occupational surname used

as a first name. Usage in both the 19th c. and 20th c. has been very occasional.

Cora (f) Greek 'maiden', a name which seems to have been invented by James Fenimore Cooper, in *The Last of the Mohicans* (1826). Cleveland Evans of Michigan reports that it was generally popular in the U.S. by 1880, by which time it was being used quietly in Britain. In the 1930s especially popular amongst middle-class black American families, but in modern times has largely been superseded by diminutives such as **Corinne** and **Coralie**.

Coral (f) Transferred use of the word as first name, dating from the 1880s and largely confined to Britain. By early users it may have been seen as a diminutive of **Cora**.

Coralie (f) French diminutive of **Cora**, but no doubt interpreted by early users as an extension of **Coral**. Use of Coralie in Britain began a few years after the introduction of Coral to the naming system. Modern American variation is **Coralee**.

Coralina (f) Adaptation of **Coral** on the analogy of **Carolina**. **Coraline** has also been used, together with the modern **Coralyn**, which uses **Carolyn** as a model. **Coralena** is also found.

Corbet(t) (m) Also **Corbitt**. Surname probably indicating an ancestor with raven-like black hair. Various forms of the name were used in the 19th c., and there was even a feminine form **Corbetta**, used very rarely.

Cordelia (f) King Lear's youngest daughter in Shakespeare's play, whose 'voice was ever soft, gentle and low; an excellent thing in woman'. Probably the same as German **Cordula**, a martyr who was a companion to St Ursula. German scholars suggest an origin from Latin *cor*, *cordis* 'heart'. Regularly but infrequently used.

Cordell (m) Surname used as a first name. The U.S. Secretary of State Cordell Hull (1871–1955), 'father of the United Nations', helped to make the name known. Originally indicated someone who made or sold cord, or rope.

Corey (m) Irish surname, sometimes indicating an ancestor whose name was **Godfrey**, used since the 1960s as a first name, especially by black American families. **Cory** is a frequent variant, and **Correy, Corrie, Corry** are found. **Corrye** has been used as a feminine form, together with **Cory Anne, Cory Lee**, etc.

Corinne (f) French adaptation of **Cora** (which French ecclesiastical authorities prefer to link with St Dioscurus rather than James Fenimore Cooper's heroine). Used in English-speaking countries since the 1860s, but modern use seems to be confined to white Americans and the English. **Corrinne** is frequently found, and other variants include **Corin, Corina, Corine, Corinn, Corinna, Correen, Correne, Corrienne, Corrin, Corrina, Corrinna, Corrine, Koreen, Korina, Korrina.**

Cornelia (f) Latin feminine form of **Cornelius**. Cornelia, wife of Titus Sempronius Gracchus, was greatly loved by the Romans, who erected a statue in her honour. Used from time to time since the 1850s. Occurs also as **Cornalia**, and in 1941 a British **Cornilear** received the name.

Cornelius (m) Latin, probably from *cornu* 'a horn'. Famous Roman clan name, and that of a centurion mentioned in the Bible (Acts 10:1.) Also the name of an early pope. In use in England by the 16th c. Irish parents used it as a substitute for **Connor**, and were still using Cornelius with some enthusiasm until the 1950s. At that point they seem to have reverted to Connor itself. Modern use of Cornelius in the U.S. is nearly always by black American parents. Appears also as **Cornilius, Cornelious, Cornelus. Cornell** is also favoured by black Americans and may be a pet form of Cornelius. In England and Wales the name has been steadily used since at least the beginning of the 19th c. Continues to be used regularly, though not quite as frequently as before 1900. The most famous bearer of the name, prob-

ably, has been Cornelius Vanderbilt (1794–1877), the American railroad magnate.

Cornell (m) Famous American surname, deriving ultimately from an English place name of several possible origins. Regularly used as a first name in the U.S., though rare in Britain. In modern times is especially favoured by black American families, who may link it with **Cornelius. Cornel** is a rare variant, though it was made well known by the actor Cornel Wilde from 1940 onwards.

Cornwallis (m) Surname originally indicating one who came from Cornwall, in England, used from time to time as a first name, especially in the 19th c.

Corona (f) Inspired by the 'coronation' of Edward VII in 1902 rather than a use of the word 'corona' as a name. **Coronar** also appeared at that time, as did **Coronetta.**

Correen (f) Also **Correne.** See Corinne.

Correy (m, f) Also **Corrie.** See Corey.

Corrin (f) Also **Corrina, Corrine, Corrinna, Corrinne.** See Corinne.

Cortez (m) Spanish place name/surname, used in the early 1980s as a first name, mainly by black American families.

Cory (m, f) Also **Corry.** See Corey.

Cosmo (m) Greek *kosmos* 'order'. Occurs in early Christian inscriptions as *Cosmas, Cosmus.* The martyred St Cosmas became the patron saint of Milan and therefore made the name well-known throughout Italy (as *Cosimo* or *Cosmo*). Introduced to Scotland in the 17th c. by the 2nd Duke of Gordon, friend of Cosimo III, Grand Duke of Tuscany. Made known by Cosmo Gordon Lang (1864–1945), Archbishop of Canterbury in 1928. Now rarely used.

Coulson (m) Surname probably linked with **Nicholas (Coll)**, used from time to time as a first name in the 19th c.

Courtney (m, f) Surname of an aristocratic British family whose ancestors came from Courtenay, in France. **Courtenay** was the usual spelling of the first name in the 19th c., but **Courtney** is now usual. Originally used as a male name, now thought of as a girl's name by white families. Black Americans continue to use it for males. **Courteney** is also found.

Craig (m) Gaelic *creag* or Welsh *craig* 'rock'. Surname which first seems to have been used as a Christian name in the early 1940s. The American actor Craig Stevens (born Gail Shekles) was in films from 1941 and no doubt helped to publicize the name. Earlier Arthur B. Reeve had created the character Craig Kennedy, a detective. The name was an immediate success in the U.S. and has subsequently spread in great numbers to all English-speaking countries.

Craven (m) Place name/surname of uncertain origin, used fairly often as a first name in the 19th c.

Crawford (m) Scottish place name and surname used as a first name, especially in Scotland. Original meaning of the name was probably 'ford where crows gather'.

Creighton (m) Place name/surname referring originally to a 'rocky place', used from time to time as a first name.

Cresswell (m) Also **Creswell**. Common English place name and surname, originally indicating a 'stream where cress grew'. Used regularly as a first name in the 19th c. and occasionally in the 20th c.

Crispin (m) Latin *crispus* 'curly'. Crispinus was a common name amongst the Christian inscriptions of the Roman Empire. St Crispin, patron saint of shoemakers, died in the 3rd c. As Shakespeare reminded us, Henry V fought a great battle on St Crispin's Day (25 October). Variant **Crispian** occurs in the Shakespearean play, and this has occasionally been used. Crispin itself well used in Britain in the 17th and 18th cc. Enjoyed something of a British revival in the 1960s and 70s, perhaps offering an alternative to **Christopher**. In earlier times there was a feminine form **Crispina**, which now seems to be obsolete.

Crista (f) See **Christa, Krista**.

Cristal (f) See **Crystal**.

Cristina (f) Occasional modern variant of **Christina**. **Cristine** also occurs for **Christine**, and **Cristopher** for **Christopher**. Pet forms of these names are also found as **Crissey, Crissie, Crissy**.

Crofton (m) Common English place name and surname of several possible origins, used from time to time as a first name.

Crosby (m) Place name/surname used as a first name in the 19th c. **Crosbie** also occurred. A name of similar origin, referring to a place where there was a public 'cross', is **Crosland**, occasionally **Crossland**. **Crossley** also belongs to this group. All used as first names in the 19th c.

Crowther (m) Surname indicating a 'fiddle-player' originally, used as a first name from time to time.

Crystal (m, f) Earliest use of this name was for men in Scotland and the north of England. Represented a diminutive of **Christopher**, and frequently appeared as **Chrystal**. This name itself had a diminutive **Christie**, or **Christy**, sometimes pronounced *chrystie*. The feminine name, which has been used intermittently since the beginning of the century, is a transferred use of the word 'crystal', with its suggestion of brightness and clarity, ultimately from Greek *krystallos* 'ice'. Has been growing in popularity in the U.S. since the 1950s, especially amongst black American families. **Cristal, Crystle** and **Crystol** are occasional variants. The earlier **Chrystal** has also reappeared as a feminine name, together with **Christal, Christel, Krystal, Krystle**, etc.

Curt (m) Variant of **Kurt**, which derives ultimately from **Konrad**. In modern times interpreted as a short form of **Curtis**, which is used far more frequently, especially in the U.S.

Curtis (m) Surname, from Old French *curteis* 'courteous', used as a first name. Used regularly in that role since the early 19th c. and especially popular since the 1950s in the U.S. Black American families in particular have favoured the name in recent years.

Cuthbert (m) Old English *cuth beorht* 'famous bright'. Formerly very popular in the north of England and Scotland, in which areas St Cuthbert was much admired. Steadily used in Britain until the 1930s, when it suffered the same fate as **Clarence**, **Cyril**, etc., and became a slight embarrassment.

Cydney (m) Presumably a deliberate re-spelling of **Sydney**. **Cylvia** also occurs, for **Sylvia**. Dickens anticipated these modern examples in his *Sketches by Boz* (1836). When the father of Simon Tuggs becomes rich, the boy announces that henceforth he will be **Cymon**.

Cynthia (f) Greek *Kynthia*, a title of the moon goddess *Artemis*, 'the goddess of *Cynthus*', from Mount *Cynthos* in the island of Delos. Literary name in the 17th c., used by Jonson, Raleigh, Spenser, etc., to address Elizabeth I. One of the classical names which the wives of U.S. plantation-owners passed on to slaves in the early 19th c. Appears frequently among slave lists of the time. In the 19th c. Mrs Gaskell named a character Cynthia in her *Wives and Daughters* (1866), but it was an intentional link with **Hyacinth**, the name of the mother. A character in the book comments that 'Cynthia seems to me such an out-of-the-way name, only fit for poetry, not for daily use.' In England it became generally popular from 1920, fading away in the 1950s. By that time extremely popular in the U.S. Pet form

Cindy subsequently replaced it, especially in Canada.

Cyprian (m) Latin *Cyprianus* 'man from Cyprus'. Common name in Christian inscriptions of the Roman Empire. St Cyprian, bishop of Carthage, was martyred in 258. Well used in Britain from the 13th c. until the 17th c. Camden included it in his list of 'usual Christian names' (1605). Rarely used in modern times, although Withycombe claims that 'it was revived by the Tractarians in the 19th c.'

Cyril (m) Greek *kyrillos*, from *kyrios* 'lord, ruler'. The name of several saints. Came into general use towards the end of the 19th c. and was decidedly popular until the 1930s. Then became a member of that unfortunate group of names which are considered to be silly for no apparent reason and its usage declined. Remains under a cloud for the moment, but is likely to return to favour in the future.

Cyrus (m) Persian *Kurush*, Hebrew *Koresh*, Greek *Kyros*, Latin *Cyrus*, name of the founder of the Persian Empire 500 BC. Traditionally interpreted as 'the sin' but this is unlikely. 'Shepherd' is an alternative meaning. The name is Biblical, O.T., e.g. 2 Chron. 36:22. Introduced by the Puritans at the end of the 16th c. but never really took hold in Britain. Formerly had far greater use in the U.S. and is still kept in the public eye by such figures as Cyrus Vance (1917–), Secretary of State to President Carter. Usual pet form is **Cy**.

D

Dacian (m) Appears to be a form of Latin *Dacianus*, 'a Dacian' – an inhabitant of the Roman province of Dacia, or what is now Rumania. Reasons why it came into use in the 1970s still unclear.

Dafydd (m) Welsh form of **David**.

Dagmar (f) Nordic version of the Slavic **Dragomira**. The meaning is disputed, possibly 'day famous', 'glory of the day'.

A royal name in Denmark, used regularly though infrequently in English-speaking countries.

Dahlia (f) Flower name used as a first name. Used intermittently since the 1920s, mainly in Britain. **Dalia** is a variant. An early literary example of the name occurs in George Meredith's novel *Rhoda Fleming* (1865), where Dahlia is the sister of the heroine, but this failed to persuade parents to use the name until fifty years later.

Daimen (m) See **Damon**. **Daemon** and **Daimon** also occur.

Daisy (f) From the flower name. Old English 'day's eye', because of its appearance and the fact that it opens in the morning. Its first use as a Christian name in England (in the 1860s) coincides with that of **Marguerite**, French 'daisy', and there is some evidence that Daisy was used as a pet form of **Margaret**. A general vogue for flower names began around that time, presumably inspired by the well-established **Rose**, and Daisy was no doubt helped by its current slang meaning − 'an excellent person or thing' − in expressions such as: 'She's the daisiest girl I've ever seen.' The name reached its peak around 1900 but has been little used since 1925. Never much used in other English-speaking countries. **Daisey** was a frequently-used 19th c. variant, and **Daisie** was sometimes used. Other forms include **Dasey**, **Dasi** (1969), **Dasie**.

Dajuan (m) See **Dejuan**.

Dale (m, f) Surname turned first name. Originally 'dweller in the dale, or valley'. First-name usage began in the 19th c. but became general in the late 1930s. The writer Dale Carnegie helped to make it widely known in the U.S. Use of the name for girls is now rare, but combined names such as **Dale Lee**, **Dale Lynn** continue to be used in the U.S. Especially popular in recent years in Australia. **Dayle** is a frequent variant.

Daley (m) See **Daly**.

Dalila (f) See **Delilah**.

Dallas (m, f) Scottish place name and surname used as a first name. Already being used as such in the 19th c., but the modern television series of this name has had no effect on the frequency of occurrence. Dallas in Texas was named for George Dallas (1792–1864), a vice-president of the U.S.A.

Daly (m) Irish surname O *Dalaigh*

'assembly' used as a first name, especially since the 1940s. Daley occurs with equal frequency, no doubt due to Daley Thompson, the decathlon athlete.

Damaris (f) Latin *Damaris*, probably a mistaken reading of Greek *damalis* 'calf'. Biblical, N.T., Acts 17, 34, where Damaris is said to be an Athenian woman who was converted by St Paul. A favourite name amongst the 17th c. Puritans, though the parish clerks of the time had difficulty with its spelling, rendering it **Tamaris**, **Damris**, **Dammeris**, **Dampris**, **Dameris**, etc. In modern times also found as **Damaras**, **Damaress**, **Damiris**, **Demaras**, **Demaris**, but now rare.

Damen (m) See **Damon**.

Damian (m) Greek *Damianos*, possibly from *damazein* 'to tame'. The Latin form of the name was borne by St **Damianus** in the 5th c., a patron of physicians. Damian was used in medieval times as an ecclesiastical name but came into general use only in the 1950s. The French form **Damien** is frequently found, while **Dameon** is a rarer modern form. **Damion** is also not uncommon, perhaps influenced by **Damon**, which also came into use in the 1950s.

Damien (m) French form of **Damian**, used since the 1950s with some frequency.

Damon (m) Form of **Damian**. Associated in modern times with the New York writer Damon Runyon, of *Guys and Dolls* fame. Regularly used since the 1950s. Occurs also as **Daemon**, **Daimen**, **Daimon**, **Daman**, **Damen**.

Dan (m) Pet form of **Daniel** used as a name in its own right. Especially popular in the 19th c., now infrequent. Kept before the public eye between 1940 and the late 1960s by the actor Dan Duryea (1907–68).

Dana (m, f) In Scandinavia a girl's name which derives from **Daniela**. In the U.S. has long been used for girls, but the surname Dana was used as a male first name in the 19th c. In Britain the male form is **Dane** and **Dana** is unknown for either sex. The actor Dana Andrews (Carver Daniel Andrews) gave the name considerable publicity after 1940, but it seems destined to revert to female use. **Danna** is a feminine variant. Dana is especially popular in compound names such as **Dana Ann, Dana Lynn, Dana Lee.** One can also notice a distinct swing from mainly white usage through the 1950s to black American usage in the 1980s.

Dane (m) Surname used as a first name. It could indicate Danish ancestors, or residence near the River Dane, in England, where Dane means 'trickling stream'. Mostly used in Britain, **Dana** being the preferred form in the U.S.

Daneen (f) See **Danette.**

Danella (f) See **Danette.**

Danette (f) Modern feminine form of **Daniel,** used in the U.S. **Danetta** is also found, together with **Daneen, Danella, Danice, Danise, Danne, Danya** and the popular **Danita.**

Daniel (m) Hebrew 'God is my judge'. Biblical, O.T., Book of Daniel. Its use in the Middle Ages is proved by surnames such as *Daniels.* Then regularly used, though slowly declining in numbers, until the end of the 19th c. From 1900–50 remained in quiet use, but by 1955 it was clearly becoming fashionable. The upward trend was still strong in the early 1970s, in both Britain and the U.S. By 1980 had passed its peak in the U.S. but was still very strong in Britain. No obvious reason for the name's sudden return to favour. The best-known bearers of the name are historical figures, such as the English novelist Daniel Defoe (1660–1731), most remembered for his *Robinson Crusoe,* and Daniel Boone (1735–1820), the American folk-hero and pioneer. A film about the latter, *Young Daniel Boone,* was released in 1950 and another, *Daniel Boone, Trail Blazer,* in 1956. A long-running television series called *Daniel Boone* began in 1964, so the public has certainly been reminded of his existence in recent years. See too

Danny. The name's main feminine forms are **Daniele, Danielle, Daniella,** with occasional variants such as **Dannielle, Daniella, Danise, Danita.** Variants of the male name include **Danyele, Danial, Danal, Daneal, Danill.**

Daniella (f) Vaguely Latinized feminine form of **Daniel,** the French **Danielle** being more common. Daniella appears only in the late 1960s, but is not infrequent. **Daniela** is a common variant.

Danielle (f) French feminine form of **Daniel.** Rare in English-speaking countries until the 1940s, then rising steadily in popularity through the '50s, '60s and '70s. Other feminine forms of the same name include **Daniela, Daniella, Daniele. Daniel** itself is occasionally given to girls, but is probably then pronounced as Danielle. Pronunciation of the latter is sometimes emphasized by the spelling, e.g. **Danyelle,** used in the U.S. in 1970, **Danyele,** used in Britain 1976.

Danita (f) Spanish-style feminine form of **Daniel,** well used in the U.S. though not as frequently as French **Danielle.** Only two occurrences of Danita have been noted in Britain (1961), but usage appeared to be increasing in the U.S. throughout the 1970s.

Danna (f) see **Dana.**

Danny (m) Pet form of **Daniel** used as a name in its own right since the 1930s. **Dannie** is a rare variant. Kept before the public eye in the 1940s and '50s, especially, by Danny Kaye (David Daniel Kaminsky). The well-loved song 'Danny Boy' seems to have been directly responsible in 1964 for the British naming of a **Daniboy** Smith. Also noted in the 1960s were two examples of the variant **D'any.**

Dante (m) Latin *durans* (Accusative *durantem*) 'enduring, obstinate' from *durare* 'to endure'. The famous Italian poet was born Durante Alighieri, Dante being a pet form. Regular use of Dante as a first name in the English-speaking world is probably entirely due to his reputation. The English painter and poet Dante Gabriel Rossetti (1828–82) was certainly named in his honour. See also **Durand.**

Daphne (f) Greek *daphnē* 'laurel'. Daphne was a nymph loved by Apollo, turned into a laurel bush when she fled him. The name is found on Christian inscriptions in early Rome. Unknown in English-speaking countries until the 18th c., when it was passed on to plantation slaves (often as **Daphney** or **Daphny**). When used in the U.S. the name remains predominantly that of black Americans. In England it was unknown until the late 19th c., when it became fairly frequent until 1935. Pet forms include **Daff** and **Daffy.**

Dara (m, f) Semitic 'pearl of wisdom'. Mentioned in 1 Chr. 2:6 in a genealogical list as a male, but now used for girls. Modern usage (1970s on) may well be a back-formation from **Darryl, Darren,** etc., in a conscious attempt to create a feminine form of such names.

Daran (m) See **Darren.**

Darby (m) See **Derby.**

Darcy (m, f) Surname used as a first name, usually deriving from the Norman place name Arcy, but also from Irish O *Dorchaidhe*, 'dark man'. Quietly used in modern times, sometimes in the form **D'Arcy** or **D'Arcie**. **Darcey** is found in the U.S., together with **Darcee, Darci,** and is usually a girl's name.

Darell (m) See **Darryl.**

Daren (m) See **Darren.**

Darin (m) See **Darren.** This spelling may be a deliberate attempt, however, to link the name with the pop singer Bobby Darin (Walden Robert Cassotto) 1936–74, who chose his stage name from a telephone directory.

Darlene (f) Presumably an adaptation of 'darling', the commonly used vocative. In use by 1937 and by 1950 had become extremely popular in the U.S. By 1980, however, had faded completely. Usage was evenly spread amongst black and white Americans. Variants such as **Darleen** and **Darlene** are found, and **Darla** is also used, alone or in combinations such as **Darla Ann, Darla Sue.**

Darnell (m) Place name which became a surname, regularly used as a first name, especially by black American families. Had become decidedly popular amongst the black community by the early 1980s. The original meaning of the place name was probably 'hidden nook'. Just possible that the surname or first name refers occasionally to the 'darnel' plant, a kind of grass which was formerly thought to have intoxicating qualities.

Daron (m) Fairly frequent variant of **Darren.**

Darrell (m) Frequently-used variant of **Darryl.** Has a feminine form **Darrellyn.**

Darren (m) Apparently an Irish surname used as a first name. Began to be used in the 1950s, when the actor Darren McGavin (1922–   ) was making regular appearances in films. Soon afterwards the television series *Bewitched*, in which the leading male character had the first name Darrin, began to be seen in the U.S. and then in Britain. (See also **Darin.**) The name appealed to British parents who wanted a 'new' first name, perhaps because of its fashionable sound – **Sharon, Karen** were amongst other popular names of the time. Has continued in use ever since, though by 1980 had clearly started to descend. Has a number of variants, especially **Darrin, Darran, Daron, Daren, Darin.** Also found are **Daran, Darien, Darron, Darryn, Darun, Daryn, Darrian. Daria** (rare) may have been seen as a feminine form. All forms of the name have been used far more intensively in Britain than in the U.S. in modern times.

Darryl (m) Surname of uncertain origin (perhaps from a Norman place name, as d'*Airel*), used as a first name. Has many variant forms, but Darryl occurs most frequently, with **Darrell, Daryl, Darrel** running close behind. An early instance was a **Darrel** Smith, named in 1866 in Britain. **Darrell** was used several times at the end of the 19th c. **Darryl** appears to date from the 1940s, and is presumably to be linked to the film producer Darryl F. Zanuck, whose name appeared prominently on cinema screens from the mid-1930s. At its most popular in the 1950s but has since faded. In the U.S. was used by both black and white families, the former always being more fond of it. Other forms include **Darral**, **Darrill**, **Darrol**, **Daryll**, **Darryll**. Occasionally used as a female name, though **Daryllyn**, **Darrellyn**, etc., are more usual in that role.

Daryn (m) See **Darren**.

Dave (m) Pet form of **David** used in its own right since the beginning of the 20th c., though never in great numbers.

Daveen (f) See **Davina**. **Davenia**, **Davena**, **Davene**, **Davenna** also occur.

David (m) Hebrew, though of disputed meaning. 'Beloved, friend' is one theory. It is also explained as a vocative roughly akin to 'darling'. Biblical, O.T., David was the young man who slew Goliath with a slingshot and later became the second King of Israel. He was the writer of the Psalms. Saint David (7th c.) became the patron saint of Wales and caused the name to be intensively used there at all times thereafter. In the surname period it led to *Davis*, *Davies*, etc. From the 12th c. David was a royal name in Scotland, and has been of lasting popularity there. In all other English-speaking countries, apart from a slight loss of favour around the turn of the 20th c., it has been extremely popular for the last hundred years. In the early 1980s it stands very high in all lists of most frequently used names (see Appendix). Pet forms include Welsh **Taffy**, **Dai**, **Davy**. Feminine forms are mainly Scottish, namely **Davina**, **Davida**. Pet form **Dave** has long been used as a name in its own right. **Davey**, **Davie** and **Davy** are also found.

Davida (f) One of the feminine forms of **David**, though **Davina** is more often used in that role.

Davina (f) Traditional Scottish feminine form of **David**. Regularly, but infrequently, used in modern times, along with more recent forms such as **Davine**, **Davinia**, **Daveen**, **Davena**, **Davenna**, **Davelle**.

Davis (m) Surname linked with **David** used from time to time as a first name. **Davison** and **Davy** also occur.

Dawn (f) Transferred use of the word, perhaps directly inspired by the use of **Aurora**, Latin 'dawn'. The Latin form of the name has been used since the 5th c., Dawn only appears in 1928, but its use rapidly increased. In the early 1980s clearly losing ground rapidly in Britain, but still well used in the U.S. The actress Dawn Addams (1930–) no doubt helped it along, together with the New Zealand-born actress Nyree Dawn Porter in the 1970s who followed a little later. To Miss Withycombe it is a '20th c. invention of novelette writers', and as such, clearly qualifies for her disapproval. One wonders what she makes of the variant forms now to be found, such as **Dawna**, **Dawne**, **Dawnetta**, **Dawnielle**, **Dawnysia**, **Dawnn**, etc. The **Dorne** who was named in 1966 was presumably being given the surname as a first name.

Dawson (m) Surname linked with **David**, used very regularly as a first name. Has continued to be so used since 1920, when a great many of the surnames used as first names in the 19th c. disappeared from the first-name scene.

Dax (m) Suddenly appeared at the end of the 1960s and was used until the early 1970s, both in the U.S. and Britain. One can only suggest a borrowing from the French place-name, Dax being well-known for its thermal waters. In that case, the name means 'of the waters', *-ax* representing Latin *aquis*, oblique form of *aqua*, water.

Dayle (m, f) Variant since the 1960s of **Dale**. **Dayl** has also been noted.

Dayna (f) Appears to be a variant of **Dana**. In use in the U.S. since the late 1970s.

Dean (m) Surname used as a first name. The surname can mean 'valley' or derive from Latin *decanus* 'leader of ten', the church officer who is in charge of several priests. First name used in the U.S. since colonial times. In the 1950s brought to the public's attention by Dean Acheson, U.S. Secretary of State 1949–53, Dean Rusk, U.S. Secretary of State in the 1960s, and Dean Martin (Dino Croccetti), the singer/actor. **Deana** is used as a feminine form.

Deana (f) Spelling variant of **Diana**, or a feminine form of **Dean**. Pronunciation of the name can therefore vary, as indicated by other forms which are found such as **Deeanna** and **Deena**.

Deandre (m) This is **André** with the fashionable De- prefix, much used in the early 1980s by black American families. See **Dejuan**.

Deane (f) Common variant, especially since the 1940s, of **Diane**.

Deangelo (m) De- + **Angelo**. Well used in the early 1980s by black American families. See also **Dejuan**.

Deanna (f) Modern form of **Diana**, made fashionable to some extent by the Canadian singer/actress Deanna Durbin (Edna Mae Durbin) from the late 1930s onwards. Now rather less used.

Deanne (f) Common variant since the 1940s of **Diane**.

Debbie (f) Pet form of **Deborah**, but much used as an independent name since the 1950s. Made well known by the actress Debbie Reynolds (born Marie Frances Reynolds). **Debby** occurs fairly frequently.

Deborah (f) Hebrew 'a bee'. The equivalent name in Greek is **Melissa**. A bee is variously said to have been symbolic of wisdom, eloquence, female perfection, industry, etc., to the ancients. Deborah is Biblical: Rebecca's faithful nurse, Gen. 35:8; a prophetess and judge in Israel, Judges 4 and 5. The name was adopted by the Puritans in the late 16th c., quietly used in the 17th c. Some interest was shown in the early part of the 18th c., but it then remained in rare use until the 1940s. The British actress Deborah Kerr began to appear in films at that time, and may have influenced use of the name. By 1950 it was certainly

one of the top names throughout the U.S. The actress **Debra** Paget (born Debralee Griffin) was by this time making the alternative modern spelling of the name more widely known. (See also **Debbie**.) Deborah reached its peak by 1960, but has tended to fade since then, in all English-speaking countries. Probably held back in the latter half of the 19th c. by Mrs Gaskell's literary creation, Deborah Jenkyns in *Cranford*. The strong-minded Miss Jenkyns liked her name to be stressed on the second syllable, and 'was not unlike the stern prophetess in some ways . . . although she would have despised the modern idea of women being equal to men. Equal, indeed! She knew they were superior.' Charlotte Yonge, writing in 1863, remarks that 'a certain amount of absurdity' is attached to the name because of its use in literature. Apart from Debra, **Debbora**, **Debbra**, **Deberah**, **Debora**, **Deborha**, **Deborrah** and **Debrah** occur as variants.

Debra (f) Modern spelling variant of **Deborah**. See further at **Deborah**.

Decima (f) Latin, feminine of *Decimus* 'tenth'. Common Roman name. Decima was the goddess who presided over childbirth. Continues to be used in modern times, although the original meaning of 'tenth child' rarely applies. Other connections with 'ten', e.g., tenth month, sometimes suggest the name, but it is also used as a pleasant-sounding word which need not have a meaning.

Decimus (m) Latin *decimus* 'tenth'. Used during the 19th c., when large families were still common, but extremely rare in the 20th c.

Declan (m) Name of a well-known Irish saint (Irish *Deaglan*) of unknown origin. Suddenly a very popular name in Ireland in the 1960s and '70s. **Decla** has been used as a feminine form.

Dee (f, m) Nickname based on any name beginning with D-, sometimes used as an independent name. Combinations such as **Dee-Ann**, **Dee Dee** also occur. The male name Dee probably represents a use of the surname or the English river name.

Deena (f) See **Dina**.

Deidre (f) See **Deirdre**.

Deirdre (f) Name of a legendary Irish heroine of great beauty, possibly meaning 'fear' or 'one who rages' according to Coghlan (*Irish Christian Names*). The name occurs in literature, e.g., W. B. Yeats' *Deirdre* (1907) and J. M. Synge's *Deirdre of the Sorrows* (1910). Fiona Macleod (William Sharp) introduced the name to Scotland in his novel *Deirdre* (1903). Not taken up until the 1920s, but it has been regularly used since then, especially in Britain. Variant forms include **Deidrie, Deidra, Deidre** and **Dierdrie**. P.G. Wodehouse commented on the problem of spelling the name correctly in *Sunset at Blandings* : 'I've often wondered how that name was spelled', said Vickey meditatively. 'I suppose you start off with a capital D and then just trust to luck'.

Dejuan (m) One of the fashionable names amongst black American families in the early 1980s. De- is an especially popular prefix, occurring in such names as **Deandre, Deangelo, Demarco, Demario, Deshawn, Dewayne**. The exact form of the prefix sometimes varies, e.g. **Dajuan** is fairly frequent, and **Dujuan, Jajuan** are found. Usually the name behind the prefix is easily recognisable. Occasionally names that happen to begin with De- are drawn into the fold, so that **Devon** is not pronounced as the English county name but as if it were -Von which happened to have a prefix. With examples like **Deon** we probably have a variant of **Dion** caused by the fashionable spelling.

Del (m, f) Pet form of names beginning with Del-, used in its own right since the 1950s. In the form **Dell**, which also occurs, it takes on the meaning of 'small valley'.

Delia (f) The classical name derives ultimately from Greek *Delos*, birthplace of the goddess Artemis. Also a pet form of Irish **Bedelia**, a form of **Bridget**, or

Cordelia, Fidelia. Well used by the pastoral poets of the 17th–18th cc. Regularly used in English-speaking countries, though never in great numbers. **Delya** is an occasional variant.

Delicia (f) Latin 'delight'. Occurs in Christian inscriptions of the Roman Empire. Found as **Delice** in the 1930s, now **Delise, Delisha**, etc. Marie Corelli published her novel *Delicia* in 1896, the story of a faithful wife and her 'cad' of a husband.

Delilah (f) Hebrew 'flirt, coquette amorous'. The mistress of Samson, who betrayed him. Biblical, O.T., Judges 16. Used to some extent by Protestants in the 16th and 17th cc., but rare in modern times. The popularity of the song 'Delilah' sung by Tom Jones appears to have had no effect on the name's use. **Dalila** is one of the variant forms occasionally found. **Lila(h)** may in some cases be seen as the diminutive form of Delilah.

Delise (f) Apparently a form of Latin **Delicia**, 'delight'. Delise occurs in the 1970s, **Delice** being an earlier form. In the U.S. **Delesha, Delisiah, Delisa, Delisha**, etc., are found. **Delys** occurs in Canada. Names beginning with De- are especially fashionable in modern times with black American parents, and forms such as Delisa may simply be **Lisa** with the favoured prefix.

Della (f) Pet form of **Adela** or **Adella** but established since the 1870s as a name in its own right. Continues to be used steadily in all English-speaking countries.

Delma (f) Probably a pet form of **Fidelma** used independently. In use since the 1940s, mainly in Britain.

Delmar (m) Common American place name used as a first name in the U.S. The usual origin is Spanish 'by the sea', though a combination of Delaware and Maryland has been suggested. Delmar in Iowa is apparently an acronym, made up of the initial letters of six women's names.

Delores (f) Presumably a mis-spelling of

Dolores originally, but becoming a standard form of the name in English-speaking countries. In Britain it has been regularly used since the 1930s. In Detroit (1960) 10 black girls and one white girl were called Delores, while 7 whites and 1 black girl were called Dolores. For the etymology see Dolores.

Delpha (f) Also **Delphe, Delphia.** See **Philadelphia.** Some examples of **Delphi** may belong here. None of the above names is used frequently.

Delphine (f) This French name is connected ultimately with Delphi, the ancient Greek town famous as the seat of the Pythian oracle. It seems likely that the place name derived from Greek *delphis* 'dolphin', the significance lying in the Greek belief that Delphi was the womb of the earth and the dolphin's shape suggesting pregnancy. *Delphinia* was applied to the goddess Artemis because of her shrine at Delphi, and Delphine may be seen as a direct descendant of that name. There was a male name *Delphinios*, Latin *Delphinus*, French *Delphin*. A 12th c. nobleman of this name assumed a dolphin as his badge, which led later to *Dauphin* 'dolphin' becoming the hereditary title of the eldest son of the French king. It may be interpreted by some parents as a flower name, connected with the delphinium, or larkspur as it is more commonly known. The flower received its name because the shape of its nectary resembled that of a dolphin. In modern times used mainly by black American parents. **Delphi** is sometimes found, perhaps as a pet form of Delphine or a direct borrowing of the place-name. As it happens, **Dolphin** has been used from time to time as a first name, but a letter from one lady who had been given that name explained that she had been born on a ship called the *Dolphin* which formerly took emigrants to Australia.

Delroy (m) Form of **Elroy** used in Britain mainly by West Indian families since the 1960s.

Delsie (f) Probably meant to be **Dulcie,** that name having been taken to be a form of **Elsie.** Occurs from time to time since the 1880s.

Delta (f) Greek *delta*, the fourth letter in the Greek alphabet. One of several that have been transferred to first-name use. See **Alpha.**

Delwyn (f) Welsh 'pretty' + 'fair'. Used in Wales from the 1920s.

Delyse (f) French form of **Delicia,** used mainly in Canada.

Delysia (f) Another form of **Delicia,** used since the 1930s.

Delyth (f) Welsh 'pretty, neat'. Usage is confined to Wales.

Demaras (f) Also **Demaris.** See **Damaris.**

Demarco (m) Also **Demario.** See **Dejuan.**

Demelza (f) Cornish place name used in modern times as a first name. Originally referred to a hill-fort. First occurs in the 1950s.

Dena (f) Perhaps to be explained as Old English *denu* 'valley'. Became more popular when **Dean** came into fashion (in the 1950s) and was no doubt seen as a feminine form of that name.

Dene (m) Fairly common modern variant of **Dean.**

Denese, Deneice (f) Variants, especially in the U.S., of **Denise.**

Denham (m) English place name/surname used as a first name. Originally a 'hamlet in a valley'. Used only sporadically.

Denholm (m) Scottish place name and surname used as a first name, though rarely. A well-known bearer of the name is the English actor Denholm Elliott.

Denice (f) Common variant, especially in the U.S. of **Denise.** Also found as **Deniece, Dennice,** etc.

Denis (m) Modern French form of **Dennis,** used regularly in English-speaking countries, but never to the extent of Dennis.

Denise (f) French *Denise*, from Latin *Dionysia*, from Greek *Dionusia*, feminine of *Dionusios* 'lame god', son of Zeus and Semele and god of wine, originally of vegetation. The Latin form of the name is common in early Roman Christian inscriptions. Camden (1605) gives **Denis** as a girl's name, which indicates that the early pronunciation of Denise in England was that of the modern male name. After the 16th c. Denise was virtually lost until it came into use again as a conscious borrowing from French in the 1920s. Became very popular in all English-speaking countries, especially in the 1950s, but lost ground after 1965. Variant spellings of the name, some reflecting a change of pronunciation from *Den-eeze* to *Den-eece*, include **Denyse, Denize, Dennise, Denese, Denice, Deneice, Deniece, Denyce**.

Dennie (f) Pet form of **Denise** and similar names, now used as a name in its own right, especially in the U.S.

Dennis (m) French *Denys*, Greek *Dionusios* 'of Dionysos'. *Dionysius* (the Latin form of his name) was the god of wine. The name (Dionysius) is Biblical, N.T., Acts 17:34, a man converted to Christianity by St Paul. Several saints bore the name, including the St Denys who became patron saint of France. Introduced by the Normans to Britain, it gave rise to many surnames, including *Dennis, Dennison, Tennyson*. Remained in common use until the 15th c., virtually disappeared in the 16th c., reappeared in the 17th c., only to fade again in the 18th c. until the beginning of the 20th c. Then became fashionable, reaching a peak in all English-speaking countries in the 1920s. Since then it has slowly faded, though it remains in use. The Dennis spelling has always been the most popular in modern times, though **Denis** and **Denys** have been used very regularly. Other variants include **Denice** (usually feminine but occasionally male), **Denies, Dennes, Dennys**. Dionysius used on very rare occasions in the 19th c. Feminine form is Denise, though Dionysia is called into use on rare occasions. The well-known bearers of the name, such as actors Dennis O'Keefe, Dennis Weaver, Dennis Price, Dennis Morgan and the singer Dennis

Day, were too late on the scene to influence the name's popularity.

Dennise (f) See Denise.

Dennison (m) Surname linked with **Dennis**, used as a first name from time to time.

Denny (m) Pet form of **Denis, Dennis** used independently, or the surname used as a first name. Regularly but infrequently used. **Dennie** appears to be used for girls.

Dennys (m) See Dennis.

Denton (m) English place name, surname 'settlement in a valley' used regularly if infrequently as a first name. Dent, a name of similar meaning, was also occasionally used as a first name in the 19th c.

Denver (m) English surname and place name, 'Dane's crossing place'. Used regularly if infrequently as a first name, especially in Britain. Denva has also been noted as a feminine form.

Denyce, Denyse (f) Variants, especially in the U.S., of Denise.

Denys (m) Old French form of **Dennis**, in regular use in English-speaking countries, but see Dennis for a fuller account.

Denzil (m) From Denzell, a place in Cornwall. Became a surname, then first name. Mainly confined to Britain, and occurring in such forms as Denzel, Denziel, Denzill and Denzyl, though Denzil is by far the commonest.

Derby (m) English place name and surname used regularly if infrequently as a first name. Originally referred to a village with a deer park. **Darby** is a rare variant. 'Darby and Joan' are the old-fashioned, loving couple who live a quiet but contented life together. First mentioned in a ballad which appeared in 1735, said to have been based on John Darby, a printer, and his wife Joan.

Derek (m) Usual modern form in Britain of **Theodoric**. Began to be used at the very end of the 19th c., its usage increasing immediately. Reached its peak in the mid-1930s and fading steadily since that time. Not as popular this century in the

U.S. (though see **Derrick**). Other forms of the name used since 1900 include **Dereck, Deric, Derick, Derik, Derreck, Derrek, Deryck, Deryk, Deryke**. The Dutch form **Dirk** has also been used. The British actors Derek Bond and Derek Farr made the name known from the 1940s onwards, and may have helped spread the name beyond Britain.

Derenda (f) Also **Derinda**. Most of the examples of these two names occur since the beginning of the 20th c., by which time **Derek** and its variants were in regular use. They are therefore probably to be explained as blends of **Derek** and the typically feminine name endings -enda/-inda. At least one **Derenda** was named in Britain in 1890, however.

Deric(k) (m) Also **Derik**. See **Derek**.

Dermot (m) Irish *Diarmuid* 'envy free'. Name of legendary Irish hero. Increasing in popularity in Ireland in the 1970s. **Dermod** and **Kermit** are amongst the name's alternative forms.

Deron (f) Also **Derran**. See **Deryn**.

Derre(c)k (m) See **Derek**.

Derren (f) Also **Derrin, Derrine**. See **Deryn**.

Derrick (m) Preferred modern spelling in the U.S. of **Derek**, used mainly in the 1980s by black American families. **Derrik** also occurs.

Derrie (m, f) Originally a pet form of such names as **Derek, Derrick, Dermot**, now occasionally used independently for both sexes, especially in the U.S.

Derry (m) Pet form of **Derek, Derrick, Dermot**, etc. used as an independent name since the 1920s. Also an Irish surname deriving from the place name, and some first-name usage may be due to transference. **Derrie** is a variant form.

Deryck (m) Spelling variant of **Derek** probably introduced by the novelist Florence Barclay in *The Rosary* (1909). This form is found soon afterwards, and continued in use until the 1960s. **Deryek, Deryk** and **Deryke** also occur.

Deryn (f) Mainly used in Wales. First appeared in the early 1950s, though isolated examples of **Derran** have been

noted in the 1940s. Davies mentions **Aderyn** as a feminine name in his *Book of Welsh Names* (1952). Examples of Aderyn are rarely found, though **Deryn** and its variants continued in regular use until the early 1970s. Davies derived the name from *aderyn* 'bird', and this is the most likely explanation of both forms. It occurred too early to have been influenced by **Darren**, and there is no reason why a name like **Derry**, used occasionally since the 1920s, should suddenly have been extended to Derryn. Many parents obviously responded to the sound of the name and did not relate it to a specific word, for while Deryn has always been the commonest form, the name also occurs as **Deron, Derren, Derrin, Derrine, Derron**. Deron and Derrin are sometimes found in the U.S., always as a male name. Such forms are probably variants of **Derwin** 'dear friend', which also occurs occasionally.

Desdemona (f) Greek *desdaimonia* 'misery'. The tragic heroine in Shakespeare's *Othello*. Little used, though occasionally found as **Desdamona, Desdemonia**, as well as in its Shakespearian form. Desdemona was made the subject of a popular song which featured in the television series *Fame* (1982) and this may affect the use of the name.

Deshawn (m) De- + **Shawn**. One of the popular names amongst black American families in the early 1980s. See **Dejuan**.

Désirée (f) French 'desired'. The Latin form **Desideratus** was a common early Christian ecclesiastical name, and this male name lives on as French **Didier**. The Puritans used **Desire** for girls, taking the name to the U.S., e.g. Desire Minter, a passenger on the *Mayflower*. In modern times Désirée remains the usual form, used especially by black American families. The most famous bearer of the name was Bernadine Eugenie Désirée Clary, who became Queen of Sweden. A fictionalized account of her life appeared in 1953, called *Désirée*, written by Annemarie

Selinko. **Desyre** appeared as a girl's name in the 1970s.

Desmond (m) Irish *Deasmhumhnaigh*, from *deas* 'south' and *Mumhan* 'Munster'. As a surname the meaning is 'descendant of a man from south Munster'. As a Christian name, was first used in Ireland, but spread to England by 1900. Became generally popular in the 1920s but has remained in very quiet use since 1930. In the U.S. favoured especially by black American parents after 1950. Usual pet form of the name is Des.

Desna (f) Appeared in the 1940s and then disappeared again. The equally mysterious **Desne** is found in the late 1930s and survived until the early 1950s. **Desney** also occurred in the 1940s and '50s. In the 19th c. an isolated example of **D'esney** has been noted, used as a first name, though it is presumably a Norman surname. *Disney* is a similar kind of surname, but does not seem to occur as a first name. Desna appears to be a blend of other names. The other forms look like a surname (in various guises) transferred to first name use.

Detta (f) Short form of Italian *Benedetta* (**Benedicta**) used as an independent name.

Devean (f) Also **Deveen, Devene**. See **Davina**.

Devon (m) English county/river (also found in the U.S.) used as a first name. Especially popular with black American families. **Devin** is a common variant, while **Devona** is used for girls. In use only since the 1960s. See also **Dejuan**.

Devorah (f) Hebrew form of **Deborah**.

Devra (f) Shortened form of Devorah, Hebrew Deborah. Its use coincided with the popularity of **Debra** in the 1950s.

Dewayne (m) De + **Wayne**. Another of the fashionable names being used by black American families in the early 1980s. See also **Dejuan**.

Dewey (m) Surname used as a first name. Derives from **Dewi**.

Dewi (m) Ancient Welsh name, traditionally rendered **David** e.g. for the patron saint. Used regularly in Wales, though not as often as **Dafydd**.

Dexter (m) Surname used as a first name. Originally it meant a 'female dyer'. In regular use, especially in Britain, since the 1940s. Also occurs in Christian inscriptions of the Roman Empire, where it derives from Latin *dexter* 'right-handed'.

Diamond (f) The jewel name. Used as a first name from the 1890s, but never as popular as e.g. **Pearl, Ruby, Beryl**.

Dian (f) Form of **Diana** or **Diane** regularly used since the 1940s.

Diana (f) Latin *Diana*, for earlier *Diviana* 'belonging to *Divia*', from *diva*, feminine of *divus* 'divine'. Goddess of the moon. Occurs in early Christian inscriptions as *Diania*. First found in the 16th c. and regularly used in all English-speaking countries. George Meredith's novel *Diana of the Crossways* (1875) had little impact on usage. The heroine of the book consistently says that she dislikes her 'pagan' name, and adds: 'To me the name is ominous of mischance.' See also **Deanna**. **Deana** and **Dianna** are other variant spellings.

Diane (f) French form of **Diana**. Diane began to be used in the 1930s. By 1950 had easily overtaken Diana in all English-speaking countries. At its peak everywhere around 1960, since when has declined rapidly. **Dianne** is fairly common as an alternative spelling. Also found are **Deane, Deanne, Deann, Dyanne**.

Dianna (f) Spelling variant of **Diana**.

Dianne (f) Spelling variant of **Diane**.

Diarmuid (m) See **Dermot**.

Dick (m) Rhyming pet name for **Richard** frequently used as a name in its own right until the 1940s, by which time the various slang meanings of the name made it difficult to use.

Dickon (m) Pet form of **Richard** dating from the 13th c. in occasional use as a first name. **Dicken** is a variant.

Didier (m) See **Desirée**.

Diedre (f) Also **Dierdre**. See **Deirdre**.

Diego (m) Spanish form of **James** used regularly if infrequently in the U.S.

Dieter (m) Modern German form of *Diether* 'people – army'. Occasionally used in English-speaking countries since the 1950s.

Digby (m) English place name 'settlement by a ditch' which became a surname, e.g. Sir Everard Digby, executed in 1606 for his part in the Gunpowder Plot. In general use as a first name, mostly in Britain, since the 1870s.

Dillon (m) Irish surname used as a first name or a variant of **Dylan**. **Dillan** also occurs. Not frequent.

Dilwyn (m) Place name (Herefordshire) 'secret or shady place'. Used in Wales as a first name since the 1920s. **Dillwyn** is also found.

Dilys (f) Welsh *dilys* 'certain, genuine, sincere'. Used in Wales and England since 1857. Trefor Rendall Davies points out that the word is used in a metrical version of the 23rd Psalm by Prys (1544–1623). **Dylis, Dyllis, Dylys** are also found.

Dina (f) Short form of names such as **Bernardina** (in which case it is pronounced **Deena**) or a variant of **Dinah**. Use of the name appears to be increasing in modern times.

Dinah (f) Hebrew 'judged, vindicated'. Biblical, O.T., the daughter of Leah and Jacob, Gen. 34. A favourite Puritan name in the 16th c., often written **Dina** (as it is today). Taken to America where it became associated strongly with the blacks of the southern States, but subsequently used as well by white families.

Dion (m) Short form of **Dionysios**, 'man from Dionysus', name of the Greek god of wine. The more familiar version of the name is **Dennis**. Dion is especially favoured by black American families and West Indians in Britain.

Dionne (f) Usual feminine form of **Dion**, though **Dionna** and **Dione** are also found. Used especially by black Americans and West Indian families in Britain. Other explanations of the name are possible: e.g. **Dione** in Greek mythology was the consort of Zeus and mother of Aphrodite. *Dionne* is also a surname,

made well-known by the Dionne quintuplets, born in 1934.

Dionysia (f) see **Denise**.

Dionysius (m) See **Dennis**.

Dirk (m) Pet form of **Diederick**, the Dutch form of **Derek** or **Derrick**. In use since the 1960s, having been publicized by the actor/writer Dirk Bogarde (Derek Gentron Gaspart Ulric van den Bogaerde).

Dives (m) This name, pronounced as two syllables, is traditionally that of the 'rich man' in the parable about the rich man and Lazarus, Luke 16. In the 19th c. it mostly occurred as **Divers**, but the occasional **Divarus, Diveros, Diverous, Diverus, Divorus** are presumably related to it.

Divina (f) Variant of **Davina**, influenced by 'divine'. Occasionally used in the 20th c. **Divinia** also occurs.

Dixie (m) Also **Dixee**. In Britain a use of the surname, said to be related to Latin words for 'I have spoken', regularly used by a chorister. Some instances may also relate to a much-admired English soccer player of former times, Dixie Dean. In the U.S. associated with the southern States because of the mid-19th c. song. Rarely used, however.

Dixon (m) Surname 'Dick's son' used as a first name with some regularity in the 19th c., but now rare.

Doctor (m) The word used as a name. Occurs very occasionally. Dickens has a character Doctor Marigold, named in honour of the doctor who assisted at his birth.

Dolly (f) Pet form of **Dorothy**, used as an independent name since the 16th c. For the form compare **Molly** from **Mary**. Dolly was used frequently in the 18th c., then faded until the end of the 19th c. Used more regularly in the 1920s, but has since slipped into the background, surfacing occasionally, e.g. Dolly Parton, the singer. **Dollie** is also found.

Dolores (f) Spanish *dolores* 'sorrows'. Part of one of the titles of the Virgin Mary, Maria de los Dolores, used as a first name. Mercedes is a similar name.

The Mexican film star Dolores del Rio helped to make the name well-known in the 1920s and '30s. Continues to be regularly used, though not frequently. See also the variant **Delores**. Pet forms **Lola** and **Lolita** are used as independent names.

Dolphin (f) See **Ocean, Delphine**.

Dolphus (m) Pet form of **Adolphus** used from time to time in its own right.

Dominic (m) Latin *dominus* 'the lord'. Common name in Christian inscriptions of the Roman Empire. Generally used from the 13th c. because of St Dominic, founder of the Order of Preachers. Mainly Roman Catholic name until the 1950s, then widely used. **Dominick** is found. Usual feminine form is the French **Dominique**, though **Dominica** also occurs.

Dominique (f) French feminine form of **Dominic**, used increasingly after the mid-1960s, especially in Britain.

Don (m) Pet form of **Donald, Donovan** used as a name in its own right, especially in the period 1925–50. **Donn** is a U.S. variant. The actor Don Ameche (1908–) is actually **Dominic** Amici.

Donald (m) Gaelic *Domhnall* 'world mighty'. Used for centuries in Scotland and associated there with the clan Donald. In the 20th c. intensively used in all English-speaking countries, at its height around 1925. Survived well until the 1950s but has since been declining. Various attempts have been made to form feminine forms, leading to **Dona, Donaldina, Donalda, Donaleen, Donelda, Donella, Donette, Donita, Donnelle**. The British actor Donald Crisp (1880–1974) may have helped spread the name from 1914 on. The American actor Donald O'Connor arrived too late to influence usage.

Donavon (m) See **Donovan**.

Donella (f) Probably a modern formation based on **Don(ald)**, creating a feminine form. Resembles Latin **Domnella**, from **Dominella** 'little mistress', from **Domina**, names that were actually used in Roman times. **Donnella, Donellia** are

variant forms. A different ending leads to **Donita**.

Donna (f) Italian *donna*, Latin *domina, domna* 'lady', originally 'mistress of the house'. The basic word is Latin *domus* 'house'. In Italian *donna* is a title of respect, not a Christian name. Occurs only in *madonna*, literally 'my lady' and used of statues representing the Virgin Mary. Donna occurred very occasionally as a first name in English-speaking countries from 1920 on. In the 1940s the actress Donna Reed (born Donna Mullenger) began to appear in films, and the name was used far more frequently from that time. Reached a peak in the U.S. in the 1950s, arriving in Britain and Australia in force some twenty years later. In recent times has become a popular element in combined names such as **Donna-Maria, Donna-Michelle**, etc.

Donna-Marie (f) 'Lady Mary', i.e., the Virgin Mary. Regularly used by British Roman Catholics, especially, since the late 1960s. **Donna-Maria** is also found.

Donnell (m) Use of the famous Irish surname as a first name, mainly by white American families.

Donnella (f) See **Donella**.

Donovan (m) Irish surname *O Donnabhain* 'dark brown' used as a first name. Its appearance coincided with an Edna Lyall novel called *Donovan* at the turn of the century. Steadily used in all English-speaking countries, and especially popular in Canada in the 1970s. **Donavon, Donoven** and **Donovon** are all found as variants.

Dora (f) Short form of such names as **Dorothy** or **Dorothea, Theodora, Isadora**. Came into use as an independent name after the publication of Dickens's *David Copperfield*. Dora Spenlow, in the novel, is a pretty but impractical girl who becomes Copperfield's 'child wife'. Especially well used in Britain and the U.S. 1875–1900. Little used since the 1930s. **Dorah** was used in the 19th c.

Dorcas (f) Greek *dorkas* 'roe or gazelle'. A translation of the Aramaic name

Tabitha. Biblical, N.T., Acts 9:36. Common name during the Roman Empire, also found as **Dorchas.** The Puritans made good use of the name in the 17th c., while in modern times it continues to be used regularly if infrequently.

Dore (m) Pet form of **Isidore**, sometimes used in its own right.

Doreen (f) Probably not directly connected with the Irish name **Doireann**, 'sullen', but formed from **Dora,** or the Dor- of **Dorothy** and -een, familiar in names such as **Kathleen, Maureen,** etc. Edna Lyall used the name in her novel *Doreen* (1894) and it began to be used from that time. By the 1920s was in the top ten list in England, but the inevitable decline followed. Currently out of favour in Britain, and never much used in the U.S. **Dorene** is found occasionally.

Doretha (f) Modern variant of **Dorothea,** used especially in the U.S. **Dorethea** is also found.

Dorette (f) Modern extension of **Dora,** used in the U.S.

Doria (f) Feminine form of **Dorian.** Rarely used, **Doris** having been preferred in that role.

Dorian (m) Greek, 'man from Doris' (a place in Central Greece). Regularly used this century, but was unknown when Oscar Wilde introduced it in his *Picture of Dorian Gray* (1891). In the U.S. now mainly used by black American families and there is some confusion as to its sex. By some parents it has been interpreted as **Dorie-Ann. Dorien** and **Dorrien** are also found, as are new feminine forms, **Doriana, Dorianne.**

Dorice (f) see **Doris.** Could conceivably be influenced by the Italian name **Doralice,** which has been used on very rare occasions.

Dorinda (f) Poetical extension of **Dora** in the 18th c., when poets and playwrights were especially fond of inventing names ending in -inda. In Farquhar's play, *The Beaux' Stratagem,* Dorinda is the lighthearted but virtuous daughter of Lady Bountiful. Seems to have been revived in the 1940s, and was still being used in the early 1970s.

Doris (f) Greek 'woman from Doris', a region of central Greece. In Greek mythology the name of the wife of Nereus, father of the Nereids. During the Roman Empire it was a common name for a freedwoman, but was virtually unknown in English-speaking countries until 1880, when it burst upon the scene. By 1900 one of the most frequently used girls' names in both the U.S. and Britain. Miss Withycombe notes that Charles Dickens had spotted the name and included it in a list of unusual names some time before 1865. Probably used between then and 1880 by a writer of romantic fiction, as yet untraced, and brought to the public's attention. **Dorothy** was already enjoying great popularity, and names like **Alice** and **Beatrice** were well established. **Dorice** was used as an alternative spelling of the name when it first appeared. The suggestion is, therefore, that a popular name-stem, Dor-, from **Dora, Dorothy** and soon to be seen in **Doreen,** etc., was given a popular ending, which also appeared in **Phyllis, Iris, Francis** and to some extent in **Agnes.** Had the name not existed in classical sources, it would probably have been invented at this time. Remained extremely popular until the 1930s but subsequently faded and now rarely used, despite the popularity of the singer/actress Doris Day in the 1950s and '60s.

Dorita (f) Spanish-style feminine variant of **Doris,** used in the U.S. and Britain this century.

Dorothea (f) Greek 'gift of God'. Latin/Greek form of **Dorothy,** which has always been more frequently used. In modern times such variants as **Dorthea, Doretha** and **Dorethea** are not infrequently found. Pet form **Thea** has also taken on a life of its own.

Dorothy (f) Greek *Dorothea* 'gift of God'. **Theodora** is the same name in reverse. A post-Biblical name; St Dorothea was martyred *circa* 303. Introduced to Britain at the end of the 15th c. and became extremely popular for the next two hundred years. By the end of the 18th c. had gone out of fashion, but re-emerged at the beginning of the present century and became very popular in all English-speaking countries. This time it lasted for a generation before beginning to lose favour. At present used only rarely. Amongst its pet forms are **Doll** (compare **Moll** from **Mary**, **Hal** from **Harry**), **Dolly, Dot, Dotty, Dothy, Dorthy, Dodo**, some of which have been used as independent names. Miss Withycombe cites evidence to show that in polite circles, at least, the 'h' in the name was not pronounced in the 18th c. She also gives a good example (Dora Wordsworth, daughter of the poet) to show that **Dora** could be used as the everyday form of Dorothy. The actress Dorothy Lamour is a well-known bearer of the name.

Dorrien (m) Variant of **Dorian. Dorien** also occurs.

Dorrit (f) Primarily a surname deriving either from **Durward** or **Dorothy**. Made famous by Charles Dickens in his novel *Little Dorrit* (1855–7) and first-name usage probably derives from it. Dorrit, **Doritt** and **Dorit** have all been used as first names, as have **Dorita** and **Doritha**.

Dorthea (f) See **Dorothea**.

Dory (m) Pet form of **Isidore**, also used as an independent name.

Dottie (f) Pet form of **Dorothy** occasionally used as a name in its own right. **Dot** also occurs.

Dougal (m) Old Irish *Dubhgall* 'black stranger', a description originally applied to the Danes by the Irish. The name was taken to Scotland and is now mainly associated with the Scottish Highlands. **Dugald** is the alternative form.

Douglas (m) Gaelic *dubhglas* 'dark blue or black water'. Common Celtic river name giving rise to place names. One such place name led to the surname of a famous Scottish family. By the 17th c. Douglas was being used as a Christian name for girls as well as boys. Camden, writing in 1605, listed it only as a girl's name 'not long made a Christian name in England'. Regularly used throughout the 19th c., then much publicized, and subsequently very popular, in the 1920s when both Douglas Fairbanks Senior and Junior were starring in many films. In the U.S., Canada and Australia reached a peak in the 1950s. Usage in the U.S. was predominantly by white American parents, and in some cases may have been a compliment to General Douglas MacArthur. Little used in any English-speaking country since 1970. Usual pet forms are **Doug** or **Dougie**, but these do not occur as independent names. **Douglass** is found as a spelling variant, and in Scotland **Douglasina** is occasionally used as a modern feminine form.

Douglasina (f) Rarely used feminine of **Douglas** found only in Scotland. Douglas was formerly used as a girl's name, but since the 17th c. has been exclusively male.

Dreena (f) Short form of **Andrena**, used mainly in Scotland. **Drena** also occurs. See also **Andrea**.

Drew (m) Pet form of **Andrew**, increasingly used as a name in its own right since the 1960s.

Drina (f) Pet form of **Alexandrina** used on rare occasions in its own right.

Drummond (m) Scottish surname of uncertain meaning used from time to time as a first name, especially in Scotland.

Drusilla (f) Latin *Drusus*, a name assumed by a Roman who killed a Gaul called *Darusus*, and continued by his family. A Drusilla (of great beauty) is to be found in the Bible, N.T., Acts 24:24, where Felix is said to have employed a magician to lure her away from her husband Aziz so that he could marry her. Formerly in regular use, but rarely employed since the early part of this century. **Drucella, Drucilla, Druscilla, Drewsila** occur as variants.

Duane (m) Irish surname *O Dubhain*

'black' used as first name. Also occurs as **Dwane**, which becomes a first name. Other modern forms are **Dwayne**, preferred in the U.S. and perhaps influenced by Dwayne Hickman, who was a child actor in the mid-1940s when the name began to be used. **Dwain**, **Dwaine**, **Duwayne** and **D'wayne** also occur.

Dudley (m) English place name and famous family name, associated especially with Robert Dudley, Earl of Leicester, Queen Elizabeth I's favourite. Regularly though infrequently used as a first name since the mid-19th c. The English comedian/pianist Dudley Moore (1939–   ) has brought the name to the public's attention in recent years.

Dugald (m) See **Dougal**.

Duke (m) Probably a pet form of **Marmaduke** originally, but also a surname used as a first name. Sometimes bestowed as a title name, Duke being the highest rank of nobility in Britain outside the Royal Family. Probably best known as the nickname of the actor John Wayne (Marion Michael Morrison, 1907–79) who took it from a pet dog, and of Duke Ellington (Edward Kennedy Ellington (1899–1974)), the leading jazz musician for fifty years.

Dulcibella (f) Latin 'sweetly beautiful'. Sometimes found as **Dulcibel**, and formerly far more frequent in its English form **Dowsabel**. The latter lost its name status and became a generic word for a sweetheart. No instances of any forms found in the present century.

Dulcie (f) Latin *dulcis* 'sweet'. *Dulcis*, *Dulcitia* were feminine names during the Roman Empire. Early use of the name in Britain led to surnames such as *Dowse*, *Dowsett*, the name having been imported in its French form, *Douce or Dowce*. Regularly used since the late 19th c., with a vogue in the 1920s and '30s. Now rarely used. **Dulce** and **Dulsie** are sometimes found.

Dulcinea (f) Spanish 'sweet, mild'. The name which Don Quixote chose to give to his loved one, the peerless Dulcinea del Toboso, who was actually Aldonca Lorenco, a different name of the same meaning. Used in Britain, e.g. Dulcenea (*sic*) Smith, born in 1883, but extremely rare.

Duncan (m) Celtic name, modern Gaelic *Donnchad* 'brown warrior'. The name of two kings of Scotland in the 11th c., one of whom was murdered by his cousin Macbeth. Surnames such as *Donecan*, *Dunkin*, etc., show that the name was being used in the Middle Ages, mostly in Scotland and Northern England. Then seems to have died out as a Christian name except in Scotland. Most used in Scotland in the 19th c. and though still used there, is becoming rare. In England and Wales Duncan had a spell of popularity 1950–70. Also occurred at that time in Australia and Canada, but rarely used in the U.S.

Dunstan (m) English place name meaning 'stony hill', but the personal name of a famous English saint who was Archbishop of Canterbury in the 10th c. Used regularly but infrequently, mainly in Britain.

Durand (m) Latin *durans* 'enduring' from *durare* 'to endure'. Rare in modern times, but the many surnames which derive from it (*Durrant*, *Durrand*, *Doran*, etc.) show its popularity in the Middle Ages. See also **Dante**.

Dustin (m) Probably the English place name/surname used as a first name, e.g. for Dustin Farnum, the American cowboy actor of silent film days. The actor Dustin Hoffman is said to have been named because his mother admired Farnum. If the place name origin is correct, the name originally meant 'dusty place', and there was some justification for the nickname which Hoffman says he had while at school, namely *Dustbin*. A more flattering origin has been claimed, however, linking the name to **Thurstan** (Thor's stone'), which led to surnames such as *Tustin*. In Britain a feminine **Dustine** is used. **Dusty** also occurs, likely to have been inspired by the English singer Dusty Springfield

(Mary O'Brien). None of these forms is common.

Dwayne (m) Preferred American form of **Duane**, especially popular in the 1960s and 70s. Always especially favoured by black American families, whites making use of the **Duane** spelling. **Dwain**, **Dwaine** and **D'wayne** also occur.

Dwight (m) English surname probably deriving from **Diot**, and ultimately from Greek **Dionysios**, name of the god of wine. Surname made famous in the U.S. by two presidents of Yale University, and more recently became known as a first name when borne by President Dwight David Eisenhower. Then came into general use in a limited way, but by the late 1970s had almost disappeared. Primarily an American name, though some instances occurred in Britain.

Dyer (m) Occupational surname used as a first name, mainly in the 19th c.

Dylan (m) Welsh name of a legendary sea-god for whom all the waves of Britain and Ireland wept when he died. Traditionally means 'son of the waves', but Trefor Davies suggests Welsh *dylanwad* 'influence'. Made well-known by the Welsh poet Dylan Thomas (1914–53), coming into general use (especially in England and Wales) after his death.

Dylis (f) Variant of Dilys. **Dyllis**, **Dylus** also occur.

Dymoke (m) Place name/surname of uncertain origin, used from time to time as a first name in the 19th c.

Dympna (f) Name of an early Irish saint, of unknown meaning, used mainly in Ireland. Occurs also as **Dymphna**.

Dyson (m) Surname ultimately linked with **Dennis**, used as a first name in the 19th c.

E

Eamon(n) (m) Irish form of **Edmund**. Made well-known in modern times by Eamon de Valera (1882–1975), the Irish president. In England and Wales the name had a minor vogue from the mid-1950s to 1970. In Ireland its use was declining by the mid-1970s. Never been commonly used elsewhere.

Ean (m) Variant of **Ian** or **Iain** found outside Scotland.

Eardley (m) Place name/surname of uncertain origin used from time to time as a first name.

Earl (m) A use of the title of nobility as a first name, or the surname turned first name. Used as a first name in Britain in the 17th c., alongside **Prince**, **Duke**, etc., and was perhaps, as Bardsley suggested, a revolt against Puritan naming habits. Earl has been particularly well used in the U.S no doubt due to the example of Earl van Dorn, Confederate leader in

the Civil War, Earl Warren, who was Chief Justice of the United States, and so on. Erle Stanley Gardner (1889–1970), creater of Perry Mason, also bore a form of the name. Nevertheless, it is tending to disappear. In the 1970s it was mainly kept alive by black American families, but they now seem to be abandoning it. **Earle** is often found, and feminine forms such as **Earlene**, **Earleen** continue to be used.

Earlene (f) Feminine form of **Earl** used mainly since the 1940s and much favoured by black American families. Variants include **Earlina**, **Earlean**, **Earline**, **Earlena**, **Earleen**, **Earlinda**.

Earnest (m) Common 19th c. variant of **Ernest**.

Eartha (f) Old English *eorthe* 'earth'. The 17th c. Puritans used **Earth** as a first name (along with **Dust**, **Ashes**) but it did not survive. The American entertainer Eartha Kitt has made this form of the name widely known, but it is rarely used.

Easter (f) In use throughout the 19th c., but it is difficult to know whether it was meant to be a season name, indicating time of birth, or whether it was a spelling variant of **Esther**. As a season name it could have been a direct translation of **Pascal** or **Pascale**, or used by analogy with **Noel**. In favour of the seasonal argument is the fact that **Christmas** was regularly used throughout the 19th c., though even that can be a transferred surname.

Eben (m) Hebrew 'stone'. Probably a shortened form of **Ebenezer** 'stone of help' via its Dutch form *Eben Haëzar*. Eben has been used in Britain since the 19th c. but is slightly more common in the U.S.

Ebenezer (m) Hebrew 'stone of help'. Biblical, O.T., Sam. 7:12, the name of the stone raised by Samuel in memory of the victory over the Philistines. Adopted by the Puritans and taken to America, where it became extremely popular, second only to **John** at one stage. Lasted through the 19th c., but began to disappear on all sides at the turn of the century. Charles Dickens had not helped the name by publishing *A Christmas Carol* in 1843, featuring the awful Ebenezer Scrooge. Variants of the name include **Ebbaneza, Ebeneezer, Ebenezar, Ebenezeer**.

Ebony (f) The word used as a first name, with reference to the intense blackness of the wood. Rapidly becoming popular throughout the 1970s amongst black families in the U.S. and beginning to occur in variant forms such as **Ebbony, Eboney, Ebonyi, Eboni** and **Ebonie**. The Paul McCartney song 'Ebony and Ivory' (1982) may help to spread the name.

Eda (f) Probably the pet form of **Edith, Edna** etc., used independently, particularly 1850–1930 when those names were popular. There was an Anglo-Saxon name Eda, meaning 'rich, happy', which may on occasions have been revived.

Eddie (m) Pet form of **Edward, Edgar,** etc., used in its own right since the 1880s, regularly but infrequently. A recent trend in the U.S. is for the name to be used for girls, either alone or in combination, e.g., **Eddie Mae**. For girls it also sometimes takes on a fanciful spelling such as **Eddye**. **Eddy** is a variant of the male name.

Eden (m, f) Hebrew 'delight, pleasantness'. For obvious reasons most people equate the name with 'Paradise'. Biblical, O.T., Genesis. The 17th c. Puritans probably began the fashion for using Biblical place names as first names, especially for women, perhaps because far more men are mentioned by name in the Bible than women. **Sharon** is the best known example today, but **Nazareth, Canaan,** etc., were formerly used. In modern times male and female Edens seem to exist in almost equal numbers.

Edgar (m) Old English 'prosperity' + 'spear'. One of the royal Anglo-Saxon names which survived the Norman Conquest. In literature the son of King Lear in Shakespeare's play, and the hero of Scott's *Bride of Lammermoor*. Well used in the last quarter of the 19th c. Now very quietly used.

Edie (f) Pet form of **Edith** used independently from 1890 but now rare.

Edith (f) Old English 'rich' + 'war'. A royal name in Anglo-Saxon times and the name of two early saints. It therefore survived the Norman Conquest and continued in Britain in regular use. Became fashionable as the 19th c. progressed, and was one of the top ten girls' names in the 1870s. Remained extremely popular until the 1930s, when it began to fade. Still in use, but becoming rare. Variant **Editha** occurred regularly in the 19th c., and **Edythe** appeared at the turn of the century. **Edyth** and **Edytha** are also found. Pet forms such as **Eda** and **Edie** were often used as names in their own right. One of the best-known name-bearers of this century was Dame Edith Evans (1888–1976), the British stage actress.

Edmee (f) French feminine of **Edmond**, occasionally used in English-speaking countries.

Edmond (m) See **Edmund**. **Edmondson** is also used as a first name from time to time.

Edmund (m) Old English 'rich protector'. The name of a 9th c. saint, king of the East Angles, whose popularity helped the name to survive the Norman Conquest. Continued to be used steadily throughout the Middle Ages, giving rise to several surnames (*Edmunds*, *Edmundson*, etc.), and remained in popular use until the end of the 19th c. Continued in use since then, especially in Ireland, while never being particularly fashionable. Has tended to be overtaken in the 20th c. by its French form, **Edmond**. In Ireland it takes the form **Eamon** or **Eamonn**, which again have tended to replace it. The surname **Edmondson** has been used from time to time as a first name. Famous bearers of the name include the English scientist Edmund Halley (1656–1742), who became Astronomer Royal. He is best remembered for having predicted the return of the comet which was subsequently named after him. Edmund Spenser (1552–99) was an English poet of note, while Edmund Kean (1787–1833) was the most celebrated Shakespearian actor of his day. In more modern times we have seen the actors Edmund Gwenn and Edmond O'Brien in countless film roles. Usual pet forms of Edmund/Edmond are **Ed**, **Ned** or **Ted**, **Eddy**, **Neddy**, etc. Some of these are used as independent names. It is Edmund, in Shakespeare's *King Lear*, with whom Goneril and Regan fall in love, causing Goneril to poison her sister, then herself, but the name has been recommended by other writers. Jane Austen writes in *Mansfield Park* that 'there is nobleness in the name of Edmund. It is a name of heroism and renown; of kings, princes and knights; and seems to breathe the spirit of chivalry and warm affections.' John

Keats also remarked in a letter to his sister: 'If my name had been Edmund, I should have been more fortunate.'

Edna (f) Hebrew *ednah* 'pleasure, delight' (the same word, perhaps, giving rise to the Garden of *Eden*). Greek *Edna*. Biblical, Apocrypha, e.g. the wife of Enoch. Ernest Weekley also suggested a derivation from **Edwina**, but Edna was in regular use before Edwina became a reasonably common name. Unrecorded in Britain until the 18th c., when it begins to occur regularly but infrequently. Quietly used in the 19th c. until it became very fashionable in the U.S. 1850–1900. Most popular in Britain around 1925, which makes it unlikely that the writer Edna Lyall, a best-selling novelist in the 1870s, was responsible for spreading the name. **Ednah** is occasionally found as a spelling variant.

Edric (m) Old English 'property-powerful'. An Anglo-Saxon personal name that did not survive the Norman Conquest, but was revived in the late 19th c. Regularly but quietly used since. **Edrick** is also found, and **Edrice** has been used as a feminine form.

Edward (m) Old English 'property guardian'. A royal name in England before the Norman Conquest, and a saintly one. Henry III then made it a royal name again in the 13th c. by giving it to his son. It then named successive kings for over a century. Camden, writing in 1605, says: 'the Christian humility of King Edward the Confessor brought such credit to the name that since that time it has been most used in all estates.' Remained extremely popular for centuries, fading only after the 1930s, but certainly not disappearing. Of the many famous men who have borne the name Edward Lear (1812–88) is held in affectionate regard by countless readers of his *Book of Nonsense*, while the actor Edward G. Robinson (1893–1973) is remembered for his individual style. The latter was born Emanuel Goldenburg and the middle initial retained the link with his original name. Pet forms of Edward include **Ned** and **Ted**, in use since the late Middle Ages and used in modern times as names in their own right. **Eddie** (or **Eddy**) dates only from the 1880s as an independent name, though it must have been used far earlier as a spoken form. It was used by Edward Israel Iskowitz (1892–1964), who became the very popular singer Eddie Cantor. Edward is one of the few popular male names that has no feminine form. Eddie has therefore been used to some extent in that role.

Edwin (m) Old English 'prosperity' + 'friend'. Revived with other Anglo-Saxon names in the 19th c. and most used 1850–75. Subsequently remained in regular use, though not frequently given. **Edwyn** often used as a variant. Normal feminine form is **Edwina**, but **Edwyna** also occurs. Confusion with **Edwy** must sometimes have led to the variant spelling.

Edwina (f) Feminine form of **Edwin**. Used more in Scotland than elsewhere. Variants of the name include **Edweena**, **Edwena**, **Edwyna**.

Edwy (m) Old English 'prosperity' + 'war'. Another Anglo-Saxon name revived to some extent in the 19th c. Now obsolete. Confusion with **Edwin** occasionally led to the form **Edwyn**.

Edyth (f) Also **Edytha**, **Edythe**. See **Edith**.

Effam (f) Formerly a short form of **Euphemia**.

Effie (f) Pet form of **Euphemia** regularly used as an independent name from 1860 onwards.

Egan (m) Irish *Mac Aodhagan* 'little fire'. Usage seems to be confined to Ireland.

Egbert (m) Old English 'bright sword'. Revived for a time in the 19th c., when Anglo-Saxon names were fashionable. Now very rare, having acquired a slightly comic feel in spite of impeccable historical associations.

Egerton (m) English place name and aristocratic surname regularly used as a first name, especially in Britain.

Egidia (f) Feminine form of *Egidius*

(**Giles**), used to some extent in Scotland in former times.

Eibhlin (f) Irish, normally anglicized as **Eileen**, but originally a form of **Helen**, or **Evelyn**.

Eiffion (m) From Eifionydd, a district in Caernarvonshire. Used in Wales in modern times, along with the feminine form **Eifiona**.

Eileen (f) From Irish **Eibhlin**, **Aibhlin**, which were probably forms of **Helen** or **Evelyn** originally. Exported to England along with a number of Irish names in the 1870s. By 1925 it ranked amongst the ten leading girls' names. Remained fashionable until the 1950s, by which time it was also being reasonably well used in the U.S. and Australia. In Scotland the variant **Aileen** has been especially well used. Other variants include **Eilean**, **Eilleen**, **Ilean**, **Ileen**, **Ileene**, **Ilene**. Usual pet forms are **Eily** or **Eiley**, which occasionally occur as independent names. *My Sister Eileen*, originally a book by Ruth McKenney, later a play and film (two versions) probably helped to spread the name.

Eiley (f) Pet form of **Eileen**.

Eiluned (f) see **Lynette**.

Eilidh (f) Gaelic form of **Helen**, occasionally used in Scotland.

Eilwen (f) Welsh, 'fair (white) brow'. In modern use in Wales. **Eilwyn** appears to be the male form of the name.

Eily (f) Pet form of **Eileen**, occasionally used as an independent name.

Eion (m) Irish form of **John**, related to Scottish **Iain**, **Ian**. Used occasionally, though forms of the variant **Sean** far outnumber it in modern times.

Eira (f) Welsh 'snow'. Regularly used in Wales this century.

Eirene (f) See **Irene**.

Eirian (f) Welsh *arian* 'silver'. Used in Wales in modern times, especially after it appeared in *A Book of Welsh Names*, by Trefor Rendall Davies (1952).

Eirlys (f) Welsh 'snowdrop'. Used in Wales in modern times. **Eiralys** also occurs.

Eirwen (f) Also **Eirwyn**. Welsh 'golden-fair'. Both forms of the name reasonably well used in Wales since the 1920s.

Eithne (f) See **Ethne**.

Elaine (f) Old French *Helaine, Elaine*, from Greek **Helen**. In Arthurian legend Elaine was the mother of Sir Galahad. Revived in Britain at the end of the 19th c. and very popular by the 1950s, especially in Scotland. Elsewhere Elaine has been quietly used. Variants **Ellaine** and **Elayne** are occasionally found. **Elaina**, influenced by **Helena**, has been used since the 1950s.

Elam (m) Biblical place name 'the highlands' used as a first name in the 19th c., though infrequently.

Elanor(e) (f) Modern variants of **Eleanor**.

Elayn(e) (f) Variant spellings of **Elaine**.

Elba (m) Name of the island to the west of Italy where Napoleon I was held prisoner 1814–15. Occasionally used as a first name.

Elbert (m) Old English 'noble bright'. A reduction of **Ethelbert**, and more usual in the form **Albert**. Revived in modern times and mainly used by black American families.

Elden (m) 19th c. variant of **Eldon**.

Eldon (m) English place name/surname originally meaning 'Ella's mound', in regular if infrequent use as a first name. An early example of a name-bearer was Sir Eldon Gorst (1861–1911), an English administrator.

Eldred (m) Old English 'old counsel'. Anglo-Saxon personal name which did not survive the Norman Conquest. Consciously revived in the mid-19th c. and used from time to time since then. Feminine **Eldreda** is rare. **Aldred** is a variant.

Eleana (f) Modern blend of **Elena** and **Eleanor** in occasional use.

Eleanor (f) Origin uncertain. It has traditionally been associated with **Helen**, which also takes the form **Ellen**. If Eleanor is Greek, then a derivation from *eleos* 'pity, mercy' is highly likely, given the French form of the name, **Eleonore**, and the Italian, **Eleanora**. This was first suggested by Professor Weekley in *Jack*

and Jill. It is supported quite independently by Alfonso Burgio in his *Dizionario dei Nomi Propri di Persona*. A derivation from Latin *lenire* 'to soothe', ultimately from *lenis* 'soft' has also been proposed, but seems far less likely. The name was brought to England by Eleanor of Acquitaine (1122–1204), wife of Henry II. Her descendant was Eleanor of Castile, wife of Edward I, whose body was conveyed to London from Herdelie when she died, 'Eleanor crosses' being erected in towns where her body rested. The last resting place before Westminster was at Charing Cross. Used with great regularity from the 12th c. onwards, also appearing as Elianor and Alienor (still a dialectal form in France). **Elinor** appeared for the first time in the 17th c., and was borne by Elinor (**Nell**) Gwyn (1650–87) the actress, dancer and one of Charles II's favourites. In Jane Austen's *Sense and Sensibility* (1796), Elinor Dashwood embodies the 'sense'. Charles Dickens also had a heroine called Elinor, but she was better known as Little Nell, of *The Old Curiosity Shop*. The various forms of Eleanor were still being very well used at the beginning of the 20th c., in the U.S. helped by the example of Eleanor Roosevelt. Usage has declined steadily since the 1930s, though it is by no means obsolete. Pet forms used independently include **Leonora, Leonore, Ella, Nora, Nell(ie)**, etc.

Eleanora (f) Infrequent variant of **Eleanor**, influenced by the Italian form of the name, **Eleonora**. Also found are **Elenora, Elenorah, Ellenora, Ellenorah**. Such names led to the pet forms **Nora** and **Norah**, which became independent.

Eleazar (m) See **Lazarus**.

Elen (f) Welsh *elen* 'nymph, angel'. Formerly used in Wales, now very rare. **Elin** is a variant.

Elena (f) Form in several European languages, e.g. Spanish, Italian, of **Helen** . Occasionally used in English-speaking countries.

Eleni (f) See **Ellen**.

Elenor (f) Common 19th c. variant of Eleanor. Elenora also occurred for Eleanora.

Elfreda (f) Variant of Elfrida which appeared at the end of the 19th c. The preferred spelling of the name in the 20th c., though infrequently used.

Elfrida (f) Old English 'elf' + 'strength'. Mainly used in the 19th c., now rare. Elfride and Alfreda are variants.

Elga (f) Form of Helga (Olga) in occasional use.

Eli (m) Hebrew 'high'. Biblical, O.T., name of the high priest of Israel, teacher of Samuel. Used in the 17th c., common in the 18th and 19th cc., much rarer since the 1930s. Sometimes found as Ely.

Elias (m) Greek form of Hebrew Elijah, 'The Lord is God'. Biblical, O.T. Elijah is the name of the great prophet, the Tishbite, 1 Kings 17:1. The name was used by Christians in Rome, e.g. Helias, a silversmith, in 406. In the 17th c. Elias and its usual variant Ellis were frequently used. All forms of the name continue to be used, but now very infrequently.

Elice (m, f) Variant of Ellis or Alice which occurs mainly in the 19th c. records. Ellice is also found.

Eliezer (m) Hebrew 'to whom God is help'. The name of twelve different men mentioned in the Bible, and in occasional use as a first name in the 19th c.

Elihu (m) Form of Elijah. Two men mentioned in the Bible bear this form of the name, which was used in the 19th c. from time to time.

Elijah (m) Hebrew 'The Lord is God'. Biblical, O.T. One of the great prophets, the Tishbite. The Greek form of the name is Elias. The English form could be said to be Ellis. All continue to be used, though rarely. Elijah was especially popular in the early part of the 19th c. In modern times black American families use it far more often than whites.

Elin (f) Welsh elen 'nymph, angel'. Also an early spelling of Ellen.

Elinda (f) Shortened form of Belinda or Melinda in occasional use.

Elinor (f) Form of Eleanor used from the 17th c. onwards. In the 19th c. Ellinor was also frequent, while Elenor and Ellenor occurred regularly. Elina, Elliner were occasionally used.

Eliot (m) Surname used as a first name, originally in Scotland, spreading through the rest of Britain from the 1960s. Ultimately a form of Eli. Well established in the U.S. in its various forms, namely Eliott, Elliot, Elliott.

Elisa (f) Pet form of Elisabeth used independently, though Eliza, from Elizabeth, has been far more popular.

Elisabeth (f) Usual form in European languages of Elizabeth. Occurs commonly in English-speaking countries.

Elise (f) French diminutive of Elisabeth. Introduced to English-speaking countries in the latter half of the 19th c. Continues in quiet use. In the U.S. Elyse is the preferred spelling.

Elisha (m) Hebrew 'God has helped'. Biblical, O.T. The disciple and successor of Elijah, the prophet. Used by the Puritans in the 17th c., and in general use throughout the 19th c. The name seemed to have disappeared but three examples of its use in the 1970s were noted. Elisher also occurs.

Elissa (f) The name by which Dido, Queen of Carthage, was known in Tyre. In modern use a form of Elizabeth. Usage began in the 1930s, influenced by the popular actress Elissa Landi (Elizabeth Zanardi-Landi), star of many films.

Elita (f) Apparently a mixture of Latin electa and French elite 'chosen'. Used since 1950, but not frequently.

Eliza (f) Short form of Elizabeth used by 16th c. poets of Queen Elizabeth I. Much used as an independent name in the 18th and 19th cc. and still in use, though now far less frequently found. Elizah sometimes occurred.

Elizabeth (f) Hebrew Elisheba, probably 'God is satisfaction, perfection, plenitude'. Biblical, O.T., the name of the wife of Aaron, Exodus 6:23, N.T., name of the mother of John the Baptist, Luke 1:60. St Elizabeth of Hungary, who died at the beginning of the 13th c., was especially popular in Europe. Born a princess, she devoted herself to the care of the poor and sick. Her great-niece, named for her, was Queen of Portugal, but devoted herself to the needy when she became a widow. These two saints were mainly responsible for the use of the name in the late Middle Ages, though it was not commonly used in England. Elizabeth I of England was probably named, as Miss Withycombe has suggested, for her great-grand-mother and grand-mother, both of whom were Elizabeths. The queen's long and successful reign was then responsible for making Elizabeth one of the three most popular names for girls (**Mary** and **Ann** being the other two). It was to remain so until the end of the 19th c. Its very success meant that many pet forms and variants had to be used to distinguish between the countless bearers of the name. Gave rise to **Bess, Bessie, Beth, Betty, Eliza, Elsie, Lisbeth, Liz, Lisa** and **Liza** amongst others, all used independently. The Spanish/Portuguese form of the name, **Isabel**, was used interchangeably with Elizabeth until the 15th c., and this in turn gave rise to many pet forms and variants. In Scotland the name developed into **Elspeth, Elspet**. Normal European spelling of the name is **Elisabeth**, often found in Britain and the U.S., together with foreign pet forms and variants such as **Bettina, Elsa, Elise, Beta, Ilse, Liese, Lisette**. Use of Elizabeth itself has been steadily declining this c., in spite of the popularity of Queen Elizabeth II, and continues to do so in the 1980s.

Elkanah (m) Hebrew, possibly 'God has created'. Several men mentioned in the O.T. bear this name, which has been used very occasionally in English-speaking countries.

Elke (f) Germanic pet form of *Adalheid* (**Alice**), made known by film stars such

as Elke Sommer (Elke Schletz). Elke is found in English-speaking countries since the 1950s.

Ella (f) Norman French *Ela, Ella, Ala*, from Old German *Alia* or *Alja*, ultimately from Old German *al* 'all entirely'. Introduced to Britain by the Normans and (according to Miss Withycombe) much used in the Middle Ages. Rare from the 16th c., though Camden (1605) lists it as a Christian name and links it with **Alice**. Reappeared in force in the 1870s in the U.S., but probably as a pet form of **Eleanor**. Now rarely used, though made well known by the very popular American poetess Ella Wheeler Wilcox (1850-1919) and the famous singer Ella Fitzgerald. The curious form **Ellaline** was in use around 1900, but quickly faded.

Ellaine (f) Variant spelling of **Elaine**.

Ellen (f) English form of **Helen**. From the 16th to the 18th c. Ellen and Helen were used in English-speaking countries with equal frequency. In Britain in the 19th c. Ellen became the fashionable form, while Helen faded away drastically. In the 20th c. the positions have been reversed in Britain, Ellen disappearing after the 1920s and Helen becoming one of the top ten names for girls. Once again fading, however, by the early 1980s. In the U.S. Helen remained the usual form until the 1950s, when Ellen became fashionable. Both forms were out of fashion by the late 1970s. For many years the best-known bearer of the name was the British actress Ellen Terry (1848–1928). The 19th c. records contain a large number of variant spellings of Ellen, including **Elen, Elin, Elyn, Elon, Ellan, Ellin, Ellon. Elena** is a form of the name in various European languages, such as Italian. **Eleni**, occasionally found in English-speaking countries, is a Greek form.

Ellenor (f) Form of **Eleanor** which occurred mainly in the 19th c., influenced by **Ellen**, a form of **Helen**, with which Eleanor has traditionally been associated. **Ellena** is also found.

Ellery (m) Surname used as a first name, though only on rare occasions. The surname can derive from Latin *hilaris* 'cheerful', or Greek *eulalia* 'sweetly speaking'. It could also be a place name by origin. In modern times associated with the fictional detective Ellery Queen, the pseudonym of Frederic Dannay and Manfred B. Lee, who wrote the stories. They borrowed Ellery from a real-life bearer of the name when naming their creation, rejecting **Wilbur** in the process.

Elli (f) Modern form of **Ella** or **Ellie**, pet form of names beginning with El-.

Ellice (m, f) See **Elice**.

Ellin (f) Common 19th c. variant of **Ellen**.

Ellinor (f) See **Eleanor**. Very common variant spelling in the 19th c.

Elliot(t) (m) Variants of **Eliot**, ultimately from **Eli**. This surname has always had a variety of spellings, all of which have regularly been used as first names. The one most frequently found is Elliott. With names of this kind there is often a family reason (e.g. mother's maiden name) which suggests its use. The actor Elliott Gould (Elliott Goldstein) has helped to make the name generally known in modern times.

Ellis (m) Middle English form of Greek *Elias*, Hebrew *Elijah*. The frequency of the surname attests to the popularity of the name in the Middle Ages. Modern use of Ellis as a first name probably reflects deliberate use of a family name. **Ellison** was also used in the 19th c., and is occasionally found in modern times.

Ellyn (f) Modern blend of **Ella** and **Lyn**, or a variant of **Ellen**. This form appeared in the U.S. in the 1950s.

Elma (f) Pet form of German **Wilhelma**, **Anselma**, etc., used independently since the mid-19th c. Miss Withycombe also gives an example of a blend using parts of **Elizabeth** and **Mary**. Now rarely found.

Elmena (f) See **Almena**.

Elmer (m) Old English *Aethelmaer* 'noble famous'. Surnames such as *Aylmer*, *Elmar* and *Elmer* show that the name

survived the Norman Conquest. Listed by Camden (1605) as 'a usual Christian name'. Recorded very rarely in Britain since then, but one of the top fifty boys' names in the U.S. at the end of the 19th c. It is commonly said to have been used in honour of two brothers, Ebenezer and Jonathan Elmer, members of Congress during the Civil War. Stewart thinks this is unlikely because they came from New Jersey and the name was more popular in 'the Middle West'. He is unable to suggest an alternative source. The novel *Elmer Gantry* (1927) by Sinclair Lewis has a hypocritical rogue as hero and may have helped to kill the name.

Elmina (f) See **Almena**.

Elnora (f) Occasional variant of **Eleanora**.

Ellie (f) Pet form of names such as **Eleanor** used independently.

Eloise (f) Made famous because of the love letters written by Eloise (or **Eloisa**) to Abelard in the 12th c. The origin of her name is disputed. Charlotte Yonge first suggested a link with the Germanic name *Helewidis*, used in Britain in the Middle Ages as **Helewise**. This gave rise to the surname *Elwes*, but some scholars would say that it did not otherwise survive. Miss Withycombe follows Yonge, but French and Italian onomatologists, supported by Ernest Weekley, prefer to link the name to **Louis**, via the Latinized form **Aloysius**. This has a feminine form **Aloysia**. French form of the name is always **Héloïse**, the Italian **Eloisa**. In English-speaking countries Eloise is preferred, Eloisa being rare. Occasional variants such as **Elouise** are found. Recently been revived to some extent.

Elon (f) Mainly 19th c. variant of **Ellen**.

Elroy (m) Variant of **Leroy** 'the king'. Usage seems to be confined to the U.S., where black American families use the name far more than whites.

Elsa (f) German diminutive of **Elisabeth**. Music-lovers associate the name with Wagner's *Lohengrin* (Elsa being his bride). In the U.S. the columnist and party-giver Elsa Maxwell (1883–1963) helped to keep the name before the public eye. The actress Elsa Lanchester (Elizabeth Sullivan) was also appearing regularly in films from the 1930s. Used infrequently in English-speaking countries.

Elsbeth (f) Variant of **Elspeth** in occasional use.

Elsie (f) From **Elspie**, pet form of **Elspeth**, itself a Scottish short form of **Elizabeth**. Has been used since the 18th c. as an independent name. The 19th c. poet Longfellow used it to name the heroine of his *Golden Legend*. Also featured in the novel *Elsie Venner* (1861) by Oliver Wendell Holmes. By the latter half of the 19th c. was one of the top names in the U.S. Re-introduced into England in the 1870s, Elsie was ranked fifth most popular name by 1900. Remained very popular until the 1920s, longer in Scotland. Now used infrequently. **Elsey** was formerly a fairly common variant.

Elspeth (f) Scottish pet form of **Elizabeth**. Sir Walter Scott used it to name several fictional characters. Well used as an independent name in Scotland since the 19th c. Elsewhere little used. A common variant is **Elspet**, and the usual pet form is **Elspie**. **Elsbeth** also occurs.

Elspie (f) Pet form of **Elspeth**.

Elton (m) English place name/surname 'Ella's settlement' used infrequently as a first name since the 1890s. Associated in modern times with the singer Elton John (Reginald Dwight) who 'borrowed' his first name from Elton Dean, the saxophone player.

Eluned (f) Welsh *eilun* 'idol, icon'. A fairly popular name with Welsh parents in the 20th c. Davies gives the name as **Eiluned** in his *Book of Welsh Names*, but Eluned is clearly preferred. **Elined** is sometimes found, capturing the pronunciation. **Luned** also occurs. Sir Thomas Malory turned the name into *Linet* in his *History of King Arthur*, which Tennyson adapted in his turn as **Lynette**.

Elva (f) Phonetic form of the traditional Irish name **Ailbhe**, Anglicized as Elva or

Olive. Used from time to time since the 1870s. Irish scholars are unable to give its origin.

Elvera (f) Variant of **Elvira**.

Elvet (m) English place name ('swan-stream') used regularly if infrequently in the 20th c. as a first name.

Elvie (f) Pet form of **Elvina** used independently since the 1920s. **Elvy** also occurs.

Elvin (m) Common variant of **Alvin**. In the U.S. both forms of the name are used more by black American parents than by whites.

Elvina (f) Feminine of **Elvin**, itself a variant of **Alvin**. Used more often than the male form in Britain. Rare elsewhere.

Elvira (f) Spanish name of uncertain origin, but possibly from the name of the Spanish town Elvira, where the first Ecumenical Council was held in 300. The name occurs in Mozart's opera *Don Giovanni*, where Elvira is deceived by him, and also in Bellini's opera *I Puritani*, Verdi's opera *Ernani* and Auber's opera *Masaniello*. In French literature **Elvire** is the wife of *Don Juan* in Molière's work of that name. Elvira is not frequently used, but is far from being obsolete; the 1968 film *Elvira Madigan* brought the name to public attention.

Elvis (m) Made world-famous by Elvis Aron Presley (1935-78). Regularly but not frequently used as a first name since the late 1950s. The entertainer's father was Vernon Elvis Presley, and the family was ultimately of Irish descent. The origin of the name, as Mrs Julie Martin, of Pontardawe, Swansea, has pointed out, is clearly the Irish saint's name **Ailbhe**. There is a place called St Elvis in Pembrokeshire, where the reference is to the patron saint of Munster. This is the St Ailbhe who is said to have baptised St David or Dewi, patron saint of Wales. As a feminine name Ailbhe was Anglicized as **Elva** (a phonetic spelling to English ears). The male name was often written **Alvy** or **Alby** in English, and was sometimes 'translated' as **Albert**, though the two names are in fact unconnected. Ailbhe seems to have been exported to the U.S. by Irish immigrants in the forms Elvis and **Alvis**, both of which appear in Newbell Puckett's lists of black and white personal names. Puckett gives Elvis as an 'unusual' name used by the whites, and dates it pre-1939. In Britain the earliest occurrences of both Elvis and Alvis, as far as we are able to trace, were in 1939, by which time the Alvis motor-car had appeared on the scene. For the probable origin of the trade name see Alvis. Elvis, then, is a possessive form which should more correctly be written Elvi's or Elvy's. The relatively quiet use of Elvis in modern times presumably stems from its overwhelming associations with pop music – Elvis Costello as well as Elvis Presley. In at least one instance, however, parents named their daughter Elizabeth Louise Victoria Isabel Simone in order to spell ELVIS with her initials.

Elwin (m) Old English *Ealdwine* 'old friend'. Probably a use of the surname rather than as a direct survival. **Elwina** (f) is found.

Elwyn (m) Probably a form of **Alwyn**, Welsh 'fair brow'. Well used in Wales in the 20th c. Occurs occasionally as **Elwin**, which has a feminine form **Elwina**.

Ely (m, f) Probably not the English place name or surname used as a first name which it appears to be. Frequency of use, especially in the 19th c., suggests that it is a variant of **Eli**. As a feminine name one should perhaps look towards **Elly** or **Ellie**.

Elyse (f) See **Elise**.

Elysia (f) Probably a back-formation from the word 'elysian', related to 'elysium', the abode of the blessed. Influenced by names such as **Elise** and **Elyse**. In use since the 1940s, but not frequent.

Emaline (f) Variant of **Emeline**.

Emanuel (m) Hebrew 'God is with us'. Biblical, O.T., Isaiah 7:14, the name given to the Messiah. Avoided by the

Puritans, but occasionally used in the 17th c. More frequent in the 18th c., regularly used through the 19th c. as Emanuel and **Emmanuel**. In the 20th c. the latter form occurs more frequently than Emanuel, but both forms are now rather rare. In the U.S. is far better known by its short form **Manuel**, which has never been frequently used in Britain. Feminine forms are **Emanuela** and **Manuela**. Pet form **Manny** is used independently on rare occasions.

Emblem (f) Obsolete form of **Emeline**.

Emblyn (f) Variant of **Emeline**. Emelen also occurs.

Emelia (f) Mainly 19th c. variant of **Amelia**.

Emeline (f) Teutonic: Old French *Ameline*, modern French *Emeline*, containing as first element Old German *amal* plus suffix *-une*. The original meaning of *amal* is much disputed, though there is a tradition that it means 'work, labour'. Introduced to Britain by the Normans in the 11th c. Became common in forms such as *Emlin*, *Emblin*, *Emblem*, all of which survive as surnames. After a period of disuse the name was restored in the 18th c. as Emeline or **Emmeline**. Helena Swan, writing in 1900, wrongly connected the name with **Emily**, and other spellings show that it was associated with **Emma**. Now appears to have become obsolete, though until the 1930s it could be found in all English-speaking countries as **Emiline, Emaline, Emblyn, Emelen, Emelyn, Emlen, Emlyn** (the Welsh name *Emlyn* is of different origin), **Emmalene, Emmaline, Emmeline, Emmiline, Emylin, Emylynn**.

Emely (f) Common 19th c. form of **Emily**.

Emelyn (f) Variant of **Emeline**.

Emerald (f) The jewel name used as a first name, though the Spanish form **Esmeralda** has been far more frequently used.

Emerson (m) 'Descendant of a man named Emery.' A surname since the 14th c. used as a first name in English-speaking countries, possibly as a tribute to Ralph Waldo Emerson (1803–1882), essayist, poet and philosopher.

Emery (m) English form of Old German *Amalric* 'noble-power'. **Emory** is often used in the U.S. Mainly a 19th c. name.

Emil (m) German form of French **Emile**, ultimately from Latin **Aemilius** (*aemulus* 'eager'). Used sporadically in Britain and the U.S. since the 1870s.

Emila (f) Common 19th c. form of **Emily**.

Emile (m) Latin *Aemilius*, a Roman clan name meaning 'eager'. Emile is the French form of the name. Also the title of a book about educational theory written by Jean-Jacques Rousseau. Made famous, too, by the French writer Emile Zola (1840–1902). Regularly but quietly used in English-speaking countries since the 1850s.

Emilia (f) Common 19th c. form of **Amelia**, influenced by **Emily**.

Emiline (f) Variant of **Emeline**.

Emily (f) Latin *Aemilia*, feminine of *Aemilius*, the name of a Roman gens or clan (commoners rather than noblemen). Common Christian name in early Roman inscriptions. Rare in English-speaking countries until the 18th c., when it was usually thought to be a form of **Amelia** (of different origin). Became very popular in the 19th c. By the 1870s it was ranked among the top names in the U.S. and Britain. Declined after 1900 until the 1970s, when it began a rapid return to favour on all sides. **Emiley** was a 19th c. variant. French form **Emilie** has also been much used.

Emlen (f) Variant of **Emeline**.

Emlyn (m, f) The male name is from the Welsh town of Castell Newydd Emlyn. Emlyn was used as a bardic name. In modern times it has been publicized by the Welsh actor and playwright, Emlyn Williams, and by the English soccer player Emlyn Hughes. Formerly used as a girl's name, Emlyn was a variant of **Emeline**.

Emma (f) Old German *ermin*, 'all-embracing', an element in names such as **Irmgard**. A royal name in England when Emma was queen to Ethelred the Unready, and later to King Canute. Its use in the Middle Ages, when it was commonly found, led to surnames such as *Emmet, Emmot*. These in turn were used as first names by the 17th c. Emma was certainly being used in the 18th c., when it was borne by the notorious Lady Emma Hamilton (1761–1815), the beautiful mistress of Lord Nelson and others. By the end of the 19th c. the name was in the British top ten, but it declined in the 20th c. It revived again in Britain in the late 1960s when Emma Peel was used as the name of a character in the television series *The Avengers*. By the early 1980s it was the most frequently used name for girls, though still unfashionable in the U.S. Its latest return to favour has also introduced a number of combined names such as **Emma-Jane, Emma-Louise, Emma-Maria**, sometimes written as one name, e.g. **Emmalinda**. The name may sometimes be given because of Jane Austen's heroine in *Emma* (1816).

Emmaline (f) Variant of **Emeline**. **Emmalene** is also found.

Emmanuel (m) Variant of **Emanuel**. Emmanuel tends to be more often used in modern times.

Emmeline (f) Variant of **Emeline**. In the 20th c. Emmeline has become the preferred spelling of the name, though seldom used.

Emmerson (m) Common variant of **Emerson**.

Emmett (f) Surname, deriving from a pet form of **Emma**, used as a first name, mainly in the 19th c. **Emmet** was also used, together with the common variant **Emmot**. In some instances it may have been used for males.

Emmie (f) Pet form of various names beginning with Em-, used in its own right regularly since the 1880s.

Emmiline (f) Variant of **Emeline**.

Emrys (m) Welsh form of **Ambrose**, ultimately from Greek *ambrosios* 'immortal'. Regularly used in Wales in the present century.

Ena (f) Short form of **Helena** or **Eugenia**, also used in Ireland as a variant of **Ethne**. In general use since the naming of Queen Victoria's grand-daughter, Princess Victoria Eugénie Julia Ena, always known as Princess Ena. She later became Queen of Spain. Now rarely found.

Enderby (m) English place name/surname, containing an Old Norse personal name, used as a first name, mainly in the 19th c.

Eneas (m) Variant of **Aeneas**.

Enid (f) Welsh *enaid* 'soul, life'. A heroine in the Arthurian legends. Tennyson published his *Idylls of the King*, which included 'Geraint and Enid', in 1859, apparently predicting within the poem that **Geraint** and Enid would be widely used to name children in the future, though he may only have meant that the members of Arthur's court would so name their children. Enid drifted into use after publication of the poem, and did not become firmly established until the 1890s. At its most popular in Britain in the 1920s, then began to fade slowly. Always rare elsewhere. Helena Swan once remarked that it was the greatest possible compliment for a woman to be called 'a second Enid', since the original was the perfect example of spotless purity.

Ennis (m) Variant of **Angus** used on rare occasions, when it has usually been the surname transferred to first-name use.

Enoch (m) Hebrew 'dedicated, consecrated'. Biblical, O.T., the father of Methuselah, Gen. 5:21. Rarely used, and more often in the north of England than in the south. Associated in Britain with the politician (John) Enoch Powell. Earlier (1864) Tennyson had associated it with his poem *Enoch Arden*, in which a seaman who has been shipwrecked returns to discover that his wife is happily married to another. He nobly goes away without revealing his identity and dies of a broken heart. Enoch enjoyed its

greatest popularity in the twenty years that followed publication of that poem. In 19th c. records often found as **Enock**.

Enos (m) Hebrew *Enosh* 'man'. The Greek form of the name was used in earlier translations of the Bible, but it now appears as **Enosh**. Biblical, O.T., Gen. 4:26, the son of Seth, grandson of Adam and Eve. Does not seem to have been used by the Puritans, but appears regularly throughout the 19th c. Rare in the present c. but still found.

Enrico (m) Italian form of **Henry**, occasionally used. Made famous by Enrico Caruso (1873–1921).

Eoghan (m) Irish form of **Eugene**. Irish parents restored it to use in 1970s, especially.

Ephie (f) Short form of **Euphemia**.

Ephraim (m) Hebrew 'fruitful'. Biblical, O.T., 'The second he (Joseph) called Ephraim, "for God has made me fruitful in the land of my affliction".' Gen. 41:52. Rare until the 18th and 19th cc., when it came into regular use. Rarely used since the 1930s, though kept alive to some extent by black American families.

Eppie (f) Pet form of **Euphemia** or **Hephzibah**, occasionally used as an independent name.

Er (m) Hebrew 'watcher'. Biblical name introduced by the Puritans in the 17th c. and still in regular if infrequent use throughout the 19th c. Now appears to be obsolete.

Erasmus (m) Greek *erasmios* 'beloved, desired'. The name of a 4th c. saint, seen in a different form in St Elmo's fire, the ball of light sometimes seen during a storm around the mast of a ship. The name was adopted by the Dutch scholar and theologist Geert Geerts (1465–1536). Used as a first name in Britain in the 17th and 18th cc. though only on rare occasions, e.g. Erasmus Darwin (1731–1802), naturalist and poet, grandfather of Charles Darwin. Used again with some regularity in the latter half of the 19th c. but now seems to be obsolete.

Eric (m) Old Norse 'ruler of all' or 'always ruler'. Not really used in English-speaking countries until the publication of *Eric, or Little by Little*, an edifying story by Frederick Farrar, in 1858. H. Rider Haggard later used it in *Eric Brighteyes*. By 1925 the name was extremely popular in Britain, though Eric Partridge (1894–1979), himself the compiler of a dictionary of first names (*Name This Child*), remarks in his entry on the name: 'By "Johns" and "Toms" and "Dons", it is often, as I discovered at school, despised as pretty-pretty.' Reached the U.S. much later, and was very high in the popularity lists of 1975. Pet form **Rick** is used independently, and the feminine forms are **Erica**, **Erika**. Eric is the usual spelling of the male name, but **Erick**, **Erik** occur. An American commentator points out that Eric may sometimes be the short form of Frederic. Perhaps this suggested the name to Frederic Farrar.

Erica (f) Feminine form of Eric. Some parents may have consciously used it because Latin *erica* is 'heather'. **Erika** has been used in Scandinavia since the early 18th c., but this form came later to English-speaking countries. Erica was almost certainly launched by Edna Lyall's novel *We Two* (1884). In the 1970s both forms of the name (especially Erika) were enjoying considerable popularity in the U.S. Swedish pet forms **Rica** and **Rika** have occasionally been given as independent names.

Erik (m) Scandinavian form of Eric, in occasional use in English-speaking countries. Feminine **Erika** is reasonably fashionable in modern times.

Erin (f) Gaelic *Eireann* 'western island', i.e. Ireland. Poetical name for Ireland, popular in modern times as a first name (though not in Ireland itself). **Erina** is also found, as are **Erinn**, **Eryn**. Typical poetic usage of the name is seen in *Cushla-ma-Chree* ('Darling of my heart') by John Curran:

Dear Erin, how sweetly thy green bosom rises!

An emerald set in the ring of the sea.

Erle (m) Variant of **Earl**, made famous by the author of the Perry Mason stories, Erle Stanley Gardner (1889–1970).

Erma (f) form of **Irma** made known by Erma Bombeck (1927–   ), American humorist.

Erna (f) Feminine of **Ernest** or the Irish name **Earnan**, from *earna* 'knowing'. Used infrequently since 1900.

Ernest (m) English form of German **Ernst**, 'earnestness, vigour'. Became extremely fashionable in the latter quarter of the 19th c. and first decades of the present c. Oscar Wilde punned on the name brilliantly in *The Importance of Being Earnest* (1895), and perhaps confused people about the spelling of the name. Appears very often as **Earnest**. Pet form **Ernie** has been used as a name in its own right, mainly this century. Normal feminine forms are **Ernestina**, **Ernestine**.

Ernestine (f) Feminine of **Ernest**, used mainly at the end of the 19th c. and in the early years of the 20th c. In the 1970s still being used to some extent by black American families. **Ernestina** is found.

Ernie (m) Pet form of **Ernest** used independently since the end of the 19th c. In Britain it is also the acronymic description of the Electronic Random Number Indicator Equipment, which selects the winning numbers in Premium Bond draws.

Errol (m) Various etymologies have been suggested for this name, which was made known throughout the world by the actor Errol Flynn (1909–59). Errol is a Scottish place name and surname, but not a common one. Not used in Scotland as a first name. *What Shall We Name The Baby?*, identified the name with **Earl**, and this explanation has been followed by many other writers. Eric Partridge quotes Loughead, one of the least reliable writers ever to deal with first names, and says that it derives ultimately from a Latin word meaning 'wanderer'. Clearly the association was with Latin *errare* 'to wander', but this is an absurdity. Johnson and Sleigh point to early forms of **Harold**, namely **Eral**, **Erall**, but this must be coincidental. The most likely source is the Scottish place name. First found in Britain in 1890 and occurred regularly, though infrequently, until the 1940s. Never common in the U.S., though it continues to be used. Feminine form **Errolyn** has been noted.

Erskine (m) Scottish place name (possibly meaning 'green ascent') and surname, used as a first name in the 20th c. Made known by the Irish writer Erskine Childers (1870–1922) and the American novelist Erskine Caldwell (1903–) The name confused Voltaire, who converted it into Hareskins.

Ervin (m) See **Irvin**. **Ervine** and **Erving** also occur.

Erwin (m) See **Irwin**.

Eryl (m, f) Mainly used in Wales, deriving from *eryl* 'watcher'. In regular use since the 1920s, though infrequently. Davies reports in his *Book of Welsh Names* that Eryl was first used by John and Dilys Glynne Jones for their daughter, born 25 January, 1893. They lived in a house called *Eryl-y-mor*. Subsequently used for boys as well as girls.

Esau (m) Hebrew 'rough, hairy'. Biblical, O.T., Gen. 25:25, 'the first came forth red, all his body like a hairy mantle; so they called him Esau. Afterward his brother came forth, and his hand had taken hold of Esau's heel; so his name was called Jacob.' In spite of this Biblical explanation, Miss Withycombe dismisses the derivation of Esau completely (and queries that of Jacob). Used in England in the 16th c., but rare until the 19th c., when it was regularly used in English-speaking countries. **Esaw** is occasionally found.

Esma (f) Variant of **Esmé**, or a conversion of that name to feminine form, since Esmé was originally a boy's name. Might also be from **Esmeralda**, a pet form used independently. Used sporadically in the 20th c.

Esmé (m, f) French, past participle of *esmer*, Latin *aestimare* 'to esteem'. Originally a male name introduced to Scotland from France by a cousin of James VI. Later taken over as a girl's name. Esmée occurs as a very definite feminine form, but is now rarely used.

Esmeralda (f) Spanish 'emerald'. A jewel name used from time to time since the 1880s. The Latin word for 'emerald' is *smaragdus*, feminine *smaragda*. Both **Smaragdus** and **Smaragda** are found as given names in Christian inscriptions of the Roman Empire. In Victor Hugo's famous novel, *The Hunchback of Notre Dame*, 'La Esmeralda' is the nickname of a principal character, derived from an amulet she wears which has a piece of green glass in it, imitating an emerald. Variant forms of the name include **Esmaralda**, **Esmarelda**, **Esmerelda**, **Esmerilda**, **Esmiralda**.

Esmond (m) Old English 'grace' + 'protection'. The name survived the Norman Conquest to become a surname, then disappeared. Reappeared in the 1890s, and it is therefore difficult to see how Thackeray's novel *Henry Esmond* (1848) could have been the reason for it, as Miss Withycombe suggests. It seems clear that the sound of the name somehow made an appeal at that time. Esmeralda had come into use in the 1880s, as had **Esmé**, **Esmée** and **Esma** appeared soon afterwards. Esmond might have seemed to be the male form of Esmé and Esmeralda. Continues to be used, though only once every few years.

Esperanza (f) Spanish 'hope'. Used occasionally in the U.S. The Romans used **Sperantia** with the same meaning. See also **Hope**.

Essie (f) Pet form of **Esther** or other names beginning with Es-, e.g. **Estelle** used in its own right. In regular but infrequent use since the 1860s, and found occasionally as **Essey** or **Essy**.

Esta (f) See **Esther**.

Estella (f) Latin *stella* 'star'. Introduced by Charles Dickens in *Great Expectations*. Miss Havisham says of her: 'One night he brought her here asleep, and I called her Estella'. There is at least a hint that the name was given because it was night and the stars were to be seen. First use of the name in Britain occurred in 1861, the year that the novel was published, but Estella is not a happy character, though beautiful, and the name was used only on rare occasions thereafter. Continues to occur but is still very infrequent. In modern times the French form of the name, **Estelle**, has been far more popular.

Estelle (f) Latin *stella*, 'star'. Introduced to Britain at the same time as **Estella**, but used more often, especially in the 20th c. The name was borne by a 3rd c. saint.

Ester (f) See **Esther**.

Esther (f) Persian 'star,' specifically 'the planet Venus'. Biblical, O.T., the Book of Esther. In the Bible she was originally a Jewish orphan called **Hadassah**, brought up by her cousin Mordecai. The name-change probably helped to conceal the fact that she was Jewish. Introduced into the harem of King Ahaseurus she quickly became his favourite and displaced Vashti, the queen. Miss Withycombe cannot accept that Esther means 'star', since the original name Hadassah means 'myrtle'. It surely cannot be a coincidence, however, that the myrtle was in ancient times the emblem of love, and sacred to Venus. The Persian name she was given simply continued the association with the goddess of love. In the 17th c. Esther and **Hester** were used interchangeably and both were well used until the end of the 19th c. In the U.S. the name was at its peak in 1900, whereas it was already declining by that time in Britain. Both forms of the name are still found, though infrequently, and Esther predominates. **Ester** was often found as a variant form, and there is a modern **Esta**.

Estrid (f) Variant form of **Astrid**.

Ethan (m) Hebrew 'firmness, constancy'. Biblical, O.T., 1 Kings 4:31. Better known in the U.S. than in Britain. Ethan Allen was a prominent leader in the American Revolutionary War. The novel by Edith Wharton, *Ethan Frome* (1911), is on the whole better known to American readers rather than British. Ethan's wife in the book is called **Zeena**, another name more likely to be found in the U.S. than in Britain.

Ethel (f) Pet form of various Old English personal names such as **Etheldred(a)**, **Ethelberta**, where Ethel- means 'noble'. The earliest example of Ethel as an independent name appears to be Ethel Smith, whose birth was registered in England in 1842. At that time Ethelinda was also in use, as was the name of St Etheldreda, though the latter had long since become more common as **Audrey**, representing its spoken form. Thackeray in *The Newcomes*, and Charlotte Yonge in *The Daisy Chain*, both had characters called or addressed as Ethel. The two novels were published 1855–6, and the name became established thereafter. By the 1870s it had become highly fashionable in all English-speaking countries, and remained so until the early 1930s. The actress Ethel Barrymore (born Ethel Blythe) kept the name before the public from 1910 onwards. Also much publicized later by the actress Ethel Merman (born Ethel Zimmerman). Now little used. In America black parents have tended to remain faithful to it. The spelling variant **Ethelle** is occasionally found.

Ethelbert (m) Old English 'noble bright'. The name of the king of Kent (560–616) converted to Christianity by St Augustine. By the 11th c. it had already developed a shorter form **Albert**. One of the Anglo-Saxon names revived in the 19th c., having been dormant for hundreds of years. Remained in fairly regular use until the 1920s, but examples of name-bearers born later than that are very hard to find.

Etheldreda (f) Latinized form of Old English *Aethelthryth* 'noble strength'.

The name of a 7th c. saint, queen of Northumbria, foundress of a convent. Regularly though infrequently given to girls in Britain; far better known in its short form, **Audrey**.

Ethelinda (f) Old German *athal linde* 'noble serpent' (i.e. 'wise'). One of the names revived in the 19th c. Variants at that time included **Ethelind, Ethelinde, Etheline, Etheleen, Ethelena, Ethelenda, Ethelina, Etholinda, Ethylinda**.

Ethelle (f) Rare variant of **Ethel**.

Ethelwyn (m) Old English *Aethel wine* 'noble friend'. Anglo-Saxon name revived with some others in the 1880s, but now rarely used. Ethelwyn was the usual modern form, but **Ethelwin, Ethelwyne** and **Ethelwynne** also occurred, sometimes being used as female names.

Ethne (f) Irish *aodhnait* 'little fire'. Feminine form of **Aidan**. Regularly used. The many variants include **Ethna, Eithne, Ethnee, Ethnea, Aithne**.

Ethylinda (f) Variant of **Ethelinda**. **Etholinda** also occurs.

Etienne (m) French form of **Stephen**, from an earlier *Estienne*. Modern French parents tend to use **Stephane**. Both forms occur rarely in English-speaking countries.

Etta (f) Pet form of names like **Henrietta, Marietta, Pauletta, Nicoletta, Lauretta**, etc., used in its own right, regularly but infrequently.

Ettie (f) Pet form of **Hetty**, itself from **Henrietta** or **Esther**, via **Hester**. Perhaps a variant of **Etta**. There is evidence, e.g. in the novels of Dickens, that names ending in -etta were often pronounced by working-class people as if ending in -ettie or -etty. Both Ettie and Etty were used as independent names from the mid-19th c. to the 1920s. Still found, but now only rarely.

Etty (f) Variant of **Ettie**. This spelling occurs with roughly equal frequency.

Euan, Euen (m) See **Ewan**.

Euclid (m) Name of a famous Greek mathematician. Used on rare occasions as a first name.

Eudora (f) Greek 'a good gift'. In Greek mythology Eudora was one of five goddesses who controlled the waves. Used to a certain extent at the end of the 19th c. when **Dora** was also in use. Eudora Welty, the American novelist, was born in 1909 but the name is now very rare.

Eugene (m) Greek *Eugenios*, from the adjective *eugenes* 'well-born'. Common early Christian name, though non-Biblical. Four popes bore it, it was a royal name in Europe (Prince Eugene of Savoy), but was little used in English speaking countries until the 19th c. By 1875 was in the U.S. top twenty. Subsequently faded, but has remained in steady use. Its pet form **Gene** took on a life of its own. A notable bearer of the name was Eugene Gladstone O'Neill, the dramatist (1888–1953), winner of the Nobel Prize for Literature in 1936.

Eugenia (f) Feminine form of **Eugene**, used regularly but infrequently in English-speaking countries.

Eugenie (f) French feminine form of **Eugene**, made well known by Empress Eugenie, wife of Napoleon III. Regularly but quietly used in English-speaking countries since the mid-19th c.

Eulalie (f) French form of **Eulalia**, Greek 'sweetly speaking'. Eulalie seems to occur more often, though both forms are extremely rare. Short form **Eula** is regularly used in the U.S.

Eunice (f) Greek *eunikē*, 'victorious'. Latin *Eunicē*, pronounced you-nice-ee. In English the name has for centuries been pronounced as you-niss for obvious reasons, although Charlotte Yonge, echoed by Miss E. G. Withycombe, considers this an unfortunate, 'lower class' pronunciation. The name is Biblical, N.T., 2 Tim. 1:5, where Eunice is the mother of Timothy. Used infrequently since the 17th c. and publicized to some extent in modern times by the British actress Eunice Gayson (born Elizabeth Grayson). In the U.S., favoured by black American parents. **Unice** has often been used as a variant spelling.

Euphan (f) Short form of **Euphemia**.

Euphemia (f) Greek *Euphēmia* 'auspicious speech', i.e., 'well spoken of'. Latin *Euphemia*. Common in early Christian inscriptions. St Euphemia was a 4th c. martyr whose cult was formerly widespread in the East. Found in Britain (as *Eufemia*) in the 12th c. By 17th c. shortened to **Effam**, later **Effie**, which was regularly used as an independent name from the 1860s. Especially well used in the 19th c. in Scotland because it was thought to translate Gaelic **Oighrig** or **Eithrig**. Still popular in 1930, but has subsequently faded. Short forms of the name include **Ephie, Euphan, Euphen, Euphie, Phemie. Fanny** was also used as a pet form.

Eustace (m) Greek *Eustachios* from *eustachus* 'fruitful'. Non-Biblical name, but used by Christians as early as the 2nd c. Introduced to Britain by the Normans. Used intermittently since the mid-19th c., mainly in Britain. Of more significance in modern times has been the use of **Stacey** or **Stacy**, which were early pet forms of Eustace and led to surnames in those forms. Feminine **Eustacia** is rarely used.

Eva (f) Hebrew *hawwah* 'life', so the name may be interpreted as 'a living being' or 'lively'. Biblical, O.T., Gen. 3:20. Used infrequently in English-speaking countries until the mid-19th c. Then became reasonably fashionable in the U.S., perhaps due to 'little Eva' in Harriet Beecher Stowe's famous anti-slavery novel, *Uncle Tom's Cabin*, though Eva in that story is a pet name for **Evangeline**. At its most popular in Britain at the turn of the century. Has since faded in all English-speaking countries, but remains well used in many European countries, e.g. Hungary, the birthplace of the actresses Eva Bartok (Eva Sjöke) and Eva Gabor, sister of Zsa Zsa Gabor (Sari Gabor).

Evadne (f) Greek. Of uncertain meaning, though in Greek *eu-* (*ev-*) denotes 'good fortune, blooming'. According to Greek mythology Evadne, the wife of Canopeus (one of the seven against Thebes) threw herself on her husband's funeral pyre. Rarely used. **Evadnie** is also recorded.

Evaline (f) Common 19th c. variant, occasionally found in the 20th c., of **Eveline**.

Evalyn (f) Variant of **Evelyn**.

Evan (m) Welsh *Ieuan*, a form of **John**. Early popularity of the name in Wales is proved by the common occurrence of *Evans* as a surname. Very regularly used in modern times, in all English-speaking countries but especially Wales, since the mid-19th c. **Evans** also occurs.

Evangelina (f) Latin form of **Evangeline**. Used only rarely.

Evangeline (f) French *Evangéline*, Latin *Evangelina*, Greek *euangelion* 'good news'. *Euangelia* occurs on a 4th c. Christian inscription. An evangelist is 'a bringer of good news'. **Evangelist** is used as a male name by Bunyan in his *Pilgrim's Progress* (1684). In Italian *Evangelista* is used. Longfellow's poem *Evangeline* (1847) introduced the name to English-speaking countries, his heroine being a French girl of beauty. Then taken up by Mrs Harriet Beecher Stowe in *Uncle Tom's Cabin* (1852), where Eva is actually Evangeline St Clare. Use of Evangeline by black American parents in former times was probably a compliment to this famous anti-slavery novel. In Britain regularly but quietly used.

Eve (f) French form of **Eva**. Always in use in English-speaking countries, but never at the top of the popularity polls. The recent popularity of **Adam** has had little influence on the use of Eve.

Eveleen (f) Mainly Irish variant of **Evelyn** in which some interest was shown in the 1950s, though Evelyn was always the preferred form. Now rare.

Evelina (f) Old German *Avelina*, a pet form of *Avi* or the male name *Avila*. Professor Weekley has also suggested a derivation from Old French *aveline* 'hazel nut', which led to place names in France and Belgium. Aveline and Eveline were well used by the Normans, imported by them into Britain, and gave rise to surnames such as *Evelyn*. In the 18th c. Fanny Burney published her successful novel *Evelina*, a typical story of a girl who suffers trials and tribulations before discovering that she is an heiress and is able to marry the lord with whom she has fallen in love. This made the name popular. The 19th c. preferred **Eveline** as a spelling, though this was overtaken by **Evelyn**. Evelina and Eveline are now rarely used.

Evelyn (m, f) Originally a male name, a use of the surname (deriving ultimately from German *Avila*). A well-known modern bearer of the male form of the name was the novelist Evelyn Waugh (1903–66). Not clear at what point the name came to be thought of as feminine, though it was probably before the turn of the century. Seen as a modern form of **Evelina** or **Eveline** and used accordingly. The interim stage, where **Evelyne** was used from the 1880s onwards, faded when the feminine status of Evelyn had become firmly established. In recent times **Evelynn** has also been used. Enjoyed most success (as a girl's name) around 1925 in Britain, and slightly earlier in the U.S. **Eva** was popular at the time, and there is little doubt that parents thought of Evelyn as a diminutive. Now rarely used.

Everard (m) Old German 'boar' + 'hard'. Personal name introduced to Britain by the Normans. Became a surname but was used as a first name by certain families, according to Camden in 1605. He specifically mentioned that the *Digby* family made use of it. Revived to some extent in the 19th c. but rare this c.

Everelda (f) Also **Everelder, Everell**. See **Averil**.

Everet(t) (m) Surname, itself a form of **Everard**, used regularly if infrequently since the 1890s as a first name. **Everitt** is a common variant, and **Everett** is found.

Everil(da) See **Averil. Everhilda** also occurs.

Everitt (m) Variant of **Everett**.

Everton (m) English place name and surname, originally a 'boar farm'. As a first name seems to have been used only from 1957. Likely that some uses have been inspired by Everton Football Club.

Evette (f) Variant of **Yvette**. Occurs only rarely in modern times.

Evie (f) Pet form of **Eva, Eve, Evelyn**, etc., used in its own right, though infrequently.

Evita (f) Spanish pet form of **Eva, Eve**. Associated in recent times with Eva Peron because of the highly successful musical, *Evita*. Mainly used in the U.S.

Evonne (f) Variant of **Yvonne** made famous in the 1970s by the Australian tennis player Evonne Goolagong. This form of the name has occasionally been used since. **Evon** also occurs.

Ewan (m) Preferred modern Scottish form of Gaelic *Eoghann*, which is of uncertain origin, though often explained as 'youth'. Also associated with **Eugene** 'well born'. Usage of the name has spread beyond Scotland since the 1950s. Also found as **Ewen, Euan, Euen, Ewhen** and **Owen**.

Ewart (m) English place name/surname regularly used as a first name. The place name meant 'homestead near a river'. The surname could be connected with **Edward** or signify a 'ewe-herder'. It could also indicate an ancestor who lived in Ewart.

Ewen (m) See **Ewan**.

Ezekiel (m) Hebrew 'May God strengthen'. Biblical, O.T., the name of one of Israel's major prophets. Used to some extent by the 17th c. Puritans and regularly if infrequently found until the end of the 19th c. At least two instances noted in the 1970s, but now rare.

Ezra (m) Hebrew 'help'. Biblical, O.T., the Book of Ezra. A 5th c. scribe. One of the O.T. names used by the 17th c. Puritans, and carried to America. Regularly used throughout the 19th c. but now found only on rare occasions. In the U.S. was made well known by Ezra Cornell (of Cornell University) and Ezra Pound (1885–1972), the poet.

Fabian (m) Roman clan, perhaps from Latin *faba* 'bean', indicating that the original bearer of the name grew or sold beans. Dr J. van der Schaar suggests alternatively a derivation 'man from Fabiae'. St Fabian was a 3rd c. pope, and the name's use in the Middle Ages led to the surname Fabian. Shakespeare has a character of the name, a servant, in *Twelfth Night*. Used rarely this century. Feminine form **Fabiana** has been noted.

Faith (f) The word used as a name. Introduced by the Puritans in the 16th c. along with other abstract 'virtue' names such as **Hope** and **Charity**. Bardsley was right to point to the influence of the Epistle to the Romans, especially 5:1–5, where words like peace, grace, rejoice, hope, tribulation, patience, etc., are used as well as faith. All these words were transferred to first-name use by the Puritans. Faith continues to be used, though not with great frequency in modern times.

Faithful (m) Puritan name that has not survived, though its equivalent is sometimes found, namely **Fidel** or **Fidelis**. Feminine **Fidelia** also occurs. These forms are from Latin *fides* 'faith'. The same word gives **Fido**, 'I am faithful', still in use as a British dog's name.

Fancy (f) See **Fiance**.

Fanny (f) Pet form of **Frances**. In use as an independent name in the 17th c. but had almost faded from sight by 1725. Then began to come back into favour, until by 1850 was one of the top twenty names in Britain, more popular temporarily than Frances itself. Then went into decline, though still to be found in great numbers in all English-speaking countries in 1900. Since about 1910 virtually extinct, the victim of slang meanings which have turned a name that Thackeray was able to describe in 1850 as 'a very pretty little name' into one which is almost impossible to use. Eric Partridge has suggested that John Cleland's notorious novel, *Memoirs of Fanny Hill*, may ultimately have been responsible for British slang usage. The milder use of 'fanny' for the buttocks, also said to derive from the name, awaits an explanation. In its heyday **Fannie** and **Fanney** frequently occurred as alternative spellings. In France Fanny is sometimes used as a pet form of **Stephanie**.

Farewell (m) The Puritans made use of this name with some regularity, and it survived until the late 19th c. in Britain. Bardsley interprets it as a 'slogan' name, retaining the original force of the phrase 'fare well' as an imperative rather than a pious hope. However, *Farewell* is also a surname which may owe its origin to a place name meaning 'beautiful spring'.

Farley (m) Place name/surname used as a first name e.g. Farley Granger (1925-), American leading man from the 1940s.

Farnham (m) Common English place name and surname, originally a 'river meadow with ferns'. Used regularly in the second half of the 19th c. as a first name, but not at all this century.

Faron (m, f) Occurred in Britain in the 1960s and '70s. Appears to be the use of a surname which has many possible origins, but perhaps of more significance was the fashionable sound of the name – **Karen**, **Sharon**, **Darren** all being in use at the time.

Farquhar (m) Gaelic *Fearcher* 'very dear one'. In occasional use in Scotland.

Farrell (m) Irish surname *O'Fearghail* 'man of valour' used regularly but infrequently as a first name. Similar surnames which occur as first names include **Farrar** and **Farrow**.

Fatima (f) Also **Fatma**, **Fatmeh**. The Prophet Mohammad's daughter, who married Ali. Favourite Arabic name now used in the U.S., especially. Original meaning unknown.

Faustina (f) Latin, derivative of *faustus* 'fortunate, lucky'. One of the commonest names in Christian inscriptions of the Roman Empire, but very rare in English-speaking countries. **Fortune** was used by the 16th c. Puritans and still occurs in modern times, together with **Fortuna**. **Lucky** also used from time to time.

Fay(e) (f) Probably a short form of **Faith**, or a use of the archaic word *fay*, used in Middle English in expressions like 'by my fay', i.e. 'by my faith'. Another word *fay* represents French *fée* 'fairy'. Came into general use in the 1920s, when the actresses Fay Compton and Fay Wray were beginning to appear regularly in films. Ten years later the actress Fay Bainter made appearances in U.S. films. In the 1940s Faye Emerson kept the name before the cinema public, and probably brought about the change in spelling, since the name is now almost always spelt Faye. One young lady, born in 1956, received the name **Fayth**, a curious etymological link.

Feargus (m) Common 19th c. variant of **Fergus**. This spelling was influenced by the Gaelic **Fearghas**.

Featherstone (m) Place name/surname, originally referring to an English place where there was a 'four-stone' structure, three uprights capped by a fourth. These are prehistoric structures ('cromlechs') presumably used for religious purposes in ancient times. Occurs from time to time as a first name in Britain.

Fedora (f) See Feodora.

Felicia (f) Feminine of Latin *Felix* 'lucky'. Found in Christian inscriptions of the Roman Empire from the 4th c. onwards. Usual form of the name in Britain in the 17th c. was **Felice**. Felice and Felicia remained throughout the 18th c., Felicia through the 19th c. Felicity has almost entirely replaced it in the 20th c., though Felicia is still found in the U.S., together with **Luckie** and **Lucky**. Variants **Phelicia** and **Philicia** also occur, serving as a reminder that in former times Felicia and **Phyllis** were often confused.

Felicity (f) Modern form of **Felicia** in Britain. In Britain a well-known bearer of the name is the actress Felicity Kendal.

Felix (m) Latin *felix* 'happy'. Very common Roman name, borne by four popes, also by St Felix after whom Felixstowe is named. Mainly used in the 19th c. Remains in use, but not frequently

found. Feminine forms include **Felicia** and **Felicity**. In literature there is the novel *Felix Holt* (1866) by George Eliot, but Pat Sullivan's cartoon series based on Felix the Cat in the 1920s is probably more widely known.

Fenella (f) Anglicized form of Gaelic *Fionnghal* 'white shoulder'. Irish form is **Finola**. Reasonably well-used in Britain from 1940. **Finella** is a variant, and the short form **Nella** occurs independently.

Fenton (m) Place name/surname ('settlement near a fen') used regularly if infrequently throughout the 19th c. as a first name. Still found, e.g. three British examples in the 1960s.

Fenwick (m) Surname well known in the north of England used as a first name. Derives from a place name, 'dairy farm in the fen'.

Feodora (f) Russian form of **Theodora** in occasional use in English-speaking countries. **Fedora** is a U.S. variant.

Ferdinand (m) Originally a Gothic name, consisting of two elements, the meaning of which is disputed. German scholars explain the name as either 'peace' or 'travel' + 'boldness'. Taken south in early times to become Spanish **Fernando**, later **Hernando**. Used there as a royal name, it was later brought back to Germany and Austria, but considered to be a foreign name until scholars uncovered its history. The Normans introduced the name to Britain in its French form **Ferrant**, though the modern French form is *Fernand*. Shakespeare twice used the name in his plays, for the king of Navarre in *Love's Labour's Lost*, and for the son of the king of Naples, Miranda's loved-one, in *The Tempest*. Was not in general use, though found regularly in 19th c. records. In the U.S., where Fernando is also kept alive, it is quietly used. In Britain it is rare. For many the name perhaps conjures up a vision of Ferdinand the Bull as portrayed by Disney, resting under a tree amongst the flowers rather than fighting in the bull-ring.

Fergus (m) Gaelic *Fearghas* 'supreme

choice'. Used mainly in Scotland and by parents of Scottish descent. Surname **Ferguson** also regularly transferred to first-name use. **Feargus** formerly a common variant.

Fern (f) The plant name. Fern Arable is a character in *Charlotte's Web* (1952) by E. B. White. Made known in Britain by Fern Britton, TV personality. **Ferne** is also found.

Fernando (m) Spanish form of **Ferdinand** used mainly in the U.S.

Fernley (m, f) English place name, 'clearing with ferns', and a long-established family name. Used as a Christian name in Britain with surprising regularity since the 1890s. **Fernleigh** also occurs. The frequency of use suggests a literary source, in print by 1891.

Fiancé (m) French word for 'betrothed', used of a man who is engaged to be married. It was borrowed in English with that sense from the mid-19th c. and was much confused with 'fancy'. From the 1850s to the end of the 19th c., Fiancé was well used as a first name. Occasional examples are found in the 20th c., together with the variant **Fiancy**. No real-life example of **Fancy** used as a girl's name has been noted though it must surely have occurred. In Thomas Hardy's *Under the Greenwood Tree* (1872) there is Fancy Day, the school-teacher. There is also a novel called *Fancy* about a girl of that name, by Robert Krepps.

Fidel (m) See **Faithful**.

Fidelma (f) Modern blend of **Fidel** and (probably) **Mary**. First recorded in 1958, and mainly used in Ireland where usage was increasing in the late 1970s. Coghlan, in *Irish Christian Names*, says that an actress named Fidelma Murphy may have helped spread the name.

Fife (m) Scottish shire name, used on rare occasions as a first name in Scotland.

Fifi (f) French pet form of **Josephine**. Used in Britain as an independent name for a girl, but rather more common as a name for French poodles.

Filomena (f) Italian form of **Philomena**.

Findlay (m) See **Finlay**.

Finella (f) Variant of **Fenella**.

Finlay (m) Gaelic *Fionnlagh* 'fair hero'. Macbeth's father, and a well-known Scottish surname. Used especially in Scotland as a first name, and found elsewhere, often in one of its variant forms **Finley**, **Findlay**, etc.

Finola (f) Anglicized form of Irish *Fionnghuala* or *Fionnuala* 'white shoulder'. Used mainly in Ireland, **Fenella** or **Finella** being used in Scotland. **Nola** and **Nuala** are pet forms occasionally used independently.

Fiona (f) Gaelic *fionn* 'fair, white'. *Fionn* occurs as an element in traditional Gaelic names such as *Fionnghuala* (**Fenella**) but Fiona itself was first used as part of his pseudonym, Fiona Macleod, by William Sharp (1855–1905). Appeared in print in 1893, but does not appear to have come into general use – at first in Scotland, later in England – until the 1930s. By 1950 very popular in Scotland; in England reached a peak around 1970. Has reached Australia and Canada but does not seem to be known in the U.S.

Firth (m) Surname used as a first name, with great regularity in the 19th c. in Britain. No examples noted this century. Originally a place name meaning 'woodland'.

Fitz (m) Norman-French, ultimately from Latin *filius*, 'son'. Common element in surnames such as *Fitzgerald*, *Fitzjohn*, etc., and not necessarily an indication of the illegitimacy of the first name-bearer. A fairly late innovation for the illegitimate sons of royalty to be given Fitz-names. Used as an independent name on several occasions since the 1950s. **Fitzarthur**, **Fitzgerald**, **Fitzjohn**, etc., also found as first names. See also **Fitzroy**.

Fitzroy (m) Surname used as a first name. Anglo-French and ultimately derives from Latin words meaning 'son of the king', with a suggestion of 'illegitimate son of the king' about it. Used as a first name since the 1840s, surprisingly often in the 1960s.

Flavia (f) Latin feminine of **Flavius**, a Roman clan name which ultimately derives from *flavus* 'yellow', indicating that the earliest bearer of the name had blond hair. Both forms of the name extremely common in Christian inscriptions of the Roman Empire, and developed into modern French **Flavien**, **Flavian** (m), **Flavie**, **Flavere** (f), as well as Italian and Spanish **Flavio**, etc. All these forms extremely rare in English-speaking countries.

Fletcher (m) Surname ('maker or seller of arrows') used as a first name. Occurs regularly in 19th c. records, but very rarely found after that.

Fleur (f) French *fleur* 'flower'. Bestowed as an 'incident' name in *The Forsyte Saga*, by John Galsworthy. Soames Forsyte and his wife are looking at their new-born daughter, ' "*Ma petite fleur*," Annette said softly. "Fleur," repeated Soames. "Fleur! we'll call her that!" ' The immensely successful 1970s television series based on the book caused the name to come into use to some extent.

Flo (f) Pet form of **Flora** or **Florence**, occasionally used in former times as an independent name. **Flow** was a rare variant.

Flora (f) Latin **flos** (Genitive *floris*) 'flower'. Roman goddess of flowers and the spring. Occurs commonly, as *Flora* or *Floria*, in early Christian inscriptions. St Flora was martyred in the 9th c. Used in Ireland and Scotland as a substitute for Gaelic *Fionnghuala* or *Fionnuala* (**Fenella**). The Scots may also have taken the name from France, where **Flore** was in use from the 17th c. Subsequently the fame of Flora Macdonald (1722–90) ensured that Flora would remain a Scottish favourite. Most used in England 1850–1900 but has since been out of fashion. Quietly used in other English-speaking countries, and even the Scots have made little use of it since the 1930s. Shares with **Florence** the pet forms **Flo**, **Florie**, **Florrie**, **Flory**, **Florry**, **Floss**, **Flossie**, **Flossy**, all of which were formerly used as independent

names. Modern adaptations include **Florann(e)**, **Florella**, **Florelle**, **Floretta**, **Florette**, and **Florine**. Sir Walter Scott has a character called **Florise** in his *Talisman*. See also **Fleur** and **Florence**. Greek equivalent to this name is **Anthea**, and there is a Welsh **Blodyn**.

Florance (f) Common 19th c. variant of **Florence**.

Florann(e) (f) Modern blend of **Flora** and **Ann(e)** in occasional use.

Flore (f) French form of **Flora**.

Florella (f) Modern adaptation of **Flora** in occasional use. **Florelle** also occurs.

Florence (m, f) Latin *Florentius*, feminine *Florentia*, from *florens*, present participle of *florēre* 'to flower'. 'Flourishing' is the literal translation of the name. Common Christian name in early inscriptions for both men and women. St Florentius was martyred in the 3rd c., and many other saints bore this name. Camden, writing in 1605, listed Florence as a male name, but it went out of fashion in England, surviving best in Ireland and to a lesser extent in Scotland. Irish usage affected by the substitution of Florence for **Finghin**, an ancient Irish name. As a female name Florence was occasionally used to honour St Florentina (7th c.), but Florence Nightingale, the famous nurse in the Crimean War in the 1850s, received the name in 1820 because she was born in the Italian city of that name. (Her older sister, born in Naples, was called **Parthenope**, an earlier name of that city.) The fame of Florence Nightingale caused the name to become very fashionable, and by 1875 it was amongst the top names for girls in Britain and the U.S. Charles Dickens's Florence Dombey in *Dombey and Son* (1848) was no doubt also a contributory factor. Remained a great favourite on all sides until the 1930s. Continues in quiet use. Pet forms of the name include **Flo**, **Florie**, **Florrie**, **Flory**, **Florry**, **Floss**, **Flossie**, **Flossy**: all were formerly used as independent names, along with the variant spelling **Florance**. **Flurry** occurs for the male name, and is associated especially with Mr Florence McCarthy Knox, in *Some Experiences of an Irish R.M.*, by Somerville and Ross (1899).

Floretta (f) Adaptation of French *fleurette* 'little flower' in occasional use. **Florette** also occurs.

Florian (m) Latin *florianus* 'flowery'. Rare name in English-speaking countries but used by families of e.g. German, Dutch, Polish, Hungarian descent.

Florida (f) Conscious borrowing from the name of the American state, or a direct use of Spanish *florida* 'flowered, flowery'. The state name given by Ponce de León in 1513 because he thought the land was flowery and because it was the Easter season – Spanish *Pasqua florida*. The Christian name is not in frequent use. All the American state names have been used from time to time as first names.

Florie (f) Pet form of **Flora** or **Florence**, occasionally found.

Florimel (f) Latin *flos, floris* 'flower' and *mel* 'honey'. Character in Spenser's *Faerie Queene*. In rare use as a Christian name.

Florina (f) Short form of **Florentina** (**Florence**) occasionally used as an independent name. **Florine** also occurs. See also **Penny**.

Florinda (f) Fanciful extension of **Flora**, used very occasionally.

Floris (f) Latin *flos* (*floris* in the Genitive case) 'flower'. In regular but occasional use in English-speaking countries. In Hungary, the Netherlands, etc., is a male name, a variant of **Florian**. Sir Walter Scott seems to have adapted this name in *The Talisman* to arrive at **Florise**.

Florrie (m, f) Pet form of **Flora** or **Florence**, used as an independent name. The male name derives only from **Florence**. **Florry** and **Flory** are variant forms, together with **Florie**, but all of these have been little used since the 1930s.

Flossie (f) Pet form of **Florence** in use

from the 1880s as an independent name. **Floss** also occurs, and **Flossy** was a variant spelling.

Flower (m,f) Now obsolete, but used in the Middle Ages, leading in some cases to the surname *Flower*. Miss Withycombe cites several 17th c. examples of the name.

Floy (f) Pet form of **Florence**. Murray Heller provides evidence of its former use as an independent name in America for black families.

Floyd (m) Surname used as a first name, either deriving from Welsh *Lloyd*, in which case it means 'grey, hoary', or from Irish name *Flood*, where its meaning is 'will (of God)'. In modern times used mainly by black American families and West Indians in Britain. Many still associate it with the former heavyweight boxing champion, Floyd Patterson.

Flurry (m) Irish pet form of **Florence** when used as a male name.

Forbes (m) Scottish place name/surname ('field, district') in occasional use, mainly in Scotland, as a first name.

Forrest (m) Surname turned first name, originally an indication of a 'dweller or worker in a forest'. Mostly used in the U.S., where early use may have been in honour of the Confederate general Nathan Bedford Forrest (1821–77), the man who advised 'Git there fuster with the mostest men'. Edwin Forrest (1806–72), the famous American tragedian, may also have inspired parents. Since 1940 the American actor Forrest Tucker has publicized the name, but it is no longer frequently used. Variant **Forest** occurs.

Forster (m) Occupational surname 'forester' used as a first name from time to time. **Forester** itself also found.

Fortunatus (m) Used occasionally in the 19th c. See **Fortune**.

Fortune (f) English version of the Roman names **Fortunatus**, feminine **Fortunata**, which are amongst the most common to occur in Christian inscriptions of the Roman Empire. Used by the Puritans of the 17th c., as Fortune, but very rare since then, instances being found only every twenty years or so. **Fortuna**, the name of a Roman goddess who was supposed to bring prosperity, is also found occasionally.

Foster (m) Common surname which has at least four possible origins, used as a first name. Occurs very regularly in all English-speaking countries. A well-known bearer of the name was John Foster Dulles (1888–1959), U.S. Secretary of State.

Fran (m, f) Pet form of **Francis** or **Frances**, occasionally used as an independent name in the U.S. Used more for boys than girls.

Francene (f) Variant spelling of **Francine**. **Francena** is also found.

Francesca (f) Italian form of **Frances**, in quiet but regular use in all English-speaking countries. The male form of the name, **Francesco**, also occurs.

Frances (f) Since the 17th c., the feminine form of **Francis**. Earlier Francis, with **Frank** as the pet form, was used for both. Frances was a very steady favourite from the 17th c. onwards. In Britain reached its peak in the 1870s and has since slowly declined. In the U.S. most used around 1900, and still one of the top twenty names in 1925. Has since been less used. Pet forms of Frances include **Fran**, **Frannie**, **Franny**, **Fanny**, **Francie**, **Frankie**, all independent names. French diminutive **Francine** also used, as are the Italian and Spanish forms of Frances, **Francesca** and **Francisca**.

Francetta (f) Diminutive form of **Frances**, in quiet but regular use by (mainly) black American parents. **Franzetta** also occurs. **Francette** is the regular French form of the name.

Francie (f) Diminutive of **Frances**, occasionally used as an independent name.

Francine (f) French diminutive of **Frances** (**Françoise**), regularly but quietly used in all English-speaking countries. Variant **Francina** also occurs, as does **Francene**.

Francis (m) Latin *Franciscus* 'a Frenchman', formerly 'a Frank' (see **Frank**). Made known in the Middle Ages by St Francis of Assisi (1182–1226), whose real name was John. His father had business dealings with France and had his son taught French so that he would be able to help him. His proficiency in the language led to the nickname. Became a royal name in France when Francis (**François**) I became king in 1515. Taken up in England by aristocratic families, e.g. Francis Russell 1527–85, Francis Drake 1545–96, Francis Bacon 1561–1626. Popular throughout the 17th c., declined slowly in the 18th c., but began to revive in the mid-19th c. From 1875–1925 reasonably fashionable in all English-speaking countries, though its pet form Frank, used as an independent name, was used more often.

Francisca (f) Spanish form of **Frances**, used mainly in the U.S. Male form of the name, **Francisco**, also occurs.

Frank (m) In modern times a pet form of **Francis** used as an independent name. In the 17th c. used also as a pet name for **Frances**. In the Middle Ages an independent name meaning 'a Frank', a member of the tribe which invaded Gaul in the 6th c. and led to its becoming *France*. The Franks probably derived their name from their chief weapon, a *franca* 'javelin', but by the 11th c. 'frank' was being used as an adjective to mean 'free', and this is normally the meaning assigned to the name. One of the top ten male names in the U.S. by 1875, and remained in the top twenty until the 1930s. In Britain reached its peak in 1900 and survived until 1940. Now only occasionally used in English-speaking countries. The singer Frank Sinatra has been one of the best-known bearers of the name in modern times.

Franco (m) Pet form of **Francesco** or **Francisco**, Italian and Spanish forms of **Francis**. Occasionally used in the U.S.

Françoise (f) French form of **Frances**, used in Britain since the 1960s.

Francyne (f) Variant of **Francine**, occasionally used in the U.S.

Frankie (m, f) Pet form of **Francis** or

Frances, used as an independent name mainly in the U.S. Variant **Frankey** also occurs.

Franklyn (m, f) Modern spelling variant of **Franklin**, used both in the U.S. and other English-speaking countries.

Franklin (m) Transferred use of the surname, which originally indicated someone who was a freeholder, a landowner of free but not noble birth. As the christian name of two Presidents (Franklin Pierce 1804–69 and Franklin Delano Roosevelt 1882–1945) it has naturally been well used in the U.S., especially in the 1930s and '40s. Also steadily but quietly used in other English-speaking countries. **Frank** is used as the pet form, and the alternative spelling **Franklyn** is not uncommon.

Franz (m) German form of **Francis**. Used occasionally in the U.S. and Britain, sometimes in honour of Franz Schubert, Franz Liszt or Franz Lehár, all famous in the musical world. In modern times made internationally famous by the German footballer, Franz Beckenbauer.

Fraser (m) From the surname, itself a form of a French place name of unknown origin, though in early times falsely derived from French *fraise* 'strawberry'. Used since at least the 1930s as a first name in Britain, Canada and Australia, especially by families with Scottish connections. **Frazer** is a variant spelling.

Fred (m) Pet form of **Frederick** used independently. Became an important name in its own right in the 19th c., continuing through to the 1930s. The well-known dancer Fred Astaire was born Frederick Austerlitz, but the actor Fred MacMurray seems to have been given that form of the name. Now rarely used.

Freda (f) Usual English form of a name which also occurs as **Frieda**, **Freida**, **Freada**, **Freeda**. Frieda possibly a separate name. Freda may be a pet form of **Winifred**, but was probably seen as a feminine form of **Fred**, which was much used at the end of the 19th c. when Freda came into frequent use. Now rarely used.

Freddie (m) Pet form of **Frederick** used independently since the late 19th c. **Freddy** was a frequent variant, but both forms now rarely used. Sometimes heard as the pet form of **Frederica**, **Frederique**, etc., and may in some cases be used for girls as a modernized **Freda** or **Frieda**.

Frederic (m) French form of **Frederick** used alongside that name while it was popular, though never to the same extent.

Frederica (f) Feminine form of **Frederic**, used mainly in the latter half of the 19th c. when Frederic was fashionable. Now rare. **Fredericka** sometimes occurred, and **Frederika** appeared briefly around 1940. French feminine **Frederique** also likely to be found in modern times. Other variants include **Fredrica**, **Fredrika** and a modern **Fredricia**.

Frederick (m) Old German 'peaceful ruler'. Rarely used until the late 18th c., when it was introduced to Britain from Germany by the royal family of the time. By the middle of the 19th c. had become immensely popular in all English-speaking countries and remained so until the 1930s. Has subsequently declined on all sides. French form **Frederic** used alongside it, but never in great numbers. Pet form **Fred** became a popular name, and the diminutives **Freddie**, **Freddy** were also used as independent names. Usual feminine forms are **Frederica** and **Frederique**, but **Fredalena**, **Fredaline**, **Fredith**, **Fredora**, **Frederickina**, **Frederine**, **Fredi**, **Fredie**, **Fredricia** and **Fredrika** are found, the last of these being a legitimate Norwegian form of the name **Frederica**. **Freda** no doubt also seen as a feminine form of Frederick. Spelling variants of the male name include the common **Fredric** and **Fredrick** and the uncommon **Frederich** (clearly influenced by German **Friedrich**) and **Fredwick**, an example of which occurs in 1977. A famous name-bearer was Frederick the

Great (1712–86), who was far from being a 'peaceful ruler'.

Frederique (f) See **Frederica**.

Fredric(k) (m) Variant forms of Frederic(k) which were well used in the 19th c. and continue to occur. These may simply be phonetic spellings, but German *Friedrich* may have had some influence, especially among settlers in the U.S. The Fredric form was adopted by the actor Fredric March, born Frederick Bickel, who was constantly seen on the screen 1930–70.

Fredrica (f) Also **Fredrika**. See **Frederica**.

Freeda (f) See **Freda**.

Freeman (m) Early use of this personal name led to the surname, which in turn is used as a first name on occasions. The 17th c. Puritans used it as a given name, clearly intending it to mean what it says. Its frequency of use in modern times suggests that some parents have also used it in that way. **Free** also occurs, and **Freedom** is almost as common as Freeman. Sometimes disguised as **Freedham**.

Freida (f) See **Freda**.

Freya (f) English form of Swedish **Freja**, earlier **Freyja**, 'noble lady'. Goddess of love and fertility in Norse mythology, ultimately the same as the goddess *Frig* whose name forms part of 'Friday'. In modern times has been given a certain amount of publicity by the archaeologist Freya Stark. Came into general use in the 1940s, but still infrequently used.

Frieda (f) Pet form of German **Friederike** (**Frederica**) used independently. In Germany also linked with **Elfrieda**. In occasional use in English-speaking countries since the 1890s, and difficult to separate from **Freda**. Phonetic form **Freeda** has been used this century, and **Freida**, **Freada** are other forms.

Friend (m) Old English *freond* 'friend'. Surname since the 12th c., used by the Puritans as a first name. Remained in regular use as such until the end of the 19th c., but now rare. **Friendship** also occurs.

Fritzroy (m) Not clear whether this is a deliberate alteration of **Fitzroy** to incorporate **Fritz**, a German pet form of **Frederick**, or whether it is a registrar's mistake. Several examples are recorded in the 1950s, '60s and '70s, which seems to suggest that it is deliberate. Fritz itself was used in the 19th c. in English-speaking countries. Later became a nickname for a German soldier.

Fuller (m) Occupational surname, regularly used as a first name in the 19th c. A feminine form **Fulleretta** was created for a young lady in 1905.

G

Gabi (f) See **Gaby**.

Gabriel (m) Hebrew 'man of God'. One of the two archangels identified in the Scriptures. Biblical, O.T., e.g. Dan. 8:16. Rare in English-speaking countries until the 18th c. Regularly used until the end of the 19th c., then very rare until a minor revival dating from the 1940s, when the feminine form **Gabrielle** became more popular. Still in use, but not frequent.

Gabriella (f) Italian feminine form of Gabriel, in regular use since the 1950s in English-speaking countries.

Gabrielle (f) French feminine of **Gabriel**, regularly used this century in English-speaking countries. Since the 1950s has met with competition from Italian **Gabriella**. Pet forms **Gaby** and **Gabi** are sometimes used independently.

Gaby (f) Pet form of **Gabrielle**, imported from Europe. Used as an independent name since the 1920s. Gabi is also found.

Gael (f) See **Gail**.

Gaenor (f) Preferred Welsh spelling of

Gaynor, though the latter is more frequently used outside Wales.

Gail (f) Pet form of **Abigail**. Burst upon the scene in the 1940s and quickly became extremely popular, especially in the U.S. and Canada. In the 1950s enjoyed a peak period in Britain as well, but never quite as popular as elsewhere in the English-speaking world. May have been launched by the American actress Gail Patrick (Margaret Fitzpatrick) who was appearing in films from 1932 onwards. She later became a successful television producer, e.g. of the *Perry Mason* series. The actress **Gale** Storm (Josephine Cottle) made her film debut in 1939. In the late 1950s she had her own television show. Variant **Gale** never as frequently used as **Gail**. **Gayle** enjoyed some success and, in Britain, **Gael** made an appearance from 1939 onwards. Difficult to know whether this is the word 'gael' being used (to indicate a Scottish highlander or an Irish Celt), or whether it is simply a variant of Gail. Of all the forms of the name, Gayle appears to be surviving most strongly in the 1980s. **Gaylene, Gayleen,** etc., were probably inspired by it.

Gaila (f) Modern variant of **Gail**, itself a pet form of **Abigail**. The fanciful spelling **Gaile** is also occasionally found.

Gaius (m) Latin, earlier *Gavius*, from *gaudere* 'to rejoice'. Roman history and Biblical – the name occurs four times in N.T. Alternative form **Caius** led to Welsh **Cai, Caio, Caw**, all occasionally used in Wales until *circa* 1900.

Gale (f) Probably variant spelling of **Gail**, rather than a use of the word.

Galen (m) Greek 'healer' or 'calm'. Name of a very distinguished physician in ancient times (130–200 AD), in occasional use as a first name, mainly in the U.S. Feminine **Galena** has been noted, but this may be a variant of Russian **Galina**, a form of **Helen**.

Gamma (f) Greek *gamma*, the third letter in the Greek alphabet, used to name a (third) child. See **Alpha**.

Gareth (m) Welsh *gwared* 'gentle, benign'. One of King Arthur's knights bore this name, a misreading originally of a name such as **Geraint**. Tennyson's poem about *Gareth and Lynette* appeared in 1872, but both Gareth and **Lynette** appear to have come into use in Britain only in the 1930s. In the top fifty list (in Britain only) in the early 1980s. Helped in modern times by the fondness for **Gary** (and for Gareth Edwards, the Welsh rugby star).

Garfield (m) Surname deriving from a place name 'field of spears' used as a first name, presumably in honour in the first place of J. A. Garfield (1831–81), 20th President of the U.S. In use since the 1880s and especially well used by black American and West Indian families. A famous name-bearer is Sir Garfield St Aubrun Sobers, the cricketer.

Garner (m) Surname used as a first name, regularly, but infrequently.

Garnet (m, f) Surname used as a first name. Original meaning of the surname probably 'shelter, protection'. Male name spread in Britain from the 1880s because of Sir Garnet Wolseley (1833–1913), creator of the modern British army. In regular, if infrequent, use since then, often as **Garnett**. As a girl's name Garnet has been used as one of the jewel names. **Garnetta** also found.

Garrard (m) Also **Garrat, Garrett**. See **Gerard**.

Garrett (m) Vernacular (medieval) pronunciation of **Gerard**. Camden includes it in his list of 'usual Christian names' in 1605. Much used in recent times in Ireland.

Garrick (m) Surname of one of the most famous actors of all time, David Garrick (1717–79), used as a first name. Original meaning of the name is 'spear' + 'rule'. The emergence of **Gary** made the name especially acceptable because of the short form, but it remains rare.

Garrie (m) Also **Garry**. See **Gary**.

Garth (m) Surname Garth originally meant 'someone in charge of a garth, or garden'. Seems to have appealed to

19th c. writers, for there are characters who bear the name in the works of George Eliot, Wilkie Collins, Charlotte Yonge, etc. The last-named author also wrote a major book on the history of Christian names, but she does not mention Garth. Began to be used as a first name very early in the 20th c. and continues in use at the present time, though not common. For some time it was the name of a cartoon character in the British daily newspaper *The Daily Mirror*, and this seems to have increased usage slightly in the 1940s. Miss Withycombe cannot really be correct in saying that the novelist Florence Barclay launched it as a first name in her novel *The Rosary* (1909), since there is clear evidence of its use before that date (e.g. Garth Smith named in 1901, another of the same name in 1906) but almost no evidence of subsequent use until the 1920s. The hero of *The Rosary* is Garth Dalmain; another character is Sir Deryck Brand, and Miss Barclay must probably be held responsible for launching *that* form of the name. Most modern commentators say that **Garth** is a form of **Gareth**, but Gareth only came into use some thirty years later.

Gary (m) Modern use entirely due to the publicity given to it by the American actor Gary Cooper. His film career began in 1927, and the name became firmly established in the 1930s. One of the most popular names in the English-speaking world from the 1950s to 1970s, but subsequently began to decline. Gary Cooper was born Frank Cooper, and the change of name was suggested by his agent, Nan Collins, who came from the town of Gary, Indiana, which had earlier been named in honour of Elmer Gary. Several possible origins of the surname, but the most likely is from **Garrett**, a form of **Gerard**. **Garry** was immediately used as a variant of Gary, and has continued to be used. **Garrie** also occurs. Formerly Gary was often rhymed with *Mary* not with *Harry*.

Gavin (m) Scottish form of **Gawain**. Since the 1960s it has spread beyond Scotland. By the early 1980s it was the 40th most popular name in England and Wales, and was being well used in Australia. Variants include **Gavan**, **Gaven** and **Gavyn**. These forms also found in the Middle Ages, but disappeared from the 17th c., except in Scotland. Miss Withycombe has pointed out that there was also an Old German name *Gawin*, Latinized to *Gavinus*, which was sometimes written as Gavin (7th c.). That name became obsolete. In a similar way there is a French surname *Gavin*, from Italian *Gavini*, where the form of the name is merely coincidental.

Gawain (m) Welsh *gwalch* 'hawk, falcon' plus a word meaning 'little' or 'white'. Famous name in literature, that of the 'courteous knight' who served King Arthur, but very rarely given as a first name in this form. Has had great success as **Gavin**.

Gay (f) Old French *gai* 'joyful'. Surname since the 12th c. Its use as a first name began in the U.S. in the 1930s; in Britain much used 1940–60. Fell out of favour everywhere when 'gay' came to mean 'homosexual'. **Gaye** frequently occurs.

Gayle (f) See **Gail**.

Gaylord (m) Surname used as a first name, but very rare. Original meaning was 'one of high spirits', Old French *gaillard*.

Gaynor (f) Phonetic form of **Gaenor**, itself from Welsh **Gwenhwyfar**, or **Guinevere**. Other forms include **Gayna**, **Gaynah**, **Gayner**. Gaynor has always been the most frequent form of the name, which was most used in the early 1970s and has subsequently faded. Does not seem to have spread beyond Britain to any noticeable extent.

Gem (f) The word converted to first-name use. Far more common in modern times in its Italian form, **Gemma**. In some instances the male name **Jem** may be intended.

Gemelle (f) Latin *Gemella*, feminine of *Gemellus*, diminutive of *geminus* 'twin'.

In early use as a Christian name but rare in modern times.

Gemma (f) In its earliest occurrences in the Middle Ages was probably the equivalent of **Jamie** or **Jaime**, namely a feminine form of **James**. In modern times it is from the Italian word for 'gem' or 'precious stone'. Long-established name in Italy, occurring in Dante's poems, and borne by St Gemma Galgani (1875–1903). This encouraged use of the name by Roman Catholic families and in the 1950s it came into more general use. By the early 1980s was rising steadily in the British top fifty list. Frequently found as **Jemma**, and may be thought of by some parents as a modern form of **Jemima**. Use of the name in Britain has probably been helped along since the 1970s by the appearances of the actresses Gemma Jones and Gemma Craven.

Gena (f) Pet form of **Eugenia**, **Virginia** used independently. **Genette** is also found.

Gene (m) Pet form of **Eugene** used in its own right since the early 20th c. Especially well used in the U.S., and made well-known by, e.g., the boxer Gene Tunney and film star Gene Kelly.

Geneva (f) Could be the Swiss place name transferred to first-name use, in which case original meaning is 'mouth (of the river'). Frequently associated with **Genevieve**, however, and comes close to that name in some languages, e.g. Spanish **Genoveva**. *Dictionnaire des Prénoms*, by Barbe and Nortel, published in 1980, accepts it as a French variant of Genevieve. Regularly but quietly used, especially in the U.S. French spelling of the place name, **Genève**, also occurs as a first name in modern times.

Genevieve (f) The language of origin, and therefore the original meaning of this name, are unclear. Said to be either Celtic or Germanic, and some scholars suggest that it contains the words 'race' (i.e. of people) and 'woman'. St Genevieve is the patron saint of Paris and the name has been well used in France. In English-speaking countries used regu-

larly but not frequently. Since 1953 it has tended to recall the film *Genevieve*, in which it was the name of a vintage car taking part in a race from London to Brighton.

Genevra (f) Presumably a form of **Guinevere**, which becomes **Ginevra** in Italian. Rarely used.

Gent (m) A use of the surname, which originally described a well-born and courteous man, a gentleman. Occurs as a first name from time to time throughout the 19th c. The similar surname **Gentle** is also found.

Genty (m) Irish surname connected with 'snow' used as a first name. In Britain used with some regularity in the 20th c.

Geoffrey (m) Old German, the second element of the name being 'peace'. The first element is of uncertain meaning. Original German name may have been *Gaufried* or *Gautfried*, but it was identified at an early date with *Gottfried* (**Godfrey**). Some early forms point to an original *Waldfried*, from *waldan*, 'governor'. Introduced by the Normans in the 11th c. and clearly very popular, judging by the number of surnames which derive from it (*Jefferies*, *Jefferson*, etc.). Remained popular until the end of the 16th c., then became rare until the latter half of the 19th c. Reappeared at first in its J- spellings, which date back to its first introduction in the Middle Ages. Geoffrey was later to become the usual British spelling, Jeffrey being preferred in the U.S. At its most popular in the 1950s in Britain, twenty years later in the U.S. and Canada. Since 1980 has been fading on all sides. A number of other variants are in use, including **Geoffery** (frequent), **Geoffry**, **Geofrey**, **Jefery**, **Jefferey**, **Jeffery** (frequent), **Jeffree**, **Jeffry**, **Jeffrie**. **Jefferson** is regularly used as a first name, **Jefferies** is occasional. Pet form **Jeff** is used independently, though **Geoff** is very rare as a name in its own right.

Geordie (m) Form of **George**, used in Britain as a generic term for a man from

Tyneside. Since the 1950s also used occasionally as a first name.

Geogan(n)a (f) Variants of **Georgiana**, used in the 19th c.

George (m) Greek *georgos* 'earthworker, husbandman, farmer'. St George was a Roman military tribune martyred in 303, his fight with the Devil having popularly become a fight with a dragon. The Crusaders were much impressed by him and brought his cult back to England. In the 14th c. Edward III made him patron saint of England. His name did not immediately come into common use, however, perhaps because of a certain hostility to non-Biblical saints. By the 16th c. it had become general and remained very popular in Britain until the 1930s, having been sustained by its royal associations for much of the time. Has subsequently gone out of fashion and is quietly used for the moment. In the U.S. it might well have become rare but for George Washington (1732–99), who caused it to be as fashionable in America as it was in Britain. There, too, the name has been declining in recent years, and by the beginning of the 1980s it was clearly unfashionable. Few pet forms, **Georgie** now being used mainly for girls, but it has given rise to a great number of feminine versions. They include **Georgia**, **Georgiana**, **Georgina**, **Georgette**, **Georgeann(e)**, etc.

Georgeana (f) Variant of **Georgiana**. **Georganna**, **Georgeanna** and **Georgana** are also found, mostly in the 19th c.

Georgeina (f) Also **Georgena**, **Georgenia**. See **Georgina**.

Georgette (f) French feminine form of **George** in which some interest has been shown in Britain since the 1940s. Also sparingly used in the U.S. The popular novelist Georgette Heyer has helped keep the name before the public eye.

Georgia (f) Normal American feminine form of **George**, **Georgina** being used in Britain. An example of Georgia as a first name occurs in a 4th c. inscription. The state of Georgia was named for George

II (1732). Georgia had become rather rare in the U.S. by 1970, whereas British parents had increased their use of the name since the early 1960s.

Georgiana (f) One of the feminine forms of **George** well used from the 18th c. until the 1890s. In use very sporadically thereafter. **Georgianna** was a frequent variant at one time, but became obsolete by the end of the 19th c. **Georganna** and **Georgeanna**, indicating the pronunciation of the name, also found while the name was in use.

Georgie (m, f) Diminutive of **George** used independently, though not infrequently, since the 1870s. Seems to have begun as a male name but has recently been used for girls.

Georgina (f) Feminine form of **George** used since the 18th c., especially in Scotland. In the rest of Britain it has had a remarkably long run, and continues to be well used in the early 1980s. Does not seem to have made an appeal outside Britain, forms like **Georgia** being preferred in the U.S. Variants include **Georgeana**, **Georgeina**, **Georgena**, **Georgiena**.

Georgine (f) Variant of **Georgina** mainly used since the late 1930s, though infrequently. **Georgene** also occurs.

Geraint (m) Welsh form of Latin *Gerontius*, itself from a Greek word meaning 'old'. Geraint is the husband of Enid in one of the Arthurian legends (see more at **Enid**). In general use in Britain since the late 1950s, having been given publicity in recent times by the opera singer Sir Geraint Evans.

Gerald (m) Old German 'spear' + 'ruler'. Became confused at an early date with **Gerard**, the more usual form. When both names were revived in the 19th c. Gerald became the more common. In Britain reached a peak in the mid-1930s, then began to wane. In the U.S. its popularity began later and lasted well into the 1960s. By the late 1970s was being kept alive by black American families, but otherwise becoming rare. Pet forms such as **Gerry**, **Jerry** and to a lesser extent, **Gerri**, have often been used independently. Variant forms include **Gerrald, Gerrold, Jerald, Jerold, Jerrold**. Normal feminine form is **Geraldine**, but in the U.S. especially **Geralyn, Geralynn, Gerilyn, Gerrilyn**, etc., are found, together with the J-variants such as **Jerilene**.

Geraldine (f) Feminine form of **Gerald**. The Earl of Surrey (1517–47) addressed many love poems to 'the fair Geraldine', who was actually Lady Elizabeth Fitzgerald. Occurs in Heywood's *The English Traveller* (17th c.) as name of a young man. Appeared in the 1840s, soon after Gerald began to be used regularly. Most used in the 1950s, but now infrequently found. Variants **Geraldene, Geralda** occur.

Gerard (m) Old German 'spear' + 'brave'. The Normans brought it to Britain and it remained in use until the 17th c. Had almost disappeared when it was revived in the mid-19th c. and came into regular use once again. Gradually increasing in popularity in all English-speaking countries, especially Ireland. Pet forms **Gerry** and **Jerry** also used independently. Some parents may use it in honour of the poet Gerard Manley Hopkins (1844–89), whose reputation continues to grow. Some of the surnames linked with Gerard, such as **Garrard, Garrat, Garrett**, are used as first names from time to time. French feminine form **Gerardine** also occurs occasionally.

Gerda (f) Norse 'protection'. Gerda is the wife of Frey or Freyr, a woman 'whose beauty was so resplendent that it illumined the whole world'. Hans Christian Andersen used the name for the little girl in *The Snow Queen*, yet it has never been much used in English-speaking countries. In Germany it is sometimes used as the pet form of Gertrude.

Geri (f) Variant of **Gerry** (f).

Germaine (f) French feminine of **Germain**, or **German** in its English form, which also indicates the meaning. Used

in English-speaking countries, especially Britain, since the 1960s, and made well-known in modern times by the feminist writer Germaine Greer.

German (m) English form of French **Germain**, Latin **Germanus**. The latter form was common in Christian inscriptions of the Roman Empire. The name of several early saints. Indicates the nationality of the original name-bearer (compare **Francis** 'a Frenchman'). Never frequently used in English-speaking countries, though the French feminine form of the name, **Germaine**, has been used recently.

Gerrald (m) See **Gerald**.

Gerrard (m) Frequent variant of **Gerard**.

Gerrold (m) See **Gerald**.

Gerry (m) Short form of **Gerald** or **Gerard**, used as an independent name, especially since the 1940s. Variant **Jerry** is the earlier form and much preferred in the U.S. **Gerrie** also occurs.

Gerry (f) Pet form of **Geraldine** used occasionally as an independent name. **Jerry** also occurs.

Gershom (m) Hebrew 'exile'. Biblical, O.T., Ex. 2:22, 'She bore a son, and he called his name Gershom; for he said "I have been a sojourner in a foreign land." ' Miss Withycombe nevertheless rejects this explanation of the name as folk-etymology and says it means 'bell'. Used by the Puritans, who would probably not have argued with the Biblical explanation, and for whom the meaning given there must have seemed apt. Brought to the U.S. and used along with other O.T. names. Still used, but rather rare. Variant forms include **Gersham, Gershon, Gerson**.

Gertie (f) Pet form of **Gertrude** used independently from the 1880s to the 1930s. Now very rare. Use of **Gerty** began slightly earlier, but the -ie spelling was preferred from 1910 onwards.

Gertina (f) Extension of **Gertie** which suddenly appealed to parents in the 1890s, but quickly faded.

Gertrude (f) Old German 'spear strength'. A 7th c. saint whose cult was widespread in the Netherlands. St Gertrude the Great was a 13th c. mystic. Camden includes the name in his 'usual Christian names' (1605), and Shakespeare brought it to the public's attention a few years earlier in *Hamlet*, where Gertrude is the Prince's mother. Infrequently used in English-speaking countries until the 1860s, when it suddenly became extremely fashionable. Reached a peak in 1900, then faded slowly during the next thirty years. Now rarely used. One of the best-known bearers of the name was the actress Gertrude Lawrence (Gertrud Alexandra Dagmar Lawrence Klasen, 1898–1952). The writer Gertrude Stein (1874–1946) was also extremely influential. Pet forms of the name include **Gert, Gertie, Gerty, Trudy, Trudie, Trudi**, all of which have been used independently.

Gerty (f) See **Gertie**.

Gervase (m) English form of Latin *Gervasius*, a martyred saint about whom nothing is known, but whose cult became popular and widespread. Original meaning equally obscure. If the name is of Old German elements, then *ger* is probably 'spear'. Always steadily used by Roman Catholic families. In the 19th c., especially, it occurred frequently in the forms **Jarvis, Jervis**. Modern French form is also found, namely **Gervais**, together with its feminine form **Gervaise**.

Gerwyn (m) Welsh, possibly 'fair love'. Used from time to time since the 1930s. **Gerwen** also occurs.

Gethin (m) Welsh *cethin* 'dusky'. Found also as **Geth, Gethen**.

Ghislaine (f) French feminine of **Ghislain**, the name of a 7th c. saint. Used in Britain in small numbers since the 1950s. The meaning is unclear, although the first element is probably Old German for 'pledge'.

Gianetta (f) Italian equivalent of **Janet**, in use since the 1950s in English-speaking countries.

Gibson (m) Surname linked with **Gilbert**, regularly used as a first name in the

19th c. and occasionally since.

Gideon (m) Hebrew 'cutter, with hand cut off'. Biblical, O.T., Judges 6:11. Hero and judge in ancient Israel. The Gideon Bibles were named because Gideon symbolizes a great work done by a few people. Regularly but quietly used as a first name in modern times.

Gifford (m) Surname originally meaning 'chubby-cheeked, bloated' used regularly if infrequently as a first name.

Gilbert (m) Old German 'pledge' + 'bright'. Brought to Britain by the Normans and a favourite in the Middle Ages. Led to many surnames such as *Gibbs, Gibson, Gibbon*, etc. Since the 17th c. used regularly, especially in Scotland and the north of England, but has died away even there since the 1950s. Has also been replaced by **Tom** in the expression 'tom-cat', formerly a 'gib-cat', **Gib** being a pet form of Gilbert. In the U.S. sometimes found in its Italian form **Gilberto** and, very rarely, in its feminine form **Gilberta**. Perhaps the best-known bearer of the name was the English writer Gilbert Keith Chesterton (1874–1936).

Gilda (f) Italian short form of **Ermenegilda**, a name known to the Anglo-Saxons as *Eormengild*, and said to have survived until the 19th c. in Britain. Miss Withycombe mentions it in her article on **Ermyntrude**. Gilda is Rigoletto's daughter in Verdi's opera, but the sudden interest in the name in the 1950s was probably due to the film *Gilda* (1946) in which Rita Hayworth played the title role.

Gildroy (m) Form of **Gilroy**. As Black says in his article on Gilroy, in *The Surnames of Scotland*, 'the hero of the well-known ballad (executed 1638) had his name changed in the low country speech to Gilderoy'. **Gilderoy** also occurs from time to time as a first name, together with **Gildero, Gildray, Gildrey, Gildri**.

Giles (m, f) French form of Latin **Egidius**, ultimately from Greek *aigidion* 'young goat'. The reference is probably to kid leather, which was used for shields. St

Giles was extremely popular in the Middle Ages, as the number of churches dedicated to him in Britain makes clear. He was especially associated with Scotland, the High Kirk in Edinburgh being dedicated to him, and the name was well used there from the 16th c. In Scotland it was always given to girls at that time, occasionally in the Latin form **Egidia**. Now reverted to male use and becoming reasonably popular in Britain in the 1970s. Very rare elsewhere. **Gyles** is occasionally found.

Gilian (f) Variant of **Gillian**.

Gill (f) Short form of **Gillian**. Commonly used in the Middle Ages, but its very popularity caused it to go out of favour from the 17th c. Began to reappear in the 1870s, but not used frequently in modern times. **Jill**, a common early variant, also made a reappearance in the 1920s. From the 1930s to the late 1970s extremely popular in all English-speaking countries, especially Australia. Subsequently tended to fade.

Gillean (m) Gaelic 'servant of St John'. The 'g' is pronounced as in 'give'. Early use of the name led to surnames such as *Gilzean*. Now rare, almost exclusive to Scotland.

Gillian (m) See **Gillean**.

Gillian (f) English form of **Juliana**. Common name in Britain in the Middle Ages, as Giliana, etc. Camden mentions that **Gilian** is legally a distinct name from Juliana (1605). In the 18th c. Juliana was the preferred form, Gillian not being revived in force until 1930. Very popular throughout the 1960s but has since faded. Variants include **Gillianne, Gillyanne, Jillian, Jillianne**. Pet forms **Gill** and **Jill** much used independently.

Gillie (f) Diminutive of **Gill**, ultimately from **Gillian**, used independently on rare occasions. **Gilly** also occurs.

Gilroy (m) Celtic surname 'servant of the red-haired man' used as a first name. Found regularly but infrequently since the beginning of the 20th c.

Gilson (m) Surname linked with **Gilbert** occasionally used as a first name.

Gina (f) Pet form of **Georgina** or **Regina**, used independently since the 1920s, especially in the 1950s. The Italian actress Gina Lollobrigida may have had some influence on its use. In Italy Gina is normally a diminutive of Luigina, ultimately from Luigi, or **Louis**.

Ginette (f) French pet form of **Genevieve**, regularly used in Britain since the 1940s. **Ginnette** and **Ginetta** also found.

Ginger (f) Use of Ginger as a first name in modern times is probably entirely due to the actress/dancer Ginger Rogers, star of many musicals in the 1930s with Fred Astaire. Born **Virginia** McMath, the Ginger was a pet form of her original name. Mainly used in the U.S. and Canada, and now very rare.

Ginny (f) Pet form of **Virginia** used independently. Not frequent.

Giovanna (f) Italian feminine of **Giovanni** (**John**), used in English-speaking countries from time to time since the 1950s.

Gipsy (m) The word used as a name. All the examples noted occur in Britain between 1880 and 1920. The first name **Romany** occurs, which a gipsy family would be more likely to use, 'gipsy' being used by outsiders. It reflects the ancient belief that all gipsies came from Egypt. Perhaps Gipsy was not a true name in the instances noted, but a description of the child entered by the registrar in the absence of other details.

Gisela (f) Primarily a German name, from Old German *gisel* (= modern German *Geisel* 'hostage, pledge'). French form of the name is **Giselle**. Gisela (pronounced with a hard *g* as in 'gas' and with the stress on the first syllable) is occasionally used in English-speaking countries.

Giselle (f) French form of **Gisela**. **Gisele** also occurs, and both forms are pronounced *Jiz-elle*. *Giselle* was the title of a ballet by Gautier (1841), and modern use of the name in English-speaking countries may derive from it.

Giuseppe (m) See **Joseph**.

Gladstone (m) Scottish surname linked

with Gledstanes in Lanarkshire. Well used as a first name in Britain from the 1860s onwards, clearly in honour of William Ewart Gladstone (1809–98), Prime Minister four times. He also gave his name to the Gladstone bag and to a type of carriage.

Gladys (f) Welsh *Gwladys*, said to be a form of **Claudia**. Camden (1605) was familiar with **Gladuse**, which he described as a 'British form of Claudia'. No trace is found of the name, however, until the 1870s, when it burst upon the scene in all English-speaking countries. At that time it clearly had an exotic strangeness about it, not to say sex-appeal. Perhaps one should re-translate it into something like **Claudine** to get its flavour. Used by several romantic novelists of the time, including Ouida (*Puck*, 1870) Anne Beale (*Gladys of Harlech*) and Edith M. Dauglish (*Gladys*). By 1900 immensely popular everywhere. Remained so until the 1930s, when reaction set in. Now very rarely given. The British actress Dame Gladys Cooper (1888–1971) was one of the most distinguished bearers of the name. Confusion over the Welsh form of the name led to the variant **Gladwys** on many occasions, but **Gladis** was surprisingly rare. **Gladness** was another very occasional variant, and perhaps indicates how the name was perceived by many parents.

Glanville (m) Norman place name which became an English surname. Occurs from time to time as a first name.

Glen (m) First occurs as a first name in the early 19th c. Probably a transferred use of the surname, which originally indicated someone who lived in a valley. Remained very rare until the 1920s, when the variant **Glenn** came into use. Both forms well used in the 1970s but seem to have faded since then, though the singer Glen Campbell is still well known.

Glenda (f) Welsh *glan* 'holy, fair' plus *da* 'good'. Dates from early 1930 (launched by actress Glenda Farrell) and was

consistently used until the mid-1960s. Subsequently became much rarer. Given wide publicity by the British actress Glenda Jackson whose film career began in the latter half of the 1960s.

Glendower (m) English form of Welsh **Glyndwr**.

Glenice (f) Variant of **Glenys** regularly used from the 1920s to the 1940s. **Glenis** lasted rather longer, until the late 1960s. Another variant, **Glenise**, in use from the 1930s to the 1950s.

Glenn (m) Modern form of **Glen**, in general use since the 1930s. The American actor Glenn Hunter (1897–1945) helped to make the name known from the 1920s, but little doubt that the Canadian-born actor Glenn Ford (1916–) was an even bigger influence. He began his screen career in the late 1930s, and had dropped his original first name Gwyllyn to become a Glenn. Another major influence on the name was the famous band-leader Glenn Miller (1904–44).

Glenna (f) Feminine form of Glenn (itself sometimes feminine) used since the 1940s.

Glennis (f) See **Glenys**.

Glenton (m) Place name/surname 'settlement in a valley' used since the 1940s as a first name, by which time **Glen(n)** had become popular. **Glentworth** occurred much earlier.

Glenville (m) Place name/surname occasionally used as a first name. **Glenvil** is also found. Both forms used rather more frequently since **Glen(n)** became more usual.

Glenys (f) Welsh *glan* 'holy, fair'. Reasonably well-used this century, especially during the 1950s, but has tended to fade since 1970. Glenys is the original Welsh form, but for many parents the name was associated with **Glen(n)**, the male name, and turned into **Glennis, Glenis. Glenice, Glennys, Glenwys, Glenyse, Glenyss, Glenise** are amongst the other variant forms.

Glinys (f) See **Glynis**.

Gloria (f) Latin *gloria* 'glory'. Ancient form of the name was **Gloriosa**. In the

17th c. **Gloriana** was the name applied by some poets to Queen Elizabeth I. G. B. Shaw seems to have been the first person to use the form Gloria, in *You Never Can Tell* (1898). Also adopted by the actress Josephine Swenson who then appeared on screen in 1915 as a Mack Sennett bathing beauty under the name of Gloria Swanson. Popular in the U.S. in the 1920s, and reached Britain rather later. Survived well into the 1960s, but then began to fade on all sides. Variants of the name include **Glory**, **Gloris**, **Glorie** and **Glori**.

Glorvina (f) Invented by the Irish writer Lady Morgan for a character in her novel *The Wild Irish Girl* (1806). Taken up by Thackeray in his *Vanity Fair* as the name of Peggy O'Dowd's sister. Coghlan says in *Irish Christian Names* that it has been used in Ireland. May have blended 'glory' and a name such as **Malvina**, though **Gloria** was not yet in use at the beginning of the 19th c.

Glory (f) English form of **Gloria**, occasionally used as a first name.

Glyn (m) Welsh *glyn* 'small valley', a word (and name) related to **Glen(n)**. Regularly used throughout the 20th c. in England and Wales, especially popular during the 1950s.

Glyndwr (m) Surname of the Welsh national hero Owain Glyndwr (1354–1416). English form of the name is **Glendower**. Commonly used as a Christian name in Wales. **Glyndor** also occurs. Normal pet form is **Glyn**, also used independently.

Glynis (f) Welsh 'little valley', allied to the Scottish name and word **Glen**. Modern spread of the name outside Wales entirely due to the publicity given to it by the British actress Glynis Johns, whose screen career began in the 1930s. Especially well used between the mid-1940s and mid-1960s. Subsequently faded from the scene. **Glynnis** was often used as a variant, and **Glinnis**, **Glinys**, **Glynes** also occurred. In some cases there may have been confusion with **Glenys**.

Godfrey (m) Old German 'god' + 'peace'. One of the names introduced to Britain in the Middle Ages which became very popular. By the 17th c. far less common, but regularly used throughout the 18th and 19th cc. Remains in use, but not often found. Professor Weekley makes the name a variant of **Geoffrey**, which in many early occurrences was certainly true.

Godwin (m) Old English 'God' or 'good' plus 'friend, protector'. Survived the Norman Conquest to become a surname and was listed by Camden (1605) as a 'usual Christian name', but it was little used. One would have expected it to be revived strongly along with other Anglo-Saxon names in the 19th c., but it remained very rare. Parents have occasionally turned to it this century.

Golden (f) A use of the word as first name. Several examples have been noted from late 19th c. records, and one occurrence in 1915. Modern form of the name, very rarely used, appears to be **Goldie**. **Golda** also found in the 1960s and '70s, presumably with reference to the former Israeli Premier, Mrs Golda Meir.

Goldie (f) Modern form of **Golden**, publicized by the actress Goldie Hawn. Rarely used.

Golding (m) Surname used as a first name from time to time. Original meaning of the name is uncertain, but may have indicated someone with 'golden' hair.

Goliath (m) Hebrew 'exile'. Biblical, O.T., 1 Sam. 17, name of the Philistine giant slain by the young David. Bardsley did not find any examples of this name amongst the Puritans, but quotes Taylor, the Water-poet, who 'seems to imply that Goliath was registered at baptism by the Puritans'. Examples occur in British registers of the 19th and 20th cc., the last one noted being in 1931. **Golliath** is also found.

Gomer (m) Mentioned in the Bible, O.T., Gen. 10:2 and occasionally used. *Gomer* also happens to be an English surname, meaning either 'good' or 'battle' plus 'famous'. In some instances it may be this surname which is being transferred to the first-name use. Usually male, but in Hosea 1:3 a woman is referred to.

Gordon (m) Famous Scottish clan name and place name, the original meaning of which is uncertain. Well used in Scotland in the 20th c. as a first name, and popular elsewhere with parents of Scottish descent. Most used from 1920 onwards, fading somewhat in England after 1940 but retained in Scotland and Canada. Sometimes found as **Gordan** or **Gorden**.

Grace (f) Latin *gratia* 'grace', found as the name of a Christian in 4th c. Rome. Independently introduced to Britain, however, by the Puritans at the end of the 16th c., the word 'grace' having great religious significance in phrases such as 'by the grace of God' and 'in the year of grace'. The Puritans brought the name to America. At the end of the 19th c. extremely popular in the U.S., and remained fashionable until the 1920s. In Scotland also well used throughout the 19th c. Scottish parents remained faithful to it until the 1950s. In England mildly fashionable 1900–25. The fame of Grace Darling's exploit in 1838, when she helped save the lives of nine shipwrecked seamen, had little effect on the English use of the name. Little used anywhere in the English-speaking world in recent years, in spite of the fame in the 1950s of the actress Grace Kelly, who then became Princess Grace of Monaco. Diminutive **Gracie** was often used as an independent name when Grace itself was popular (see Gracie). Spelling variant **Gracey** also found.

Gracey (f) Occasional variant of Gracie (see).

Gracie (f) Diminutive of Grace formerly used as an independent name. Made well known by the English singer and comedienne Gracie Fields (1898–1979) (born Grace Stansfield).

Graeme (m) Form of Graham used almost exclusively in Scotland or by

Scottish parents living elsewhere. This spelling of the name first appears in a work on family history by William Buchanan in the 18th c. Gradually more widely used, mainly since the 1920s.

Graham (m) Originally an English place name, 'Granta's homestead', but early became a Scottish clan name and surname. Occurs consistently in Scottish history since the 12th c. As a first name also most used in Scotland, but became very popular in the rest of Britain in the 1950s. Also a success with Scottish families abroad, especially in Australia. Does not seem to have appealed to American parents, and signs now that it is reverting to being a purely Scottish first name. **Grahame** and **Graeme** are the usual variants.

Grahame (m) This spelling of Graham was extremely rare until the 1920s, when **Graeme** became frequent. The final -e presumably came from that form of the name.

Grania (f) Based on the Irish word for 'love'. In Ireland in the 1970s it was being well used in its Irish form **Grainne**. Occurs also as **Grainnia**.

Grant (m) Surname used as a first name. Original meaning is 'tall', French *grand*. Surname was established in Scotland at an early date, and Scottish parents have always been fond of using family names as first names. In this case, however, Canadian or American parents seem to have started the trend. In the U.S. usage may have been in honour of Ulysses S. Grant (1822–85), 18th President of the U.S. Continues to be regularly, if quietly, used.

Grantley (m) English place name/surname 'Granta's meadow' used as a first name. Regular if infrequent use since the 1860s. **Grantly** also occurs.

Granville (m) Common French place name which became an English surname. Regularly used as a first name in the U.S. and Britain, though examples are difficult to find after the 1960s. Variants include **Granvil**, **Granvile**, **Granvill**, **Grenvil**, **Grenville**.

Gray (m) Use of the surname as a first name. Original reference would have been to gray hair. Other surnames containing this element occur in modern times as first names, e.g., **Graydon**, **Grayson**, though **Grayham** is probably a spelling variant of **Graham**.

Greenwood (m) Place name/surname used with great regularity as a first name throughout the 19th c. The frequency of occurrence suggests that in some instances at least the name was used for its pleasant meaning, without family reference. **Greener** was also in use in the 19th c., while **Green** and **Greenshaw** occurred very occasionally.

Greer (f) Form of **Gregor**. First-name usage in modern times entirely due to the Anglo-Irish actress Greer Garson, regularly on the screen from 1939. Greer was the family name of her mother, Nina Greer. Not often found.

Greeta (f) Occasional variant of **Greta**.

Greg (m) Pet form of **Gregor** and **Gregory** used independently, mainly since the 1950s. **Gregg** is a frequent variant. **Greig** is rare, but is also ultimately from Gregor(y).

Gregor (m) Early form of **Gregory**, also the form of that name in languages such as German and Norwegian. Early use in Scotland led to surnames such as *Macgregor*. Gregory has been the usual modern form, but Gregor is found since the 1920s, especially in Scotland.

Gregory (m) Greek *Gregorios* from *gregoros* 'watchful'. Post-Biblical name, common in the Roman Empire. It named sixteen popes. Common in Britain in the Middle Ages but faded between the 16th and 18th cc. Used infrequently in the 19th c., and in the 20th c. quietly used until the 1940s, when it was probably the actor Gregory Peck who made it fashionable. Popular everywhere through the 1950s but subsequently waned. Pet forms **Greg** and **Gregg**, especially the latter, have been well used as independent names since the 1950s. **Gregor** is used in Scotland, and the foreign form **Grigor** is found.

Grenville (m) Common variant of **Granville**. **Grenvil** is also found.

Gresham (m) Place name/surname used as a first name, mainly in the 19th c. Refers to a hamlet with grazing land around it.

Greta (f) Pet form of **Margaret** in several languages, especially German. Swedish scholars describe it as a German import. In modern times internationally associated with Greta Garbo (Greta Lovisa Gustaffson at birth, though making use of other pseudonyms from time to time, such as Harriet Brown). Her legendary film career spanned roughly twenty years, from the 1920s to 1940. In use in English-speaking countries from the 1880s, but Miss Garbo caused it to be most used in the 1930s. Now rarely found.

Gretchen (f) German pet form of **Margarete** (**Margaret**) used as an independent name in English-speaking countries since the late 19th c.

Grethel (f) German diminutive of **Margarete**. The name of the lady who narrates the tales of the Grimm brothers. Used on rare occasions this century. **Gretel** also occurs, presumably with reference to the *Hansel and Gretel* story.

Gretna (f) Scottish village, Gretna Green, formerly famous as the place to which runaway English couples went to be married under Scottish law. Use of Gretna as a first name (a rare occurrence) presumably recalls such a marital trip.

Gretta (f) Variant of **Greta** by origin, though indicating a different pronunciation.

Greville (m) Surname (from a Norman place name) used as a first name, regularly but infrequently.

Griffith (m) English form of Welsh **Gruffydd**, usually explained as 'strong, powerful' plus 'chief' or 'fighter'. Early use led to the surnames *Griffith*, *Griffiths*. Used as a first name from the 16th c. to the end of the 18th c., then became infrequent. Still found, but rather rare.

Grigor (m) The form in some languages,

e.g. Ukrainian, Bulgarian, of **Gregory**. Occasionally found.

Grimshaw (m) Surname derived from a place name referring originally to a rather sinister copse. Used as a first name mainly in the 19th c.

Griselda (f) The German *Lexikon der Vornamen* explains this as an Italian name of unknown origin. The standard Italian work on first names explains it as a German name, a view followed by most English authorities. Probably had an original meaning of 'grey battle-maid'. Its literary history is well-known, Boccaccio having told the story of the perfect wife whose patience was sorely tried by her husband in the *Decameron*. Chaucer re-told the tale, and the patience of a Griselda became proverbial in the Middle Ages. Philip Massinger makes a typical reference to the name in the 17th c.:

> shall you sit puling (crying),
> Like a patient Grizzle, and be laughed
> at?

Survived in Scotland until the 18th c., but rare in all English-speaking countries since the beginning of the 19th c. By this time 'to grizzle' had taken on the meaning of 'whining, sulking'. Mainly found in modern times in its short form, **Zelda**, used independently since the beginning of the 20th c.

Grover (m) Surname originally indicating someone who lived in a 'grove', regularly used as a first name in the U.S. because of President Grover Cleveland (1837–1908). Still being fairly well used in the 1940s but rare in modern times. Very occasionally used in Britain.

Guildford (m) Place name 'ford with golden flowers' which became a surname, used regularly as a first name in the 19th c. **Guilford** also occurs.

Guinevere (f) French form of Welsh Gwenhwyfar, the wife of King Arthur. Far more familiar in modern times as **Jennifer**, but Guinevere is found on rare occasions.

Gus (m) Pet form of **Augustus** or **Augustin(e)**. Occasionally used as an independent name, e.g. two instances in Detroit, 1965.

Gussie (f) Pet form of **Augusta** or **Augustina**, occasionally used as an independent name.

Gusta (f) German short form of **Augusta** used independently.

Gustave (m) French form of Swedish **Gustav**, **Gustaf**, earlier Götstaf, 'staff of the gods'. Royal name in Sweden which spread through Europe in the 17th c. Used in Britain mainly in the 19th c., often as Latin **Gustavus**. Rare elsewhere.

Guy (m) Germanic *Wido*, Italian/Spanish *Guido*, of uncertain origin. A 12th c. saint bore the name, and it was in early use. The Guy Fawkes episode in England in 1605 disgraced the name and it was not used for two hundred years. Revived in the mid-19th c. and became popular at first in the U.S., but never so popular that it could become the general word for a man. This is thought to have happened because of the Hebrew word *goy* 'gentile'. In Britain used fairly strongly from the 1950s to the late 1970s. In the U.S. recent usage has been markedly by white parents rather than black. Use of the name in Scott's *Guy Mannering* (1815) and *The Heir of Redcliffe* (1853), by Charlotte Yonge, appeared to have very little influence on its popularity.

Gwen (f) Short form of names such as **Gwendolen**, **Gwenllian**, etc., used in its own right since the 1880s. Welsh *gwen* can mean 'white, fair' or 'blessed'. Never intensively used and rare since the early 1960s.

Gwenda (f) Welsh *gwen* 'fair' and *da* 'good'. Regularly used until the 1960s, now rare. **Glenda** came rather later and may have been suggested by this name.

Gwendolen (f) Welsh *gwen* 'fair, blessed' and *dolen* 'ring, bow'. Ancient Welsh name which seems to have been introduced in modern times by George Eliot in her novel *Daniel Deronda*, published in instalments between 1874–76. Gwendoline, however, had begun to be used in the 1860s and became the most popular form of a name which also appeared as **Gwendolyn**, later **Gwendolene, Gwendolin, Gwendolyne**. Even more recent variants are **Gwendolynn, Gwendolynne**. By the 1960s Gwendolyn was being very well used by black American families, roughly ten times as often as by white families. Now infrequently used.

Gwendoline (f) By far the most popular form in Britain of **Gwendolen**, at a peak in the 1920s but now quietly used.

Gwendolyn (f) Preferred form of **Gwendolen** in the U.S. and Canada. See Gwendolen.

Gweneth (f) See Gwyneth.

Gwenllian (f) Welsh *gwen* 'white, fair' and *llaian* 'flaxen'. Royal name in Wales in the 12th c., used in modern times until the 1930s, when it appears to have become obsolete again.

Gwenneth (f) See Gwyneth.

Gwennie (f) Pet form of any of the Welsh names beginning with Gwen-, such as **Gwendolen (Gwendoline), Gwenfrewi**, etc. Used independently this century until the 1930s. **Gwenny** also occurs, but rarely.

Gwenyth (f) See Gwyneth.

Gwilym (m) Welsh form of **William**,

showing the influence of French **Guillaume**. Regularly used in Wales since the 1870s.

Gwladys (f) Welsh form of **Gladys**. Traditionally said to translate *Claudia*, but may be from Welsh *gwlad*, a territory, and *gwledig*, the ruler of such a territory. Gwladys would be a feminine form of the latter word. Used in Wales from 1877 to the 1920s, when it became rare.

Gwyn (m) Welsh 'fair, blessed'. Used mainly in Wales, but also in England, since the beginning of the 20th c.

Gwyneth (f) Welsh *gwynaeth* 'happiness, felicity'. Much used in England and Wales this century, especially in the 1930s and '40s. Found as **Gwynneth** (frequently), and by confusion with the many Welsh names beginning Gwen-, as **Gwenyth, Gweneth, Gwenith, Gwenneth, Gwennyth**. Welsh **Gwynedd** also occurs.

Gwynfor (m) Welsh *gwyn* 'fair, good' + *ior* 'lord'. A 20th c. innovation used in Wales and made well-known by the president of Plaid Cymru (the Welsh Nationalist Party), Gwynfor Evans. Feminine form **Gwynfa** is also found.

Gwynne (f) Feminine form of **Gwyn**.

Gwynneth (f) See Gwyneth.

Gyles (m) Variant of Giles.

H

Hadassah (f) Hebrew 'myrtle'. Biblical, O.T., Book of Esther. Esther's original name. The myrtle was a symbol of love in ancient times, sacred to Venus. The name was therefore translated by a Persian word meaning 'star', specifically 'the planet Venus', namely **Esther**. Hadassah itself used by the 17th c. Puritans. Occurs very rarely in modern times.

Haddon (m) English place name/surname 'hill with heather' used as a first name. Regular but infrequent. **Haden, Hadon**, etc., also occur but may be variants of

Hadyn, Haydn, since official records do not indicate how the names are meant to be pronounced.

Hadrian (m) Old Roman spelling of **Adrian**, used by the Emperor Hadrian, responsible for Hadrian's Wall in Britain. Has been used (almost exclusively in Britain) since the 1960s as a variant of Adrian.

Hadyn (m) In regular use in the 20th c., especially in Wales. Individual pronunciation of the same varies, and it can be linked with **Haddon** or **Haydon** (**Hayden**). In some instances may be a variant of **Haydn**. None of these forms is Welsh, but Trefor Jones has suggested that Welsh parents link the name with Celtic **Aidan**.

Hagar (f) Hebrew 'forsaken'. Biblical, O.T., Gen. 16:1. Sarah's handmaid, an Egyptian girl. When Sarah despaired of having a child she sent Hagar to her husband, Abraham. The law of the time said that any children born to Hagar would be Sarah's. Hagar duly had a son, but Sarah responded to the situation much as a modern wife might do. Abraham was forced to send both Hagar and her son away. Used regularly though infrequently throughout the 19th c. but seems to have disappeared since the 1920s. The form **Haggar** is found.

Haidee (f) Probably from the Greek word for 'modest'. There is much about her in Byron's *Don Juan*, which was probably responsible for bringing the name into occasional use from the 1820s onwards. Used again since the 1960s, probably because it is thought to be a variant of **Heidi**.

Hailey (f) See **Hayley**.

Hal (m) Diminutive of **Henry** or **Harry**, used independently from time to time since the turn of the century. For the form compare **Molly** from **Mary**, **Sally** from **Sarah**, etc.

Halcyon (f) Greek *halkyon* 'mythical bird' identified with the kingfisher. 'Halcyon days' means a period of calmness. Used as a first name on rare occasions.

Haley (f) See **Hayley**.

Halford (m) English place name/surname used from time to time as a first name. Originally refers to a 'ford in a valley'.

Halina (f) Polish/Russian form of **Helen** in occasional use in English-speaking countries.

Hall (m) Surname, indicating someone who worked at the 'hall,' used as a first name. All the instances noted occur in the 19th c.

Ham (m) Hebrew: connected with *hamam* 'to be hot'. Biblical, O.T.,

Gen. 5:32. Noah's son. Rarely used.

Hamilton (m) Place name and aristocratic surname used regularly as a first name from the beginning of the 19th c., especially in Scotland. Hamilton Fish, U.S. Secretary of State 1869–77, encouraged use of the name by American parents.

Hamish (m) Phonetic spelling of Gaelic **Sheumais**, vocative case of **Seumas**, or **James**. Very rarely used outside Scotland, where it ranked 78th in 1958.

Hamlet (m) The famous Hamlet, mythical or semi-historical prince of Denmark, is *Amleth* in the original text of *Saxo Grammaticus*, the first writer to tell the tale. Represents an Old Norse name *Amlothi* or *Amblothi*, which does not seem to have survived in any form. English translators of *Saxo* used a name that was familiar to them, namely Hamlet, a diminutive of Old German *Heimo*. Basic meaning is the same as in the word 'hamlet' meaning a village, where 'ham' is 'home'. The Normans had introduced the name to Britain as **Hamo** or **Hamon**, and other diminutive forms, many of which led to surnames, were *Hamelot, Hamnet, Hamlin, Hamblin, Hamonet*. In common use in Britain from the 16th c. to the 18th c. Found irregularly throughout the 19th c. and very rarely used in the 20th c. Professor Weekley comments on the curious disappearance of a name that was formerly so common, and which remains so well known. As an example of its commonness, he quotes a 17th c. clergyman, the Rev. Hamlet Marshall, who lived with his nephew Hamlet Joyce and left legacies to Hamlet Pickerin and Hamlet Duncalf. His son Hamlet Marshall was executor of his will. The form **Hamnet**, which Shakespeare himself used to name his son, also seems to have disappeared in modern times. Surnames **Hammond, Hammet, Hamlyn, Hamlin**, all used as first names in the 19th c., are no longer used in that role, though the writer Hammond Innes keeps one of them before the public eye.

113

Hamlyn (m) See **Hamlet**. **Hammond** and **Hamnet** also occur.

Handel (m) Surname of the composer George Frederick Handel (1685–1759) used as a first name regularly, if infrequently in the latter half of the 19th c., rarely since the 1920s. The German family name is usually referred to a diminutive of **Hans** (**Johannes**). In Dickens's *Great Expectations* it is the nickname given to Pip by Herbert Pocket, the allusion being to *The Harmonious Blacksmith* and the fact that Pip had been apprenticed to a blacksmith.

Handley (m) Also **Hanley**. Surnames derived from a place name 'high-wood clearing', used from time to time as first names.

Hank (m) Diminutive of **Henry**, probably influenced by the Dutch diminutive of **Hendrik**, namely **Hannek**. Used on very rare occasions as an independent name, and mainly in the U.S.

Hannah (f) Hebrew 'grace, favour'. Biblical, O.T., 1 Samuel 1:2. The wife of Elkanah and the mother of the prophet Samuel. Very popular in Britain from the beginning of the 17th c. until the end of the 19th c. Ranked 7th 1750–1800 and still in the top twenty in 1875. This makes Miss Withycombe's statement about the name having been 'in regular, though not frequent, use' (since the 17th c.) seem rather strange. After a period of disuse, there were signs of renewed interest in Hannah at the beginning of the 1970s. Never used to any great extent in other English-speaking countries, though the Greek/Latin **Anna**, French **Anne** and English **Ann** have been immensely popular. Hannah is sometimes a pet form of **Johanna**.

Hannibal (m) One of the most illustrious generals of antiquity, of unknown meaning. Still in use in Britain in the 19th c., the last example (of several) having been noted in 1897.

Hans (m) Form of **John** in several languages, e.g. German, Dutch, in occasional use in English-speaking countries.

Hanson (m) Surname of several possible meanings, regularly used as a first name in the 19th c., but rare since.

Happy (m, f) The word used as a name. Usage frequent throughout the 19th c., but 20th c. parents have preferred to use other language forms such as **Felicity**, **Felix**.

Harcourt (m) Norman place name and aristocratic English surname in occasional use as a first name.

Hardy (m) Surname 'hardy, courageous' used as a first name, regularly if infrequently since the 1840s. Modern use possibly influenced by the German actor Hardy Kruger, seen on screen since 1957.

Hargreaves (m) Place name 'grove with hares' which became a surname, regularly used as a first name in the 19th c. Hargrave also occurred.

Harlan (m) Old German 'army land'. Mainly a surname, but in occasional use as a first name, e.g. Harlan Bushfield, U.S. Senator.

Harley (m) Place name/surname used very regularly as a first name in all English-speaking countries. In Britain especially associated with Harley Street, in London, where many of the leading medical consultants have their offices. It was named after Edward Harley, who compiled the Harleian Library, now in the British Museum. Originally referred to a 'hare wood'.

Harman (m) See **Herman**.

Harold (m) Old English 'army power', two common elements in Anglo-Saxon names. The second element can also be interpreted as 'ruler'. **Walter** contains the same two name elements in reverse. The Anglo-Saxon name would probably have died out, but the similar name **Harald**, from Old Norse, was introduced to Britain by the Anglo-Danes. Even this did not prevent the name lapsing into obscurity for several centuries, until it was revived halfway through the 19th c. Then became extremely popular, reaching a peak in all English-speaking countries around 1900. Since then a consistent decline in the use of the name. Now rarely bestowed. Even the fact that it was borne by two Prime Ministers in modern times, Harold Macmillan and Harold Wilson, failed to save it in Britain. Variant **Harrold** was often used, but Scandinavian **Harald** remained rare. Attempts to create feminine forms for the name have resulted in **Haralda** and **Haroldene**.

Haroldene (f) 20th c. feminine form of **Harold**, rarely used.

Harper (m) Occupational surname 'harp-player' or 'harp-maker', occasionally used as a first name.

Harrie (m) 19th c. variant of **Harry**, **Harray**, **Harrey**, **Harri** were also found occasionally.

Harriet (f) Feminine form of **Harry**, and the usual popular spoken form of **Henrietta** in former times. Infrequently used in the 17th c., but extremely well used throughout the 18th and 19th cc. After 1900 virtually disappeared, though a minor revival of interest in the 1970s. Of the famous women who have borne the name Harriet Beecher Stowe is by far the best-known. Her novel, *Uncle Tom's Cabin*, remains one of the all-time best-sellers in the English language. Has a number of variant forms, including the common **Harriett**, **Harriette**, **Harriot**, **Harriott**. **Harrietta** was occasionally used to link more closely with Henrietta in the 19th c. Pet forms **Hatty** and **Hattie** were used independently to some extent at the end of the 19th c., and Hattie in particular was revived with Harriet in the 1960s and '70s. In the U.S. black American families mainly used the names at that time.

Harrington (m) Place name and surname of several possible origins, used from time to time in the 19th c. as a first name.

Harriot(t) (f) Common variants of **Harriet**. The English poet George Crabbe, for instance, celebrated the Harriot who 'was in truth/A tall fair beauty in the bloom of youth.'

Harris (m) Surname 'son of **Harry**' used

as a first name. Frequent 1860–1920, when Harry was well used; now rare.

Harrison (m) Surname 'Harry's son' used as a first name. More frequently used, over a longer period, than **Harris**. Occurred with great regularity during the 19th c., but rare since the 1940s. Benjamin Harrison (1833–1901), 23rd President of the U.S., presumably influenced the use of the name while in office.

Harrold (m) Common 19th c. variant of **Harold**.

Harry (m) Normal colloquial form of **Henry** when the latter name was introduced to Britain by the Normans. English-speakers had difficulty coping with the nasal sound of French **Henri** and turned it into the easier Herry or Harry. The written form of the name in the Middle Ages remained Henry or the Latin *Henricus*. The frequency of use at the time is reflected by the commonness of surnames which derive from it, such as *Harris*, *Harrison*. Very popular in the latter half of the 19th c. and lasted well into the 1930s, though declining steadily from the 1880s. In modern times Harry and Henry are used equally, but in the first fifty years of the 19th c. Harry was rare, while Henry was common. Harry came into its own as a normal written form from 1850 onwards, but still only achieved equal status with Henry in the 1920s in terms of frequency of use. **Harrie**, **Harrey** are found as variant forms. **Harriet**, **Harriot(t)** are the usual feminine forms.

Hartley (m) English place name/surname 'stag wood' or 'stag hill' used as a first name. Used with great regularity in Britain throughout the 19th c. but rare since the 1920s. The poet S. T. Coleridge names his son Hartley in honour of David Hartley (1705–57), the philosopher. More recently publicized by Sir Hartley Shawcross, the British jurist who was, among other things, the chief prosecutor at the Nuremberg Trials 1945–6.

Harvey (m) English form of French

Herve, itself from Celtic *haer* 'strong' and *ber* 'ardent', according to *Dictionnaire des Prénoms* (1980), or 'battle ardent' according to *Dictionnaire des Noms de Famille et Prénoms de France* (1951). The name of a Breton saint in the 6th c., introduced to Britain by the Normans. Used during the surname period, then fell into disuse until revived in the 19th c. At the beginning of the 1970s was being used more frequently in Britain than at any other time, but had fallen away again by the end of the decade. Continues to be used in all English-speaking countries, but quietly. The play *Harvey*, later a film with James Stewart playing the lead (1950), was written by Mary Chase in the mid-1940s. In that Harvey is the name of the invisible man-sized rabbit who is the great friend of Elwood P. Dowd. By a happy coincidence it is also Mr Dowd's favourite name. For a long and whimsical discussion of various aspects of this name see the opening chapters of *A Name To Conjure With*, by G. B. Stern.

Harwood (m) Place name/surname, originally 'hare wood', used occasionally as a first name.

Hattie (f) Usual pet form of Harriet, used independently to some extent, mainly at the end of the 19th c. **Hatty** also occurs. See **Harriet**.

Havelock (m) Old Norse 'sea-sport'. A use of the English surname as first name, mainly in the 19th c.

Hawthorn (m) Common place name and surname regularly used as a first name in the 19th c. **Hawthorne** also found. Referred to a place where hawthorns grew.

Hayden (m) Place name/surname in regular use as a first name. See **Haydn**.

Haydn (f) Appears to be the family name of the Austrian composer Joseph Haydn (1732–1809), normally pronounced *High-den*. But the variants **Hayden** and **Haydon** have always been used alongside it to indicate the pronunciation which is usual in Wales, where the name

is mainly used. In his *Book of Welsh Names* Trefor Jones was convinced that Welsh parents saw all three forms as variants of the Celtic **Aidan**. In regular use in the 20th c. and is the most frequently-used spelling of the name. The spelling link with the composer is probably regarded as a bonus.

Haydon (m) Place name/surname used as a first name. The original form of the first name, but now more usual as **Haydn**.

Hayley (f) English place name/surname 'hay-meadow' used as a first name. Rarely used in the U.S., but the modern spread of the name in Britain – by 1980 it was well into the top fifty – is entirely due to the actress Hayley Mills, daughter of John Mills, whose screen career began in 1959. In general use from 1961. Often written as **Haley**, a better-known form of the surname. Other variants include **Hailey, Halie, Haylee**.

Hayward (m) Surname indicating a 'bailiff' originally, used as a first name in the 19th c.

Hayyim (m) See **Hyman**.

Hazel (f) Tree name, used as a first name since 1890 when botanical names became fashionable. Most popular in the U.S. around 1900, in Britain 1925–60. Occurs also as **Hazell, Hazelle, Hazael, Hazal** and in extended forms such as **Hazeline, Hazelgrove**.

Headley (m) See **Hedley**.

Heath (m) Surname used as a first name. Probably first used in the U.S. in honour of William Heath, an officer in the Revolutionary Army. In Britain it came into use in the 1950s, well before Edward Heath became Prime Minister in 1970. Continued to be steadily used while he was in power, but did not markedly increase in numbers. Also popular in Australia throughout the 1970s. Presumably seen as a male form of **Heather**.

Heather (f) Plant name used as a first name. Usually associated with 'heath', though the *Oxford English Dictionary* queries this. In use since the 1880s but reached a peak in Britain in the 1950s and '60s. In the U.S. and Canada it arrived in force rather later and was being used intensively in the mid-1970s. The Latin name for heather is *erica*. **Erica** may occasionally be used with this in mind, though is usually seen as a feminine of **Eric**.

Heaton (m) Common English place name and surname, alluding to a 'high place' originally. Regularly used as a first name in the 19th c.

Hebe (f) Greek *Hebe* 'youth', name of the goddess of youth. Used in the latter half of the 19th c., but then disappeared.

Heber (m) Hebrew 'fellowship'. Biblical, O.T., e.g. Judges 4:11. Bardsley found the name in use amongst the Puritans, and it continued to be used very regularly until the 1920s. Has since become extremely rare. **Hebor** is a variant form.

Hector (m) Greek *hector* 'holding fast'. Probably means 'prop' or 'stay'. Priam's son, and one of the heroes of Homer's *Iliad*. Had a sudden burst of popularity in Britain at the end of the 19th c., but little used this century. In Scotland was used as a substitute for **Eachdoin** 'horse lord', when Gaelic names were not acceptable to the authorities.

Hedley (m) Place name/surname 'clearing overgrown with heather' used regularly as a first name, especially in Britain. Use began in the 1840s, and there was a distinct flurry of interest in the name around 1900. Since then has continued to be used steadily, but quietly. Variant **Headley** is not uncommon, and **Hedly** is found. Not much used in the U.S.

Hedwig (f) German 'struggle, strife'. Best-known in English-speaking countries in its various pet forms, **Hedy**, **Hedda**, **Hetta**.

Hedy (f) Pet form of the German name Hedwig, made famous in the 1930s and '40s by the Austrian actress Hedy Lamarr (Hedwig Kiesler). A few parents in English-speaking countries made use of the name.

Heidi (f) German pet form of **Adelheid** (Adelaide). Popular independent name

in German-speaking countries in the 20th c., probably influenced by Johanna Spyri's children's classic *Heidi*, first published in 1881. In the U.S. and Britain it became highly fashionable in the 1970s. **Heide** is occasionally found, and **Hiedi** occurs.

Helen (f) Greek *Helene*, feminine of *Helenos* 'the bright one, shining one'. Occurs in Christian inscriptions of the Roman Empire. The fame of St Helena, mother of Constantine the Great, did much to spread the name in early times, but as Professor Weekley puts it: 'The fame of the saint has been helped by that of a sinner, the most beautiful woman of antiquity.' The latter is the subject of one of the best-known quotations in English: 'Was this the face that launched a thousand ships/And burnt the topless towers of Ilium?' (Christopher Marlowe, *Doctor Faustus*). **Ellen** was the usual colloquial form of Helen in former times, though Helen predominated as the form in the 17th c., Ellen in the 18th. In the 19th c. Helen was used only once for every ten occurrences of Ellen in Britain, though Helen remained the usual form in the U.S. By the 1950s Ellen was enjoying great popularity in the U.S., whereas Helen was re-emerging in Britain. Helen went on to reach the top ten in Britain in the 1970s, but the early 1980s showed clear signs of retreat. In the U.S. in the 1980s being little used. **Helena** has always been a usual variant, and the French form **Hélène** has been steadily used since the 1880s. **Hellen**, showing the influence of Ellen, is regularly found in birth records. Polish/Russian **Halina** sometimes occurs, as does the Hungarian **Ilona**. Pet form **Lena** has taken on a life of its own as an independent name.

Helena (f) See **Helen**.

Hélène (f) French form of **Helen**, used regularly if infrequently since the 1880s.

Helenor (f) Blend of **Helen** and **Eleanor** used in the 19th c. **Hellenor** has also been used.

Helga (f) Nordic name probably deriving

from a word meaning 'holy'. Russian form is **Olga**. Used on rare occasions in English-speaking countries.

Hellen (f) Common variant, especially in the 19th c., of **Helen**.

Helliwell (m) Place name/surname originally indicating a 'holy well' used as a first name. **Hellewell** and **Hallewell** also occur.

Héloise (f) French form of **Eloise**. Used from time to time, and some interest shown in the 1970s.

Henderson (m) Surname 'son of **Henry**' used as a first name. Occurs regularly but not frequently. In the U.S. black American families use it most often.

Heneage (m) Probably a form of the Irish family name *O'hEineachain*, or **Henaghan**, used as a first name. Publicized and used in the 19th c. after the showing of Gainsborough's portrait group 'Heneage Lloyd and his sister' from the late 18th c. onwards. Now very rare anywhere.

Henerietta (f) See **Henrietta**.

Henery (m) Form of **Henry** used by British parents in the 19th c. from time to time, indicating the common pronunciation of the name at the time.

Henley (m) English place name/surname used from time to time as a first name, mainly in Britain. Originally meant a 'high-clearing', but associated in modern times with the annual regatta held at Henley-on-Thames in Oxfordshire. The major rowing events there are regarded unofficially as world championships.

Henri (m) French form of **Henry**, used from time to time in English-speaking countries.

Henrietta (f) Normal English form of the French feminine **Henriette**, itself from **Henri** (**Henry**). Introduced to Britain by Henriette Marie, daughter of Henri IV of France and Mary de Medici, who became the wife of King Charles I of England. In England she was known as Henrietta Maria. The name did not become generally fashionable until the 1870s, but after a brief period it faded once more into the background. Now

found regularly but infrequently in all English-speaking countries. The spelling Henriette has always been rare, while the 19th c. saw several forms such as **Henerietta**, **Heneretta** and the like which reflect the popular pronunciation at the time of **Henry** (often found as **Henery**). Variant **Henryetta** is also found from time to time. Pet forms **Hetty**, **Etta** and **Henny** are occasionally used independently. In modern times pronounced as spelled. Normal colloquial pronunciation in the 17th c. would have made the name sound like **Harriet**. See **Harry**.

Henrik (m) Swedish form of **Henry** occasionally used in English-speaking countries. Feminine **Henrika** is also found.

Henry (m) Old German *Heimerich* 'home ruler'. Some German scholars suggest that this may have merged with another name *Haganrich*, where the first element means 'hedge'. Introduced to Britain by the Normans in the 11th c., usually pronounced as **Harry** or **Herry** by English-speakers. Spelling influenced by French **Henri**, Latin **Henricus**. A royal name in Britain from the 11th c. to the 16th c. and one of the commonest names in use. Remained so until the 1920s, but then began to fade quickly. In the 1980s little used in any English-speaking country. Borne by many famous men, e.g. Henry Wadsworth Longfellow (1807–82), the poet, Henry James (1843–1916) the writer, Henry L. Mencken (1880–1956) the authority on American English, and Henry Fonda the actor (1905–1982). Spanish form **Enrique** is used in the U.S., and the Italian **Enrico** is used. Pet form **Hal** (compare **Sally** from **Sarah**, **Molly** from **Mary**) occasionally occurs in its own right, but **Hank** seems to be used in speech but not in formal records. Harry is not really a pet form of the name but its normal English form. Main feminine forms of the name are **Henrietta** and **Henriette**, **Harriet**, **Harriette**.

Henryk (m) Form of **Henry** in several languages, e.g. Polish. Occasionally used in

English-speaking countries. **Henrik** is the Swedish form rather than a spelling variant.

Hephzibah (f) Hebrew 'my delight is in her'. Biblical, O.T., 2 Kings 21:1. At Isaiah 62:4 occurs: 'You shall no more be termed Forsaken (Hebrew *Azubah*) . . . but you shall be called My delight is in her (Hebrew *Hephzibah*).' Popular name with the Puritans of the 17th c., then in regular if infrequent use until the early part of the 20th c. In George Eliot's *Silas Marner* (1861) Silas suggests using this name for the baby he has adopted. 'That's a hard name,' said Dolly. Silas explains that his sister, who bore the name, was always called **Eppie**. Eppie has in fact been used as a name in its own right. Other pet forms include **Hepsey**, **Hepsie**, **Hepsy**, also used rarely as independent names. In *Pollyanna* (1913), the highly successful novel by Eleanor H. Porter, Mrs White is called Hephzibah. 'Her husband calls her "Hep", and she doesn't like it. She says when he calls out "Hep Hep" she feels just as if the next minute he was going to yell "Hurrah!" ' These two quotations hint at the reasons for the name's virtual disappearance in modern times. Its 'hardness' is attested to by the many variant forms it took in the official registers, including **Hephsibah**, **Hephzabah**, **Hephzibeth**, **Hepzabah**, **Hepzibah**. The last of these was used to name a girl born in 1975, first sign of the name for over fifty years in British records.

Hepsey (f) Pet form of **Hephzibah** used independently. **Hepsie** and **Hepsy** also occur.

Hepzibah (f) See **Hephzibah**.

Herald (m) Surname used as a first name. Originally refers to a **Harold** rather than someone who held the office of 'herald'.

Herbert (m) Old German 'army' plus 'bright, shining'. Introduced to Britain by the Normans but not commonly used after the 13th c. Reappeared at the beginning of the 19th c. and steadily increased in popularity until the turn of the century. Still being well used in the 1920s, though declining, and by the end of the 1930s was infrequent. Since the 1960s rarely used. Amongst the eminent men who have borne the name are Herbert C. Hoover (1874–1964), 31st President of the U.S., Herbert George Wells (1866–1946), the English writer, and the actors Herbert Beerbohm Tree (1853–1917) and Herbert Lom. These two English actors were in fact of German and Czech descent respectively: Herbert Beerbohm adopted the surname Tree to translate the original meaning of his family name Beerbohm ('pear tree'), while Herbert Lom was born Herbert Charles Angelo Kuchacevich ze Schluderpacheru.

Hercules (m) Greek *Heracles*, Latin *Hercules*, of unknown meaning, 'glory of Hera (a goddess)' being the most likely possibility. In Greek mythology the son of Zeus and Alkmene. In the Shetland Islands used as a substitute for the Scandinavian **Hakon**. Elsewhere used on very rare occasions. Agatha Christie helped to make the French form of the name well-known with her character **Hercule** Poirot.

Hereward (m) Old English 'army – defence'. Made famous by Hereward the Wake (i.e. the vigilant). Charles Kingsley wrote a novel about him in 1865, but the name has been remarkably little used at any time since the 11th c.

Herman (m) Old German 'army' plus 'man'. The Normans introduced the name to Britain where it was widespread enough during the surname period to cause names such as *Herman*, *Hermon*, *Harman*, etc., to become fixed as family names. Camden, writing in 1605, lists only Harman and Hermon in his 'usual Christian names'. Herman was revived in the mid-19th c. and used regularly, especially in the U.S., where it reached 36th position by 1875. Remained in the U.S. top fifty until the turn of the century but subsequently declined steadily. Infrequent in Britain throughout this period. Now rarely used in any English-speaking country. Probably kept alive in most people's minds by the American writer Herman Melville (1819–91), of *Moby Dick* fame. While in use, frequently found as **Hermann**, the modern German form, and as **Hermon**. Rarer variants were **Harman** and **Hermann**. French form of the name is **Armand** (though French commentators insist on linking Armand with **Hartmann**). Armand is used occasionally in English-speaking countries, together with Spanish **Armando**.

Hermia (f) Contracted form of **Hermione**. On the rare occasions that the name is used parents probably have Shakespeare's *Midsummer Night's Dream* in mind, where one of the principal characters bears the name.

Hermione (f) Greek derivative of Hermes, the messenger of the gods. Mainly occurs in literature, e.g., Shakespeare's *Winter's Tale* and the novels of Sir Walter Scott. Publicized in Britain in modern times by the actresses Hermione Baddeley and Hermione Gingold, but remains rare.

Hermon (m) See **Herman**.

Hervey (m) Variant of **Harvey** perhaps influenced by the original French form *Hervé*. Regularly used in the 19th c. but rare today. Dr Johnson made the well-known remark: 'call a dog Hervey and I shall love him.' He was alluding to a man who had befriended him in need, Harry Hervey.

Hester (f) Variant of **Esther**. Form of the name borne by Hester Prynne, in Nathaniel Hawthorne's *Scarlet Letter*. May well have been used symbolically by Hawthorne to suggest a woman dedicated to love. Hester's daughter, **Pearl**, is certainly named in the book because she is 'her mother's only treasure'. Pet forms **Hetty**, **Hettie** and occasionally **Hetta** have all been used independently.

Hetta (f) German pet form of **Hedwig**, 'battle – battle'. Used in the 19th c. Modern parents prefer the variant Hedy.

Hettie (f) Pet form of **Hester** and **Henrietta** used in its own right from the mid-19th c. until the 1930s, but now rare. **Hetty** also occurs.

Hetty (f) See **Hettie**.

Heulwen (f) Welsh 'sunshine'. Used in Wales, though not frequently, since the 1930s.

Hew (m) Welsh variant of **Huw**, a form of **Hugh**. In use on rare occasions since the 1940s.

Hewitt (m) Aristocratic English surname, usually linked with **Hugh**, used as a first name. The similar names **Hewlett** and **Hewson** also occur as first names from time to time.

Hezekiah (m) Hebrew 'May Jehovah strengthen'. Biblical, O.T., 2 Kings 18:1. The king of Judah. Used irregularly throughout the 19th c. but rare in modern times, though a Hezekiah Smith was named in Britain in 1976.

Hiedi (f) See **Heidi**.

Hilary (m, f) Latin *Hilarius* from *hilaris* 'cheerful'. A papal name and that of a 4th c. saint. Used in Britain until the 17th c. but was always male, though a feminine *Hilaria* had been recorded in Christian inscriptions of the 5th c. The male form continued to be used elsewhere, e.g. France, as **Hilaire**, but when revived in English-speaking countries in the 1890s considered to be a female name. As such reached a peak in the 1950s and '60s, but has since faded. Variants include **Hillary**, **Hillery**, **Hilarie**.

Hilda (f) Short form of one of the many Old German names beginning with *Hilde-* 'battle'. A 7th c. abbess at Whitby, St Hilda. Used in the Middle Ages and revived in the 1860s, first appearance of the name being about a year after the publication of Nathaniel Hawthorne's *The Marble Faun*, in which Hilda is an artist and native of New England. By 1900 also enjoying a great success in Britain, lasting until the late 1930s, since when the name has been given only on rare occasions. In

Britain always more frequently used in
the north of England.

Hildegarde (f) Old German 'war strong-
hold'. An 11th c. saint, a mystic. Occasionally used in modern times especially
by those of German descent, e.g. Hildegarde Neff (Hildegard Knef), the
German actress in Hollywood from the
1940s. **Hildagard, Hildagarde** are
found.

Hildred (f) Old English 'battle-counsel'.
Revived with other Anglo-Saxon names
in the 19th c. (from the 1880s), and
used until 1920. Now very rare.

Hillary (m, f) See Hilary. **Hillery** also occurs.

Hilma (f) Scandinavian short form of
Wilhelmina, recorded in Sweden since
the 19th c. and noted in English-
speaking countries since 1920. Other
Scandinavian forms include **Helma,
Hjälma, Helmy, Helmi.**

Hilton (m) English place name and surname, used as a first name. Found regularly since the 1860s, though never in
great numbers. Recent usage seems to
have been mainly by black American
families and West Indians. **Hylton** is a
fairly frequent variant.

Hippolyta (f) Greek feminine form of
Hippolytus. The name refers to 'horses'
but the second element is much disputed. The reference may be to horses
which are 'loose' or stampeding'. In Greek
legend she was Queen of the Amazons. In *A Midsummer Night's Dream*
Shakespeare links her with Theseus,
though the Greeks themselves usually
said that it was her sister Antiope who
married Theseus. Rarely used in
English-speaking countries. The male
name is used in Europe (French **Hippo-
lyte**, Italian **Ippolito**) because of a famous saint who bore the name.

Hiram (m) Hebrew 'My Brother is on
high'. Biblical, O.T., 1 Kings 5:10 refers
to King Hiram of Tyre. Elsewhere in the
Bible the name is given as **Hirom** and
Huram. Well used throughout the 19th
c. together with other O.T. names, but
rare since the 1930s. Sometimes spelt
Hyrum.

Hobart (m) Form of **Hubert** used rather
more in the U.S. than Britain. The screen
career of Hobart Bosworth began in
1909, and he continued to appear in
'talkies' until the early 1940s.

Hodgson (m) Surname, linked with
Roger, used as a first name. The similar
surname **Hobson**, from **Robert**, also
occurs as a first name from time to time.

Holden (m) Place name/surname 'hollow
valley' used very regularly as a first
name in the 19th c. Has been associated
this century with the actor William
Holden (1918–81), born William Bee-
dle: the real name sounded too much
like an insect for comfort, hence the
change.

Holland (m) Common English place name
and surname, used from time to time as
a first name. Originally refers to land on
rising ground.

Hollie (f) See **Holly**.

Hollis (f) Surname used as a first name,
regularly but infrequently. Original
meaning indicates that its bearer lived
near holly bushes or a holm-oak. Recent
interest in the name probably linked to
fortunes of **Holly**.

Holly (f) Plant name used as a first name.
Came into regular use at the beginning
of the century, but had faded by 1915.
Revived again strongly in the early
1960s and continues to be well used. In
the U.S., especially, has taken on a variety of forms, including **Holli, Hollie** and
Holley, and is frequently used as part of
a double name such as **Holly-Ann**.
Perhaps to be thought of as a seasonal
name, such as **Noel, Noelle, Carol**, etc.,
associated with Christmas. The pattern
of usage suggests strongly that John
Galsworthy's character of the name in
The Forsyte Saga contributed a great
deal, first by means of the book, later
because of its televised version. In the
book Jolly and Holly are son and
daughter of Jolyon and Hélène Forsyte.

Holmes (m) Surname derived from a
place name of several possible meanings, regularly used as a first name in the
19th c. and occasionally found in the

20th c. The English actor Holmes Herbert was formerly a well-known bearer of the name, though born Edward Sanger. Unlikely to be given with reference to the fictional detective (and no real-life examples of **Sherlock** have been noted).

Homer (m) Greek *homeros* 'hostage, pledge'. The name of the poet (*Iliad*, *The Odyssey*) used as a first name. Common practice to give black slaves classical names, but according to the Puckett lists Homer was not one of them, or certainly not frequent. H. L. Mencken mentions the popularity of Homer in the U.S. but suggests no reason for it. Certainly used far more in the U.S. than elsewhere, and at all levels of society e.g., by several senators. Continues to be used, though quietly. In Britain all instances of the name occur in the 19th c., but it was never common. May on occasions be a use of the English surname, identical with *Holmer*.

Honor (f) Usual modern form of Latin *Honoria*, feminine of *Honorius* 'man of honour'. Roman form of the name was always **Honoria** but the Normans introduced it to Britain as Honor or **Honora**. The Puritans often turned it into **Honour**. Honor probably survives because of Honor Blackman, the British actress whose impact came with appearances in the film *Goldfinger* (1964) and the TV series *The Avengers* (1960–3). Occurs regularly in Britain, but seems to be unknown elsewhere. **Honner, Honnor, Honnour, Honoure** also occur.

Honora (f) Anglo-Norman form of Latin *Honoria*. See **Honor**. **Honorah** is found regularly, showing the influence of names such as **Hannah, Deborah, Sarah**.

Honoria (f) Usual Roman form of **Honor**, meaning 'woman of honour'. Both spellings used in the 18th c., but Honoria now very rare. A French diminutive **Honorine**, the name of a martyr, has also been used in Britain, but on rare occasions.

Honour (f) English form of Latin *Honoria*. See **Honor**. Occasional attempts to disguise the word slightly, or turn it into a name form, are found in **Honnour, Honoure**.

Hope (f) The word used as a first name. Popular with the 16th c. Puritans, who often used phrasal names such as Hope-on-High, Hope-Still, Hope-Well as well as Hope itself. They were also fond of **Hopeful**. Although now always feminine when used, formerly used for males as well. Also something of a tradition for girl triplets to be named **Faith, Hope** and **Charity**. Modern usage mainly confined to the U.S., where **Esperanza** also occurs. **Esperance** is the French form of the name.

Hopkin (m) A pet form of Robert, used very regularly as a first name throughout the 19th c., especially in Wales.

Horace (m) Latin *Horatius*, the name of a Roman clan made famous by the Roman poet *Quintus Horatius Flaccus* (Horace). Often the spoken form of **Horatio**, e.g. Horatio Nelson liked to be called Horace as a boy. In Britain the name was most successful from the 1870s to 1900. Has remained in consistent use, but is not frequent. Never as popular in the U.S. as in Britain, but used quietly by black American families in modern times. Borne by the U.S. journalist and political leader Horace Greeley (1811–72), remembered today because of the advice he gave: 'Go West, young man, and grow up with the country.'

Horatia (f) Feminine of **Horatio** or *Horatius*. Recorded in Christian inscriptions of the Roman Empire, but introduced to the British public by Admiral Lord Horatio Nelson (1758–1805). He and Lady Hamilton gave this name to their daughter. Used in the 19th c. until the 1870s, but then virtually disappeared.

Horatio (m) Form of *Horatius*, a Roman clan name, perhaps influenced by Italian *Orazio*. In use in England amongst aristocratic families before Shakespeare used the name for a character in *Hamlet*. Continued to be so used and was given to Horatio Nelson, destined to become one of the greatest British national heroes. After his death in 1805 at the Battle of Trafalgar his name became rather more widespread, but it eventually had a far more general success in Britain as **Horace** around 1900. One can compare the relatively restrained use of **Winston** with that of Horatio to show that a name-bearer's popularity does not always lead to that name becoming fashionable. A feminine form **Horatia**. Colloquial pet form of the name usually **Orry** or **Horry**, though Emily Lawless, in her novel *Hurrish*, says that **Hurrish** was a colloquial form in Ireland. One should also note the character in Samuel Lover's *Handy Andy* who was named after Lord Nelson, but whose friends changed the Horatio into **Ratty**.

Hortensia (f) Latin feminine of *Hortensius*, a Roman clan name of unknown origin. Also a flower name, named after **Hortense** Lepante in the 18th c. Occasionally used in the 19th c.

Howard (m) Surname used as a first name. Origin uncertain. May indicate someone who was the guardian of a fence or enclosure, someone who looked after sheep or pigs, or someone who bore a Germanic name meaning 'heart, mind' plus 'brave, hardy'. In Britain the name is decidedly aristocratic, and the *Oxford Dictionary of English Christian Names* falls into the trap of assuming that the name belongs with other such names, used to bring a little distinction into the lives of lesser people by being adopted as first names. Statistical evidence makes it clear, however, that Howard was used intensively in the U.S. long before it reached Britain in any numbers, probably in honour of Oliver Otis Howard (1830–1909), an officer in the Civil War and founder of Howard University. Ranked 22nd in the U.S. in the 1870s, and still in 48th place in 1950. Helped perhaps by the fame of the millionaire recluse Howard Hughes. In Britain only just reaching its peak at that time, probably due to parental admiration for the singer Howard Keel (Harold Keel). Since the 1970s it has been quietly used in all English-speaking countries.

Howell (m) Form of Welsh **Hywel** 'eminent'. Sparingly used since the 1850s, occurring also as **Howel**.

Hubert (m) Old German *Hugibert* 'mind' plus 'bright, shining'. An 8th c. saint, patron of hunters. Its use in the Middle Ages led to several surnames, e.g. the old Mother Hubbard who looked in a cupboard had an ancestor who was a Hubert. Mainly used 1875–1925. Remains in use but is infrequent. **Hubbard** itself was occasionally used as a first name in the 19th c.

Hudson (m) Surname linked with **Hugh** or **Richard**, used as a first name in the 19th c. and again in the 1970s, though not in great numbers.

Hugh (m) Old German 'mind, soul, thought'. Introduced by the Normans and very popular in the Middle Ages, as the frequency of related surnames such as *Hughes*, *Howe*, *Howse*, etc., demonstrates. Continued to be very popular until the 17th c., but usage gradually declined. Used continuously since the beginning of the 19th c. while never being especially fashionable. Had almost disappeared in Britain by the 1950s but showing signs of a minor revival in the early 1980s. In the U.S. at that time was still being very quietly used. Irish parents have been amongst the most frequent users of the name in the 20th c. A Welsh form **Huw** is used from time to time, and **Hew** occurs. Latin **Hugo** used regularly if infrequently. Pet forms such as **Huey**, **Hughey**, **Hughie**, **Hughy** also occur independently. Surname **Hughes** also found as a first name on infrequent occasions. **Hughina**, as a feminine form, occurs mainly in Scotland. Hugh Griffith and Hugh Williams are

123

amongst the well-known bearers of the name, both being British actors.

Hughie (m) Pet form of **Hugh** used independently from time to time. Well publicized in the 1960s by the Canadian actor and television quiz-master Hughie Green. **Hughey, Huey, Hughy** also occur.

Hugo (m) Latin form of **Hugh**, revived in the 1860s and regularly if infrequently used since then.

Huldah (f) Hebrew 'weasel' or 'mole'. Biblical, O.T., 2 Kings 22:14, the name of a prophetess. Used very rarely in English-speaking countries. The form **Hulda** is sometimes found, said to be a separate Scandinavian name, but it may be that writers such as Roland Otterbjörk, in *Svenska Fornamn*, have simply failed to identify the Hebrew original. Its use in Scandinavia seems to date only from the beginning of the 19th c., which makes an Old Norse original highly unlikely. Hulda is a well-known name in Germany, thanks to a popular song which asked: '*Ist denn kein Stuhl da, Stuhl da, Stuhl da, für meine Hulda, Hulda, Hulda?*' but it is considered to be rather comic.

Humbert (m) Old German 'Hun' or 'giant' plus 'famous'. Rarely used in English-speaking countries – even more rarely after the publication of Vladimir Nabokov's *Lolita* (1960) with its confessions by Humbert Humbert.

Humphrey (m) There was an Old English name, cognate with Old German *Hunfrid*, modern German *Hunfried*, where the first element is of uncertain meaning. The second element means 'peace'. The Normans used the name as *Onfroi* but it was *Humfrey, Humfrye*, etc., in medieval English records. Camden lists it as Humfrey in 1605 and interprets it as 'house-peace'. This inspires him to say: 'a lovely and happy name if it could turn home-wars between man and wife into peace.' Latinized as *Onuphrius*, an Egyptian saint of the 5th c., which is presumably what caused the -ph- spellings to appear. These arrived late on the scene, but **Humphrey** was established by the beginning of the 18th c. Steadily but infrequently used since the beginning of the 19th c., though rare since the 1960s. Well-known thanks to the American actor Humphrey Bogart (1899–1957) and the British musician Humphrey Lyttleton. Variants such as **Humphery** and **Humphry** are found, but no trace in modern times of the original -f- spelling, even though the -ph- was described long ago by Charlotte Yonge in her *History of Christian Names* as 'barbarous'.

Hunter (m) Surname, originally indicating a 'huntsman', used as a first name, especially in Scotland. Not in frequent use.

Huntly (m) English and Scottish place name (taken to Scotland by the Earls of Huntly) originally 'hunting meadow'. In occasional use as a first name.

Hurbert (m) 19th c. variant of **Herbert**.

Hutchinson (m) Surname linked with **Hugh** used in the 19th c. as a first name.

Huw (m) Welsh form of **Hugh**, used mainly since the 1940s.

Hyacinth (m, f) A 3rd c. saint bore this flower name, which in Greek mythology was named for Hyacinthus, a youth beloved by Apollo. The flower is said to have sprung from his blood. Used in the 19th c., and seems to have been linked with other flower names being used for girls. Mrs Gaskell has a character of the name in her *Wives and Daughters* (1866) who calls her daughter **Cynthia** in order to link with it.

Hylda (f) Occasional variant of **Hilda**.

Hylton (m) Variant of **Hilton** in use since the 1870s.

Hyman (m) Hebrew 'life'. Masculine equivalent of **Eve**. Used almost exclusively by Jewish families, and found also as **Chaim, Hayyim, Hymen**. Pet forms **Hymie** and **Hy** also occur. Hyman the usual form in English-speaking countries since the 1880s.

Hypatia (f) Greek *hypatos* 'highest'. In

later Greek *hypatia* was used for 'consulate'. The 5th c. philosopher and mathematician Hypatia was killed by a mob of Christian fanatics. She was the subject of a novel by Charles Kingsley (1883) which caused some 19th c.

usage.

Hyrum (m) See **Hiram**.

Hywel (m) Welsh 'eminent, conspicuous'. Used since the 1950s in this form and made known by the actor Hywel Bennett (1944–   ).

I

Iago (m) Form of **James** or **Jacob** in several languages, e.g. Welsh, also a dialectal form in Spanish and Italian of those names. In modern times used as **Jago**, the Cornish variant. Naturally associated in English-speaking countries with the character in Shakespeare's *Othello*, a malevolent, evil man.

Iain (m) Scottish Gaelic form of **John**. The more 'correct' form of the name for Scottish parents, but **Ian** has always been used in far greater numbers. Dates only from the last part of the 19th c.

Ian (m) Modern Scottish form of **John**, unknown there until the last part of the 19th c. Then became immensely popular and spread to the rest of Britain. In England and Wales, for instance, one of the top names of the 1960s. Steadily declining since then. Also found in Canada and Australia but has made relatively little impression in the U.S., despite the fame of the writer Ian Fleming, creator of James Bond.

Ianthe (f) Greek 'violet flower'. Appealed to the romantic poets of the 19th c., including Byron and Shelley. The latter gave the name to one of the characters in his *Queen Mab* and also to his daughter. Used in the latter half of the 19th c., and sudden interest also shown in the 1970s. Occurs incidentally in Ovid's *Metamorphoses*, where she marries Iphis. Iphis was actually a girl, but had been brought up as a boy by the mother. The mother prayed hard, and Iphis was changed into a man on the day of his wedding.

Icarus (m) Greek 'dedicated to the

moon-goddess Car'. The son of Daedalus who flew too near the sun so that the wax on the wings his father had made for him melted. He plunged into what was later called the Icarian sea. Rarely used, but an Icarus Smith was named in Britain in 1963.

Ichabod (m) Hebrew *Ikabhoth* 'where is the glory?', usually translated as 'the glory has departed'. Biblical, O.T., 1 Sam. 4:21. Introduced into U.S. and Britain in the 17th c. In modern times best known as the name of the schoolmaster in Washington Irving's *Legend of Sleepy Hollow*, filmed by Walt Disney.

Ida (f) German pet form of names beginning with *Ida*, none of which are in current use. German scholars also suggest a link with **Adelheid** (**Adelaide**). Meaning of the name far from clear. 'Youthful' or 'labour' has been suggested. Became very popular in the U.S. from the 1870s to 1900 and then made an impact in Britain. Fading steadily since the 1920s in all English-speaking countries. One well-known bearer of the name is the British actress, later director, Ida Lupino. Ida is the heroine of Tennyson's poem *The Princess* (1874). Gilbert and Sullivan enthusiasts associate the name with the operetta *Princess Ida* (1884).

Idris (m) Welsh *iud* 'lord' *ris* 'ardent, impulsive'. Ancient Welsh name revived in the mid-19th c. Used very regularly until the 1920s, but infrequent thereafter.

Idwal (m) Welsh *iud* 'lord' *(g)wal* 'wall, rampart'. Occurs in Welsh history as early as the 10th c; occasionally used in modern times.

leasha (f) Also **Ieashia, Ieesha, Ieeshia, Iesha.** See **Aisha.**

Iestin (f) Welsh feminine form of **Iestyn** (**Justin**). More commonly found as **Jestine.**

Iestyn (m) Welsh form of **Justin.** Rarely used. **Jestyn** also found.

Ieuan (m) Welsh form of **John** used in Wales since the beginning of the 20th c., but rarely.

Ifor (m) In Wales this name is identified with Welsh *ior* 'lord', but see **Ivor.** Used occasionally by Welsh parents.

Ignace (m) French form of **Ignatious.**

Ignatious (m) Usual English spelling of Greek *Ignatios.* Etymology unknown. In early use as a Christian name, as evidenced by Ignatius, Bishop of Antioch in the 2nd c. Later made famous by St Ignatius de Loyola (1548–99), founder of the Society of Jesus. Never frequent in English-speaking countries. When it does occur also likely to be as **Ignatius** or **Ignacious.** See also **Inigo.**

Igor (m) Russian form of Scandinavian *Ingvar*, earlier *Yngvar* 'Ing's warrior'. See also **Inga.** Surnames such as *Inger, Inker* and *Ingerson* derive from it. Particularly well known in musical circles thanks to the composer Igor Stravinsky, the violinist Igor Oistrakh and the opera by Borodin, *Prince Igor.* Occasionally used in the U.S. and Britain.

Ike (m) Pet form of **Isaac** used independently, though not frequently. Associated in modern times with Dwight D. Eisenhower (1890–1969), 34th President of the U.S., whose nickname it was.

Ileen(e) (f) Spelling variants of **Eileen** or **Aileen. Ilean** and **Ilene** also occur.

Illingworth (m) From the place name Illingworth in Yorkshire, 'Illa's enclosure'. Surname used as a Christian name, fairly common in late 19th c. northern England.

Ilma (f) Pet form of **Wilma** used on rare occasions in its own right.

Ilona (f) Hungarian form of **Helen,** in use in English-speaking countries since

the 1940s. The Hungarian-born actress Ilona Massey (Ilona Hajmassy, 1912–74) was appearing in Hollywood films from 1937 onwards, and may have helped spread the name. *Ilona*, the novel by Hans Habe, first published in English in the 1960s, may also have been responsible for some usage.

Ilse (f) German pet form of **Elisabeth,** especially popular in Germany in the 19th c. Occasionally used in English-speaking countries. The form of the name is a half-way stage between Elisabeth and **Isabel,** since there was presumably a development to **Ilsabet. Ilsa** also occurs.

Ima (f) Form of **Emma,** rarely used. A famous bearer of the name was Ima Hogg, of Houston, Texas.

Imalda (f) See **Imelda.**

Imelda (f) Italian and Swiss form of German *Irmhild* 'all-embracing battle'. Imelda Lambertini, Virgin of Bologna, was a 14th c. saint who made the name suitable for Roman Catholic use. Most used in Britain after the First World War. When the name first came into use it was usually spelt **Imalda** and both spellings still occur.

Immanuel (m) See **Emanuel.**

Imogen (f) Name of the heroine of Shakespeare's *Cymbeline.* Interpreted as Latin *imo-gens* 'last born', but actually a misprint in the Folio for *Innogen*, which is how the name appears in Holinshed, Shakespeare's source. Innogen probably derived from Latin *innocens* 'innocent'. Rarely used until the 20th c., but now occurs as Imogen, **Imogine, Imogene,** the latter form made known by the American comedienne, Imogene Coca.

Ina (f) Pet form of names ending in *ina*, such as **Georgina, Clementina, Martina, Christina, Bettina, Edwina,** etc., used as a name in its own right. Regular but infrequent since the 1860s. **Ena** is a similar name.

India (f) The country name as a first name. In special cases used because of family connections with the country (e.g. Lord

Mountbatten's grand-daughter) but the regular use of the name in the U.S. was inspired by India Wilkes in *Gone With the Wind* (1939).

Ines (f) Italian diminutive of **Agnese** (**Agnes**). In the English-speaking world the Spanish form **Inez** is more common.

Inez (f) Spanish form of **Agnes**, regularly but quietly used in Britain and the U.S.

Inga (f) Nordic: shortened form of **Ingeborg**, '*Ing's* protection'. *Ing* in Norse mythology was the god of fertility, peace and prosperity: his name is an element in **Ingvar**, **Ingrid**, etc. Inga was one of the Norse names formerly used in Scotland. Used intermittently in England, regularly in the U.S. and Canada amongst those of Scandinavian descent.

Inge (f) Pet form of German **Ingeborg** used independently. In use since the late 1940s, but infrequently.

Ingeborg (f) Nordic, '*Ing's* protection'. Formerly used in Scotland and occasionally in England. Introduced to the U.S. by Scandinavian settlers. See also **Inga**.

Ingham (m) English place name/surname used with some regularity as a first name in the 19th c., but now rare.

Ingraham (m) See **Ingram**.

Ingram (m) Teutonic: Old German *Engel-* or *Ingelramnus* 'Anglian raven'. Used as a Christian name in Britain until 17th c. Modern usage derives from the surname. **Ingraham** is also found.

Ingrid (f) Old Norse '*Ing*', the name of a god, and 'beautiful'. In modern use, undoubtedly inspired by the screen appearances of the Swedish actress Ingrid Bergman from 1940 onwards. Had a mild vogue in the 1960s and '70s, but has since faded again on all sides.

Ingvar (m) Scandinavian name meaning '*Ing's* warrior'. See **Igor**.

Inigo (m) St **Ignatius** of Loyola, founder of the Society of Jesus, was otherwise known as Inigo, which appears to be a Spanish or Basque form of the name, *via* Eneco. Borne by the father of the famous architect Inigo Jones (1573–1652) and passed on to the son. Used on very

rare occasions in modern times.

Innes (m) Celtic: Gaelic *innes* 'island'. Scottish place name then surname, used as a Scottish Christian name, generally for boys, sometimes for girls. Now also used in the U.S. **Innis** is found.

Iola (f) Greek 'dawn cloud'. Hercules fell in love with Princess Iole. Modern usage appears to be confined to Wales, which suggests a feminine form of **Iolo**, a diminutive of **Iorwerth** (**Yorath**).

Iolanthe (f) See **Yolande**. The name of the Gilbertian opera (1882), but very rarely used as a first name.

Iona (f) Island in the Hebrides where St Columba founded a monastery in 563. Used especially in Scotland as a first name, infrequently but regularly. Ivor Brown wrote perceptively in his book *A Charm of Names*: 'the smaller islands have been taken up for Christian names on their merits of appearance when one sees them and of music when one hears them.'

Ione (f) Greek *ion* 'violet'. Flower name used very rarely as a first name.

Iorwerth (m) Celtic: Welsh *iŏr* 'lord' and *gwerth* 'worth'. **Yorath** is the English spelling. Used as a substitute for **Edward** in Wales. **Iolo** is a diminutive.

Ira (m) Hebrew 'watchful'. Biblical, O.T., 2 Sam. 23:26, one of King David's captains. Used regularly but not frequently since the 19th c. Ira D. Sankey (1840–1908), the evangelist, may have influenced U.S. usage.

Irena (f) Common variant of **Irene**.

Irene (f) Greek *Eirene* 'peace'. Irene is the Latin form. One of the commonest Christian names during the Roman Empire, and the name of a 4th c. saint. Unknown, however, in English-speaking countries until the middle of the 19th c. George Stewart, in *American Given Names*, seems to think it was the pedantic English who introduced the name and insisted on pronouncing it in the Greek way, as three syllables. First became popular, however, in the U.S., reaching the top fifty in 1900. Reached a peak in Britain some twenty-five years later and then declined steadily until the 1960s. Since then rarely used. *I-reen* has long been the normal pronunciation thanks to a musical and popular song which established it as such. Often found as **Irena**, a form it takes in Slavic languages. Some parents have returned to the original Greek **Eirene**, while others, perhaps influenced by **Eileen**, have favoured **Eireen**. On rare occasions has been spelt **Irenee** or **Irenie** in order to force the three-syllable spoken form. Pet forms **Rene** (**Renie, Renee, Rena**) have often been used independently. A well-known Irene in modern times is the actress Irene Dunne, a leading lady of the 1930s and '40s.

Iris (f) Goddess of the rainbow in Greek mythology, but probably more generally known as a plant name. Came into use in Britain, especially, with other flower names in the 1890s. Use increased steadily until the 1920s, but very rare everywhere since the 1960s. The British novelist Iris Murdoch has kept it before the public in recent years.

Irma (f) Pet form of German names beginning with *Irm-* such as *Irmgard*. Represents Old German *irmin* 'whole, universal'. Used regularly but infrequently from the 1890s to 1940. Many people associate it with Shirley MacLaine who played the title-role in the film *Irma la Douce*. **Erma** is also found.

Irvin(e) (m) Also **Irving**. These are Scottish place names/surnames, regularly if occasionally used as first names since the latter half of the 19th c. The most famous Irving is the song-writer Irving Berlin (Israel Baline), whose surname was changed accidentally by a printer and whose first name was chosen to make him more English.

Irwin (m) Old English 'boar' plus 'friend'. One of the Old English names revived from the 1860s. Used regularly until the 1940s, though never in great numbers. **Erwin** is also found, and in some cases the name is confused with **Irvin. Irwyn** is a rare variant.

Isa (f) Pet form of **Isabel(la)**, used chiefly

in Scotland as an independent name. Some usage in England 1900–30.

Isaac (m) Hebrew 'May God laugh, be kind'. Biblical O.T. Gen. 21:3. 'Abraham was a hundred years old when his son Isaac was born to him. And Sarah said, "God has made laughter for me; everyone who hears will laugh over me." ' A favourite amongst the 17th c. Puritans. Very popular throughout the 18th c., and remained in very general use throughout the 18th c. Since 1950 used far more rarely. The famous treatise *The Compleat Angler* (1653) was written by Izaak Walton, and this form of the name is sometimes found. An even more famous bearer of the name was Sir Isaac Newton (1642–1727), the mathematician and philosopher who described the laws of motion and gravity. Pet form **Ike** is used independently, as is **Zak** (since 1965), though the latter is also from **Zachary**.

Isabel (f) Spanish/Portuguese form of **Elizabeth**, used interchangeably with that name until the 16th c. but long regarded as independent. In modern times most used 1875–1900, though there was a slight resurgence in the 1950s. Continues to be used, though quietly. **Isabell** has frequently been used as a variant, influenced no doubt by **Isabella**. French form **Isabelle** has also been much used. The spelling **Isobel**, rarely **Isobell, Isobelle**, appeared in the 1870s, and has been much used this century. Usual pet forms of the name are **Bel(le), Ib(bie), Isa, Sib, Tib(by)**. Of these **Bel(le)** and **Isa** have been most used.

Isabella (f) Italian form of **Elizabeth**. Very popular in Britain throughout the 19th c. and continuing until the 1930s, later in Scotland. Never as popular in the U.S., where Elizabeth has remained the usual form. Pet form **Bella** was much used as a name in its own right. Isabella still found, but becoming rare.

Isabelle (f) See **Isabel**.

Isador (m) Variant of **Isidore**.

Isadora (f) Greek, feminine of **Isidore**,

and more correctly **Isidora**, but Isadora was made world-famous by the dancer Isadora Duncan, 1878–1927. Rarely used nowadays.

Isaiah (m) Hebrew 'Jehovah is salvation'. Biblical, O.T., Book of Isaiah, one of the great Hebrew prophets. Adopted by the 17th c. Puritans and brought to the U.S. along with other O.T. names. Revived to some extent in the 19th c. Black Americans often use pronunciation *I-zay-uh* with spelling **Isaiah**.

Ishbel (f) Scottish form of **Isabel** influenced by Gaelic **Iseabail**. Occurs from time to time, usually in Scotland but also in England.

Isidora (f) Feminine of **Isidore**. See also **Isadora**.

Isidore (m) Greek *Isidōros* 'gift of Isis', a common ancient Greek name. *Isidorus* is found as the name of a 6th c. Christian in Rome. St Isidore of Seville, 'the schoolmaster of the Middle Ages', died 636. Other saints bear the name, including St Isidore the Ploughman, patron saint of Madrid. Adopted by Spanish Jews, whom St Isidore of Seville tried to convert. Used in the U.S. and Britain, mainly by Jews, since the 19th c. Forms of the name include **Isidor, Isador, Dore, Dorian, Dory, Issy, Izzy**. Feminine is **Isidora**, or **Isadora**.

Isla (f) Scottish river name used as a first name. Publicized in Britain in the late 1970s by the Scottish television personality Isla St Clair. Pronounced *Eye-la*, which seems to disprove the theory sometimes advanced that the name is connected with **Isabel**.

Ismay (f) Of unknown origin. Reaney connects the surname *Ismay* with an Old German name that has not survived, with a possible meaning 'might'. In later use some confusion with **Esmée** is possible. Used very rarely.

Isobel (f) Common variant of **Isabel**, mainly used this century. **Isobell** and **Isobelle** also found on rare occasions.

Isolda (f) Form of **Isolde** used from time to time in English-speaking countries, presumably in modern times with refer-

ence to Wagner's opera *Tristan and Isolde*. Also occurs in different versions of the legend as **Ysolde, Ysonde, Yseult, Isold, Isolte, Yseulte**. In early English records often **Isot** or **Izot**, reflecting phonetically the French forms of the name. The name is impossible to explain because it is not clear whether it is German or Celtic. Tristan is usually **Tristram** in English. In the standard version of the tale he falls in love with Ysolde the Fair, but she marries King Mark. He therefore marries another young lady called Ysolde for the sake of her name, but does not live with her.

Israel (m) The name given to Jacob by God after Jacob had spent three days 'wrestling with the Lord'. See O.T., Gen. 35:10. Possible meanings are 'May God show his strength' or 'May God reign'. Later came to mean 'the Jewish nation', and took on a new significance in 1948 with the founding of the state of Israel. The 17th c. Puritans made use of the name, and it was in general use along with all other O.T. names throughout the 19th c. Far less commonly bestowed as a first name in the 20th c., though Jewish families remain faithful to it. Pet form **Issy** has occasionally been used independently.

Issy (m) Pet form of **Isidore, Israel**, sometimes used as an independent name.

Ita (f) Old Irish *itu* 'thirst'. Irish saint who was head of a school in County Limerick in the 6th c. Amongst her pupils is said to have been St Brendan. Regularly used in Ireland, or by Irish parents living elsewhere, but otherwise rare.

Ithel (m) Welsh 'generous/bountiful lord'. Ancient Welsh name in occasional modern use.

Iva (f) Probably a short form of **Ivana**, the feminine form of **Ivan**. Weidenham mentions that there is a Cornish martyr named Iva (*Baptismal Names*) but writers who have dealt in detail with Cornish names make no mention of her. May occasionally represent a form of **Eva**, or be a variant of **Ivah**, a Biblical place name which is occasionally used as a first name.

Ivah (f) Place name mentioned in the Bible, O.T., 2 Kings 18:34, used on rare occasions as a first name. **Sharon** is another Biblical place name used in this way.

Ivan (m) Form of **John** in several languages, especially Russian. Steadily used in English-speaking countries since the end of the 19th c., but never fashionable, or only to the extent that Russian names have become fashionable in a mild way from time to time, bringing renewed interest in **Natasha**, **Olga**, **Vera**, **Sonia**, etc.

Iver (m) Variant of **Ivor** perhaps influenced by the Scottish last name *MacIver* 'son of Ivor'.

Iverna (f) Old Latin form of a lost Celtic name which also gave modern Irish **Erin** and was corrupted to **Hibernia**. Therefore a rather esoteric reference to Ireland. Variant **Juverna** has also been used, but both forms are rare.

Ives (m) Variant of **Ivo** used mainly in the 19th c., but never with great frequency.

Ivie (f) Variant of **Ivy**. **Ivey** also occurs.

Ivo (m) Teutonic *Iv* 'yew wood'. Latin *Ivo*, Old French *Ive*, *Yve(s)*, *Ivon*. Yew wood was used to make bows, and the name may have signified 'archer'. Very common among the Normans and Bretons. Brought to England at the Norman Conquest: now very rare.

Ivon (m) French variant of **Yves**, but in some instances probably a spelling variant of **Yvonne**.

Ivor (m) Old Norse *Ivarr*, possibly connected with *Ingvar*. The name of a god in this personal name, but its meaning is obscure. Used especially in Scotland and Ireland, regularly but infrequently. In Wales usually becomes **Ifor**, but one famous Welshman bore it as Ivor and made it famous, namely Ivor Novello (1893–1951). He was born David Ivor Davies and borrowed the Novello from his mother, who bore it as a middle name because her father had admired an Italian singer of that name.

Ivorine (f) This occurs as a trade name for a substance imitating ivory, but probably used as a feminine form of **Ivor**. Not frequent. **Ivoreen** is also found.

Ivory (m, f) The word used as a first name. Recorded first in 1905, and now used mainly by black American families. Male and female usage is roughly equal.

Ivy (f) Plant name used as a first name. Introduced in the 1860s when such names began to become fashionable. Very popular 1900–25 but has since faded, perhaps because its 'clinging' image is no longer felt to be suitable. In Scotland found regularly as a male name, a pet form of **Ivor**.

Izaak (m) See **Isaac**.

Izzy (m) Pet form of **Isidore**, used as a name in its own right.

J

Jabez (m) Hebrew, Biblical, O.T. 1 Chron. 4:9; 'his mother called his name Jabez, saying, "Because I bore him in pain." ' Used fairly frequently in Britain throughout the 18th and 19th cc., but rare since the 1930s in all English-speaking countries. Variants **Jabes**, **Jabesh** and **Jabus** are found.

Jacalyn (f) Modern variant of **Jacqueline**.

Jacinta (f) Greek *Hyakinthos*, Latin *Hyacinthus* 'iris, larkspur'. Originally a

male name, e.g. the Roman martyred in 257 whose relics were discovered in the cemetery of St Basilla at Rome in 1845. Feminine form Hyacintha (e.g. St Hyacintha Mariscotti, d. 1640) became **Jacinthe** in French, **Jacinta** in Spanish. The latter has become the usual modern form in the U.S. and Britain. **Jacinth** and **Jacintha** are also found.

Jack (m) Pet form of **John** which developed in the Middle Ages by way of

Jan + Kin which became **Jackin**. By a
parallel development **Jon** + **Kin** led to
Jock. A full philological study of the
name was carried out by E. W. B.
Nicholson in 1892. French **Jacques** was
less of an influence than its form might
suggest since it was often pronounced
Jake. Nevertheless, in terms of usage,
the two names have long been considered as equivalents. Normal written
form of the name was John until the
mid-19th c, when Jack began to appear
in baptismal records. Slowly became
more popular, reaching a peak in all
English-speaking countries in the
1920s. Since then has been fading.
Associated with many well-known
actors and entertainers, including Jack
Benny (1894–1974), born Benjamin
Kubelsky, Jack Buchanan
(1891–1957), Jack Carson (1910–63),
Jack Hawkins (1910–73), and Jack
Lemmon. Pet forms **Jackie** and **Jacky**
occasionally used, though these have
now become mainly female.

Jackie (m) Diminutive of **Jack** used independently. Now rare, having been taken
over as a girl's name, but associated in
the 1920s and '30s with such actors as
Jackie Coogan, Jackie Cooper and Jackie Gleason. Perhaps significant that the
first two of these achieved most success
as child actors. Their image, created in
part by their name, did not survive too
well in the adult world.

Jackie (f) Pet form of **Jacqueline** used
independently since the 1930s, especially when Jacqueline itself was in
fashion. Jackie always the most frequent spelling, but **Jackey, Jacki, Jacky,
Jacquey, Jacqui** and **Jaquie** are found.

Jackson (m) Use of the surname 'son of
Jack' as first name. Occurs regularly in
the U.S. and Britain. In many instances
probably a maiden name being put to
good use, but may sometimes honour
famous bearers of the surname, such as
Andrew Jackson (1767–1845), 7th
President of the U.S., and Confederate
general Thomas 'Stonewall' Jackson
(1824–63).

Jacky (f) See **Jackie**.

Jacob (m) Arabic 'Let God protect', but
often explained as Hebrew 'heel', i.e.
'supplanter'. Greek form was *Iakobos*,
the later Latin form *Jacomus*, leading to
James. Biblical, O.T., Gen. 25:26. Difficult to know how commonly Jacob
was used in earlier times, since the Latin
form *Jacobus* which appears in formal
documents was also used for James.
Jacob probably rare, used mainly by
Jewish families. Steadily used throughout the 18th and 19th cc. and now
gaining ground in the U.S. Pet form
Jake has aroused interest as a name in
its own right since the 1960s. Feminine **Jacobina** occasionally found
in Scotland, but no trace now of the
earlier **Jacoba**.

Jacobina (f) Feminine of **Jacob** (**James**)
used occasionally in Scotland.

Jacqueline (f) French feminine diminutive of **Jacques** (**James**). Introduced to
Britain at an early date and found infrequently in records of the 17th c. and
before. Revived at the beginning of the
20th c. and by 1925 was one of the top
fifty names in the U.S. In Britain reached
its peak in the 1950s and '60s. Fading on
all sides in recent years. One problem
with the name, it seems, is its spelling.
The following variants are amongst
those found in the U.S. and Britain –
some of them are deliberate attempts to
blend existing names, others are simply
ways of representing the name phonetically: Jacalyn (fairly frequent), Jackalin,
Jacaline, Jackalyn, Jackeline, Jaclyn,
Jaclynn, Jacolyn, Jacqualine, Jacqualyn,
Jacqualynn, Jacquelean, Jacquelene,
Jacquelin, Jacquelyn (very frequent),
Jacquelyne, Jacquelynn, Jacquiline,
Jacquline, Jacqulynn, Jaculine, Jakelyn,
Jaqueline (frequent), Jaquelline.

Jacquelyn (f) See **Jacqueline**. The Jacquelyn spelling was introduced in the
1930s and has been much used.

Jacques (m) French form of **James** or
Jacob, formerly one of the commonest
first names used in France. Occurs from
time to time in English-speaking countries.

Jade (f) Precious stone name used in Britain in the 1970s. There was another word 'jade' which was formerly commonly used as a contemptuous name for a horse or a woman. 'You jade' was an insult similar to 'you hussy', still used as such in 19th c. literature. In modern times the variant **Jayde** has appeared in first-name use.

Jael (f) Hebrew 'antelope'. Biblical, O.T., a lady who abused traditional ideas of hospitality by killing her guest, Sisera. Occasionally used in the 19th c.

Jago (m) Cornish form of **James**. In Welsh the name becomes **Iago** and there is a Breton form **Jagu**. Has suddenly become rather fashionable in Britain since the early 1970s.

Jaime (m, f) The form of **James** in Spanish and Portuguese, and in occasional use as a male name in English-speaking countries. Since the early 1970s increasingly used for girls. See also **Jamie**.

Jaine (f) Variant of **Jane** which appeared in the 1960s but then seems to have disappeared.

Jake (m) Pet form of **Jacob** used independently. Publicized in Britain since the 1960s by the singer Jake Thackray, and parents seem to have responded to it with enthusiasm. Little used elsewhere.

Jamal (m) Based on the Arabic word for 'handsome'. Much used by black American families in the early 1980s. Variants include **Jamaal, Jamahl, Jamall, Jameel, Jamel, Jamele, Jamell, Jamelle, Jamiel, Jamil.**

Jamar (m) Well used by black American families in the early 1980s. Probably makes use of two popular name elements, Ja- (used as a prefix in recent times in names like **Jajuan, Japual**) and -mar, also popular as **Lamar** and to a lesser extent as **Demar**. **Jamarr** is also found.

James (m) Late Latin *Jacomus*, an altered form of *Jacobus*, ultimately from Hebrew. For the meaning see **Jacob**. Biblical, N.T., the name of two Apostles. (Jacob was used as the O.T. version of the name.) In use in the Middle Ages, but its real popularity began with the accession of James Stuart to the throne of England in 1603. One of the most popular names for men in all English-speaking countries since that time, though some reaction against it in the 1960s. Apart from its Biblical and royal associations, has been borne by many well-known men, including the Irish writer James Joyce (1882–1941) and 20th c. actors such as James Cagney, James Stewart, James Mason, James Robertson Justice, James Dean. Also associated with the fictional character James Bond. Apart from **Jim, Jimmy, Jimmie**, other pet forms of the name have taken on an independent existence, especially **Jamie (Jaime**, etc.). These have also been used as feminine forms, replacing the earlier **Jamesina**. Other modern feminine forms (of **James** or **Jamal**) include **Jametta, Jamille, Jamelia, Jamila, Jamell.**

Jamesina (f) Traditional feminine form of **James**, now largely replaced by **Jamie, Jaime**. See also **James** for other modern feminine variants.

Jamie (m, f) Scottish diminutive of **James**, quietly used until the early 1960s as a boy's name. Then came into fashion, especially in the U.S., as a girl's name. Signs by 1980 that the peak period of use had passed. Use of the name in the television series *The Bionic Woman* undoubtedly had some influence, both on **Jaime** and Jamie. **Jayme, Jaymee** and **Jaymie** are also found.

Jamieson (m) Surname, linked with **James**, used as a first name. **Jameson** also occurs from time to time.

Jan (m) Form of **John** in several languages, e.g. Polish, Czech, Dutch, and once a variant used in Britain. Modern use of the name probably reflects a borrowing from another language rather than a revival of the obsolete English form. Pronunciation should be *Yan*.

Jan (f) Pet form of **Janet** used independently. In regular but quiet use since the beginning of the 20th c.

Jana (f) Form of **Jane** in several Central European languages. Used in the U.S. since the 1950s, but not in great numbers. Pronounced *Yana*.

Jane (f) Form of Latin **Johanna**, feminine of Johannes (**John**). The earlier form was **Joan**, but Jane overtook it in popularity from the 16th c. onwards. In Britain, especially, one of the top names throughout the 18th and 19th cc. In the U.S. it reached its peak in the period 1920–50 (used almost exclusively by white parents), which caused a minor revival of popularity in Britian in the 1960s. Declined on all sides since then, but remains a favourite middle name. Associated with many fictional heroines in the 18th c., (and with the great writer of fiction, Jane Austen, 1775–1815), and in more recent times with actresses such as Jane Wyman (Sarah Jane Faulks). Modern variants of the name are **Jayne** and **Jaine**, and the many diminutives include **Janell, Janene, Janessa, Janet, Janetta, Janey, Janice, Janina, Janine, Janis, Janise, Janita, Jaynie**. Has a Gaelic form **Sine**, usually spelt phonetically as **Sheena** (though **Sheenagh, Sheenah, Shena, Sheona, Shiona** also occur). All these forms have been increasingly used in Scotland, especially, but spreading through the rest of Britain, since the 1950s.

Janelle (f) Diminutive of **Jane**, in use by 1950 in the U.S. Quietly but consistently used since then, also in the forms **Janel** and **Janell**. A Janel Smith was named in Britain in 1951 and Janell appeared there in the 1960s.

Janene (f) Variant of **Janine** used regularly since the 1950s.

Janet (f) Diminutive of **Jane**. It was earlier **Janeta**, which occurs very rarely in modern times, and **Janetta**, frequently found in the 19th c. and intermittently in the 20th c. Alongside these forms **Jenet(te), Jennet(t), Jennette, Jennetta** and **Jenetta** have been well used. **Jonet** survived only until the 18th c. Janet was mainly a Scottish name in the 19th c. Came into wider use in the 20th c., and

at its peak in all English-speaking countries in the 1950s. **Janette**, in imitation of French **Jeannette**, was by that time a frequent variant. All forms of the name going out of fashion since the 1960s. Considerably helped along in the 1920s and '30s by the actress Janet Gaynor (Laura Gainer). Janet Blair and Janet Leigh made a contribution later, but the name was already very fashionable when they began to appear on the screen. In Scotland only, Janets have traditionally been addressed as **Jess, Jessie** or **Jessy, Jennie** or **Jenny**. All these pet forms have been used as independent names, though they have other possible origins. The same is true of **Netta** and **Nita**, used in their own right as well as being diminutives of Janet. Spelling variants **Janett, Jannet** are regularly found.

Janetta (f) Latinized form of **Janet** used regularly in the 19th c., less frequently in the 20th c., when it has been largely replaced by the form **Jannetta**. **Janeta** also occurs.

Janette (f) Variant of **Janet**, influenced by French **Jeannette**, popular in the 1950s when Janette Scott was a child star.

Janey (f) See **Janie**.

Janice (f) Diminutive of **Jane**, first recorded as the name of a character in a popular novel by Paul Leicester Ford, *Janice Meredith* (1899). By 1916 used in Britain as **Janis**, a form which occurs regularly. Came into general use by the early 1930s. By 1950 popular in all English-speaking countries, remaining fashionable until the beginning of the 1970s. Since then declining steadily. **Jannice** is a rare variant, and **Janise** is occasionally found.

Janie (f) Pet form of **Jane** used as an independent name since the 1870s with some regularity. **Janey** occurs less frequently.

Janine (f) Probably a phonetic form of French **Jeannine**, but occasionally a pet form of **Jan**. Regularly used since the 1930s. **Jannine** is a fairly frequent variant.

Janis (f) See **Janice**.

Janita (f) Simplified form of **Juanita** in use since the 1930s. **Jannita** also occurs.

Janna (f) Apparently a contraction of **Johanna**. Used on rare occasions since 1960.

Jannet (f) See **Janet**. **Jannetta**, **Jannice**, **Jannine**, etc., occur for **Janetta**, **Janice**, **Janine**.

Janson (m) Surname linked with **Jan** (**John**) used as a first name in modern times. Similar names used since the 1940s include **Jansen**, **Jantzen**, **Janzen**.

Japheth (m) Hebrew *Yepheth*, Greek *Iapheth*, Latin *Japheth*, 'enlargement', 'may he expand'. Biblical, O.T., Gen. 9:27; eldest son of Noah, whose descendants were supposed to have peopled Europe and N. Asia. Introduced by Puritans in 17th c. and often confused with **Jephthah**. Now rarely used.

Jaqueline (f) See **Jacqueline**.

Jared (m) Accadian 'servant'. Biblical, O.T., Gen 5:15. Used by the Puritans, but then very rare until the mid-1960s. *The Big Valley* changed all that from 1965. Barbara Stanwyck's children in the American TV series included a **Jarrod**, a suave sophisticated lawyer. **Jared**, **Jarod**, **Jarrod** and, a little later, **Jarred** came into regular use from that time, mainly in Britain. **Jarrod** is in fact a surname deriving from **Gerald**.

Jarvis (m) Use of the surname as first name, or a phonetic form of **Gervase**, from which the surname in any case usually derives. Regularly found, if infrequently. Variant **Jervis** occurs rather less often.

Jasmine (f) Persian *yasemin*, Arabic *yāsamin*, French *jasmin* (*jasmine* is the French feminine form). One of the flower names in vogue at the end of the 19th c. Began to be used from about 1930, possibly because of a popular play by James Elroy Flecker (1884–1915), *Hassan*, first produced posthumously in 1922, and revived in 1951. Heroine of the play is **Yasmin**, a form of the name often used. **Jasmin**,

Yasmine and **Yasmina** also occur.

Jason (m) A form used by translators of the Bible to represent Greek *Eason*, itself a form of Hebrew **Joshua**. The translators were no doubt familiar with Jason, the leader of the Argonauts, whose name should correctly be written *Iason*. In the Bible Jason is the host to St Paul at Thessalonica (Acts 17:5). Occurs as a first name in Britain from the 17th c. onwards. Regularly but quietly used in the 20th c. until the mid-1950s, when it began to appear on all sides. By the mid-1970s had registered a phenomenal success in all English-speaking countries. Its moment now seems to have passed, and usage has been declining steadily since 1980. The reasons for its success are not clear, but one can look for evidence about how it was brought to the attention of young parents. The actor Jason Robards appeared in a few films in the 1920s and '30s, and his son followed him at the end of the 1950s; a film version of *Jason and the Argonauts* was released in 1963, by which time the name was already showing all the signs of becoming fashionable; there were also television series, such as the American *Room 222*, in which one of the more admirable students was called Jason, *Here Come the Brides*, another American series which featured three lumberjack heroes called Jason, Joshua and Jeremy – many young ladies watching the series, according to a correspondent, stored the name of their favourite character for future use – and the British series, *Jason King*, again gave the name a great deal of publicity. However, no amount of publicity will cause a name to be used so intensively unless something about it appeals strongly. In some families the name was interpreted by fathers whose own name began with 'J' as meaning 'J's son'. Variant **Jayson** was occasionally used to support this. The name has also caused a violent reaction the other way. Clearly it is a name one loves or hates, judging by the comments in a great many parental letters received in recent years.

Jasper (m) Of unknown origin, possibly Persian 'treasure holder'. Traditionally one of the three kings, or 'wise men', who came to Bethlehem to worship the infant Christ. In Germany the name became **Kaspar** or **Caspar**, in French **Gaspard**. Therefore found in some English records as Caspar or Gaspar. Early use led to surnames such as *Jasper* and *Jesperson*. Used regularly but quietly since the 16th c. Has acquired a curious reputation in Britain, including a silent-film image of the villainous would-be seducer Sir Jasper, perhaps suggested by the song 'Oh, Sir Jasper, do not touch me.' In literature the poet Southey created a **Jaspar** who was a highway robber and murderer, and Fielding has a Sir Jasper in *The Mock Doctor* who is made to look foolish. Dickens tells us of Jasper Packlemerton, one of the chief figures in Mrs Jarley's wax-works exhibition (*The Old Curiosity Shop*): 'Jasper courted and married fourteen wives, and destroyed them all by tickling the soles of their feet when they were asleep.' Found amongst the slave lists of the early 19th c., which has led to the suggestion that a particular slave named Jasper who was renowned for his musical and dancing abilities gave rise to the word 'jazz'. The earlier slang meaning of that word, however, had more to do with sexual than musical prowess.

Javan (m) Biblical, Gen. 10:2 where Javan is the son of Japheth. Elsewhere Javan is a place name and is usually translated as 'Greece,' e.g., Isaiah 66:19. In recent use, and also seen as **Javon**, **Javin**. Still a rare name, however.

Jay (m, f) Latin: Late Latin *gaius*, Old French *jay*, 'the jay bird, chatterer'. Gaius was a Roman personal name, from *gaudere* 'to rejoice'. The bird may have been given the name in the same way that *Jack*, *Robin*, etc., were given to others. Used in medieval times, leading to surnames such as *Jay, Jaye, Jeays, Jeyes,* etc. Now rare in Britain, more common in the U.S. and Canada as both a boy's and girl's name, often as a diminutive of names beginning with the letter J. Jaye also occurs.

Jayme(e) (f) See **Jamie**. Jaymie also occurs.

Jayne (f) Variant of **Jane** in early use, e.g. eight examples in the Leeds parish register of 1625, but associated in modern times with the actress Jayne Mansfield (born Vera Jayne Palmer, Mansfield was her married name, 1932–67). This form of Jane reached a minor peak in the 1960s.

Jayson (m) Variant of **Jason** used since the 1960s.

Jean (f) Old French *Jehane*, ultimately from Latin *Johanna*, feminine of *Johannes* (**John**). Popular in Scotland long before it became generally known. In the mid-19th c. in the Scottish top twenty, though **Jane** was still more popular in Scotland at that time. Elsewhere remained rare until the 1880s. Then began to become fashionable, and by 1920 was being very well used in all English-speaking countries. Reached a peak on all sides in the 1930s, then began to decline slowly. By the late 1970s rarely used. Well-known bearers of the name included the American actresses Jean Arthur and Jean Harlow, constantly on cinema screens throughout the 1930s, and later the British actress Jean Simmons. While the name was at its most popular a certain amount of interest was shown in its French form, **Jeanne. Jeane** also occurred regularly, as parents confused the two names. Diminutive forms include **Jeanette, Jeanie, Jeanine, Jeanetta, Jeannetta, Jeannette, Jeannie, Jeannine, Jeannie.** Rarer variants are **Jeana** (perhaps a deliberate variant of **Gina**), **Jeanna, Jeannah.**

Jeanetta (f) Latinized variant of **Jeanette** used rather infrequently. **Jeannetta** also occurred in the 19th c. but does not seem to have survived.

Jeanette (f) Diminutive of **Jean** used mainly in Scotland originally. **Jane** and **Janet** (often **Janette**) used there, and natural that the popular **Jean** should also take the diminutive form Jeanette. Variant **Jeannette** almost as frequently used. **Jennet(t)**, **Jennette**, **Jenet(t)**, **Jenette** all in very early use in Scotland, to some extent replaced by the Jeanette/Jeannette spellings. Associated throughout the 1930s and '40s with the actress/singer Jeanette MacDonald, the frequent screen partner of Nelson Eddy.

Jeanie (f) Pet form of **Jean** in use as an independent name since the mid-19th c., though later overtaken in popularity by **Jeannie**. The famous song 'I dream of Jeanie with the light brown hair' was written by Stephen Foster.

Jeanine (f) See **Jeannine**.

Jeanne (f) French feminine form of **Jean** (**John**), traditionally translated as **Joan** but popularly seen as a French form of the feminine name **Jean**. Used to some extent in English-speaking countries when Joan and Jean were at their most popular, 1920–55. Most famous bearer of the name was Jeanne d'Arc (Joan of Arc).

Jeannetta (f) See **Jeanetta**.

Jeannette (f) See **Jeanette**.

Jeannie (f) Diminutive of **Jean** or **Jeanne**, used as a name in its own right since the 1880s. **Jeanie** used earlier and has continued alongside it, but Jeannie has been used more frequently. Much publicized in the 1950s by the British actress and entertainer Jeannie Carson (Jean Shufflebottom).

Jeannine (f) French diminutive of **Jeanne** (**Jean** or **Jane**). In use since the 1930s in English-speaking countries, and well used in the 1980s. Often found as **Jeanine**, while **Jenine**, **Jennine**, probably represent the same name in phonetic spellings. Even more common are variants **Janine** and **Jannine**. Although all forms probably derive from the original Jeannine, some of the variants may be subject to spelling pronunciations.

Jed (m) Pet form of **Jedidiah**.

Jedidiah (m) Semitic: Hebrew 'friend (beloved) of the Lord'. Biblical, O.T., a name given by the prophet Nathan to Solomon. Introduced by the Puritans in the 17th c. and used intermittently until the present day. Pet form **Jed** sometimes occurs as an independent name.

Jeff (m) Pet form of **Jeffrey/Geoffrey** rarely used as an independent name before the 1950s. The American actor Jeff Chandler (Ira Grossel) then began to appear on the screen regularly and may well have influenced usage.

Jefferson (m) Surname 'son of Geoffrey or Jeffrey' used regularly since the beginning of the 19th c. in all English-speaking countries. In the U.S. must often have been used to honour Thomas Jefferson (1743–1826), 3rd President of the U.S. Its regular use in Britain reflects its convenience as an alternative to Geoffrey or Jeffrey. Jefferson Davis was President of the Confederate States of America 1861–65.

Jeffery (m) See **Geoffrey**. **Jefery**, **Jefferey**, **Jeffree** also occur.

Jeffrey (m) Normal spelling in the U.S. and Canada of **Geoffrey**, very popular in the 1970s. See **Geoffrey** for the history of the name. **Jeffry** also fairly common.

Jehu (m) Hebrew 'The Lord is He'. Biblical, O.T., 2 Kings 9:20. Name of a cruel and unscrupulous man of great personal ambition. Used, perhaps surprisingly, by the 17th c. Puritans. Still in use in the first half of the 19th c., but extremely rare in the 20th c.

Jem (m) Pet form of **James** regularly used as an independent name in the latter half of the 19th c., but now very rarely found.

Jemima (f) Hebrew 'dove'. Biblical, O.T., Job 42:14. One of the daughters of Job. Used by the Puritans, along with the names of her sisters, **Keziah** and **Kerenhappuch**. It may have seemed significant to those 17th c. parents that the names of Job's daughters had been carefully recorded in the Bible, while the names of his seven sons were omitted.

Job also treated his daughters as if they were sons when he made his will. The girls were renowned for their beauty, but were obviously unusual in other ways. At its most popular from the end of the 18th c. to the mid-19th c. Continues to be quietly used. **Jemmima** and **Jemimah** are found. Countless children know the name through *The Tale of Jemima Puddleduck* (1908) by Beatrix Potter. In the U.S. used as a substitute for Jesus in expletives, leading in turn to 'jiminy' and tending to conjure up image of Aunt Jemima, a black cook. Pet forms of the name, **Jemmy** and **Mima**, have been used independently.

Jemma (f) Frequently-used modern variant of **Gemma**.

Jemmy (m, f) Pet form of **James**, a variant of **Jimmy**, or a pet form of **Jemima**. Occurs rarely as an independent name, perhaps because in Britain it is associated strongly with the burglar's crowbar, 'jemmy' in Britain, a 'jimmy' in the U.S.

Jenefer (f) Variant of **Jennifer** in use since the 1930s. **Jennefer** also occurs.

Jenet(te) (f) Variants of **Janet**, influenced by **Jeannette**.

Jenifer (f) Cornish spelling of **Jennifer**. In general use since the 1930s, but much rarer than **Jennifer**.

Jenine (f) Modern name, used from the 1970s onwards, perhaps a diminutive of **Jennie** or a phonetic form of **Jeannine**. **Jennine** is also found.

Jenkin (m) Diminutive of **Jen**, itself a form of **John**, so that **Jenkin** means 'little John'. Known mainly as a surname but used since the mid-19th c. as a first name, infrequently. **Jenkyn** also occurs.

Jenna (f) Latinized form of **Jennie/Jenny**. Greatly increased usage mid-1980s due to Jenna Wade, character in *Dallas*. **Jena** also occurred.

Jennet(t) (f) Variants of **Janet** used with great regularity in the 19th c., but now rather rare. **Jennette** was also used. It may be that **Jeannette** was the name parents had in mind.

Jennetta (f) Variant of **Janetta, Jannetta**.

Jenney (f) See **Jennie**.

Jennie (f) Until the 1930s always a pet form of **Jane** or **Janet** (in Scotland). In more recent times usually a pet form of **Jennifer**. **Jenny** has always been as frequently used as **Jennie**. **Jenney** occurs regularly, and **Jenni** appeared in the 1960s. **Jennie/Jenny** popular as an independent name since at least the beginning of the 18th c. All forms continue to be used regularly.

Jennifer (f) Welsh *Gwenhwyfar* 'fair, white' + 'yielding, smooth'. The name of King Arthur's queen. Has many forms, including **Guinevere, Guenever, Guinever, Guenievre, Gueanor, Guener, Gaynor, Gweniver, Jenifer**. Latter forms were especially Cornish, and it was in Cornwall that the name was mostly used in the 18th c. Had previously reached Scotland in the forms **Wannore, Wannour, Wander**. Survives there as the surname *Wanders*. Miss Withycombe also mentions Scottish **Vanora**, but this appears to be totally obsolete. **Jenny, Jenney** and **Jennie** all in use throughout the 19th c. as independent names, but they derived from **Janet**. Noel Coward named a character Jennifer in *The Young Idea* (1923). This immediately attracted the attention of parents and the name began to be used throughout Britain. By 1950 in 6th position in the British popularity chart, but has subsequently declined. Also reached Australia by the 1950s and became very popular. During the 1940s the actress Jennifer Jones gave the name considerable publicity. She was born Phyllis Isley, and David Selznick's organization is said to have spent nearly a year thinking up her new name. They chose well, for the name then became extremely popular in the U.S. and Canada, reaching number one position by the mid-1970s. The immensely successful book and film *Love Story*, with its heroine Jennifer Cavilleri, did the name no harm in the early 1970s. Has probably passed its peak in the U.S. and usage will decline through the 1980s.

Jenny (f) See **Jennie**.

Jephthah (m) Hebrew 'whom God sets free'. Biblical, O.T., name of the unhappy man, driven from home by his brothers because of his illegitimacy, who became a guerilla leader, then the chief of the Gileadites. Before a battle he vowed to sacrifice whoever should first emerge from his door to greet him if he returned victorious. When he did return his only daughter was the first to emerge. She bravely accepted her fate. Occasionally used in the 19th c., sometimes occuring as **Jephtha, Jeptha**.

Jerald (m) Modern variant of **Gerald**, in regular use in the U.S. in the 1960s.

Jeraldine (f) See **Geraldine**.

Jeremiah (m) Hebrew 'Jehovah is high' or 'Jehovah exalts'. Biblical, O.T., the Book of Jeremiah. He has been called 'the most interesting personality in the history of Israel', and was a renowned prophet. The Greek/Latin form of the name, **Jeremias**, in early use as a Christian name, revived to some extent by the Puritans in the 17th c. **Jeremy** was established early as the normal spoken form of the name, but Jeremiah is usual written form in records until modern times, when Jeremy has become fashionable. Miss Withycombe is right to say that Jeremiah has always been popular in Ireland (though showing signs of fading out there in the 1970s). Especially well used there in the 1950s. Irish fondness for the name apparently based on a belief that the prophet visited the country at some time. Also used in Ireland as the English form of **Diarmaid**, or **Dermot**, though the latter used more frequently as Jeremiah fades. Pet form **Jerry** occurs as a name in its own right, though infrequently.

Jeremy (m) English form of **Jeremiah**, used in the N.T. Rarely used until the 1920s, Jeremiah being more usual. By 1950 was clearly becoming fashionable on all sides. In Britain reached a peak in the mid-1960s and has been declining since then. In the U.S. use of the name

was still increasing at the beginning of the 1980s, boosted by the television series *Here Come the Brides*, which also had a dramatic effect too on **Jason** and **Joshua**. Best-known English bearer of the name perhaps the rather eccentric philosopher Jeremy Bentham (1748–1832), whose preserved corpse can still be seen at University College London. In *The Tale of Jeremy Fisher*, by Beatrix Potter, Jeremy is the frog who is fortunately not eaten by the trout because he is wearing his mackintosh.

Jeri (f) See **Gerry**.

Jermaine (m) Appears to be a form of French **Germain**, Latin *Germanus*, the name of several saints. Originally indicated someone who came from Germany. Normal English form of the name, used to some extent in the 19th c., was **German**. Jermain W. Loguen (1813–72) was a black Methodist minister whose autobiography was a classic in anti-slavery literature. Jermaine Jackson (1954–), older brother of Michael Jackson, has helped popularize the name with black families since the early 1970s. Whites have tended to ignore it. The name has been little used in Britain. American variants include **Jermane, Jamaine, Germaine**, though the last of these is actually a French feminine form.

Jerold (m) Modern variant of **Gerald**. **Jerrold** also occurs.

Jerome (m) Greek: *Ieronumos* 'sacred name', Latin *Hieronymus*, Italian *Geronimo*, French *Jerôme*. St Jerome (340–420) was responsible for an important Latin translation of the Bible. *Jeronimus* occurs in England 1206, and Camden lists *Hierome* in 1605. Fairly common in the 16th c. and revived in the 19th c. Jerome K. Jerome made his name well known in 1889 with the publication of his *Three Men In A Boat*. The composer Jerome Kern (1885–1945) also kept the name before the public. **Jerry** is usual pet form of the name.

Jerrold (m) Use of the surname as first name or a variant of **Gerald**. The surname indicates that an ancestor was called Gerald.

Jerry (f) See **Gerry** (f).

Jerry (m) Short form of **Jeremiah** or a variant of **Gerry**. Used infrequently as an independent name since the 19th c., though now made well-known by the actor Jerry Lewis (Joseph Levitch) and the mouse who torments Tom in the popular Tom and Jerry cartoons.

Jervis (m) See **Jarvis**.

Jess (m, f) Pet form of **Jesse**, **Jessie** or **Jessica** used independently. In Scotland a pet form of **Janet**.

Jessamine (f) Earlier spelling of the flower name **Jasmine**, used in Britain as a Christian name 1900–20. Later Jasmin(e) and **Yasmin**(e) became more usual. **Jessie** used as a pet form. Variants include **Jessamy**, **Jessamyn**, **Jessemine**, **Jessimine**.

Jesse (m) Hebrew 'Jehovah exists'. Greek *Iessai*, Latin *Jesse*. Biblical O.T. The father of King David. Used with reasonable frequency in the 18th c., regularly if infrequently since then. Pet form **Jess** often used independently, and many now pronounce Jesse as Jess instead of Jess-ee. In the 19th c. the outlaw Jesse James made the name notorious. Redeemed by the athlete Jesse Owens who became world-famous for his record-breaking feats at the 1936 Berlin Olympics. Used by both black and white American families and found also as **Jessie**, **Jessey**.

Jessey (m, f) Variant spelling, no longer in favour but formerly common, of **Jessie**.

Jessica (f) Hebrew 'he beholds'. Biblical, O.T., Gen. 11:29; *Iscah*, or *Jesca* in early translations. Shakespeare turned this into Jessica in the *Merchant of Venice* and used it for the daughter of Shylock the Jew. Until recently considered to be a Jewish name, but by the 1970s had become generally popular, especially with white American parents. The actress Jessica Lange (1949–   ) has helped make it known recently.

Jessie (m, f) In the U.S. a variant of **Jesse**. In Scotland a pet form of **Janet**. In all English-speaking countries a pet form of **Jessica**, used as an independent name. Has its own pet form, **Jess**, and variants **Jessy** and **Jessey** were common in the 19th c.

Jestina (f) Form of **Justina** influenced strongly by Welsh **Iestin**, the feminine of **Iestyn** (**Justin**). Used in Wales at the end of the 19th c. and revived there in the 1960s.

Jethro (m) Hebrew 'pre-eminence'. Biblical, O.T., Exod. 18:6; the father-in-law of Moses. In regular use until the 1870s, having been introduced in the late 16th c. The rock music group Jethro Tull aroused some British interest in the early 1970s.

Jewel (f) Modern use of the word as a first name. Far more frequent in the U.S. than in Britain, and often found as **Jewell**. First occurrences of the name were in the 1930s, ten years later in Britain. Rare variant is **Jewelle**. Noticeable that **Joelle** also began to be used when Jewel first appeared.

Jezebel (f) Hebrew 'chaste, unmarried'. Biblical, O.T., the wife of Ahab, who was damned by the Puritans as a 'painted lady'. She eventually met her death with some bravery, but remains a hated figure, her name well known but impossible to use. Nevertheless, a Jezebel Smith was named in Britain in 1851. A popular song 'Jezebel' in modern times, sung by Frankie Laine, failed to remove the taboo on the name.

Jill (f) Usual modern form of **Gill**, both being pet forms of **Gillian** used independently. Early popularity of Jill is shown by such traditional rhymes as 'Jack and Jill went up the hill'. Out of favour from the 17th c., but revived from the 1920s. Then began to enjoy a spell of great popularity in all English-speaking countries, especially Australia.

Jillian (f) Variant of **Gillian**. **Jillianne** also occurs.

Jim (m) Pet form of **James**, used as an independent name with great regularity since the mid-19th c., though never in great numbers.

Jimmie (m,f) See **Jimmy**. In the 1970s mainly black families were using this spelling for both sexes.

Jimmy (m) Pet form of **James** used independently since the end of the 19th c. Occurs regularly, along with the rather more popular **Jim** and the occasional variant **Jimmie**. Associated with entertainers such as Jimmy 'Schnozzle' Durante (1893–1980), the comedian, and, in Britain, Jimmy Edwards and Jimmy Young.

Jinny (f) Probably a pet form of **Jane** or a variant of **Jenny**. Used mainly in the 19th c., never frequently. Use of the name by British miners for the stationary engine that draws trucks up an inclined plane was no doubt suggested by the second syllable of 'engine'. **Jinney** and **Jinnie** also occur as first names on rare occasions. In some instances may be a pet form of **Virginia**.

Jo (f) Pet form of **Josephine**, **Joanna**, etc., used as a name in its own right. Sparingly used in the 19th c., more frequently found 1940–60. Now rare.

Joah (m) Hebrew 'Jehovah (is) brother'. Biblical, O.T., the name of several men. Not mentioned by Bardsley in his book about Puritan names, and examples are very hard to find in the 18th c. Certainly in regular use, however, throughout the 19th c.

Joan (f) Contraction of Latin **Johanna**, feminine of **Johannes** (**John**). In the Middle Ages seems to have been pronounced as John, and was as commonly used as that name. Various factors caused it to go out of favour in the 17th c. Camden, writing in 1605, observes: 'In latter years some of the better and nicer sort, misliking Joan, have mollified the name of Joan into **Jane**.' Shakespeare uses the name to refer to the commonest type of woman, at the other end of the social scale from a 'lady'. Use of the name inevitably declined, with Jane replacing it. In the latter half of the 19th c. examples are

very difficult to find, and it looked as if it would become obsolete. Between 1900 and 1925 it staged an amazing comeback to become one of the most popular names in the English-speaking world by 1925. Its new-found popularity lasted for some twenty years, but by 1950 once again rapidly declining in use. In the 1980s rarely used. The reasons for resurgence in the early part of the century are not clear. Well-known actresses such as Joan Crawford (Lucille le Sueur), Joan Fontaine (Joan de Havilland), Joan Bennett, Joan Blondell and Joan Collins came on the scene too late to have been responsible. The answer might lie in the brilliantly-named film *Joan the Woman* (1916), in which Geraldine Farrar played the title-role, Joan of Arc. (G. B. Shaw's play, *St Joan*, on the same theme, was not staged until 1924.)

Joanna (f) Contracted form of Latin **Johanna**, feminine of **Johannes** (**John**). Regularly used throughout the 19th c. Used in increasing numbers in the 1920s when **Joan** became popular, and still more when **Joan** began to go out of fashion and alternatives were needed. In the U.S. reached a peak in 1950 and started to decline from that point. Still rising in Britain in 1980 though a long way to go before matching the popularity of **Joanne**. Variant forms of the name include **Joana**, **Joannah**, **Jo Anna**.

Joanne (f) French contracted form of Latin **Johanna**, feminine of **Johannes** (**John**). Returned to favour in the U.S. in the 1920s, along with **Joan**. Well used until the mid-1950s, by which time it was beginning to be used in rapidly increasing numbers in Britain. Reached third position in the British popularity charts in 1975 before beginning to decline. By that time in the U.S. had become a rare name again. Popular variants in modern times have included **Jo-Ann**, **Joann**, **Jo'anne**, **Jo-anne**, **Joeanne**.

Job (m) Hebrew, of uncertain meaning. Perhaps 'the afflicted' or 'the persecuted'. Biblical, O.T., Book of Job. The man who endured much suffering with great patience, hence the proverbial 'patience of Job'. The phrase 'Job's comforter' refers to someone who comforts you when you are suffering by reminding you that you were responsible for your own problems. Used by the Puritans in spite of its melancholy associations, or perhaps, as Professor Weekley has suggested, because of them, since the Puritans often humbled themselves in every way. More surprisingly, it continued in general use throughout the 18th c. and was reasonably fashionable in the first half of the 19th c. Steadily but quietly used since 1900. Pronunciation sometimes emphasized by **Jobe** spelling (**Joab**, Hebrew 'Jehovah is father' is separate name). Also a modern tendency to distinguish between the name and the word 'job' by extending the first name to **Jobey, Jobie** or **Joby**.

Jobey (m) See **Job**. **Jobie** and **Joby** also occur.

Jocelyn (m, f) Old German, of uncertain meaning but probably connected with the tribal name of the Goths. The Normans introduced the name to Britain in the 11th c. They connected the name with the Breton **Judocus**, which had become **Josse** in normal speech. This would link the name etymologically to **Joyce**, which is probably what English-speaking parents did at the beginning of the 20th c. when they began to use the name for girls. In the Middle Ages the name was always male, and its frequent use gave rise to several surnames, including *Gosling*. Quietly but regularly used this century. **Jocelin, Joceline, Joclyn, Josalene, Joscelin, Joscelyn, Joseline, Joselyn, Joselyne, Josiline, Josline, Josslyn** are some of the variant forms.

Jock (m) An English term for a Scotsman and a U.S. term for an athlete but extremely rare as a real first name. First applied to seamen of the north of England, 'Jock' being a common name

of the people of Northumberland, according to Grose's *Dictionary of the Vulgar Tongue* in the late 18th c. The men were probably called **John** officially, but known as **Jack**, which became Jock in the local pronunciation. Never given as a first name by Scottish parents.

Jodie (f) Jodie, Jodi and Jody are pet forms of **Judith** or **Joanna** (compare **Dodie** from **Dorothy**). Popular since the 1950s in the U.S. and Canada, e.g. the actress Jodie Foster. Amongst the top ten girls' names in the 1970s in Canada and Australia. At the time these forms had not spread to Britain. Jody is occasionally male, presumably from **Joseph** or **Jude**.

Joe (m) Pet form of **Joseph**, long used as an independent name. Continues to be regularly if quietly used in all English-speaking countries.

Joel (m) Hebrew 'Jehovah is the Lord'. Biblical, O.T., Book of Joel. The name of several men mentioned in the Bible, and that of the second of the twelve prophets. In quiet but regular use since the 16th c. Associated with the American actor Joel McCrea and more recently with Joel Grey (of *Cabaret*). Another well-known bearer of the name was Joel Chandler Harris (1848–1908), author of the *Uncle Remus* stories.

Joella (f) See **Joellen**.

Joelle (f) French feminine form of **Joel**, but see **Joellen**.

Joellen (f) Modern blend of names beginning with *Jo-* and **Ellen**, popular in the U.S. in the 1940s. By the 1950s occurring more often as **Joella**. This in turn changed by the 1960s into the French feminine of Joel, namely **Joelle**. Reached Britain in the latter form by the 1970s. All forms of the name appear to have slipped into the background again in the 1980s.

Joey (m) Diminutive of **Joe**, itself from **Joseph**, used regularly as an independent name. By the 1960s being clearly favoured by black American parents.

Joffre (m) Surname of Joseph Jacques Césaire Joffre (1852–1931), Marshal of France and French commander-in-chief in World War One. Used as a first name by some British families 1914–16.

Johan (m, f) Form of *Johannes* (John), used in countries such as Holland and occasionally in English-speaking countries. In Scotland a form of **Joan** at the beginning of the 20th c., a clipped form of **Johanna**.

Johann (m) German clipped form of *Johannes* used since the 1950s in English-speaking countries. One of the replacement forms of **John** in modern times.

John (m) Hebrew *Yohanan* 'Jehovah has been gracious'. Greek *Jōannes*, Low Latin *Joannes*, Medieval Latin *Johannes*. Biblical O.T. *Johanan*, N.T. *John*. Of particular Christian significance as the name of John the Baptist (and therefore particularly suitable for baptism) and of John the Evangelist. Common name in Christian inscriptions of the Roman Empire, and the name of seven popes from the 6th c. Brought to Britain by the Normans in the 11th c., though it had been used on rare occasions in the Old English period. Early English forms, influenced by French, included *Johan*, *Jehan*, *Jean*, *Jon*, *Jan*. Flemish immigrants introduced forms such as *Hann* and *Jen*, together with their diminutive forms -kin, -cock, etc. Usual English pet form of John was **Jack**, and the use of all these names in the surname-formation period led to a wide variety of forms ranging from *Johnson*, *Jones*, *Jenkins*, *Hanson* to *Jackson* and *Hancock*. From the 16th c. until the 1950s John was consistently the most commonly-used name for boys in all English-speaking countries. Since that time has clearly been dropping out of favour, though alternative forms of the name have increased in use. See, for instance, the entries under **Ian**, **Iain**, **Sean**, **Jon**. The slang meaning of 'john' may have contributed to its decline. Unlike the two other outstandingly popular male Christian names – **William** and **Thomas** – John's influence has been greatly extended for centuries by the use of many feminine forms. These include **Jane**, **Jean**, **Joan**, **Joanna**, **Johanna**, **Janet**, **Jeanne**, **Sheona**, **Sheena**, etc. Seems likely that John will continue to decline in use in the immediate future, since there is a widespread tendency to turn away from traditional name forms. (*Johannes* and *Hans* in Germany, for example, have similarly been put aside in recent years, and the traditional names for girls, **Mary**, **Elizabeth** and **Margaret** are all out of favour.) Influence of the name will continue to be felt in the use of its more exotic forms, such as **Shaun** and **Joanne**.

Johnathan (m) See **Jonathan**.

Johnnie (m, f) See **Johnny**.

Johnny (m, f) Diminutive of **John** used as an independent name. In the 1980s used almost equally for boys and girls, especially in the U.S. Johnny is the most popular spelling, but **Johnnie** is very frequent. **Johnie** and **Johny** are also found, together with the variants **Jonnie**, **Jonney**, **Jonny**, **Johney**.

Johnson (m) Common surname, linked with **John**, used very regularly as a first name, especially in the 19th c.

Joi (f) Variant of **Joy**, influenced by French *joie* 'joy', much used by black American families in the early 1980s. Joie itself is sometimes found.

Jolean (f) Also **Joleen**. See **Jolene**.

Jolene (f) Modern blend of two fashionable name elements, *Jo*- and -*lene* to form a new name. Appeared in the U.S. in the early 1940s and gradually established itself. By the mid-1960s used in Britain. Ten years later the forms **Joleen** and **Jolean** had reached Britain. American parents also experimented in the 1940s with similar blends, such as **Jolyn**, **Jolynne**, **Jolinda**, but none has continued to be used regularly.

Jolie (f) French word for 'pretty' used as a first name. Occurs rarely in both British and U.S. records since the late 1960s, but with no indication as to its pronunciation. **Joley** also occurs, and **Jolly** has been used, the latter probably being inspired by the example of Jolly Forsyte, son of Jolyon in the *Forsyte Saga*. **Jolie** may, however, be a spelling variant of **Julie**.

Jolinda (f) See **Jolene**.

Jolyn(ne) (f) See **Jolene**.

Jolyon (m) Northern English form of **Julian**, made well known by the novelist John Galsworthy in *The Forsyte Saga* (1922). Came into sporadic use, and was then boosted by the television version of the book in the late 1960s. Modern variants of the name include **Jolean**, **Joleen**, **Jolian**.

Jon (m) Early variant spelling of **John** re-introduced in modern times to give a fresh look to an old name. No doubt **Jonathan** has been an influence, since many people consider it to be a fanciful form of John. Reappeared in the late 1920s and has steadily increased in numbers since then.

Jonah (m) Hebrew *Yonah* 'dove, pigeon', literally 'the moaning one'. Greek *Iones*, Late Latin *Jonas*. Biblical, O.T. The Book of Jonah tells the story of Jonah being thrown overboard and swallowed by a whale. Also associated with bad luck, and by the 19th c. had become synonymous with 'jinx'. In spite of this, has been regularly used as a Christian name, though never in great numbers. Latin form of the name **Jonas** more frequently found in English-speaking countries. In Britain often associated with Jonah Barrington, the squash player.

Jonas (m) Latin form of **Jonah**. Always the more popular form of the name in English-speaking countries. See further at **Jonah**.

Jonathan (m) Hebrew 'Jehovah has given' or 'Jehovah's gift'. **Nathaniel** and **Nathan** are names with a similar meaning, as is the Greek **Theodore**. Jonathan is Biblical, O.T., 2 Sam. 1:4. Best known as the friend of King David, and literary allusions to 'David and Jonathan' as the

symbol of true friendship were common in previous centuries. Rarely used until the 17th c. but then very popular, especially when carried over to America. At the Siege of Boston the British applied the name 'Brother Jonathan' to any American, or to the country as a whole, though the nickname had originally applied to Jonathan Trumbull, Governor of Connecticut. The nickname had the effect of causing Jonathan to go out of fashion, both in the U.S. and Britain, though it remained in quiet use. Rediscovered in the 1940s as parents looked for an alternative to **John**. Still being very well used at the beginning of the 1980s. Inevitable confusion with John, so that **Johnathan** is frequently found as a variant. **Jonathon** is also very common. Other variants include **Jonathen**, **Jonothon**, **Jonothan**. Short form **Jon** often used independently. One of the best-known bearers of the name was the satirical writer Jonathan Swift (1667–1745), best remembered for his *Gulliver's Travels*.

Jonella (f) Modern blend of **Jon** and **Ella** to make a new name. Used sporadically in the U.S. mainly in the 1960s.

Joni (f) Modern feminine form of **Jon**. Used with some frequency in the 1960s in the U.S. Also occurs in Britain. Pronounced **Joanie** (e.g. by singer Joni Mitchell (1943 –   ) or *Jonnie* and also spelt as **Johnnie**, **Jonnie**.

Jonnie (f) See **Joni**.

Jonquil (f) Flower name used as a first name. Introduced only in the 1940s and used throughout the 1950s in Britain. Then seems to have disappeared. Possibly seen as a feminine form of Jon.

Jordan (m,f) Name of the River Jordan: Hebrew *yārdan* 'to descend'. Used as a Christian name by returning Crusaders who brought back with them Jordan water for the baptism of their children. Popularity of the name in the Middle Ages shown by surnames such as *Judd*, *Jutte*, *Jurd* and *Jordan*. The Christian name was revived to some extent in the 19th c. and is now often feminine.

José (m) Spanish form of **Joseph**, used mainly in the U.S. by Spanish-speaking families.

Joseph (m) Hebrew 'Jehovah adds'. Biblical, O.T., Gen. 30:24, the name of the patriarch; N.T., Mat. 1:18, name of the husband of the Virgin Mary. The meaning of the name was probably a reference to large families. Joseph was the twelfth son of Jacob. In the Middle Ages was a Jewish name, but became far more generally used in the 17th c. Extremely well used throughout the 19th c. but has declined since the beginning of the 20th c. in Britain. By 1981 also showing signs of fading in the U.S., but still being used by both white and black American parents in considerable numbers. Irish parents remained faithful to it rather more than the English and Welsh. In Scotland well used until the 1950s but subsequently declined. **Joe** and **Joey** are used to some extent as names in their own right. Foreign forms include Polish/German **Josef**, Spanish **José**, Italian **Giuseppe**, together with pet forms such as Spanish **Che**, German **Sepp**. Joseph Cotten is one of the best-known actors to have borne the name. Also the name of Joseph Addison (1672–1719) essayist, Joseph Conrad (1857–1924) writer, Joseph Haydn (1732–1809) composer, and Joseph Lister (1827–1912) the founder of antiseptic surgery. In literature Joseph Andrews is the hero of a novel of that name by Henry Fielding. Normal feminine form of the name is French **Josephine**, but **Josepha**, **Josephe**, **Josette** also occur, together with the pet form **Josie**. In the 19th c. sometimes recorded in its Latin form, **Josephus**.

Josephine (f) French diminutive of **Josèphe**, feminine of **Joseph**. Pet name of Napoleon's wife, the Empress Marie Josèphe Rose. Its use in English-speaking countries began during her life-time, in the early years of the 19th c. Especially popular in Ireland 1920-50, with a corresponding peak of interest in the rest of Britain at that time. Quietly used elsewhere and probably not helped by the well-known phrase 'Not tonight Josephine.' Latinized **Josephina** is sometimes found, together with the variant **Josephene**. Pet form **Josie** has been much used as a name in its own right. French diminutive **Fifi** found only rarely as a girl's name, though well used for pets.

Josette (f) French feminine form of **Josephine** used in Britain since the 1940s.

Josh (m) Pet form of **Joshua** or **Josiah** used independently on rare occasions, though usage may well increase through the 1980s as Joshua rises in the popularity charts. The English novelist Horace Vachell found an original way to describe a 'pet name' or 'diminutive' in *The Disappearance of Martha Penny*: 'Josh was Mrs White's *nom de caresse* for Mr White, who had been baptised Joshua.'

Joshua (m) Hebrew 'Jehovah saves' or 'is generous'. **Jesus** is another form of the same name. Joshua is Biblical, O.T., the successor to Moses who led the Israelites into the Promised Land. Little used until the 18th c., when it became frequent until the middle of the 19th c. In Britain has remained in quiet use since then, whereas it has been highly fashionable in the U.S. and Canada since the 1960s, amongst white families at least. Reintroduced there by the television series *Here Come the Brides*, and now has a Western flavour. Historically speaking, the best-known bearer of the name was Joshua Reynolds (1732–93), the English portrait painter.

Josiah (m) Hebrew 'Jehovah supports'. Biblical, O.T., an upright king of Judah. Appears as **Josias** in the N.T. Rarely used in the 16th and 17th cc., but regular throughout the 18th c. Then continued in regular but infrequent usage until the 1940s, since when it has been rare. Josias used occasionally in the 19th c. but appears to be obsolete, though a **Jozias** Smith was named in

Britain in 1947. Kept before the public to some extent by Josiah Wedgwood (1730–95) and the company he founded to produce high-quality pottery. The Wedgwood family is reported to make use of the first name still and to use **Josh** as a pet form. The latter has been used on rare occasions as an independent name. **Si** is another pet form.

Josie (f) Pet form of **Josephine** used regularly if infrequently as a name in its own right since the beginning of the 20th c.

Jotham (m) Semitic (Hebrew *Jōthām* 'Jehovah is perfect'). Biblical, O.T., the youngest son of Gideon; also a king of Judah (Judges 9:5; Isaiah 1:1). Rarely used.

Joy (f) The word used as a name. Such usage began in the Middle Ages, and Reaney records at least one example of the name being given to a man. In the 17th c. the Puritans made limited use of Joy, sometimes as part of phrasal names such as *Joy-in-sorrow*. Modern use of the name began again in the 1880s and reached a minor peak in Britain in the 1950s. This was some time after **Joyce** had been fashionable, and it seems unlikely that Joy was ever thought of as a pet form of Joyce when given as a first name. French form **Joie** has been used as a name, and **Joye, Joi, Joya** are found, especially in the U.S.

Joyce (m, f) The personal name in early use was apparently Celtic, borne by a 7th c. Breton prince and saint, **Judocus**, Latinized as **Judocius**. In ordinary speech became **Josse, Jos, Joisse, Jouusse**, etc. Early forms of the name became fossilized in the French place names Saint-Josse and Saint-Judoce. Also found in the Netherlands as **Joost** (though **Joos** is a form of **Jozef**). Judocus is one of the possible origins of the surname *Joyce*, another being the Latin feminine name **Jocosa** 'merry, joyful'. The surname survived the Middle Ages, the masculine first name becoming virtually obsolete and the feminine name extremely rare. In Mrs Henry Wood's novel *East Lynne* (1861) there

is a Joyce Hallijohn. Her name is commented on by Captain Levison: 'Joyce. I never heard such a name. Is it a Christian or surname?' Joyce's name at that time was probably as unusual as that of her half-sister in the novel, **Aphrodite**. In 1897 Bardsley commented that the Puritans used Joyce but he clearly considered that the name became totally obsolete soon afterward, for he writes: '*Joyce* fought hard, but it was useless.' As it happens, the name was beginning to be used again when Bardsley wrote those words, and it very quickly became fashionable in Britain. By 1925 was in 3rd position, but then began to fade. By the 1980s once again a rarely used name. Reasonably well used throughout the 20th c. in the U.S., though never as popular as in Britain. The revival of the name had probably been brought about by popular novelists such as Edna Lyall (e.g. in her novel *In the Golden Days* (1885)).

Joycelyn (f) Diminutive of **Joyce** heavily influenced by **Jocelyn**, used this century with some regularity.

Juan (m) Spanish form of **John**, used regularly in the U.S. but rarely in other English-speaking countries. **Juana** and **Juanita** are the usual feminine forms.

Juanita (f) Spanish **Juana**, feminine of **Juan = John**, with diminutive ending. Pronounced Hwa-Nee-ta. Introduced into the U.S. at the beginning of the 20th c. and reasonably well used, especially in the 1950s. Pet form **Nita** occurs in Britain and the U.S. as an independent name.

Jubal (m) Hebrew 'ramshorn', used as a trumpet. The word 'jubilee' is from the same root. Biblical, O.T., said in Genesis to be the inventor of the flute and the lyre. Used to some extent in the 19th c. **Jubilee** itself has been used as a first name in Britain, e.g. in 1887 and 1897, when Queen Victoria celebrated her fiftieth and sixtieth jubilees.

Judas (m) See **Jude**.

Jude (m) Hebrew 'praise'. Biblical, O.T. and N.T., e.g. Gen. 29:35 'she conceived again and bore a son, and said, "This time I will praise the Lord"; therefore she called his name **Judah**.' Greek form of this name is **Judas**, but this is associated strongly with Judas Iscariot, the betrayer of Christ. If it were not for him the name would almost certainly have been well used in all English-speaking countries, since it names several other men in the Bible, including one of Christ's brothers. Also the name of another of the Apostles, the writer of the Epistle of Jude in the N.T. In literature Jude Fawley is the unhappy hero of Thomas Hardy's novel *Jude the Obscure*, which must have further dampened any enthusiasm for the name. Very rarely used in the 20th c., though two boys, one white and one black, received the name in 1977 according to the Detroit records. This modern flicker of interest in the name may well have been caused by the highly successful Beatles' song *Hey Jude*!

Judith (f) Hebrew *Yehudith* 'Jewish, Jewess'. Biblical, O.T., Gen. 26:34, Esau's wife. Also the *Book of Judith* in the Apocrypha. Had a minor spell of popularity in the 18th c., but otherwise infrequently used until 1925. Then rose steadily in the popularity charts in all English-speaking countries, especially in Australia. Also used more densely in the U.S. than in Britain. Since the 1950s has fallen away, largely replaced in Australia by forms of **Jody**. Jody has also increased in use in other English-speaking countries, but not to the same extent. Pet form **Judy** continues to be used steadily, though not in great numbers, on all sides.

Judy (f) Pet form of **Judith** used independently since the 18th c. By 1850 had disappeared, probably because of its slang meaning 'a girl of loose morals.' Reappeared in the 1920s and steadily used since in all English-speaking countries, especially the U.S. and Canada. Sometimes found as **Judie** or **Judi**. In Australia, especially, overtaken by the variant form **Jody** (**Jodi**, **Jodie**).

Jules (m) French form of **Julius**, rarely used in English-speaking countries.

Julia (f) Latin feminine of **Julius**. Common as a Christian name in Roman times but rare in English-speaking countries until the 18th c. Then regularly and frequently used throughout the 19th c. After a quiet period 1900–30 became fairly popular once again 1945–75, but was quickly overtaken, and virtually eclipsed, by its French form **Julie**. Continues to be used very regularly but remains outside the top fifty names in all English-speaking countries.

Julian (m) Derivative of **Julius** through the Latin **Julianus**. Julianus fairly common amongst early Christians. Julian was made known as the name of several saints, especially St Julian the Hospitaller, patron of innkeepers, travellers, boatmen, etc. In early records difficult to distinguish between Julian and **Juliana**, both being recorded frequently as Julian, though the feminine version was pronounced **Gillian**. Appears regularly from the 18th c., though infrequently. In Britain began to be used in earnest in the 1950s, with numbers increasing steadily into the 1970s when it levelled out. Sometimes used in the French form **Julien**, and variants such as **Julion**, **Julyan** have been noted, the latter perhaps a deliberate reminder of the name's link with the month of July, named for Julius Caesar. Variant **Jolyon** also used in modern times.

Juliana (f) Latin feminine of *Julianus*, from *Julius*, the Roman clan name. Very common name amongst the early Christians. A 4th c. saint bore the name. Usual pronunciation of the name when introduced to Britain in the late Middle Ages led to the form **Gillian**, which soon overtook Juliana. Original name revived in the 18th c. and in sporadic use ever since. Likely to live on in the future in another of its forms, **Liana** (**Liane**, **Lianne**, **Lianna**, etc.).

Julianne (f) Modern feminine of **Julian**, re-interpreting **Juliana**. In use since the late 1950s. **Julie-Ann**, **Juliane**, **Julieann**,

Julie-Anne (frequent) and **Julieanne** also used.

Julie (f) French feminine of Latin **Julius**. Began to be used in English-speaking countries in the 1920s and quickly became popular on all sides. One of the most popular names for a girl in the U.S. and Britain in the mid-1970s, but has since declined. In the 1960s publicized by the actresses Julie Andrews and Julie Harris. Julie Andrews was born Julia Wells and adopted the more fashionable version of her first name. Diminutive **Juliet** was used more often as Julie became popular (often as **Juliette**), and **Julie-Ann**(e) was especially favoured. In the U.S. both Julie and Julia seem to have appealed almost exclusively to white parents.

Julie-Ann(e) (f) See **Julianne**.

Julien (m) French form of **Julian**. Regularly but quietly used, especially in Britain.

Julienne (f) French feminine form of **Julien**, or **Julian** as it usually is in English-speaking countries. Enjoyed a minor vogue from the 1930s to the late 1950s, but very rare since.

Juliet (f) English adaptation of Italian **Giuletta**, a diminutive of **Giulia** (**Julia**), Associated with Shakespeare's Juliet, beloved of Romeo. Shakespeare used the name again in *Measure for Measure*, but Juliet Capulet is known to all. To her Shakespeare gave the famous speech which includes the phrase: 'What's in a name?' This is often taken to indicate that Shakespeare thought that names were unimportant, though in context it is clear that for all Juliet's desperate attempt to reason along those lines, she knows just how important they are. Quietly used until recent times, but the popularity of **Julie** from the 1950s onwards caused it to be used far more frequently. In Britain often found in its French form **Juliette**. Other variants include **Juliett** and **Julietta**.

Juliette (f) French form of **Juliet**, used in the 1960s and '70s when **Julie** was at its most popular. **Julietta** also found.

Julio (m) Spanish form of **Julius** used to some extent in the U.S.

Julitta (f) Diminutive of **Julia**. St Julitta was martyred at Caesarea in 303, but her name is very rarely used.

Julius (m) Roman clan name which the Romans themselves derived from Greek *ioulos* 'downy (bearded)' but which probably derived from *Jovilios* 'descended from Jove'. Common Christian name in Roman times, e.g. Pope Julius I 337–352. Always famous because of Gaius Julius Caesar, but very rarely used as a first name in English-speaking countries until the 19th c. Then used regularly until the early part of the 20th c. when it once again became very rare. Revived to some extent in the 1940s and continues to be used, especially by Jewish families. Derivative **Julian** has been rather more frequently used. French form **Jules** is occasionally met with, and Spanish **Julio** occurs in the U.S. Black American families sometimes use variants such as **Julious, Julias, Julas**. Used to some extent in the days of slavery, perhaps inspired by the common use of **Caesar** for male slaves.

June (f) Name of the month used as a first name. Consistently used since 1919, especially in Britain, where it was most popular in the 1950s. See **April** for fuller discussion of month names.

Junior (m) Used in Britain as a first name throughout the 1960s and into the early '70s. Possible that British parents misunderstood American vocative usage and thought that Junior was a first name. In the U.S. associated with Junior Samples (1927–83), a 'country bumpkin' comedian.

Junita (f) Simplified form of **Juanita** used occasionally in modern times. **Janita** developed in a similar way.

Justin (m) Latin *justus* 'just'. Common Christian name in early Rome, together with its feminine **Justina**. St Justin Martyr (11th c.) the greatest of the early Christian apologists. *Justinus* is found in Britain in the 14th c. In the 20th c. used in Ireland but hardly at all elsewhere until the 1970s, when it suddenly became very popular in Britain, America, Canada and Australia. **Justyn** also occurs. Justin will be especially well used in the U.S. throughout the 1980s.

Justina (f) Early feminine form in Latin of **Justin**. Justina occurs frequently as a Christian name in inscriptions of the Roman Empire. A St Justina in the 6th c. was greatly revered in Padua, where a church was built in her honour. In modern times, however, French form **Justine** rather more fashionable.

Justine (f) French feminine form of **Justin**. **Justina** was the more usual form until the 1960s. Lawrence Durrell's novel *Justine*, part of his *Alexandria Quartet* (1960) may have influenced use of the name.

K

Kai (f) Probably a short form of **Kylie** also found as **Ky** and **Kye**. Also a spelling variant of **Kay**. Very recently appeared in the U.S., where it is used by black American parents, but established in Britain by the 1960s. American usage may have been influenced by Sue Browder, author of *The New Age Baby Name Book*. She states that Kai is Hawaian for 'sea' or 'sea-water', its meaning in many Hawaian place names.

Kalvin (m) Form of **Calvin** in use since the 1960s.

Kandi (f) Also **Kandy**. Forms of **Candy** in use since the late 1950s.

Kane (m) Celtic; a contraction of *Mac-Cathain* 'son of *Cathain*' from *cath* 'warrior', or from the French place name *Caen*, Latin 'field of combat'. The surname which derives from these various sources has became a popular Christian name since 1960 in Australia. Kane Richmond (born Frederick Bowditch 1906-73) was in many second feature films from 1930.

Kara (f) Probably spelling variant of **Cara**, influenced by the popularity in modern times of **Karen** or the general fondness for K- spellings. Especially well used in the U.S. and may be an independent pet form of **Katherine**.

Karan (f) Variant of **Karen** in regular if infrequent use since the mid-1950s.

Karel (m) Dutch form of **Charles**. See also Carol.

Karen (f) Danish short form of **Katarina** which began to be used regularly in the 1930s in English-speaking countries, at first by Danish settlers in the U.S., where it had an immense success in the 1950s and '60s. Its success in Britain came only a few years later, reaching a peak in the 1960s. Since then there has been a reaction and the name is fading on all sides. Hard to find a specific reason for the sudden dramatic rise in popularity in all English-speaking countries. The sound of the name obviously struck a fashionable note. Names like **Sharon**, **Darren** also became far more popular during the period when Karen was being well used. The 'sound' theory is perhaps supported by the fact that the name has been used in a number of forms which seem to indicate that it had been heard by parents, but not seen. They often wrote it as **Karan**, **Karon**, **Karyn**, or used C- spellings, such as **Caren**, **Carin**, **Caron**, **Caronne**, **Carren**, **Carrin**, **Carron**, **Caryn**. Variant **Karin** is a legitimate Swedish form of the name, and by Swedish settlers in the U.S. it must have been used quite deliberately. For others it was no doubt simply a spelling alternative. In its various forms, the name has been given to thousands of young ladies born since 1945 in the various English-speaking countries. In the 1977 edition of *The Oxford Dictionary of English Christian Names* we are told that it is a name 'sometimes met with'. It is indeed. The same source is more helpful in mentioning the use of the name in a strip cartoon in the 1940s, featured in the British newspaper *The Daily Mirror*.

There is some evidence that Karen spread upwards through the social classes instead of downwards, as is more usual, so the cartoon character may well have been influential in the case of British parents.

Karena (f) Variant of **Karina**, influenced by **Karen**, in use since the 1960s. **Carina** also occurs.

Karenza (f) Form of the Cornish name **Kerensa** or **Kerenza** 'love, affection', influenced by **Karen**. A girl named Karenza is the daughter-heroine in Denys Val Baker's *Don't Lose Your Cool, Dad*. Used sporadically since 1950, rather more often than the correct form.

Karey (f) See **Karrie**.

Kari(e) (f) See **Karrie**.

Karin (f) Swedish equivalent of Danish **Karen**, far less frequently used than the Danish form. See **Karen** for a fuller discussion.

Karina (f) Variant of **Carina** or a shortened form of **Katarina**, or perhaps **Karin** with the traditional feminine -a ending. In use since the 1940s but now quietly used.

Karl (m) See **Carl**.

Karla (f See **Carla**.

Karleen (f) Also **Karlene, Karline, Karli, Karlie,** See **Carlene**.

Karol (m) Form of **Charles** in Polish and other languages. Found from time to time in English-speaking countries, and may be used on occasion to honour Pope John-Paul II.

Karrie (f) Form of **Carrie** which appeared in the 1960s. **Karie** is found as early as 1906 and **Kari** appeared in the 1950s. **Karey** and **Karry** occurred in the 1970s. For a discussion of possible confusion between Carrie and Kerry see **Kerry**.

Karyn (f) Spelling variant of **Karen** in occasional use.

Katarina (f) Form in several countries, e.g. Sweden, of **Catherine** or **Katherine**. Occasionally used in English-speaking countries.

Kate (f) Pet form of **Catherine/Katherine** since the Middle Ages, and long used as a name in its own right. Especially popular in the 1870s.

Katerina (f) Early Latin form of **Catherine/Katherine**, occasionally used in modern times.

Katey (f) See **Katie**.

Katharine (f) Old-established and frequently used variant of **Catherine/Katherine**. For the history and development see **Catherine**. Probably most associated in modern times with the actress Katharine Hepburn, whose highly successful film career began in the 1930s.

Katherine (f) For the history and development of the name see **Catherine**. The usual modern spelling of the name in the U.S. and Canada, Catherine being preferred in Britain. By chance is especially associated with two writers of short stories, namely the American Katherine Ann Porter and the New Zealand-born Katherine Mansfield, though the latter was actually Kathleen Mansfield Beauchamp.

Katheryn (f) Variant of **Kathryn** used since the 1950s. See also **Catherine**.

Kathleen (f) English form of Irish **Caitlin**, ultimately a form of **Catherine**. In use since the 1840s outside Ireland. At its most popular in Britain in the 1920s, but reached its greatest height in the U.S. only in the 1950s. The popular song 'I'll take you home again, Kathleen' was first heard in the 1870s. The actress Kathleen Harrison helped to make the name known from the 1930s onwards. Probably benefited most, however, from the general liking from 1920 on for Irish names such as **Eileen, Maureen, Doreen. Irene,** in its new two-syllable pronunciation, also a great success in the 1920s and probably thought of as being an Irish name. Still being used in the early 1980s, though more in the U.S. at that time than in Ireland. See under **Catherine** for the many variant forms.

Kathlyn (f) Blend of **Kathleen** and **Kathryn**, used regularly but with no great frequency since 1910.

Kathrine (f) Variant of **Katharine/ Katherine** much used since the 1860s.

Kathryn (f) Form of **Catherine/Katherine** already being used by 1912, but became common in the 1940s when the singer/actress Kathryn Grayson appeared on the screen. Now one of the commonest spellings of the name, especially in the U.S. and Canada. Miss Grayson was born Zelma Hedrick.

Kathy (f) One of the pet forms of **Catherine/Katherine** used as an independent name, especially since the 1950s. Publicized then by the British singer Kathy Kirby.

Katie (f) Diminutive of **Kate**, ultimately of **Katherine** or **Kathleen**, used independently since the mid-19th c. Katie is the usual form, but **Katey** and **Katy** occur regularly.

Katrina (f) Modern phonetic form of **Catriona** or **Katarina**, especially popular with black American families.

Katrine (f) Name of a Scottish loch, or form of **Catriona** (**Catherine**), in use since 1870s

Katy (f) See **Katie**.

Kay (m) Old Welsh **Cai**, Cornish **Kay** from Latin **Caius**. See **Gaius**. In ancient use but extremely rare in modern times.

Kay (f) Pet form of names beginning with K-, used in its own right since the 1880s, though in regular use only since the 1930s. **Kaye** used rather more often in the 19th c. but rarer in modern times. Much publicized throughout the 1940s and '50s by the British actress Kay Kendall (1926–59), born Justine McCarthy. Reached a minor peak of usage in Britain in the mid-1960s.

Kayley (f) Also **Kayleigh**. Form of **Kylie**, or an adaptation of **Kay** by analogy with **Keeley**. See also **Kelly**.

Kazia (f) Mainly 19th c. variant of **Keziah**.

Keeley (f) Another form of the Irish surname **Kelly**. See **Kelly** for details. Other variants are **Kealey, Kealy, Keelie, Keellie, Keely, Keighley**, though **Keiley, Keilly, Keily** are probably variants of **Kylie**.

Keir (m) Gaelic **cair** 'swarthy, dusky', or from a place name. Scottish surname occasionally used as a Christian name in Britain. Made known by the politician James Keir Hardie (1856–1915).

Keira (f) Feminine form of **Kieran**.

Keiran (m) See **Kieran**. **Keiron** also occurs, **Keiren** is rare.

Keisha (f) Probably a back-formation from **Lakeisha**, since the latter name was first used at the end of the 1960s by black American families. By the early 1980s Lakeisha had given birth to many variant forms, such as **Lakisha, Lakeesha, Lakesha, Lakesia, Lakeysha, Lakeyshia, Lakiesha, Laqueisha, Laquesha, Laquisha**. Keisha had likewise led to **Kecia, Keesha, Kesha, Keshia, Keysha, Kiesha, Kisha**, and to diminutives such as **Kishanda**. Original name possibly **Aisha/Ayesha**, which was linked to the fashionable prefix La- by the bridging sound 'k' to give Lakeisha/Lakisha.

Keith (m) Scottish place name of uncertain origin, possibly meaning 'wood'. Became a surname, then a first name. Rather like **Kenneth**, it was taken up by parents outside Scotland in the latter part of the 19th c. Slowly increased in popularity, reaching its peak in Britain in the 1950s. At its height in the U.S. some ten years later, but fading since 1970. Remarkable in the way it has avoided variant forms, though a **Keath** was named in 1944 in Britain. Feminine forms also extremely hard to find. One girl was named Keith in the U.S. in 1965, and a few years earlier a girl was named **Keita**. It is said that many pairs of cats in London have been named Keith and **Prowse**, an allusion to a theatre ticket agency which advertises with the slogan: 'You want the best seats – we have them.'

Kelda (f) Appeared in the 1960s and still being used in the 1970s, though only in Britain. Presumably helped by the popularity of names such as **Kelly**. Origin is a mystery. An Old Norse word **kelda** meaning a 'spring' became an element in several English place-names, but that must be coincidental. Definitely not a

Scandinavian personal name. The nearest one can get to it in personal name terms is **Kelday**, an old Orkney family name which has on rare occasions been used as a first name. Listed in the influential *What Shall We Name the Baby* (1935), by Winthrop Ames, though no evidence to show that the name was actually being used at that time. Authors of subsequent books have also listed it, giving it a printed 'authority' which is hardly justified.

Kellie (f) Also Kelley. See Kelly.

Kelly (f,m) Irish surname used as a first name, originally for boys, and still occasionally male. Probably derives from *O Ceallaigh* 'strife', the personal name *Ceallach* usually being interpreted as 'the warlike one'. There are also Scottish places called Kelly where a derivation from Pictish 'holly' or 'wood' has been suggested. An immense success in recent times, reaching its peak in 1970 in the U.S. and Canada, in 1981 in Britain (4th place). The various forms in use make it clear that parents have been responding to an overall shape and sound rather than to the family name. Individual preferences in spelling and slightly variant pronunciations are shown in the following: **Kealey, Kayley, Kaylee, Kealy, Keelie, Keely, Kieli, Kieley, Kiley, Kelley, Kellie, Keighley, Keiley, Keily, Keilly.** In some instances it merges with the mainly Australian **Kylie**, also found as **Kylee**. The male name **Kyle** is occasionally used for girls. Few of the above forms found as first names in the English-speaking world before the late 1950s. They probably divide into three basic names which may be grouped under the main spellings, namely Kelly, Kylie and Keeley. The obvious reasons for the sudden interest in the various names are not clear. Although not used in great numbers, the male name Kyle came into use first of all, in the late 1940s; it would therefore seem that this was first borrowed, then adapted, for feminine use. The adaptation may have

been suggested by Grace Kelly, who played a leading role in the film *High Society* (1956). The names of the character she portrayed in the film, **Tracy Samantha**, were certainly taken up.

Kelly-Ann(e) (f) Popular name combination in the 1970s.

Kelsey (m) English place name and surname used as a first name in modern times, but infrequently. Original meaning of the name is probably 'Ceol's island'. **Kelsie** occurs, and **Kelcey** is used for girls. Mainly modern and found mostly in the Southern states of the U.S., but a Kelsey Smith was named in England in 1871, and a Kelsie in 1917. **Kelsa** also occurs in the 1970s, probably an attempt to form a feminine name from Kelsey.

Kelvin (m) Celtic: a Scottish river name of uncertain origin used as a Christian name mainly in Britain and Canada in the 1920s. The British physicist, William Thomson (1824–1907), raised to the peerage in 1892 as Baron Kelvin of Largs may have contributed to the use of the name. **Kelvyn** is the usual variant.

Ken (m) Pet form of **Kenneth** used in modern times as a name in its own right. **Kenn** is also found.

Kendall (m) Surname, from the place name Kendal (Westmorland, England) meaning 'valley of the river Kent', used as a Christian name since the mid-19th c. **Kendal** itself is used, and **Kendell** is a rare variant.

Kendra (f) Probably a blend of **Kenneth** and **Alexandra** or **Sandra**. Enjoyed a spell of minor popularity in the U.S. in the late 1940s, but only appeared in the late 1960s in Britain. Black American parents are now especially fond of it.

Kendrick (m) See Kenrick.

Kenelm (m) Old English *cene* 'brave' and *helm* 'helmet'. Name of a 9th c. saint venerated in the Middle Ages. Recorded as a Christian name in current use by Camden (1605). Still used occasionally.

Kennedy (m) Irish surname *O Cinneide*, from *ceann* 'head' and *eidigh* 'ugly', in occasional use in modern times as a first name. Found in all English-speaking countries.

Kenneth (m) English form of two Gaelic names, *Coinneach* 'fair one' and *Cinaed* 'fire-sprung'. Formerly a Scottish name, its early use being captured in the surname *MacKenzie*, but it was taken up more generally in the 1870s. Began to be a fashionable name in Britain at the start of the 20th c., and at its height in the 1920s and '30s. Reached the U.S. rather later, scoring its greatest success throughout the 1950s and '60s. Since 1970 fading on all sides. **Kennith** is found as a variant, and pet forms **Ken** and **Kenny** have been used sporadically as independent names. **Kennice, Kenia, Kena** and **Kenza** are amongst the feminine forms which have been created, though none used with any great frequency. **Kendra** may have been interpreted by some parents as a feminine form of Kenneth. Associated in Britain with Kenneth Grahame (1859–1932), author of *Wind in the Willows* and with actors Kenneth More (1914–82), Kenneth Williams and Kenneth Griffith. In fiction there is a Sir Kenneth in Scott's *Talisman*, really the Prince Royal of Scotland in disguise. Will probably revert in the future to being purely Scottish again, but the authors of the *Harrap Book of Boys and Girls Names*, published in 1973, could hardly have been more wrong when they said 'Most modern bearers are of Scottish origin or extraction.' That statement could correctly have been made in 1873, but it will be well into the 21st century before it becomes true again.

Kenny (m) Pet form of **Kenneth**, used infrequently as a name in its own right. **Kennie** also occurs, but usually a feminine form.

Kenrick (m) Celtic: Welsh *Cynwrig* 'chief hero'. Old English also had *Cynric* 'royal ruler'. These personal names survived only in surname form until the 19th c., then became first names. Other spellings include **Kenric, Kendrick, Kenerick, Kerrick**.

Kent (m) Place name, English county of Kent, of disputed origin, possibly 'rim, border'. Became a surname which has been used in modern times as a Christian name, especially in the U.S. and Canada.

Kentigern (m) Celtic: possibly 'chief lord'. Glasgow's patron saint and used as a Christian name there mainly in the 16th and 17th cc. In modern times the saint's nickname **Mungo** has been preferred.

Kenton (m) Common place name of several different origins which became a surname. Now used regularly as a first name (since the 1950s), especially in Britain, but also in the U.S.

Keren (f) Short form of **Kerenhappuch**, used as an independent name. No connection with **Karen**.

Kerenhappuch (f) Hebrew 'horn of antimony (eyelash dye)', presumably drawing attention to the beautiful eyes of the bearer. Biblical, O.T., the third daughter of Job (Job 42:14). Introduced by the Puritans in the 17th c. and still found in the 20th c. in the U.S. and Britain, usually reduced ·to **Keren**.

Kerensa (f) Also **Kerenza**. Cornish name meaning 'love, affection.' Much liked by novelists who are using a Cornish setting, e.g. by Victoria Holt in *The Legend of the Seventh Virgin*. Used since the early 1970s, but more often in its variant form **Karenza**.

Keri(e) (f) See **Kerry**.

Kermit (m) Variant of the Irish name **Dermot**, now little used though made famous recently by Kermit the Frog in *The Muppets*.

Kerr (m) Scottish surname, derived from a place-name, used especially in Scotland as a first name, though infrequently.

Kerrick (m) See **Kenrick**.

Kerri(e) (f) See **Kerry**.

Kerry (m, f) The Irish county, originally the place of 'Ciar's people', used as a first name. At first a male name used in Australia (in the 1940s) but now considered to be a girl's name. Popularity was still rising as such in 1980, though only in Britain. In the U.S. used quietly. Kerry is the most usual form, but it occurs frequently as **Kerrie** and **Kerri. Keri** came into use surprisingly early, and has continued. **Kerie** is another variant, as are **Keree, Kerrey.** The female name may be from **Carrie.** The male name may originally have been a re-spelling of Welsh *Ceri.*

Kerry-Ann (f) Popular double name used since the 1960s. Also found as **Kerri-Ann, Kerrianne, Kerryann, Kerry-Anne.**

Kersti(e) (f) See **Kirsty.**

Kerwin (m) Probably from Irish *O Ciardhubhain* 'dark' or 'black'. Used from time to time in the 20th c. Also occurs as **Kervin** in the U.S. **Kerwaine** has also been noted.

Kes (m) The name of Billy Casper's pet kestrel in Barry Hines's novel *A Kestrel for a Knave,* later made into the British film *Kes.* Clearly the name was derived from the word 'kestrel' itself. Taken up and used by some British parents as a first name in the 1970s.

Kester (m) Colloquial form of **Christopher** in early times, occasionally brought into use this century.

Keturah (f) Hebrew *Qeturah* 'incense'. Biblical O.T., name of the second wife of Abraham (Gen. 25:1). Introduced in the 17th c. by the Puritans. Used frequently until the 20th c.

Kevan (m) Normally a variant of **Kevin** but can be the Scottish surname used as a first name.

Keverne (m) See **Kevin.**

Kevin (m) Irish *Caomhin* 'handsome at birth'. Irish saint. Exclusively Irish until the 1920s. By 1945 rapidly coming into fashion in Britain, and picking up in the U.S. Still being well-used in the early 1980s, but had passed its peak by about 1965, having been extremely successful in all English-speaking countries. **Kevan** is often found, occasionally before Kevin became popular, in which case it is probably a transferred use of the Scottish surname rather than a spelling variant of Kevin. **Kevyn** also occurs,

though infrequently. Variant **Keverne,** used in the 1950s, and '60s, shows the influence of the Irish surname. **Keva** also appeared in the 1970s, presumably based on the name and turning it into a feminine form.

Kezia(h) (f) Hebrew *qetziah* 'cassia'. Biblical, O.T., one of the daughters of Job. First used by the 17th c. Puritans; a favourite name of the 18th c. and common in the 19th c. Quietly used since. Taken to Georgia in 1735 by Keziah Wesley, sister of John Wesley. Became a popular slave name there (cf. **Wesley),** often in its pet forms **Kizzie,** or **Kissie.**

Kiana (f) Also **Quiana, Quianna.** Probably a modernised form of **Anna,** using a fashionable prefix. Used in its various forms by black American families in the early 1980s. Pet form **Kia** also well used in its own right.

Kiara (f) Feminine form of **Kiaran,** name of a 7th c. Irish saint sometimes confused with the earlier St **Kieran.** Infrequently used.

Kiera (f) Feminine form of **Kieran.**

Kieran (m) Irish *Ciaran* 'dark, black'. Two early Irish saints. Began to be used again by Irish parents, especially, in the 1950s. By the 1970s clearly becoming fashionable in its various forms, which include **Kieron, Keiran, Keiren, Keiron, Kieren, Kyran.** The Kieran spelling is technically more 'correct', but it seems likely that the 'o' spellings, Kieron and Keiron, will become the more usual. This points to the influence of the Irish actor Kieron Moore (Kieron O'Hanrahan), who has been giving the name publicity by his screen appearances since the 1940s. **Kiera** and **Keira** have been used as feminine forms. Noted in the U.S. in the 1970s but not yet as well established.

Kilian (m) Irish *ceallach* 'strife'. Variant of *Cillian* or *Killian,* the name of an Irish saint. In occasional modern use.

Kim (f) Pet form of **Kimberley** or **Kimberly** used as a name in its own right. Kim is the hero of a famous novel by Rudyard Kipling, published in 1901.

His real name is **Kimball** O'Hara. The book does not seem to have had much influence on the name, other than to cause it to be used occasionally as a male name. It was really launched by Eda Ferber's *Showboat* (1926), later filmed three times, in which there is a female character called Kim. Use of the name picked up considerably because of the publicity given to Kim Novak in the early 1950s. Miss Novak had also adopted the name, having been given the name Marilyn by her parents. Another actress, Kim Stanley, later came along to reinforce the name. Miss Stanley was originally Patricia Kimberly Reid. In Britain Kim climbed steadily into the 1960s, then faded. In the U.S. Kim was reasonably well used, but it was **Kimberley** which really rocketed up the popularity charts.

Kimba (f) See **Kimberley**. Kimber also occurs.

Kimball (m) See **Kim**.

Kimberley (m, f) Town in South Africa associated with diamonds and hence, perhaps, with wealth and luxury in general. The town was named for Lord Kimberley, who in turn bore a surname which derived from an English place name. Original meaning was 'land belonging to *Cyneburg*'. In 1900 Kimberley was a well-known name to the British public, since British soldiers were fighting there. Many boys received the name at that time to commemorate their fathers' activities, and in some instances, the place where they had died. The male name no longer used after 1905, however. When it re-emerged in the 1940s it had become a girl's name and was more usual in its U.S. spelling, **Kimberly**, or in its short form of **Kim**. In the U.S. and Canada, Kimberly went on to become one of the most frequently used names in the 1960s and 70s. By 1980, though it was still being well used, it was clearly fading from the scene at great speed. The name's standard form in modern times, in all English-speaking countries, is definitely Kimberly, with Kimberley accounting for only one instance in twelve in the U.S., rather more in Britain. Many other variants are found, however, including the frequent **Kimberlee**, as well as **Kimbely, Kimberely, Kimberlea, Kimberlei, Kimberli, Kimberlie, Kimba Lee, Kimbley**. The back-formations **Kimber** and **Kimba** have been used, and the extended form **Kimberlyn** was not uncommon. Apart from the independent use of the pet form **Kim**, there was a noticeable liking for the combination **Kim Marie**. This sometimes became **Kimarie**. One can also note the use of **Kimette, Kimiko, Kimmie** and **Kimmy**. In a few instances, Kimberly was still being used in the late 1960s as a male name. See also **Kim**.

Kimberly (f) Usual modern form of **Kimberley**, but see under that name and **Kim**.

Kimberlyn (f) See **Kimberley**.

Kim Marie (f) See **Kimberley**.

King (m) Old English *cyning* 'king'. Surname since the 13th c. As a modern first name is especially associated with black Americans, many of whom use it to commemorate Dr Martin Luther King (1929–68). Previously a slave name, one bestowed ironically by sailors on the slave ships or by plantation owners. Dickens comments in *Our Mutual Friend*: 'there's usually a King George, or a King Boy, or a King Sambo, or a King Bill, or Bull, or Rum, or Junk, or whatever name the sailors may have happened to give him.' 'Where?' asked Rokesmith. 'Anywhere in Africa. Pretty well everywhere, I may say; for black kings are cheap.' One bearer of the name was King Camp Gillette, first president of Gillette Industries and the man who patented disposable razor blades in 1902. Even better known was the film director King Vidor.

Kingsley (m) Common English place name 'king's wood or clearing' which became a surname. First-name usage began in the life-time of Charles Kingsley (1819–75), author of *The Water Babies* and *Westward Ho!* Continued regularly, if infrequently. Kingsley Martin (1897–1969), editor of the *New Statesman* (1931-62), kept it in the public eye, followed by the English novelist Kingsley Amis in the 1950s. Well used until 1970, but seems to have disappeared since. At least one instance of its use for a girl has been noted. Does not seem to have reached the U.S.

Kirby (m, f) English place name, simplification of Kirkby, 'church farm or village'; also a surname. Used as a Christian name in the 19th c.

Kirk (m) Old Norse *kirkja* 'church'. Early surname recorded as a Christian name in Britain in the 1860s. Revived in the 1940s after being much publicized by the actor Kirk Douglas, who adopted that name (he was born Issur Danielovitch Demsky) in 1941.

Kirsten (f) Norwegian and Danish form of **Christine** used 1940–80 in English-speaking countries other than Scotland, where the name has been in regular use for a much longer period. Swedish form **Kersten** is also found, but rarely. Other spelling variants include **Kerstine**, **Kersten**, **Keirstan**, **Kirsteen** (frequent), **Kirstien**, **Kirstin** (frequent), **Kirstine**, **Kirston**, **Kirstyn**.

Kirstie (f) See Kirsty.

Kirstin (f) See Kerstin, Kirsten.

Kirsty (f) Scottish pet form of **Christine**. Since the 1950s has been taken up outside Scotland. By 1980 had edged its way into the top fifty names for girls in England and Wales. Variant forms include **Kirstie**, **Kirsti**, **Kerstie**. The influence of **Kerstin** and **Kirsten** has led to **Kirstyn**. **Kyrsty** is also found. In the U.S. not yet as popular, and the forms Kirstie, Kirsti seem to be preferred. A character in R. L. Stevenson's *Weir of Hermiston* is addressed as 'Miss Kirstie'. She immediately asks the speaker to call her 'Miss **Christina**, if you please. I canna bear the contraction.' Modern parents obviously have other views.

Kirstyn (f) See Kirsty, Kirsten, Kerstin.

Kirton (m) Common English place name 'settlement with a church' which became a surname. Used regularly if infrequently as a first name since the mid-19th c.

Kissie (f) Pet form of **Keziah**.

Kit (m) Early pet form of **Christopher**, used on rare occasions as an independent name. Well-known bearer of the name was Kit Carson (1809–68), the trapper and Indian agent. The island in the West Indies, discovered by Christopher Columbus, St Kitts, was named for himself and his patron saint.

Kitty (f) Early pet form of **Katharine**, later **Kathleen**, used independently. Reasonably popular until the 16th c., by which time it had become a term for a 'loose woman'. Returned to use in the 18th c. and was used regularly until the 1930s. Subsequently became rather rare.

Kizzy (f) Made famous in modern times by Alex Haley's novel *Roots*. In the book the name is explained by the hero Kunta as 'you sit down' or 'you stay put' in the Mandinka language. Kunta sees this as meaning that 'unlike Bell's previous two babies, this child would never get sold away'. But Kizzy, **Kizzie**, **Kissie**, etc. were common slave names and are far more likely to have derived from **Keziah**.

Knight (m) Surname used as a first name. Similar surnames such as **Knightley**, **Knightly** have also been pressed into service.

Kody (m,f) Also **Kodee**, **Kodi**, **Kodie**. Forms of **Cody** in modern use.

Korina (f) See Corinne.

Kris (m) Pet form of **Kristian** or **Kristofer** used independently. Usage in the 1970s probably due to popularity of the actor/ singer Kris Kristofferson.

Krista (f) Czech, Estonian and Latvian form of **Christina** or **Christine**, or variant of **Christa**. Well used in the U.S. since the mid-1960s, especially by white Americans.

Kristen (f) Mixture of **Kirsten** and **Kristina** or **Kristine**. Brings about a Scandinavian-looking name that is not actually used in Scandinavia. Used mostly in the U.S. since the 1960s. **Kristan** also occurs.

Kristi(e) See **Kristy**.

Kristian (m) Danish form of **Christian**, long-established as a royal name there. Used in English-speaking countries in increasing numbers since 1960.

Kristin (f) Shortened form of **Kristina** or **Kristine** perhaps influenced by Swedish **Kerstin**. Fairly well used, especially in the U.S., 1940–80.

Kristina (f) Swedish form of **Christina** used increasingly in English-speaking countries since the early 1950s. **Krystina** and **Krystyna** also occur, being the Czech and Polish forms respectively.

Kristine (f) Form of **Christine** in several languages, e.g. Norwegian. Used in English-speaking countries since the 1940s (mainly U.S. and Canada), reaching Britain in the 1960s. Kristine has been the more popular form in the U.S., while **Kristina** has been more frequently used in Britain. Both names almost exclusively used by white families. By the beginning of the 1980s they had clearly passed their peak and were fading quickly.

Kristopher (m) Form of **Christopher** influenced by Scandinavian **Kristofer**.

Kristy (f) Pet form of **Kristen**, **Kristina**, etc., used independently, especially in the 1970s. In the U.S. the form **Kristi** is also very popular, though **Kristie** is second choice in Britain.

Krystina (f) See **Kristina**.

Krystle (f) Form of **Crystal** borne by character in TV series *Dynasty*, played by Linda Evans.

Kurt (m) German diminutive of **Konrad**, used in English-speaking countries (along with its variant **Curt**) since the 1950s.

Kyla (f) Apparently a feminine form of **Kyle** used occasionally in modern times in the U.S.

Kyle (m, f) Irish surname but originally a Scottish surname deriving from a place name. Original Gaelic word means 'a strait, narrow piece of land', though Johnston suggested in his *Place-Names of Scotland* a possible link with 'Old King Cole'. Place name probably helped to give rise to the legend about the supposed king. If the place took its name from the nearby river, a tributary of the Ayr, the meaning would still be 'narrow', though the reference would be to the narrowness of the stream. Introduced in the U.S. in the late 1940s as a first name and used quietly since then. May have influenced the later use of several feminine names (see **Kelly**), itself being used on occasions to name girls.

Kylie (f) From the language of the Aborigines of Western Australia. Listed in a vocabulary of 1832 as 'curl, curled stick or boomerang'. Its use as a girl's Christian name has been confined almost exclusively to Australia, where in 1975 it was the third most frequently used name for girls born that year. **Kellie** was also popular there at the same time, and for the possible link between the names, see **Kelly**.

Kym (f) See **Kim** and **Kimberley**.

Kyra (f) Greek, feminine of *kyrios* 'lord'. Thus a feminine form of **Cyril**. In the U.S. used consistently, if infrequently, by black American families. Also used regularly in Britain since the 1960s.

Kyran (m) Early variant of **Kieran** used by one of the Irish saints of that name. Occurs as a modern variant.

L

Laban (m) Hebrew *laban* 'white'. Biblical, O.T., Gen. 24:32, the name of Laban the Syrian, brother of Rebecca, Isaac's wife. Introduced in the 17th c. with other O.T. names and used intermittently since, especially in the 19th c.

Lacey (m) Surname deriving from a French place name, used as a first name. Occurs regularly in the 19th c., rarely in the 20th c. Variant **Lacy** also found.

Lachlan (m) Gaelic **Lachlann** or **Lachunn**. Probable meaning is 'fjordland', i.e. Norway. Very rarely used outside Scotland, where it was ranked 35th in 1858, but 92nd in 1935.

Lachlanina (f) Scottish feminine form of Lachlan, very rarely used.

Lacy (m) See Lacey.

Ladonna (f) This is **Donna** with the La-prefix. The latter is immensely popular with black American families in the early 1980s. The range of names in use is indicated below: Labrenda, Lacara, Lachana, Lachelle, Lachina, Lachonda, Lachresa, Lacole, Lacoria, Lacrecia, Lacyndora, Ladaisha, Ladawn, Ladiva, Ladon, Ladonne, Ladonya, Lafondra, Lajessica, Lajoia, Lajuliette, Lakaiya, Lakea, Lakecia, Lakedia, Lakeesh, Lakeisha, Lakendria, Lakenya, Lakesha, Lakesia, Lakeysha, Lakia, Lakida, Lakila, Lakisha, Lakita, Lakiya, Lakresha, Lakrisha, Lakshana, Lameeka, Lamonica, Lanata, Lanecia, Laneetra, Laneisha, Lanetta, Lanette, Laniece, Lanisha, Lanora, Lapaula, Laqualia, Laquana, Laquanda, Laquarius, Laqueena, Laquela, Laquesha, Laqueta, Laquilla, Laquinda, Laquisha, Laquita, Larena, Laresa, Laresha, Laretha, Larinda, Larissa, Larita, Laseana, Lashana, Lashanda, Lashanna, Lashannon, Lashanta, Lasharon, Lashaun, Lashauna, Lashaunda, Lashaunia, Lashaunta, Lashawn, Lashawna, Lashawnda, Lashea, Lasheba, Lasheele, Lashell, Lashenia, Lasherri, Lashon, Lashona, Lashonda, Lashunda, Lashundra, Lasonda, Lasonya, Lastarr, Lataisha, Latania, Latanya, Latarisha, Latarra, Latasha, Latashia, Latavis, Lateisha, Latenna, Latesha, Latia, Laticia, Latina, Latisha, Lativia, Latoia, Latona, Latonia, Latonya, Latora, Latosha, Latoshia, Latoya, Latoyia, Latrecia, Latrice, Latricia, Latrina, Latrisha, Lavanna, Laveda, Laverne, Lavetta, Lavon, Lavonne, Lawanda, Lawanna, Lawanza. In all cases the prefix is presumably sounded, since names like Laura and Lauren are not much favoured by black Americans. Although the range of names is very great, a few of the above are used far more intensively than the rest, namely **Lakeisha/Lakisha**, **Latasha**, **Latisha**, **Latonya**, **Latoya**, **Latrice**.

Lady (f) A 'title' name, occasionally used in the 20th century. Around 1900 it was used in Britain by Smith families in particular, with special reference to Ladysmith, a place in South Africa of significance in the Boer War. In the U.S. Lady is one of the most popular names for a female dog.

Laetitia (f) Very rare form of **Letitia**.

Lafayette (m) The surname was made famous in American history by General Marie Joseph Paul Yves Roch Gilbert du Motier, Marquis de Lafayette (1757–1834). He joined Washington's army in 1777 and was wounded at Brandywine. His triumphal tour of the U.S. 1824–5 made his name known on all sides. Used regularly if infrequently ever since, though only in the U.S. Pet forms are Fate and Lafe.

Laila (f) See Leila.

Lakeisha (f) Also **Lakisha**, which is used in almost equal numbers by black American families in the early 1980s. This is the fashionable prefix La-used with a second element, possibly Aisha or Aiesha/Ayesha, which is also fashionable. See also **Ladonna** and **Keisha**.

Lalage (f) Greek *lalage* from *lalagein* 'to babble'. *Lalein* is 'to talk, prattle'. The name was used by the Roman poet Horace, and has appealed to poets and writers ever since. W. E. Henley begins

157

his *Ballad of Ladies' Names* with the words:

Brown's for Lalage, Jones for Lelia,
Robinson's bosom for Beatrice
glows. . .

but the number of Brown families who have named a daughter Lalage must be very small indeed. Coleridge had earlier asked in poetry whether his loved one wished to be called 'Lalage, Neaera, Chloris, Sappho, Lesbia, or Doris, Arethusa or Lucrece?' She sensibly replied: 'Choose thou whatever suits the line. . . Only, only call me Thine.' More recently the name occurred in John Fowles's immensely successful novel *The French Lieutenant's Woman*. ' "Lalage." She pronounced it as a dactyl, the "g" hard. (Mr Rossetti) proposed the name. He is her godfather. I know it is strange.' Evidence of modern use is extremely hard to come by, but Lallie and Lally have been used.

Lallie (f) Pet form of Lalage used independently. Lally also occurs, but both forms are rare.

Lambert (m) Old German 'land bright'. The 7th c. saint Lambert was especially venerated in Flanders and the name introduced to England from there. Gave rise to several surnames, such as *Lambert*, *Lambard*, *Lampard*, etc. (though some such names can have a different origin). Remained very popular throughout the 16th c., regularly if less frequently used through the 18th and 19th cc. In the 19th c. became rather rare, though there was a flurry of interest in the 1880s. Rarely used since the 1920s. Possibly died away at the beginning of the 19th c. because it was most associated at that time with Daniel Lambert, who died in 1809 as the fattest man in England. He weighed 739 pounds.

Lamont (m) Surname used as a first name. First-name usage occurred mainly in the 1940s and only in the U.S. Best-known bearer of the family name at that time was probably Thomas Lamont, the American banker and benefactor of Harvard University. Original meaning of the surname was 'lawman'.

Lana (f) Short form of Alana. Much publicized by the actress Lana Turner, who changed her Christian name from Julia in 1935. There is a word 'lanate', which means 'having a woolly covering' (from Latin *lana* 'wool'), but apt though this description might be for a star who made sweaters famous, it was presumably a coincidence.

Lance (m) Pet form of Lancelot used independently. First appears in the 1880s, but at its most popular in the 1940s and '50s, first in the U.S., later in Britain. Launce is occasionally found.

Lancelot (m) Usual English form of Launcelot, a major figure in the Arthurian legends. The tale was composed in the 12th c. in Latin, and soon appeared in French and English versions. Miss Withycombe would derive the name from an Old German Lanzo. In the 17th c. Camden thought the name had simply been invented by one of the early writers, a view supported by Professor Weekley. Eric Partridge gives by far the most convincing explanation, which links the name with the commonly used Norman personal name Ancel 'servant'. This had a diminutive form Ancelot, and also a feminine Ancelle. The French surnames *Lancel*, *Lancelle* make it clear that the name was often used with the definite article. By coincidence, the Shakespearean Lancelot, or Launcelot, *is* a servant in *The Merchant of Venice*. Introduced with some regularity in English-speaking countries in the early 19th c., continued to be used regularly if infrequently until the 1940s, but has since become very rare. In modern times short form Lance has been more successful. Launcelot has been used less often than Lancelot. Minor variants include Lancelott, Lancelet, Launclet. One modern bearer of the name whose writings are well-known is Lancelot Hogben, author of *Mathematics for the Millions*.

Lane (m) English surname originally indicating somebody who lived near a lane. In regular but quiet use since the 1940s in the U.S., but not yet recorded in Britain. American families also use the variant **Layne**. Listed in 1935 in *What Shall We Name the Baby?*, by Winthrop Ames.

Lara (f) In Roman mythology alternative name for Larunda or Lala, supposedly a nymph deprived by Jupiter of her tongue for having betrayed him to Juno. Used in modern Italy, where it is explained as a pet form of **Larisa** or **Larissa**, the name of a Greek martyr. Modern use in English-speaking countries probably stems from the character in Boris Pasternak's novel *Doctor Zhivago* (filmed in 1965). Byron's poem *Lara* is his sequel to *The Corsair*, Lara being the name assumed by the hero after the death of Medora.

Laraine (f) Modern variant of **Loraine/Lorraine**, in use since the early 1940s. Larraine also occurs. Ivor Morris suggests derivation from French *la reine* 'the queen' and compares Leroy.

Larissa (f) Latin *hilaris* 'laughing, cheerful'. Probably adaptation of Russian **Larisa**. A U.S. commentator suggests that the name has been used as the feminine of **Larry**. In use only since the 1960s.

Lark (f) From the name of the bird (perhaps by mistaken analogy with **Robin**, which derives from **Robert** as a Christian name). Also a family name and transference may have occurred. Used as a first name mainly in the U.S. in the 1950s.

Larraine (f) Variant of **Loraine/Lorraine** in use since the 1940s. In the 1970s this form preferred to **Laraine**.

Larry (m) Pet form of **Laurence** or **Lawrence**, used independently since the beginning of the 20th c. Especially popular in the U.S. in the 1950s. In Britain used far more quietly.

Lars (m) Normal Swedish form of **Laurence**. The reduction occurred in stages,

Laurens becoming *Lauris*, then *Laris*, then *Lars*. This form of the name occasionally used in English-speaking countries.

Latasha (f) La- plus **Tasha**, presumably from **Natasha**. See also **Ladonna**. In frequent use amongst black American families in the early 1980s.

Latisha (f) Modern form of **Letitia** used mainly by black American families. **Tisha** also occurs as an independent name.

Latonia (f) Variant of **Latonya**.

Latona (f) See **Latonya**.

Latonya (f) **Tonya** with the fashionable **La-** prefix, used almost exclusively by black American families. **Latonia** also occurs, and the name occasionally becomes **Latona**. In the latter form it was known to the Romans as the mother of a goddess, but that is almost certainly a coincidence. Compare **Lasonia**, **Lasonya**, **Latanya**, etc., all well used by the black community.

Latoya (f) Modern name, used almost exclusively by black American families or West Indians in Britain. Appears to be a simplified form of **Latonya**.

Latrice (f) Probably La- (see **Ladonna**) with a second element which ultimately derives from **Patrice/Patricia**. Well used by black American families in the early 1980s.

Launcelot (m) See **Lancelot**.

Laura (f) Latin feminine of *laurus* 'bay, laurel'. In Roman times the male name **Laurus** is found, but not Laura. Feminine forms at that time were **Lauricia**, **Laurina** and **Laurentia**. The significance of the laurel lay in the use of its leaves to decorate a victor or otherwise distinguished person. The sense of the name is indicated in a phrase like 'poet *laureate*'. Made famous by the 14th c. Italian poet Petrarch, who addressed countless sonnets to a lady of the name. If she was a real person, she was probably Laura de Noves, who married Hugues de Sade and had eleven children by him before dying of the plague. Petrarch's relationship with her was almost certainly purely poetical, and as Byron cynically remarked:

Think you, if Laura had been Petrarch's wife,
He would have written sonnets all his life?

The name was well established in England by the 16th c., but only as **Lora**. Became rare by the 18th c. but was revived strongly in the mid-19th c. By 1875 one of the top fifty names in Britain and the U.S. In the American top fifty ever since (which can be said of few names) but in Britain it tailed off at the beginning of the 20th c. A film and popular song called *Laura* reintroduced the name to Britain in the 1940s. Then slowly came into fashion and reached the top ten by the early 1980s, looking set to continue rising. In the U.S. and Britain Laura is almost exclusively a white name, being ignored almost completely by black families. Early form Lora used sporadically in the 19th c. in Britain, and still found in the U.S., though the pet form **Lori** is more common. An old pet form of Laura was **Lolly** (compare **Mary-Molly, Sarah-Sally**), but this appears to be obsolete. **Low** was also used, along with **Lor**. The latter still survives. In English literature Laura has been much celebrated by poets, probably in imitation of Petrarch.

Lauraine (f) Variant of **Loraine/Lorraine** in occasional use since the 1940s.

Laurance (m) Fairly frequent variant of **Laurence** or **Lawrence**.

Laureen (f) Diminutive of **Laura** in use since the 1940s. **Loreen** also occurs, as do **Laurene, Laurine, Lorene**, but Laureen remains the most frequent from.

Laurel (f) Botanical name, for the bay-tree, used as a first name. The pattern of usage shows that it owes more to a fondness for **Laura** and its derivatives than to the fashion for plant names which was at one time prevalent. Introduced as a first name in the 19th c. but most used in the 1940s and '50s in the U.S. and Canada. Also found as **Laural**.

On rare occasions has been used as a boy's name, perhaps in such instances being derived from the surname.

Lauren (f, m) Diminutive of **Laura** or a newly-formed feminine version of **Laurence**. Seems to have been suggested by Howard Hawks in the early 1940s for Lauren Bacall, who was previously Betty Jean Bacal (she added the extra -1 to change the pronunciation). Immediately after her first screen appearance in 1944, a great many Laurens were named in the U.S., most of them girls. Had been used a few years earlier as a male name, a variant of **Loren**, from **Lorenz**, or **Lorenzo**. With the advent of Lauren as a girl's name, parents began to use Loren as a girl's name as well. By 1970 both forms of the name were still being used for both sexes, but Lauren was predominantly the feminine form, Loren the male form. In the early 1980s Loren had almost disappeared, while Lauren was still in use for girls, both in the U.S. and Britain. The name arrived rather later in Britain, and was most used in the 1960s.

Laurena (f) Variant of **Laurina**.

Laurence (m) Latin *Laurentius* 'from Laurentium', a maritime city in Latium, a few miles south of Rome. The city took its name from the laurels that grew abundantly in the area. Common name (as Laurentius) amongst the early Christians, and the name of a favourite saint in medieval Europe, martyred in the 3rd c. Introduced to Britain by the Normans in the 11th c. and frequently used from the 12th c. Gave rise to many surnames, including *Larkins, Laurie, Law, Lawrence, Lowry*, etc. Remained in constant use, though declined steadily after the 16th c. until the end of the 19th c., when it began a fashionable run in the U.S. From 1900–70 was extremely popular in the U.S., though usually spelt **Lawrence**. During the same period the two forms of the name were used consistently but quietly in Britain, with a minor peak in the 1950s. Lawrence has been slightly the more popular form in Britain in modern times, with **Laurance** occurring regularly as a variant. Amongst the famous men who have borne the name one may number Laurence Sterne (1713–68), author of *Tristram Shandy*, the actor Laurence Olivier (Lord Olivier), who has publicized the name since the 1930s, and Laurence Harvey (Larushka Mischa Skikne), who publicized the name during the 1960s. Main pet forms of the name are **Larry** (rarely **Larrie**), **Laurie** (rarely **Lauri**), **Lawrie**, all independent names. Early feminine forms were **Lauricia**, **Laurina** and **Laurentia**. Later feminine forms have been heavily influenced by Laura, which may itself have derived from Laurence, but was probably from **Laurus**, a male name used by the Romans. Of the foreign forms of the name, Spanish/Italian **Lorenzo** has been most used in English-speaking countries, but German **Lorenz**, Swedish **Lars** also occur, together with the derivative **Loren**. In Ireland Laurence has been used to translate the Irish name *Lorcan* 'fierce', though its correct Irish form is *Labhras*. Lorcan ua Tuathail was the 12th c. archbishop of Dublin, better known perhaps as St Laurence O'Toole. Regard for him has kept Laurence in steady use in Ireland, where the pet name is said by several commentators to be **Lanty**. Woulfe states clearly that this is in fact from **Laughlin** or **Leachlainn**.

Laurene (f) See Laureen.

Lauretta (f) Diminutive of Laura used consistently though infrequently since 1850, found later as **Loretta** and later still as **Lorretta**. Clearly in use before the 19th c., since Sheridan made much of it in his play *St Patrick's Day* (1775): 'Lauretta! aye, you would have her called so; but for my part I never knew any good come of giving girls these heathen Christian names. . . . I always knew Lauretta was a runaway name.'

Laurette (f) Diminutive of French Laure (Laura), used only rarely. Lorette and Lorrette also occur.

Lauri (f) Pet form of Laura in modern use, especially in the U.S. and Canada. Occasionally male, from Laurence.

Lauriane (f) French diminutive of Laure (Laura) which has been re-interpreted in English-speaking countries, especially the U.S. and Canada, as Lori Ann. Laurianne occurs rarely, and Lauriane itself is rare.

Laurice (f) See Loris.

Laurie (m, f) Originally a pet form of Laurence or Lawrence. Since the 1940s has become predominantly a girl's name, a pet form of Laura used in its own right. The male name, especially in Scotland, often occurs as Lawrie. The girl's name, used far more often in the U.S. than in Britain, is frequently Lori. Other variants of the feminine name include **Lauri**, **Laury**, **Loree**, **Lorey**, **Lorie**, **Lorri**, **Lorrie**, **Lory**, **Lorry**. All these forms found most frequently around 1960, and in the U.S. and Canada rather than Britain.

Laurina (f) Feminine form of *Laurentius* (Laurence) in use amongst the Romans. Appeared in Britain in the 1840s and quietly but regularly used ever since. Also occurs as **Lorina**, **Lorena**, **Laurena**. None of these forms seems to have appealed to American parents in modern times.

Laurinda (f) Diminutive of Laura in occasional use.

Laurine (f) See Laureen.

Laurraine (f) Variant of Lorraine occasionally used in the 1970s.

Lavenia (f) See Lavinia. Lavena also occurs.

Laverne (f) Probably a form of Laverna influenced by the Californian place name La Verne (mistakenly thought by the namer to be Spanish for 'the green'), also a place in Texas called Lavernia. Laverna was the Roman goddess of thieves and impostors; in that form used on very rare occasions. Usually occurs as Laverne, and nearly always used in the U.S. by black families. Sometimes spelt like the place name as La Verne, and Lavern is found. Occurs from time to time as a male name. In Britain used only since the 1950s.

Lavinia (f) The daughter of King Latinus, last wife of Aeneas, according to Livy and Virgil. Some scholars believe that such a person did not exist, and that Lavinia merely personified Latin territory. Could also be a feminine form of her father's name, Latinus. Found in Christian inscriptions, e.g., *Labinia*, *virgo dei*, Rome, 409 AD. Came into use with other classical names after the Renaissance. Popular in the 18th c. after the Scottish poet James Thomson (1700–48) retold in his *Seasons* the biblical story of Boaz and Ruth under the names of Palemon and Lavinia. Lavina has long been a variant. Other forms include **Levenia, Levener, Lavena, Lavenia, Laviner, Lavinie, Levina, Levinia, Livinia, Lovenah, Loveviner, Lovina, Lovinia,** but the name is not used intensively in modern times.

Lavon (m, f) H. L. Mencken reported on the use of this 'made-up' name amongst the Mormons. By the 1950s the form **Lavonne** had been developed for girls, and was even being used by black American parents to name their sons by 1960. But by 1980 both forms of the name had become rare. No trace of either of them at any time in Britain.

Lawrance (m) Variant of **Lawrence/** Laurence which occurs regularly since the beginning of the 19th c.

Lawrence (m) For the history of the name see **Laurence**. Lawrence is the usual modern form, by a very wide margin in the U.S. and Canada, but by a narrow margin only in Britain. The -w- spellings seem to occur from the 15th c. onwards in both surname and first name.

Lawrie (m) Mainly Scottish pet form of Lawrence, used infrequently as an independent name.

Lawson (m) Aristocratic English surname used with great regularity as a first name. Original meaning is 'son of Laurence'. Introduced in the 1850s and consistently used since.

Lawton (m) English place name 'settlement on a hill' which became a surname. Used regularly as a first name in the 19th c., but rare since.

Layla (f) Has appeared with some frequency since the late 1960s, though it seems to be confined to Britain. Probably a form of **Leila**.

Layne (f) See **Lane**.

Layton (m) English place name and surname used as a first name. Used as such in the 1870s, but later took on the more common place name form **Leighton** and was used more intensively (in Britain at least). Since the 1950s has also occurred in yet another place name form, **Leyton**. Publicized in Britain since the 1970s by two sportsmen, the darts player Leighton Rees and the soccer player Leighton James.

Lazarus (m) Greek form of Hebrew *El'azar* (*Eleazar*) 'God (my) help'. Biblical, N.T., name of the brother of Martha and Mary, also of a beggar, the only man individually named in the parables. Listed as a Christian name by Camden (1605) but Eleazar was the commoner form in the 18th c. Returned in the 19th c. but now almost obsolete.

Lea (f) For the Romans this was a feminine form of Leo, but in modern times it is often a variant of **Leah** or **Lee** (**Leigh**). Increasingly used since the 1960s.

Leah (f) Hebrew 'wild cow' or 'weary', or Assyrian 'mistress'. Biblical, O.T., Gen. 29:23. Jacob thinks he is going to marry Leah's sister, Rachel, but their father secretly tells Leah to put on the bridal veil. The Roman name **Lea**, feminine of Leo, is not connected. Introduced into England by the Puritans in the late 16th c. Fairly common in the 18th c. and regularly used everywhere until the 1930s. Revived again in Britain in the 1970s.

Leanda (f) Feminine form of **Leander**. Very rarely used until the 1960s, more frequent in the 1970s. **Leeanda** also occurs. Reappearance of the name coincides with interest in **Lee-Ann** in its various forms. American parents show a slight preference for **Leandra**.

Leander (m) Greek, *Leiandros* 'lion man', Latin *Leander*. The name of the young man in Greek mythology who nightly swam across the Hellespont to visit Hero in Sestos. Recorded as a Christian name in inscriptions of the 5th c. St Leander was a 7th c. bishop of Seville. Regularly used in Britain but more popular in the U.S., especially among black American families. Very occasionally used for girls, e.g. Leander Reynolds born in Oxford, 1982.

Leandra (f) Feminine form of **Leander**, quietly used in modern times and more in the U.S. than in Britain.

Leanne (f) See **Lianne**.

Leanora (f) See **Leonora**.

Lee (m, f) Common English surname deriving from a place name element 'wood', 'clearing', 'meadow'. Originally used in the U.S. in honour of General Robert E. Lee (1807–70). Publicized by the actors Lee J. Cobb (Leo Jacoby), and to a lesser extent by Lee Bowman from the mid-1930s onwards. In the 1950s Lee Marvin began his screen career, and may have been responsible for the name reaching its mild peak in the U.S. and Canada at that time. In Britain it became one of the top ten names in the early 1980s. In the U.S. it had already faded by 1960. Predominantly used for males, but popular as a girl's name in the U.S. as Lee Ann. Variant **Leigh**, in regular use since 1950, perhaps influenced by the actress Vivien Leigh, tends to be used for girls, but an independent study carried out by C. V. Appleton on Lee and its variants revealed that all forms of the name (including **Lea**) can be used for both sexes. Usage of the name in the U.S., especially, may have been negatively influenced by the publicity that surrounded Lee Harvey Oswald after he assassinated President Kennedy.

Leeann (f) Often written as Lee Ann. Leeanne and Lee Anne also occur, and Leigh Ann is found. See **Lianne**.

Leesa (f) Form of Lisa in use since the

1960s. Perhaps regarded as a feminine form of Lee.

Leigh (m, f) Variant of **Lee**. Mainly used for girls, but see the discussion under Lee. **Leighann(e)** has been used since the 1960s.

Leighton (m) See **Layton**.

Leila (f) Arabic '(dark as) night'. Dr Brewer describes her as 'the Oriental type of female loveliness, chastity and impassioned affection'. Name borrowed by Lord Byron in *The Giaour* (1813), and used for the beautiful slave girl. He also used the name again in *Don Juan* (1824) for a young Turkish child. In 1838 Lord Lytton published his novel *Leila*. Not until the 1860s, however, that the name began to be used with any regularity in Britain. Has continued to be used very quietly, occurring also as Lila, Leilah, Lilah, Laila. Layla, which has appeared since the late 1960s, is probably the same name with a different pronunciation.

Leisa (f) Form of Lisa presumably intended to emphasize that the pronunciation of Liza is required. Appeared in the late 1960s and occurred regularly until the mid-1970s.

Lela (f) Variant of Lelia.

Leland (m) Use of the American place name (Missouri and Michigan) or surname as a first name. Best-known bearer of the name was Charles Leland (1824–1903), but he published much under the pseudonym Hans Breitmann. Mainly used in the 1940s and almost unknown outside the U.S.

Lelia (f) Latin, from the Roman family name *Laelius*, feminine Laelia (Lelia). Laelia occurs in Christian inscriptions of the late 4th c. Came to Britain in the mid-19th c. from France after the publication in 1833 of George Sand's popular love story *Lélia*. Used intermittently since. Lilia is a common variant, and Lela, Lellia are found.

Lemmy (m) Usual pet form of **Lemuel**, though Lemy and Lemmie also occur. Has continued in modern use to some extent, whereas Lemuel virtually disappeared in the 1930s.

Lemuel (m) Hebrew 'devoted, or belonging, to God'. Biblical, O.T., Prov. 31:1, the name of a king. Probably better known as the name of the hero of *Gulliver's Travels*, by Jonathan Swift. Rarely used until the 1840s, when it came into regular, though infrequent, use until the 1930s. Since then the name seems to have disappeared, though pet forms **Lemmy**, **Lemy**, **Lemmie** continue to be used as independent names.

Lemy (m) See **Lemmy**.

Len (m) Pet form of **Leonard**, which is often spelt **Lennard** or **Lenard**. Used as an independent name in this century. Associated with writer Len Deighton.

Lena (f) Pet form of names ending in -lena, especially **Helena**. Used regularly since the 1860s in its own right and especially popular in Britain 1900–25. More recently associated with the singer Lena Horne, who helped the name along in the U.S. in the 1940s.

Lenard (m) See **Leonard**.

Lenda (f) Feminine form of **Leonard** regularly if infrequently used in the 20th c. In use before **Glenda** appeared on the scene, but the ending could have been suggested by **Brenda**, **Gwenda**, etc.

Lenna (f) Feminine form of **Leonard** used from time to time. May be a variant of **Leona**.

Lennard (m) See **Leonard**.

Lennox (m, f) Scottish place name and aristocratic surname used as a first name, mainly in Scotland. Original meaning of the name has to do with an abundance of elm trees. **Lenox** is a legitimate variant, and was established in the U.S. by James Lenox, founder of the Lenox Library (now part of the New York Public Library).

Lenny (m) Also **Lennie**. Pet forms of **Leonard** used independently. **Leny** was the earlier form.

Lenor (f) Modern form of **Lenore** used since 1970 in English-speaking countries.

Lenora (f) Form of **Eleanor** used in countries such as Russia, according to *Foreign Versions of English Names*, a book compiled by the U.S. Immigration and Naturalization Service. Used in English-speaking countries from time to time, sometimes found as **Lenorah**.

Lenore (f) Germanic variant of **Eleanor** occasionally used in English-speaking countries.

Leo (m) Latin *leo*, Greek *leon* 'lion'. Occurs very frequently amongst Christian inscriptions of the Roman Empire. The name of thirteen early popes. Used fairly often until the 18th c. Then made a mild comeback in the 1870s and was reasonably well used until the 1920s. The British actor Leo Genn has given the name much publicity since the mid-1930s, as has Leo G. Carroll in the U.S. Leo Gorcey, one of the original Dead-End kids, began his American film career at the same time. More recently has been associated with the popular singer Leo Sayer, born Gerard Hughes Sayer.

Leon (m) The Greek form of Leo, 'lion'. Regularly used from the 1880s, in Britain, but earlier in the U.S. One of the top thirty names in the U.S. by the 1870s, remaining very popular for a generation. Since then has continued to be used far more frequently in the U.S. than in Britain, though had faded considerably by the beginning of the 1980s. Publicized by the American actor Leon Ames, seen in the cinema since the 1930s and in television series such as *Life With Father*, *Father of the Bride*.

Leona (f) Normal American feminine of **Leon**, adapted from Latin **Leonia**. First came into use in the 1870s, but rare until the 1940s. In Britain **Leonie** has been preferred, though Leona has also occurred regularly since the 1940s.

Leonard (m) Old German *Leonhard* 'strong as a lion'. The name of a popular 5th c. saint to whom many churches were dedicated. Rarely used as an English first name until the 18th c., though its occurrence in the Middle Ages led to surnames such as *Leonard*, *Lennard*. Used throughout the 19th c., but infrequently. Then became reasonably fashionable 1900–30. Has since waned.

One well-known bearer of the name is the composer/conductor Leonard Bernstein. Pet form **Len** occurs from time to time as an independent name, along with **Lenny, Lennie, Leny**. **Lena** may be used on some occasions as a feminine form. Others include **Lenda, Leneen, Lenette, Lenia, Lenna, Lennah**. Variants **Lenard** and **Lennard** occur regularly.

Leone (f) See **Leonie**.

Leonie (f) French feminine form of **Leon**. An early Latin form **Leonia** was used by early Christians. Leonie seems to have been brought back to England by soldiers who fought in the First World War. Used regularly if infrequently ever since, though only in Britain, American parents remaining faithful to the earlier **Leona**. Leone has also been used, and **Leoni** occurs. Rarer variants include **Leonicia, Leoline, Leonine, Leontine**.

Leonora (f) Short form of **Eleanora** (**Eleonore** in its French form, **Eleonora** in Italian). In Beethoven's opera she is the heroine who assumes the name *Fidelio*. In *Il Trovatore* by Verdi, Leonora is the tragic heroine. Yet another Leonora is the king's mistress in Donizetti's opera *La Favorita*. In real life the name is consistently used, though never in great numbers in any particular year. Sometimes occurs in its German form **Leonore**, and the variants **Leanora** and **Leanore** are found, clearly influenced by **Eleanora**. **Nora** is a pet form of the name. American parents no doubt associate it frequently with **Leon**.

Leopold (m) Old German *Luitpold* 'people bold'. At an early stage the name became Leopold in German under the influence of Latin/Greek names such as **Leo, Leon, Leonhard** (**Leonard**). The name of an Austrian saint, and much favoured by the Austrian aristocracy. Queen Victoria named one of her sons Leopold as a compliment to her Belgian uncle who bore the name. Since the 1860s regularly but quietly used in England, though it picked up to some extent towards the end of the 19th c. Else-

where has had little impact.

Leroy (m) Old French 'the king'. Surname originally given to someone connected with the king's household as a servant, or to someone who played the part of a king in one of the medieval pageants. As a first name well-used in the U.S. in the late 19th c., edging its way into the top fifty in 1875. Thereafter it declined, though still in evidence in the U.S. at the beginning of the 1980s. Black American families remained especially faithful to the name after it had passed its peak, so that in modern times it is thought of as a typically black name. Used in Britain at the beginning of the 20th c. but made no real impact until the 1950s. Use of the name has steadily increased since then, mainly amongst the West Indian community. Also written as **Le'Roy** and **Le Roy**. Variant **Elroy** is very rare in Britain.

Les (m) Pet form of **Leslie** or **Lester**, rarely used in its own right.

Lesley (f) See **Leslie**.

Leslie (m, f) Scottish place name of uncertain meaning, which became a family name, then first name. Appeared as a first name in the 18th c., when Robert Burns wrote of a 'bonnie Lesley' in one of his poems. Lesley was an early spelling (one of many) of the surname, but Burns's use of it for a girl established it as the normal feminine form of Leslie in Britain. Male name Leslie began to become fashionable towards the end of the 19th c. in Britain. Reached its peak by 1925, and already fading when actors such as Leslie Banks and Leslie Howard began to appear on the screen. The popularity of Leslie Howard, e.g. in *Gone With the Wind* (1939), helped to maintain the name reasonably well through the 1940s. In the U.S., where the name had never been as popular as in Britain, he was probably responsible for its considerable increase in usage in the early 1940s. At this time the girl's name Lesley began to be fashionable in Britain, rising to a peak in the early 1960s. By 1960 the name was also being used more for girls than for boys in the U.S. The American spelling of the feminine name remained Leslie, probably under the influence of the French actress Leslie Caron, on screen from 1951 (e.g. in *Gigi*, *An American In Paris*). Miss Caron also caused spelling confusion in Britain, and many girls were now called Leslie for the first time. Not clear why Leslie Caron was given the name, but French dictionaries now list it and link it with **Elisabeth,** probably confusing it with German names such as Liesl. The British-born comedian Bob Hope was forced to abandon his real first name, Leslie, when he came to the U.S. and discovered that it was pronounced Less-lie instead of Lez-lie. His name thus became Less Hope, or worse still, Hope Less. In Britain the well-known disc-jockey Jimmy Young also abandoned the Leslie which his parents gave him. Humphrey Bogart had a more positive attitude to the name and gave it to his daughter, as a compliment to Leslie Howard who helped him when he was still unknown. Now little used as either a male or female name, but is found in modern birth records in variant forms which include **Leslee, Lesli, Lesly, Lesslie, Leslye.** Pet form **Les** occurs very rarely as an independent name.

Lester (m) Phonetic form of the English place name *Leicester*, which became a surname. Consistently used as a first name since the 1840s. In Britain it is widely associated with the jockey Lester Piggott. Also made widely known by the Canadian Prime Minister Lester B. Pearson, in the 1960s. In the U.S. and Canada was being well used throughout the 1940s, but has faded since. Also at its height in Australia at that time.

Leta (f) Latin, feminine of *laetus* 'glad'. Found during the Roman Empire. Used sporadically since the 1870s.

Letitia (f) Latin *laetitia* 'gladness'. The English vernacular form in the Middle Ages was **Lettice.** Use of the name and its diminutives at that time led to sur-

names such as *Letson*, *Letts*, *Lettice*, etc. Remained in constant use since the 12th c., though never fashionable. In the 20th c. even less often used, but modern instances are always of Letitia, not Lettice. The latter form was common in the 19th c. and lasted until 1920. Variant **Lettuce** occurred, but very rarely. **Lettitia** was sometimes found, no doubt influenced by the pet forms **Lettie, Letty,** which were used fairly well as independent names from the latter half of the 19th c. to the 1930s. Miss Withycombe remarks that **Laetitia** replaced Lettice from the 18th c. onwards. Birth records make it quite clear, however, that Letitia and Lettice continued in popular use for at least another century, and that Laetitia has only been used on very rare occasions. Girls bearing the name were sometimes known as **Tish,** and **Tisha** has in fact appeared in the U.S. as an independent name in recent years, used especially by black American families. They also turn the name into **Latisha,** or use that spelling as a variant of Letitia. They are certainly aware of Letitia, and continue to use it quietly, sometimes in another variant form **Leticia.**

Lettice (f) Normal vernacular form of **Letitia** until the 1920s.

Lettie (f) See Letty.

Lettuce (f) See Letitia.

Letty (f) Pet form of **Letitia** or **Violette** used as an independent name from the 1840s until the 1930s. Letty was the usual form, Lettie being less frequently used. Both forms survive in modern times, mainly amongst black families in the U.S., and there is now a slight preference for Lettie.

Levenia (f) 19th c. variant of **Lavinia.** Levener also occurred.

Levi (m) Hebrew 'attached', from a word meaning 'to adhere'. Biblical, O.T., the name of Jacob's son by Leah. In the N.T. the Apostle Matthew is also called Levi. At Gen. 29:34 we are told that Leah chose the name because she hoped her husband would now be joined to her more closely because she had borne him three sons. She had good reason to think that Jacob loved Rachel more than her. Levi has been in constant, if infrequent, use since the 17th c. In the 1970s both British and American parents seemed to prefer the spelling **Levy**, but the name was clearly alive and well.

Levinia (f) Common 19th c. variant of **Lavinia**. Variant form **Levina**, just as Lavinia was often found as **Lavina**.

Levy (m) Form of **Levi** well used in the 1970s. The surname *Levy* is not usually from the Hebrew name, but from Old English *Leofwig* 'beloved warrior'.

Lewellen (m) Also **Lewellin**. See **Llewellyn**.

Lewin (m) Old English *leofwine* 'beloved friend'. The personal name only survived the Norman Conquest as a surname, which has been regularly used as a first name in modern times, though mainly in the 19th c.

Lewis (m) For the early history of the name see **Louis**. Steadily but quietly used in Britain since the Middle Ages. Especially popular in Wales, where it was interpreted as a simplified form of **Llewelyn**. In the U.S. enjoyed a run of popularity in the 1870s, when the French form Louis was re-introduced, but by 1900 Louis had taken over completely and Lewis faded. In English literature made famous by Lewis Carroll (Charles Lutwidge Dodgson) whose *Alice in Wonderland* appeared in 1865. The Lewis of his pen-name was an adaptation of his real middle name, Lutwidge.

Lex (m) Short form of **Alex**, itself from **Alexander**. Made known by the actor Lex Barker (1919–73), who appeared in five of the Tarzan films, but used very rarely.

Leyland (m) Place name 'untilled land' which became a surname, used from time to time as a first name.

Leyton (m) See **Layton**.

Lia (f) Italian form of **Leah**. Appears for the first time in the 1970s in English-speaking countries.

Liam (m) Pet form of **William** which originated in Ireland. Predominantly Irish name, but since 1930 has also been used in Scotland and England.

Lian (f) Pet form of **Gillian** used independently since the 1970s, and apparently only in Britain. **Lianne, Leanne**, etc., are preferred in the U.S. and Canada.

Liana (f) Pet form of **Juliana, Liliana, Emiliana**, etc., used mainly in Italy, occasionally in English-speaking countries.

Lianne (f) Pet form of **Julianne** used independently. Re-interpreted in modern time as **Lee Ann, Lee Anne, Leigh Ann**. Liane occurs regularly, and **Leanne** is frequent. None of these forms much used until the 1940s, when they began to appear in the U.S. In Britain they remained rare until the 1960s.

Libby (f) Pet form of **Elizabeth**, occasionally used independently. **Libbie** also occurs. The actress Libby Holman and comedienne Libby Morris have helped make the name known.

Liberty (m, f) The word used as a name. **Freedom** has been used slightly more often, but Liberty was preferred in the 1970s, probably because of the acceptable pet-form **Libby**.

Liesa (f) German pet form of **Elisabeth**, used occasionally in English-speaking countries. **Liese** also occurs.

Liesl (f) German pet form of **Elisabeth**, in use since the 1960s. Found also as **Liesel** and **Lisel**.

Lila(h) (f) See **Leila**.

Lilac (f) Plant name, occasionally used as a first name.

Lilia (f) Latin *lilia* 'lilies', plural of *lilium*. See **Lily**.

Lilian (f) Ultimately from the flower name, 'lily', through Italian **Liliana**. See **Lily**. Lilian has been the usual British spelling of the name, **Lillian** being preferred in the U.S. In Britain it was most used 1890–1920, but has been rarely given since the 1930s.

Lilias (f) Gaelic *Lileas*, a form of **Lilian**. **Lillias** also occurs. Both forms usually found in Scotland, but they were regular, if infrequent, throughout the 19th c. in England. See also **Lily**.

Lilith (f) The name of a female demon in Jewish folk-lore. Biblical O.T., Is. 34:14. Traditionally translated 'night monster' but probably derives from Sumerian *lilla* 'ghost'. Said to have been Adam's first wife. She refused to obey him and turned into a demon. Later accounts make her a vampire who preyed on children and men sleeping alone. Rarely given as a first name. The Gaelic *Lilidh* is not connected, being a translation of **Lily**.

Lilia (f) Simplified form of **Lilia** or pet form of **Elizabeth**. In regular but infrequent use since the 1850s. See also **Lily**.

Lilley (f) Fairly common 19th c. variant of **Lily**. No doubt influenced by the surname which has this form. The surname is either from a place name, or from **Elizabeth**.

Lilli (f) German pet form of **Elisabeth**, rarely used in English-speaking countries. Made well-known by the wartime song 'Lilli Marlene'.

Lillia (f) 19th c. variant of **Lilia**.

Lillian (f) Preferred form in the U.S. of **Lilian**. See also **Lily**. Most used in the U.S. from the 1890s to 1930. Now very rarely used. At one time associated with the famous star of silent films Lillian Gish (Lillian de Guiche).

Lillias (f) See **Lilias**.

Lillie (f) Variant of **Lily** most used in the U.S. in the 1870s. Occurred in Britain at the same time, and remained in use until the 1920s. Very rarely used since.

Lilly (f) In the 1870s used as frequently as **Lily**, but the latter form soon prevailed. Rarely used in the 20th c.

Lily (f) The name of the flower used as a first name. In some instances, especially in early use, it may derive from **Elizabeth**. It is clear, however, that Lily was not in frequent use as a pet form of Elizabeth since it occurs only rarely in 18th c. records, at a time when other pet forms of Elizabeth (such as **Betty**) appear in great numbers. The lily has long been significant in Christian art, representing

purity. The ancient Hebrews used the flower name as a personal name (see **Susannah**). There was also a 9th c. martyr, **Liliosa**, whose name in Spanish derived from Latin *lilium* 'lily'. In Italian this became **Liliana** at an early date, which accounts for English **Lilian**. The Spanish Liliosa probably gave rise to the Scottish **Lilias**, Gaelic *Lileas*. The martyr may have received her name in reference to Christ's words: 'Consider the lilies of the field, how they grow; they neither toil nor spin; yet I tell you, even Solomon in all his glory was not arrayed like one of these' (Matt. 6:28). Some 19th c. parents certainly had these N.T. words in mind, since they used **Lilia** as their preferred form of the name, the Latin plural form of *lilium*. Simplified form of Lilia, **Lillia**, also appeared in the 19th c. and remained in steady use. In some cases this may be a form of **Lila**(Leila). Most of the forms mentioned above, together with their many variants such as **Lilie, Lilium, Lilley, Lillia, Lillian, Lillias, Lillie, Lilly**, came into regular use in the 1850s. Lily at its most popular in Britain (Lillie being preferred in the U.S.) around 1900, with a rapid decline thereafter. Now very rarely used. At one time there was a popular music-hall song 'Lily of Laguna'.

Lina (f) Originally a pet form of **Adelina, Emelina, Carolina, Angelina, Selina,** etc. Used steadily as an independent name since the mid-19th c.

Lincoln (m) English place name, 'Roman colony at the pool', and surname. As a Christian name it originally paid homage to the 16th President of the U.S.A., Abraham Lincoln (1809–65) but does not seem to have been frequently used. In Britain it was first used in the 1860s and has been steadily, if infrequently, used since.

Linda (f) In its earliest occurrences, an element in many Germanic names (such as **Traudlinde, Friedlinde, Ermelinde, Gotelinde, Sieglinde, Heimlinde, Ermlinde, Gunlinde, Gerlinde**) where *-linde*/*linda* meant 'serpent', a symbol of wisdom. By the 19th c., in English-speaking countries, seen as a pet-form of **Belinda, Malinda, Melinda, Rosalinda,** used independently. Later associated with Spanish *linda*, feminine of *lindo* 'pretty'. Extremely fashionable in the U.S. in the late 1930s. By the time actresses such as Linda Darnell (Manetta Eloisa Darnell) and Linda Christian (Blanca Rosa Welter) had begun to appear on screen in the 1940s, the name was already becoming more popular by the minute. They probably helped to spread the name to other English-speaking countries, and throughout the 1950s it enjoyed an immense success on all sides. By 1960 fading quickly in Britain. A few years later it began to decline rapidly in the U.S. and Canada. At the beginning of the 1980s was being very quietly used once again. While at its height it was frequently found as **Lynda.** As this began to fade the name's pet forms **Lyn, Lynn** and **Lynne** became mildly fashionable in their own right. Diminutives such as **Lindy, Lindey, Lindie, Lyndi, Lyndy** were also used. Rarer variants included **Lin, Linn, Lynnda.**

Linden (m, f) Variant of **Lyndon,** presumably influenced by German *Linden* 'lime-trees', which occurs in well-known German songs.

Lindon (m) See **Lyndon.**

Lindsay (m, f) Scottish surname deriving from a place name. Until the 1930s predominantly a male name. By the 1950s being used for both sexes in roughly equal numbers, nearly always as Lindsay for boys, but in a number of forms for girls. In the early 1980s the name (if one considers it to be one name with variants rather than a number of names) was in the British top twenty as a girl's name, but had faded as a boy's name. American parents were also showing a great deal of interest in it as a girl's name. Variants include the following: **Lindsey** (frequent), **Lynsey** (frequent), **Lyndsey** (frequent), **Linsey, Linzi, Lindsaye, Lindsie, Lindsy, Lindzi, Lindzy, Linzey, Linzie, Lynsday, Lyndsy, Lyn-**

say, **Lynsie, Linsay.** The British film director Lindsay Anderson is a well-known (male) bearer of the name.

Lindsey (f) Frequent variant of **Lindsay.** Usually a feminine form, occasionally male.

Lindy (f) Pet form of **Linda** in use as an independent name since the 1940s.

Linette (f) See **Lynette.**

Linnell (f) See **Lynnell. Linell** also occurs.

Linnette (f) See **Lynette.**

Linnie (f) Pet form of names such as **Caroline, Emmeline, Pauline,** used as an independent name, especially 1900–20.

Linsay (f) See **Lindsay. Linsey** also occurs.

Linton (m) See **Lynton.**

Linus (m) Greek 'flax'. Little used, and probably best known because of the character in the Peanuts cartoons by Charles Schultz.

Lionel (m) Latin *leonellus* 'little lion'. Its use in the Middle Ages led to surnames such as *Lyall, Lyell.* Remained in steady but infrequent use ever since, with a spell of mild popularity in the 1920s and '30s. That may have been due to the publicity given to the name by the actor Lionel Barrymore (1878–1954).

Lisa (f) Pet form of **Elisabeth** (**Elizabeth**) used as a name in its own right. One of the most popular names in all English-speaking countries in the early 1980s, though it was extremely rare until the 1950s. Before that its use was mainly confined to Spain and Germany. Possible that its present popularity was helped by the song *Mona Lisa,* one of Nat 'King' Cole's great hits.

Lisanne (f) See **Lizanne.**

Lisbeth (f) Pet form of **Elizabeth,** or its European form **Elisabeth,** used independently. **Lizbeth** is slightly more common.

Lisa-Marie (f) This combination name has been used with considerable frequency since the 1960s. **Lisa-Jane** is also popular.

Lisette (f) French diminutive of **Elisabeth,** in use in Britain since the 1950s.

Lister (m) The surname 'a dyer' used as a first name. Regularly used in the 19th c., but it was curiously *less* used as the fame of Joseph Lister (1827-1912), the English surgeon who made such a contribution to antiseptic surgery, became more widespread. Rare in modern times.

Lita (f) Pet form of **Roselita, Lolita, Carmelita, Julita**, etc., used independently. Introduced in the 1930s and used rather more frequently in the 1950s and '60s.

Livinia (f) Occasional 19th c. variant of **Lavinia**.

Liz (f) Pet form of **Elizabeth**, used on rare occasions in its own right.

Liza (f) Pet form of **Elizabeth**, rarely used as an independent name until the 1960s. Then became reasonably popular, as did **Lisa**. Liza Minnelli is a well-known bearer of the name.

Lizanne (f) Modern blend of **Liz** (**Elizabeth**) and **Anne** used since the 1940s. **Lisanne** also occurs.

Lizbeth (f) Shortened form of **Elizabeth** used from time to time as an independent name, especially since 1950.

Lizzie (f) Pet form of **Elizabeth** used consistently as an independent name from the 1850s to the 1920s. **Lizzy** was a frequently-found alternative. **Lizzey, Lizey** and **Lizie** were also found. No examples of any of the forms found since the 1940s.

Llewellyn (m) Usual modern form of Welsh **Llywelyn**. The traditional derivation is 'lion-likeness'. Davies dismisses this in his *Book of Welsh Names* on the grounds that lions are not indigenous to Wales. He forgets that names such as **Leo, Leon** and **Leonard**, all based on 'lion', have been in use for centuries in countries where lions are not frequent. However, his alternative suggestion that Llewellyn is from Welsh *llyw* 'leader' makes sense. The name is usually found only in Wales, and occurs as **Llewelyn, Llewllyn, Llewelin, Llewelleyn, Lewellen, Lewellin**. Rarely used since the 1940s.

Llinos (f) Welsh 'linnet'. Used in Wales since the 1960s, possibly as a translation of the name **Linette**.

Lloyd (m) Welsh *llwyd* 'grey, holy'. Common Welsh surname and Christian name which has spread to all English-speaking countries. Especially popular during the 1940s in the U.S., probably helped along by the constant screen appearances at that time of Lloyd Nolan and Lloyd Bridges. In Britain the name enjoyed a mild spell of popularity in the 1960s. Associated there with the former Prime Minister David Lloyd George (1863–1945). **Loyd** also occurs.

Lois (f) Presumed to be a Greek name. Biblical, N.T., name of Timothy's grandmother (2 Tim. 1:5). Possibly used by Puritans and brought to America: Stewart lists a New England example in the 1680s. In modern times has been thought of as deriving from **Louisa** via such forms as Italian **Eloisa**, French **Heloise**. Especially popular in the U.S. 1900–25.

Lola (f) Pet form of **Dolores** used independently. Perhaps best known because of Lola Montez, the Irish dancer (1818–61) and mistress of Louis I of Bavaria. She was born Marie Dolores Eliza Roseanna Gilbert. The name continues to be steadily used in both the U.S. and Britain.

Lolita (f) Diminutive of **Dolores** (**Lola**). Continues to be steadily used, especially in the U.S., but for many is mainly associated with the novel of the same name by Vladimir Nabokov (1958) which concerns the love affair between Professor Humbert and the 12-year-old Lolita of the title.

Lomas (m) Place name/surname in occasional use as a first name.

Lona (f) Form of **Leona** or a short form of **Ilona, Apollonia**. Some parents may have the word 'lone' or 'alone' in mind when using it. Used regularly but infrequently since the beginning of the 20th c.

Lonnie (m) Pet form of **Alonzo** used independently. Associated in modern times with the singer Lonnie Donegan. Used regularly in the U.S. in the 1980s, though not in great numbers.

Lora (f) Provençal spelling of **Laura** according to Charlotte Yonge. Introduced to England in the 14th c. and remained the normal spelling of the name for at least two centuries. Now very rare in Britain but still used in the U.S.

Loraine (f) Common variant of **Lorraine**.

Lorane (f) Diminutive of **Lora** influenced heavily by **Lorraine**. Used in the 1960s for the first time.

Lord (m) Lord was regularly used as a first name, in Britain especially, until the 1920s, which suggests that it was the surname being brought into the first-name stock. Parents could hardly have been unaware, however, that it would make their sons sound like titled gentlemen.

Loreen (f) See **Laureen**.

Loren (m) Short form of German **Lorenz** or Spanish/Italian **Lorenzo**. Introduced in the U.S. in the early 1940s. Also used to some extent for girls after 1944, being considered a variant of **Lauren**, but by 1970 had established itself as a male form again. Lauren has also been used as a male name, but is now very rare in that role.

Lorena (f) Variant of **Laurena**, infrequently used. The lack of interest is perhaps surprising, especially in the U.S., in view of Margaret Mitchell's comments in *Gone With the Wind*: the child of Scarlett and Frank was 'named Ella Lorena . . . Lorena because it was the most fashionable name of the day for girls, even as Robert E. Lee and Stonewall Jackson were popular for boys and Abraham Lincoln and Emancipation for negro children.' Elsewhere in the novel she talks of a song in which 'Lorena's lost love' is mentioned. However, available lists of names being used at the time of the Civil War do not mention it. Johnny Cash has made a recording of the song.

Lorene (f) See **Laureen**.

Lorette (f) See **Laurette**.

Lorenza (f) Feminine form of **Lorenzo**, infrequently used.

Lorenzo (m) Spanish/Italian form of **Laurence/Lawrence**. In Shakespeare's *Merchant of Venice* Lorenzo is the young man with whom Shylock's daughter, Jessica, elopes. In modern times is most used in the U.S. Pet form **Renzo** is occasionally used independently.

Loretta (f) This variant of **Lauretta** first occurred in the 1870s, but it was clearly brought to life by the American actress Loretta Young (Gretchen Young), whose film career began in 1928. Consistently used, though not in great numbers, since the early 1930s. Some parents (Roman Catholics) may have linked the name with the Italian place-name Loretto, a place of pilgrimage for centuries. **Lorretta** also occurs.

Lori (f) Pet form of **Laura**. Extremely popular in the U.S. and Canada around 1960, especially in the combination **Lori Ann(e)**. Occurred even more often as **Laurie**, less frequently as **Lauri**. All forms used far more often by whites than blacks.

Lorin (m) Occasional variant of **Loren**. Seems to be favoured by Jewish families in the U.S.

Lorina (f) Variant of **Lorena/Laurina**.

Lorinda (f) Diminutive of **Laura**, *via* **Lori**. Lorinda is used from time to time, more often than its associated form **Laurinda**. **Lorrinda** also occurs.

Loris (f) Variant of **Laurice** or **Lauricia**, the latter being a feminine form of **Laurence** which was used during the Roman Empire. Loris is the more usual form, but is infrequently used.

Lorna (f) Made famous by R. D. Blackmore's novel *Lorna Doone* (1869). He based the name on the Scottish place-name Lorn. The MacDougalls of Lorn were famous in former times, and Lorna Doone is eventually found to be Lady Lorna Dugal. First used a few years after the publication of the book and in regular use ever since, especially in Scotland. Lorn and Lorne are also found there, the latter occasionally being used to name boys. Regularly but quietly used in the U.S.

Lorne (m, f) See Lorna.

Lorraine (f) The spelling of this name naturally links it with the French province, and there are various reasons why that link should be a valid one. Parents who look upon this as a French first name which they are borrowing owe the name ultimately to *Jeanne la Lorraine*, or Joan of Arc, who was born in Lorraine. Some Scottish parents used the name at an early date knowing that the mother of Mary Queen of Scots was Mary of Lorraine. *Lorraine, Lorrain, Lorain* are also Scottish surnames, indicating that the original name-bearers came from that part of France. The use of surnames as first names is a long-established tradition in Scotland. But the possibility exists that Lorraine and its variants **Loraine, Lorain, Lorane, Lorayne, Lorrain, Lorrane, Lorrayne**, etc., came about as independent diminutives of **Lora**, and that the name was associated with the French place name afterwards. In English-speaking countries the name (in any of its forms) was rarely used in the 19th c., though Stewart mentions American examples in the 1820s. In Britain they are easier to find after 1870. Usage was sporadic until the mid-1930s, when the name clearly began to come into fashion in both the U.S. and Britain. The name's popularity reached a peak in the U.S. in the 1940s, in Britain in the '60s and '70s, Scottish parents using it far more often than the English and Welsh. Irish parents discovered the name late, and were using it intensively in the 1970s. By the beginning of the 1980s, however, all forms of the name were fading very quickly.

Lorrayne (f) Also **Lorayne**. Variants of **Lorraine** which appeared in the 1960s.

Lorretta (f) Variant of **Lauretta/Loretta** which appeared in the 1960s and is used infrequently.

Lorrette (f) See **Laurette**.

Lorrie (f) See **Laurie**. **Lorry** also occurs.

Lot (m) Hebrew 'covering'. Biblical, O.T., perhaps best known because his wife was turned into a pillar of salt when she insisted on looking over her shoulder. The Puritans do not seem to have used the name, perhaps aware of Lot's selfishness and worldly character, but it was used very regularly throughout the 19th c. Now appears to be obsolete.

Lottie (f) Pet form of **Charlotte** or **Charlotta**, frequently used in the 19th c. as an independent name. **Lotty, Lottey** and **Lotte** also occur.

Lou (m) Pet form of **Louis** used as a name in its own right, mainly in the U.S. Publicized during the 1940s and early 1950s by the actor Lou Costello (Louis Cristillo) of the Abbot and Costello comedy team.

Lou (f) Pet form of **Louisa** or **Louise** used as a name in its own right, mainly in the U.S. Also a popular element in combined names such as **Louann, Louella, Louetta**.

Louann (f) Combination of **Lou** (usually from **Louise**) and **Ann**. Mainly an American name of the 1940s, occurring also as **Louanne, Luann, Luanne**.

Louella (f) Blend of **Lou** (usually from **Louisa**) and **Ella**. Made famous by the Hollywood gossip columnist Louella Parsons (Louella Oettinger, 1880–1972), but by the 1940s American parents were showing a clear preference for the variant **Luella**. By 1950 both forms of the name were being used very rarely.

Louie (m) Phonetic form of **Louis**, used fairly frequently since Louis was reintroduced to the English-speaking world in the 19th c.

Louis (m) French form of an Old German name *Hlutwig* 'famous in battle', Modern German **Ludwig**. Borne by the Frankish kings who ruled over kingdoms in Gaul and Germany from AD 500. The German name had been Latinized as **Ludovicus**, then turned by the French into **Clovis**, Louis. As Louis it became the name of eighteen kings of France from the 8th c. onwards. The Normans introduced the name to Britain in the 11th c., but it quickly took the English form **Lewis**. Louis was re-introduced into English-speaking countries in the mid-19th c. It kept its French pronunciation and was often written as **Louie**. Became extremely fashionable in the U.S. by the 1870s, and remained one of the top thirty names until the late 1920s. Subsequently faded. Associated by many with the great jazz trumpeter Louis Armstrong. Pet form **Lou** has been used independently, and the feminine forms **Louisa** and **Louise** have been popular.

Louisa (f) Latinized feminine form of **Louis**. Regularly used in the 18th c. and extremely fashionable in the 1870s in all English-speaking countries. Later largely replaced by its French form **Louise**, though Louisa has survived in modest use. Best-known bearer of the name was probably Louisa M. Alcott (1832–88), author of *Little Women*. Spanish form of the name, **Luisa**, is used from time to time, and pet forms such as **Lulu, Lulie, Lula** have been used as names in their own right.

Louise (f) French feminine form of **Louis**. In the U.S. the name became very popular at the end of the 19th c. and almost replaced the earlier form **Louisa**. Remained in the American top fifty until 1930, when it faded. In Britain it had been quietly used throughout that period, began to become fashionable in the mid-1950s, and by the early 1980s was in twelfth position. No signs of a similar revival in the U.S. at the time. British awareness of the name possibly stimulated by a popular song called *Louise* sung by Maurice Chevalier.

Louiza (f) Variant of **Louisa** which occurred regularly in the 19th c.

Louse (f) Presumably an error for **Louise**, though according to official records a Louse Smith was named in Britain in 1973. In modern times such errors are slips of the official pen. In former times, when a large number of parents registering a birth were illiterate and had to rely on the registrar, mistakes could occur if the official was unfamiliar with the

name. Thus a **Murder** Smith was registered because the English official did not know of the Scottish name **Murdo**.

Louvain (m) The name of this Belgian city has been used by British parents as a first name since 1915. Soldiers who fought there in World War One probably first made use of it. Its further use in the 1940s suggests that World War Two battles also led to its being given to English children. Some evidence, however, that it is now used independently as a first name, its place name origins having been put aside.

Love (m,f) Probably the surname used as a first name or the word when used by the Puritans in the 17th c. Found in 19th c. records, along with such names as **Loveday, Lovey, Lovie,** which are also transferred surnames.

Lovell (m) Surname derived from a French nickname 'wolf-cub' used as a first name. Used mainly in the 19th c., rarely found in the 20th c. **Lovel** was also used.

Lovina (f) Probably a variant of **Lavinia**, since **Lovinia** also occurs. Both forms were used from time to time in the 19th c.

Low (f) Pet form of **Laura** in the 19th c. and occasionally used independently.

Loyd (m) Variant of **Lloyd** which has occurred since the 14th c. Used again during the 1940s when Lloyd was popular in the U.S.

Luan (f) Form of **Louann** which reached Britain in the 1970s. Subsequently used there more often than **Luane, Luanne, Louanne, Louann.**

Lucas (m) Latin form of **Luke**, a contraction of **Lucanus**, 'man from Lucania', a place in Southern Italy. Almost exclusively a surname form until the 1930s. Increasingly used as a first name in Britain since the late 1960s, when Luke began to become fashionable, but not yet in the U.S.

Lucetta (f) Diminutive of **Lucia** or **Lucy**, used to some extent in the 19th c., but extremely rare since the 1920s. French form **Lucette** also occurred, but was never common.

Lucia (f) Latin feminine of the Roman clan name *Lucius*, derived from *lux* 'light'. Used frequently by early Christians. Saint Lucia, martyred at the beginning of the 4th c., was a popular medieval saint whose name was used in England as **Luce**, later **Lucy**. Camden, in 1605, lists **Lucia** as a 'usual Christian name' of the time and suggests that it was 'a name first given to them that were born when daylight first appeared'. Became very rare until the beginning of the 20th c. Used rather more frequently as Lucy has returned to favour (in Britain), since 1970. Given rise to many diminutive forms, including **Lucetta, Lucilla, Lucille, Lucina, Lucinda**. Lucia remains the modern Italian form of the name, and is known to opera lovers because of Donizetti's *Lucia di Lammermoor* (1835), based on Sir Walter Scott's novel *The Bride of Lammermoor*. Scott calls her Lucy Ashton.

Lucian (m) From Latin *Lucianus*, itself from **Lucius**. Very rarely used in English-speaking countries, though two instances of **Luciano**, the Italian form of the name, have been noted in Britain since 1960. Spanish form **Lucio** occasionally occurs in the U.S.

Lucie (f) French form of **Lucia** or **Lucy**. Used infrequently in English-speaking countries in the 19th c., seemingly not influenced by the example of Lucie Manette, the loving, golden-haired, blue-eyed daughter of Dr Mannette in Dickens's *Tale of Two Cities* (1859). In Britain use of this form has considerably increased since the late 1960s, when Lucy began to return to favour.

Lucien (m) French form of **Lucius** and the more usual form of the name in English-speaking countries in the 20th c. Since the late 1960s the feminine form **Lucienne** has been used increasingly, though only as yet in Britain.

Lucilla (f) See **Lucille**.

Lucille (f) French form of Latin **Lucilla**, a diminutive of **Lucia**. Lucilla well used by

early Christians of the Roman Empire; began to be used in Britain in the 1840s and has continued infrequently since then, though rare in modern times. Lucille first appeared in the 1880s and has been considerably more popular this century, especially from the mid-1950s. In the U.S. the name began to become fashionable in 1940 and was much used for the next fifteen years. It is fairly clear that this was due to Lucille Ball, the comedienne who appeared regularly in films from the early 1930s and then in a television series, *I Love Lucy*, popular in both the U.S. and Britain.

Lucina (f) Originally a derivative of Latin *lucus* 'grove' but the Romans themselves soon associated it with *lux* 'light', since it was the name of the goddess of childbirth, 'she who brings into the light'. Commonly used by the Romans. Appeared in England in the 18th c. Since the 19th c. seems to have become obsolete. In early records is occasionally found as **Lucinna**.

Lucinda (f) Derivative of **Lucia**. A girl of the name appears in *Don Quixote*, by Cervantes (1605). Molière used the name as **Lucinde** in *L'Amour Médicin* and *Le Médicin Malgré Lui*, both written in the 1660s. Taken up by English poets such as Thomson in *The Seasons* (1728) and became fairly popular in the 18th c. because of its fashionable ending (**Belinda, Malinda**, etc., were being much used at the time). Used regularly if infrequently ever since. In the U.S. became more popular when **Lucille** was being much used in the 1940s and early '50s. Pet form **Cindy** used as a name in its own right.

Lucio (m) See **Lucian**.

Lucius (m) Latin *lux* 'light'. Roman first name (*praenomen*) well used by early Christians, though not as frequently as the feminine form **Lucia**. A mythical king of Britain, **Lucius**, is said to have abdicated and become a missionary in Switzerland. Name occurs in several of Shakespeare's plays. Very little used in English-speaking countries, especially in the 20th c. Some instances are found from the 1840s onwards.

Lucky (f) Sometimes used for a girl born on Friday 13th. Luckie is found. See also Felicia.

Lucrece (f) see Lucretia.

Lucretia (f) Latin feminine form of *Lucretius*, a Roman clan name of unknown origin. Lucretia, the wife of the Roman Collatinus, was raped by Sextus. She told her husband and father what had happened and stabbed herself in their presence. The subject was dealt with by Shakespeare in *The Rape of Lucrece* (Lucrece being the French form of the name). Another well-known form of the name, but one not used in English-speaking countries, is the Italian Lucrezia, made infamous by Lucrezia di Borgia. Lucretia, always in that form, occurred regularly if infrequently in the 19th c., then virtually disappeared in the 1920s. Resurfaced in the 1960s and is in occasional modern use, sometimes in the phonetic form Lucrisha. In the U.S. is usually used by black American families.

Lucy (f) Normal English form of Lucia since the Middle Ages, though formerly common as Luce. Commonly used until the end of the 16th c., but infrequent in the 17th c. Revived and used consistently throughout the 18th and 19th cc., enjoying its most popular spell in the 1870s in Britain, a generation later in the U.S. Then faded away, only to be revived again in the 1970s in Britain, where usage was still increasing at the beginning of the 1980s. Associated with Lucy Stone (1818–93), the American reformer and prominent advocate of women's rights. It also brings to mind Lucy Lockitt, the foolish young lady in Gay's *Beggar's Opera* (1727). The Lucy who features in Fielding's *The Virgin Unmasked* (1740) has rather more sense. Goldsmith was of the opinion that the ballad *Lucy and Colin*, written in 1720 by Thomas Tickell, was the best in the language.

Ludovic (m) For the early history of the

name see Louis. Used mainly in Scotland and associated with author/broadcaster Ludovic Kennedy (1919–   ).

Luella (f) Later form of Louella, well used in the U.S. in the 1940s but it then seems to have disappeared.

Luigi (m) Italian form of Louis. Occasionally used in English-speaking countries.

Luis (m) Spanish form of Louis/Lewis, used mainly in the U.S. in the 1950s.

Luke (m) Greek *Loukas* 'from Lucania', Lucania being a district in Southern Italy. Biblical, N.T., where St Luke the Evangelist is the author of the Gospel and the Acts of the Apostles. Introduced to Britain by the Normans, and its use in the Middle Ages gave rise to many surnames such as *Luke*, *Lucas*, *Luck*, etc. Since the 14th c. quietly used in English-speaking countries, though became fashionable in Britain in the late 1960s and has continued to rise in popularity since. By the early 1980s had entered the top fifty list in Britain. Even more popular in Australia during the 1970s and may well spread to other English-speaking countries. Lucas is another form of the name.

Lulu (f) Re-duplicated pet form of Lucy and Louisa in the U.S. in the 1870s when the two full names were popular. Remained very rare in Britain.

Luned (f) See Eluned.

Luther (m) Modern use of this first name is entirely due to Martin Luther (1483–1546), the German religious reformer and translator of the Bible. His translation was also an important literary influence in its own right. The surname, which Martin Luther's father wrote as Luder, derives from Old German *Liuther* or *Lothar*. The original meaning could have been 'people' + 'army' or 'famous people'. In modern times closely associated with Martin Luther King (1929–1968) and has been used by black American families.

Lydia (f) Greek 'woman of Lydia', a region of Asia. Biblical, N.T., Acts 16:14. Occurred fairly frequently in the 17th c.

and popular throughout the 18th and 19th cc. Remains in consistent use in modern times, though not especially fashionable. Most associated with the delightful Lydia Languish in Sheridan's play *The Rivals* (1775), who is always reading sensational novels and moulding her behaviour on them. In Jane Austen's *Pride and Prejudice* (1813) Lydia is the young sister who elopes with Wickham.

Lyla (f) Occasional variant of **Leila**.

Lyle (m) Place name/surname which originally indicated someone who lived on an island, used as a first name regularly in the U.S. and Canada since the 1930s. Most used in the 1950s, but there is a character of the name in *Olive*, by Mrs Craik (1826–87), where it is said to be a name which 'exactly suited the pretty, delicate younger brother'.

Lyman (m) A surname, possibly 'valley dweller'.

Lyn (f) See **Lynn(e)**.

Lynda (f) See **Linda**. This form appears in 1896 but has been used mostly since the 1940s.

Lyndal(l) (m) English place name 'lime tree valley' used occasionally as a first name, especially since **Linda**, **Lynda** became fashionable in the 1940s.

Lyndon (m) English place name 'hill with lime trees' which became a surname. Used as a first name regularly throughout the 19th c. (from the 1840s), and with increasing frequency in the 20th c. In modern times associated with Lyndon B. Johnson, 36th President of the U.S.A. Pet forms **Lyn**, **Lynn** are occasionally used independently, though these are predominantly feminine forms. Later variants of the name have included **Lynden** (from the late 1940s), **Lindon**, **Linden** both in use since the 1880s but infrequent) and the rare **Lindan**.

Lyndsay (f) Frequent variant of **Lindsay**, usually feminine, occasionally male. **Lyndsey** and **Lyndsy** are also found.

Lynelle (f) See **Lynnell**.

Lynette (f) French form of Welsh **Eiluned**,

'idol, icon'. This form of the name derives directly from Tennyson's *Idylls of the King*, which relates the Arthurian legend. **Linet** was an earlier form, but this usually appears now as **Linette**. The name generally has been fairly popular since **Lyn(n)** became fashionable in the 1940s, and the variants **Linnet**, **Linnette**, **Lynnette** and **Lynetta** are also used.

Lynn(e) (f) Pet forms of **Linda** used in their own right, mainly since the 1940s. Both used with almost equal frequency in Britain, Lynn much preferred in the U.S. and Canada. Lyn has also been used to some extent in Britain, rarely elsewhere, and **Lin(n)** is a rare variant. Early bearer of the name was Lynn Fontanne, who was mainly a stage-actress but made rare screen appearances, beginning in 1926. Lynn Bari (Marjorie Bitzer) was often listed among the screen credits from 1933 onwards and may have helped publicize the name. By the early 1980s little used in any of the English-speaking countries.

Lynnell (f) Diminutive of **Lyn/Lynn/ Lynne** in use since the 1940s, mainly in the U.S. **Lynelle** occurs and has also been used in Britain. Other American variants include **Linell**, **Linnell**, **Lynell**.

Lynnette (f) See **Lynette**.

Lynsey (f) Frequent variant of **Lindsay**, usually feminine, occasionally male. **Lynsay** and **Lynsie** also occur.

Lynton (m) Place name deriving from the River Lyn 'torrent'. This form of the name in regular use in Britain since the 1930s. Previously found regularly as **Linton**, a common English place name of several possible origins. The first name may derive directly from the place names, or from the surnames which also derived from the place names.

Lynwen (f) Welsh 'fair image'. **Lynwyn** is also found. Occasionally used in Wales.

Lyra (f) Greek 'lyre'. In use in the 1840s in Britain, but rarely used since. There is a character named Lyra in *Cass Timberlane*, by Sinclair Lewis. Various name books also mention **Lyris**, but no real-life examples noted.

M

Mabel (f) Shortened form of **Amabel** originally, later thought to be French *ma belle* 'my beautiful one'. Therefore often written as **Mabelle**. However, other variants, such as **Mable, Maybel, Maybell, Maybelle**, show that the name had taken on the pronunciation *May-bull* by the mid-19th c., and this became standard. The name enjoyed a great success in the U.S. from the 1870s, until at least 1900. By that time it was being intensively used in Britain, and continued to be popular until the early 1920s. Then went out of fashion and is now rare in all English-speaking countries. Moviebuffs associate the name with Mabel Normand, a comedienne in silent film days. At one time she was Chaplin's co-star.

Mabelle (f) French 'my beautiful one', though in some cases this was a fanciful spelling of **Mabel**, from **Amabel**. Used infrequently 1860–1930.

Mable (f) Frequent variant of **Mabel**.

Macdonald (m) Scottish surname 'son of Donald' used from time to time as a first name since the 1880s. **McDonald** also occurs.

Madaline (f) Frequent variant of **Madeline**.

Madeleine (f) French form of **Magdalen(e)**. Came into use in English-speaking countries in the 1930s, **Madeline** having previously been the preferred form. This may have had something to do with the many screen appearances of Madeleine Carroll (Marie Madeleine Bernadette O'Carroll), which began in 1928. By 1960 Madeleine had become the usual form of the name in Britain, though by that time American parents, who had remained far more faithful to Madeline, had almost stopped using the name. Since 1980 has been very quietly used in all English-speaking countries, Roman Catholic families making most use of it.

Madeline (f) English form of French Madeleine, itself from **Magdalen(e)**. Became quite popular around 1900. In Britain it tended to be replaced in the 1930s by the French Madeleine, but U.S. parents continued to use it. Has always had a wide variety of spellings and pronunciations. Once the middle 'g' had been lost, there was doubt about the final sound, whether it should rhyme with 'din', 'dane', or 'dine'. The first part of the name had also tended to become Maud- rather than Mad-. The following forms, which have all been officially used as first names, indicate the confusion: **Madaleine, Madaliene, Madaline, Madalyn, Madalyne, Maddaline, Madelain, Madelaine, Madelene, Madeliene, Madelin, Madelyn, Madelyne, Madelynne, Madoline, Madilyn, Madlen, Madlyn, Madylon, Madellen, Maudlin**. Preference for a final -a sound, as in **Magdelena**, has led to **Madalaina, Maddelena, Madelina**, the last being the most frequent. For further variants with 'g' see **Magdalen(e)**. The English poets, at least, have been consistent in their use of the name. Keats makes Madeline the heroine of his *Eve of St Agnes*, and Tennyson has a poem addressed to Madeline, who was 'ever varying'. Both poets rhyme the name with 'thine'.

Madge (f) Pet form of **Margaret** through Margery. Came into use at the beginning of the 20th c. and mildly popular in the 1920s.

Mae (f) Variant of **May**. Made known in the 1920s by Mae Murray (Marie Adrienne Koenig), a leading lady in many silent films. In the 1930s Mae West made it famous. Little used in Britain, but reasonably popular in the U.S. until the 1950s.

Magdalen(e) (f) From the name of *St Mary Magdalene*, where the second part of the name indicates that she came from Magdala, a place named for its 'tower'. Introduced into the U.K. from France in the Middle Ages, the sound of the 'g' having already been lost, leading to **Madeline, Madeleine**. In modern times a spelling pronunciation is usual, as it is in **Agnes**, formerly pronounced *Annis*, or *Anyes*. Madeleine was further reduced in sound to give 'maudlin', and the tearful pictures of the saint led to a meaning of over-indulgent sadness. The occurrence of Magdalen or Magdalene in early records therefore gives no exact indication of how the name was being spoken. These may have been written forms of Madeline and Madeleine, which remain the most popular forms, though there are many others. Common variants of the name with the 'g' in the spelling include **Magdaline, Magdelene, Magdlen, Magdelena, Magdalena, Magdelina**. In spite of these many variants, the name has been used very quietly (if one considers that Magdalen(e) and Madel(e)ine are separate names, pronounced differently since the beginning of the 19th c.). German pet form **Magda** is found on very rare occasions, and **Lena** is used.

Maggie (f) Pet form of **Margaret**, especially popular as an independent name in the latter part of the 19th c. **Maggy** also occurred. Rarely used now as a name in its own right, though a spoken diminutive.

Magnolia (f) From the tree. In Edna Ferber's *Showboat* Magnolia is known as **Nola, Nollie** or **Maggie**. Occasionally used.

Magnus (m) Latin *magnus* 'great'. This became a royal name in Norway and Denmark in the 11th c. and was later taken to Scotland, where it became **Manus** in Gaelic. Both forms are quietly used in Scotland, and increased interest in Magnus has been shown in England since 1970. This is presumably due to the publicity given to the television personalities Magnus Magnusson and Magnus Pyke. Occasional variants are found, such as **Magnes, Manius, Manyus**.

Mahala (f) Hebrew 'tenderness'. Biblical O.T., probably the same as **Mahlah** mentioned at Numbers 26:33. Regularly used in the 19th c. and has survived best in modern times in the U.S., though used only rarely since the 1930s. Found in various forms, e.g. **Mahalia** as borne

by Mahalia Jackson, the singer of spirituals. Other variants include **Mahalah, Mahalar, Mahela, Mahelea, Mehala, Mehalah, Mehalia**.

Maidie (f) A use of the word, meaning 'little maid', as a first name. In *Iolanthe*, by Gilbert and Sullivan, a character sings: 'Yours will be the charming maidie.' In such a context 'maidie' could easily be mistaken for a name. The novels of Thomas Hardy contain many examples of the similar 'maidy' used as a vocative. Used as a first name in Britain reasonably frequently until 1930. Resurfaced again briefly in the 1960s, but is a rarely used name.

Mair (f) Welsh form of **Mary**. Regularly used in Wales.

Maire (f) Gaelic form of **Mary**. See also **Mhairi**.

Mairona (f) Diminutive of Irish **Maire** (**Mary**) which appeared in the 1940s but appears to have faded almost immediately.

Mairwen (f) Welsh *Mair* 'Mary' + *wen* 'fair, beautiful'. Used in Wales since the 1930s.

Maisie (f) Scottish pet form of **Margery**, influenced by its Gaelic form **Marsail**. **Mysie** was another form of the name. Maisie came into general use at the beginning of the 20th c. and was especially popular in the 1920s and '30s. Rare since the 1960s. Variant forms include **Maisey, Maisy, Maizie, Maysie, Mazey, Mazie**.

Maitland (m) Norman place name which became an aristocratic British surname. Used regularly, though not in great numbers, as a first name since the 1850s.

Major (m) Use of the surname or military title as a first name. Bardsley says that the name was common in the 17th c. in the north of England. Daniel Defoe has a character called Major Jack in his *Life of Colonel Jack* (1722): 'a Major of the Guards was the father of the child, but she was obliged to conceal the name.' Bardsley suggests instead that the name was used to defy openly the Puritans, who had condemned the use of titles of all kinds. Whatever the reason for the use of the name, examples are easily found in Britain from the 16th c. through to the 1930s. Then disappeared abruptly in the mid-1930s whereas previously it occurred every few years. In the U.S. the name lives on, favoured especially by black American families. The last example noted was a boy born in Detroit in 1978.

Majorie (f) This variant of **Marjorie** appeared in the 1880s and was found regularly until the 1920s. The fact that the male name **Major** was in regular use throughout that period is presumably coincidental.

Malachi (m) Hebrew 'my messenger'. Biblical, O.T., Book of Malachi. He was the last of the minor prophets. Used very rarely. In Ireland usually becomes **Malachy**, the form used by an early Irish saint.

Malcolm (m) Gaelic *Maol Caluim* 'servant of (St) Columba'. A royal name in Scotland and much used there until recent times. Malcolm was the eldest son of Duncan and was staying with him at Macbeth's castle when the latter murdered the king. When Macbeth himself was slain the prince became Malcolm III. Outside Scotland the name began to become popular in England around 1930. Reached a peak of popularity in 1950 but declined thereafter. Known in the U.S. because of the exploits of Sir Malcolm Campbell (1885–1949), who set various speed records, and latterly associated with Malcolm X. American parents use the name quietly but steadily. Rare variant **Malcom** is found.

Maldwyn (m) Welsh form of **Baldwin** 'bold friend'. The Welsh name for the county of Montgomeryshire. In use as a first name, especially for boys born in that county, since the beginning of the 20th c.

Malena (f) Danish pet form of **Magdalene**, occasionally used in English-speaking countries.

Malinda (f) See **Melinda**.

Malina (f) Form of **Magdalene**, influenced by Swedish **Malin** and Danish **Malena**. Infrequently used.

Mallory (m) French 'unlucky, unfortunate'. Nickname which became a surname, and now used from time to time as a first name.

Mally (f) Earlier form of **Molly**. Survived until the mid-19th c. but is now obsolete.

Malonza (f) Three instances of this name have been noted since the 1920s. Presumably a place name transferred to first name use.

Malvern (m) The name of an English beauty spot, the Malvern hills (from Welsh words meaning 'bare hill'), used as a first name in Britain from time to time. Earliest example noted is in 1912, but none recorded after 1951.

Malvin (m) Variant of **Melvin** in use since the 1940s.

Malvina (f) Invented by James Macpherson in the 18th c. for his Ossianic poems. Miss Withycombe has suggested that Gaelic words meaning 'smooth brow' may have inspired the name. When it came into use in the 19th c. it took on the variant form **Melvina**, which in recent times has been the preferred form. Melvina in its turn gave rise to the male name **Melvin**, first used in the 1870s but not in any great numbers until the 1950s. As Melvin became more popular the male name **Malvin** appeared for the first time. In 1982 the public suddenly became aware of the Falkland Islands, known to Argentina as The Malvinas. The Spanish name is a corruption of French Malouines, ultimately from the place name St Malo.

Mamie (f) Pet form of names beginning with M-, especially **Mary**. An extension of **May**. Used independently but very infrequent since the 1920s. **Mamy** is a variant.

Manasseh (m) Hebrew 'causing to forget'. Biblical, O.T., e.g. Gen. 41:51, the elder son of Joseph. Used until the end of the 19th c.

Manda (f) Pet form of **Amanda** first used

in the late 19th c. In the 1960s and '70s re-introduced occasionally as a variant of **Mandy**.

Mandi(e) (f) See **Amanda**.

Mandy (f) Usual spelling of the pet form of **Amanda** or **Miranda** when used as an independent name. Came into use in the 1940s and became especially popular in Britain in the '60s and '70s. Also enjoyed great success in Australia and Canada, no doubt influenced by the child star Mandy Miller (1944–   ).

Manfred (m) Old German 'man peace'. Originally introduced to Britain by the Normans. Rarely used. Associated in modern times with the pop group Manfred Mann.

Manley (m) Surname which probably meant that the original bearer of the name was 'manly'. Used as a first name in the 19th c., but no 20th c. examples have been noted.

Mansel (m) Surname of different origins (e.g. from a French place name or residence in a manse), regularly if infrequently used as a first name. Mansel is the usual form, but **Mansell** is also found.

Mansfield (m) English place name of uncertain origin which became a surname. Used irregularly since the 1860s as a first name.

Manuel (m) Spanish pet form of **Emanuel**, more frequently used in the U.S. than Britain (where it is associated in modern times with a comic figure in *Fawlty Towers*). Feminine form of the name is **Manuela**.

Manuela (f) Feminine form of **Manuel**, used infrequently in English-speaking countries.

Manus (m) See **Magnus**.

Mara (f) Hebrew 'bitter'. Biblical, O.T., Ruth 1:20. 'Do not call me **Naomi** ('pleasant'), call me Mara, for the Almighty has dealt very bitterly with me.' Found from time to time in modern records in both the U.S. and Britain, also as **Marah**.

Maralyn (f) Frequent variant of **Marilyn**. **Maralin, Maralyne, Maralynn** also occur.

Maranda (f) Variant of **Miranda**.

Marbella (f) Shortened form of Latin *Mariabella* 'beautiful **Mary**'. **Marable** was the 17th c. form.

Marc (m) French form of **Mark**. Used since the 1950s as a variant of Mark, especially as parents became aware of how frequently that name was being used.

Marcel (m) French form of Latin *Marcellus*, a diminutive of **Marcus**. First appeared in Britain in the 19th c. as **Marcell**, but used only rarely. In the 20th c. has been used more regularly, especially in the U.S. where it is favoured by black American families, but by no means exclusive to them. **Marcelle** is normally a feminine form, but has been used occasionally for boys. Marcel and Marcell are also on rare occasions used for girls. Other male forms in use include the Italian **Marcello** and the original Latin **Marcellus**.

Marcella (f) Latin feminine of **Marcellus**, a diminutive of **Marcus**. In regular use in all English-speaking countries since the 1860s. The most famous Marcella is probably 'the most beautiful creature ever sent into the world', in *Don Quixote* by Cervantes. Every young man falls in love with her, but she turns them all away. One of her lovers dies of disappointment, and the local shepherds write on his tombstone that Marcella is 'the common enemy of man, whose beauty and cruelty are both in the extreme.' Found in modern times as **Marcela** and **Marsella**. See also **Marcelle**.

Marcelle (f) French feminine form of **Marcel**, but used on rare occasions for boys. In regular if infrequent use in all English-speaking countries since the 1920s, but never as popular as **Marcella**. In the U.S. other feminine forms have come into use in modern times, including **Marcelyn, Marceline, Marcellin**.

Marcene (f) Feminine form of **Marc**, or a development from **Marcia**, used in the U.S. in the 1940s and '50s when Marcia was at its most popular. **Marcine** is a variant, and **Marcena, Marcina** are also found.

March (m) Probably a transferred use of the surname *March* 'dweller by a boundary' rather than the name of the month. Not frequently used. See also **April**.

Marcia (f) Latin feminine of *Marcius*, a Roman name related to **Marcus** and ultimately to Mars, the Roman god of war. Commonly used by the early Christians, but almost unknown in English-speaking countries before the late 19th c. Never especially popular in Britain, but enjoyed considerable success in the U.S. and Canada in the 1940s and '50s. By 1960 had clearly faded. In modern times the phonetic form **Marsha** has been almost as frequently used, in the U.S. especially, as Marcia itself. Pet forms **Marcie, Marcy, Marci** have all been used as names in their own right, and several diminutive forms have emerged, such as **Marcilyn, Marcene, Marcena, Marcine, Marcina**. The name has also been blended to give **Marciann, Marcianna**, etc. Marcia became popular at roughly the same time as **Mark**, so one did not become popular because of the other.

Marci(e) (f) See Marcy.

Marcine (f) See Marcene.

Marco (m) Italian form of **Mark**. Well-established in the U.S., and used to some extent in Britain since the 1960s.

Marcus (m) The Roman name, ultimately from Mars, the Roman god of war, from which English **Mark** was derived. Commonly used by the earliest Christians, but came into use in English-speaking countries only in the mid-19th c. Then used very quietly until Mark's immense popularity caused it to become far more popular in its turn. This happened only in the early 1970s, by which time Mark was so frequently used that parents were looking for alternatives. It was at this time that they also turned to **Marc**. In the U.S. Marcus has been especially favoured in recent years by black American families,

though whites have also used it. By 1980 showing signs of settling back into relative obscurity again.

Marcy (f) Pet form of **Marcia** used independently in the U.S. in the 1940s and '50s. Rare in Britain. **Marcie** and **Marci** also occur, and Marcy is still in use, though infrequently.

Mardi (f) French 'Tuesday'. A name in recent use in the U.S., perhaps inspired by the Mardi Gras festival in New Orleans, or by the example of the actress **Tuesday** Weld (Susan Ker Weld). Herman Melville has a novel called *Mardi*.

Maree (f) Modern phonetic form of French **Marie** used since the 1940s, especially in Australia.

Marella (f) Blend of **Mary** and **Ella**. The name was listed (surprisingly) by Weidenham in his *Baptismal Names* (1931) and in *What to Name the Baby?* (1935). Used only occasionally, and also found as **Marelle**.

Maretta (f) English variant of French **Marietta**, in regular use since the 1860s, though infrequently. **Marette** is a rare variant. In Britain Maretta has been used more often than Marietta, but the French version of the name is preferred in the U.S.

Margaret (f) Greek *margaron* 'pearl'. Latin **Margarita**, French **Marguerite**. The name of a very popular 3rd c. saint. In the Middle Ages the name was common as *Marget, Margret, Margat*. Of these **Margret** still being commonly used in the 19th c., **Margrett** being a variant. Margaret was introduced to Scotland in the 11th c. and went on to become 'the national Scottish female name', as Charlotte Yonge called it in the 19th c. Even in the 1980s about one woman in twenty born in Scotland bears the name, though young Scottish parents are now looking elsewhere. In other English-speaking countries the name was outstandingly popular from the 17th c. onwards, usually running second only to **Mary** in Britain, and high in the popularity lists in the U.S. Began to fade in the 1960s. By the early 1980s being little used in most English-speaking countries. Variants and foreign forms of the name that have been used in English-speaking countries include **Margareta, Margarete, Margaretha, Margarethe, Margarett, Margaretta, Margarette, Margarita, Margarite, Margeret, Margeretta, Margerita, Margharita, Margherita, Margot, Margretta, Margrita, Marguarita, Marguarite, Marguaretta, Marguerette, Marguerita, Marguerite, Margurita, Margurite. Marjorie, Marjory, Margery,** etc., also derive from Margaret, as do the pet forms **Madge, Maggie, Meg, Meggie, Maisie, Mysie, Peg, Peggy.** Meg also gave rise to the Welsh diminutive **Megan** which has been well used. Amongst the famous bearers of the name in the 20th c. have been the British actresses Margaret Leighton, Margaret Lockwood (Margaret Day), and Margaret Rutherford. It has also been distinguished as the name of Britain's first woman Prime Minister, Margaret Thatcher.

Margareta (f) The form in several European languages e.g. German, of **Margaret.** Used occasionally in English-speaking countries.

Margaretta (f) Form of **Margaret** much used in English-speaking countries. Shows the clear influence of various European versions of Margaret, such as **Margareta, Margarita,** while changing the pronunciation of the penultimate syllable.

Margarita (f) The form of **Margaret** in many languages, e.g. Spanish, regularly used this century in all English-speaking countries, though not in great numbers.

Margeret (f) Variant of **Margaret** in regular use, no doubt influenced by **Margery.**

Margery (f) French *Margerie*, an early spoken form of **Marguerite** (**Margaret**). When the name appeared in England in the 12th c. it was also spelt **Marjory, Margorie, Margorie, Margory.** The remarks of Camden (1605) and others make it clear that Margery was felt to be

an independent name, not a form of Margaret, from an early date. Use of the name in the surname period had led to family names such as *Margary, Margison.* Remained in use quietly until the end of the 19th c., when it became decidely popular in the U.S., **Marjorie** being the preferred form. This also became the usual form of the name in Britain when the name rose to popularity in the 1920s. Remained popular in all English-speaking countries until the late 1930s, but suffered from the increased usage in domestic life of margarine, the butter-substitute. This was promptly pronounced as if it were *marjarine*, and often abbreviated to 'marge', which was already established as a pet form of the name. Now little used in any of its forms, though when it does occur it is usually as Marjorie.

Margherita (f) Italian form of **Margaret,** used from time to time in English-speaking countries.

Margo (f) Phonetic form of French **Margot**, ultimately from **Margaret.** Used in Scotland and Australia especially, but also in the U.S.

Margorie (f) Reasonably common variant of **Marjorie**, influenced by **Margery.** Margory has also been steadily used.

Margot (f) French form of **Margaret** usually pronounced, and often written, as **Margo.** Some speakers pronounce the name in the German way, sounding the final 't'. Used mainly in the U.S., Scotland and Australia. In England the name has been quietly used in the 20th c., and very rarely since the 1960s. Made famous by the English ballet dancer Dame Margot Fonteyn (Margaret Hookham).

Margret (f) Medieval form of **Margaret** regularly used in the 19th c. Occasionally found in more recent use, also as **Margarett. Margretta** is found as a variant of **Margaretta.**

Marguerita (f) Latinized form of **Marguerite** consistently used since the 1880s, though never in great numbers. **Margarita** has been the slightly more common form of the name.

Marguerite (f) French form of **Margaret;** also a flower name. Probably used most frequently because of its floral meaning, since it came into use at the same time as **Daisy.** Appeared in the 1860s and used steadily since then. Most popular 1920–50 in Britain, and well used in the U.S. in the 1940s.

Margurite (f) This cross between **Margaret** and **Marguerite** occurs regularly in records since the 1880s, though not in great numbers.

Mari (f) Occasional modern variant of **Marie.**

Maria (f) Latin form of **Mary,** also the normal form of that name in several European languages. Maria was the written form of Mary in Latin records in early times, but became a spoken form in the 18th c. Remained popular until the 1870s, then faded. Recovered in the 1940s, especially in the U.S. Considerably boosted in the 1960s, probably helped by the song 'Maria' from *West Side Story* (1961), the modern version of *Romeo and Juliet.* The usual pronunciation of the name has led to the variant **Marea.** In the 19th c. the pronunciation Mar-eye-ah was often used, though some remarks made by Thackeray in *Pendennis* make it clear that this was considered to be uneducated and a sign of low social rank. **Mariah** was a fairly common variant in the 19th c. **Mariae** is also found.

Mariam (f) The form of **Mary** used in the Greek translation of the Bible. **Miriam** is another form of the name. Never frequently used, but found regularly in the 19th c. and on rare occasions in modern times.

Marian (f) English form of **Marion,** in use since the Middle Ages. There was a natural tendency to interpret Marion as a blend of **Mary** and **Ann.** Such a blend actually existed in French as **Marianne,** Marion having a slightly different origin. Well used in the Middle Ages, a famous early name-bearer being Maid Marion, Robin Hood's partner. In the 18th c. Mary Ann was used instead of

Marian, but the latter name returned to use by the 1840s. Quietly but steadily used ever since. During the 19th c. sometimes given a Latinized form, as **Mariana.** Other variants include **Mariane** and **Mariann.**

Marianna (f) Latinized form of **Marianne** used mainly in the 19th c.

Marianne (f) French blend of **Marie** and **Anne,** first used in Britain in the 18th c. Mildly popular in the first half of the 19th c. In Jane Austen's novel *Sense and Sensibility* it is Marianne Dashwood who displays the sensibility of the title, though sense prevails in the end. Then virtually disappeared for a hundred years. Reappeared in the early 1950s and steadily used since. In the 1960s Marianne Faithfull was a well-known British actress.

Marie (f) French form of **Mary.** Also the earlier form of the name in England until the Authorized Version of the Bible established Mary as the English spelling. Began to be used again in English-speaking countries in the mid-19th c. In the U.S. it remained for a long time a popular alternative to Mary, a role played by **Maria** in Britain. British parents then rediscovered the name in the 1960s, and by 1970 were using Marie more often than Mary. Still hovering at the bottom of the British top fifty list in the early 1980s. This renewal of interest possibly brought about by use of the name in several popular songs of the time. In the U.S., by 1980, being very quietly used.

Mariel (f) Diminutive of **Marie.** In France and the Netherlands usually spelt **Marielle.** In Italy becomes **Mariella.** **Mariela** is also found. These various forms occur occasionally in English-speaking countries.

Marietta (f) French diminutive of **Marie,** used in English-speaking countries since the 1850s. This is the usual form of the name in the U.S. Occurs also in Britain, but there has been a preference there for **Maretta. Mariette** is a rare variant.

Marigold (f) The flower name '(the Virgin) **Mary** + gold'. Regularly but quietly used as a first name in the 20th c., mainly in Britain.

Marilyn (f) Blend of **Mary** and **Ellen** or a use of Mary plus the popular name element -lyn. One of the earliest users of the name was Marilyn Miller, the musical star of the 1920s (born Mary Ellen Reynolds). Almost certainly her influence made Marilyn a popular success in the U.S. in the 1920s and '30s. In the early 1940s Marilyn Maxwell (Marvel Maxwell) began to appear regularly on cinema screens. By this time Marilyn had reached Britain and was rapidly becoming extremely popular. Reached its peak in 1950, but British parents turned away from it at that point. By 1950 use of the name in the U.S. also declining steadily, despite screen appearances of Marilyn Monroe from 1948 through the 1950s (she had been re-named by a casting agent who had Marilyn Miller in mind). Variant forms include **Marillyn, Marilynn, Marilynne, Maralyn** (frequent), **Maralyne, Maralynn, Maralin, Marrilyn, Marrilynn, Marrilynne, Marolyn, Marylin, Marylyn** (frequent), **Merilyn.**

Marina (f) Latin feminine of *Marinus*, which was possibly a diminutive of *Marius* and not necessarily connected with Latin *mare* 'the sea'. That has been the natural supposition for centuries, and Shakespeare certainly thought of it in that way. In *Pericles* he tells us that his princess is 'Call'd Marina, for I was born at sea'. Minor flurry of interest in the name in the 1930s when Princess Marina of Greece married Prince George. Since the 1950s steadily but quietly used in all English-speaking countries. Variant **Marena** has been noted.

Marinda (f) Diminutive of **Mary** using a popular feminine suffix, in occasional use since the 1860s.

Mario (m) Italian form of Latin *Marius*, a Roman clan name probably connected with *Mars*, the god of war. Well used by black American families in modern

times, and used regularly in Britain since the 1950s. **Marius** is used more rarely, though the actor Marius Goring has made the name well known in Britain.

Marion (f) French diminutive of **Marie**, introduced to England by the Normans in the Middle Ages. Quickly given the English form **Marian**, which in turn was interpreted as **Mary Ann** by the end of the 18th c. Marion was rediscovered towards the middle of the 19th c. By the 1870s was being reasonably well used, and remained so for a hundred years. Still in use in all English-speaking countries, though not in great numbers. Marion still tends to be used rather more often than Marian. The well-known example of Marion Michael Morrison, who later became John Wayne, shows that the name can occasionally be used for men. In that role it probably represents a transferred surname.

Maris (f) Latin, from the phrase *stella maris* 'star of the sea', one of the titles of the Virgin Mary. Seems to have been used for the first time in the 1920s but has never been frequent. The later **Marisa** and **Marise** may represent direct developments from the name.

Marisa (f) Variant of **Marise** which came into regular use in the 1950s. Could also represent a development of **Maris**. **Marisha** also appeared in the 1960s.

Marise (f) Form of **Mary** influenced by the Dutch pet form **Maryse** and the Swiss **Marisa**, or a development from **Maris**. Infrequently used.

Marissa (f) Variant of **Marisa** used since the 1950s, though infrequently.

Marita (f) Probably a diminutive of **Mary** by analogy with **Anita, Rosita,** etc. To the Romans Marita was the feminine of Latin *maritus* and meant 'married woman'. Used steadily in modern times.

Marius (m) See Mario.

Marjorie (f) By far the most popular form, especially in the U.S., of the name that began life as **Margerie** in French, a popular form of **Marguerite**. The earliest English form in the Middle Ages was **Margery**. In Britain the spelling

Marjory has also been well used. For details of the name's usage and its decline see **Margery**. **Marjery** and **Marjori** are also found.

Mark (m) English form of Latin **Marcus**, a Roman *praenomen* ultimately from Mars, the Roman god of war. Biblical, N.T., St Mark the Evangelist. Not in common use in the Middle Ages, so that surnames deriving from it (*Marke*, etc.) are rare. In more general use in the 17th c. and remained so until the beginning of the 19th c. Then used very infrequently until the early 1950s, when it suddenly became extremely fashionable in all English-speaking countries. In the U.S. faded considerably since the late 1970s. In Britain still intensively used in 1980, but showing the first signs of a loss of popularity. Strongly associated with Mark Twain (1835–1910), author of *The Adventures of Tom Sawyer* and *Huckleberry Finn*. As is well-known, the writer was actually Samuel L. Clemens, and took his pen-name from a call used by Mississippi boatmen: 'Mark twain' indicated that the water was to be two fathoms deep. It could hardly have been Mark Twain who caused the name to leap into popularity in the 1950s, however, and no one has so far been able to explain why it happened.

Markham (m) Place name 'homestead on the boundary' which became a surname, used occasionally as a first name. The surname **Marks**, which sometimes has much the same original meaning as Markham, but can also link with **Marcus**, also occurs as a first name.

Marla (f) Back-formation from **Marlene** first used in the U.S. in the early 1940s. Reasonably well used until the end of the 1970s, but now rare. British parents on the whole do not seem to have been aware of the name, though one English girl received the name in 1977.

Marleen (f) Common variant of **Marlene** 1930–60, but now rarely used.

Marlena (f) Occasional variant of **Marlene**, reflecting the original German pronunciation of that name.

Marlene (f) Blend of **Maria** and **Magdalene**, used by the German actress Marlene Dietrich as her stage name. Her film career began in the 1920s, and the name first began to be used in English-speaking countries in the 1930s. At its height in the 1940s and '50s but has subsequently faded. The popular wartime song 'Lili Marlene' no doubt influenced usage. Some parents used phonetic spellings to indicate their preferred pronunciation of the name. **Marlaina**, for instance, roughly keeps the pronunciation of the original German name. **Marlane** and **Marlaine** differentiate the name from **Marleen**, a common variant, and **Marline**, also fairly frequent. The latter form seems to have given rise to **Marlin**, later **Marlyn**, **Marlyne**, and by this time the name is becoming confused with **Marilyn**. Another development in the 1940s was the use of **Marla** as a shortened form of the name. This survived well in the U.S. until the late 1970s. **Marlea**, **Marlee**, **Marley**, **Marlie** also began to be used in the 1940s but did not survive.

Marlea (f) Pet form of **Marlene** used during the 1940s in the U.S. Variants were **Marlee**, **Marley**, **Marlie**, all used in roughly equal numbers, and all of which seem to have faded in the 1950s.

Marlin (m, f) See **Marlyn**.

Marline (f) Variant of **Marlene**, used fairly frequently while that name was popular. Pronunciation is usually as *Marleen*.

Marlo (f) Apparently a variant of the surname *Marlowe* used as a first name. Sudden flurry of interest around 1970, especially by black American families. **Marlow** also used for girls at that time, and **Marlowe** occasionally used for boys. Marlo could have been seen as a feminine form of **Marlon**, or as a pet form of **Marlene**. In any case, the name disappeared almost as quickly as it had come.

Marlon (m) Modern use of this name is entirely due to the actor Marlon Brando, whose screen appearances began in 1950. The actor's family is said to be of French origin. Marlon is not a French first name, and the closest one can get to it in a French context is the family name *Marlin*, indicating an ancestor whose name was **Merlin**. In the U.S. has been used almost exclusively by black families since the 1960s. First recorded in Britain in 1963.

Marlyn (f) Variant of **Marlene**, strongly influenced by **Marilyn**, which appeared in the U.S. in the early 1940s and was used until the 1960s. **Marlin** appeared slightly earlier than Marlyn, and may have derived from **Marline**, another variant of **Marlene**.

Marmaduke (m) Of uncertain origin, though Irish *Maelmaedoc* 'servant of St Maedoc' or an Irish name *Meriaduc* have been suggested as possible sources for the name. Mainly used in Yorkshire and found regularly between the 16th c. and 18th c. Used irregularly throughout the 19th c., but disappeared at the beginning of the 20th c., other than as the name of a large dog who features in a popular British cartoon strip. Pet form of the name is **Duke**, used on very rare occasions as a name in its own right.

Marna (f) Otterbjörk, in his *Svenska Förnamm*, gives this as a form of **Marina** and compares it with **Karna** from **Karina**, **Elna** from **Elina**. Being used in the U.S. by the early 1940s, presumably by families of Scandinavian descent. **Marne, Marni, Marnie, Marney** and the like appeared after the 1964 release of the Hitchcock thriller *Marnie*, with Tippi Hedren in the title role. Marnie, in particular enjoyed a period of mild popularity for ten years. These are all presumably pet forms of the same name, and could have been influenced by **Marnia**, the name listed by Winthrop Ames in *What Shall We Name the Baby?* (1935). Ames also gave the explanation that the name was a form of Marina. Sue Browder has also claimed that Marni is a Hebrew name meaning 'to rejoice'. Marni is the form of the name used by Marni

Nixon, the singer who has dubbed the voices of many film stars in various films.

Marrianne (f) See **Marianne**. Most of the names that normally have a single 'r' are also found with 'rr', e.g. **Marrian, Marrietta, Marrilyn, Marrina, Marrion**.

Marsden (m) Common English place name 'boundary valley' and surname, regularly used in the 19th c. (though infrequently) as a first name.

Marsha (f) Phonetic form of **Marcia** in use in the U.S. since the 1920s. In Britain appeared for the first time in the 1940s, a hundred years later than the first appearance of Marcia. American parents have used Marsha almost as often as Marcia in modern times, though both forms of the name have faded since 1960. **Marshia** is occasionally found.

Marshall (m) Germanic, but introduced to England as a Norman term, the original meaning being 'horse-servant'. Covered a wide range of functions from a farrier to a high officer of state. The word became an occupational surname, especially frequent in Scotland, and in use as a first name since at least the beginning of the 19th c. Still used regularly in all English-speaking countries. **Marshal** is an occasional variant.

Marston (m) Place name/surname, originally indicating residence near a marshy place, used as a first name, though infrequently.

Marten (m) Probably a variant of **Martin** rather than the animal which is akin to the weasel. This form of the name occurs in the 1940s and '50s.

Martha (f) Aramaic 'lady, mistress of the house'. Biblical, N.T., Luke 10:38. The image of the Biblical Martha is of a hard-working, rather anxious housewife, and she became the patron saint of house-bound wives. Very popular from the 16th c. to the beginning of the 20th c. in Britain, when it lost favour and has never recovered. In the U.S. strongly associated with the first First Lady, Martha Washington, and its popularity continued into the 1950s.

Subsequently faded. Sometimes found in its Italian form **Marta**, also in pet forms such as **Marti, Martie, Marty**. Earlier pet forms **Mattie, Matty** have also been used independently. Occasional extensions of the name such as **Marthena** seem to suggest that it may later have become confused with **Martina**. The French **Marthe** is rare.

Martin (m) Latin *Martinus*, a diminutive of *Martius*, from *Mars*, the god of war. Common name amongst early Christians of the Roman Empire and made famous by St Martin of Tours, who lived in the 4th c. Frequent use of the name in the Middle Ages accounts for the commonness of the surname *Martin*. Continued in popular use from the 16th c. to the 18th c. Regularly used throughout the 19th c., but became noticeably popular only in the 1950s. In the 1980s clearly fading rapidly. In American history it is associated with Martin van Buren, 8th President of the U.S.A. In literature it recalls *Martin Chuzzlewit*, the novel by Charles Dickens, whose hero is snobbish and rather foolish for most of the story. The book did not encourage parents to use the name. During its fashionable spell in the 1950s and '60s it often occurred as **Martyn**. Feminine forms **Martine** and **Martina** also became reasonably popular at that time.

Martina (f) Latin feminine of **Martin**, used mainly in the 1950s and '60s. Best-known bearer, however, is probably the Czech-born tennis player Martina Navratilova.

Martine (f) French feminine form of **Martin**. Came into use to some extent in the 1950s and '60s but subsequently faded.

Marty (m, f) Pet form of **Martin**, but sometimes from **Martha**. Adopted by the British pop singer Reginald Smith, who became Marty Wilde, but used mainly in the U.S. as a girl's name.

Martyn (m) Common variant of **Martin** in use since the 1930s.

Marvin (m) From the Old Welsh name **Merfin** or **Merfyn**, the name of a 9th c.

king. It is *not* the same name as **Mervyn**, but the meaning is uncertain. Taken up in the U.S. in the 19th c. Rose steadily in popularity and reached a peak in the 1920s. Faded slowly, and becoming rare in the early 1980s. Black American families had tended to remain faithful to it longer than most, and almost made the name their own from the mid-1960s. Used only rarely in Britain, though belated signs of interest being shown in the late 1970s. Variant forms of the name include **Marvyn** and **Marvine**, but these are rarely used. No one has been able to suggest why the name reappeared in the 19th c. and appealed so much to American parents while British parents virtually ignored it. *Marvin* is a surname, and someone bearing the name may have inspired its use.

Mary (f) See **Miriam** for meaning. Mary is the English form of Greek **Maria**, itself a form of **Miriam**. As the name of the Blessed Virgin, Mary was at first considered to be too holy for ordinary use. Began to be used in England in the 12th c., and by the 16th c. was the most frequently used name for girls. For nearly three hundred years its only real rivals were **Margaret** and **Ann**. This popularity was matched in other Christian countries, where **Maria** or **Marie** was as frequent as Mary in English-speaking countries. Charlotte Yonge reports on a saying: 'To seek Maria in Ravenna.' The meaning was 'to look for a needle in a haystack.' Ways had to be found to distinguish between all the girls called Mary, and many pet-forms were used. These included **Mal** and **Mally** (compare **Sal** and **Sally** from **Sarah**), which later became **Moll** and **Molly**, then **Polly**. **May, Minnie, Mamie** have been other pet forms used independently. American parents remained completely faithful to Mary until the 1950s, but it then began to fade rapidly as a first name. No doubt the name is preserved as a middle name in countless families, as it is in Britain, but by 1980 it had become unusual to hear girls in kindergarten actually answering to the name. British parents had turned away from it by the 1940s, and by 1980 it was no longer among the top fifty girls' names. The name has many royal associations, as well as Christian, and it has been borne by many famous women. The Canadian actress Mary Pickford was outstanding among them, rightly known at one time in her career as the 'world's sweetheart'. Miss Pickford had chosen to become a Mary – she was born Gladys Smith. Many poets have celebrated the special significance and sound of Mary. For Byron it was a 'magic' name. Oliver Wendell Holmes, in his poem *L'Inconnue*, had this to say:

And she to whom it once was given.
Was half of earth and half of heaven.

The name will obviously remain a special one, but for the moment it does not seem to have the right image in the minds of young parents.

Mary-Ann(e) (f) Blend of **Mary** and **Ann** or **Anne** which became common in the 18th c. After 1900 it virtually disappeared until the 1950s. **Mary-Ann**, especially, well used in the 1960s, but a slackening of interest since. Parents probably think they are restoring **Marian** to its original form by using the compound name, though that was actually Mary with a diminutive ending -on, which gave rise to **Marion.**

Marylyn (f) Frequent variant of **Marilyn**. **Marylyn** is also found.

Masie (f) Common variant of **Maisie**.

Mason (m) Surname, indicating an ancestor who was a stone-mason, regularly if infrequently used as a first name since the 1840s.

Mathew (m) Common variant of **Matthew**.

Matilda (f) Old German *Mahthild(is)* 'mighty in battle'. Introduced to Britain by the wife of William the Conqueror in the 11th c. Normal spoken form of the name seems to have been **Maud**, and pet forms such as **Tilly** were in use. Matilda

itself little used after the 13th c., but revived in the 18th c. In Britain it continued to be popular in the first half of the 19th c., but subsequently declined. Never especially popular in the U.S., but continues to be used occasionally, as it does in other English-speaking countries. The famous song 'Waltzing Matilda' refers to an Australian slang expression and originally meant to carry one's personal possessions rolled up in a bundle.

Matthew (m) Hebrew 'gift of the Lord'. Biblical, N.T., the name of the Apostle and Evangelist. The commonness of surnames such as *Matthews*, *Mayhew*, *Matheson*, etc., all testify to the frequency of use in the Middle Ages. Remained in frequent use until the beginning of the 19th c., when it faded into the background, always present in official records of births, but obviously not especially fashionable. After the beginning of the 20th c. the name faded still further. On the point of disappearing in the 1940s when it suffered a sudden and dramatic change of fortune, both in the U.S. and Britain. By the late 1970s one of the most frequently-used names in the English-speaking world. In the early 1980s appeared to have passed its peak in the U.S. and was fading quickly. In Britain it was leading the field amongst male names by a substantial margin. Not clear what brought about the change of fortune, but the name had survived most strongly in Scotland before it was rediscovered by American and British parents. Variant **Mathew** is often used, and the diminutive **Matt** is occasionally found as an independent name. Perhaps worth noting that Matthew (and **Mark**) rose sharply in popularity as **John** fell from its leading position. Perhaps as Matthew and Mark fall from favour, parents will turn to **Luke**. There are clear signs that British parents are already doing so.

Matthias (m) Greek and Latin form of **Matthew**. The name of the disciple who was chosen by lot to replace Judas Iscariot. Little is heard of him after that. Used since the 17th c., very regularly, but at no time in great numbers. **Mathias** is found as a variant. Use of Matthias in the U.S. no doubt owes something to the influence of German settlers, since it has remained the normal form of Matthew in German-speaking countries.

Mattie (f) Pet form of **Matilda** used independently. In common use in the 18th c. but then rare until 1940, when it began to appear in the U.S. again. Remained in use until the 1950s before fading. Matilda itself did not come back into favour at the time, and the reason for the reappearance of the pet name has not been explained.

Maud (f) Early contracted form of **Matilda**. Old German *Mahthild* became in French *Mahault*, *Maheut*, *Maheud*, *Maud*. The name's use in the Middle Ages, after its introduction to England by the Normans, led to surnames such as *Maudson*, *Mawson*. Camden mentioned Maud as a 'usual Christian name' in 1605, but it was being rarely used at that time. Revived strongly in the 1840s, often as **Maude**, and given impetus by Tennyson's poem *Maud*, published in 1855. The poem was made widely known by its musical version, 'Come Into the Garden, Maud.' At its most popular from the 1870s to 1910 in all English-speaking countries, though more used in Britain than elsewhere. Then faded, and since the 1950s extremely rarely used. Pet form **Maudie** sometimes given as an independent name while the name was being used.

Maura (f) Phonetic form of **Moira**, Irish **Maire** (**Mary**). The name of two saints. In modern times has been most used in Ireland, with occasional usage elsewhere in the English-speaking world.

Maureen (f) Irish *Mairin*, diminutive of *Maire* (**Mary**). Came into use at the end of the 19th c. and at its most popular 1925–55 in Britain, 1945–65 in the U.S. Now quietly used. Amongst the best known name-bearers has been Maureen O'Sullivan, the Irish star whose screen career began in 1930 and continued for forty years. She is the mother of Mia Farrow. Maureen O'Hara (Maureen Fitzsimmons) began her career rather later but also enjoyed great success. Variants of the name include **Moreen**, **Moureen**, **Maurene**, **Maurine**, **Morreen**, **Mureen**.

Maurice (m) Latin *Mauritius* 'Moorish, dark-skinned'. The name of an early saint, and used by Christians of the Roman Empire. The Normans introduced the name to Britain, and its common use led to surnames such as *Morris*, *Morse*, *Morcock*. Remained popular until the 17th c., then faded until the middle of the 19th c. At its peak in the U.S. in the 1870s, but most used in Britain 1910–40. Popularity of the French entertainer Maurice Chevalier helped it from 1930 onwards. British cinema audiences also associated it with the actor Maurice Denham. Irish parents used the name in former times as a substitute for *Muirgheas* 'sea-choice', and the name was popular in Ireland before it reached the rest of Britain. **Morris**, now the normal form of the surname, has been used very frequently for the first name. Variants include **Morice**, **Moris**, **Morrice**, **Morriss**, **Morry**. **Moss**, one of the Irish pet forms of the name, occurs independently. Since the 1960s black American families have shown a particular liking for the name.

Maven (f) Also **Mavin**, **Mavine**, **Mavon**. **Mabyn** is probably also from the same name, Irish **Maeve** (*Meadhbh*), name of a 1st c. queen, but of unknown meaning.

Mavis (f) Poetical word for the songthrush which suddenly appeared as a first name in the 1890s. Marie Corelli was probably responsible, using it to name a character in her novel *The Sorrows of Satan* (1894). Reached its height in Britain in 1935 but has since become rare. Sometimes found in official records as **Mayvis** or **Mavies**. Little used in the U.S.

Max (m) Pet form of **Maximillian, Maxwell** or **Maxine** used as a name in its own right. Occurs first in the 1880s and at its most popular in Britain in the 1930s, though never especially frequent. Use of the name followed a similar pattern in the U.S. Well-known bearers of the name include Sir Max Beerbohm (1872–1956), the English essayist and critic, Max Miller (Harold Sargent), and Max Wall (Maxwell Lorimer), both actor-comedians, and Max Bygraves, the British entertainer.

Maxime (m) Latin *Maximus* 'the greatest', a very common Roman name much used by early Christians. Also the modern French form of the name which is occasionally used in English-speaking countries.

Maxine (f) Modern feminine form of **Max** which appeared in the late 1930s. Reasonably well used from 1950 to the late 1970s, especially in Britain, but appears to have faded. Miss Withycombe makes the rather extraordinary statement that Maxine is 'a favourite modern French girl's name'. In fact the name will not be found in any French name dictionary, and French people consider it to be an English name. The Romans used a female name **Maxima** 'greatest' which failed to survive in French, though there is a male name **Maxime**, from Latin *maximus*. Also found in English-speaking countries as **Maxene, Maxeen, Maxina, Maxena.**

Maxwell (m) Scottish place name and surname regularly used as a first name. Original meaning of the name was probably 'Maccus's well'. Especially well used in Scotland, but made known in the U.S. by such men as Maxwell Anderson (1888–1959), the playwright whose works were often made into films.

May (f) In the Middle Ages probably a form of **Matthew** (**Mayhew**). Its use led to the surname *May*. When the name came back into use in the 19th c. it was as a pet form of **Mary** or other names beginning with M-. Probably not thought of as a use of the month name until the 1920s, by which time **Avril, April** and **June** were being used (see **April**). Extremely popular in the U.S. in the 1870s, and in Britain at its peak around 1900. Now rarely used. **Mae** has been the main variant form, and the name has been extended in the U.S. to form new names such as **Mayberry, Maybeth, Maydee, Mayelene, Mayella, Mayetta.** In Britain **Mayday, Mayrene** and **Mayvoureen** have been used. **Maybel(le)** also occurs, a variant of **Mabel**, as **Mayvis, Maysie** are variants of **Mavis, Maisie.**

Maya (f) Looks like the name of the Indian tribe in South America and southern Mexico, but may simply be **May** given a modern look. Used in the early 1980s by both black and white Americans.

Maynard (m) English surname 'strength-hard' used regularly if infrequently as a first name since the 1870s.

Mazey (f) Fairly frequent variant of **Maisie. Mazie** also occurs.

McDonald (m) See **Macdonald.**

Meagan (f) American variant of **Megan. Meaghan** also occurs.

Medina (f) Arabic 'city'. Place name used as a first name. The original city, north of Mecca, is where the Prophet Mohammad died, but there are many places of this name in the U.S.

Medora (f) The name of the heroine in Byron's poem *The Corsair* (1814). Sophy Moody suggested that it meant 'mother's gift'. It has occasionally been used in Britain as a first name.

Meg (f) Pet form of **Margaret**. Formerly much used in Scotland. Sir Walter Scott has several characters in his novels who bear the name. As an independent name it has mostly been used as **Meggie** or **Megan.**

Megan (f) Welsh pet form of **Margaret**, adapting the old-established **Meggie**. Received publicity early in the 20th c. when Lloyd George became Prime Minister in England, since he had used the name for his daughter. Has been steadily used and has spread to all English-speaking countries, often taking the form **Meghan, Meagan, Meaghan** in the U.S. This is due to the insistence by several otherwise reliable name commentators that the name has an Irish origin. In Britain the name is usually pronounced Meg (to rhyme with 'peg') plus -an. U.S. bearers of the name sometimes prefer Meegan or May-gan.

Meggie (f) Diminutive of **Margaret** which came into use as a name in its own right in the 1870s and was well-used for a generation. **Meggy** was a common variant, but both forms seem to have disappeared.

Meghan (f) U.S. variant of **Megan**.

Mehala(h) (f) Also **Mehalia**. See **Mahala**.

Mehetabel (f) Hebrew 'God does good'. Biblical, O.T., the name of two women mentioned there. Mehetabel is occasionally found in 19th c. records.

Meirion (m) Welsh name of the county of Merioneth. **Meirionwen** and **Meirionfa** are feminine forms. **Merion** and **Merrion** also occur.

Mel (m, f) Pet form of names beginning *Mel-* used independently.

Melanie (f) Greek *melaina*, feminine of *melas* 'black, dark-complexioned'. Earliest form of the Christian name was **Melania**, borne by two saints. In use in Britain by the 17th c., especially in Cornwall. Remained a rare name, however, until the heroine of *Gone With the Wind*, Melanie Hamilton, caused it to come into fashion in all English-speaking countries. Its rise began in 1940, but by 1980 there were signs that it was fading rapidly on all sides. Used in many variant forms, including **Melaine, Melane, Melani, Melany, Mellanie, Melloney, Mellony, Melonie, Melony**.

Melantha (f) Form of **Melanie**. A character of this name appears in Dryden's *Marriage à la Mode* (1672). Rarely used.

Melba (f) Use of this first name was entirely due to the Australian operatic soprano Nellie Melba, born Helen Mitchell (1861–1931). The stage name was suggested by Melbourne, the city from which she came. Melba has lived on as a name because of the peach-Melba, created in the singer's honour by Escoffier, chef at the Savoy Hotel in London in 1892. Melba first appeared as a Christian name in 1913. Has continued to be used, in Britain and the U.S., though now very rare.

Melbourne (m) Place name of several possible origins which became an aristocratic surname, used from time to time as a first name since the 1880s. May occasionally be a direct borrowing from the Australian city.

Meleta (f) Occasional variant of **Melita**.

Melia (f) Pet form of **Amelia** used since the 1950s in its own right, though infrequently.

Melicent (f) See **Millicent**.

Melina (f) Greek *meli* 'honey' with a diminutive ending, or a pet form of **Carmelina, Emmelina**, etc. Used independently since the 19th c., but had virtually disappeared before the Greek actress Melina Mercouri began to appear regularly on the cinema screen in the mid-1950s. Now occasionally found, together with its variant **Meleana**.

Melinda (f) Latin *mel* 'honey' plus *-inda*, a highly fashionable name element in the 18th c. Many new names were formed with it on the analogy of **Belinda**, such as **Clarinda, Dorinda, Florinda**, etc. The name was mainly in literary use until the 1840s, when it came into regular use as a first name. **Malinda** is a frequent variant. **Melinder, Mellinda, Melynda** are also found.

Meliora (f) Latin *melior* 'better.' Melior occurs as both family name and given name in Christian inscriptions of the Roman Empire. A St Meliorius gave his name to a church in Cornwall, which may account for the tradition that Meliora is an exclusively Cornish name. In fact it was generally used by the Puritans in the 16th and 17th cc., often as **Melyor, Mellear** etc. By the 19th c. it had acquired its final -a and was regarded, according to Mrs Craik's remark in her best-selling novel *Olive*, as 'eccentric'. But wherever Meliora went, Mrs Craik tells us, 'she always brought "better things" – at least in anticipation.' The name is now rare.

Melissa (f) Greek *melissa* 'bee'. Used as a personal name in early Greece, and occasionally found in Christian inscriptions of the Roman Empire. Used in Italy in the 16th c. in poetry, together with **Melisso**, the name of Melissa's father. Became one of the top girls' names in America in the early 1970s. Usage increased considerably at that time in Britain, but it did not achieve such a high placing in the most popular name-lists. Often found as **Mellissa**. **Melisa** and **Mellisa** are occasional variants. Steady use of the name in the 19th c. probably due to use in Charles Dickens's *The Old Curiosity Shop* (1841), Tennyson's poem *Princess* (1847) and Gilbert and Sullivan's *Princess Ida* (1884).

Melita (f) Greek *meli* (genitive *melitos*), Latin *mel, mellis* 'honey'. (Latin *mellitus*, feminine *mellita* 'sweet as honey'.) It can also derive from Greek *Melite*, Latin *Melita* 'the island of Malta'. Used as a first name since the 1860s.

Mellanie (f) Frequent variant of **Melanie**.

Mellicent (f) See **Millicent**.

Mellissa (f) Common variant of **Melissa**. **Mellisa** also occurs.

Melloney (f) Fairly frequent variant of **Melanie**. **Mellony** is also found.

Melody (f) The word used as a name. Reaney records a 13th c. example leading to the surname *Melody*, but it was clearly not a common name. An 18th c. example was Melody Franklin of Dunton, in Buckinghamshire, whose daughter Melody married Thomas Dunklin. Came into general use in the 1940s and reasonably well used since in both the U.S. and Britain. Often found as **Melodie**, but the early Latin form **Melodia** appears to be obsolete.

Melonie (f) Frequent variant of **Melanie**. **Melony** also occurs.

Melva (f) First listed by Charlotte Yonge in the 19th c., described as a male name and meaning 'chief.' In modern times always a girl's name, usually explained as a contracted form of **Melvina**. Melvina itself is a variant of **Malvina**, a name invented in the 18th c. by James Macpherson (1736–96) in his Ossianic poems. *What Shall We Name the Baby?* (1935) gave both Melva and Malva as girls' names, but although examples of Melva are easily found both in the U.S. and Britain, Malva appears not to have been used. New male names were derived from Malvina and Melvina, namely **Melvin** (later also **Melvyn**) and **Malvin**, and Melva may on occasion have been a back-formation from the male name. Melva was mainly used in the 1930s and '40s.

Melville (m) Surname deriving from a French place name, used regularly as a first name since the 1890s. The British actor Melville Cooper kept the name before cinema audiences during his long career. In quiet but infrequent use in all English-speaking countries.

Melvin (m) A back-formation from **Melvina**, itself from **Malvina**. The Scottish surname, however, which is also used as a first name, is a form of **Melville**. In use since the 1870s but most popular in the 1950s and '60s, especially in the form of **Melvyn**. Publicized in Britain by the writer and television presenter Melvyn Bragg, earlier in the U.S. by the actor Melvyn Douglas. The film producer/director Mel Brooks was born Melvin Kaminsky.

Melvina (f) Variant of **Malvina**.

Melvyn (m) Variant of **Melvin**.

Mena (f) In some cases a variant of **Mina**, but Mena is a German/Dutch pet form of various names which begin with *Mein-*, such as *Meinhild*, where the meaning is 'strength'. Occurs regularly but infrequently in English-speaking countries.

Menna (f) Variant of **Mena** in countries where that name is used (i.e., Germany, Netherlands), but Menna is also used regularly in Wales in modern times. Welsh writers on names are unable to explain its origin.

Menty (f) Found on rare occasions in the 19th c., and a sudden flurry of interest in it in Britain in the 1960s, though that proved to be short-lived. **Mentie** also occurs in 19th c. records, where both forms are probably variants of **Minty**. The latter name was revived to some extent in the 1950s and may account for the slightly later Menty examples, for which no other explanation can be suggested.

Merab (f) Hebrew 'multiplication'. Biblical, O.T., the elder daughter of Saul who was promised in marriage to whoever should slay Goliath, though this promise was not kept. Used regularly during the 19th c. but now very rare.

Mercedes (f) Spanish *merced* 'grace, mercy'. From one of the titles of the Virgin Mary, *Maria de las Mercedes*, 'Our Lady of the Mercies'. Usually a Roman Catholic name. Pet forms include **Mercy** and **Sadie**.

Mercia (f) The name of a kingdom in Anglo-Saxon England, roughly covering the Midlands. Used as a first name since the beginning of the 20th c., regularly if infrequently and mainly in Britain. Some parents may have seen it as a 'Latinized' form of **Mercy**. A magazine article reports an interview with Mercia Harrison, wife of the actor Rex Harrison.

Mercy (f) The word used as a name. One of the 'virtue' names introduced by the Puritans in the 17th c. In regular use until the 1950s, but more recent examples are very hard to find. The 19th c. pet name seems to have been **Merry**, and the name itself was sometimes found as **Mercey**.

Meredith (m, f) Old Welsh 'great chief'. A male name in the 19th c. and still thought of as such in Wales. Elsewhere the attitude to the name is perhaps that of Margaret Forster in her novel *Georgy Girl*: 'Meredith's real name was Mary, but she wasn't having any of that. She needed something much more original and pretty, so she chose Meredith and it sounded suitably soft and caressing on the lips of her numerous boyfriends.' Many parents seem to share the view that Meredith is a suitably feminine name (unless they are called *Smith*, for Smith families avoid it) and it has been well used in recent years in all English-speaking countries. Found also as **Merridith**, **Meridith** and **Meridath**. Pet form **Merry** is used as a name in its own right.

Meriel (f) Early variant of **Muriel** which was re-introduced in the 1920s and used regularly if infrequently since. Also occurs as **Merial**, **Meriol**, **Merrial**, **Merriel**.

Merilyn (f) Extended form of **Merril** or **Meryl**, in use since the 1930s. **Merrilyn** is also found, but less frequently. **Merralyn** has also been used. **Merlyn** began to appear in the 1930s as a variant of **Merlin**, and the two names seem to have been confused to some extent.

Merina (f) Fairly frequent variant of **Marina**.

Merle (f) French *merle* 'blackbird'. Mainly came into use when Merle Oberon (Estelle Merle O'Brien Thompson) began to appear on cinema screens in the early 1930s. At the time names like **Meryl**, **Meriel** and **Muriel** were fashionable. **Merlin** was also in use. Merle seems to have lapsed since the 1960s. Occasionally a male name, e.g. Merle Haggard, country and western singer.

Merlin (m, f) The male name arose due to a misunderstanding. See **Mervyn**. The girl's name may be from the bird, which is a small falcon, but its use was probably suggested by **Merle**, **Merilyn**, etc. Since the 1930s girls have often been given the name in its variant form **Merlyn** in an attempt to distinguish their sex. Neither form of the name is used frequently, and the first examples noted (at first for males) occur in the early years of the 20th c.

Merrick (m) English form of Welsh **Meurig**, itself a variant of **Maurice**. Merrick is the usual form of the name, though **Meyrick** is also used. Meurig occurs rarely. All forms used on rare occasions in the 19th c., but Merrick especially has been used with some frequency since 1900.

Merriel (f) See **Meriel**.

Merrill (f) Common variant of **Meryl**, especially in the U.S. Found also as **Merril, Merel, Meril**. In use since the 1930s.

Merrion (m) See **Meirion**.

Merry (f) Pet form of **Mercy**, used by Dickens to name one of the Pecksniff daughters in *Martin Chuzzlewit*. She is an unsympathetic character who makes a disastrous marriage, so she has not inspired many namesakes. In recent times has been more used in the U.S. than elsewhere, especially in the 1950s. Some usage may derive from the surname *Merry*, in existence since the 12th c.

Merton (m) English place name/surname, originally indicating residence near a 'mere' or lake, used from time to time as a first name.

Merville (f) Mrs Merville Hasler reports its first name use since 1841, imported from French court by the Amott family. The name originally referred to a 'minor' village, not one which was near the 'sea'.

Mervin (m) Usual form in the U.S., and a variant in Britain, of **Mervyn**.

Mervyn (m) Welsh *Myrddin*, probably meant for the town known in English as Carmarthen (in Welsh as Caerfyrddin). The wizard at King Arthur's court was known as *Myrddin Emrys* in Welsh, which probably meant that he was Emrys from Carmarthen. This name was Latinized as **Merlin Ambrosius**, and it was assumed by later writers that Merlin was his personal name. Mervyn is an English form of Myrddin, which meant 'sea hill' as part of the place name. Strictly speaking, Mervyn is also the 'correct' English form of the wizard Merlin's name. Began to be used in Wales in the 1870s, and steadily used since. It made a bid for general popular-

ity in Britain from the 1930s onwards, but was not over-successful. In the U.S. the name has also been used quietly, Mervin being the preferred form. From a historical point of view, **Marvin** is a different name, but the two forms have probably been confused in modern times.

Meryl (f) Phonetic form of **Muriel**, or its old-established variant **Meriel**. Meryl appeared at the beginning of the 20th c. and has been used steadily since then, especially in Wales. Occurs in many variant spellings, including **Merel, Merial, Meril, Meriol, Merril, Merrill, Merrall, Meryle, Meryll**. Also has diminutive forms such as **Merelyn, Merilyn**. In some instances the name merges with **Merle** or **Merlin**, and in the U.S., where Merrill is a popular form, the name has been extended to **Merrily, Merrilee**, etc. Associated in the 1980s with Meryl Streep, the actress.

Meshach (m) Of unknown origin. Biblical, O.T., the name of one of Daniel's three friends. Occasionally used in the 19th c.

Meta (f) German pet form from **Margareta**. Highly popular in Germany in the late 19th and early 20th cc. but now rare. Used occasionally in English-speaking countries between the 1880s and the early 1920s.

Meyrick (m) Form of Welsh **Meurig**. See **Merrick**.

Mhairi (f) Vocative form of Gaelic **Mairi** (**Mary**). **Mhari, Mharie** and **Mhairie** also occur in Scotland. The name is pronounced *Va-hri* with the stress on the first syllable. The names **Varey** and **Varie**, used in the 19th c., are therefore likely to be phonetic forms of Mhairi.

Mia (f) Italian/Spanish 'my', and perhaps used as a name due to a misunderstanding of the Italian phrase *Cara mia*, 'my dear'. Use of the name has notably increased since the American actress Mia Farrow (1945–   ) began to appear in films from 1964 on, especially after *Rosemary's Baby* (1968).

Michael (m) The Greek form of a Hebrew name meaning 'who is like the Lord?'

Biblical, O.T., the name of the archangel, the angelic head of the Israelites. Several men in the Bible bear the name. In the Middle Ages its pronunciation was close to French **Michel**, leading to **Mitchell**, now mainly a surname but still well used as a first name. Well used until the beginning of the 19th c., when it became decidedly unfashionable. Returned to favour in the 1920s and by 1950 was one of the most intensively used names in the English-speaking world. In the early 1980s still being very well used but beginning to fade quickly on all sides. Used in great numbers in Ireland at least a generation before American and English parents rediscovered it. Irish fondness for the name, at a time when it was temporarily a rather rare name elsewhere, had caused *Mick* to become a generic word for an Irishman. The name is no longer used in Ireland with such intensity: it began to go out of fashion there earlier than anywhere else. One possible reason for the name's return to favour is its use in J. M. Barrie's immensely successful entertainment *Peter Pan*. Michael is one of the Darling children. There is certainly no doubt that use of **Wendy** began with this play, which was first seen in 1904. The other children were **Moira**, **Angela** and **John**. John was naturally already highly popular. Moira and Angela were both rare names in 1904 but were used far more in the years that followed. Michael is a rather unusual word by English standards, but variant spellings are remarkably few in official records. **Micael** occurs, and **Michal** is found, but that may represent a deliberate use of the Polish or other version of the name. **Micheal** occurs, and **Mikel** has appeared since 1960, though not in great numbers. Pet forms **Mick**, **Micky**, **Mike** are not frequently used as independent names. **Mitch** is extremely rare in that role. The name's main feminine form has been French **Michèle**, later **Michelle**. **Michaela** is also used to some

extent, especially in Britain. The actors Michael Redgrave and Michael Caine (Maurice Micklewhite) have helped to keep the name before the public eye, but in recent years, with the name heard on all sides, that has hardly been necessary.

Michaela (f) Feminine form of **Michael** used increasingly in Britain since the mid-1950s. Pronounced *Mi-kay-la* or *My-kay-la* and found also as **Micaela**, **Michaella**, **Michala**, **Mickala**, **Mykela**.

Michal (m) Form of **Michael** in languages such as Polish and Czech. Occasionally used in English-speaking countries.

Michala (f) Frequent variant of **Michaela**.

Michele (m) Italian form of **Michael**, occasionally used in English-speaking countries.

Michèle (f) French feminine form of **Michel** (**Michael**). Appeared in the U.S. in the early 1940s and in Britain a year or two later. Immediate success in the U.S., but steadily overtaken by its variant **Michelle**. By the late 1950s Michelle was the usual spelling and it has since come to be considered the norm, the Beatles' song 'Michelle' having been an influence. Other variants of the name in English-speaking countries include **Michela**, which leans towards the Scottish **Michaela**, **Michell** and the masculine form **Michel**, used for girls.

Michelle (f) Since the late 1950s the usual spelling of French **Michèle** in English-speaking countries. Both forms of the name were introduced to Britain and the U.S. in the early 1940s and became an immediate success in the U.S. Only a mild impact in Britain until the Beatles' song 'Michelle' was released in the mid-1960s. Then became one of the top ten names, and was still to be found in the British top twenty in 1980, though it had clearly passed its peak. The song had meanwhile given a further boost to the name in the U.S., but by the early 1970s it was beginning to fade there. Not clear why the name came into fashion though the French actress Michèle Morgan began to appear in films from 1940 onwards.

Mick (m) Pet form of **Michael** much used as a spoken form but very rarely given as a first name. The avoidance of Mick is no doubt because of the offensive slang use of the name for an Irishman. The diminutives **Mickey** (the usual spelling) and **Micky** *are* used as independent names in the U.S. but not in Britain. The British phrase 'take the mickey', in the sense of 'jeer at', does not help this form of the name. Mickey was nevertheless adopted by Joe Yule when he became Mickey Rooney in the early 1930s. Another successful film star who started his career at that time was Mickey Mouse. Mickey Spillane was a successful crime writer.

Middleton (m) Common place name/surname, originally indicating a farm in the 'middle' of others, regularly used as a first name in the 19th c.

Mignon (f) French *mignon* 'cute'. Not a name in France, but used as such by Goethe in his *Wilhelm Meister's Apprenticeship* (1796). Victor Hugo made her into the **Esmeralda** of his *Notre Dame*, while Thomas's opera *Mignon* is based on the character. Has a diminutive form, **Mignonette**, which one could roughly translate as 'cutey-pie', or 'little darling'. Both forms have been used in English-speaking countries, together with phonetic spellings which attempt to capture the pronunciation of the names, e.g., **Minnionette**, **Minnonette**. The problem is that the name suggests a 'little minion', which hardly pleases anyone.

Miguel (m) Spanish form of **Michael**, used from time to time in English-speaking countries, especially the U.S.

Mike (m) Normal pet form of **Michael**, very rare in its own right until the 1940s and used only occasionally since.

Milbrough (m) English place name/surname indicating a 'middle borough', used as a first name in the 19th c., together with its variant **Milborough**.

Mildred (f) Old English 'mild strength'. The name of a popular 8th c. saint, but did not survive the Norman Conquest as a name in ordinary use. Discovered again in the 17th c. and mildly popular in the 18th c. Its popularity rose throughout the 19th c., especially in the U.S., where it became one of the top ten names in 1900. Remained very popular in the U.S. for the next thirty years, but used infrequently since 1930. Never as popular in Britain. Pet forms **Millie**, **Milley**, **Milly** have been used independently.

Miles (m) Of uncertain origin. Old German **Milo** 'generous' was one source of the name. Also a common short form of **Emile**. In early French *Mihiel*, later *Miel*, were forms of **Michael**. This was suggested as the origin of Miles in the 17th c. essay on first names by William Camden; a suggestion later supported by Professor Weekley. In some cases the surname *Miles* is from the Latin word for 'soldier', and this is therefore another possible origin. In Ireland Miles (or **Myles**) has long been used to Anglicize such names as *Maeleachlainn* (*Malachy*), *Maolmhuire*, *Maolmordha*. At its most popular until the end of the 18th c. In consistent use since the beginning of the 19th c. but has not been fashionable at any time. In U.S. history it is associated with Miles Standish, one of the Puritans who helped found New England – though his first name was not favoured by the stricter Puritans. In Britain the name suggests the actor/writer Miles Malleson (1888–1969) and the satirical writer Miles Kington. Occasional attempts to form a feminine name from Miles have led to **Milessa**, **Mileta**, **Milena**. Myles has led to **Mylea**, **Mylie**, **Mylinda**.

Milley (f) Variant of **Millie**.

Millicent (f) French *Melisent*, *Melisande*, from Old German *Amalswint* 'noble strength'. Introduced to Britain by the Normans but was being little used by the 16th c. Use of the name increased steadily from the beginning of the 17th c., and eventually achieved a minor peak of popularity around 1900, though only in Britain. Faded thereafter, though the British singer/actress Millicent Martin was responsible for slightly increased usage of the name in the 1960s. The spoken form of the name which had been introduced in the 12th c. appeared to survive until the 19th c. for the name is often found as **Melicent** or **Mellicent**. One girl born in 1841 received the name **Meliscent**, a hybrid which suggests a meaning 'scent of honey'. Pet form of the name was **Millie**, shared with **Mildred**.

Millie (f) Pet form of **Mildred** or **Millicent** used independently. In use since the 1860s, but now rare. In some cases girls called **Amelia** or **Emily** were addressed by this name. The name **Milliestone** was used by a British family in 1903, presumably for a daughter whom they felt would be a millstone. The name probably was for her.

Mills (m) The surname, linked with a 'mill' originally because of residence near one, though it may occasionally have been a form of **Miles**, used as a first name in the 19th c.

Milly (f) See **Millie**.

Milo (m) Old German name adopted by the French, established in English-speaking countries as **Miles** or **Myles**. Still occasionally used in modern times, mainly in Ireland. See **Miles**.

Milson (m) Surname, 'son of Miles' or 'son of Miller', used as a first name in the 19th c.

Milton (m) Common English place name and surname, originally indicating a 'settlement near a mill' or a 'middle settlement'. The surname is especially associated with the poet John Milton (1608–74). In regular use as a first name since the beginning of the 19th c., and made well known by such name-bearers as Milton Obote, President of Uganda, and Milton Berle (Mendel Berlinger), the television comedian.

Mima (f) Pet form of **Jemima** used independently on rare occasions.

Mimi (f) Pet form of **Mary** or other names beginning with M-, probably arising from infant attempts to pronounce such names. First use of the name coincided with the first production of Puccini's opera *La Bohème*, in which Mimi is the heroine whose 'tiny hand is frozen'. Used sporadically since then. **Mimie** is also found.

Mina (f) Pet form of names like **Wilhelmina, Carmina**, etc., used independently, mainly in the 19th c. Very rarely used since the 1930s.

Mindy (f) Appeared in the U.S. in some numbers in the 1960s but has since faded. Seems to be a pet form of **Malinda** or **Melinda**, perhaps **Miranda**, though Otterbjörk records **Minda** in use in Sweden in 1899. He is unable to explain its origin.

Minerva (f) Old Latin *Menerva*, Roman goddess of wisdom. Usually linked to Latin root *men-* 'mind'. Came into use in the 1860s and regularly used until 1920, though not in great numbers. Now rare. The unusual **Minivera**, used in Britain in 1885, was probably a blend of Minerva and the then popular **Minnie**.

Minette (f) Diminutive of **Mina**, itself from names like **Wilhelmina, Carmina**, etc. Also the nickname of **Henriette**, Duchess of Orléans and daughter of Charles I. Used on rare occasions, also as **Minetta**.

Minie (f) See **Minnie**.

Minna (f) Probably a pet form of **Wilhelmina**, a name which was well used in Scotland in the 19th c. Sir Walter Scott used Minna as the name of a beautiful girl in *The Pirate*, published in 1821, but it only came into general use when **Minnie** was becoming popular. Used from the 1850s until 1920, but seems to have become obsolete.

Minnie (f) Pet form of **Wilhelmina**. In general use *before* **Minna**, and **Minerva** came at least ten years later, so those names could not have been responsible for it originally. There is a tradition that Minnie was also a pet form of **Mary**, but no evidence supports that idea. Came into general use in the 1850s and immediately became fashionable. At its height in the 1870s in both Britain and the U.S., surviving well until about 1910. Subsequently faded almost completely, though still used on rare occasions. During its period of popularity found also as **Minie, Minne, Minny**. Occasionally, in the 1880s, extended to **Minniehaha**, though Longfellow had written:

From the waterfall, he named her,
Minnehaha, Laughing Water.

Minty (f) Pet form of **Aminta** or **Araminta**. Sudden revival of interest in the name in the 1950s, having first appeared briefly in the 1860s, but quickly faded into the background again.

Mira (f) Variant of **Myra** frequently used in the 19th c., but used only occasionally in the 20th c. **Mirah** was also used, but appears to be obsolete. Mira must have been pronounced by some namebearers to rhyme with 'mirror'. Sometimes written as **Mirra**, and the form **Miram**, influenced by **Miriam**, came into use in the 1840s. Myra itself could have been pronounced with the short vowel sound, since **Myriam** was sometimes used as the written form of Miriam.

Mirabel (f) Latin *mirabilis* 'wonderful'. A Latin name invented in England in the 12th c., much as **Miranda** was later invented by Shakespeare. Used enough during the Middle Ages to give rise to surnames such as *Marrable*, but became rare after the 14th c. By the 17th c. it was being used for men. In Fletcher's *Wild-goose Chase* (1652), Mirabel is the wild goose of the title who loves the women and leaves them until he is trapped by Oriana. In Farquhar's *The Inconstant* (1702) there is again a Mirabel who is trapped into marriage by an Oriana. In Congreve's *Way of the World* Edward Mirabell is the hero. Meanwhile Spenser, in his *Faerie Queene*, had created **Mirabella** as a truly feminine form of the name. The name now appears to be obsolete, though literary references continue. In Hugh

Walpole's novel *Rogue Herries* (1930), for instance, there is a **Mirabell** who is complimented on her 'pretty name'. She replies: 'No, it is a crazy name. My mother had it from a play. It is a man's name.'

Miram (f) Form of **Miriam** influenced by **Mira** which appeared in the 1840s but seems to have disappeared in the 1860s.

Miranda (f) Latin *miranda* 'fit to be admired', feminine gerundive of *mirare* 'to wonder at'. Invented by Shakespeare as the name of his heroine in *The Tempest*. In the play he also gave the perfect formula for asking someone's name: 'I do beseech you, chiefly that I may set it in my prayers, what is your name?' When Miranda answers Ferdinand's question, there follows a typical Shakespearian pun: 'Admir'd Miranda, Indeed the top of admiration.' Has been used consistently, though quietly, enjoying a minor spell of popularity in the 1960s, more in Britain than the U.S. Pet forms usually **Mandy** (**Mandi, Mandie**) in Britain, **Randy** (**Randi, Randie**) in the U.S.

Mirham (f) see **Miriam**.

Miriam (f) Early form of the Hebrew name which had the structure *M-r-y-m* and which in different translations of the Bible, and applied to different Biblical figures, became variously Miriam, Mary, Mariam, Mariamne, Miryam. The meaning of the name is unknown. One school of thought links the name with Hebrew **Marah** 'bitterness', but that seems most unconvincing. 'Rebellion' or 'rebelliousness' is another traditional meaning often assigned to the name. Miss Withycombe favoured 'wished-for child'. At one time it was fashionable to link the name with 'sea' in some way. Latest scholarship, reported in Odelain and Séguineau's *Dictionary of Proper Names and Places in the Bible,* favours 'seeress' or 'lady'. Miriam is usually associated with the sister of Moses, a prophetess. Began to be used in the 18th c. and remained in very steady usage until the 1960s. In spite of a general fashion for O.T. names, it then seems to have faded in all English-speaking countries, though Jewish families remain faithful to it. Was most intensively used around 1900 in the U.S. **Mirriam** was sometimes used in the 19th c. and **Miriama** was the name given to a British girl in 1955. It was presumably indistinct hearing of the name which led to the form **Mirian**, which occurs very regularly in the 19th c. records. This also gave rise to **Mirrian, Miriaenne, Miriain**. Miriam was also confused with **Mira** to some extent, which was presumably pronounced by some name-bearers to rhyme almost with 'mirror', since it was sometimes spelt as **Mirra**. The blended form of Mira and Miriam was **Miram**, used especially between the 1840s and 1860s. Another curiosity was **Mirham**, which was used occasionally between 1900 and the mid-1930s.

Mirian (f) Presumably a variant based on a mis-hearing of **Miriam**. Occurs with surprising frequency in official records of the 19th c., and examples are found in the early 20th c. Perhaps the reason lies in the fact that -an is a common ending of feminine names, while -am is usually a masculine ending.

Mishka (m) Russian pet form of **Michael** used to some extent in English-speaking countries since the 1960s. Found also as **Mischca**.

Mitchell (m) Surname deriving either from **Michael** or a word meaning 'big', in regular use as a first name since the 1840s. In the U.S. it was used in some numbers in the 1940s and by 1960 was decidedly popular. Has since faded. Use of the name in Britain remained steady but quiet throughout that period. **Mitchel** is often found, but the pet form **Mitch** is very rare as an independent name. A feminine **Mitchelle** appeared in the 1970s.

Mitzi (f) German pet form of **Maria**. Use of the name has probably been influenced by the actress Mitzi Gaynor (Francesca Mitzi Marlene deChamey von Gerber).

Mizela (f) Also **Mizella**. These names have been occasionally used this century and are an etymological mystery, unless they are phonetic variants of **Marcella, Marcelle, Michelle**. In support of that argument one may point to **Masella, Mazella, Mazala, Mazila, Marcalla, Marsella**, all recorded in the 19th c. after Marcella had come into regular use. By the turn of the century one finds **Mesella, Messella, Mezillah**. These then appear to have developed into Mizella, Mizela, **Mizelli, Mizelly, Myzel, Marzalie**. Pet forms **Mizzie** and **Messie** also occur as independent names in the 1940s and '50s. **Mizelle** first appeared in the 1870s but has been re-used in more recent times. Most of the names quoted above are unrecorded in name dictionaries or other reference works, and the evidence does point to their being misunderstandings of names that have been heard but not seen.

Modesty (f) English form of Latin **Modesta**, feminine of **Modestus**, both used as Christian names during the Roman Empire. Modesty does not seem to have been used by the Puritans, fond though they were of 'virtue' names, perhaps because there were saints of the Catholic Church who bore the name. In modern times it is mostly associated with the British cartoon character Modesty Blaise; instances of first-name use are very hard to find. **Modestina** is occasionally used. **Modestine** is perhaps too closely identified with the name of the donkey on which R. L. Stevenson made his *Travels With A Donkey* to be used as a first name, attractive though it is.

Mohammed (m) Also **Mohamad, Mohamed, Mohammad, Muhammad, Mahomet**. Arabic 'greatly praised'. Name of the Prophet of Islam. Use has slightly increased in the U.S. in the early 1980s. In Britain in infrequent use since the 1960s.

Moira (f) Phonetic form of Irish **Maire** (**Mary**) used more in Scotland in the

20th c. than elsewhere. The Scottish-born ballet-dancer Moira Shearer (Moira King) and the South African actress Moira Lister made the name well-known in the 1940s, and it enjoyed a spell of popularity in England until 1950. Rarely used in the U.S. but continues to be quietly used in Britain. **Moyra** is a common variant.

Molly (f) Pet form of **Mary** used independently. The name was earlier **Mally** (compare **Sally** from **Sarah**), a form which survived until the mid-19th c. Molly was very popular in the 18th c. but virtually disappeared in the 19th c. 'Papa likes Molly,' says a character in Mrs Gaskell's novel *Wives and Daughters* (1855), and she is told in reply: 'That's right. Keep to the good old fashions, my dear.' But by that time a 'moll' had acquired various undesirable meanings both in Britain and the U.S., and it was impossible for parents to use it. Its reappearance coincided with the end of the 19th c., and in the mid-1930s it was beginning to be used in considerable numbers. There was a movement away from it at that point, however, and now it is again a rarely given name. Used steadily but quietly in the U.S. this century. **Mollie** is a common variant, and **Molley** is occasionally found. The name has a definite suggestion of Irishness about it, partly due to the traditional song 'Cockles and Mussels,' in which Molly Malone is the central personage, partly to its association with the Molly Maguires, the 19th c. American secret society.

Mona (f) Irish *Muadhnait*, a diminutive of *muadh* 'noble'. The name of an Irish saint which began to be used in the 1860s in England as well as Ireland. The American actress Mona Freeman helped to make the name more widely known from the 1940s onwards: in her case the name was a pet form of **Monica**. Mona continues to be used steadily but quietly in all English-speaking countries. In Britain it is also known as the Latin name of the Isle of Man and Manx parents occa-

sionally use it for that reason.

Monday (m) See **Tuesday**.

Monica (f) Of uncertain origin. Suggestions include a derivation from Greek *monos* 'alone', Latin *monere* 'to advise' or Latin *nonnica*, from *nonna* 'nun'. The name came into use because of St Monica, who was from Africa, and may have originated in an African language. Has primarily been used by Roman Catholics, though in more general use in the 1920s. At its height in Britain in the 1950s, rather later in the U.S. Andrea Newman, in *A Bouquet of Barbed Wire* (1969), commented: 'Now Monica . . . what image does that conjure up? The hockey-field. The swimming bath. The gymnasium. Tennis courts and netball and lacrosse'. These associations, in Britain at least, with a frighteningly healthy, pig-tailed girl owe much to stories by Angela Brazil and others. Since the 1950s, perhaps in an attempt to escape this image, other forms of the name have been used, namely German **Monika** (which does not escape it) and French **Monique** (which does).

Monique (f) French form of **Monica**, in regular use in the U.S. and Britain since the 1950s. French bearers of the name are often called **Mique**.

Montague (m) Surname deriving from a French place name, used regularly as a first name since the beginning of the 19th c. Use of the name has decreased noticeably since the late 1950s. *Montague* was Romeo's family name in Shakespeare's *Romeo and Juliet*, and the cause of all the trouble, since Juliet was a *Capulet*. But as Juliet says:

'What's Montague? It is not hand, nor foot,
Nor arm, nor face, nor any other part
Belonging to a man. O, be some other name.'

Variant **Montagu** has been frequently used. Pet form **Monty**, which is not exclusively from this name, also occurs in its own right. In passing one can note

that Montague has been used as a first
name in English-speaking countries far
more often than **Romeo**. **Juliet** has of
course been commonly used, *Capulet*
not.

Monty (m) Usually a pet form of **Montague** or **Montagu**, used in its own right.
During the Second World War the name
was closely associated with Field
Marshal Lord Montgomery, and some
British parents may have used the name
in his honour. Began to be used in the
1920s, and there was no noticeable
upsurge in interest in the 1940s.

Morag (f) Diminutive of Gaelic *mor*
'great'. In this form the name is almost
exclusively Scottish. Continues in quiet
use in Scotland. Formerly considered to
be the equivalent of **Sarah**.

Moray (m) Scottish place name and surname in occasional use as a first name,
both in Scotland and elsewhere. **Murray**
is a variant.

Mordecai (m) Of uncertain meaning.
Biblical, O.T., the cousin and foster-
father of **Esther**. A popular name
amongst the Puritans and used until the
end of the 19th c. Now very rare.

Moreen (f) Frequent variant of **Maureen**.

Morfydd (f) Ancient Welsh name of
uncertain meaning, used again in Wales
1900–30 but now out of favour. **Mor-
fudd** was a variant.

Morgan (m,f) Welsh *mawr* 'great' and
can 'bright'. A personal name since the
7th c. and well established in Wales
as a surname as well as a first name.
Continues to be used very steadily
as a first name, without ever being especially fashionable. The rare feminine
form **Morganetta** was used to name a
baby born in 1912. Morgan itself is
feminine in Sir Thomas Malory's *History of Prince Arthur* (1470), and this
has now become normal usage in the
U.S.

Moria (f) Probably feminine of Greek
moros 'simpleton' as used by Ben Jonson to name a character in *Cynthia's
Revels* who 'talks anything of anything'.
Modern instances of the name may be

mis-spellings of **Maria** or **Moira**.

Morice (m) Early variant of **Maurice**, still
in very occasional use. **Morrice** is a rare
variant.

Morley (m) Common English place name
'moor clearing' which became a surname. Used regularly if infrequently as a
first name.

Morna (f) Gaelic *muirne* 'beloved, gentle'.
This form of the name is quietly used,
mainly in Scotland. More frequent as
Myrna.

Morris (m) Variant of **Maurice**. At one
time used as frequently as Maurice for
the first name, but now mainly thought
of as the surname. **Moris** and **Moriss**
also occurred as first names in the
19th c., while surnames such as **Morrison**, **Morriss**, **Morrisson** were also
transferred to first-name use from time
to time.

Mortimer (m) Surname derived from a
French place name meaning 'dead
water', i.e. a stagnant pool, or lake.
Used regularly in the 19th c., and on
very rare occasions in the 20th c., as a
first name. Made well-known by the
English archaeologist Sir Mortimer
Wheeler.

Morton (m) Common English place
name/surname 'village on a moor' used
as a first name. In regular use since the
1850s, though infrequent. In the U.S.
especially well favoured by Jewish
families. In former times used as a
replacement for **Moses**.

Morven (f) Gaelic 'big mountain peak'.
The name of Scottish mountains transferred to first-name use, but so far only
by Scottish parents.

Morwenna (f) Welsh *morwyn* 'maiden'.
Used in Wales since the 1940s and
becoming more popular in the early
1970s.

Moses (m) Of disputed origin. Possibly
Hebrew 'delivered (from water)'. Also
frequently explained as Egyptian 'child,
son'. Biblical, O.T., the name of the
liberator of Israel and their law-giver.
The name was of particular significance
to Jewish families from early times, but

came into more general use in the 17th c. when the Puritans turned to O.T. names. Remained relatively common until the end of the 19th c., then became very infrequent. Jewish families sometimes use it in the form **Moshe**. Moss is another variant.

Moss (m) Surname used as a first name. The surname usually means 'descendant of Moses'. Used regularly in the 19th c. but now rare. In some instances it may have represented the pet form of Maurice.

Mostyn (m) Welsh place name/surname used in modern times as a first name. Originally referred to a 'fortress in a field'.

Moureen (f) Fairly common variant of Maureen.

Moya (f) Appears to be a form of **Moira**, which often occurs as **Moyra**. Used fairly regularly in Britain in the 20th c., especially since the 1940s.

Moyna (f) Variant of **Mona** or an adaptation of the common Irish place name Moyne, which referred originally to a small area of flat land. A minor vogue for this name in the 1930s but it subsequently disappeared.

Moyra (f) Common variant of **Moira**.

Muir (m) Mainly a Scottish surname, 'dweller by the moor', but used occasionally as a first name.

Mungo (m) Gaelic 'amiable'. The nickname of St Kentigern, patron saint of Glasgow. Used mostly in that area of Scotland and by those of Scottish descent, but not frequently.

Munro (m) Scottish surname of uncertain origin in occasional use as a first name. Found also as **Monro** and **Munroe**.

Murdoch (m) Gaelic *Muireach* 'mariner' or *Murchadh* 'sea warrior'. Mainly used in Scotland, often as **Murdo**. Its unfamiliarity can cause problems: see Louse.

Muriel (f) Irish *Muirgheal* 'sea-bright'. The name may have been common to Celtic languages, being found in early times in Brittany and Wales as well as Ireland. Generally popular in the Middle Ages and gave rise to surnames such as *Merrall*, *Murrell*, etc. Then became rare until the 1870s. It is the 'rather peculiar' name of a character in Mrs Craik's best-selling novel *John Halifax, Gentleman*. Despite that authorial description of it, plus the fact that the bearer of the name in the story is blind, from 1870 onwards it slowly became more common, reaching a peak of popularity in Britain in 1925. By 1940, however, had faded away almost completely. The screen appearances of the British actress Muriel Pavlov came rather too late to influence its use. In the U.S. used reasonably well in the 1930s and early 1940s but now rare. Variants include **Murial**, **Murielle**.

Murray (m) Variant of **Moray** by origin, but Murray is by far the commoner spelling of the name. Occurs also as **Murrey**, **Murry**. Steadily used by parents of Scottish descent, e.g. in Canada, since the 1870s.

Mycala (f) Also **Myckala**, **Mykela**. Modern forms of **Michaela** in occasional use, mainly in Britain.

Myer (m) Surname of various possible origins (e.g. 'dweller near a marsh', 'physician', 'bailiff') used regularly as a first name from the 1870s until the early part of the 20th c. The last recorded instance in England is of a Myer Smith who was named in 1913. The First World War began a year later, and the name was probably felt to be too close for comfort to the common German surname *Maier*, which has the variant forms *Meyer*, *Mayer*. Myers occurs rarely.

Myfanwy (f) Welsh 'my fine one, my rare one'. Popular name in Wales since the 1880s. Occasionally as **Myfannwy**.

Myles (m) Variant of **Miles**, especially common in Ireland.

Myra (f) Invented by the 17th c. English poet Fulke Greville (1554–1618) for use in his love poems. He perhaps based it on Latin *myron* 'sweet-smelling oil', creating a feminine form of **Myron**. It has also been suggested that he simply rearranged the letters of **Mary**. He could also, like Shakespeare with the name **Miranda**, have been thinking of a name which would mean 'admirable'. Came into general use only in the 1830s, frequently as **Mira**, occasionally as **Mirah**. Steadily used since then, with Scottish parents displaying a special fondness for it.

Myria (f) Probably a variant of **Maria**, a name which was recorded by one registrar in the 19th c. as **Mrrya**.

Myriam (f) Occasional variant of **Miriam**.

Myrna (f) Gaelic *muirne*, 'beloved, gentle'. Modern use of the name is almost certainly due to the publicity given to it from the mid-1920s onwards by the actress Myrna Loy (Myrna Williams). Most used in the 1930s and '40s. Variants of the name include **Muirna, Morna, Murnia**.

Myron (m) Greek *myron* 'sweet-smelling oil'. The name of a famous Greek sculptor who is best known for his 'Discus Thrower'. Most used in the U.S. in modern times, especially in the 1940s. Still steadily used, mainly by black American families.

Myrtle (f) The plant name used as a first name. Usage began in the 1850s, but increased markedly in the 1880s. Then enjoyed a mild spell of popularity, more in Britain than the U.S., until the 1930s. Rarely used since 1960 in any English-speaking country. **Myrtilla**, used as a personal name in 5th c. Rome, was used very occasionally in the 19th c.

Mysie (f) Variant of **Maisie**. Formerly in use in Scotland but now appears to be obsolete. Characters who bear the name occur in literature, especially the novels of Sir Walter Scott.

N

Nada (f) Form of **Nadia**, from the Russian word for 'hope'. In occasional use since the beginning of the 20th c. H. Rider Haggard's *Nada the Lily* was published in 1892.

Nadene (f) Frequent variant of **Nadine**.

Nadia (f) Russian *nadezhda* 'hope'. Nadia was the name of Lenin's wife, which presumably made it an acceptable name in the U.S.S.R. The earlier form of the name used in English-speaking countries was **Nada**, which appeared as early as 1908. Nadia became frequent in the 1960s and has continued to be steadily used in both Britain and the U.S. **Nadya** and **Nadja** are variants. **Nadine** is the French form of the name. The Russian equivalent of **Faith** has also been well used in English-speaking countries – see **Vera**.

Nadine (f) French diminutive of **Nada**, or **Nadia**. May also have arisen from a pet form of **Bernadette**. In regular use in English-speaking countries since the 1890s. Interest in it has increased since the 1940s, since when it has often been used as **Nadene**. **Nadeen** and **Nadena** are rarer variants.

Nan (f) Pet form of **Ann** occasionally used as an independent name in modern times. In the 18th c. it was extremely popular, but it acquired the slang meaning 'grand-mother', which it has retained.

Nance (f) Form of **Nancy** occasionally used as an independent name.

Nanci(e) (f) Modern spelling variants of **Nancy**.

Nancy (f) Originally a pet form of **Ann** or **Anne**, but long considered an independent name. Began to be used as such in increasing numbers at the end of the 18th c. in Britain, remaining steadily in use until the 1930s. Then little used until the early 1970s, when there were signs of renewed interest in it. In the U.S. it became very popular around 1920, appealing mainly to white parents, and was still in the American top ten in 1950. Canadian parents were also using it a great deal during this period. Since the 1960s has been unfashionable.

Nanette (f) Diminutive of **Nan**, which also occurs as **Nannette**. Used in English-speaking countries since the beginning of the 20th c., though never in great numbers. Associated with the British actress Nanette Newman.

Nanny (f) Pet form of **Ann** or **Anne**, formerly in frequent use as an independent name and often used interchangeably with **Nancy**. Became the general term for a child's nurse at the beginning of the 20th c. and this seems to have caused the Christian name to become obsolete. Nanny goats (and billy goats) have been so-called since the end of the 18th c. **Nannie** is another spelling, and there is a comment in *Lorna Doone*, by R. D. Blackmore: 'Uncle Reuben would always call her "Nannie"; he said that "Annie" was too fine and Frenchified for us.'

Naomi (f) Hebrew 'pleasantness, delight'. Biblical, O.T., the name of the mother-in-law of Ruth. In regular use in all English-speaking countries since the 18th c. Distinct interest in the name in Britain around 1970. Variant **Naomie** appeared at this time. In the 19th c. the name was occasionally turned into **Naomia**. Helena Swan was right to say in her article on the name (*Girls' Christian Names*, 1900): 'it has never been widely adopted either in everyday life or literature.' She wondered why it had not been more widely used, given the beauty of the name itself and its Biblical associations. Naomi Jacob has been well-known as a novelist since the 1930s.

Napoleon (m) Occasionally used in the 19th c., especially between 1840–80. Made famous, of course, by Napoleon Bonaparte (1769–1821). French scholars believe it to be an ancient Germanic name which was changed by popular etymology because of the double influence of *Napoli* (Naples) and *leone* 'lion'. The name certainly did not mean

'lion from Naples', but its original meaning remains obscure. In modern times is occasionally used by black American families.

Napthali (m) Hebrew 'I have fought'. Biblical, O.T., name of the fifth son of Jacob. Occasionally used in the 19th c.

Narcissus (m) Greek *narkissos* 'daffodil'. The name of a beautiful Greek youth who fell in love with his own reflection. In early use as a Christian name, together with its feminine form *Narcissa*. St Narcissus was bishop of Jerusalem in the 2nd c. Rarely used in modern times.

Narelle (f) Of unknown origin, used in Australia in modern times but not in other English-speaking countries. May therefore derive from an Aboriginal word such as *narang* 'little'. Mrs Cecily Dynes, who makes a special study of Australian personal names, has also suggested in a private communication that it may derive from a trade name, that of a perfume. The modern use of **Chanel** in the U.S. perhaps lends support to that theory.

Nat (m) Diminutive of **Nathaniel**, **Nathan** in occasional use as an independent name.

Natacha (f) See **Natasha**. Natacha is the usual spelling of the name in France.

Natalie (f) Latin *natale domini* 'birthday of the Lord', i.e. 'Christmas Day'. The spelling has been influenced by French **Nathalie**. The form of the name used by the earliest Christians was **Natalia**, e.g. St Natalia, wife of St Adrian, who was martyred in the 4th c. This form continues to be used on rare occasions, together with **Natalya**, which appeared in the 1960s. Natalie first appeared in the 1880s but was very quietly used until the late 1960s in Britain, some years earlier in the U.S. It seems likely that the actress Natalie Wood (Natasha Gurdin, 1938–81), was responsible for bringing the name to the public's attention. Her screen appearances began in the 1940s, and by 1960 she was very well known. In the early 1980s Natalie was in fifteenth place in the popularity chart in Britain. In the U.S. it was being used far more quietly by that time, never having been quite such a success. Occasional variants of the name include **Natalee, Natelie**.

Natasha (f) One of the many Russian forms of **Natalie**, meaning 'Christmas Day'. Used in English-speaking countries on rare occasions since the beginning of the 20th c. Usage increased fairly dramatically in the late 1960s when a television version of Tolstoy's *War and Peace* was seen. By 1980, however, there were signs that the name was once again receding into the background. Pet form **Tasha** used independently during the 1970s, but now also fading. Natasha seems to have made a particularly strong impression in Australia during the 1970s. **Natacha** is used from time to time, as is **Natashia**.

Nathalie (f) French form of the name that in English-speaking countries is far more commonly spelt **Natalie**. The 'h' of Nathalie is in any case silent. First used in Britain in the 1860s, but remained a very rare name for a hundred years until the popularity of Natalie caused it to be used rather more often. See further at **Natalie**.

Nathan (m) Hebrew 'He has given'. Biblical, O.T., 2 Sam. 7:2, the name of a prophet. Used rarely until the 18th c. Then came into regular use, with a sudden increase of interest in it on all sides in the 1960s. In Britain was still one of the top fifty names in 1980, and Australian parents were still using it well. White rather than black American parents responded to it from the 1950s onwards.

Nathaniel (m) Hebrew 'God has given'. **Nathanael** is the Greek and Latin form of the name. Biblical, N.T., the name of one of the Apostles, John 1:45. Came into use in the 17th c. and was reasonably well used until the end of the 18th c. In constant use since then, but never especially fashionable. In recent times black American parents have

shown a particular liking for it and have almost made the name their own. The name's other associations are mainly American, e.g. Nathaniel Hawthorne (1804–64) the author, Natty Bumpo, scout and pioneer, the original of James Fenimore Cooper's *Deerslayer*, and Nathanael West (Nathan Weinstein) another well-known writer.

Nayland (m) English place name/surname 'dweller at the island' used as a first name. In regular but infrequent use since the 1920s in Britain.

Neal(e) (m) Common variants of **Neil** in use since the 1940s.

Ned (m) Pet name from **Edward** or **Edmond** used since the 14th c., and given as an independent name since the 1850s. In steady but infrequent use since then.

Nehemiah (m) Hebrew 'the Lord comforts'. Biblical, O.T., the name of a prophet. One of the O.T. names used by the Puritans in the 17th c. Regularly used until the 1920s, after which it became very rare.

Neil (m) Irish genitive **Neill** or **Niall**, from *niadh* 'champion'. The name was Latinized as *Nigellus*, so that it was later thought to derive from Latin *niger* 'black'. The Latin form also led to the variant form **Nigel**. In the 19th c. Neil was predominantly a Scottish name. Used sporadically in the rest of Britain but only became really popular in the 1950s. Reached a peak in the 1970s and still in the British top twenty in the early 1980s. This popularity was not reflected in the U.S., though the name was given a definite boost in 1969 when Neil Armstrong stepped onto the moon's surface. The singer Neil Diamond and playwright Neil Simon have also kept the name before the public eye. Variants of the name include **Niall, Neill, Neal, Neale, Nial, Nialle, Niel. Niels** and **Nils** are also found, but they are Danish and Swedish forms of **Nicholas**.

Neila (f) Modern feminine form of **Neil** rarely used. **Neilla** also occurs.

Neilson (m) Surname linked with **Neil**,

regularly used as a first name since the 1920s.

Nelia (f) Pet form of **Cornelia** in modern use as an independent name.

Nell (f) Pet form of **Helen, Eleanor, Elinor**, etc., used independently since at least the 17th c. Dickens's Little Nell in *The Old Curiosity Shop* was an Elinor; Nell (Gwynn(e)) was also an Eleanor or Elinor. Nell has been rarely used this century, its own diminutive forms **Nelly, Nellie, Nella** being preferred. Nelley was also common in the 19th c.

Nellie (f) Diminutive of **Nell**, ultimately from **Helen, Eleanor**, etc., used independently. Especially popular from the 1860s to the 1930s, now rare. **Nelly** is as often found; **Nelley** was regular in the 19th c. Dame Nellie Melba, the opera singer, was Helen Porter Amstrong (1861–1931).

Nelson (m) A surname 'son of Neil' used as a first name. Famous in British history because of Lord Nelson (1758–1805), the English admiral who defeated the French and Spanish off Cape Trafalgar in 1805, though he was killed in action. As a first name it has been made well known by such men as Nelson Rockefeller, governor of New York, the publisher Nelson Doubleday and the singer Nelson Eddy. Never especially fashionable but it continues to be steadily used in all English-speaking countries.

Neptune (m) The chief sea-divinity of the Romans. A name given usually to a child born at sea. See **Ocean**.

Nerida (f) Greek *Nereis*, genitive *Nereidos* 'sea nymph'. In occasional use, along with its variants **Nerina** and **Nerissa**. Nerissa is known in *The Merchant of Venice* as the witty and clever waiting-woman who works for Portia.

Nerissa (f) See **Nerida**.

Nerys (f) Welsh feminine adaptation of *ner* 'lord', a recent innovation which is gaining favour in Wales. Publicized by the actress Nerys Hughes (1941–).

Nessie (f) Scottish diminutive of **Agnes**. Occasionally used as an independent name until the 1930s, when it was playfully applied to the Loch Ness Monster.

Nest (f) Welsh diminutive of **Agnes**, now usually **Nesta**. One bearer of the name, grandmother of Gerald the Welshman and mistress of Henry I of England, was famous for her beauty.

Nesta (f) Welsh pet form of **Agnes**. Regularly used as a name in its own right. In earlier times it was always written as Nest.

Neta (f) Pet form of **Agneta**, itself derived from **Agnes**. Used only occasionally as an independent name.

Netta (f) Pet form of **Annetta** or names ending in -ette. As a name in its own right it is quietly used.

Nettie (f) Pet form of names such as **Jeannette, Annette**. Found as an independent name 1880–1920, but never in frequent use. **Netty** was an occasional variant.

Neva (f) Probably from Spanish *nieve* 'snow', ultimately Latin *nix, nivis* 'snow'. Also an American place name, the name of a river in Russia and of a mountain in Switzerland. Used as a first name since the 19th c.

Nevada (f) From the name of the American state, Spanish 'snowed upon, snowy'. Used in Britain as well as the U.S.

Nevil (m) Frequent variant of **Neville** in Britain.

Neville (m) A Norman surname from a French place name meaning 'new town'. Came into use in Britain as a first name in the 1860s (earlier uses being extremely rare). Use of the name increased slightly in the 1920s, and reached a minor peak in Britain in the mid-1950s. Never especially popular elsewhere, though black American parents occasionally use it. In Britain the forms **Nevil, Nevill, Nevile** are also found. British usage was undoubtedly influenced by (Arthur) Neville Chamberlain, Prime Minister in 1937. In the U.S. the actor Neville Brand received much publicity in the 1940s as one of America's most decorated soldiers.

Nevin (m) Irish *Naomhan, Naomhain*, a

diminutive of *naomh* 'holy'. The name
of an Irish saint in occasional use. Irish
reference books usually give it in the
form **Nevan**, but Nevin is the form actually used by parents. The surname
Niven derives from the same name, and
is occasionally used as a first name.

Newel(l) (m) Surnames which have more
than one possible origin (one of them
being a variant of **Noel**), used from time
to time as first names.

Newman (m) This surname, indicating a
newcomer to a district, was used very
regularly as a first name in Britain in the
19th c. It is probably significant that the
earliest example found is in 1844, a few
years after the publication of *Nicholas
Nickleby*, by Charles Dickens. In that
novel there is a character called Newman Noggs, hardly a heroic person
although he turns out well in the end.
Families in which Newman was a
maiden name, or was otherwise mean-
ingful, were probably encouraged to use
it because of the fictional example.
Much less frequently used in the 20th c.,
though an example was noted in the
1970s.

Newton (m) Common place name 'new
settlement' and surname, used regularly
as a first name from the 1840s to 1920.
Used in the U.S. into the 1940s, then
seems to have died out. In *Sons and
Lovers*, by D. H. Lawrence, there is a
Newton who 'is a big jolly fellow, with a
touch of the bounder about him', a
friend of Paul Morel's.

Niall (m) Irish, derived from *niadh*
'champion'. In its genitive form it
becomes **Neill**, which has given rise to
Neil, the usual form of the name.
Thought of in modern times as Irish.
Certainly used in Ireland (and Scotland), but in the 1970s Irish parents
were clearly using Neil far more often
than Niall.

Nichola (f) See Nicola. **Nichol** also occurs
for Nicole.

Nicholas (m) Greek *Nikolaos* 'victory
people' or 'prevailing among the people'. Biblical, N.T., Acts 6:5, where

Nicolaus is mentioned as a deacon. The
5th c. patron saint of children was St
Nicholas, still revered today as Santa
Claus. Five popes bore the name
Nicholas, and it was widely used in the
Middle Ages. The common surnames
Nichols, *Nicholson*, etc., reflect its use
at the time. Much used in the 16th and
17th cc. and almost disappeared in the
18th c. Reappeared at the beginning of
the 19th c. but again almost disappeared after 1850, despite Dickens's
novel *Nicholas Nickleby* (1838–9)
which showed its young hero in a good
light. Remained in very quiet use until
the late 1930s, when it began to arouse
interest in all English-speaking countries. Went on to have most success in
Britain in the mid-1970s, though never
as popular there as the feminine form
Nicola. By the early 1980s was fading
on all sides. **Colin** was originally a pet
form of Nicholas, but has long been
regarded as independent. **Nick** is infrequently used as a name in its own right.

Nichole (f) Modern variant in English-
speaking countries of Nicole. Nicholette
also occurs for Nicolette.

Nicholson (m) Surname linked with
Nicholas, used in the 19th c. as a first
name, though infrequently.

Nick (m) Pet form of Nicholas used independently. Rare in Britain and infrequent in the U.S. The name is associated
with Nick Carter, a fictional detective,
also the pen-name of the various
authors who wrote the stories, beginning at the end of the 19th c.

Nicki (f) Pet form of Nicola or Nicole
used independently. In use since the
1960s. Nickie also occurs.

Nickola (f) See Nicola.

Nickolas (m) Variant of Nicholas in regular if infrequent use since the 1930s.

Nicky (f) Pet form of Nicola or Nicole
used independently. Well used in the
1970s.

Nicodemus (m) Greek *Nikodemus* 'vic-
tory of the people'. Biblical, N.T.,
John 3:1., the name of a Jewish leader.
Used very rarely in English-speaking

countries, perhaps because of the reference to it in Laurence Sterne's *Tristram Shandy*. In a famous passage about the influence of Christian names on those who bear them he asks: 'how many might have done well had they not been Nicodemus'd into nothing.' It is not clear whether Sterne considered Nicodemus to be a silly name, or whether he associated it with Old Nick, the Devil.

Nicol (m, f) Usual written form of **Nicholas** in the Middle Ages. Occasionally used as the male name in modern times, e.g. in Scotland, but since 1960 has been more frequent as a variant spelling of **Nicole**.

Nicola (f) Italian form of **Nicholas**, but interpreted in Britain, especially, as a feminine form of that name. First appeared in both Britain and the U.S. around 1940. By 1950 had begun an upward rise through the British popularity charts, bringing it to third place in the mid-1970s. By 1980 it was in ninth place and had clearly passed its peak. Elsewhere, in other English-speaking countries, a clear preference had been shown for the French feminine form **Nicole**, though this did not begin to become really popular until the 1960s. British parents have often used **Nichola** as a variant. **Nickola** and **Nicolla** are also found. Pet forms **Nicki**, **Nickie**, **Nicky** have been frequently given as independent names. The popular variant **Nikola** has also led to **Niki**, **Nikki** and **Nikky** being used as names in their own right. **Nykola** occurs, but is rare. The pet forms make use of a sound that clearly appealed to young parents at the time, since various forms of **Vicki** were intensively used during the same period. **Nicola** may have been started on its fashionable run by the increased use of **Nicholas** in the 1940s, but its popularity quickly outstripped that of the male name.

Nicole (f) French feminine form of **Nicholas**. Also a diminutive form **Nicolette**. Had a very considerable suc-

cess in the U.S., Canada and Australia in the 1970s, **Nicola** being preferred at that time in Britain. At the beginning of the 1980s was still being well used, but had passed its peak. **Nichole, Nichol, Nickol, Nickole, Nicol, Nicolle, Nikole** all occur as variants. Various pet forms such as **Nicki**, **Nikki** have not been as frequently used in the U.S. as in Britain (where **Vicki, Vikki**, etc., have also been more popular). On the other hand, American parents have made almost exclusive use of modern diminutive forms such as **Nicholyn, Nicolena, Nicolene, Nicolina, Nicoline, Nicolyn**.

Nicoletta (f) Italian feminine form of **Nicola (Nicholas)**. French **Nicolette** is preferred in English-speaking countries.

Nicolette (f) French feminine form of **Nicholas**. Used in Britain and the U.S. in the late 1930s and continuously since, though not in great numbers. **Nicholette** is an occasional variant. Pet form **Colette** has also been well used as an independent name since the 1940s.

Niel (m) Common variant of **Neil** until the late 1960s, by which time Neil had become thoroughly established in all English-speaking countries. Niel was possibly influenced by the Latin form of the name, *Nigellus*, which gave rise to **Nigel**.

Nigel (m) Back-formation from Latin *Nigellus*, or **Neil**. Almost unknown in the U.S. In Britain quietly used from the Middle Ages onwards, but became decidedly popular in the 1940s. Reached a peak in the early 1960s and fading since. All the well-known bearers of the names are British. They include the writer Nigel Balchin and actors Nigel Bruce, Nigel Davenport and Nigel Patrick. Occasional variants of the name include **Nigal, Nigiel, Nigil**.

Nikki (f) Pet form of **Nicola (Nikola)**, occasionally of **Nicole**, used mainly in Britain since 1960. Nikki is the usual spelling, **Niki** is reasonably frequent, **Nikky** occurs occasionally.

Nikola (f) Variant of **Nicola**, fairly popular in Britain since the 1940s.

Nikolas (m) Probably a spelling variant of **Nicholas**, though it is the normal form of that name in languages such as Bulgarian.

Nimrod (m) Hebrew, traditionally said to mean 'rebel'. Biblical, O.T., Gen. 10:8, where he is 'the mighty hunter'. In rare use as a first name, but in regular use as a name for British naval warships since 1795.

Nina (f) Russian pet form of **Annina**, **Anninka** (**Ann**), or of names such as **Janina**, **Antonina**. Regularly but quietly used as an independent name. Signs of increased usage in the 1970s.

Ninette (f) Diminutive of **Nina** in occasional use in modern times. **Ninetta** is also found, together with **Ninita** in the U.S.

Ninian (m) The name of a 5th c. Scottish saint. Its meaning is unknown. Much used in Scotland in the 16th c. and before, but rarely used in modern times.

Nipton (m) The name of a place on the Isle of Wight, occasionally used by British parents as a first name.

Nita (f) Spanish pet form of names such as **Anita**, **Juanita**, **Benita**. Regularly but quietly used in Britain and the U.S.

Niven (m) See **Nevin**.

Noah (m) Hebrew name of uncertain origin. 'Rest' is often suggested; 'long-lived' is another possibility, and 'motion' or 'wandering' yet another. Biblical, O.T., the man who built the famous ark. In continuous use since the 17th c. in all English-speaking countries, but never especially fashionable. Noah Webster (1758–1843) was the great authority on American grammar and spelling, and compiler of a dictionary which has remained a standard reference work in its many revised forms ever since its first appearance in 1822. To cinema audiences the name was associated in silent screen days with Noah Beery, and later with his son Noah Beery Jr.

Noble (m) A use of the word or the surname as a first name. The first name appeared in the 1840s and was regularly used throughout the 19th c. In the 20th c. the name has been used more in the U.S. than Britain (where it was used until the early 1930s).

Noel (m, f) French 'Christmas'. *Nowel* or *Nowell* was the usual spelling in the Middle Ages, which accounts for the surnames. Originally used for both sexes, but by the 17th c. was more usually male. In the 19th c. it was not frequent, perhaps because **Christmas** was still in regular use for boys. Since the beginning of the 20th c. Noel has been steadily used, though never especially fashionable. The best-known bearer of the name has been the British actor Noel Coward (1899–1973), but his popularity in the 1930s had only a marginal effect on the name's use. Usual feminine form of the name is **Noelle**, though **Noeleen** has been well used since the 1960s. Variants include **Noela**, **Noeline**, **Noella**, **Noleen**. Many parents prefer the Latin forms **Natalie** or **Natalia**, or the Russian **Natasha**. **Carole(e)** is also used on occasion for girls born during the Christmas season, though the word and the name derive from different sources. It may be the use of **Nowell** in Christmas carols, however, that leads to that form of the name being used, as it is occasionally. Parents may also be making a transferred use of the surname.

Noeleen (f) Usual form in Britain of **Noelene** as used in Australia. Dates from the 1960s in England. The earlier form of the name was **Noeline**, used in the 1940s. All are feminine forms of **Noel**, and none, as yet, seems to be used in the U.S.

Noella (f) Latinized feminine form of **Noel**, in occasional use since the 1920s. **Noela** is also found.

Noelle (f) French feminine form of **Noel**, in use since the 1950s but rare since the 1960s.

Nola (f) Pet form of **Finola**, though interpreted by some parents as a feminine form of **Nolan**. Also the name of an Italian town, associated by ecclesiastical tradition with the invention of church bells; this has led some writers to explain the meaning of the first name as 'bell' or 'Italian town' (c.f. **Florence**, **Venice**). Well used in Britain since 1940.

Nolan (m) The Irish surname O *Nuallain*, based on *nuall* 'shout' i.e., 'famous'. In use as a first name since the end of the 19th c., but especially popular in the 1970s. **Nolen** is a variant.

Noleen (f) Diminutive of **Nola** or a variant of **Noelene**. Rarely used.

Nollie (f) A pet form of **Magnolia** in Edna Ferber's *Showboat*

Nona (f) Latin *nona*, feminine of *nonus* 'ninth'. Originally given to a child who was the ninth in the family. Also to a child born in the ninth month or on the ninth day of the month. Used regularly if infrequently since the 1880s.

Nora (f) Pet form of **Eleanora**, **Honora**, etc., used as a name in its own right. Especially popular from the 1870s to the 1920s, but now much rarer. **Norah** is frequently found. There is a Nora in Ibsen's play *A Doll's House* (1879).

Norbert (m) Old German 'famous in the North'. The name of an 11th c. saint. In regular use in English-speaking countries since the 1890s. Between 1940 and 1960 it was well used in the U.S. but rather rare in Britain.

Noreen (f) Diminutive of **Nora** first used in Ireland, where Nora is usually a form of **Honora**. Later spread and took on variant forms such as **Norene**, **Noreena**, **Norina**, **Norine**.

Norma (f) Latin *norma* 'pattern, model'. The name of an opera by Bellini, first performed in 1831. Used spasmodically thereafter until the 1920s, when the American actress Norma Shearer made it famous. Remained fashionable until the 1950s but now little used. Especially popular in Scotland, where it was probably considered to be a feminine form of **Norman**.

Norman (m) Old English 'man from the North, e.g. a Norwegian'. A personal name in the Middle Ages before and

after the Normans had invaded England, in 1066. They themselves were from Normandy, and were Scandinavian settlers in France. Rarely used after the 14th c. until revived in the mid-19th c. Then gradually became popular and reached its peak in all English-speaking countries in 1925. Since then it has been fading and is now little used. The Scots had kept the name alive at a time when it was virtually obsolete elsewhere, and it was probably Scottish instances of the name which inspired novelists such as Lord Lytton to use it in *The Sea Captain* (1839). Charlotte Yonge made use of it in *The Daisy Chain* (1856), and these literary references were probably enough to launch it into more general use. In modern times the name is associated with, say, the American writer Norman Mailer, or the British actor Norman Wisdom.

Norna (f) The name of one of the Fates in Scandinavian mythology. Occurs in Sir Walter Scott's *The Pirate* (1821). Rarely used as a first name.

Norrie (m) Pet form of **Norman**, **Norris**, **Norton** in occasional use as an independent name.

Norris (m) The normal meaning of the personal name, used in the Middle Ages, was 'northerner', but the surname can also derive from French *nourrice* 'nurse'. As a first name has been in regular if infrequent use since the beginning of the 19th c. in all English-speaking countries. Occasionally occurs as **Noris**, **Norice**, **Norreys**, **Norriss**. In modern times is associated with Norris McWhirter, editor of the *Guinness Book of Records*.

Norton (m) English place name 'northern settlement' which became a surname. In regular if infrequent use as a first name since the 1840s.

Norval (m) Appears in a play called *Douglas*, by John Home (1722–1808), where Norval is a shepherd who adopts a foundling in whom he calls young Norval. The child is son of a Scottish nobleman. Occasionally used as a first name. In the

U.S. is more frequent as **Norville, Norvel, Norvell**.

Nova (f) Latin *nova*, feminine of *novus* 'new'. In use since 1930s, when the British actress Nova Pilbeam regularly appeared on screen. She had family associations with Nova Scotia.

Nowell (m) Occasional variant of Noel.

Nuala (f) Pet form of Irish *Fionnuala* 'white shoulder' used independently. See **Finola**.

Nydia (f) The name of the blind flower girl and street singer in Lord Lytton's *Last Days of Pompeii* (1834). Rarely used. Could have been a changed form

of **Nadia** or **Lydia**, though its form suggests a link with Latin *nidus* 'nest'. This could have been suggested in turn by **Nest**, a Welsh pet form of **Agnes**.

Nye (m) Pet form of **Aneurin**, very rare as an independent name.

Nyree (f) Phonetic form of Maori *Ngaire*. Publicized by the New Zealand actress Nyree Dawn Porter, especially after her appearance in the TV series *The Forsyte Saga* (1967). Taken up almost immediately and used through the 1970s, though never with great frequency. Does not seem to have appealed to American parents.

O

Obadiah (m) Hebrew 'servant of God'. Biblical, O.T., the name of one of the minor Hebrew prophets. In common use in the 17th and 18th cc., then used fairly regularly throughout the 19th c. 20th c. Examples are slightly easier to find in the U.S. than in Britain, but it is not often used.

Oberon (m) See **Auberon**.

Ocean (m, f) A use of the word as a first name, especially for a child born at sea. The custom of naming children in this way dates at least from the voyage of the *Mayflower* in 1620. Oceanus Hopkins was named during that journey. As Bardsley has pointed out, other names in use amongst the Puritans reflect birth at sea: **Sea-Born, Sea-Mercy** and names like **Bonaventure**, taken directly from the name of the ship on which the child was born. Later emigrants to Australia likewise bestowed names like **Dolphin** on children who were born during the voyage on the ship of that name. In an article in *Doctors Only*, Dr David Aitken mentioned the following additional names that were inspired by birth at sea: **Neptune, Atlantic, Sou'wester,** and **Challenger, Pilgrim, Himalaya, Orontes,**

Berengaria, Exeter, Tremendous (names of the ships).

Octavia (f) Latin *Octavia*, feminine of *octavus* 'eighth'. A common Christian name in Roman times. Octavia was the sister of the Emperor Augustus, which may have caused the name to be used without numerical reference (i.e. the eighth child in the family, born in the eighth month, etc.). Mainly used in the 19th c. and very rare in modern times.

Octavius (m) Latin *Octavius*, from *octavus* 'eighth'. The name of a Roman clan, of which the emperor Augustus was the most famous member. Brought into use in the mid-19th c. and used regularly until the beginning of the 20th c. Very rare in modern times, but black American parents turn to it on occasion.

Odell (m) English place name 'woad hill' and surname, used as a first name mainly in the U.S., seldom in Britain. On rare occasions the name is given to girls, though they usually receive a feminine form of the name such as **Odella**, or **Odelyn**. French feminine names **Odile** and **Odette** may also be thought of as being linked with Odell, though from an etymological point of view they are unconnected.

Odessa (f) The Russian city of this name was thought to have been associated with a Greek *Odessos*. When used as a first name in modern times (only in the U.S.) it is no doubt thought of as a feminine form of *Odysseus*, name of the hero of Homer's epic poem *The Odyssey*.

Odette (f) French feminine diminutive of Germanic **Odo** 'riches'. Used in English-speaking countries since the 1930s. During the Second World War was made famous by the courage of Odette Brailly, who risked her life in France to supply information to the Allies.

Odile (f) French feminine diminutive of **Odo** 'riches'. Made known in English-speaking countries by the French actress Odile Versois (Militza de Poliakoff-Baidarov) from the mid-1940s, but not widely used. In the U.S. seen as a feminine form of **Odell**.

Odo (m) See **Otto**.

Ogden (m) Place name 'oak valley' and surname used as a first name. Occurs regularly if infrequently in the 19th c. but very rarely used in the 20th c., though Ogden Nash, the prolific verse-writer, made it well known.

Olaf (m) See **Olave** and **Aulay**. Mainly used in Scotland, but rare.

Olave (m) Old Norse 'forefather, ancestor'. The usual form in English-speaking countries of this Scandinavian name, which is also found as **Ola, Olaf, Olav, Olavus, Ole, Olef, Olle, Olof, Olov, Oluf** in the Scandinavian countries themselves. Seems to have been taken to Ireland by the Norsemen where it became *Amhlaoibh* (the Norse form of the name having been *Anleifr*). Olave represents the Anglicized form of *Amhlaoibh*. In Scotland the original name was turned into Gaelic *Amhlaibh* and ultimately became **Aulay**.

Olga (f) Russian form of **Helga** 'holy'. A 10th c. saint bore the name. Regularly used in English-speaking countries since the 1870s, though less often since 1970.

Olif(fe) (f) A use of the surnames, which derive from **Olive**, as first names. Occasionally Old Norse *Olafr* is the source, see **Olave**.

Olinda (f) Feminine form of Italian **Olindo**, said to be the name of a Greek city *Olinthos*. Used on rare occasions in English-speaking countries. Olindo was used by Tasso in his *Jerusalem Delivered* (1575).

Olive (f) Latin *oliva* 'olive'. The olive has for long been a symbol of peace. *Oliva* was used in the Middle Ages, *Oliff* being the English form. This gave rise to surnames such as *Oliffe, Oliff* which have occasionally been re-used as first names in modern times. Olive came into fashion at the end of the 19th c. along with other botanical names, remaining popular until the early 1930s. From that time on **Olivia** became the more popular form, especially in the U.S. Olive gave rise to a diminutive form **Olivette**, regularly used 1910–25.

Oliver (m) French **Olivier** is the source of this name, which the French themselves usually explain as being a male form of **Olive**. But whereas Olive clearly derived from a Roman name **Oliva**, no trace has been found of a Roman *Olivarius*. The name first occurs in an Old French epic where all the names around it are of Teutonic origin. Miss Withycombe therefore suggested plausibly a derivation from Old German *Alfihar* 'elf-host'. Professor Weekley is amongst those who favour a derivation from Old Norse *Olafr* (see **Olave**). The name was borne by Oliver Cromwell (1599–1658), who became Lord Protector of England. After the Restoration of the Monarchy (1660) the name was little used, especially in Ireland, where Cromwell was hated, yet it was the name given to Oliver Goldsmith (1730–74) by his Irish father. This may reflect the influence of Oliver Plunket (1629–81), made a saint in 1920. Dickens's *Oliver Twist* was published in 1837–8 but had little influence on the name's use, though it became slightly more popular in the latter half of the 19th c. In modern times it has been associated with Oliver Hardy, the fat member of the Laurel and Hardy team in many comedy films. Oliver Reed has possibly had more influence on the name's use since 1960, and a character in a British television series *Rings On Their Fingers* certainly seems to have given the name a boost in Britain in the late 1970s.

Olivette (f) Diminutive of **Olive** used between 1910 and 1925. Earlier form was **Olivet**.

Olivia (f) Italian form of **Olive**. Oliver Goldsmith made it the name of a character in *The Vicar of Wakefield* (1766), no doubt influenced by his own name, but he makes the Vicar remark that it is a romantic name, chosen by his wife after reading a novel. Shakespeare also used the name in *Twelfth Night*, but it seems to have been Goldsmith, who used the name again in his *Good-Natured Man* (1768), who made Olivia fashionable in the 18th c. In recent times more frequently used in the U.S. than in Britain, especially since Olivia de Havilland began to appear on cinema screens in the mid-1930s.

Olivier (m) French form of **Oliver**, occasionally used in English-speaking countries.

Ollie (m, f) Pet form of names such as **Oliver** when used for men, **Olivia** when used for women. In modern times Ollie is used rather more often for girls than boys, and more often in the U.S. than Britain.

Olwen (f) Welsh *ol* 'footprint, track' + *(g)wen* 'white'. In Welsh legend a beautiful maiden. Wherever she trod four white clover sprang from the ground. Used very regularly in Wales, and by families of Welsh descent living elsewhere, since the end of the 19th c. Found with almost equal frequency as **Olwyn**, occasionally as **Olwin** or **Olwyne**.

Oma (f) Taken to be the feminine form of **Omar** by all the reference works which

mention it. Used infrequently in the U.S.

Omar (m) Hebrew 'eloquent'. Biblical, O.T., Gen. 36:11. Mainly associated with Edward Fitzgerald's free translation of Omar Khayyam's *Rubaiyat* in 1859. Used very infrequently until modern times, when black American parents have shown a marked interest in it. A well-known modern bearer of the name was General Omar Nelson Bradley, famous during World War Two. The actor and bridge-player Omar Sharif currently keeps the name before the public.

Omega (f) Greek *omega*, name of the last letter of the Greek alphabet and used symbolically to mean 'the end'. Its use as a first name may indicate the parents' intention to have no further children. See also **Alpha**.

Ona (f) Probably a pet form of a name ending in *-ona*, such as **Leona**, **Ilona**, **Mona**, **Ramona**, **Nona**, **Rona**, **Verona**. It might occasionally be a variant of **Oona**. Made known by the American actress Ona Munson, and used from time to time, mainly in the U.S.

Onita (f) Pet form of **Antonita** occasionally used in its own right. Usage seems to be confined to the U.S.

Oonagh (f) An Irish form of **Una**. Not often used, but found more frequently from the 1950s to the late 1960s, perhaps because of Oonagh Chaplin, wife of Charlie Chaplin. **Oona** and **Oonie** also occur, the latter influenced by **Uny** and **Unity**, both having been used to anglicize the name.

Opal (f) The name of the precious stone used as a first name. Used very infrequently.

Ophelia (f) Greek *opheleia* 'help, aid', though the original use of *Ofelia* by a 16th c. Italian poet may have been influenced by a Roman family name *Ofellius*. Ophelia in Shakespeare's *Hamlet* is the beautiful daughter of Polonius. Hamlet falls in love with her, but his behaviour to her causes her loss of reason. Used from time to time, especially in the latter half of the 19th c. In modern times black American families usually make use of it.

Ora (f) Pet form of **Cora, Dora, Lora, Nora,** etc., used independently, or perhaps from the Latin expression formerly used in Roman Catholic churches *Ora pro nobis,* 'pray for us'. Ora was being used in the 1940s and '50s, especially by black American families, occasionally for boys as well as girls.

Oran (m) Irish *Odhran* from *odhar* 'green'. The name of nine Irish saints, but used rather rarely.

Orange (m) Rare use of the word as first name. Other fruity names include **Cherry, Berry** and at least one **Apple** Smith named in 1972. (The Roman name **Pomona** is also found). Girls who answer to **Prune** are usually **Prunella** on their birth certificates. **Peach** does not seem to have been used as a first name, though **Melba** has, and **Peaches** was given to two black American girls in 1981. In the U.S.A. new feminine form **Orangetta** has been developed.

Oren (m) See **Orin**.

Oriana (f) Latin, formed from the participle *oriens* (from *oriri* 'to rise) and meaning 'dawn, sunrise'. Mainly a literary name but occasionally used as a first name. Elizabeth I was frequently referred to as 'the peerless Oriana' in contemporary poems. In Fletcher's *The Wild Goose Chase* and Farquhar's *The Inconstant* there are women who bear the name. She also appears as a teasing, tormenting, brilliant woman in Beaumont and Fletcher's *The Woman-hater.* Tennyson attempted to revive the name in the 19th c. with his *Ballad of Oriana,* but his heroine is accidentally killed and the poem is a lament for her death. Such a theme did not inspire parents to use the name.

Oriel (f) Probably a form of **Auriel,** the spelling influenced in Britain, perhaps, by Oriel College, Oxford. The college takes its name from Latin *oriolum* 'gallery, porch', but there was a medieval personal name, *Orieldis* or *Aurildis,*

which came from Old German and meant 'fire-strife'. It was that name in the Middle Ages which led to the surname *Oriel.* Auriel and Oriel were revived at roughly the same time, at the beginning of the 20th c., and were clearly heard by parents as the same name. The Au- spelling was the first to appear in official records, but one cannot be sure which name was a variant of the other. **Oriole** is an occasional variant.

Orin (m) Used by Eugene O'Neill in *Mourning Becomes Electra* as a deliberate link, it has been suggested, with Greek **Orestes.** More often spelt **Orrin** when used in modern times. **Oren** also occurs, and there may be confusion with **Oran.** George Bernard Shaw invented the feminine name **Orinthia** in *The Apple Cart,* two years before O'Neill's play. In the 17th c. the poet Cowley made use of another feminine name which appears to belong to the same group, **Orinda,** though this may have been a shortening of **Dorinda.**

Oria (f) Irish *Orfhlaith* 'golden lady'. Modern Irish name clearly increasing in popularity in the late 1970s and beginning to spread outside Ireland. Also occurs as **Orlagh.**

Orland (m) Form of **Orlando** now used in the U.S.

Orlando (m) Italian form of **Roland.** Used in the latter half of the 19th c. with some regularity, but rarely since the 1920s. A literary name, e.g. Ariosto's poem *Orlando Furioso.* Also the name of a central character in Shakespeare's *As You Like It.*

Ormerod (m) English place name/ surname 'Orm's clearing' used regularly in Britain as a first name during the latter half of the 19th c. **Ormrod** occurs as a variant.

Ormond(e) (m) Irish surname derived from *O Ruaidh* 'red' used from time to time as a first name.

Orpah (f) Hebrew, of uncertain meaning. Biblical, O.T., Ruth 1:44. In very rare use. In the 19th c. it was turned into **Orpha** and **Orphy.**

Orrin (m) See **Orin**.

Orris (m) Probably a form of **Horace** when used in early records. **Orriss** also occurs.

Orson (m) French *Ourson*, Latin *Ursinus*, a diminutive of *ursus* 'bear'. Feminine form of the name is **Ursula**. Shakespeare uses an Italian form **Orsino** in his *Twelfth Night*. Dickens seems to have expected his readers to recognize the allusion to Orson in *The Child's Story*: 'They had plenty of the finest toys in the world, and the most astonishing picture books: all about . . . blue-beards and bean-stalks and riches and caverns and forests and caverns and Valentines and Orsons.' The reference is to a 15th c. story about the brothers Valentine and Orson. Orson was carried off by a bear and brought up as one of its cubs. He grew up to become the Wild Man of the Forest and the terror of France, but his brother reclaimed him. An Orson figures in a 19th c. story by Dr Wolcot, *Orson and Ellen*. He is a young man who dislikes matrimony ('The man who can buy milk is a fool to keep a cow' is one of his favourite sayings), but he eventually marries Ellen. Orson has been made famous, of course, by the actor/writer/producer Orson Welles, but it is used rarely in any English-speaking country.

Orval (m) French place name and surname, but probably represents a variant of **Orville** when used in the U.S.

Orville (m) Apparently invented by Fanny Burney in her novel *Evelina* (1779). Lord Orville is the 'handsome, gallant, polite and ardent' hero of the novel. The parents of Orville Wright (1871–1948), the aviation pioneer, named him in honour of a Unitarian minister, Orville Dewey. Used infrequently in English-speaking countries.

Osbert (m) Old English 'god-bright'. One of the names that survived the Norman Conquest, though not used in great numbers. Revived to some extent in the 19th c., but has almost disappeared since the 1930s.

Osborn(e) (m) Old English 'god-bear'. The Normans used a cognate name from Scandinavia, which meant that Osborn(e) survived the Conquest. Its use as a personal name in the Middle Ages led to surnames such as *Osborn(e)*, *Osburn*, etc. When used again as a first name in the 19th c. it was probably a conscious use of a surname. Osborne was the usual form, and usage was very regular until the end of the century. The fact that Queen Victoria often stayed in Osborne House on the Isle of Wight may have had some bearing on the matter. Use of Osborn(e) as a first name faded early in the 20th c., but it reappeared in the 1940s in the U.S., rather later in Britain, and often as **Osbourn** or **Osburn**. **Osbon** and **Osbern** are other modern variants. In the U.S. is favoured by black American families.

Oscar (m) Old English 'god-spear'. The name did not survive the Norman conquest, but was revived by James Macpherson (1736–96) for his Ossianic poems. These were poems which Macpherson claimed to have translated from the Gaelic of a poet called Ossian. Whatever their origin, Napoleon was amongst their admirers. He gave the name to his godson, who became King of Sweden. Oscar Wilde's father, an eye-surgeon, treated Oscar II of Sweden, which led to the naming of the playwright. Oscar Wilde was publicly disgraced in 1895. Oscar had been frequently used before that time, especially in the 1870s in the U.S., but the scandal did not help matters. Used very quietly ever since, its best-known modern bearer being Oscar Hammerstein II, whose musical partnership with Richard Rodgers produced *South Pacific* and other shows. The name is now associated with the award made by the Academy of Motion Picture Arts and Sciences to outstanding members of the profession. It is said to have been named in 1931 when the Academy's librarian remarked that the statuette reminded her of her uncle Oscar.

Osmond (m) Old English 'god-protector'. An Anglo-Saxon name which survived the Norman Conquest because the Normans used a cognate name from Old Norse, *Asmundr*. Use in the Middle Ages led to surnames such as *Osmond*, *Osman*, *Osmint*, but the name faded by the 14th c. The fashion for Old English names caused it to be partially revived in the latter half of the 19th c. Used regularly until the 1930s, but rare since. Variants of the name include **Osman, Osmand, Osmund.**

Osten, Ostin (m) Variants (19th c.) of **Austin.**

Oswald (m) Old English 'god-power'. The Normans used a similar name deriving from Old Norse. Would probably have survived the Norman Conquest in any case, since it was the name of St Oswald, King of Northumbria in the 7th c. Another St Oswald lived in the 10th c. Use of the name in the Middle Ages led to surnames such as *Oswell* and *Oswill*. Oswell, especially, was used with some regularity in the 19th c. as a first name, together with **Oswall** and **Oswold.** Oswald is the name of a minor character in *King Lear* by William Shakespeare, but the name is rarely given in modern times in any English-speaking country.

Oswin (m) Old English 'god-friend'. Anglo-Saxon name that did not long survive the Norman Conquest, though the surname *Oswin* shows that it was still used until at least the beginning of the 13th c. Revived as a first name in the latter part of the 19th c. and used regularly until the 1920s.

Osyth (f) The name of a 7th c. queen and saint, earlier *Osgith*, of unknown meaning. Occasionally used as a first name in modern times, especially in the early 20th c.

Otho (m) See Otto.

Otis (m) A use of the surname, which derives in turn from **Otto.** Used far more regularly in the U.S. than in Britain, and is a particular favourite with black American families. It was originally given in honour of James Otis (1725–83), the American patriot. It was Elisha Graves Otis (1811–61) who invented the elevator and made possible the development of New York with its skyscrapers. Used on rare occasions for girls.

Otto (m) Old German *Ot-*, from *Autha* 'possessions'. Short form of names beginning with *Ot-* originally, but long established in Germany as a name in its own right. A famous name in the latter half of the 19th c. because of Otto von Bismarck, Germany's 'Iron Chancellor'. At that time the name was regularly used in English-speaking countries. In Britain the name has been rarely used since 1900. In the U.S. German immigrants continued to make use of it until the early 1940s. Anti-German feeling then made it a difficult name to use, and it does not seem to have come back into use later. **Odo** and **Otho** are variants of the name.

Ouida (f) Babyish mispronunciation of **Louise.** Used as a pseudonym by the novelist Marie Louise de la Ramée (1839–1908) and as a first name by admirers soon after her death. Another instance of the first name was noted in the 1950s.

Owain (m) Welsh form of Owen. In regular use, but in modern times Owen is the preferred spelling.

Owen (m) Welsh **Owain,** a form of Latin *Eugenius*, Greek *eugenes* 'well-born'. A very common name in early Welsh history and the name of the 14th c. hero Owain Glyndwr, or Owen Glendower. Rarely used in the 16th c. and 17th c., but regularly used throughout the 18th c. Used very steadily since then, while never being especially fashionable, in all English-speaking countries. In Wales a feminine form **Owena** is used on rare occasions.

P

Paddy (m) Pet form of **Patrick** (Gaelic **Padraig**) and a generic term for an Irishman. Occasionally used as an independent name.

Padraig (m) Irish form of **Patrick**, used in ever-increasing numbers in the 1970s in the Republic, though rarely elsewhere.

Page (f) Variant of **Paige**. **Paget**, a surname deriving from the same source, is also used on occasions as a first name.

Paige (f) As a surname Paige indicates an ancestor who was a 'page' in the Middle Ages. Regularly used in the U.S. as a first name, usually for girls, occasionally for boys. **Page** also occurs.

Painter (m) Occupational surname used as a first name from time to time.

Palmer (m) Surname, originally indicating a pilgrim, one who carried a palm branch, used as a first name on infrequent occasions.

Pamela (f) First used by Sir Philip Sidney in his *Arcadia* (1590). If he invented it, it is not clear what meaning he intended the name to have, though a derivation from Greek 'all honey', i.e. 'all sweetness', is possible. Not in general use when Samuel Richardson used it as the name of his servant-girl heroine, Pamela Andrews, in his best-selling novel *Pamela* (1740). Pronunciation of the name in the 18th c. varied between *Pam-eela* and the modern *Pam-ella*. Traces of the early pronunciation are probably to be found in the 19th c. variants **Pamelia** and **Pamilia**. Used consistently but infrequently throughout the 19th c. and began to be fashionable in the 1920s. Peak period of usage in all English-speaking countries in the 1950s and '60s, since when the name has faded. It is fitting, given its literary associations in its early days, that the name should have been borne by successful writers such as Pamela Frankau, Pamela Hansford Johnson, Pamela Moore. Occasionally found as **Pamala**, **Pamella**, **Pamila**, **Pammala**. Pet form **Pam** is also used as a name in its own right.

Pansy (f) Flower name used as a first name, mainly in Britain from the 1880s. Rare since the 1930s. The first British use of the name that has been noted was a Pansy Smith named in 1882. Henry James published his *Portrait of a Lady* in 1881, and Pansy in the novel is the daughter of Osmond, who is described as having exquisite taste in all things. Pansy was not one of the more popular flower names used as a first name, however, either in Britain or the U.S.

Paris (m) The name of the man who eloped with Helen of Troy and brought about the Trojan War. *Paris* is also an English and French surname. It can indicate that the original name-bearer came from the French capital city, but more often it represents a form of French **Patrice** (**Patrick**). As Professor Dauzat pointed out, Parisians rarely left the city to live elsewhere, though Paris was always full of people who bore the names of the places they had left. Used in Britain in the 19th c. but appears to be obsolete. In the U.S. is in regular use, favoured especially by black American parents.

Parker (m) Surname indicating a 'keeper of a park' which was used with great regularity in the 19th c. as a first name but has been rare since the beginning of the 20th c. American parents have remained more faithful to it than those in other English-speaking countries.

Parry (m) Surname, deriving from Welsh *ap* Harry 'son of Harry', in occasional use as a first name.

Parthenia (f) Greek *parthenos* 'virgin, maiden'. The Parthenon, in Athens, was the temple of Athena Parthenos, i.e., Athena the maiden goddess. A correspondent mentions a Parthenia named *ca.* 1811 in North Carolina, known as **Theny**. Occurs in various forms, such as **Parthena, Parthina, Pathania, Pathena, Pathenia, Pathina**, most of which occurred at the end of the 19th c., but the name is still used on rare occasions, e.g. as **Parthine**.

Pascal (m) French 'Easter child'. In use

since the 1960s. **Easter** was used as a first name throughout the 19th c., but in many instances it was probably just a variant of **Esther**. The name **Pascow** or **Pascoe** was formerly used in Cornwall, *Pask* being the Cornish word for 'Easter'. A **Pasko** Smith was named in 1959.

Pascale (f) French feminine of **Pascal**, used since the 1960s in English-speaking countries.

Pat (m, f) Pet form of **Patrick** or **Patricia** used in its own right, but rarely since the early 1970s.

Pathania (f) Also **Pathena**, **Pathenia**, **Pathina**. See **Parthenia**.

Patience (f) The word used as a name. One of the 'virtues' favoured by the Puritans in the 16th c. In regular use ever since and associated with the popular poet Patience Strong (Winifred May). *Patience* is also the heroine of the Gilbert and Sullivan opera of that name. **Patient** was used occasionally in the 19th c.

Patrice (f) French form of **Patricia**. Used far more in the U.S. than in Britain, and has been publicized by the actress Patrice Wymore and opera singer Patrice Munsel.

Patricia (f) Latin feminine of *Patricius* 'noble'. Recorded in the 6th c. and the name of the 7th c. nun, St Patricia, patron of Naples. Very rarely used in English-speaking countries until the beginning of the 20th c. Associated at that time with Princess Patricia, granddaugher of Queen Victoria. Quickly became highly fashionable in both Britain and the U.S. Reached a peak in Britain in the 1930s and lasted until the end of the 1960s before fading drastically. It followed a similar pattern in the U.S. but lasted even longer. By 1980 it was being used rather quietly on all sides. Usual pet form at first was **Pat** or **Patty**, which was already in use as a pet form of **Martha**, or **Matilda**. Later the forms **Tricia** and **Trisha** became popular as names in their own right. The British actress Patricia Roc was amongst the best-known bearers of the name in

the 1940s, though she came on the scene too late to claim credit for the name's intensive use. She herself was born Felicia Riese. The American actress Patricia Neal became well-known from 1950 onwards.

Patrick (m) Latin *Patricius* 'noble man'. A common name amongst the early Christians. The 5th c. St Patrick became patron of Ireland. One of the Gaelic forms of the name was *Patair*, which caused the name to become confused in Scotland, especially, with **Peter**. Well used in Ireland after 1600, and continued to be one of the most popular Irish names for boys until recently. This led to **Pat** and **Paddy** becoming generic terms for Irishmen. In the early 1980s Irish parents were increasingly turning to **Padraig**, the usual form of the name in Erse, as use of Patrick itself declined. In England Patrick did not come into general use until the 18th c. At its peak 1935–70. American parents also used it mainly between those dates, but by the early 1980s use of the name was declining rapidly on all sides. Some well-known bearers of the name include actor/singer Pat Boone, and actors Patrick O'Neal in the U.S. and Patrick Cargill in Britain. Patrick has also been very popular in recent years in countries such as France and Germany.

Patsy (m, f) Usually a pet form of **Patricia**, occasionally of **Patrick**, used in its own right, though rarely in the U.S. where 'a patsy' is someone who is duped or victimized. In Britain the name occurs regularly since the beginning of the 20th c.

Patti (f) Pet form of **Patricia** in regular use, especially in the U.S., since the late 1940s. The singer Patti Page (Clara Ann Fowler) has helped to spread the name.

Patty (f) Pet form of various names, such as **Martha** and **Matilda**, *via* **Matty**, and later, from the beginning of the 20th c., **Patricia**. Used as an independent name in the 1840s, long before Patricia came into general use, but has faded since the

1920s. **Pattie** was a common variant, **Pattey** occasional.

Paul (m) Latin *paulus* 'small'. Paulus was the surname of the Aemilian family. Biblical, N.T., St Paul the Apostle. One of the commonest names amongst the early Christians. Its use in medieval England led to surnames such as *Pole* and *Powell*. Not particularly common in the 16th or 17th cc., but came back into use in the 18th c. By the end of the 19th c. it was very popular in the U.S., whereas in Britain it was being used very quietly. American parents continued to use it as one of their favourite names until the mid-1970s, but they then began to leave it aside. British parents only discovered the name again in the 1920s, by 1950 it was very popular, and by the 1980s it was second only to **Matthew** in the British top fifty. By that time parents were becoming aware of its popularity, and this would normally lead to its going out of fashion. American fondness for the name in the 19th c. was probably due to Paul Revere (1735–1818), whose famous ride to warn his countrymen of the advancing British soldiers was celebrated in verse by Longfellow. Other well-known modern bearers of the name include actors Paul Newman, Paul Douglas, Paul Carpenter and Paul Scofield, and singers Paul McCartney and Paul Anka. Feminine forms of the name include **Paula**, **Paule**, **Pauleen**, **Paulene**, **Paulette**, **Paulina**, **Pauline**, **Paulyne**. Italian **Paolo** and Spanish **Pablo** are sometimes used in the U.S. Appears to have no pet forms, probably one of the reasons for its popularity.

Paula (f) Latin feminine of *paulus* 'small'. Used by early Christians, but almost unknown in English-speaking countries until the 1920s. Until then it had been primarily a German name, being especially well used in Germany at the end of the 19th c. A. W. Pinero used the name for the title role in his *Second Mrs Tanqueray* (1893), but at the time this had as little effect on name usage as **Ellean**, which was the name he gave to another

character. Reached a peak of popularity in the U.S. in the 1950s and '60s. In Britain it arrived rather later, being most used in the 1970s. Actresses who helped to publicize the name include Paula Raymond and Paula Prentiss.

Paulann (f) Blend of **Paula** and **Ann** used since the 1940s mainly in the U.S.

Pauleen (f) Variant of **Pauline** regularly used since the 1930s.

Paulette (f) French feminine diminutive of **Paul** in use in English-speaking countries since the 1920s. Much publicized from 1931 onwards by actress Paulette Goddard (Marion Levy), who helped make the name reasonably popular in the U.S. in the 1940s. In Britain the name is still in regular use, as it is in the U.S., but it has never been especially popular. **Pauletta** is occasionally used.

Paulina (f) Latin feminine of *Paulinus*, diminutive of *Paulus* 'little'. A common name amongst the early Christians and the name of a 3rd c. saint. Shakespeare has a Paulina in his *Winter's Tale* (1604), but the name was not being used in England in the 17th c. Revived in the 19th c. and used regularly in all English-speaking countries, though never in great numbers. In modern times seldom used, French **Pauline** being much preferred.

Pauline (f) French form of **Paulina**. Came into use in English-speaking countries in the 19th c. At first, as with **Paul**, far more popular in the U.S. than in Britain. At its peak in the U.S. 1870–1900, and quietly used ever since. British parents began to use the name seriously in the 1920s. It reached a peak of popularity in the 1950s and has faded since then, though Paul continued to be very well used. Also occurs as **Pauleen** and **Paulene**.

Paxton (m) English place name and surname used as a first name from time to time. Found in both Britain and the U.S.

Peace (f) The word 'peace' (ultimately from Latin *pax*) used as an abstract virtue name by the Puritans in the 17th c. Did not survive as well as **Faith**, **Hope**, etc., and rare in modern times. The name can be compared to **Irene, Solomon, Salome, Frieda**, etc., which are based on the word for peace in Greek, Hebrew and German. **Fred** derives also from the Germanic *frithu* 'peace', connected etymologically with the word 'friend'.

Pearce (m) Surname derived from **Piers** (Peter) used from time to time as a first name. See also **Pierce, Pearson**.

Pearl (f) The word used as a name. Could be considered an English form of **Margaret**. In Hawthorne's *The Scarlet Letter* (1850) it is the name given by Hester to her daughter, 'as being of great price – purchased with all she had – her mother's only treasure'. Came into general use in the 1860s and used regularly ever since, reaching a minor peak in the 1920s. The novelist Pearl S. Buck helped to make it well known, and the entertainer Pearl Bailey has done much to keep it before the public eye. Pearl White was earlier a famous star of silent films, in such series as *The Perils of Pauline*. The name has also given rise to such forms as **Pearla, Pearleen, Pearley, Pearlie, Pearline, Pearly, Pearle, Pearlena, Perl, Perlie, Perly, Purly**.

Pearle (f) Variant of **Pearl** regularly used in the U.S. British parents occasionally use **Pearla**, and more often, **Pearly**.

Pearline (f) Development of **Pearl** on the analogy of **Pauline** and similar names, in regular use in both Britain and the U.S. since the 1930s.

Pearson (m) Surname 'son of **Piers** (Peter)' used as a first name, especially in the 19th c. Rare since the 1920s. **Pierson** also occurs.

Pedro (m) Spanish form of **Peter**, used in the U.S.

Peggie (f) See **Peggy**.

Peggotty (f) Surname of Clara Peggotty, the faithful nurse of *David Copperfield* in Dickens's novel of that name. In the novel she is always addressed by her surname because the name of her mistress is also Clara. Occasionally taken to be a fanciful form of **Peggy**, and indeed

is listed as such in Partridge's *Name This Child*. Found also as **Peggetty**.

Peggy (f) Originally a pet form of **Margaret**, *via* **Maggie, Meggie**, but in use in its own right since the 18th c., when it was very popular. Then went out of fashion completely until 1910 onwards. Until the mid-1930s highly popular in Britain, though much less so in the U.S. In modern times seldom used. Famous bearers of the name include the British actress Dame Peggy Ashcroft and the American actress Peggy Wood. **Peggie** is a 20th c. variant, regularly used while the name was popular. **Peggey** also occurs.

Pelham (m) English place name 'Peola's residence'. The surname of a distinguished English family with a branch in New England. Made known as a first name by Pelham Grenville Wodehouse, the humorous writer (1881–1975).

Penelope (f) Greek *Penelopeia*, traditionally associated with *pene* 'a bobbin', presumably with reference to the thread on the bobbin. While Penelope's husband, Ulysses, was absent and presumed to be dead, she was besieged by would-be wooers. She told them that she could not consider another husband until she had finished weaving a shroud for her father-in-law. Penelope worked on the tapestry every day, but every night she unpicked what she had done. Camden, writing in 1605, connected her name instead with Greek *penelops*, a kind of bird, saying that she received the name because she loved and fed such birds. Came into use in Britain in the 16th c. and regularly used until the end of the 18th c. Used only sporadically from 1800 until the 1940s, when it became mildly fashionable. At its height in the 1950s and '60s but later faded. Much the same pattern in the U.S., though the name was not as intensively used as in Britain. American parents began to use the pet form **Penny** as an independent name in the 1930s, though not in significant numbers until the mid-1940s. By 1950 Penny was being well used in Britain and it remained in use until the early 1980s. Coghlan says that in Ireland another pet form of the name is **Nappy**, but his own statistical tables show that the name has in any case been little used there this century.

Penny (f) Usual pet form of **Penelope**, used independently since the late 1930s in the U.S., rather later in Britain (though isolated examples are found in the 19th c.). **Pennie** is an infrequent variant, as is **Penney**. The name is unlikely to represent a use of the word for a coin, since money-names have never been in fashion. **Cash** has reportedly been used as a male first name, however, and it is possible that the 'florin', while it was still in use, suggested **Florine** and **Florina** to the British parents who used those names in the 19th c. **Lolly**, which in Britain is slang for 'money', is a nickname for **Laura** or **Laurence** when it is heard. **Bob** is of course from **Robert**, but once again its British slang meaning was a 'shilling'. Dickens was therefore able to comment in *A Christmas Carol* that 'Bob had but fifteen "Bob" a week himself; he pocketed on Saturdays but fifteen copies of his Christian name.' A similar play on words would be possible, presumably, with **Bill**, using its slang meaning of a hundred dollars. Finally, **Buck** is probably another accidental money-name, since it was probably used in its sense 'a dashing fellow, a dandy', rather than its slang sense of 'dollar' when it was first used as a given name.

Pepita (f) Spanish diminutive of Josefina (**Josephine**), *via* Italian Giuseppe (**Joseph**) and its short forms **Peppo**, **Peppe**. The male Spanish forms are respectively **Jose**, **Pepe** and **Pepito**. Pepita has long been recognized as an independent name and is used in English-speaking countries, especially the U.S.

Percival (m) Invented by the 12th c. poet Crestien de Troyes for a mythical knight associated with King Arthur. The name perhaps meant 'pierce vale', i.e. 'one who breaks through into the valley', but none of the Arthurian names have satisfactory etymologies. Troyes may have found a Celtic (Welsh) name, which he transposed into a French form. In modern Welsh Percival becomes **Peredur**, but this is probably not old enough to have been, as Professor Dauzat suggests, the original name. Percival was being used in Britain throughout the 16th and 17th cc., and it became reasonably frequent in the 18th c. Rose in popularity in the 19th c. and reached its peak in 1900. Subsequently declined and is now rarely used in Britain. In the early 1980s black American parents were still using it occasionally. Tennyson's *Idylls* contains a section devoted to 'Sir Percival', and this may have helped spread the name after 1860. Early German form of the name was **Parzival**, though Wagner makes it *Parsifal* for his opera. **Perceval** is the normal French spelling of the name, and is found as a variant in Britain.

Percy (m) Norman place name which became an aristocratic English surname. Then used within the family as a first name. The poet Percy Bysshe Shelley (1792–1822), who was vaguely connected with the Percys, made the name more widely known. In 1839 Lord Lytton was able to use it for one of his aristocratic characters in *The Sea-Captain*, a novel which was widely read. By 1875 the name was becoming very popular, and it reached a peak in Britain in 1900. **Percival** was also at its peak at that time, and there is not the slightest doubt that Percy was generally interpreted as a pet form of the longer name. Both names faded quickly and are now rarely used, though Percy continues to find favour with black American parents. Variants of the name include **Pearcy**, **Pearcey**, **Percey**.

Perdita (f) Latin, feminine of the past participle of *perdere* 'to lose'. The name was created by Shakespeare in *The Winter's Tale*: 'For the babe is counted *lost* for ever, Perdita I prithee call't'. Rarely used.

Peregrine (m) Latin *peregrinus* 'traveller, stranger, pilgrim.' *Peregrinus* and *Peregrina* are common names in the Christian inscriptions of the Roman Empire, and at least three male saints bore the name. Tobias Smollett's hero *Peregrine Pickle* in his novel of that name (1751) was certainly not a saint, but the name was well-used in the 18th c. Became rare in the 19th c. and has remained so. Pet form **Perry** was first used independently in the 1840s.

Peronelle (f) Petronella was reduced in the Middle Ages to forms such as **Peronel** and **Pernel**, the latter being written as **Pernelle** in France. Peronelle seems to be a French form of Peronel, and both forms have been used occasionally in modern times.

Perry (m) Originally a pet form of **Peregrine**. The first name can also be a use of the surname *Perry* which indicates an ancestor who lived near a pear tree. Modern use of the name stems from the fictional lawyer-detective Perry Mason, created by Erle Stanley Gardner in 1933 and later made widely known by television series. The singer Perry Como has been the other main impetus for the name's greatly increased usage since the 1940s. He was originally Nick Perido, and Perry was probably chosen to keep a link with his family name. In the early 1980s Perry was still being used quietly, but its period of popularity had clearly passed.

Peta (f) Feminine form of Peter used regularly in Britain and Australia since the 1930s, but seemingly unknown in the U.S.

Peter (m) Greek *petros* 'stone, rock'. This was the name used to translate **Cephas**, the Aramaic name that Jesus gave to Simon son of Jonas. Biblical, N.T., e.g. John 1:42, Mat. 4:18. The Normans introduced the name to England in the Middle Ages as **Piers**, **Pierce**, etc. This would have been Latinized as *Petrus*, from which form Peter became established in the late Middle Ages. Anti-Catholic feeling kept the name in the

background for a century or so, but it was steadily used from the 16th c. onwards. Not being used with great intensity at the beginning of the 20th c., but became fashionable very soon afterwards and remained so until the late 1970s in Britain. In the U.S. its rise to popularity began around 1930, and it was highly fashionable for at least thirty years. Still in use in all English-speaking countries, but no longer in great numbers. Miss Withycombe is probably right to suggest that the vogue for Peter in the 20th c. was begun by J. M. Barrie's play *Peter Pan* (1904). The influence of the play is clearly demonstrated by the success of **Wendy**, a name which Barrie invented. Peter has been coincidentally a highly successful thespian name in other ways, since actors like Peter Finch, Peter Lorre, Peter O'Toole, Peter Sellers, Peter Ustinov are amongst those who have borne it. Pet form **Pete** is sometimes used independently (and was possibly the name intended by the parents who named their son Peat in 1862). Petar, Peterr, Petre occur occasionally. Feminine forms of the name include **Peta**, **Petena**, **Peterina**, **Peternella**, **Petra**, **Petrina**, **Petrona**, **Petronella**, **Petronilla**. **Petula** may also belong here.

Petra (f) Latin 'stone'. Modern feminine form of Peter, known to the Romans only as a place-name. In regular use only since the 1960s.

Petrice (f) Modern feminine form of Peter, influenced by **Petra**.

Petrina (f) Modern feminine form of Peter, in use since the 1940s. Petra came into use rather later.

Petronella (f) Latin *Petronilla*, a feminine diminutive of the Roman clan name *Petronius*. As **Petronilla** the name was used by the early Christians. St Petronilla was formerly regarded as the daughter of St Peter. Petronella has been used in Britain since the 1940s, though not in great numbers. Examples have also been noted in the U.S.

Petula (f) In use since the British actress

and singer Petula Clark appeared on the screen in 1944. Its form suggests a derivation from Latin *petulantia* 'sauciness'. Seems to have faded since the early 1970s.

Peyton (m) Place name and surname used as a first name. Its use, almost exclusively in the U.S., was established long before the immensely successful novel, film and television series *Peyton Place*. Peyton Randolph (1721–75) was the first president of the Continental Congress in 1774. Used spasmodically in the U.S. ever since.

Pharaoh (m) Generic title of the ancient Egyptian kings. Used as a first name from time to time in the 19th c., sometimes in the form **Pharoah**. A more recent example was noted in the U.S. in 1970.

Phebe (f) See **Phoebe**.

Phelan (m) Irish surname 'wolf' used as a first name, mainly in the U.S. Features in a short story by O. Henry, *Between Rounds*, about an Irish couple who fight constantly. They quarrel about what the son they might have had six years ago would have been called Phelan or Pat.

Phemie (f) Pet form of **Euphemia**.

Pheobe (f) Common variant of **Phoebe** in the 19th c. especially. **Pheoby** is also found.

Phil (m) Usual pet form of **Philip**, used in its own right since the 1870s, but infrequently.

Philadelphia (f) Greek 'brotherly love'. Biblical, O.T., Rev. 3:7, the name of a city founded by Attalus II in Lydia. Bardsley suggests that William Penn might have founded the American city 'after a friend or kinswoman', since the name was very common amongst the Puritans. Penn certainly took the name directly from the Biblical place name and because of its meaning; he would never have named a place for a person. The whole point of his number names for streets (*First Avenue*, etc.,) was to avoid commemorating people in the giving of names. As a girl's name Philadelphia continued to be used until the end

of the 19th c., very regularly, but never in great numbers. Then disappeared, though it may have survived to some extent as **Delphia, Delphe, Delphi,** all used more recently.

Philander (m) Greek *philandros* 'fond of men' or a woman 'fond of her husband'. Used from time to time in the 19th c., but the name has come to suggest a philanderer, a man who flirts lightly with women, having no serious intentions towards them. This is rather a slur on the original Philander described by Ariosto in *Orlando Furioso*, who was quick to leave the house where he was a guest when Gabrina, the wife of his host, made advances to him. She later tricked him into killing her husband and made him marry her.

Philemon (m) Greek *philema* 'a kiss'. Biblical, N.T., St Paul's letter to Philemon. In Britain mainly used in the 19th c. though never in great numbers. In modern times still in use in the U.S., though very infrequently.

Philip (m) Greek *Philippos* 'fond of horses'. Biblical, N.T., e.g. Mat. 10:3, the name of one of the Apostles. In common use amongst the early Christians. Its use in medieval times is reflected in the commonness of surnames such as *Phillips, Philps, Phipps*, etc. From the 16th c. onwards one of the more densely used male names in Britain, but faded into the background to some extent throughout the 19th c. Usage increased again in the 1920s and continued until the 1960s, when the name was at its peak. Since then it has faded considerably. Roughly the same pattern in the U.S., except that the name became popular rather earlier in the century and faded sooner. In the early 1980s it was still being used in all English-speaking countries, but in ever-decreasing numbers. While Philip has usually been the more common form, **Phillip** has long been a popular variant. Also found are **Philipp, Philippe, Phillippe**. Surname **Phillips** has been used from time to time as a first name. Best-known modern bearer of the name is Prince Philip, husband of Queen Elizabeth II, while in literature the name suggests Philip Pirrip, or Pip, of Dickens's *Great Expectations*. Pip is still one of the name's pet forms, but does not seem to be given as an independent name. Flip is a similar nickname. The short form **Phil** has been used as a name in its own right since the 1870s. **Philippa** is the usual feminine form of the name, found also as **Phillippa**, **Philipa**, **Phillipa** and in its pet form **Pippa**. **Phillipina** has also been used.

Philippa (f) Normal feminine form of **Philip**, though **Phillipa** and **Phillippa** are common variants. Miss Withycombe provides ample evidence to show that in former times women whose name was recorded in Latin documents as Philippa were actually addressed as **Philip**. By the 19th c., however, the name was spoken as written. Used throughout the 19th c., though never in great numbers, and reached its mild peak only in the 1970s. By 1980 there were signs that it was retreating into the background again. In the U.S., however, the name is used very quietly.

Philippe (m) French form of **Philip**. Occasionally used in English-speaking countries, and is found also as **Phillippe** and **Phillipe**.

Philis (f) Fairly common 19th c. variant of **Phyllis**.

Phillip (m) Very common variant of **Philip**.

Phillipa (f) Frequent variant of **Philippa**.

Phillipe (m) See **Philip**, **Philippe**.

Phillipina (f) Diminutive of **Phillipa** used irregularly between the 1870s and the 1920s.

Phillips (m) See **Philip**.

Phillippa (f) Frequent variant of **Philippa**.

Phillis (f) Normal form of **Phyllis** in the 17th and 18th cc. A common variant in Britain until 1930. Still used infrequently in the U.S. in the early 1980s.

Philomena (f) Greek *philoumene* 'beloved'. Used by early Christians of the Roman Empire but appeared in English-speaking countries only in the latter half of the 19th c. Used far more frequently in the 20th c., especially in Scotland and Australia. Remains a rare name in the U.S. Sometimes found as **Philomene**, **Philomina** or in its Italian form **Filomena**.

Phineas (m) The language of origin and meaning of this name is uncertain, though it is often said to be Hebrew and to mean 'oracle'. It is Biblical, O.T., 1 Sam. 1:3. The Puritans adopted it and it was used fairly regularly until the end of the 19th c. Later examples are extremely rare. Associated with Phineas T. Barnum (1810–91), America's great showman.

Phoebe (f) Greek *Phoibe*, feminine of *phoibos* 'pure, bright'. In Greek mythology Phoebe was the goddess of the moon. Biblical, N.T., Romans 16:1. First used in English-speaking countries in the 16th c., but not regularly used until the 18th c. At its most popular in the 1870s but faded steadily afterwards. Some translations of the Bible used the form **Phebe**, and this has therefore been a long-standing variant of the name. Eric Partridge considers it to be a pet form of Phoebe which is pronounced as *Feeb*, but this nickname, sometimes extended playfully to *Feeble*, applies to both spellings. Many other variants are found, including **Pheabe**, **Pheaby**, **Pheba**, **Pheby**, **Pheobe**, **Pheoby**, **Phobe**, **Phoeboe**, **Phoeby**. The Phobe examples occur in the 19th c., before *phobias* began to be commonly known to the layman.

Phoeboe (f) Variant of **Phoebe** which occurred on more than one occasion in the 19th c. This form is disconcerting at first glance, though the logic is that if *oe* is to be pronounced *ee* in the first syllable, then why should it not be pronounced in that way in the second syllable?

Phthisis (m) Greek 'wasting, consumption'. Not a name in frequent use, but a Phthisis Smith was named in Britain in 1915.

Phylis (f) Common variant of **Phyllis**.

Phyllida (f) Modern form of **Phillida**, itself a form of **Phyllis** which was used by 16th c. poets and writers. Lyly has a character of the name in his *Galathea* (1592), a play in which two girls both disguise themselves as men and fall in love with each other, each thinking that the other is a man. Used occasionally since the 1930s.

Phyllis (f) Greek *phullis* 'foliage, leafy branch'. In Greek mythology Phyllis changed into a tree after her death. To the classical poets Phyllis was the typical name for a country maiden, a tradition the 17th c. poets inherited. In general use in the 18th c., though often confused with *Felis*, a form of **Felicia**. Usage slowly increased in the 19th c., reaching a peak in 1925. Faded sharply in the 1930s and little used since. The earlier spelling was **Phillis** and this still occurs in the U.S., though very rare in Britain since the 1930s. Other forms of the name include **Philis**, **Philliss**, **Phillys**, **Phylis**, **Phylliss**. In the 1920s the name was made well-known by one of Mack Sennet's bathing beauties, Phyllis Haver. Phyllis Calvert (Phyllis Bickle) was probably the best-known bearer of the name in the 1940s and '50s.

Pierce (m) Surname deriving from **Piers** (Peter). The usual form of Piers in the 19th c., and still used occasionally as a first name.

Piercy (m) Surname meaning 'pierce hedge', possibly a nickname for a poacher, used regularly if infrequently in the 19th c. as a first name, when Pierce was also in regular use. Piercey is also found.

Pierre (m) French form of **Peter**, used in English-speaking countries with some regularity since the 1920s. In recent times especially favoured by black American parents.

Piers (m) The normal medieval form of **Peter**, influenced by French **Pierre**. Its early use led to the common surnames *Pierce*, *Pearson*, etc. The famous satirical poem, *Piers Plowman*, written in the 14th c. by William Langland, was not published until 1550. Almost disappeared for two hundred years but began to be used again in the 18th c. as Piers and Peers. In the 19th c. Pierce was the usual form, though the name was infrequently used. Piers was once again restored in the 1930s and has been used regularly since, especially in Britain.

Pippa (f) Pet form of **Philippa**, used increasingly since 1960 as an independent name, though only in Britain.

Piran (m) The name of a Cornish saint, looked upon as the patron of miners and by some as the patron saint of Cornwall, used occasionally as a first name. In Cornish place names the name occurs as **Perran**. **Pieran** also occurs, and the name is in fact probably a form of **Piers** or **Peter**.

Pixie (f) The word used as a name. Pixies tend to be associated with Ireland, but the name occurs more often in the U.S. Used especially in the 1930s and '40s.

Plato (m) The name of the famous Greek philosopher used from time to time as a first name, more frequently in the 19th c.

Pleasance (f) An archaic word meaning 'pleasure, delight' used as a first name. Used mainly in the 19th c., though the last recorded example was in 1942. **Pleasence** and **Pleasants** are also found in early records. The earlier form seems to have been **Pleasant**. Dickens has a character of that name in *Our Mutual Friend*, and rather cruelly makes her an especially ugly girl.

Polly (f) Originally a pet form of **Mary**, *via* **Mal**, **Mally**, **Molly**. Used as a name in its own right since the 18th c. but infrequent since the beginning of the 20th c. Gay gave the name to the heroine of his *Beggar's Opera* (1727). **Poll** or **Polly** has been associated with 'parrot' since the 17th c., which has probably restricted its use for girls. It was the name adopted by the American singer Nellie Burgin when she became Polly Bergen and began to appear in films from 1950. **Pollie** has often been used as a variant spelling, and **Polley** occurs.

Pollyanna (f) Compound of **Polly** and **Anna** used by Eleanor H. Porter to name the heroine of her children's novel *Pollyanna*. She explains that Pollyanna's mother chose the name in honour of her two sisters, Polly and Anna. The young lady's aunt refers to it as a 'ridiculous' name until its bearer arrives and wins her affections. Modern parents have tended to prefer **Pollyann**, but both forms remain rare.

Poppy (f) One of the flower names introduced in England at the end of the 19th c. Most used in the 1920s but occasionally used in modern times. **Pollie** also occurs.

Porter (m) Surname, meaning a 'gatekeeper', used as a first name. Used mainly in the 19th c.

Portia (f) Latin *Porcia*, feminine of *Porcius*, a Roman clan name of unknown meaning. Shakespeare mentions Portia, the wife of Marcus Brutus, who killed herself by taking hot coals into her mouth, but his more famous character of the name is Portia in *The Merchant of Venice*, who saves Antonio's life by pointing out that Shylock's 'pound of flesh' gave him no right to a single drop of Antonio's blood. In occasional use in English-speaking countries, with black American parents favouring it rather more than whites.

Precious (m, f) The word used as a name. Not frequently used, but made well known in Britain by such popular figures as the weight-lifter Precious Mackenzie, and the singer/dancer Precious Wilson. The black entertainer, interviewed as she was about to appear in her own television show, began by saying: 'Despite what you may think, the name is not an assumed one. My mother wanted one child, preferably a girl, so when I arrived she was overjoyed.'

Preston (m) Common English place name 'priest's settlement' which became a surname, regularly used as a first

name. The surname could also derive from 'priest's song'. Use as a first name began in the 1860s and has continued regularly if infrequently ever since.

Price (m) Welsh surname *ap Rhys* 'son of Rhys regularly used as a first name in the 19th c., but rarely in the 20th c.

Pricilla (f) See **Priscilla**.

Priestley (m) Place name/surname, 'priest's clearing', used as a first name, especially in the 19th c. **Priestly** also occurred.

Primrose (f) Flower name used as a first name, especially in Britain since the 1880s. Often given to children born on April 19, Primrose Day. Also a transferred surname.

Primula (f) Latin diminutive of *Primus*, *Prima* 'first', common names amongst the early Christians. Use of Primula in modern times is a borrowing from the flower name, named from the phrase *primula veris* 'first flower of spring'. The similar name **Primrose** has been far more often used.

Prince (m) The word used as a first name. *Principius* is found fairly frequently amongst the Christian inscriptions of the Roman Empire. *Prince* became a surname by 1400, indicating someone who worked in a prince's household, someone who had the manners of a prince or someone who had played the part of a prince in a medieval pageant. Some uses of the first name in modern times may therefore be transferred from the family name. In the U.S. Prince was a common name for male slaves, far too common for all the bearers of the name to have been princes in their original homelands. The name lives on in the U.S., especially in black American families where it has often been borne for several generations. In Britain rare as a first name since 1910.

Princess (f) The word used as a name. Never as frequently used as **Prince**, but still commonly used especially in the U.S. In Margaret Laurence's novel *The Diviners* the girl who bears this name is usually called **Prin**.

Priscilla (f) Latin feminine diminutive from *priscus* 'old, primitive'. Biblical, N.T., Acts 18:26. The name of an early saint and commonly used by both Romans and early Christians. The Puritans took up the name in earnest and it was at its most popular in the 17th c. Faded in the 18th c., became regular in the 19th c., faded again after 1960, having been regularly if quietly used since 1900. In literature the name is best known in Longfellow's poem *The Courtship of Miles Standish*. Standish asks John Alden to plead his cause with the lovely Priscilla. John does so, though he himself loves Priscilla and she loves him. They eventually marry when Standish is killed in battle. Earlier pet forms of the name were **Priss** and **Prissy**. More recently **Cilla** has been made known by the English actress/singer Cilla Black (Priscilla Maria Veronica White). In official records the name also occurs as **Pricilla, Precilla, Prescilla, Priscella, Prissilla**.

Prudence (f) A use of the word as name. As Camden pointed out in the 17th c., Prudence is roughly the equivalent of Greek **Sophia**. *Prudentius* was a Christian Latin poet of the 4th c. Also a Latin feminine form *Prudentia*, but not in frequent use. The Puritans favoured the name along with other 'virtues' and it was popular in the 16th and 17th cc. Used regularly but infrequently ever since, mainly in Britain. Lord Lytton has a Prudence in his novel *The Sea-Captain* (1839) who is supposed to protect Violet from the attentions of strange men. One of them conveniently causes her to go blind temporarily by putting two golden coins over her eyes. Pet forms of the name are **Pru** or **Prue**, used independently on rare occasions.

Prue (f) Pet form of **Prudence**, used occasionally as a name in its own right.

Prunella (f) Latin diminutive of *prunum*, giving a meaning of 'little plum'. Flurry of interest in the name in the 1850s, and again in the 1930s, though nothing was seen or heard of it in the years between. The British actress Prunella Scales has given it publicity recently, but it remains rare in all English-speaking countries.

Pryce (m) See **Price**.

Q

Queen (f) The title used as a name. Usage began in the 1880s and was regular until the 1920s. In Britain, especially, there was later a shift to **Queenie**, though Queen continued to be used occasionally. Variant **Queena** found in the U.S.

Queenie (f) 'Queen' adapted to first name use. Appeared in the 1890s and especially popular before 1930. **Queen** also used, though less often. Other variants were **Queeny** and **Queenation** (used in 1839). Alongside these forms were the Latin **Regina** 'queen', well known in the 19th c. because Queen Victoria was often referred to on statues and the like as *Victoria regina*. Much rarer has been the use of French **Reine** 'queen', though it certainly occurs. Regina and its variants are more popular in the U.S., but variants of Queen used there include **Queena, Queeneste, Queenette**.

Quentin (m) The usual spelling in England and the U.S. of **Quintin**. Quentin was the form of the name used to translate *Quinctian* (Latin *Quinctinus*), the name of an early saint, patron of Kirkmahoe in Scotland. Sir Walter Scott may have known the name in that connection. He used the Quentin variant to name the hero of his historical novel *Quentin Durward* (1823). Quentin is regularly used, but never with great intensity.

Quiana (f) See **Kiana**. **Quianna** also occurs.

Quincy (m) French place name, originally indicating an 'estate belonging to Quintus', which became an English surname. Made famous by John Quincy Adams (1767–1848), sixth President of the U.S.A., and quietly used as a first name, almost exclusively in the U.S., since his time. Recently used primarily by black American families.

Quinn (m) Irish surname of several possible origins, used from time to time in the U.S., especially, as a first name.

Quintin (m) Latin *Quintinus*, diminutive of *Quintus* 'fifth'. The Romans used the feminine form *Quinta* more frequently. Quintin is used regularly if infrequently in English-speaking countries, often as **Quentin**. Other variants include **Quinten, Quinton** and the short form **Quint**, which occurs in the U.S. Quinta does not seem to be used in modern times as a feminine form, but **Quintina, Quintona, Quintonice, Quinella, Quinetta**, etc., are amongst feminine forms which occur infrequently in the U.S.

Quinton (m) Modern variant of **Quintin** which has firmly established itself in English-speaking countries.

R

Rab (m) Scottish diminutive form of Robert, occasionally used independently. **Rabbie** also occurs, **Rabi** and **Raby** perhaps being variants in their turn of that form.

Rabbi (m) Appears to be the religious title *Rabbi*, given to a trained religious leader and teacher of Jewish law. Used regularly, if infrequently, as a first name in Britain, the last known examples occurring in 1944, 1948, 1955 and 1960. Reuben and Blanche Brookes do not mention the name as a possibility in their *Guide to Jewish Names*. It is just possible that in some instances, at least, **Rabbie** is the intended name (see **Rab**). Dean is, of course, much used as a first name, though normally without religious significance, and instances of **Pope** and **Prior** have been noted. These again probably reflect transferred use of surnames. Very rare in U.S.

Rabbie (m) Diminutive of **Rab**, itself a form of **Rob**, from Robert. Almost exclusively a Scottish name, given only rarely in its own right. **Raby** also occurred in the 19th c. In some cases **Rabbi** may be intended for Rabbie.

Rachel (f) Hebrew 'ewe'. Biblical, O.T., name of the wife of Jacob. The Puritans made use of the name in the 16th and 17th cc., and it became generally popular in the 18th c. Remained in regular use until the late 1960s, then suddenly became extremely fashionable on all sides. In the early 1980s was still being intensively used, though perhaps past its peak. A Rachel is a well-drawn character in Dickens' *Hard Times*. The late Welsh actress Rachel Roberts helped to publicize the name from the 1950s. Variant **Rachael** appeared in the 17th c. and is still regularly used. Presumably influenced by other Hebrew names such as **Michael** and **Raphael**, but there is in fact no justification for the *-ael* ending in Rachel. **Racheal** occurs fairly often, and modern variants include **Rachelle, Rachele, Rachell**.

Rachelle (f) Modern variant of **Rachel** which looks French but is unknown in France. Appeared in the U.S. in the 1930s and reached Britain by the 1940s. Many name-bearers pronounce it as *Ra-shell*, and **Shell(e)y** is used in the U.S. as a pet name. Seems to have died out in the early 1970s. The inspiration for it may have been Italian **Rachele**. Parents probably thought it was a French form (such as **Michele**) which had Rachelle as a variant.

Radcliff(e) (m) English place name/

surname used from time to time as a first name. Originally indicating a settlement near a 'red cliff'.

Radford (m) Common English place name 'reedy ford' which became a surname. In occasional use as a first name.

Rae (f) Pet form of **Rachel**, used as a name in its own right since 1918. Steadily but quietly used in recent times. Favoured as an element in compound names such as **Rae Ann, Rae Lynn, Rae Louise**.

Raelene (f) Extended form of **Rae**, using the popular feminine ending *-lene*, which has been especially popular in Australia since 1950.

Rafael (m) See **Raphael**.

Raina (f) A Russian form of **Regina**, or feminine of **Rainer** (**Rayner**). The form **Rayna** is found in the U.S., where the name first began to appear in the early 1940s. Rayna may belong to the group of names which are clearly feminine forms of **Ray**, such as **Rayann, Rayetta, Raylene, Raynette, Rayona**. In some instances parents appear to have taken the word 'rain' and formed a feminine name. **Rainell** and **Rainelle** are found, and names such as **Rainbow** and **Rainy** have been used in the past. Raina could therefore be a disguised use of the word, an explanation that could also apply to **Raine** which appeared in the late 1960s. Raina seems to have settled down as a standard name, especially in the U.S. where it was still being steadily used in the early 1980s. New forms were still occurring, however (e.g. **Raenah**), which seem to indicate that parents like the sound of the name and are not over-concerned with the form it takes.

Raine (f) May be phonetic form of **Reine** or variant of **Raina**. Appeared in Britain in the late 1960s and occurred during the 1970s.

Rainer (m) German form of **Rayner**.

Raleigh (m) Place name and surname, in occasional use as a first name. The famous bearer of the name in English history was Sir Walter Raleigh (1552–1618), after whom the city in North Carolina was named. Use of Raleigh in the U.S., which is more frequent than in Britain, possibly derives from the city.

Ralph (m) Common to several languages in ancient times, e.g. *Rathulfr* in Old Norse, *Raedwulf* in Old English, composed of elements meaning 'counsel' and 'wolf'. In the Middle Ages it occurred in such forms as *Radulf, Raulf, Raul*. Diminutives such as *Raulin* led to surnames like *Rawlings, Rawlingson*. By the 16th c. had settled down as **Ralf**, but this was still Latinized as **Radolphus**. The Latin form caused **Ralph** to become the usual spelling in the 18th c., when the name was still very well used. Pronunciation of the name was *Rafe*, which was still to be heard until the beginning of the 20th c. In Britain quietly used throughout the 19th c., but reached a minor peak of popularity in the 1920s. Still in use in all English-speaking countries, having enjoyed a much greater spell of success in the U.S. American parents made it one of their top thirty names from the 1870s to the 1920s, and it was very well used in the U.S. until the mid-1950s. Modern French form of the name, **Raoul**, is used from time to time. **Ralf** is a rare variant, as is **Rafe**, used to indicate that the older pronunciation is preferred. Feminine form **Ralphina** has been used on rare occasions, and the pet form **Ralphie** has been given as an independent name. Two well-known name-bearers are Ralph Waldo Emerson (1803-82), the philosopher and poet, and the British actor Sir Ralph Richardson.

Ralphina (f) Feminine form of **Ralph** used as early as the 1870s but rarely since. **Ralphine** has also been used in the U.S., though Ralph itself has been used rather more often as a feminine name.

Ralston (m) Scottish and English place name, probably from the Old Norse personal name *Hróaldr* + *tun* 'settlement'. A surname since the 13th c. now being used as a first name.

Ramon (m) Spanish form of **Raymond**

used mainly in the U.S. In Britain appeared for the first time in the 1920s.

Ramona (f) Feminine form of **Ramon**. Used mainly in the U.S., and associated by many with Helen Hunt Jackson's novel *Ramona* (1884).

Ramond (m) Variant of **Raymond** in occasional use, possibly influenced by Spanish **Ramon**.

Ramsay (m) Common English place name and aristocratic Scottish surname, used as a first name. Found in the 19th c., but British use mainly in the 1920s when Ramsay Macdonald (1866–1937) became Prime Minister. Ramsey is also found.

Ramsden (m) Place name 'valley with rams' or 'valley where wild garlic grows', which became a surname, used as a first name in the 19th c. with great regularity.

Ramsey (m) Variant of **Ramsay**.

Ranald (m) Old English 'power-might'. Variant of **Ronald** which was formerly well used in Scotland. Still in occasional use.

Randal(l) (m) For the early history of the name see **Randolph**. Randal or Randall was well used in the Middle Ages, giving rise to many surnames such as *Randall, Randell, Randle*. Faded after the 14th c., though it never became obsolete. Both forms considerably revived in the 1860s, being reinforced later by **Randle, Randel, Randol, Randell**. In its various forms popular in the U.S. in the 1950s and '60s. Randall was the usual form, with the pet form **Randy** being frequently used as a name in its own right. American parents had tended to look elsewhere by the early 1980s, though Randy was still in use. In Britain the name occurs from time to time, though almost never as Randy.

Randee (f) See **Randy**.

Randel(l) (m) Variants of **Randal(l)** used mainly in the U.S.

Randi (f) Form of **Randy** in use since the 1950s, mainly in the U.S. Randee also occurs. Originally a pet form of **Miranda**.

Randle (m) Fairly common variant of **Randal(l)**.

Randolph (m) Old English *Randwulf* 'shield-wolf'. The Normans used a similar name derived from Old Norse. In the Middle Ages the spoken form of the name was either *Ranulf* or *Randal*. These were Latinized as *Ranulfus/Ranulphus* and *Randulfus/Randulphus*. Randal survived best, together with its Latin forms. The latter seem to have suggested a 'correct' form of the name in English to 18th c. scholars, and Randolph appeared for the first time. Then quietly used in the 19th c. and continues to be infrequently used. The actor Randolph Scott (Randolph Crane) gave the name considerable publicity from the 1930s onwards, but had little influence on the name's use. In the U.S. **Randall** has been the successful form of the name.

Randy (m,f) The male name is mainly a pet form of **Randall** used independently. Can also derive from **Randolph**. The feminine form, sometimes written **Randi** or **Randee** to distinguish it, is a pet form of **Miranda**. Randey is also found. Use of both names has been far more common in the U.S. than in Britain, probably because the word 'randy' is more commonly used in Britain to describe a lecherous person.

Ransome (m) The surname, derived from **Randolph**, used as a first name. Associated with the English children's writer Arthur Ransome (1884–1967), author of *Swallows and Amazons*.

Raoul (m) French form of **Ralph**, occasionally used in English-speaking countries in modern times.

Raphael (m) Hebrew 'God cures' or 'God has healed'. The name of one of the archangels. Used fairly well in the 16th and 17th cc., then revived in the late 19th c. Used very infrequently since then. In the U.S. especially is found in its Spanish form **Rafael**. Feminine forms **Raphaela** and **Rafaela** also occur. Associated strongly with the Italian painter Raffaelo Sanzio (1483–1520), and the name may occasionally be given in admiration of his works.

Raquel (f) Spanish/Portuguese form of **Rachel**, used mainly in the U.S. In Britain used mainly in the 1960s when the actress Raquel Welch (Raquel Tejada) first made her appearance on screen.

Rashida (f) Apparently a form of the Turkish name **Rashid**, which Elsdon C. Smith explains as 'the rightly guided'. Now in use amongst black American families, also in the forms **Rasheda, Rasheeda, Rasheedah, Rasheida**.

Raul (m) Spanish form of **Ralph**, used to some extent in the U.S.

Raven (f) See **Robin**.

Rawdon (m) Place name/surname, originally meaning 'rough hill', used as a first name since the 1870s. Famous literary example of the name in Thackeray's *Vanity Fair*, where Rawdon Crawley is the husband of Becky Sharp. He is portrayed as a rather amiable idiot, a great sportsman and dandy, popular but limited in his conversation and thinking.

Rawson (m) Surname linked with **Raoul** or **Roland**, regularly used as a first name in the 19th c.

Ray (m) Pet form of **Raymond** used independently. Especially popular in the U.S. at the beginning of the 20th c. The actor Ray Milland (Reginald Truscott-Jones) helped to keep the name before the public eye from the 1930s.

Raye (f) Variant of **Rae**, pet form of **Rachel**, used only rarely. Sometimes extended into forms such as **Raycene, Rayma, Raynette, Rayna, Raynelle, Rayleen, Raylena, Rayona**, especially in the U.S.

Rayment (m) Surname form of **Raymond** used occasionally as a first name.

Raymond (m) Old German 'counsel-protection'. This was another of the Germanic names used by the Normans and taken to England by them in the 11th c. Its use during the Middle Ages is reflected in modern surnames such as *Raymond*, *Rayment*. As a first name extremely rare until the 1840s. Then steadily became more popular, becom-

ing one of the top twenty male names in the U.S. by 1900. Remained in intensive use in the U.S. until the mid-1960s, but had greatly diminished by the early 1980s. In Britain was at its peak in the mid-1930s, with a subsequent slow decline. The Canadian actor Raymond Massey made the name well known from 1930 onwards, while another Canadian, Raymond Burr, later became very well known as Perry Mason in the television series of that name. Spanish form **Ramon** is used both in the U.S. and Britain, Italian **Raimondo** is rarer. French feminine **Raymonde** occurs occasionally. Also found are the variants **Raymund** and **Raymunde**, presumably influenced by modern German **Raimund** or Latin *Raimundus*. **Raimunde** is a feminine form in German.

Raymonde (f) French feminine form of **Raymond** in occasional use.

Raymund(e) (m) See **Raymond**.

Rayner (m) Use of the surname as first name. Derives from an Old German personal name which meant 'mighty army'. The Normans introduced the name to Britain, and it lives on as a modern French first name **Rainier** (also a surname). A 12th c. saint bore the name and became patron of Pisa in Italy. Italian form of the name is **Ranieri**. **Rainer** is another form of the name, borne by the German lyric poet Rainer Maria Rilke (1875–1926). Rayner has been in use as a first name since the 1860s but never with great intensity. Found also as **Rainor** and **Raynor**.

Rea (f) Pet form of **Andrea** used independently. Not in frequent use. In some cases **Rhea** may be intended. There is a similar name **Ria**.

Read (m) Variant of **Reed** or **Reid**.

Rebbie (f) Pet form of **Rebecca** used independently on rare occasions. **Reby** and **Rebi** also occur.

Rebecca (f) Hebrew name of uncertain origin. The usual explanation is 'noose' or a joining cord of some kind. Biblical,

O.T., the name of the wife of Isaac, mother of Jacob and Esau. Came into frequent use in the 16th c. and remained popular until the end of the 19th c. Then went out of fashion until it revived in the U.S. in the 1930s. Went on to reach a peak in the U.S. in the 1960s. Revival began in Britain only in the late 1960s, and its success was greater. By 1980 was in fifth position in the British popularity chart, whereas it had clearly faded by that time in the U.S. A Rebecca plays an important part in Sir Walter Scott's novel *Ivanhoe*, though her rival Rowena fares better in that she marries the hero. Accordingly, the novel increased the use of Rowena rather than Rebecca. Becky Sharp in Thackeray's *Vanity Fair*, though one of the major characters of English literature, was again not inspiring for parents. Kate Douglas's *Rebecca of Sunnybrook Farm* (1903) was a more positive influence, and the novelist Cicily Isabel Fairfield helped remind the public of the name when she became Rebecca West in 1911. Quite clear that the major influence on the name, however, was the novel *Rebecca*, by Daphne du Maurier, which Alfred Hitchcock turned into an excellent film in 1940. Rebecca is the Latin form of the name. Greek form **Rebekka** is sometimes found, while the form of the name used in the Authorized Version of the Bible, **Rebekah**, has naturally been used a great deal. Also found on occasion as **Rebbecca, Rebeca, Rebeccah, Rebecka, Rebeckah. Rebbie** and **Becky**, the pet forms, are used independently.

Reby (f) See **Rebbie**.

Redmond (m) Irish *Raemonn*, a form of **Raymond**. Rarely used.

Redvers (m) Aristocratic English family name, ultimately from a Norman place name, used as a first name. Introduced at the turn of the century in Britain when General Sir Redvers Henry Buller became supreme commander of the British troops at the start of the Boer War in 1899. At that time was one of the 50 most popular male names being used in Britain. Remains in use in Britain, but now very infrequent.

Reece (m) See **Rhys**.

Reed (m) Surname, which usually means 'red, red-haired', used as a first name, mainly in the U.S. **Reid** is also used, and **Read** occurs.

Reenie (f) Variant of **Renie**.

Rees (m) Frequently used variant of **Rhys**. **Reese** and **Reece** also occur.

Reg (m) Pet form of **Reginald** used in its own right on rare occasions.

Regan (m, f) The male name is from the Irish surname *O'Riagain* 'descendant of the little king'. The female name is presumably taken from Shakespeare's *King Lear*, where Regan is one of the king's ungrateful daughters. In use since the 1940s in the U.S., rather later in Britain. Used more often for men than women.

Reggie (m) Pet form of **Reginald** used independently since the 1880s, but rare since the 1940s. **Regie** is a variant.

Regina (f) Latin 'queen'. Use of the name has roughly paralleled that of **Queenie**, **Queen**, etc. in Britain. In the U.S. Regina is far more popular. Variants include **Regena, Reginia, Regiena, Reginia, Reginna**.

Reginald (m) For the origin of the name see **Reynold**, which probably represented the normal spoken form of the name in the Middle Ages, *Reginaldus* appearing as its Latin form on occasion. Almost disappeared by the 18th c., but restored slowly from the 1830s. Usage increased throughout the 19th c., and by 1900 it was very popular in Britain. Steadily faded since 1930. American parents did not take to the name during this period. George R. Stewart remarks that 'Reggie became in fact the prime example of an over-pretentious, decadent, or un-American name.' H. L. Mencken describes it as an 'aristocratic' name, one that the name-bearer 'is likely to have to defend with his fists', in the same group as **Algernon, Percy** and **Cecil**. This was at one time true, perhaps, of **Reggie**, but certainly does not apply to a modern British **Reg**.

There could perhaps be no more striking an example of the different images evoked by the same name in different societies, and for that matter, amongst different ethnic groups. For if white Americans have shown no liking for Reginald in modern times, black American families certainly have. In 1960, for instance, in the city of Detroit, Reginald was used to name 55 boys, 53 of them black, 2 white. In the same city in 1981, 23 boys received the name, all of them black. Some of the blame for Reginald's poor image in the U.S. may perhaps be heaped on the shoulders of the British actor Reginald Gardiner, regularly seen as an 'amiable silly ass' from the mid-1930s. Reginald Denny, Reginald Owen and Reginald Beckwith were other British actors who had successful careers. Probably the best-known American bearer of the name has been the baseball star Reggie Jackson, who was no doubt responsible for making the name so popular with black American families.

Reid (m) Use of the surname as a first name, the original meaning being 'red, red-haired'. Reid is usually a Scottish surname, but the first name is used mainly in the U.S.

Rena (f) Pet form of names ending in -rena, such as Irena, Serena, Verena, Lorena. Used regularly if infrequently from the 1860s to the 1960s.

Renata (f) See Renée.

Renatus (m) See Réné (m).

Rene (f) Pet form of Irene used regularly but infrequently in its own right.

René (m) French 're-born', modelled on Latin *Renatus* a frequent name in Christian inscriptions of the Roman Empire. Renatus was used for a while by the Puritans in the 17th c. René has been in steady use in English-speaking countries since the beginning of the 20th c.

Renée (f) Feminine form of French Réné 're-born'. The Latin name was Renata, used by the early Roman Christians, taken up temporarily by the 17th c. Puritans, and still occasionally used in

modern times. Has had most success in Australia, where it was especially popular in the 1970s. Elsewhere steadily but quietly used. English pronunciation of the name has led to variants such as Rennie, Renie, Renay, Renny, Reney. In some cases these may represent Réné rather than Renée.

Renie (f) Pet form of Irene used independently or a variant of Rennie. Came into use in the 1890s but rarely used since the 1930s.

Renita (f) Variant of Renata or based on Latin *renitor*, 'to resist, to be firm, self-poised' (though *renita* would not be the correct adjectival form). Mostly used by black American families in the early 1980s, and occurs also as Reneeta.

Rennie (f) See Renée. Renie and Renny are variants.

Renzo (m) Pet form of Lorenzo occasionally used independently in the U.S.

Reta (f) Pet form of Margareta used independently since the 19th c., but Rita has been the preferred form.

Reuben (m) Hebrew 'behold a son!' Biblical, O.T., the name of Jacob's eldest son. Later became the name of one of the tribes of Israel. By the 18th c. was in general use in England, clearly not confined to Jewish families. Used regularly ever since, though not in great numbers, and rather more in the 19th c. than in the 20th c. Also found as Reuban, Reubin, Reuven, Ruben, Rubin, Rueben.

Reva (f) Apparently an anagram of Vera. Rarely used.

Rex (m) Latin *rex* 'king'. Feminine form Regina came into use rather earlier. Found at the end of the 19th c., but mainly used in the 20th c., rarely since the 1960s. The best-known bearer of the name is the actor Rex Harrison (Rex being a pet form of his real first name Reginald (Carey)).

Reynold (m) Popular form in the Middle Ages of a name common in several European languages. In Old English it was *Regenweald*, Old German had *Raginwald*, the Old Norse form was

Rögnvaldr. The elements of the name mean 'counsel' and 'power'. Apart from Reynold (and associated surnames such as *Reynolds*), these names developed into **Reginald** and **Ronald**, as well as *Renault* — one of the many modern French forms, and *Reinold*, one of the German forms. Reynold itself became uncommon as a first name after the 15th c. and had almost disappeared by the 18th c. The partial revival of the name since the 1860s may represent a transferred use of the surname. In the early 1980s black American families were keeping the name alive, perhaps as an offshoot of their pronounced liking for Reginald. They were also using forms such as **Reinaldo, Renaldo, Renauld, Renault, Reynaldo**, though none of them in large numbers.

Rhian (f) Welsh *rhiain* 'maiden'. Used regularly in Wales, especially since the 1950s.

Rhiannon (f) Welsh *rhianon* 'nymph, goddess'. Popular in Wales in recent times. Occurs also as **Rhianon**.

Rhoades (m) See Rhodes.

Rhoda (f) Greek *rhodon* 'rose'. Latin *Rhoda* meant 'woman from *Rhodes* (the island of roses'). Biblical, N.T., Acts 12:13. Came into general use in the 18th c. and regularly used throughout the 19th c., reaching a minor peak 1870–1900. The television *Rhoda* reminded audiences of the name in the 1970s, but the name is now very quietly used. In the 19th c., especially, often found as **Roda**.

Rhodes (m) Distinctly popular during the 1870s, before Cecil Rhodes (1853–1902) had made his name. Had been in use in a mild way since the 1830s, sometimes appearing as **Rhoades**. The name may have been borrowed from the Aegean island of Rhodes, but the reason for the particular interest in it, which lasted for ten years and has never been renewed, is far from clear.

Rhodri (m) Welsh *rhod* 'circle, disc, orb', plus *rhi* 'ruler'. The 'circle' probably refers to a crown or other symbol of royalty. The name of a 9th c. Welsh king, re-introduced in Wales in modern times.

Rhona (f) A name of uncertain origin which began to be used in Britain in the 1870s. The name **Rona** appeared at the same time and it is therefore reasonable to connect the two, especially since both were much used in Scotland. This would make the origin of the name a Scottish place name, itself derived from Old Norse *hraun-ey* 'rough isle'. Miss Withycombe suggests a connection with Welsh **Rhonwen**, but no Welsh writer on names has ever suggested that Rhona is Welsh. In Britain both forms are used regularly, though not frequently. Rona is usual in the U.S.

Rhonda (f) Appears to be a simplification of the Welsh place name *Rhondda*, derived in turn from the river which runs through the Rhondda Valley. Original meaning of the name, applied to the river, is 'noisy one'. One example of Rhonda as a first name has been noted in 1917, but most use of the name was made after the early 1940s, when Rhonda Fleming (born Marilyn Louis) appeared regularly on cinema screens.

Rhonwen (f) Welsh name consisting of two elements, the second being 'fair'. The first may be *rhon* 'pike, lance' meant to be interpreted metaphorically as 'slender'. Used only in Wales.

Rhys (m) Welsh 'ardour'. A name famous in Welsh history. General use in Wales in early times led to surnames such as *Reece, Rees, Rice, Price* (ap *Rhys* 'son of Rhys). Continues to be steadily used in Wales.

Ria (f) Pet form of **Maria, Victoria**, etc., used independently. May in some cases be a phonetic rendering of **Rhea**.

Rica (f) See Erica.

Ricardo (m) Spanish/Portuguese form of **Richard**, used in English-speaking countries since the end of the 19th c. Always used more in the U.S. than Britain, but British parents suddenly showed interest in it from 1960 onwards, having ignored it for fifty years.

Riccardo (m) Italian form of **Richard**. Used very occasionally in English-speaking countries, Spanish **Ricardo** being far more frequent.

Rice (m) See **Rhys**.

Richard (m) Old German 'ruler-hard', i.e. 'strong ruler'. A favourite with the Normans, who introduced it to Britain in the 11th c. Its intensive usage from that time is reflected in the large number of surnames which it brought into being, many based on the wide variety of pet forms of Richard. The most popular of these were **Rich, Hitch, Rick, Hick, Dick**. Typical surnames include *Dickens, Dickinson, Dixon, Hicks, Hitchcock, Richards, Rix*. The most famous early bearer of the name was King Richard I of England, known as Richard the Lion-Heart. One of the commonest names in the English-speaking world until the 19th c., when it faded somewhat on all sides. In the 1890s it appeared to be heading for obscurity, but then suddenly and strongly revived, first in the U.S., later in Britain. By 1925 it was completely restored to favour in the U.S., whereas the upward turn in its fortunes did not happen in Britain until the late 1930s. By the early 1980s the name had faded dramatically in the U.S. and had dropped out of the British top ten. The pattern of usage means that the average American who is a Richard will be rather older than his British counterpart. Well-known actors include Richard Burton, Richard Todd, Richard Widmark, Richard Attenborough, Richard Basehart, Richard Chamberlain. While it is true that the use of Richard declined sharply after Richard Nixon's resignation as President of the U.S. all the evidence suggests that the name was in decline anyway at that time in the U.S. because of changing fashions. Other forms of Richard in modern use include **Ricardo** and **Riccardo, Ricky**. Feminine forms are **Richenda, Richmal, Rikki, Ricarda**.

Richenda (f) Appears to be a feminine form of **Richard** using *Rich-* and a variant of the common feminine ending *-inda*. Found from time to time, beginning in the 1850s. Charlotte Yonge, in the 1860s, mentions a **Richenza** 'sometimes used in England as the feminine of Richard', but she may have mis-read Richenda.

Richie (m) Mainly Scottish pet form of **Richard**, more often found as **Ritchie**. In modern times often associated with the former Australian cricketer, now commentator, Richie Benaud.

Richmal (f) The Revd. J. G. Edward of Week St. Mary draws our attention to *History Today* (August, 1986) in which the name is explained as a blend of Richard and Mary. In the 20th c. made well known in Britain by the writer of the *William* books, Richmal Crompton (Richmal C Lamburn).

Richmond (m) Originally a French place name meaning a 'hill richly covered in vegetation'. The place name was transferred to Britain and became an aristocratic surname. Used fairly frequently as a first name since the 1840s in both Britain and the U.S.

Rick (m) Also **Rik**. Pet forms of Eric, Richard, Derek, Derrick used as names. In modern times mostly used in the U.S. and Canada, remaining rare in Britain. By 1960 the various pet forms of Rick, Ricky, Rickey, etc., were being more frequently used than Rick itself.

Rickey (m) See **Ricky**.

Ricki(e) (m, f) As male names these are variants of **Ricky**. In Britain, especially, they have been well used for girls since the 1950s, also as **Rikki, Rikky**, perhaps forms of Erica, Frederica, Richarda etc. Probably the sound of the names rather than the possible origin appealed to British parents, since Nickie (Nicky, Nikki) and Vickie (Vicky, Vikki) were being well used at the same time. **Ricquie** also occurs.

Ricky (m) Pet form of **Richard** or **Derek/Derrick** used independently. Rick and Ricky began to be used in the U.S. in the early 1940s and for some time were equally popular. Both at their peak in the 1950s, and by 1960 Ricky was clearly the preferred form. **Rickey** was also being well used, and **Rickie, Ricki** were occasionally found. All forms of the name began to fade in the U.S. during the 1960s. Ricky had reached Britain in the late 1940s and became more frequent in the 1960s. By 1970 was beginning to disappear again.

Rika (f) See **Erica**.

Rikki (f) Modern pet form of **Erica, Ricarda, Frederica,** etc., in use since the 1950s. **Rikky** also occurs.

Riley (m) Irish surname 'valiant' used as a first name. As a first name, always in this form, although the surname is often found as **Reilly**. Used with some frequency as a first name since the 1840s, and found in all English-speaking countries.

Rina (f) Pet form of **Katrina, Marina, Sabrina, Karina,** etc., used as an independent name. Found since the 1920s in Britain and the U.S., though never in great numbers.

Rita (f) Pet form of **Margarita, Dorita,** etc. used independently since the turn of the century. High in the popularity charts by 1930, before the actress Rita Hayworth (Margarita Carmen Cansino) began to appear in films, but she probably helped to maintain the name into the 1950s. Now rarely used. **Reta** was actually first used in 1867, but has never been as frequent as Rita.

Ritchi (m) See **Richie**.

Roald (m) Scandinavian name composed of words meaning 'fame' and 'power'. Made famous by the Norwegian polar explorer Roald Amundsen (1872–1928), and more recently by the writer Roald Dahl. Used only occasionally in English-speaking countries.

Rob(b) (m) Pet forms of **Robert** used independently, though infrequently, especially in Scotland. The fame of Rob Roy, the Scottish outlaw whose exploits were later chronicled by Sir Walter Scott, sometimes causes the two names to be used together.

Robbie (m) Diminutive of **Robert** used mainly in Scotland, occasionally given as a name in its own right.

Robbin (f) Form of **Robin** used more in the U.S. than Britain, especially in the 1950s. The spelling was probably deliberately changed to distinguish it from the male name.

Robert (m) Old English *Hreodbeorht* 'fame-bright'. The Normans used a similar name from Old German, and used it in far greater numbers. Although they did not therefore introduce the name to Britain, it was their liking for it which caused Robert to be very well used in the Middle Ages. Because so many men bore it a number of different pet forms were necessary. **Rob**, by the usual rhyming process, led to **Hob, Dob, Nob** and later, **Bob**. These took on diminutive forms and gave rise to forms such as **Robin, Dobbin**. The popularity of all forms of the name in the surname period (11th c. to the 14th c.) is attested to by family names such as *Dobson, Hobbs, Hopkins, Roberts, Robeson,* etc. Robert was early established in Scotland by Robert the Bruce, Robert I of Scotland and a national hero, and has remained a great favourite there, as in all English-speaking countries. In the early 1980s showing signs of a slight reduction in use in most regions. Many famous men have borne the name, amongst whom one may number Robert Burns, the Scottish poet; General Robert E. Lee; the writer Robert Louis Stevenson; actors Robert Taylor, Robert Morley, Robert Ryan, Robert Wagner, Robert Newton, Robert Young, Robert Donat, Robert Beatty, Robert Mitchum, Robert Redford. Feminine forms of the name include **Roberta, Robin, Robyn, Robbin, Robertina, Robina, Robena**.

Roberta (f) Feminine form of **Robert** first used in the 1870s and continuously since then. In the 1950s the name was being used far more often in the U.S. than in Britain. By 1980 had faded on all sides. Jerome Kern wrote a light opera

Roberta which included the song 'Smoke Gets in Your Eyes'. A well-known bearer of the name is Roberta Peters of the Metropolitan Opera.

Robertina (f) Feminine of **Robert** used mainly in Scotland, though rarely in modern times. **Robertena** also occurs.

Roberto (m) Spanish/Italian form of **Robert**, used regularly in the U.S. and occasionally, since the 1960s, in Britain.

Roberts (m) The surname linked with **Robert** used as a first name. The similar name **Robertson** also occurs as a first name.

Robin (m, f) For many centuries this was a pet form of **Robert** and exclusively a male name. Girls were given the name **Robina** from the 1840s onwards, and that form continued to be used until recent times. But by 1940 Robin was being occasionally used for girls, perhaps being identified with the bird-name. There was some precedent for transferring bird-names to the stock of first names. **Mavis** ('song-thrush') was already in use, as was **Merlin**. **Biddy** and **Polly** accidentally fall into such a category by their form, as do **Finch, Jay, Martin, Oriole, Peregrine**. A **Raven** Smith was named in 1860, and a **Starling** Smith in 1862. Modern use of Robin, however, does not yet seem to have inspired parents to turn to bird names in a more general way. Having begun to see Robin for girls, parents soon began to spell it differently in an effort to distinguish the feminine form of the name. **Robyn** appeared by the mid-1940s. **Robbin** also came into use. The change of spelling is probably no longer necessary, since Robin is now not given to boys. As a name for girls it appears to have passed its peak of popularity on all sides, and is now used infrequently. The most famous person to have borne the name remains the English outlaw Robin Hood. See also **Christopher**.

Robina (f) Feminine form of **Robin**, itself a pet form of **Robert**, in consistent use from the 1840s until recent times. **Robena** and **Robine** occur as variants.

Robinson (m) The surname 'son of Robert' used as a first name. Especially popular throughout the 19th c. but now rarely given as a first name. Daniel Defoe's novel *Robinson Crusoe*, sometimes said to be the first novel written in English, was published in 1719. Defoe begins the story by explaining that Robinson was the maiden name of Robinson Crusoe's mother.

Robson (m) The surname 'son of Robert' used as a first name. More frequent in the 19th c. but continues to be used regularly if infrequently.

Robyn (f) Form of **Robin** in use since the 1940s.

Rocco (m) The Italian form of a Germanic name meaning 'repose'. The name of a 14th c. saint. Developed into French *Roch*, Spanish *Roque*, Dutch *Rochus, Rokus, Rook*. Used steadily but quietly in the U.S. See also **Rocky**.

Rochelle (f) French place name, also found in the U.S., meaning 'little rock'. Well used in the U.S. as a first name by 1940 and became decidedly popular throughout the 1940s and '50s. Then began to fade, and by the early 1980s being quietly used. Reached Britain in the late 1950s but used infrequently. Nurnberg and Rosenblum suggest that Rochelle may have been suggested by **Rachelle**, but statistics show that the form Rachelle was suggested by Rochelle. In the early 1940s was being used more intensively, and that remained the case for the next twenty years. **Rochele** and **Roshele** are occasional variants, and **Shelley** is used as a pet name.

Rocky (m) The word used as a name. The name first appeared in the 1950s and was clearly a reference to the American heavyweight boxing champion Rocky Marciano (Rocco Francis Marchegiano). Still in use in the early 1980s in the U.S., having been much publicized by a successful series of films since 1976 starring Sylvester Stallone.

Roda (f) Mainly 19th c. variant of **Rhoda**.

Rod(dy) (m) See **Rodney, Roderick**.

Roderick (m) Old German *Hrodric*
(Modern German *Roderich*) 'fame-
rule'. Taken up by the Scots who used it
to Anglicize Gaelic *Ruairidh* 'red'. They
used it most in the 19th c., though there
were signs of a revival there in the
1970s. In the rest of Britain it reached a
minor peak in the mid-1950s. Never
particularly fashionable in the other
English-speaking countries. Tobias
Smollett created a character of the name
in his *Roderick Random* (1748), but the
hero of that novel was not especially
admirable. Henry James gave us
Roderick Hudson (1876), his first novel
and certainly not his best. In *The Lady
of the Lake* (1810) Sir Walter Scott
describes Roderick Dhu, an outlaw and
bandit. A well-known bearer of the
name is the actor Roddy McDowell.
Roddy is in fact used as an independent
name. Variants of Roderick include the
common **Roderic** and the occasional
Rodric, Rodrick. Spanish **Rodrigo**
occurs from time to time, and in the U.S.
the surname **Rodriguez (Rodrigues)**
'son of Rodrigo' is also used as a first
name.

Rodger (m) Common variant of **Roger**,
influenced by the surname form.

Rodney (m) English place name and surname used as a first name. Made famous
by Admiral George Brydges, Lord Rodney (1719–92). A number of ships of the
Royal Navy were named after him, the
last being a battleship of 1925. The first
name began to be used in the 1850s and
slowly established itself. At its most
popular in Britain in the 1950s, by
which time it was even more popular in
the U.S. In Britain the name faded from
1960, but it continued to be more intensively used in the U.S. until 1965, when
it also began to decline. Always
appealed to black American families as
well as white, and in the early 1980s
black Americans were using the name
most. One of the best-known bearers of
the name is the actor Rod Steiger. In
fiction there is the central character of

Conan Doyle's novel *Rodney Stone*
(1896).

Rodolph (m) Variant of **Rudolph**.

Rodric(k) (m) Variants of **Roderick** used
mainly in the U.S.

Rodrigo (m) Spanish form of **Roderick**
used from time to time in English-
speaking countries.

Roger (m) A name common to several
Germanic languages, e.g., Old English
Hrothgar, Old German *Hrodgar*, composed of elements meaning 'fame' and
'spear'. Roger was the Norman form of
the name, introduced to Britain in the
12th c. Became very popular and rhyming pet forms were soon being used,
Hodge and *Dodge*. These led to modern
surnames such as *Hodges, Dodgson*,
while Roger itself led to *Rogers, Rodgers*, etc. Slowly lost favour through the
16th and 17th cc., then faded until it
had almost disappeared at the beginning
of the 19th c. Recovered around 1840
and remained in quiet use until the
1950s when it was at its peak on all
sides. Still used in all English-speaking
countries, but is out of fashion. A distinguished early bearer of the name was the
English philosopher Roger Bacon
(1214–94). More recently the name has
been associated with the actor Roger
Moore. In radio communications
'Roger' was used to mean 'Received and
understood', the name being chosen
because of its initial letter. There seems
to have been no special reason for naming the skull and cross-bones, the traditional pirate flag, the Jolly Roger. Variants of Roger include the common
Rodger and rare forms such as **Rogar,
Rogre**. In the U.S., especially, the surname **Rogers** is used as a first name.

Rogers (m) Use of the surname 'descendant of **Roger**' as a first name. More
common in the U.S. than in Britain.
A famous name-bearer is Rogers
Hornsby, the baseball player.

Rohan (m) Irish surname used as a first
name, in use as such since the 1960s.
Probably from Irish *ruadhan* 'red'.
Rowan was in earlier use, and Rohan

may have been seen as a variant of that name.

Roisin (f) Irish diminutive of **Rois** (**Rosa**) in use since the 1930s. Usually translated **Rosaleen**, or given the phonetic form **Rosheen**.

Roland (m) Old German *Hrodland*, probably 'famous land'. The nephew of Charlemagne, brave and loyal, has been the hero of many romances, especially Theroulde's *Chanson de Roland* and Ariosto's *Orlando Furioso*, **Orlando** being the Italian form of Roland. Popular in the Middle Ages and led to surnames such as *Rowland, Rolland*. **Rowland** seems to have been the 17th c. form of the name, used by Shakespeare in four of his plays, especially *As You Like It*. This continued to be usual, until the taste for restoring old names and spellings re-introduced Roland in the 18th c. Rowland remained the rather more popular spelling until the 1870s, since when Roland has established itself firmly, especially in the U.S., as the usual form of the name. At its height in Britain in the 1920s and reached a minor peak in the U.S. in the 1940s. **Rolland** and **Rolando** have been amongst the American variants, while occasional use has been made in Britain of the French feminine form **Rolande**.

Rolande (f) French feminine form of **Roland** in occasional use.

Rolf (m) Scandinavian form of **Rudolph**. Steadily but quietly used in English-speaking countries since the 1860s. Variants include **Rolfe, Rolph**.

Rolland (m) Mainly U.S. variant of **Roland**.

Rollie (m) Variant of **Rolly**. This spelling is also used occasionally for girls in the U.S.

Rollo (m) Pet form of **Roland, Rudolph** or **Ralph** used independently, though only on rare occasions. Swedish form of the name is **Rolle**.

Rolly (m) Pet form of **Roland** used independently from time to time. **Rolla** and **Rollie** also occur.

Rolph (m) Variant of **Rolf**, ultimately a form of **Rudolph**.

Roma (f) Italian name of the city of Rome, used as a first name with great regularity since the 1880s. **Florence** had long been in use when Roma first appeared, and **Venice** was already known as a first name. George Eliot created the name *Romola* for her novel and its heroine, based on Latin *Romula* 'a woman of Rome', but the name does not seem to have been used in real life.

Romaine (f) French feminine of **Romain**, 'Roman'. Used occasionally in English-speaking countries, and found also as **Romayne**.

Romany (m) The name of the gypsy language and a word used for 'gipsy' brought into first-name use since the 1960s, though infrequently. Possibly a misunderstanding of phrases like 'Romany Joe', where Joe was the name and Romany the generic description. In the Romany language *rom* means 'man, husband'.

Romeo (m) Italian 'pilgrim who had visited Rome'. Since Shakespeare's *Romeo and Juliet* (1598) a generic name for a young lover. Used rather more often in the U.S. than in Britain, but not with great frequency in any English-speaking country.

Romy (f) Pet form of **Rosemarie**, made known by the Austrian film star Romy Schneider (Rosemarie Albach-Retty). First use of the name in English-speaking countries dates from the appearance of her first film in the early 1960s. **Romi** is sometimes used as a variant.

Ron (m) Pet form of **Ronald** used independently. Not frequent. **Ronn** is mainly U.S. usage.

Rona (f) see **Rhona**.

Ronald (m) For the origin of the name see **Reynold**. Ronald probably derives directly from the Old Norse form of that name *Rögnvaldr*. First used intensively in Scotland but spread to the rest of the English-speaking world from the end of the 19th c. In Britain at the height of fashion in the 1920s and '30s. American parents came to the name slightly later, in the 1940s and '50s. In the early 1980s was being used far more in the U.S. than in Britain, presumably due to President Ronald Reagan. However, the name had clearly passed its fashionable peak in all English-speaking countries by that time. Biggest influence probably the British actor Ronald Colman (1891–1958), on screen regularly from 1919. **Ranald** was formerly used in Scotland, especially as a variant of Ronald, and is still found occasionally.

Ronan (m) Irish 'little seal' according to Ronan Coghlan, in his *Irish Christian Names*. Well used in Ireland in the 1970s, having been known in Irish legend for many centuries.

Ronelle (f) Modern diminutive of **Rona** in occasional use. **Ronella** has also been used.

Ronna (f) Modern feminine form of **Ronald** which was being reasonably well used around 1950 in the U.S. **Ronne** was also used on occasion.

Ronnette (f) Modern feminine form of **Ronald** used in the U.S.

Ronnie (m) Pet form of **Ronald** used as a name in its own right. In regular but infrequent use this century. Since the 1960s **Ronni**, **Roni** and occasionally **Ronnie** itself have been used for girls, especially in the U.S. **Ronney** and **Ronny** are variants.

Rory (m) Gaelic *Ruairidh* 'red'. Almost exclusively a Scottish name until Rory Calhoun (born Francis Timothy Durgin) began to appear regularly on the cinema screen in the 1940s. Since the 1940s it has remained in quiet use in all English-speaking countries.

Rosa (f) Latin *rosa* 'rose'. The written form of **Rose** in Latin documents from the Middle Ages onwards, but used as a name in its own right at the beginning of the 19th c. At its most popular in the 1870s, but at no time displaced Rose as the usual form. Dickens has a Rosa Dartle in his *David Copperfield*, but his description of her would not have inspired parents to use the name. He

tells us she was a 'little dilapidated – like a house – with having been so long to let'. He makes amends in *Bleak House*, where Rosa is a shy village beauty.

Rosabella (f) A name formed in the mid-19th c. to mean 'beautiful rose'. Used with some regularity until the 1920s. Variants **Rosabel**, **Rosabell**, **Rosabelle** all came into use later, but Rosabella remained the usual form.

Rosalee (f) Variant of **Rosalie** in use since the 1960s in Britain, though it was being used in the 1940s in the U.S. **Rosalea** also occurs.

Rosaleen (f) Irish diminutive of **Rosa**, in use since the 1930s. In Ireland occurs also as **Roisin**. Ronan Coghlan tells us that the phrase 'dark Rosaleen' was 'used as a figurative name for Ireland in a celebrated poem'. He forgets to name the poem. **Rosalene** is also found. Both forms of the name had found their way to the U.S. by the 1940s.

Rosalia (f) The name of an Italian saint of the 12th c. whose name is connected with Latin *rosa* 'rose'. *Rosalia* is the name of a ceremony in which rose-garlands were hung on tombs, but the name could easily be a form of *Rosaria* 'rose-garden', since the change from 'r' to 'l' in such words is common. In English-speaking countries it has been more common in its French form **Rosalie**, but Rosalia was used regularly in the 19th c. Rare since the 1920s. **Rosella** may be a variant form, via **Roselia** which was used in the 19th c.

Rosalie (f) French form of **Rosalia**, in regular use since the 1850s. In modern times also occurs as **Rosalea**, **Rosalee**, though the latter form gets uncomfortably close to Cockney rhyming slang 'Rosy Lee', used for a 'cup of tea'.

Rosalin (f) Variant of **Roseline** in use since the 1920s though infrequently.

Rosalina (f) Latinized form of **Rosaline**, used mainly in the latter part of the 19th c. Presumably formed on the analogy of **Caroline-Carolina**, **Ernestine-Ernestina**, **Clementine-Clementina**, **Christine-Christina**, etc., and pronounced in the same way as Carolina.

Rosalind (f) The English poet Edmund Spenser made use of this name in his *Shepherd's Calendar*, explaining that it was 'a fained (invented) name, which, being well ordered, will bewray (betray) the verie name of his love and mistresse, whom by that name he coloureth.' The lady in question was Rosa Daniel, and Rosalind was a simple anagram of her name. Thomas Lodge took the name from Spenser and used it as **Rosalynde** in his *Rosalynde, Eupheus Golden Legacy* (1590), a romance which Shakespeare then turned into dramatic form in *As You Like It*. The immediate source of the name in English-speaking countries is thus from Spenser via Shakespeare. The question is: was Spenser aware of the German name Rosalinde? Rosalinde did in fact already exist when he made use of it. Its origin is disputed. Traditionally the first element has been explained as Old German *Hros* 'horse'. Drosdowski prefers a derivation from Germanic *Hroth* 'fame', and has been supported by more recent German name-scholars. The second element of the name can likewise be explained either as 'shield' (made from *lime* wood) or as 'serpent'. To add to the minor confusion, the name was taken to Spain where it was identified with Spanish *linda* 'pretty', the whole name being taken to mean 'pretty rose'. This does indeed seem rather more suitable for a young lady than 'horse-serpent'. Came into general use in the 1860s which may indicate that the immediate source was Thackeray's novel *The Newcomes*, published in the 1850s. In recent times most used in the 1950s and '60s. The actress Rosalind Russell had made parents aware of the name from the mid-1930s onwards.

Rosalinda (f) Occasional variant of Rosalind.

Rosalinde (f) German form of Rosalind, in occasional use.

Rosaline (f) Probably a variant of Rosalind (German *Rosalinde*). Shakespeare uses the name twice in his plays – as a waiting-lady in *Love's Labour's Lost*, and (referred to but does not appear) in *Romeo and Juliet* (the girl whom Romeo loved before he met Juliet). Consistently used since the 1840s, though never especially fashionable. Different bearers of the name pronounce it in different ways, though its normal sound is indicated by the common variants **Rosalin**, **Rosalyn**, **Rosalynne**, **Roselin**, **Roselyn**, together with the later development **Roslyn**. **Rosilyn** is also found, as are **Rozalyn**, **Rozlyn**.

Rosalyn (f) Modern form of Rosaline in use since the 1920s. Used more often than Rosaline itself. Other forms are **Rosalyne** (rare), **Rosalynn**, **Rosalynne**, **Roselyn**, **Rosilyn**, **Roslyn**, **Roslyne**, **Roslynn**.

Rosalynd (f) Modern variant of Rosalind in occasional use.

Rosalyn(ne) (f) See Rosalyn.

Rosamond (f) The more usual spelling of Rosamund since the beginning of the 19th c., especially in the U.S. Traditionally Rosamund is the name given by Henry II to his mistress Jane Clifford. Queen Eleanor compelled her to swallow poison. Her story appealed much to writers from the 16th c. onwards, e.g. Swinburne's *Rosamond* (1861) and Tennyson's *Fair Rosamond* (1879).

Rosamund (f) The Normans brought Rosamund to Britain in the 11th c., having inherited an Old German name of disputed origin. Modern German scholars explain the first element as 'fame' and the second as 'protection'. Other scholars, such as Miss E. G. Withycombe, believe that the first element of the name is 'horse'. The original meaning was forgotten when the name reached Britain and it was re-interpreted as Latin *rosa mundi* 'rose of the world' or *rosa munda* 'pure, clean rose'. These two Latin meanings have been standard ones for some 500 years, and no doubt explain the name's continued use throughout that period. Rosamond has been the rather more usual spelling of the name since the beginning of the 19th c., but both forms have been rarely used since the 1960s.

Rosan (f) See Rosanne.

Rosana (f) Blend of Rose and Anna, used sporadically throughout the 19th c. but now obsolete. First occurrence of the name is in Richard Johnson's *Famous Historie of the Seven Champions of Christendom* (1617), in which Rosana helps St George.

Rosann (f) See Rosanne.

Rosanna (f) Blend of Rose and Anna which was in use by the end of the 18th c. Became decidedly popular around 1850 for at least a generation. Still used, though not in great numbers. In terms of frequency, Rosanna has been the usual form of the name, but Rosana, Rosannah, Roseana, Roseanna, Roseannah, Rosehanah, Rosehannah, Rozanna all occur. The Rosanne variants are treated separately. Brewer cites an example of Rosana in a minor literary source in the early 17th c., but it almost certainly had no effect on later usage.

Rosannah (f) Common 19th c. variant of Rosanna but seemingly obsolete since 1930. The spelling was possibly influenced by Hannah.

Rosanne (f) Blend of Rose and Anne, imitating the similar Rosanna. The forms of the name with -a were far more usual in the 19th c. Roseann and Rosan were used before Rosanne appeared together with Rosann in the 1860s, but none with any great frequency. Very distinct renewal of interest in Rosanne and its variants in the 1940s. Rosanne became the usual form, Roseann supported it, and a new form, Roseanne, appeared in the 1960s and has remained in use. Many American parents write the two names separately as Rose Ann, or Rose Anne but use them as one name.

Rose (f) For 500 years this name has been identified with the flower. The name which the Normans had actually brought to England in the 13th c., at first found as *Royse*, *Roes*, *Roys*, etc., derived from an Old German name *Hrodohaidis*, composed of elements meaning 'fame' and 'kind'. The second element *-haidis* is the same as *-hood* in a word like 'knighthood', i.e. it refers to the state of being a knight, or in the case of the personal name, the state of being famous. However, this sense had probably been forgotten by the Normans themselves, and ordinary Englishmen decided that the name they heard being used was the flower name. Proof of this comes in the Latin form *Rosa*, always used for Rose in formal documents. Rose was used infrequently until the 18th c., then became popular throughout the 19th c., reaching its height in all English-speaking countries around 1900. Then began to fade on all sides. Remains in use, but is now infrequent. Has been especially productive of diminutive forms which are listed separately.

Roseana (f) A 19th c. variant of Rosanna.

Roseann (f) See Rosanne.

Roseanna(h) (f) Common variants of Rosanna, especially in the 19th c. Occasionally occurs in modern times.

Roseanne (f) See Rosanne.

Rosehannah (f) Blend of Rose and Hannah used regularly in the 19th c. The name imitated Rosanna. Rosehanah was also found.

Rosella (f) See Rosalia.

Roselin (f) Variant of Rosaline, used only occasionally.

Roselind (f) Occasional variant of Rosalind.

Roseline (f) Fairly common variant of Rosaline/Rosalyn, with perhaps a changed pronunciation of the first syllable from *Roz-* to *Rose-*. Found from the 1890s, but has never been particularly fashionable.

Rosella (f) Diminutive of Rose in use since the 1850s, though never in great numbers. May also be a variant of Rosalia which came into use slightly earlier.

242

Roselyn (f) Fairly common variant of **Rosaline/Rosalyn**, in use since the 1880s. The change in spelling may indicate a preferred pronunciation of the first syllable as *Rose-* instead of *Roz*.

Rosemarie (f) Variant of **Rosemary** which appeared in the 1920s. Later boosted by a popular musical in which the central character was Rose Marie. A Latin form of Rosemarie (which is now used in France for Rosemary) has occasionally been used, namely **Rosemaria**.

Rosemary (f) Introduced as one of the 'flower' names in the 1890s. Its origin looks obvious, but it is in fact an alteration of *rosemarine* 'dew of the sea'. Latin *ros* 'dew' naturally looked like 'rose' to English eyes, especially as part of a flower name, and **Mary** was more familiar than Latin *marinus*. The first name steadily became more popular on all sides after its introduction, and was at its height of popularity between 1935 and 1955. Has since tended to fade. Rosemary Clooney, the American singer, helped to publicize the name in the 1950s.

Rosena (f) Fairly common variant of **Rosina**, especially in the early part of the 19th c. **Rosenah** also occurred.

Rosetta (f) Italian diminutive of **Rose**. The name appealed to 18th c. writers. Rosetta is the heroine of Bickerstaff's *Love in a Village* (1763) and of Moore's *The Foundling* (1748). Consistently used throughout the 19th c. Usage may have been influenced by the fame of the Rosetta Stone, which supplied the key to the Egyptian hieroglyphics in the 1820s, and takes its name from a city near the mouth of the Nile. Now rarely used. The former variant **Rosette** has disappeared.

Rosey (f) See **Rosie**.

Rosheen (f) Phonetic form of Irish **Roisin** (**Rosaleen**) in use since the 1960s.

Roshelle (f) See **Rochelle**.

Rosie (f) Pet form of **Rose**, **Rosalind**, etc. used since the 1860s. The earliest form of the name seems to have been **Rosy**, but it was used infrequently and disappeared in the 1920s. **Rosey** also made

an early appearance, and was used more frequently than **Rosy**, but it too lasted only until the 1920s. Rosie came on the scene late, but soon became the most frequent form, especially between the end of the 19th c. and 1925. Continues to be used regularly, if infrequently.

Rosilyn (f) Occasional variant of **Rosalyn**.

Rosina (f) Italian diminutive of **Rosa** (**Rose**), established in English-speaking countries since the beginning of the 19th c. Especially popular in the latter half of the 19th c., and well used until the 1920s. Still in regular use, but infrequently. Perhaps the best-known bearer of the name is Rosina in Rossini's opera *The Barber of Seville* (1816), which may have been responsible for introducing the name.

Rosita (f) Spanish diminutive of **Rosa** used occasionally in English-speaking countries since the 1940s.

Roslyn (f) Modern form of **Rosaline** via **Rosalyn**. In use since the early years of the 20th c. and well used in most English-speaking countries, especially in the 1950s and '60s. Also found as **Roslynn**, **Roslyne**, **Roslin**, **Rozlyn**.

Ross (m) Scottish place name and surname used as a first name. The original meaning can be 'cape' or 'promontory', or the surname can derive from a word meaning 'red'. Established as a first name since at least the 1840s. Steadily if quietly used in modern times in all English-speaking countries. Terence Rattigan's play *Ross* is about Lawrence of Arabia, who enlisted in the Royal Air Force in 1922 as T. E. Ross. The American film producer Ross Hunter is a well-known bearer of the first name.

Rossalyn (f) Also **Rosselyn**. See **Rosslyn**.

Rosslyn (m,f) As a male name in Scotland a use of the place name. Also a feminine variant of **Roslyn**. The first name has been in use since the early part of the 20th c., and in that respect coincides with Roslyn, but the different pronunciation of Rosslyn, and its almost exclusive use by Scottish parents, entitles it to be considered as a separate name. Found occasionally as **Rossalyn, Rosselyn, Rosslynn.**

Rosy (f) See **Rosie.**

Rowan (m) Irish *Ruadhan*, diminutive of *Ruadh* 'red'. Irish parents do not seem to use the name a great deal, which suggests that some parents identify the name with the rowan tree, or mountain ash, which is commonly found in Scotland. Has occurred regularly in Britain since the 1950s.

Rowena (f) Probably the same name as **Rhonwen.** Sir Walter Scott made it the name of the Saxon girl who marries *Ivanhoe*, in the novel of that name (1820). Gradually came into general use in the 19th c. and consistently used since, especially in the 1950s, and slightly more often in Britain than in the U.S.

Rowland (m) Long-standing variant of **Roland.** Could be said to be the English form of French Roland, but the latter spelling is now mainly used. Surnames **Rowlands** and **Rowlandson** also occur as first names.

Rowley (m) English place name 'rough clearing' which became a surname, occasionally used as a first name.

Roxana (f) Latin form of a name which was probably Persian, meaning 'the dawn'. The Greek form is **Roxane,** which is also used. The name of the Persian wife of Alexander the Great, a violently jealous woman who stabbed her rival. Nathaniel Lee wrote a play on the subject, *Alexander the Great* (1678), and according to theatrical legend actresses playing the part of Roxana have on at least two occasions stabbed their fellow-actresses in earnest during the play because of real-life jealousies. Daniel Defoe wrote a novel *Roxana* (1724). Used more often in the U.S. in modern times than in other English-speaking countries, the preferred spellings now being **Roxanna, Roxanne.** Also found are **Roxann, Roxianne** and the pet forms **Roxie, Roxy.**

Roy (m) Originally this name was from

Gaelic *ruadh* 'red'. Some parents may see it as a pet form of **Royal, Royden, Roydon, Royston,** etc. and others probably connect it with **Elroy, Leroy,** where Roy means 'king'. In the U.S. was most used around 1900, though still being well used in the 1940s. In Britain became fashionable slightly later, reaching a peak in the mid-1930s. Survived in frequent use until the 1960s. Is still given, but now clearly out of fashion in all English-speaking countries. Associated in the 1940s and '50s with the singing cowboy Roy Rogers (Leonard Slye).

Royal (m) The word or surname used as a first name. The density of usage in the U.S., e.g. in the 1940s, strongly suggests that the word was being used for its commendatory meaning. Very occasionally used for a girl, and other feminine forms include **Royalyn, Royalene.**

Royce (m) English surname of uncertain origin, possibly deriving from an Old German feminine name *Hrodohaidis* 'fame-kind'. Used as a first name since the end of the 19th c., mainly in the 1920s and '30s. Most associated with the Rolls-Royce company, formed by the Hon. C. S. Rolls and F. H. Royce in 1904.

Royden (m) Common English place name and surname regularly used this century as a first name. **Roydon** is a variant, and occurs in equal numbers. In place names of this type, 'roy' refers to 'rye'. Roydon is therefore a 'hill where rye grows'. Neither form of the name occurs frequently.

Roystan (m) Occasional variant of **Royston.**

Royston (m) English place name and surname used as a first name. The same place name in different parts of the country had different origins. First-name usage in Britain began in the 1890s and has been very consistent since then, with a distinct increase in parental interest in the name around 1935. American parents do not seem to have discovered the name as yet.

244

Roza (f) Variant of **Rosa** in occasional use since the 1840s.

Rozena (f) Modern variant of **Rosina** in occasional use.

Rozlyn (f) See **Roslyn**.

Ruben (m) German and Spanish form of **Reuben**, used very regularly in English-speaking countries.

Rubie (f) See **Ruby**.

Rubina (f) Either a feminine of **Reuben**, which sometimes occurs as **Rubin**, or a diminutive of **Ruby**. Only came into use after Ruby had been established as a 'jewel' name in the 1870s. **Robina** was well-established by that time and could have acted as a model. Variants include most of the spellings of Reuben with the -*a* ending, namely **Reubena**, **Reubina**, **Rubena** (**Rubenia**), but **Rubyna** also occurs to show the Ruby connection. **Rubine** is also found, but Rubina has always been the most usual spelling of the name. Never used in great numbers.

Ruby (f) The word used as a first name, inspired by a general fashion for 'jewel' names. Came into use in the 1870s and reached a minor peak of popularity 1900–25 in Britain, rather later in the U.S. In the 1930s associated with the singer/dancer Ruby Keeler (Ethel Keeler). **Rubie** has been used as a variant. **Rubye** is also found, together with **Rubey**. In some cases **Rubina** is a diminutive form.

Rudi (m) Variant of **Rudy**, itself from **Rudolph**.

Rudolf (m) The form in several European languages of **Rudolph**. In occasional use.

Rudolph (m) Old German *Hrudolf* 'fame-wolf'. Used in the 19th c., but it was Rudolph Valentino (Rodolpho Alfonzo Raffaelo Pierre Filibert Gugliemi di Valentina d'Antonguolla) who caused it to be used more intensely in the 1920s. In Britain it remained almost unused after his death in 1926 for some thirty years, but it re-appeared in the 1950s. Then killed off as a legitimate first name in Britain by a song which featured 'Rudolph, the red-nosed reindeer'. Continued to be used steadily though quietly in the U.S. **Rudolphus** is used on rare occasions, and **Rudolf**, the form of the name in several European languages, is a variant. Scandinavian form of Rudolph is **Rolf**, often used together with **Rolfe**, **Rolph**. **Rodolph** is another variant. In the U.S. the comedian, former crooner Rudy Vallee (Hubert Vallee) caused **Rudy** to be well used, though the name is rare in Britain. The best-known Rudolph in recent times has been the Russian-born ballet-dancer Rudolph Nureyev.

Rudy (m) Pet form of **Rudolph** used independently.

Rueben (m) See **Reuben**.

Rufus (m) Latin *rufus* 'red, red-haired'. *Rufus*, *Rufius* and *Rufinus* were common Roman names used by the early Christians. In English history is associated with William II, second son of William the Conqueror, known as William Rufus because of the colour of his hair. In Britain was well used throughout the 19th c., but rare since the early years of the 20th c. In the U.S. now mainly used by black American families.

Rupert (m) German form of **Robert**. The name was made known in England in the 17th c. by Prince Rupert (or **Ruprecht**), the nephew of Charles I, who served his uncle as a military commander. Mildly used in the 18th c., and more consistently in the 19th c. Continues to be mildly used in both Britain and the U.S. In modern times it is associated with Rupert of Hentzau, in the popular novels of Anthony Hope. The English poet Rupert Brooke (1887–1915) became instantly famous in the First World War, mainly for his sonnet 'If I Should Die. . .' British children may associate the name with the adventures of the cartoon character Rupert the Bear.

Russel (m) Frequent variant of **Russell**. A well-known bearer of the name is Russel Crouse, co-author of *Life With Father*.

Russell (m) Surname of French origin deriving from the nickname of a red-haired or red-faced man, used as a first name. Such usage began in the U.S. in the late 17th c. after the admired Lord William Russell was beheaded, but American parents used the name most intensively in the early years of the 20th c. The surname is a common one in the U.S. and several eminent people have borne it. At its height in all English-speaking countries in the 1950s. In the U.S. faded very considerably by the early 1980s; in Britain still being fairly well used. **Russel** is a common variant, and the pet form **Russ** is used as a name in its own right from time to time, mainly in the U.S.

Rusty (m) This nickname for a person with red hair is occasionally used as a first name, especially in the U.S.

Ruth (f) Hebrew, Probably 'friend, companion'. Biblical, O.T., The Book of Ruth. The archaic word 'ruth' means 'pity' or 'remorse', as it does in 'ruthless', but the word is not connected with the name. Ruth came into use in the 17th c. especially amongst the migrating Puritans, since the Biblical Ruth also left her homeland. Remained in very steady use, and was helped along by Mrs Gaskell's novel *Ruth* (1835). At its most popular in English-speaking countries 1890–1920, but especially in the U.S. Continues to be steadily used in modern times. Had a special attraction for 19th c. poets. The best-known poems about Ruth are by Wordsworth, Thomas Hood and Mrs Hemans. Some parents have tried to improve an already beautiful name by using such forms as **Ruthalma, Ruthella, Ruthetta, Ruthina, Ruthine. Ruthann(e)** has been very well used in the U.S., together with the diminutive form **Ruthie**. Scottish parents occasionally make use of **Ruthven**, an aristocratic family name.

Ruthann(e) Blends of **Ruth** and **Ann** or **Anne** used mainly in the U.S.

Ruthie (f) Pet form of **Ruth** used in its own right, mainly in the U.S.

Ruthven (f) Aristocratic Scottish surname, used on rare occasions as a first name. After a treasonable conspiracy an Act of Parliament was passed in 1600 ordering 'that the surname of Ruthven shall now and in all time coming be extinguished and abolished for ever'. The ban on the name was lifted by Parliament in 1641.

Ryan (m) Common Irish surname of unknown meaning, used as a first name. Usage does not seem to have begun in Ireland. A Ryan Smith was named in Britain in 1939, and examples of the first name are found in the U.S. in the early 1940s. By 1960 quietly but steadily used in both Britain and the U.S. When Ryan O'Neal appeared in *Love Story* in 1970 the name then became considerably more popular. In the early 1980s it was difficult to predict whether the name would fade or become still more popular.

S

Saba (f) A name used by the essayist and wit Sydney Smith (1776–1845) for his eldest daughter (c. 1800) in an effort to find something striking to go with *Smith*. Possibly he took the name from the Bible, where Saba is an alternative form of Sheba, a region of southern Arabia. The fabulously rich Queen of Sheba who visited Solomon (1 Kings 10) is elsewhere called the Queen of Saba. Very rarely used, however, as a first name.

Sabina (f) Feminine of Latin *Sabinus*, 'a Sabine', i.e. one of the people from central Italy later united with the Romans. Common early Christian name, e.g. St Sabina, a noble Roman maiden. In continuous use since the 17th c., while never being especially fashionable. Examples have been difficult to find, however, since the 1940s. In the U.S. Sabrina has tended to displace Sabina since that time. French form **Sabine** occurs occasionally, and pet form **Bina** is used independently.

Sabra (f) Of unknown origin. In the 13th c. *Golden Legend* Sabra is the daughter of *Ptolemy*, king of Egypt. She was rescued by St George from the dragon, or giant, and later married him. Used occasionally in England as a girl's name, especially in the 19th c., when it was sometimes spelt **Sabrah**. Not the same name as **Sabre** (Sabrina). Also occurs in the U.S. in the 1940s.

Sabrina (f) Roman name for the River Severn, in England. Ekwall, in his *English River Names*, thinks that Severn is a Celtic name but is unable to explain it. The legendary explanation for Sabrina is that she was the daughter of King Locrine by his mistress Estrildis. Queen Guendolen's fury led to her assembling an army to make war on her husband, who was slain. Guendolen then had Sabrina and Estrildis thrown into the river which from that time was called Sabrina. The poet Milton, in *Comus*, and the playwright Fletcher, in *The Faithful Shepherdess*, refer to the legend. In modern times there has been a play *Sab-*

rina Fair by Samuel Taylor, and a film called *Sabrina*. In Britain the name was used throughout the 19th c. but has been very rarely used in the 20th c. In the U.S. it was being steadily used in the 1970s and early 1980s.

Sacha (m) Russian pet form of **Alexander** in use since the late 1960s. Much publicized by the French entertainer Sacha Distel.

Sadie (f) Originally a pet form of **Sarah**, but used as a name in its own right from the end of the 19th c. In the early 1980s, however, it is very quietly used.

Sadler (m) The occupational surname, 'maker of saddles', used fairly regularly as a first name in the 19th c. and occasionally since.

Saffron (f) Flower or colour name which appeared briefly in the late 1960s but now seems to have faded.

Sagar (m) Old English *Sigehere* 'victory people'. Common name in the Middle Ages which gave rise to many surnames (*Segar*, *Sagar*, *Sayer*, etc.). Used very rarely in modern times.

Saidee (f) Presumably a fanciful form of Sadie. Occurs on occasion in the 19th c.

Saint (f) The word used as a first name. Several examples occurred between the 1840s and 1880s, but parents then seem to have abandoned it.

Salena (f) Variant of Selina. Salina is also found.

Salley (f) Mainly 19th c. variant of **Sally**, perhaps influenced by Henry Carey's famous song 'Sally in our Alley'.

Sallianne (f) Form of Sally-Anne used to some extent in the 1960s and '70s. **Sallian** is also used occasionally.

Sallie (f) Modern variant of **Sally**, found fairly often.

Sally (f) Originally a pet form of **Sarah** (compare **Mally** from **Mary**, **Hal** from **Harry**). Used as a name in its own right since the 18th c., when it was very popular. Faded away in the 19th c. and reappeared only in the 1920s, when it was reasonably popular in the U.S. American parents used the name well from then until the 1960s. In Britain the name was at its most popular in the 1960s but subsequently faded. **Sallie** is a fairly frequent variant in modern times, while **Salley** was used in the 19th c. Parents have sometimes lined **Selina** with Sally to produce forms such as **Salina, Salena.**

Sally-Ann(e) (f) The following forms of this name occur: **Sally-Ann, Sallyann, Sally-Anne, Sallyanne, Sallianne, Sallian.** An American example of Sally-Ann was noted in 1940, and a Sallyann was named in Britain in 1942, but there seems little doubt that the appearances on the cinema screen of Sally-Ann Howes, at first as a child actress in the 1940s, gave the name a great impetus. By the early 1980s all forms of the name had faded in the U.S., but Sally-Anne and Sallyanne were still being quietly used in Britain.

Salome (f) Hebrew 'peace'. Biblical, N.T. One of the women who ministered to Jesus, and possibly the sister of the Virgin Mary. Under normal circumstances her name would have been greatly used in the Christian world, but it was also a favourite in the Herodian family. In particular it was borne by the daughter of Herodias, the girl who danced before her step-father King Herod on his birthday and greatly pleased him so that he offered her anything she wished. Salome applied to her mother for guidance, and it was she who told her to ask for the head of St John the Baptist on a platter. John had displeased Herodias by condemning her second marriage. The story of the dancing and its tragic sequel is told in the Gospels of both Matthew and Mark, neither of whom mention Salome's name. Nevertheless, Salome's association with this incident caused the name to be avoided until the 18th c. Then regularly used throughout the 19th c., but now very rarely used in any English-speaking country. Oscar Wilde wrote a play called *Salome* in 1893, produced in Paris in 1896, but not presented in England until 1931. Richard Strauss based an opera on the play.

The name is sometimes found as **Saloma.**

Salvador (m) Spanish form of Italian Salvatore. Rarely used in the U.S. or Britain.

Salvatore (m) Italian form of Latin *Salvator* 'one who saves', a title applied to Jesus Christ in the Vulgate Bible. Well used in the U.S. in the 1940s and '50s, and still in use, but not in great numbers. Rarely used in Britain.

Sam (m) Pet form of **Samuel, Samson,** etc., used as a name in its own right. Especially popular in the 1870s. Remains in use in all English-speaking countries in a quiet way.

Samantha (f) Almost certainly a feminine form of **Samuel.** Heller's *Black Names in America,* which deals with names in use from the 17th c., contains lists of 'unusual' names used by both black and white families. Samantha occurs in both, along with other feminine forms based on the same name: **Samella, Samuela, Samuella, Samarthur, Samaria, Samarie, Samentha.** It is also clear that *-antha* was thought of as a viable feminine ending. **Iantha** occurs in the lists, presumably adapting the Greek name **Ianthe.** Also there are names like **Armantha, Salantha, Pantha.** All these names were used in a society (in the Southern states of America) which placed a high value on names which would individualize the name-bearer. Samantha seems to have struck a chord which caused parents to use it more often than some of the other inventions of the 18th c. It was picked up by the author Marietta Holley, responsible for a series of books which were published in the 1880s. These no doubt caused the name to be used occasionally. The film *High Society*, released in 1956, had a major influence on the use of the name. The film was a remake of *The Philadelphia Story* (1940) in which Katharine Hepburn played Tracy Lord. In *High Society* Grace Kelly became Tracy *Samantha* Lord and there was a Cole Porter song 'I Love You, Samantha'.

Within a year or two Samantha began to appear regularly in the U.S. In Britain it appeared in records regularly from 1961 onwards. This seems to suggest that teenage girls who had seen *High Society* or liked the song stored the name for use when they became mothers a few years later, a not uncommon phenomenon. Use of Samantha increased from 1964 onwards, though by no means dramatically, when the television series *Bewitched* was released. In this Elizabeth Montgomery played the part of Samantha, the witch. In the U.S. the series had the effect of associating Samantha with cats, because of the witchcraft, and it became a well-used cat name. When the series was released in Britain a year of so later the British public simply had their liking for the name reinforced and began to use it in great numbers. The name reached the top twenty by 1975, but in the early 1980s was clearly fading, though still being used in substantial numbers. American parents, meanwhile, were steadily increasing their use of the name in the early 1980s. The British actress Samantha Eggar, named in 1939, has also helped the name along since her first screen appearrance in 1962. Sometimes found in the variant forms **Samanntha**, **Symantha**.

Sammy (m) Pet form of **Samuel** or **Samson** used as a name in its own right, especially since the 1950s.

Sampson (m) See **Samson**.

Samson (m) Hebrew *Shimshon*, from *shemesh* 'sun'. Biblical, O.T., Judges 13, the man of enormous strength, champion of the Israelites against the Philistines. Also the name of an important 6th c. saint who took the name to Brittany. The use of the name by the Normans may have been due to him. Samson was a popular figure in the medieval mystery plays, which according to Miss Withycombe caused some usage in the 12th c. Again prominent in the 16th and 17th cc., but became

infrequent in the 18th c. In the early 1980s it remains in use in both Britain and the U.S., but is rather rare. Variant **Sampson** was extremely common until the end of the 19th c. but Samson seems to have been the preferred 20th c. form.

Samuel (m) Hebrew probably 'name of God' but meaning disputed. Biblical, O.T., 1 Sam.1:20. Rare name in England until the 17th c., when it was in general use. It later became decidedly popular, and remained so until the beginning of the 20th c. In the U.S. it faded very slowly, being reasonably well used until the late 1920s. Since then it has remained in very steady use in all English-speaking countries with minor fluctuations. In the early 1980s it was clearly not fashionable, since it was not in the top fifty boys' names list, but it was being used by enough parents to show that it was still a thoroughly acceptable name. Some of the famous men who have borne this name include Dr Samuel Johnson, the lexicographer; Samuel Taylor Coleridge, the poet; Samuel Adams, the American patriot. A more modern example is Samuel Goldwyn, the film producer. In literature Samuel was the first name of the immortal Mr Pickwick, also that of his servant Sam Weller in Dickens's *Pickwick Papers*. The generic name Uncle Sam, used of America, is usually explained as a playful expansion of the initials U.S. **Sam**, **Sammy** and to a lesser extent, **Sammie**, have been used as names in their own right. The boy named **Same** Smith, born in 1864, was probably meant to be a **Sammy**. For the feminine forms of the name see **Samantha**.

Sanchia (f) Spanish, from Latin *sancta* 'holy'. Also occurs as **Sancha** and **Sancia**. Used mainly by Roman Catholics in memory of an early saint, but none of these forms is frequently found in English-speaking countries.

Sanders (m) Surname deriving from **Alexander** used occasionally as a first name. **Sanderson** was used even more frequently as a first name in the 19th c.

Other surnames which derive from Alexander and which have been used as first names in modern times include **Saunders**, **Saunderson**.

Sandie (f) Pet form of **Sandra** used independently. Sandie has been the usual form in Britain where it was publicized in the 1970s by the singer Sandie Shaw, but **Sandy** is used in the U.S.

Sandra (f) Pet form of **Alessandra** (**Alexandra**). A character of this name in *Jacob's Room* (1922) by Virginia Woolf. Introduced generally in the 1930s, it became popular very rapidly. An immense success in all English-speaking countries throughout the 1950s especially. Then began to fade, and by the early 1980s was being little used. No one has explained why the name came into use when it did, and whether its success was due to a particular name-bearer. Main variant of the name, in the U.S. only, has been **Saundra**. **Sandria** and **Sandrea** occur from time to time, and diminutive forms such as **Sandrina**, **Sandrell** are found. **Zandra** is used surprisingly little.

Sandy (m, f) Originally a pet form of **Alexander** especially well used in Scotland. (In the form **Sawny** it became the general nickname for a Scotsman.) In modern times a pet form of **Sandra**, used as an independent feminine name. Appears also as **Sandie**, **Sandi**. See also **Sandie**.

Sapphire (f) Hebrew *sappir* 'lapis lazuli'. Biblical N.T., Acts 5:1: *Sapphira* is the wife of Ananias. In modern times no doubt identified with the jewel name sapphire. Rarely used.

Sara (f) See **Sarah**. Sara is the form of the name in several languages and has been used since the 1850s.

Sarah (f) Hebrew 'princess'. Biblical, O.T., the wife of Abraham. Not commonly used in Britain until the 16th c., then extremely popular until the beginning of the 20th c. Then faded drastically in Britain, though American parents continued to use it reasonably well. Strongly revived on all sides in the early 1960s. Still being intensively used in the early 1980s after at least ten years near the top of the popularity charts. Can be expected to decline during the 1980s. Borne by the famous actress Sarah Bernhardt, but Sarah Miles probably had more to do with its revival in the 1960s. In the 18th c. one of the most famous actresses was Sarah Siddons. Has not been used for many literary characters, though Dickens immortalized the dreadful Mrs Sarah Gamp, the drunken midwife, in *Martin Chuzzlewit*. **Sara** is the Greek form of Sarah, and the normal spelling of the name in languages such as French. Sara is also well used in modern times. Those who bear the name either pronounce it as Sarah, or make it sound different by rhyming the first syllable with 'far,' instead of 'fair'. The Biblical Sarah herself only took that form of the name when she was ninety years old. We are told in Genesis 17:15– 'And God said to Abraham, 'As for Sarai your wife, you shall not call her name Sarai, but Sarah shall be her name.' **Sarai** has nevertheless been used as a modern first name. Its meaning was possibly 'contentious'. **Sally** was an early pet form of Sarah, while **Sadie** was used later. Variants are rare, but include **Zara** and **Zarah**. The Spanish diminutive **Sarita** also occurs as **Zarita** and **Saritia**. **Sarena** and **Sarina** are found.

Sarah-Jane (f) Combination of **Sarah** and **Jane**, especially popular since the late 1960s in Britain. Found also as **Sarah-jane**, **Sarah-jayne**, and in the variant forms **Sara-Jane**, **Sarajane**.

Sarann (f) Spoken form of **Sarah-Ann** in 19th c., now used occasionally.

Sargent (m) Occupational surname, 'legal officer', used as a first name. Occurs mostly in the 19th c., also in the forms **Sargant**, **Sargeant**, **Sarjent**, **Sergeant**.

Sarina (f) Modern diminutive of **Sara(h)** in occasional use. **Sarena** is also used.

Sarita (f) Spanish diminutive of **Sara** in occasional use. Occurs also as **Zarita**.

Saritia (f) Variant of **Sarita** in occasional modern use.

Sarra (f) Modern variant of **Sara** used in the 1970s.

Sasha (m,f) Also **Sascha**. Pet forms of **Alexandra**, **Alexander** in use since late 1960s.

Saskia (f) Dutch name borne by the wife of Rembrandt. Dr J. van der Schaar suggests in his *Woordenboek van Voornamen* that it is linked to 'Saxon'. Used in Britain, especially in the 1970s.

Saul (m) Hebrew 'asked for'. Biblical, O.T., name of the first king of Israel. Also the original Hebrew name of the Apostle whose Latin name is Paul, and is always known as such. Little used in English-speaking countries; regularly but infrequently used in the second half of the 19th c., then disappeared until the 1960s, and in the early 1980s was being very quietly used in both Britain and the U.S. The novelist Saul Bellow has kept the name before the public in modern times.

Saunders (m) Also **Saunderson**. See **Sanders**.

Saundra (f) Common variant of **Sandra** in the U.S., but not used in Britain.

Savilla (m) French place name and surname regularly used as a first name in the 19th c. Found also as **Savile**, **Savil**, **Savill**.

Savina (f) Variant of **Sabina**. Sabina was the more usual form of the name in early times, but Savina seems to have been used in Italy. Used occasionally since the 1850s, mostly by Roman Catholics.

Sawn(e)y (m) Scottish form of **Sandy** which became a derisive general nickname for a Scotsman in the 18th c.

Saxon (m) The name of an early Germanic tribe, perhaps derived from a word meaning 'axe, knife'. Use of Saxon as a first name since the 1880s probably represents a transferred use of the surname.

Scarlett (f) Surname indicating someone who wore or dealt in 'scarlet', a kind of cloth. In Margaret Mitchell's *Gone With the Wind* Katie Scarlett O'Hara,

always called Scarlett, has the middle name because it was her grandmother's maiden name. Scarlett, and **Scarlet**, have been used mildly in the U.S. since the novel and film appeared in 1939, but the Biblical associations with the 'scarlet woman', the mother of harlots, are still strong. (The powerful description of the scarlet woman is found in the N.T., Rev. 17:3.)

Scilla (f) Pet form of **Priscilla**.

Scott (m) Surname, indicating 'a Scot', used as a first name. The Scots originally came from Ireland, so the name is particularly suitable for boys of either Scottish or Irish descent. Very rarely used as a first name in Britain until the late 1940s. Then came into regular use and was at its peak in the 1970s. Still being well used in the early 1980s but showing signs of fading. In the U.S. it began to be used in earnest in the late 1930s. Usage increased steadily into the early 1970s. Then began to fade, though still very much in evidence in the early 1980s. Popular in the U.S. almost exclusively with white families. Scott was probably started on its way by the novelist Scott Fitzgerald (Francis Scott Key Fitzgerald, 1896–1940). The actor Scott Brady (Gerald Tierney) helped it through the 1950s. Variant **Scot** occurs from time to time.

Seamore (m) Also **Seamor**, **Seamour**. See **Seymour**.

Seamus (m) Irish form of **James**. Pronunciation of the name is indicated by the phonetic form **Shamus** which is occasionally used. Used in Ireland since the 1940s and in the rest of Britain since the 1950s. Rare in the U.S.

Sean (m) Irish form of **John**, in use in Ireland and elsewhere since the 1920s, rare before that period. One famous bearer of the name, however, was the playwright Sean O'Casey (1880–1964). Became far more popular throughout the 1960s and '70s as a result of Sean Connery's appearances in the early James Bond films. Connery himself adopted Sean as a stage name in favour of his real name Thomas. Sean has remained the usual spelling in the U.S., with **Shawn** running second. In Britain **Shaun** had become the predominant spelling by 1970, with Sean in second place. All forms of the name have now passed their peak.

Seaton (m) English place name 'settlement near the sea', also a surname. In occasional use as a first name. Variant Seton also occurs.

Sebastian (m) Latin *Sebastianus* 'man from Sebastia', a city in Asia Minor. Common name amongst the early Christians, and the name of a famous saint of the 3rd c. The use of the name in medieval times gave rise to such surnames as *Bastian* but by the 17th c. it was being rarely used. Shakespeare obviously thought of it as a suitably foreign name and used it in *Twelfth Night* and *The Tempest*. Other 17th c. playwrights, such as Fletcher and Dryden, also made use of it. In Britain it occurred a few times in the 19th c., but did not come into regular use until the 1940s. Continues to be used, having been much publicized in the 1970s and early 1980s by the athlete Sebastian Coe. Still rarely used in the U.S. French form of the name, **Sebastien**, occurs from time to time. **Bastian** now appears to be obsolete as a first name, **Seb** being used as a pet name.

Sebert (m) Surname 'sea-bright' occasionally used as a first name.

Sebina (f) Variant of **Sabina** used in the 19th c.

Sebra (f) Spelling variant of **Sabra** mainly used in the 19th c.

Seelia (f) See **Celia**.

Sefton (m) Place name 'settlement in the rushes' which became a surname, used as a first name, regularly but infrequently, since the 1870s.

Selah (m) One of the more curious Biblical names, introduced by the Puritans and still found in the early 20th c. The word 'selah' occurs seventy-one times in the Psalms. It is thought to be a musical term, indicating a pause in the

singing which would be filled with instrumental music.

Selby (m) English place name 'willow farm', also a surname, used regularly since the 1870s as a first name, though never in great numbers. Usually male, but a **Selby-Ann** (f) was named in 1944.

Selena (f) Common variant of **Selina**.

Selia (f) 19th c. variant of **Celia**. **Seelia** was also used.

Selina (f) Form of Greek *Selene*, the goddess of the moon. The name has sometimes been referred to French **Céline**, a pet form of **Marceline**, but the S-spelling predominates throughout the 19th c., when the name was very popular. Its popularity was probably due to Selina, Countess of Huntingdon, who died in 1791 having devoted her life and considerable fortune to the Methodists. Frequent variant in the 19th c. was **Selena**. Also in use were **Salina**, **Salena**, **Salinah**, **Celina**, **Cellina**. In the early 1980s Selina and Selena continue to be quietly used in both Britain and the U.S.

Selinda (f) Development of **Selina** in the 19th c. when names like **Belinda**, **Melinda** were being well used. Smollett has a **Celinda** in his *Count Fathom* (1754).

Selma (f) Short form of **Anselma**, but also occurs as a place name in Macpherson's Ossianic poems (1765) and its use sometimes derives from that source. Well used in modern times in Scandinavian countries (e.g. Selma Lagerlöf, winner of the Nobel Prize for Literature, 1909), but rare in Britain and the U.S.A. **Zelma** also occurs.

Selvin (m) Surname, variant of **Selwyn**, used from time to time as a first name.

Selwyn (m) Probably from Latin *Silvanus* 'of the woods, savage, wild'. Surname was in use in Gloucestershire by the 13th c., often written as *Selveyn*. The more obvious explanation, which would derive Selwyn from Old English *selewine* 'hall-friend', is marred by the fact that no such name is recorded in Anglo-Saxon times. A formation in the Middle Ages is out of the question. Not

used as a first name until the 1840s.
Welsh parents responded to it well since
it had all the characteristics of a Welsh
name. They saw the name as composed
of *sel* 'ardour' and *wyn* 'fair, white', and
compared it with names like **Sulwyn**,
borne by an early saint. Selwyn became
more widely known in the latter half of
the 19th c. because of George Selwyn,
Bishop of New Zealand (1809–78).
Selwyn College, Cambridge was named
for him. Later the name was associated
with Selwyn Lloyd, the British politician. In modern times is quietly used in
both Britain and the U.S., black American families favouring it more than
white families.

Senga (f) Reversed form of **Agnes**, used
regularly but infrequently in Scotland.

Seonaid (f) Scottish Gaelic form of **Janet**,
little used other than by Scottish parents. See also **Sinead**.

Sepp (m) See **Joseph**.

September (f) The name of the month
used as a first name. See **April**.

Septimus (m) Latin *septimus* 'seventh'.
Feminine form of **Septima** has also been
used, but Septimus occurs far more
often. Both names were mainly used in
the 19th c. Septimus continued to be
used until the 1930s, but very rarely
used since.

Seraphina (f) Latin form of a Hebrew
name meaning 'ardent'. A 13th c. saint
whose name is used on rare occasions.
Seraphine also occurs.

Serena (f) Latin feminine of *Serenus*
'calm'. The name of an early saint and
common amongst the Christians of the
Roman Empire. Rare in English-
speaking countries until the 18th c.
Then faded, but was revived in the
mid-19th c. Used with some consistency
since the 1920s. Found also as **Serene**,
Sereena, **Serenah**, **Serenna** and more
commonly as **Serina**.

Serge (m) French form of Latin *Sergius*.
Russian **Sergei** also occurs. See **Sergio**.

Sergeant (m) See **Sargent**.

Sergio (m) Italian form of Latin *Sergius*, a
Roman clan name possibly connected

originally with 'servant'. The name of
several saints and an early pope. Used
quietly but steadily in the U.S. Rare in
Britain. French form **Serge** is occasionally used. Saint Sergius is especially
popular in Russia, and Russian bearers
of the name include Sergei Rach-
maninoff, Sergei Prokofiev and Sergei
Eisenstein. **Sergei** has been noted in the
U.S.

Serina (f) See **Serena**.

Seth (m) Hebrew 'to put, set'. Normally
explained as 'appointed' because of the
passage in the O.T., Gen. 4:25, 'she
bore a son and called his name Seth, for
she said, "God has appointed for me
another child".' Seth was the third son
of Adam and Eve. The name was
reasonably well used from the 18th c.
until the end of the 19th c., with a particular flurry of interest around 1850.
This was just before the publication of
George Eliot's novel *Adam Bede*, in
which there is a character called Seth.
Usage increased throughout the 1970s
and though in the early 1980s it was
very rarely used in Britain, there were
distinct signs of interest being shown in
it in the U.S.

Seumas (m) Occasional variant of
Seamus.

Sevilla (f) Spanish form of **Sibylla**. Borne
by an early saint and is occasionally
used. Spanish place name **Seville** is also
transferred to first-name use from time
to time. In this case the original meaning
is probably 'lower, beneath'.

Seward (m) Surname 'sea guardian' or
'victory-guardian' used as a first name,
especially at the end of the 19th c.

Seymour (m) Norman place name and
aristocratic English surname, regularly
used as a first name, especially in the
19th c. Much rarer in modern times.
A well-known bearer of the name was
the actor/writer Sir Seymour Hicks
(1871–1949). In 19th c. records the
name also occurs as **Seamor, Seamore,
Seamour**.

Shadrach (m) Biblical name of uncertain
origin. The Babylonian name of

Hananiah, one of Daniel's three companions, and may well have contained a reference to Aku, the sun-god. The Puritans made good use of the name from the 16th c., and it was still being well used in the 19th c. Rather rare since the 1920s. **Shadrack** was an early variant form which continued to be used alongside Shadrach.

Shafaye (f) Faye with the fashionable Sha- prefix which was being intensively used by black American parents in the early 1980s. Some of the names making use of the prefix, used in 1981, were **Shajuan, Shajuana, Shakeena, Shakela, Shaketa, Shakeya, Shakia, Shakilah, Shakina, Shakirah, Shakirra, Shaita, Shalanda, Shalaun, Shalay, Shalaya, Shalena, Shaleta, Shaletta, Shalika, Shalinda, Shalisa, Shalonda, Shalonde. Shalyn, Shameka, Shamica, Shamika, Shamita.** Of these, Shamika and its variants were especially popular. See also **Shan**.

Shamus (m) Phonetic form of Irish Seamus. This spelling is seldom used.

Shan (f) Phonetic form of Welsh Sian in use since the mid-1950s. Parents might have also seen it as a pet form of **Shannon**, which had also developed into **Shanna** by the 1940s. In support of this view, the variant **Shann** was actually in use as a girl's name several years before Shan appeared. Again, it is possible that the name was thought of as a feminine form of **Shane** or **Shayne**, which came into use after 1953. **Shani** appeared at the same time as Shan and survived rather better, but that may be a separate name. In the U.S. especially, Shan is clearly a fashionable sound in feminine names for the 1980s. The following forms were amongst those used to name girls in 1981: **Shana, Shanae, Shanay, Shanda, Shane, Shanea, Shaneen, Shaneka, Shanekia, Shanel, Shanell, Shanelle, Shanequa, Shanetha, Shanethis, Shanetta, Shanette, Shani, Shania, Shanicka, Shanida, Shanika, Shanisha, Shanita, Shanitha, Shanitra, Shanna, Shannan, Shannel, Shanta,** **Shante, Shanteka, Shantia, Shantilli, Shantina, Shantrice.** All of these were used by black American families, and one or two, such as Shanna, Shana, were also used by whites. White Americans made use of **Shannon** far more often than black families in the same year, so they were also expressing their liking for the sound in a more conservative way – using one name a great deal rather than many different names. In Britain, in the early 1980s, no evidence that Shan is fashionable as a name or a sound, though **Shannie** is in occasional use.

Shana (f) Variant of **Shan**, or a feminine form of **Shawn** (Sean). **Shannah** is a rare variant.

Shanay (f) Presumably a development of Shan. **Shanae** also occurs. Used only in the U.S.

Shane (m) Anglicized form of Irish Sean (**John**). Had almost disappeared as a first name by the beginning of the 20th c., though it occurred from time to time, especially in Ireland. Mainly known as a surname, and probably thought of as a surname being used as a first name until 1953, when the film *Shane* was released. In Britain the name immediately began to be used again in steadily increasing numbers, and enjoyed considerable popularity throughout the 1970s. Indications early in the 1980s that it had passed its peak. Also used in the U.S. since the film was released, but does not seem to have had the same success. Occasionally Shane is feminine, a phonetic rendering of Welsh **Sian**.

Shanell (f) Usual spelling of a name which also occurs as **Shanel, Shanelle, Shannel.** All are variants of **Chanel**, a much advertised French perfume and now a first name used by black American families.

Shani (f) Sue Browder listed this name in her *New Age Baby Name Book* (1974), and said quite correctly that in Swahili the word means 'wonderful, marvellous'. She did not unfortunately account for the name's sudden appearance in

Britain in the mid-1950s and its subsequent use both in the U.S. and Britain. Probably seen by many parents as a pet form of **Shannon** or **Shan**. Still being used in the early 1980s, though not in great numbers.

Shanika (f) Probably a development of **Shan** or **Shani**. Occurs also as **Shanicka**, **Shaneka**, **Shanekia**. All forms are used exclusively for the moment by black American families.

Shanita (f) Appears to be a newly-formed name using two popular name-elements, **Shan-** and **-ita**. Appeared for the first time in the late 1970s and is having a considerable success in the U.S. amongst black American families in the early 1980s.

Shanna (f) Probably a back-formation from **Shannon**. In the early 1980s it was being used by both black and white families in the U.S., but was still unknown in Britain.

Shannon (m, f) Celtic river name meaning 'old one', i.e. an ancient divinity. Also an Irish place name and surname. Began to be used as a first name (for girls) in the U.S. in the late 1930s. By 1947 had also appeared in Britain. Use of the name increased very slowly but steadily, and by 1960 it was occasionally found as a boy's name. In the early 1980s the name was still found in Britain, but only on rare occasions. In the U.S. it had become more popular, mainly for girls, but black American families were using the name in almost equal numbers for their sons as well as their daughters. Also found as **Shanon**, **Shannan**.

Shanta (f) Also **Shante**, **Chanta**, **Chante**. These appear to be pet forms of **Chantal**, the original French form of the name which often becomes **Chantel**, **Chantell**, **Chantelle**, **Shantale**, **Shantel**, **Shantele**, **Shantelle** in the U.S., especially, used as independent names. Shanta and Shante were being well used in the early 1980s by black American parents.

Shantel (f) Also **Shantele**, **Shantell**, **Shantelle**. These are phonetic variants of **Chantal**, all being used in the early 1980s by black American parents.

Shara (f) Pet form of **Sharon** used independently in the 1960s.

Sharan (f) See **Sharon**. **Sharen** is also found.

Shari (f) Pet form of **Sharon** used mainly in the U.S. in the 1940s and '50s. **Sharie** also occurs.

Sharlene (f) Form of **Charlene** used by e.g. Sharlene Wells ('Miss America' 1985).

Sharmain(e) (f) Phonetic form of **Charmain(e)**. **Sharmane** also occurs.

Sharolyn (f) Recent innovation, appearing in the 1970s, based on **Sharon** and the popular ending -lyn.

Sharon (f) Hebrew 'the plain'. Biblical, O.T., the name of a fertile plain between Jaffa and Mount Carmel. Not a personal name in the Bible, though there are references to 'the rose of Sharon', a beautiful shepherdess, in the Song of Songs. 'Rose of Sharon' itself became **Rosasharn** in John Steinbeck's *Grapes of Wrath* (1939), but Sharon was by this time already in use for girls. Sinclair Lewis makes no comment on the name being unusual, for instance, when a character in his *Elmer Gantry* (1927) changes her name from Katie Jonas to Sharon Falconer. The name steadily became more popular in the U.S. after the publication of Lewis's novel, and was at its peak in the 1950s. British parents first noticed the name in the 1930s, but did not turn to it in force until the 1950s. At its height in Britain in the early 1970s, but subsequently faded sharply. By the early 1980s was being quietly used in all English-speaking countries. Main variant of the name is **Sharron**, but the following have also occurred: **Sharan**, **Sharane**, **Sharin**, **Sharen**, **Sharyn**. Mainly American variants are **Shaaron**, **Sharene**, **Sharone**, **Sharran**, **Sharren**, **Sharronne**. Pet forms **Shari**, **Sharie** and **Shara** have been used to some extent as names in their own right.

Sharonda (f) Diminutive of **Sharon**, favoured by black American parents in the early 1980s. **Sharronda** also occurs. **Sharona** is a similar name.

Sharron (f) Common variant of **Sharon**.

Shaun (m) Phonetic form of Irish **Sean**, and by 1970 the usual spelling of the name in England.

Shauna (f) Feminine form of **Shaun** used to some extent since the 1950s. Also found are **Shaune, Shauneen, Shaunette**. In the U.S. Shaun itself is used fairly often as a girl's name.

Shavon(ne) (f) Frequently used variants in the U.S. of **Siobhan**.

Shaw (m) Common place name 'wood' and surname, used infrequently as a first name since the 1840s.

Shawn (m) See **Sean**. Especially popular variant of the name in the U.S.

Shayla (f) Modern form of **Sheila** used mainly by black American families.

Shayne (m) Fairly frequent variant of **Shane**.

Sheba (f) Pet form of **Bathsheba**, used as a name in its own right. Associated also with the Queen of Sheba (see **Saba**).

Sheela(g)h (f) Alternative spelling of **Sheila**.

Sheena (f) Phonetic form of Gaelic **Sine**, the Scottish form of **Jean** or **Jane**. Sheena is the usual spelling, but **Sheenagh, Sheenah, Shena, Sheona** and **Shiona** are found. Used more generally since the 1950s, and appearing by the 1970s in the U.S.

Sheila (f) Anglicization of Irish **Sile**, itself a form of **Celia**. Extensively used in Britain and Canada 1920–50, its peak period being in the 1930s. Never as popular in the U.S. The Australian slang term for a girl, *sheila*, is said by Eric Partridge to derive from *shaler* ('a sheller'), not from the personal name. Sheila was used mainly in Australia in the 1920s: the slang term pre-dates it. Other spellings include **Shiela, Sheelagh, Sheelah, Sheilah, Shelagh, Shelia. Shelah** is a separate name.

Shelah (m) Hebrew 'request, petition'. Biblical, O.T., Gen 38:5. Youngest son of Judah. Very rarely used. Occasion-

ally as a feminine name, a spelling variant of **Sheila**.

Sheldon (m) Place name 'valley with steep sides', also a surname, used as a first name regularly in the U.S. since the late 1940s, in Britain since the 1960s. Reasonably popular until the early 1970s but has since faded.

Shelia (f) Alternative spelling of **Sheila**.

Shelley (m, f) English place name 'meadow on a slope or ledge', also a surname, used as a first name. Began to be used for boys in the 19th c., though never common, and continued as a male name until the 1940s. By that time being used far more frequently for girls, and male usage faded completely. The girl's name was probably an independent formation from **Shirley**, as it certainly was in the case of the actress Shelley Winters (Shirley Schrift), whose screen career began in the 1940s. Miss Winters helped to establish the name as feminine, and was no doubt responsible in some measure for its increased usage. Shelley remains the usual form of the name, but **Shelly, Shellie** and **Shelli** are also in use.

Shelton (m) Common English place name/surname, originally referring to a settlement on a high plateau, used as a first name from time to time.

Shem (m) Hebrew 'renown'. Biblical, O.T., the name of Noah's eldest son. Never well used in English-speaking countries.

Shena (f) See **Sheena**.

Sheona (f) See **Sheena**.

Shepherd (m) Occupational surname used as a first name. Especially well used as such in the 19th c., also in its variant forms **Shephard, Sheppard**. Rarely used as a first name in modern times.

Sheralyn (f) For the development of the name see **Cheryl**. Sheralyn was one of the more popular Sh- spellings.

Sheree (f) Popular variant of **Cherie** since the 1950s. **Sherree** is also found.

Shereen (f) Also **Sherene**. A modern development from **Sheri**, ultimately from **Cherie**. **Chereen** also occurs. Some parents prefer forms such as **Shereena, Sherena, Sherina.**

Sheri (f) Phonetic variant of **Cherie**, used mainly in the U.S. **Sherie** is occasionally found.

Sheridan (m) Irish surname made famous by the playwright Richard Brinsley Sheridan (1751–1816), in use as a first name since the 1860s. In Britain has been used far more regularly since the 1940s. Publicized in recent times by Sheridan Morley, the writer-son of actor Robert Morley. Occurs less often in the U.S., though Senator Sheridan Downey made it more widely known. **Sheridon** is also found, and the name has been turned into the feminine form **Sheridawn**. The back-formation **Sherida** has also been used for girls.

Sherie (f) Modern form of **Cherie**, in use since the 1950s. **Sheri** also occurs.

Sherilyn (f) Phonetic change of **Cherilyn**. First used in the 1950s, and variously spelt as **Sherralyn, Sherralynn, Sherry-lyn**, etc.

Sherleen (f) Modern development of **Shirley**. **Sherline, Sherlean, Shirleen, Shirlene** also occur.

Sherley (f) Variant of **Shirley**.

Sheron (f) Fairly frequent modern variant of **Sharon**, an alternative to **Sherryn, Sheren**, etc., which are also found.

Sherralyn (f) See **Sherilyn**. **Sherralynn** also occurs.

Sherree (f) See **Sheree**.

Sherri (f) Phonetic variant of **Cherie**, used mainly in the U.S. **Sherrie** is a rarely used alternative.

Sherry (f) Phonetic reading of French *chèrie* 'dear one', influenced by the name of the drink. In the 1970s the name was being used far more in the U.S. than in Britain. Adapted in recent years to **Shericia, Sherilyn, Sherrita, Sheryl**, etc.

Sheryl (f) See **Cheryl**.

Sherryn (f) Modern extension of **Sherry**, appearing only in the 1970s. Popularity of **Sharon** is a clear influence, giving rise to variants such as **Sheron, Sheren, Sharyn.**

Shevon(ne) (f) Variants of **Siobhan**.

Shiela (f) Alternative spelling of **Sheila**.

Shiona (f) See **Sheena**.

Shirley (f) Common English place name, 'bright clearing', also an aristocratic family name. Charlotte Bronte's novel *Shirley* (1849) used the name for the heroine, though the fictional parents had the name in mind for a son. Shirley had earlier been used as a male name, and is still sometimes male, but when it came into general use in the 1860s it was as a girl's name. At its most popular in the U.S. in the 1920s and '30s, and interest had begun to be shown in it in Britain. The popularity of the name rocketed overnight, however, when parents were exposed to the child star Shirley Temple in 1932. By 1950 the name had considerably faded, but there was a temporary revival in the 1960s, perhaps due to such actresses as Shirley Maclaine, Shirley Eaton, Shirley Jones and Shirley Knight. This revival was not matched in the U.S., the name having been very well used during its slow run-down in the 1940s and '50s. In the 1980s it is rarely used. Variants of the name include **Sherley, Sherlie, Shirlee, Shirlie, Shirly, Shurley, Shurly.** Names which appear to be developments of Shirley include **Sherline, Shirlean, Shirleen, Shirlene, Shirlynn.**

Shivon (f) See **Siobhan**.

Sholto (m) Gaelic 'sower, propagator'. Occurs in Scottish clan histories and used rarely as a modern first name.

Shona (f) Phonetic form of Gaelic **Seonaid**, a feminine form of **John** and therefore the equivalent of **Joan, Jean** or **Jane**. Well used in Britain since the 1940s. In the U.S. used quietly in the early 1980s. **Shonagh, Shonah, Shone**, etc., are amongst the variants used by Scottish parents.

Shoshana (f) Also **Shoshanna, Shushana.** Hebrew forms of **Susannah**, in occasional modern use.

Sian (f) Welsh form of **Jane**, regularly used since the 1940s. Found also in the phonetic form **Shan** and **Shane**.

Siarl (m) Welsh form of **Charles**. Used occasionally.

Sibby (f) Pet form of **Sibyl** in occasional use as an independent name.

Sibella (f) Form of Latin *Sibylla* used mainly in the 19th c. See also **Sibyl**.

Sibyl (f) Medieval Latin *Sibylla*, Greek *Sibulla*, name of the mythological priestess who uttered the ancient oracles. A 'sibyl' therefore came to mean a 'prophetess'. Introduced to Britain by the Normans and well used in the Middle Ages, as surnames such as *Sibley*, *Sibson*, *Sibbs*, etc., show. Continued in use, but rather rare after the 17th c. Variant **Sybil** has been more popular since the beginning of the 19th c., and was the form used by Benjamin Disraeli for his novel *Sybil* (1845). The novel may have influenced usage, since Sybil gradually became more popular as the 19th c. wore on. At its height 1900–25, then faded. In the early 1980s rarely used as either Sibyl or Sybil. Most associated with the British actress Dame Sybil Thorndike. Occasional variants of the name include **Sibbill**, **Sibell**, **Sybel**, **Sybille**. Latinized form of the name appears as **Sibbella**, **Sibella**, **Sibilla**, **Sibylla**, **Sybilla**, **Sybella**.

Sid (m) Pet form of **Sidney** used independently. Rare since the beginning of the 20th c. **Siddie** and **Siddy** are also found. **Syd** is very rare.

Sidney (m) Dr Reaney is at pains to dismiss the accepted derivation of this name in his *Origin of English Surnames*. It has long been derived from a French place-name *Saint-Denis*, an explanation accepted by such authorities as Bardsley, Professor Weekley and E. G. Withycombe. The reason for this ready acceptance lies in the fact that many Norman French surnames are indeed derived from villages named for saints, and these names usually changed their form fairly drastically when pronounced by Englishmen. Bardsley cites such examples as *Sinclair* from St Clair, *Semple* from St Paul, *Sandeman* from St Amand, *Seymour* from St Maur, *Semper*

from St Pierre, *Somers* from St Omer, and so on. *Saint-Denis*, and even more commonly, *Saindenis*, exist as modern French surnames. It is therefore very likely that bearers of such names came to England in the Middle Ages, and that the name was anglicized along with those of similar type. Reaney himself notes someone who was presumably of Norman descent who appeared as Roger de Sancto Dionisio in 1212. There seems to be every reason, therefore, for supposing that some Sydney families owe their name to an ancestor who came from a place called Saint-Denis. What Dr Reaney *is* able to show is that the famous Sidney family who were especially prominent in the 16th and 17th cc. did not owe *their* name to such an ancestor. It came from a place in Surrey which was recorded in 1280 as *La Sydenye*, and which the Sidneys owned. Place-name scholars derive the name from Old English words meaning 'wide well-watered land'. The first name appeared for the first time in the 18th c., but was not in general use until the 19th c. Became very fashionable in the second half of the century, and reached a peak of popularity in 1900 in all English-speaking countries. By this time Sydney was in very common use as a variant, and was the form of the name used by Charles Dickens in his *Tale of Two Cities* (1859) for Sydney Carton, the man who sacrifices himself nobly at the end of the novel ('It is a far, far better thing I do than I have ever done'). The British entertainer Sid Field was famous in his time, and the actor Sidney Poitier has been well known since the 1950s. This may partly account for the continued favour shown to Sidney by black American families in the early 1980s, whereas everyone else seems to have put it aside.

Sidonia (f) Latin 'woman from Sidon'. Occurs very rarely. Sometimes appears in its French form **Sidonie**, or in its English form **Sidony**, but these are very rare. Probably the early use of these female names, however, led to the belief that **Sidney** was also a female name. Still used as such on occasions.

Sidwell (m) English place name/surname originally referring to a 'broad stream', used as a first name on occasions since the 1880s.

Sigmund (m) German 'victory-shield'. **Sigismund** was listed by Camden in 1605 as a 'usual Christian name', but there is no evidence that the name was in use in England at the time. Used occasionally in modern times in the U.S. and Britain, perhaps with reference to **Siegmund** in Wagner's opera *Die Walküre*, or to Sigmund Freud (1856–1939), the Austrian founder of psychoanalysis.

Silas (m) Greek contraction of *Silouanos*, a form of Latin **Silvanus**. Biblical, N.T., Acts 15:22. Came into general use in the 17th c. and regularly, though quietly, used until the 1920s. Since that time has been used rather more often in the U.S. than in Britain, though it has not been fashionable. In literature the name at once suggests George Eliot's novel *Silas Marner* (1861), though the character who gives his name to the story is not the kind of hero who inspires namesakes.

Síle (f) Irish form of **Celia** or **Cecilia**, but **Julia** is sometimes used as the English equivalent. Síle is rendered phonetically as **Sheila**, **Sheelagh**, etc.

Silence (f) A popular name amongst the Puritans, usually given to girls, very occasionally to boys. Commonly abbreviated to **Sill**. Translated into Latin it became **Tace** – 'be silent', which Camden, writing in 1605, thought was 'a fit name to admonish that sex of silence.' Tace in its turn developed into **Tacey**, a name still in use. The ultimate origin of this name was undoubtedly the admonition of St Paul: 'Let the women learn in silence, with all subjection.' Silence was still in use in the 19th c., but no examples noted since 1875.

Silva (f) Latin 'wood'. The name of a saint, and occasionally used in this form, especially in the 19th c. Far more usual as **Sylvia**.

Silvana (f) See **Silvanus**.

Silvanus (m) Latin 'living in a wood' or 'presiding over woods'. Biblical, N.T., 2 Cor. 1:19, the name of one of St Paul's companions. In general use by the 18th c., often as **Sylvanus**, but has never been fashionable. Feminine form of **Silvania** is rarely used, though a variant **Silvana** suddenly appeared in the late 1960s, both in the U.S. and Britain. It did not seem to survive into the 1970s.

Silvester (m) Latin 'woody, rural', from *silva* 'wood'. Common name amongst the early Christians, and the name of three popes. Consistently, but quietly, used in English-speaking countries since the 16th c. Since the 18th c. **Sylvester** has been the preferred spelling, and is certainly the form of the name used in the 1980s. It was also the form used by the cartoon cat who chased Tweetie Pie for twenty years from the 1940s in a great many animated films. Silvester and Sylvester have become rare names in Britain since the late 1960s. Brought to public attention in the 1970s by the actor Sylvester Stallone in the 'Rocky' films, though in fact in the U.S. Sylvester is now used almost exclusively by black American families. The English version of the name, **Woody**, is also used to some extent in the U.S., e.g. Woody Allen the film actor and director.

Silvia (f) Latin feminine of *Silvius*, a name borne by many kings of Alba. It derives from *silva* 'wood'. Rhea Silvia is the nature goddess who was supposedly the mother of Romulus and Remus, founders of Rome. Shakespeare made Silvia a noble-woman in his *Two Gentlemen of Verona* (1594). The play includes the famous song 'Who is Silvia?'. Many other English poets and playwrights have made use of the name, often in its long-standing variant form **Sylvia**. When the name came into general use in the mid-19th c. it was Sylvia which soon predominated. Became a great success in Britain in the 1930s, some ten years later in the U.S. Subsequently faded, and by the early 1980s was being little used.

Simeon (m) Hebrew 'hearkening, listening attentively'. Biblical, O.T., Gen. 29:33, 'The Lord hath heard that I am hated, He hath therefore given me this son also: and she called his name Simeon.' (Hebrew *shimon* 'hearing.') Regularly if infrequently used from the 16th c. until the 1920s. Now rarely used in any English-speaking country.

Simon (m) The N.T. version of **Simeon**, perhaps identified with the Greek name Simon from *simos* 'snub-nosed'. A name associated with many Biblical personages, especially the Apostle Simon Peter. Its frequent use in the Middle Ages gave rise to many surnames, including the common *Simpson*, *Simms*, *Simmonds*, etc. Very well used until the beginning of the 19th c. Almost disappeared by the 1850s, but began to be used again in the 1920s. Extremely popular around 1970 in Britain, but subsequently faded. American parents never seem to have taken to it. George Stewart suggests that the villainous Simon Legree in *Uncle Tom's Cabin* (1859) may have been responsible for that. A more modern literary connection is with Simon Templar, the creation of Leslie Charteris. It is possible that the popularity of the 'Saint' books began the fashionable run of the name in Britain from the mid-1930s. Pet form **Sim** has been used independently, and **Simm** occurs. Surnames **Simms**, **Simpson** and **Simson** have been used as first names. Usual modern feminine form is French **Simone**. **Simmina** has been used, and modern **Simonne** is found.

Simona (f) Variant in the U.S. of **Simone**.

Simone (f) French feminine form of **Simon**, in use in English-speaking countries since the 1940s. The French actress Simone Signoret has helped to make the name known internationally. In the U.S. the name is especially favoured now by black American families, many of whom prefer the form **Simona**. **Simonia** also occurs, and **Simonne** is a rare variant.

Simpson (m) Surname 'son of Simon'

used from time to time since the 1850s as a first name.

Sina(h) (f) Probably forms of Gaelic **Sine**, which normally becomes **Sheena**. Sina and Sinah were used in Britain between the 1890s and 1920s to some extent.

Sinclair (m) Form of St Clair, a French place name in honour of the saint, also a surname, especially common in Scotland. Used as a first name since the 1870s, though never in great numbers, and associated with the novelist Sinclair Lewis (1885–1951).

Sindy (f) Variant of **Cindy** in use since the 1950s.

Sinead (f) Irish form of **Janet**, much used by Irish parents in the mid-1970s. Publicized to some extent by the actress Sinead Cusack, daughter of Cyril Cusack. Scottish form of this name, less frequently used, is **Seonaid**.

Siobahn (f) Also **Sioban**, **Siobhian**, **Siobhian**. Variants of **Siobhan** in modern use.

Siobhan (f) Irish form of **Joan**. Normally pronounced *Sh'vawn*, with the stress on the second syllable. Made known internationally by Siobhan McKenna, the actress, but outside Ireland phonetic forms of the name tend to be used more often than Siobhan itself. Variants include **Shavon**, **Shavone**, **Shavonne**, **Sheryvonn**, **Shevon**, **Shivohn**, **Shy-vonia** (all used in the U.S. in 1981). Other variants include **Shervan**, **Shevonne** and probably the following *Ch-* spellings, again used in the U.S. in 1981: **Charvon**, **Chavon**, **Chavonn**, **Chavonne**, **Cheavon**, **Chevon**, **Chevonne**, **Chivon**. All these forms appear to show parents responding favourably to the sound of a name without being too sure as to its original spelling. The most frequent variants are **Shavonne** and **Shavon** – likely to become the normal forms.

Sion (m) Welsh form of **John** in occasional use.

Sir (m) The social title used as a first name. Nine British examples have been noted since the 1840s, mainly in the 1950s, and '60s.

Sissie (f) Pet form of **Cecilia** used independently from the 1890s, but rare after the 1920s. The name was killed off when 'sissy' or 'cissy' was applied to an effeminate boy or man as a term of abuse. In the 19th c. the name also occurred as **Sisie, Sissey, Sissy**.

Smith (m) The occupational surname used as a first name. Usage was very regular in the 19th c., especially by families whose surname was Smith. One boy born in 1858 had another surname as middle name, so that he rejoiced in the full title of Smith Follows Smith. The last British example of Smith as a first name was noted in 1929, though a Smythe Smith was named in 1931. An American example was noted in the early 1940s.

Snowdrop (f) The name of the flower used as a first name, mainly between the 1890s and the 1920s, but never one of the more popular names of this kind.

Sofia (f) The form of **Sophia** in several languages, e.g. Spanish, Italian. Used from time to time, especially in the U.S.

Soloman (m) Common 19th c. variant of **Solomon**. The spelling was suddenly used again in the 1970s, when the change in spelling may have been deliberate to give the name the meaning of a lone wolf (*Solo-man*).

Solomon (m) Hebrew *Shelomah* from *shalom* 'peace'. Greek *Solomon, Salomon*, Late Latin *Solomon*, Old French *Salomon*. Biblical, O.T., Solomon, King of Israel and Judah and wisest of men. The medieval form of the name in England was Salamon, hence the surnames *Salmon, Sammon*, etc. Solomon was reasonably well used in the 18th c. and continued to be regularly, if quietly, used until the 1940s. Especially associated with Jewish families. Feminine form of the name is **Salome**.

Sonia (f) Russian diminutive form of **Sophia**. This is the normal spelling of the name in Britain, where it has been in use since the beginning of the 20th c., becoming steadily more popular. **Sonya** is the usual spelling in the U.S., and

Sonja is a frequent variant everywhere. Stephen McKenna's novel *Sonia*, published in 1917, went through a great many editions and probably helped to establish the name. Sonja Henie, the Norwegian skating star, later spread that form of the name by her film appearances in the 1940s and '50s.

Sonja (f) Scandinavian form of **Sonia**.

Sonny (m) The common term of address, not necessarily to one's own son, used as a first name. The name is recorded before Al Jolson's appearance in the film *Sonny Boy* (1929), where he sang his famous song of that name, but the song undoubtedly boosted the first name. Continues to be used occasionally in modern times, sometimes spelt **Sonnie**. **Sunny** has also been used as a first name.

Sonya (f) Usual form in the U.S. of **Sonia**.

Sophia (f) Greek 'wisdom'. First used in England in the 17th c. and well used until the 1870s. Has continued to be used since then, though French **Sophie** has been much preferred in modern times. In the U.S., however, Sophia has remained in use very steadily since the 1940s and Sophie is rare. The Italian actress Sophia Loren is the best-known modern bearer of the name. St Sophia is the name of the celebrated mosque in Istambul, formerly a Christian church and bearing the name of an early saint. Sonia is a Russian diminutive of this name.

Sophie (f) French form of **Sophia**, and the preferred form of the name in Britain in modern times. In use since the 1920s, but became more popular in the late 1960s. Still reasonably well used in the early 1980s and showing signs of becoming yet more popular. Made famous in the 1930s by the singer Sophie Tucker, the 'red-hot mamma' of vaudeville (born Sophia Abuza, 1884–1966).

Sophronia (f) Greek 'prudent, self-controlled'. A feminine form of *Sophronius*, a name borne by several saints. Rarely used in English-speaking countries, though occasionally appears in the

19th c. records in such forms as **Soffrona**. Charles Dickens seems to have been especially fond of the name. A Sophronia Jobson is mentioned in his essay on Mormons, *Bound for the Great Salt Lake*. In *Our Mutual Friend* it is Sophronia Akershem who marries Mr Lammle – to their mutual regret. In *The Old Curiosity Shop* it becomes necessary to name the girl who acts as a domestic slave to Sampson and Sally Brass, and whom they have not bothered to name ('What does your mistress call you when she wants you?' 'A little devil'). Dick Swiveller, who eventually becomes her husband, gives some thought to the matter. 'After casting about for some time for a name which should be worthy of her, he decided in favour of Sophronia Sphynx, as being euphonious and genteel, and furthermore indicative of mystery.'

Sophy (f) Pet form of **Sophia** regularly used in the 19th c. In modern times is an occasional variant of French **Sophie**.

Sorcha (f) Irish 'bright'. Old Irish name now being used again by Irish parents. **Sarah** is used as its English equivalent, though **Claire** would be a closer translation. Pronounced **Surracha**.

Soraya (f) Persian name of unknown meaning, made known by the former wife of the Shah of Persia. Used in English-speaking countries since the 1960s. Wilfried Seibicke also reports on its use in Germany.

Sorrel (f,m) Appeared in the 1940s and used infrequently since, sometimes as **Sorrell** or **Sorrelle**. It can be a male name – e.g. Sorrell Booke (Boss Hogg in the TV series *The Dukes of Hazzard*). Sorrel is a common wild plant, so it could be considered a botanical name. It also describes a reddish-brown or light-chestnut colour. In Noel Coward's *Hay Fever* (1925) there is a Sorel Bliss.

Spencer (m) Occupational surname referring to a 'dispenser of provisions' within a household, a steward or butler, used as a first name. The surname is closely associated with the Churchill family: Sir Winston Churchill was Winston Leonard Spencer Churchill. The first name immediately suggests the actor Spencer Tracy, popular from 1930 onwards. Spencer has been in continuous use as a first name since the beginning of the 19th c. In Britain was especially well used during the 1970s, but has tended to fade since then. In the U.S. it continues to be used quietly but steadily. **Spenser** is a rare variant, and **Spence** occurs.

Spoors (m) Occupational surname 'man who made spurs' used occasionally as a first name. All the examples found are 20th c.

Squire (m) Surname originally indicating a young gentleman who accompanied a knight, a shield-bearer. Melvyn Hirst of Coventry makes a good case for attributing early use to admiration of John Squire, an officer who fought at Waterloo (1815). Squire was first used regularly and reasonably frequently throughout the 19th c. Rare soon after the start of the 20th c.

Stacey (m, f) Used as a male name originally, probably a use of the surname, deriving from **Eustace**. The later use of the name for girls probably identified the name with a pet form of **Anastasia**. The girl's name has been popular since the 1970s, and is often found as **Staci**, **Stacie**, **Stacy**.

Stacia (f) Recent variant of **Stacy** or **Stacie**.

Staci(e) (f) Pet forms of **Anastasia** used independently. Popular since the 1970s.

Stacy (m, f) See Stacey.

Stafford (m) English place name 'ford near a landing-place' and an aristocratic English surname, used as a first name regularly but infrequently since the 1840s. Associated with the British statesman Sir Stafford Cripps (1889–1952), but is used also in the U.S.

Stamford (m) The surname is a variant of **Stanford**. Also regularly used as a first name and still brought into use on infrequent occasions.

Stanford (m) Common English place name and surname, deriving from 'stony ford'. Used with some regularity in all English-speaking countries since the 1890s. In the U.S. it is especially associated with Leland Stanford (1824–93), founder of Stanford University in California.

Stanislaus (m) Latin form of Polish Stanislaw. The second element of the name is 'glory', but the first element is of uncertain origin. It may mean 'camp'. Occurs from time to time in English-speaking countries, though there has long been a tendency to anglicize it to Stanley. Feminine form Stanislawa is rare. French form of the name is Stanislas.

Stanley (m) Common English place name 'stony clearing', also an aristocratic surname, used as a first name since the 18th c. In the 1870s the search of Henry Stanley for Dr David Livingstone caught the public's imagination both in Britain and the U.S., and Stanley became decidedly more popular as a first name. In fact it was one of the best-used names in all English-speaking countries between the 1880s and the 1920s. Famous name-bearers include the British Prime Minister Stanley Baldwin (1867–1947), the outstanding English soccer player Stanley Matthews, and actors Stanley Baker, Stanley Holloway and Stan Laurel. Pet form Stan, seldom used independently, made it possible for surnames such as Stancie, Stanborough Stancombe, Stanhope, Stannard, Stansfield, Stanton to be brought into use as first names, though none of these became very general.

Stannard (m) Mainly Suffolk surname, 'stone-hard', used as a first name occasionally. Similar names are Stansfield, the original surname of the popular British entertainer Gracie Fields, and Stanton, meaning 'stony field' and 'stony place'. Both also occur as first names from time to time.

Stanton (m) English place name 'stony ground settlement', also a surname, used as a first name on rare occasions since the 1860s.

Star (f) In modern use, occasionally as Starr, when it may refer to Ringo Starr, the former 'Beatle'. It translates Esther, Estelle, Stella. See also Astra.

Starkie (m) The surname 'courageous' used as a first name, though rarely.

Starling (f) See Robin.

Stasia (f) Recent variant of Stacy or Stacie.

Stefan (m) The form of Stephen or Steven in several languages, e.g. Swedish, German, Russian, used in English-speaking countries since the 1940s, though infrequently.

Stefanie (f) Feminine form of Stefan used occasionally in English-speaking countries since the 1940s.

Stella (f) Latin *stella* 'star'. Used by Sir Philip Sidney in a famous series of sonnets 'Astrophel to Stella' written between 1580–84. 'Stella' was really a young lady called Penelope. 'Astrophel' was intended to have the meaning 'lover of stars'. In the 18th c. Jonathan Swift published his *Journal to Stella*, where 'Stella' was Esther Johnson. Esther means 'star' in Persian. Roman Catholics associated the name with the Virgin Mary, one of her titles being *stella maris*, 'star of the sea'. Very popular in the U.S. in the 1870s. Reached a peak in Britain much later, in the 1920s. Continues to be used with great regularity, but now found much less frequently. Estelle may be said to be the more modern form of the name, while Star itself has been used in the 1970s, occasionally as Starr.

Stephan (m) European form of Stephen, regularly used in English-speaking countries, though at times it may be an accidental variant of Stephen.

Stephanie (f) Feminine form of French Stephan (Stephen). *Stephana* and *Stephania* were the forms used by the early Christians. Stephanie began to be used in English-speaking countries in the 1920s and became more popular as

Stephen/Steven rose in the popularity charts. Did not have as much success as the male forms of the name, but still being well used in both the U.S. and Britain in the early 1980s. **Stefanie** is a common variant. Other forms include **Stefani, Stephany, Stephenie, Stephne, Stephney, Stephannie.** One of the French pet forms of the name is **Fanny.**

Stephanus (m) Latin form of **Stephen.** Used very infrequently.

Stephen (m) Greek *Stephanos* 'crown'. Biblical, N.T., Acts 7:59, the name of the first Christian martyr. A common name amongst the early Christians. Rare in England before the Norman Conquest, but its popularity from the 12th c. is reflected in the many surnames which derive from it. These include *Stevens, Stevenson, Steen,* etc. *Stevyn* was a common form of the name during the surname period (before 1400). Remained very popular until the end of the 18th c. In use throughout the 19th c., then declined to an all-time low in the 1920s. Revived strongly in the 1940s and went on to be one of the most popular names in the English-speaking world in the 1950s. Its popularity continued throughout the 1960s. Began to fade in the U.S. in the early 1970s, but was still the most popular name for boys in Britain until 1975. By the early 1980s clear signs that use of the name was declining on all sides, though it was still being well used. When the name was revived in modern times the spelling Stephen predominated at first. **Steven** steadily became more usual, especially in the U.S. By 1950 the two spellings were found in equal numbers in the U.S., whereas British parents still used Stephen nearly ten times as often at that time. By 1960 Steven had outstripped Stephen in the U.S. and has remained the usual form of the name. In Britain the -v- spelling continued to be used more frequently, and by 1980 Stephen and Steven were being used equally by British parents. In modern times many of the best-known bearers of the name

have used the short form **Steve,** which must have helped establish Steven as the normal form. Well known Stephens include writers Stephen Vincent Benet (1898–1943) and Stephen Crane (1871–1900). In literature there is Stephen Dedalus in James Joyce's *Ulysses,* and less importantly, Stephen Blackpool in Dickens's *Hard Times.* Foreign forms of Stephen are sometimes used in English-speaking countries, especially **Stefan, Stephan.** French **Etienne** is rarely found. Variant forms include the fairly common **Stevan** and modern **Stephon.** Surnames based on Stephen are often pressed into use as first names: **Stephens, Stephenson, Stevens, Stevenson, Stevinson.** French **Stephanie** is the usual feminine form, but **Stefanie** and **Stevie** are also well used. Rarer feminine adaptations include **Stephannie, Stephena, Stephene.**

Stephena (f) Rarely used feminine form of **Stephen. Stephene** also occurs.

Stephenie (f) Variant of French **Stephanie** used from time to time.

Stephens (m) Surname used as a first name on infrequent occasions. In the 19th c. **Stephenson** was regularly used as a first name.

Sterling (m) The word meaning 'of excellent quality' used as a first name, or a use of the surname as first name. Occurs more regularly in the U.S. than in Britain. The actor Sterling Hayden (John Hamilton) helped to make the name known from the 1940s. In Britain tends to be spelt **Stirling,** as with Stirling Moss, the former racing driver. This form of the name probably derives from the Scottish place name and surname.

Stevan (m) Fairly common modern variant of **Steven.**

Steve (m) Pet form of **Steven** (**Stephen**) used independently since the 1930s. Boosted in the early 1950s by such actors as Steve Brodie and Steve Cochran, and even more in the 1960s by Steve McQueen.

Steven (m) See **Stephen.**

Stevens (m) Surname used as a first name

on rare occasions. **Stevenson** was used in the 19th c.

Stevie (f) Feminine form of **Steven** in use since the 1960s. The best-known bearer of the name was the poetess Stevie Smith.

Steward (m) Surname used as a first name, especially in the 19th c. The name is an English form of **Stuart**.

Stewart (m) See **Stuart**. In early use and has been used as a variant of Stuart since the beginning of the 19th c. Both forms have existed as surnames since the 14th c. One well-known bearer in modern times has been the actor Stewart Granger, who was forced to change his name from James Stewart because another famous actor bore that name.

Stirling (m) See **Sterling**.

St John (m) The name of the saint together with the title has been in regular if infrequent use in Britain, mainly amongst Roman Catholic families, since the 1880s. It occurs far more often as a middle name. The normal pronunciation has led to the modern phonetic forms **Sinjon, Sinjun**, both of which have been used since 1960. Compare **Sinclair** from St Clair.

Storm (f) The word or surname 'stormy-tempered' used as a first name. The English novelist Storm Jameson has made the name well known, but it is used very rarely.

Stuart (m) Old English *stigweard* 'steward, keeper of the household'. *Steward* became *Stewart* in Scotland, but was adopted in the Frenchified spelling Stuart by Mary Queen of Scots. The Stuarts were the ruling house in Scotland from 1371, and in England from 1714. Use of Stuart and **Stewart** (see) as first names became general in the early 19th c. Both forms of the name were equally used until the 1950s, when a very clear preference was shown on all sides for Stuart. Became popular first of all in Scotland, but reached a peak of considerable popularity in the rest of Britain around 1970. Has subsequently faded. In the U.S. the name was at its

height in the 1960s, but by the 1980s was being very quietly used.

Sue (f) Pet form of **Susan, Susannah, Suzanne**, etc., used independently, mainly since the 1950s.

Sugden (m) Place name/surname originally referring to a valley where sows were kept, regularly used as a first name in the 19th c.

Sukey (f) Also **Suky, Sukie**. Popular pet forms of **Susan** in the 18th c. which were not revived when Susan again became very popular in the 20th c. One curious measure of the name's former popularity is provided by Don H. Kennedy's excellent book *Ship Names*. He notes that twenty ships called *Sukey* were registered in American ports at the end of the 18th c. Seven British ships, built between 1759 and 1773, also received the name.

Sullivan (m) Irish surname 'black-eyed' or 'hawk-eyed' used as a first name. Usage began in the 1930s and continues infrequently.

Sulwyn (m) Welsh 'sun-fair'. Occasionally used in Wales. A feminine form **Sulwen**.

Sunny (m) The word used as a first name, or a variant of the much commoner **Sonny**. See also **Samson**.

Susan (f) The short form of **Susannah**. Popular name in the 18th c., but generally declining throughout the 19th c. By the 1920s at a very low ebb, but parents began to be interested in it in the early 1930s. Rapidly became extremely popular in all English-speaking countries, and throughout the 1950s and '60s was one of the most intensively used names in all of them. Someone must have brought the name to the attention of young parents on both sides of the Atlantic at the same time, around 1930, but no one has been able to suggest who it was. The actresses Susan Hayward, Susan Hampshire, Susan Strasberg all came on the scene rather too late to have started the fashion. Susan Hayward in fact dropped her original name Edythe Marrener when she began her screen career in 1938. Variants include **Susann, Suson, Suzan**, together with the many forms of French **Suzanne**. The name was still being used in the early 1980s, though only by white parents. Even when at its most popular, black American parents had virtually ignored it.

Susana(h) (f) Variant of **Susannah** in use since the 1840s. Susanah is the usual spelling.

Susanna (f) Latin form of **Susannah**. Very frequent variant since the beginning of the 19th c.

Susannah (f) Hebrew 'lily'. Biblical, N.T., Luke 8:3, but mainly associated with the Apocryphal story of Susannah and the Elders. Two 'elders of the people' who lusted after the beautiful wife of Joachim but were repulsed by her, falsely accused her of adultery. She was sentenced to death, but Daniel stepped in and insisted that the two Elders be examined separately. Their contradictory stories proved them liars, and it was they, not Susannah, who were put to death. Very popular name from the 16th to the 18th c. Declined in use throughout the 19th c. and has been used infrequently since, though the short form **Susan** has been extremely popular in modern times. Susannah has been the usual form of the full name, the final -h reflecting the feeling that Jewish names should end with this letter. Latin form **Susanna** has, however, always been a well-used variant. Rarer variants include **Susana, Susanah, Suzana. Suzanna** has been used very regularly since the 1930s, with its own variant **Suzannah**. Some parents try to get nearer to the original Hebrew form of the name by using **Shushana** or **Shoshanna**. One of the best known bearers of the name is the British actress Susannah York. **Susan** and **Suzanne** and their many variants are treated separately. Pet forms **Sue** and **Susie** have also been well used as names in their own right. Older pet form was **Sukie** or **Suky**.

Susanne (f) German variant of French **Suzanne** reasonably well used since the

1930s, especially when **Susan** was being intensively used in the 1950s. **Susann** also occurs.

Susette (f) Occasional variant of **Suzette**. Susette is the German form of the French diminutive.

Susey (f) Common 19th c. variant of **Susie**.

Susie (f) Pet form of **Susan** or **Susannah** used independently since the 1860s. Susie has been the most popular form of the name, but it occurs also as **Susey, Susy, Suzie, Suzy**.

Susy (f) Common 19th c. variant of **Susie**.

Suszanne (f) Occasional variant of **Suzanne**.

Sutcliffe (m) Place name/surname, originally 'southern cliff', used as a first name from time to time.

Suzan (f) Variant of **Susan**, influenced by French **Suzanne** and perhaps meant to be pronounced in the French way, with the stress on the second syllable. This form appeared in the 1940s but has been rare since 1970. **Suzane** and, more frequently, **Suzann** are also found.

Suzana (f) See **Suzanna(h)**.

Suzanna (f) Variant of **Susannah** influenced by French **Suzanne**. In regular use since the 1930s, and found also as **Suzannah, Suzana**.

Suzanne (f) French form of **Susan**. In regular use since the beginning of the 20th c. but more intensively so in the U.S. than in Britain. American parents used it in great numbers when Susan was at its height, throughout the 1940s, '50s and '60s. It faded there when Susan faded. In Britain it tended to be used after Susan had faded, so that it reached its minor peak in the early 1970s. By the early 1980s it was showing all the signs of receding into the background in all English-speaking countries. Variants **Suzan, Suzane** and **Suzann** occur fairly often, as do **Susanne, Susann**. Rarer variants are **Suzzanne, Suzzane**, both used since 1960.

Suzette (f) French diminutive of **Suzanne** used in English-speaking countries since the 1940s. Strongly associated with the *crêpe Suzette*, a pancake with an orange sauce.

Suzy (f) Variant of **Susie** used mainly since the 1960s. **Suzie** also occurs.

Suzzanne (f) See **Suzanne**. **Suzzane** also occurs.

Swaley (m) Surname derived from a place name/river name, used from time to time as a first name. Original meaning is probably 'winding stream'. Also found are **Swailey, Swale, Swales**.

Swinbourne (m) English place name/ surname, originally referring to a 'brook used by swine'. Found as a first name in the 19th c., together with similar names such as **Swinborne, Swinburne, Swindel, Swinfen, Swinford, Swinton**.

Sybel (f) Formerly a fairly common variant of **Sibyl/Sybil**.

Sybella (f) Form of Latin *Sibylla* in occasional use. See also **Sibyl**.

Sybil (f) For the origin of the name see **Sibyl**, though Sybil has been the commonest form since the beginning of the 19th c.

Sybilla (f) Common variant of Latin *Sibylla* in the 19th c. See also **Sibyl**.

Sydney (m) Very common variant of **Sidney**.

Sydonia (f) See **Sidonia**. **Sydonah** also occurs.

Sylvanus (m) Occasional variant of **Silvanus**.

Sylvester (m) See **Silvester**.

Sylvia (f) See **Silvia**, the original form of the name, though Sylvia has been the usual spelling in modern times.

Symon (m) Modern variant of **Simon**, in use since the 1950s.

Syndonia (f) Variant of **Sidonia**. Miss E. G. Withycombe offers the proof of the link between the two names, quoting **Sindonia**, but the form in 19th c. records is always with the -y-.

T

Tabatha (f) Modern variant of **Tabitha**.

Tabitha (f) Aramaic 'gazelle'. Biblical, N.T., Acts 9:36, where the name is the equivalent of Greek **Dorcas**. Introduced in the 17th c. and fairly frequently used until the beginning of the 20th c. Seems to have died out in Britain soon after Beatrix Potter had introduced the character Tabitha Twitchet the cat, obviously playing on the idea of 'tabby cat'. Reappeared in Britain in the 1960s as **Tabatha**, probably picked up from the sequel to the television series *Bewitched* (the name of Samantha's daughter). The same series reintroduced the name to American parents, where the name has occurred since the 1960s as Tabitha, Tabatha, **Tabotha**.

Tacey (f) See **Silence**.

Talbot (m) Surname of unknown origin, regularly used as a first name since the middle of the 19th c., though less so since the beginning of the 20th c. There was once a kind of dog called a 'talbot', but it was probably the aristocratic family which gave its name to the dog, not *vice versa*.

Taliesin (m) Welsh 'radiant brow'. The name of a famous 6th c. poet, occasionally used in modern times in Wales.

Talisha (f) Probably a changed form of **Talitha** to create a new name. **Talicia** is also found. Both forms are used mainly by black American families.

Talitha (f) Aramaic 'little girl'. Biblical, N.T., Mark 5:41, 'Taking her by the hand he said to her, "Talitha cumi"; which means, "Little girl, I say to you, arise." ' The name has been in use since 1800. In 1862 *The Times* noted a girl who had been called Talitha-Cumi. Talitha is not frequently used, but modern examples are easily found in the U.S., especially amongst the black community. **Taletha** occurs, and **Taleta** is probably a variant.

Tallulah (f) American Indian place name which probably meant 'running water'. Tallulah Falls, in Georgia, is one of the scenic wonders of the American South. It was the name of Tallulah Bankhead's paternal grandmother and passed on to the actress when she was born in 1902. In her autobiography Miss Bankhead wrote that the name had 'been no handicap to me. It has been argued that had I been christened **Jane** or **Julia** it is unlikely I would ever have gotten out of Huntsville, Alabama, place of my birth.' However, she admits that as a child the name embarrassed her and she once changed it to **Elizabeth** when she moved to another school. Ethel Barrymore also advised her to change it to **Barbara** or **Mary**. All this advice was rightly ignored, and during her long career Miss Bankhead received many letters from her fans about her name. An Irish poet told her it meant a 'colleen' in Gaelic, while in Israel the name was said to mean 'precipice' or 'rocky'. Although the name is closely associated with Tallulah Bankhead, it was clearly in more general use at one time. It appears in comparative lists of white names used in the American South before 1930 in Heller's *Black Names in America*.

Tamar (f) Hebrew 'date palm'. A favourite name in the East, suggesting beauty and gracefulness. Biblical, O.T., the name of several women. In regular use since the 16th c., though since the 1930s it has been virtually replaced by its Russian form **Tamara**. Early records record the name in forms such as **Tamah**, **Tamer**, **Tamor**, **Tamour**, **Tayma**, **Thama**, **Thamar**, **Thamer**.

Tamara (f) Russian form of **Tamar**. Queen Tamara was ruler of Georgia in the 12th c. Occurs frequently in Russian literature, and notably in a poem by Lermontov. Began to be used in English-speaking countries in the 1930s and attracted the interest of parents in 1970s to a considerable extent. In the 1980s is quietly used in Britain, while black American parents especially favour

it. Occurs also as **Tamarra**, **Tammara**, **Tammera**, **Tamra**, **Tamyra**.

Tamaris (f) See **Damaris**.

Tamasin(e) (f) Modern forms of **Tamsin** used mainly in Britain.

Tamer (f) See **Tamar**. Occurs very regularly in 19th c. records.

Tammie (f) See **Tammy** (f). **Tami** and **Tamie** also occur.

Tammy (m) Pet form of **Tammas**, the Lowland Scots form of **Thomas**, used independently. Now rarely used for men. See **Tammy** (f).

Tammy (f) Pet form of **Tamara**, **Tameka**, **Tamika**, **Tamsin**, etc., used as a name in its own right. Appeared suddenly in the U.S. in 1957. Reached Britain by the early 1960s. Well used until 1975, then faded in the U.S. and Britain. Still found in considerable numbers in the early 1980s, but had clearly passed its peak. **Tammie** is a fairly frequent variant. **Tami** and **Tamie** also occur. A popular song called *Tammy* had a considerable impact on the use of the name.

Tamor (f) See **Tamar**. **Tamour** also occurs.

Tamsin (f) Early pet form of **Thomasin**. The name is thought of as Cornish because it appears to have survived in Cornwall at a time when it was virtually obsolete elsewhere. Isolated examples of Tamsin and **Tamzen** are found in the mid-19th c., but the real revival of the name in Britain began in the late 1950s. Tamsin became the usual modern form, but variants include **Tamasin**, **Tamasine**, **Tamsyn**, **Tamzin**. **Tasmin** and **Tasmine** are also found in modern times, and may be deliberate or accidental variants of Tamsin. In the early 1980s British parents were still using the name quietly. Remains rare elsewhere.

Tana (f) Apparently a pet form of **Tania/Tanya**, used infrequently as a name in its own right.

Tania (f) See **Tanya**.

Tanis (f) First appears in *Babbit* (1923) by Sinclair Lewis and has since been used occasionally in both Britain and the U.S. Suggestions as to its origin include an alteration of **Tania**, a Biblical place name, a variant of **Tansy** (**Athanasius**), or a use of the Irish surname Tansey.

Tanisha (f) This name is possibly linked to a Hausa day-name, given to children born on a Monday, but as with so many of the names popular in modern times with black American families, its origin is obscure. No doubt about the name's popularity, however, in the early 1980s. Tanisha is the usual form, but it occurs also as **Taneisha, Tanesha, Taneshea, Taneshia, Tanicha, Taniesha, Tanish, Tenecia, Teneisha, Tenesha, Teniesha, Tenisha.**

Tanith (f) The name of the goddess of love in Carthage. Has been noted in Britain in the 1970s, while **Tanitha** occurs in the U.S. **Tanita** is also found. These may simply be 'invented' modern names based on **Tania**. None is frequently used as yet.

Tanja (f) See **Tanya**.

Tansy (f) The name of the flower, ultimately from Greek *athanasia* 'immortality', used as a first name in both Britain and the U.S., especially since 1960. Tansy seems to have appealed to writers of fiction. One novel of the name, by Tickner Edwardes, published in 1921, contains the comment: ''Tis a queer name for a Christian woman.' 'It is a nickname she gave herself when she was a child. It should be Nancy by rights.' In another novel called *Tansy* Maureen Peters says that 'Tansy was not a real name at all. It was not a decent God-fearing name.' The explanation given for the name in this book is that the mother had worn a wreath of tansy flowers on the day of her marriage, and had counted off her children of the future on the blossoms.

Tanya (f) Abbreviated form of Russian **Tatiana**, a feminine of **Tatianus**, diminutive of **Tatius**, the name of a king of the Sabines (Titus Tatius). In modern Italian this name is **Tazio**. Tatiana is occasionally used in English-speaking countries – more in the U.S. than Britain – but Tanya and its variants have been

regularly used since 1940, and with considerable frequency in the 1970s. In the early 1980s it was clearly going out of fashion. Tanya has been the most popular spelling in modern times, with **Tania** the main variant. Other forms include **Tana, Tanja, Tannia, Tarnia, Tarnya.**

Tara (f) From an Irish word meaning 'hill'. There are several places called Tara in Ireland, the most famous being in County Meath. According to Irish legend the ancient Irish kings resided in Tara's halls, i.e., in the fortress or castle built at Tara. The poet Thomas Moore made much of the name in his *Irish Melodies* (1814). In recent years it has named a major character in the TV series *All My Children*. By 1940 the first name Tara was in use in the U.S. Use of the name has been increasing very slowly in America ever since. In Britain the name was introduced in the late 1960s (by *The Avengers* on TV) and became popular, though by the early 1980s it appeared to have passed its peak.

Taran (f) See **Taryn**.

Tarin(a) (f) See **Taryn**.

Tarnia (f) See **Tanya**. **Tarnya** also occurs.

Tarry (m) Probably a variant of **Terry** rather than a use of the word 'tarry' as a name. Occurs only rarely.

Taryn (f) Innovation of the 1970s, presumably extending **Tara** with a fashionable name sound. **Tarryn** also occurs, as do **Taran** and **Tarin**. **Taryna, Tarina** extend the name still further. The various forms of the name are now being used in the U.S. and Britain.

Tasha (f) Pet form of **Natasha** used to some extent in the 1970s. The immediate source of the name was a television version of Tolstoy's *War and Peace*.

Taylor (m) Occupational surname used as a first name. In Britain it was used fairly often in the 19th c. but has been rare in the 20th c. In the U.S. the name is best known as that of the authoress (Janet) Taylor Caldwell.

Teasdale (m) Place name connected with the River Tees which became a surname, used occasionally as a first name.

Ted (m) Pet form of **Edward** since the Middle Ages. Used as a name in its own right since the 1860s, regularly but infrequently. **Teddie**, more often **Teddy**, is also found, but this has been associated with **Theodore** since the time of President Roosevelt.

Teena (f) Variant of **Tina** in use since the early 1960s. **Tena** also occurs.

Tegan (f) Celtic, variant of Cornish **Tegen**, 'ornament, pretty little thing'. A character from *Dr Who* TV series.

Tegwen (f) Welsh *teg* 'beautiful' + (g)*wen* 'fair'. Usage in the 20th c. has been regular but sporadic. Most used in Wales in the 1920s. **Tegwyn** was also found.

Telford (m) Norman surname, originally indicating one who could 'cut iron', i.e., pierce a knight's armour, used from time to time as a first name.

Temperance (f) The word used as a name. Highly popular amongst the Puritans of the 16th and 17th cc. but then faded. Revived and used throughout the 19th c.

Tempest (m) Probably a use of the surname as a first name, though it appears to be a use of the word and belongs to a 'weather' group of names. The latter would include **Storm, Gale, Raine, Sunny**, all of which have been used as first names. H. E. Bates has a short story about a **Breeze** Anstey, a young lady whose name does not suit her personality, but no real-life example of the name has been noted.

Temple (m) Surname used occasionally as a first name. The surname is one which was often given to foundlings left at the Temple Church in London.

Tena (f) See **Tina**.

Tenisha (f) See **Tanisha**. **Tenecia, Teneisha, Tenesha**, etc., also occur.

Tennant (m) Surname, meaning 'a tenant', used occasionally as a first name. **Tennent** also occurs, as does **Tenant** itself.

Tennessee (m) The name of the U.S. State used as a first name. Made well-known in that role by the American dramatist Tennessee Williams (Thomas Lanier Williams). Occasionally used, including a British example in 1937. Tennessee Williams was himself born in Mississippi, but his family had many connections with Tennessee in earlier times.

Tenny (m) Surname, 'descendant of Denis', used from time to time as a first name. **Tennie** also occurs.

Tennyson (m) Surname of Alfred, Lord Tennyson (1809–92), the poet, used as a first name in Britain in the early 20th c. The surname ultimately derives from **Dennis**.

Terall (f) Extended form of **Terry**, (**Teri, Terri, Terrie**, etc) used mainly in the U.S. since the 1940s. Probably influenced by names like **Beryl, Meryl**. Terall occurs in such variant spellings as **Terral, Terrall, Terrell, Terryl, Teryl, Terriel. Terelyn, Terilyn**, etc., also occur, and the Terall variants could be shortened forms of these.

Terance (m) Form of **Terence** in regular use since the beginning of the 20th c.

Terasa (f) See **Teresa**.

Teree (f) Variant of **Terry** in occasional modern use. **Terree** also occurs.

Terena (f) Feminine form of **Terence** which seems to have been created in the late 1930s. In the 1940s it was being used in the U.S. as both Terena and Terina. British parents soon began to use the name, and usage increased slightly in the 1950s. Terena became the usual form, but **Tereena, Terrena, Terrina** are also found. By the early 1980s examples of any of these were very hard to find anywhere, presumably because Terence had also declined.

Terence (m) Latin *Terentius*, the name of a Roman clan, made famous by the writer Publius Terentius (Terence). Common name amongst the early Christians but rare in English-speaking countries until the 1870s. Irish parents used it as an English form of the native name *Turlough*, but by the beginning of the 20th c. this connection was probably forgotten. In Britain the name slowly became more fashionable until it reached a peak in the 1950s, since when it has faded. In the U.S. the name has been used very consistently, though it has tended to change its form. The original Terence at first gave way to Terrence, but by the early 1980s Terrance was clearly the most popular spelling. Terance also occurs. The name was formerly used by both white and black Americans, but since the 1970s black American families have remained faithful to it. Pet form Terry has been much used as an independent name. Occasional attempts to create a feminine form of the name have led to Tereena, Terelyn, Terena, Terencena, Terenne, Terrene, Terrina, Terrosina, Terrylle. The playwright Terence Rattigan is one of the best-known bearers of the name.

Teresa (f) The origin of this name is not known, though two possible explanations are that it derives from Greek *Therasia*, the name of two islands, or from Greek *theros* 'summer, harvest'. If the first derivation is correct then the original bearer of the name would have been a 'woman of Therasia'. Made famous by St Teresa of Avila (1515–82) and later by St Thérèse of Lisieux (1873–97), 'the Little Flower'. It was probably Irish parents who introduced the name to the rest of Britain and carried it to the U.S., where it began to be used steadily, though at first infrequently, in the early 19th c. In the U.S. was at its most popular in the early 1960s, **Theresa** being by far the more popular spelling. Reached its peak in Britain in the early 1970s, Teresa being the preferred spelling. In the early 1980s both forms were still being reasonably well used in all English-speaking countries. Other modern variants include Terese, Teressa, Terise, Terrise, Theressa, Tressa, Trisa. Terasa occurs, indicating a preference in pronunciation (*ay* in the second syllable). Older variants include Teresia, Tereza, Terresia, Terricia, Theresia, Thereza, Treaser, Tresa, Treza. The following pet forms of the name have all been used independently: Tess, Tessa, Tessie, Teri, Terri, Terrie, Terry, Tracey, Tracy. The American actress Teresa Wright is a well-known bearer of the name.

Térèse (f) Modern variant of Teresa influenced by **Thérèse**. Used mainly in the 1960s, in the U.S. rather than Britain.

Teresita (f) Spanish diminutive of Teresa used infrequently in the U.S.

Teressa (f) Variant of Teresa in use since the 1960s.

Teri (f) Occasional variant of Terri.

Terina (f) See Terena.

Terrance (m) Usual form of Terence in the early 1980s amongst black American families.

Terrence (m) Popular modern form of Terence.

Terri (f) Pet form of Teresa, well used in its own right since the early 1940s in the U.S. Appeared in Britain in the mid-1950s, but by the early 1980s British parents appeared to be turning away from it, whereas American parents still used it regularly. **Terrie** is equally common.

Terry (m) Until the beginning of the 20th c. the occurrences of this name probably reflect a use of the surname *Terry*, a form of **Theodore**. Later use represents the pet form of Terence used independently. The name was most used in the 1950s and '60s. Faded subsequently, perhaps because the feminine form of the name had also been well used.

Terry (f) Pet form of Teresa used independently since the late 1930s. Especially popular in the U.S. in the 1940s, together with its variants Teri, Terree, Terri, Terrie.

Terryl (m) Extended form of Terry used in the 1950s and '60s, mainly by black American parents. The name was perhaps suggested by **Darryl**.

Tersia (f) Also Terza. See Thirza.

Tertius (m) Latin *tertius* 'third'. A name given to a third son, **Tertia** being used for the third girl. Very rarely used.

Tess (f) Pet form of **Teresa** in occasional use as an independent name. The unfortunate heroine of Thomas Hardy's novel *Tess of the D'Urbervilles* did not encourage parents to use her name.

Tessa (f) Pet form of **Teresa** used only occasionally since the beginning of the 20th c. The name occurred earlier in literature in an Italian context, e.g. the Tessa in George Eliot's novel *Romola* (1862) and another in Gilbert and Sullivan's *The Gondoliers* (1889). Burgio, an Italian writer on names, suggests that early instances of the name represent an abbreviation of *Contessa*. Tessa has never been especially popular in English-speaking countries and is rarely used in modern times.

Tessie (f) Diminutive of **Tessa**, rarely used. Made well-known by the British music-hall singer 'Two-ton' Tessie O'Shea.

Tetty (f) Pet form of **Elizabeth** used e.g. by Dr Johnson to his wife in the 18th c. Rare as an independent name.

Tex (m) Back-formation from Texas or Texan, in occasional use as a first name, mainly in the U.S. Made well known by the singing cowboy Tex Ritter (Woodward Ritter) in the late 1930s and '40s.

Thaddeus (m) The Aramaic name of one of the Apostles, mentioned by Matthew and Mark. In Luke he is Judas, son of James. Thaddeus was presumably a surname to distinguish him from Judas Iscariot. There are different theories about the original meaning of the name, but no general agreement amongst scholars. The name has rarely been used in Britain, though it was formerly used in Ireland to anglicize *Tadhg*. Reasonably well used in the U.S. around 1970, occurring also as **Thaddius**. Pet form **Thad** also in use as an independent name.

Thalia (f) Greek *Thaleia* 'bloom, plenty'. The Muse of Comedy in Greek mythology, and one of the three Graces. Occasionally used since the 1930s.

Thamar (f) Mainly 19th c. variant of **Tamar**. **Thama** and **Thamer** also occur.

Thea (f) Pet form of **Dorothea** now used as a name in its own right.

Thekla (f) Greek *theocleia* 'god-famed'. St Thekla was the first virgin martyr, but her name is rarely used in English-speaking countries.

Thelma (f) Invented by the novelist Marie Corelli for the heroine of her novel *Thelma* (1887). It is presumably based on Greek *thelema* 'will'. Began to be used in the 1890s and was especially popular in Britain in the 1920s and '30s. The best-known bearer of the name is Thelma Ritter, the actress and comedienne, whose screen career began in the late 1940s. In the 1980s the name is quietly used, mostly by black American parents.

Theo (m) Pet form of **Theophilus, Theodore**, used independently from time to time since the 1880s.

Theobald (m) Germanic 'people-bold'. Early pronunciation of this name was Tibald, and many modern surnames which begin with *Tibb-* can be derived from it. Seems to have faded after the 17th c. An attempt was made to resurrect it in Britain in the 19th c., but did not succeed. Seldom if ever used in modern times.

Theodora (f) Feminine form of **Theodore**. **Dorothea** contains the same elements in reverse order. The use of the name has almost exactly paralleled that of Theodore, except that it faded rather earlier in both Britain and the U.S.

Theodore (m) Greek *theodoros* 'God's gift'. Common name in the Christian inscriptions of the Roman Empire, and the name of several saints. Used regularly if infrequently in English-speaking countries from the 17th c. onwards. In Britain rather rarely used since the 1930s. The much greater use of the name in the U.S. in modern times has been due to President Theodore Roosevelt (1858–1919). The novelist Theodore Dreiser has also kept the name before the public. In the early 1980s it was still being regularly used in the U.S. (in almost equal numbers by white and black parents). In Britain by 1980 the name had become rare. Welsh variant of the name is **Tudor**. Pet forms are **Ted** or **Theo**.

Theodoric (m) Old German 'ruler of the people'. It became **Dietrich**, Dutch **Diederic** and English **Derek/Derrick**, and is known to English-speaking countries primarily in the latter forms.

Theodosia (f) Greek 'God's gift'. The name of a 4th c. saint. First found in Britain in the 17th c. It became slightly more common in the 18th c., and was regularly used throughout the 19th c. Then became virtually obsolete, though an isolated instance of the name was noted in 1940.

Theophilus (m) Greek *Theophilos* 'friend of God'. Biblical, N.T. The Acts of the Apostles and St Luke are addressed to a Theophilus. The name was well used in the 17th c. but gradually declined through the 18th and 19th cc. Rarely used in modern times. Even rarer now is the feminine form **Theophila**, which was occasionally used in the 19th c.

Theresa (f) Usual form in the U.S. of Teresa. See that name for a full discussion.

Thérèse (f) French form of **Teresa**, made famous by St Thérèse of Lisieux, 'the Little Flower'. This form of the name regularly used in English-speaking countries since the 1920s.

Theresia (f) See **Teresa**.

Theressa (f) See **Teresa/Teressa**.

Thersa (f) Also **Thersea**, **Therza**. See **Thirza**.

Thetis (f) Greek *tithemi* 'to dispose'. The name of the mother of Achilles. Rarely used.

Thirza (f) Greek 'pleasant'. Biblical, O.T., Numbers 27:1. Occasionally used in the 17th c. Found regularly but infrequently throughout the 19th c. and continued in use until 1950. Appears in 19th c. records in such variant forms as **Thersa**, **Thersea**, **Therza**, **Thirsa**, **Thursa**, **Thurza**, **Tirza**, **Tirzah**.

Thomas (m) Aramaic 'twin'. Biblical, N.T., name of one of the twelve Apostles, referred to three times in St John

as 'Thomas, called the twin'. Used by priests before the Norman Conquest but not in general use until Thomas à Beckett (1118–70) made it famous. His murder in Canterbury Cathedral caused Canterbury to become a centre of pilgrimage, while Thomas became one of the most frequently used names in the English-speaking world for centuries. In Britain it faded sharply from the 1920s, though there were signs of a possible revival in the early 1980s. Still being fairly well used in the U.S. at that time, but nevertheless at its lowest point in the popularity polls since records began. **Tomas**, the form of the name in several languages, is sometimes used, and the pet forms **Tom**, **Tommy** (**Tommey**, **Tomey**), **Thom** have long been used as names in their own right. Feminine forms include **Tomina**, **Tommina**, **Thomasina**, **Thomasin**, **Thomasine**, **Thomasena**, **Tamsin**, etc. Several of the surnames which are linked with the name occur as first names, e.g., **Thompson**, **Thomson**, **Tomson**. A great many famous men have borne the name, including the American presidents Thomas Jefferson (1743–1826) and Thomas Woodrow Wilson (1856–1924). Writers who have borne the name include Thomas Hardy and T. S. Eliot. Thomas Alva Edison (1847–1931) is another famous namebearer, but the name does not seem to have been an especially lucky one for actors.

Thomasena (f) See **Thomasina**.

Thomasin (f) Feminine form of **Thomas** in use by the 15th c. Camden, writing in 1605, mentions that the name had already developed into *Tamesin*. Lyford (1655) also gives it as *Thamasin* in its variant form. Neither Tamesin nor Thamasin seems to have survived, but Thomasin and **Thomazin** were in use in the 1830s, along with **Thomason**, which was probably a variant of the first name rather than a transferred use of the surname. **Thomazine** occurs in the 1840s, and **Thomazine** was restored to fairly regular use from 1850. **Thomasina** then appeared in the 1860s and was the form which survived best, being regularly used until the 1960s. Probably faded then because **Tamsin** and its variants had become the fashionable forms, in Britain at least. American parents still continue to make modest use of Thomasina, Thomasine and Thomazine in modern times, together with an occasional **Thomasa**. British parents since the late 1950s have very clearly favoured Tamsin, **Tamsyn**, Tamzen, **Tamzin**, forms which seem to be unknown in the U.S. They survived longest in Cornwall, though they were not originally Cornish. One reason for the early use of Thomasin might lie in the traditional belief that the Apostle Thomas had a twin sister. In literature there is Thomasin Yeobright in Thomas Hardy's *Return of the Native* (1878).

Thomasina (f) Latinized form of **Thomasin**, restored to use in the 1860s. Used regularly until displaced in Britain by **Tamsin** in the 1960s. Continues to be quietly used in the U.S.

Thomasine (f) Variant of **Thomasin** used very regularly between the 1850s and 1900. Still occurs in the early 1980s in the U.S.

Thomason (m) Also **Thomeson**, **Thomison**. See **Thompson**.

Thomazin(e) (f) Variants of **Thomasin** used in the 19th c.

Thompson (m) Surname 'son of Tom' used as a first name. Common as a first name throughout the 19th c., but usage suddenly ceased at the beginning of the 20th c. **Thomson**, **Thomeson**, **Thomison**, **Thomason**, **Tomson** were also used, but no instances have been noted, in Britain or the U.S., since 1904. Some of the 19th c. instances, used for girls, are variants of **Thomasin**.

Thora (f) Variant of **Thyra** in occasional use. The British actress Thora Hird is the best-known bearer of the name.

Thorley (m) Place name 'thorn clearing' and surname used from time to time,

especially in the 19th c., as a first name. **Thornley** was also found.

Thornton (m) Common English place name 'settlement amongst thorns', also a surname, used with some regularity as a first name since the 1830s. The best-known bearer of the name is the writer Thornton Wilder.

Thursday (m) See **Tuesday**.

Thurston (m) Surname 'Thor's stone' used as a first name, mainly in the 19th c. Thurston has been the more usual form, but **Thurstan** also occurs. **Thurstain** is a rare variant. Little used in modern times, except in Canada.

Thurza (f) Fairly common variant of **Thirza**. **Thursa** also occurs.

Thyra (f) Earlier form of a name which in Scandinavia is now usually **Tyra**. It is thought to mean 'Thor-battle'. Rarely used in English-speaking countries.

Thyrza (f) See **Thirza**.

Tia (f) This appears to be the Spanish word for 'aunt'. The liqueur *Tia Maria* is widely known, and some parents possibly interpret Tia as the first name, with Maria as another given name. In the U.S., where Tia is now being well used, especially by black American parents, it may be a short form of **Tiana** or **Tiara**, also popular names amongst black American families in the early 1980s. Used in the U.S. since the 1940s. First appeared in Britain in the early 1960s.

Tiffany (f) Greek *Theophania* 'manifestation of God'. The Old French form was *Tifaine*. Originally a name given to girls born on the Epiphany (January 6), but it became almost obsolete until the 1960s. The film *Breakfast at Tiffany's* (1961) made the name of the fashionable New York jeweller's widely known, and managed to associate the name with Audrey Hepburn, and with luxury. Parents quickly responded and by the late 1970s it was being especially well used by black American families, often in variant forms such as **Tifani**, **Tiffani**, **Tiffini**, **Tiffiny**, **Tiffanie**, **Tiffiney**, **Tiffaney**, **Tiffney**.

Tilda (f) Pet form of **Matilda** used on rare occasions.

Tilden (m) Surname from a place name 'fertile valley', regularly used as a first name during the 19th c.

Tilly (f) Pet form of **Matilda** used in the Middle Ages to some extent and reintroduced at the end of the 19th c. Used in modern times, though rarely. Also found as **Tilley, Tillie**.

Tim (m) Pet form of **Timothy** used independently. In regular but quiet use since the 1850s.

Timmy (m) Pet form of **Timothy** used independently mainly in the 1960s, and in the U.S. rather than Britain. **Timmie** is a rare variant.

Timothy (m) Greek *Timotheos* 'honouring God'. Biblical, N.T. St Timothy was the companion of St Paul. Fairly common name amongst the early Christians. Rarely used in England in the 16th and 17th cc. but became more usual in the 18th c. In regular if infrequent use until the mid-1930s, when it became fashionable. Reached a peak in Britain and the U.S. in the 1960s, and in the early 1980s was still being fairly well used in both countries, though slipping out of fashion. **Timmothy** occurs as a rare variant, as does **Timothey**. **Tim** is sometimes used as a name in its own right, and **Timmy** occurs. **Timmie** is rare. The name seems to have defied the parents who like to create a feminine form, though **Timothea** has been noted, together with one example (in the U.S.) of **Timaula**. Dickens has made Tiny Tim well known, the crippled son of Bob Cratchit in the Christmas stories. He also gave the name to the fat clerk of the Cheeryble brothers in *Nicholas Nickleby*.

Tina (f) Pet form of **Christina, Clementina, Martina, Albertina, Ernestina, Bettina**, etc., used in its own right since the beginning of the 20th c., but at its most popular in all English-speaking countries throughout the 1960s. By the early 1980s had clearly faded on all sides. Tina has been the usual modern form,

but **Teena, Tena** occur.

Tirza(h) (f) Variants of **Thirza**.

Tisha (f) Ultimately a pet form of **Letitia**. It may have been responsible for, or be a back-formation from, **Latisha**.

Titus (m) Roman personal name of unknown meaning. Biblical, N.T., 2 Cor 2:13. Name of a Gentile disciple of St Paul. Well used in the 18th and 19th cc. In the U.S. still in occasional use, especially by black American parents. In Longfellow's *Golden Legend* Titus is a penitent thief who is promised a place in paradise by Jesus. In English history Titus Oates was the inventor of The Popish Plot in 1678. He swore that he had discovered a plot which could put England under the command of the pope, at the expense of many Protestant lives. This caused many Roman Catholics to be put to death for alleged conspiracy. Oates was eventually whipped and imprisoned for his lies. Italian/Spanish form of this name is **Tito**, which occurs very rarely in English-speaking countries.

Tobias (m) Hebrew 'God is good'. Biblical, O.T., Neh. 2:10. The name was well used in the 16th c., then reappeared in the early 19th c. and has continued to be used steadily but quietly since. Since the 1950s there has been a tendency to use the pet form **Toby** as an independent name. Tobias Smollett (1721–71) was one of the major 18th c. novelists, though not as gifted as Laurence Sterne, who created at that time Uncle Toby in his *Tristram Shandy*. Shakespeare also gave us Sir Toby Belch in his *Twelfth Night*, while Dickens has Toby Veck in *The Chimes*. Since the 19th c. Toby has been the traditional name of a small dog incorporated into *Punch and Judy* performances. The choice of name is presumably a reference to the apocryphal *Book of Tobit*, in which Tobias, the son of Tobit, is said to have a dog. Tobias's dog, by humorous tradition, is called *Moreover*: 'Moreover the dog went with him.' A toby jug, or Toby Philpot, derives its name from the name of a character in an 18th c. play, *Poor Soldier*.

Toby (m) Pet form of **Tobias** used independently. **Tobi** also occurs.

Todd (m) Surname 'fox-hunter' used as a first name. Todd is now the usual form, though the name appeared in the U.S. in the late 1930s as **Tod**. **Todor** exists in Hungarian as a form of **Teodor** (**Theodore**), but this is merely coincidental. President Abraham Lincoln married Mary Todd and named his son Robert Todd Lincoln, but it is difficult to see how this fact could have caused Todd to become rather fashionable in the U.S. around 1970. By 1980 it was once again out of fashion. In Britain the name was mainly used in the 1960s.

Tom (m) Pet form of **Thomas** used in its own right since the 18th c. At its most popular in the 1870s. In the early 1980s it was being quietly used in Britain and the U.S., though only white American families seem to favour it. **Thom** occurs occasionally.

Tomasina (f) Also **Tomasine**. See **Thomasina**.

Tommie (m, f) Variant of **Tommy** used mainly in the U.S. in modern times. Usage favours the masculine name about three times as often as the feminine name, though the latter is well established. American girls have been called Tommie since at least 1940.

Tommina (f) Feminine form of **Thomas** in occasional use. **Tomina** also occurs.

Tommy (m) Pet form of **Thomas**, used very rarely in the 19th c. as a name in its own right, but far more common since the 1940s. Tommy Atkins was the generic name for a private soldier in the British army, hence 'tommy' came to mean 'soldier'. **Tommie** occurs regularly in the U.S. but is rare in Britain. **Tomey** and **Tommey** are older variants.

Toney (m) See **Tony**.

Toni (f) Pet form of **Antonia** or **Antoinette**, used as a name in its own right since the 1940s. In the early 1980s was being used slightly more in the U.S. than in Britain. **Tonie** is an infrequent variant.

Tonia (f) Pet form of **Antonia** used independently. In regular but quiet use since the 1930s. Taken up in the early 1950s by black American families, especially, who quickly showed a preference for the spelling **Tonya**. **Tonja** also occurs but is rare, and **Tonyia** is found. Tonya appeared in Britain in the 1960s and tended to replace Tonia. In the U.S. the name reached its peak in 1970. Still being well used in 1980, but fading.

Tonja (f) See **Tonia**.

Tony (m) Pet form of **Antony** used independently since the beginning of the 20th c., though in significant numbers only since the 1930s. In modern times black American parents have naturally made good use of the name, since they are also fond of **Antony**, **Antonio** and **Antoine**. The name is sometimes given to girls, though the usual feminine form is **Toni**. Tony Curtis (Bernard Schwarz), Tony Martin (Alfred Norris), Tony Randall and Tony Hancock are amongst the actors who have helped make the name known.

Tonya (f) Preferred modern spelling of **Tonia**, a pet form of **Antonia** or **Antoinette**. Black American families have shown particular interest in this name since the 1950s. **Tonja** also occurs.

Topsy (f) The name of a black slave girl in Harriet Beecher Stowe's *Uncle Tom's Cabin* (1852), used intermittently, mainly in the 19th c. Sometimes found as **Toppsy**, **Topsey**, **Topsie**. Occurs in Heller's lists of unusual names in *Black Names in America*. Another name in the slave lists gives a clue as to its possible origin, namely **Topsail**. We have the documentary evidence of a seaman who regularly transported slaves that names such as **Main-Stay**, **Rope-Yarn** 'and various other sea-phrases' were given to slaves while they were on board. Some of these names obviously stuck. It is easy to see how Topsail would have become Topsy in normal speech. It is therefore likely that Mrs Stowe had known a real slave who bore the name.

Torquil (m) Old Norse name which contains the name of the god *Thor* and a second element which is obscure, though it is often said to be 'kettle', i.e. 'cauldron'. In early use in Britain, responsible for many surnames such as *Thirkell*, *Thurkle*. In modern times has been mainly associated with Scotland, and is often looked upon as vaguely aristocratic. Used only rarely.

Totty (f) Pet form of **Charlotte**. **Tottie** is also found. Used in the 19th c. when Charlotte was a popular name.

Tracey (f) Common variant of **Tracy** since 1940. Previously a variant of the male name. **Tracee** is a rare modern variant.

Traci(e) (f) Variants of **Tracy**.

Tracy (m) Norman place name which became an English surname, occasionally used as a first name, especially in the 19th c. A literary example occurs in Dickens's *The Pickwick Papers*. Tracy Tupman is the member of the Pickwick Club who likes food and ladies, but settles for the former. Never frequent in the 19th c., and since the 1950s has been entirely overtaken by the feminine name. **Tracey** was the usual variant.

Tracy (f) Helena Swan, writing in 1900, mentions Tracy as a pet form of **Teresa**, echoing Charlotte Yonge's opinion of the 1860s. The intervening stages from Teresa to Tracy are perhaps marked by **Treza**, used to name girls in 1847 and 1862, **Treesy** (1884), **Treacy** (1898). These forms were very rare as names in their own right, but perhaps indicate the kind of pet forms of Teresa which were being used in some families. The modern run of Tracy (**Tracey**, **Traci**, **Tracie**, **Trasey**) began in the U.S. in the early 1940s. This seems to indicate a direct link with the film *The Philadelphia Story* (1940), in which Katharine Hepburn was the idle heiress Tracy Lord. Remained in very quiet use in the U.S., and was very rare in Britain, until 1956. At that point the re-make of *The Philadelphia Story* was released as *High Society*, with Grace Kelly as Tracy

Samantha Lord. This film did much to establish Tracy far more firmly, and also seems to have had an important effect on **Samantha** and **Kelly** as girls' names. Tracy and its variants went on to be used very intensively in all English-speaking countries, reaching a peak around 1970. All forms of the name have since faded. Some parents, e.g. the actress Jean Simmons, had Spencer Tracy in mind when giving the name.

Travis (m) The surname, which probably indicated someone who was a 'toll-collector', used as a first name. Infrequently used in Britain but well used in the U.S. and Australia. **Travers** is a variant form of the surname which also occurs as a first name.

Trayton (m) Appears to be a place name/surname, with a meaning something like 'settlement near trees', but no traces of such a place name have been found, and the surname is very rare, if it exists at all. Trayton nevertheless occurs regularly as a first name throughout the 19th c., and was last used in that role in the 1930s.

Treena (f) See **Trina**.

Trefor (m) Welsh form of **Trevor**. In steady use in Wales since 1900.

Trena (f) See **Trina**.

Trent (m) English river name, place name and surname used regularly but infrequently in the U.S. as a first name.

Tresa (f) See **Teresa**.

Trevor (m) Normal English form of Welsh **Trefor**, which was a place name before it became a personal name. The meaning is either 'great homestead' or 'sea homestead'. First began to be used in the 1860s but reached its peak in Britain a hundred years later, being popular throughout the 1950s and '60s. The name was already becoming more popular when the actor Trevor Howard began his screen career in the 1940s, but he helped to make it more widely known. By the early 1980s Trevor was being quietly used in Britain, while in the U.S., where the name has never been a favourite, it continued to be used from time to time. Is occasionally found as

Trevar, Trever, and attempts to create a feminine form of the name have led to Trevina, Treva.

Treza (f) See Tresa.

Tricia (f) Pet form of Patricia (occasionally Beatrice), used as a name in its own right since the 1950s. Trichia is also found, and Trisha is frequent.

Trina (f) Pet form of Katrina, Catrina, Catriona in use as an independent name since the 1940s. Treena, Trena, Treina are found, but are less common. Black American parents are especially fond of the name. It has developed its own diminutives, such as Trinette, Trinita.

Trisha (f) Phonetic form of Tricia in use since the late 1960s.

Trissie (f) Pet form of Beatrice which has occasionally been used independently. Tris also occurs, together with the extended form Trissina.

Tristan (m) Dauzat explains this name as Pictish Drustan, which became Dristan. Folk-etymology caused the name to become Tristan by association with French triste 'sad', a meaning which seemed appropriate to the legendary knight who loved Iseult. Usual form of the name in English has been Tristram, but Wagner's opera Tristan und Isolde has kept that form of the name before the public's eye. In Britain much publicity was given in recent times to the island Tristan da Cunha, named for a Portuguese admiral, whose inhabitants were forced to take refuge in Britain in 1961 because of a volcanic eruption. Use of the name has slightly increased in Britain since then, also because of the attention focused on one of the characters in the books by James Herriot.

Tristram (m) English form of Tristan. Made famous by the 18th c. novelist Laurence Sterne, author of Tristram Shandy. There is a famous passage in this book in which we learn of Walter Shandy's theories about the importance of first names, and how they affect the characters of those who bear them. The worst name in the universe, according to Walter Shandy, is Tristram, and it is typical of the novel's humour that Shandy's son comes to be baptized with this name by accident. The name is occasionally used in modern times because of its other literary connections. The tale of Tristram and Iseult is parallel to, but much older than, that of Launcelot and Guinevere. Matthew Arnold tells part of the story in his poem Tristram and Iseult (1852). Swinburne also tackled the subject in his Tristram of Lyonesse (1882). Tristram Coffin won the Pulitzer Poetry Prize in 1936, while Tristram E. (Tris) Speaker is a member of the National Baseball Hall of Fame.

Trixie (f) Pet form of Beatrix (Beatrice) used as a name in its own right.

Troy (m) In the 18th c. this was a common name amongst black slaves, as were names such as York, London, Aberdeen, Paris, etc. It is clear that plantation owners often used well known place names when they exercised their assumed right to re-name their charges. As it happens, Troy could have other origins. It is the anglicized version of the Irish surname O Troighthigh, from a word meaning 'foot-soldier'. It is also a surname deriving from Troyes in France. Troy is also the name of several towns in the U.S. which adopted the famous classical place name. The American actor Merle Johnson became Troy Donohue when he began his screen career in the late 1950s, and he probably made the name reasonably fashionable in both Britain and the U.S. for the next twenty years. In the early 1980s it was still being fairly well used in the U.S., but had faded in Britain. Troi also occurs.

Trudy (f) Pet form of names such as Gertrude, Ermintrude, or one of the Germanic names beginning with Trud-. Appeared in English-speaking countries in the mid-1940s (extremely rare before that) and has been used steadily since. Trudie and Trudi are common variants.

Tryphena (f) Greek Tryphaina from tryphe 'delicacy'. Biblical, N.T., Romans 16:12. In regular use from the

16th c. until the beginning of the 20th c., though never especially fashionable. Very rarely used since the 1930s. Found also as **Triphena, Tryphana, Triphenia, Tryphina, Tryphene**.

Tudor (m) Welsh form of **Theodore**. Henry VII was the first king of the Tudor dynasty, which ended with Queen Elizabeth I. Tudor lives on as a modern surname, found chiefly in Wales. The first name is used regularly but infrequently, the first example noted being 1888.

Tuesday (f) The day name used as a first name. The occurrences are modern and have no doubt been inspired by the actress Tuesday Weld, born a Susan. She has explained the name in different ways at different times, but it was possibly a childish corruption of her real first name. Day names are not common in English-speaking countries, though they are normal in some parts of Africa. In former times black slaves sometimes bore such names, which were misunderstood by the plantation owners. The common slave name **Coffee**, for instance, was almost certainly **Kofi**, given to a boy born on a Friday. Days in the year which have special names to themselves do lend those names to children born on them (e.g. **Natalie, Natasha** – Christmas Day), but the ordinary weekdays are rare. A **Monday** Smith was named in 1883, and a **Thursday** Smith in 1868. British examples of a **Friday** and **Sunday** are both found in the 1960s and again may be due indirectly to Tuesday Weld, who first appeared on screen in the 1950s. **Saturday** Keith is a character in *Poet's Pub* (1929) by Eric

Linklater and the name may occur in real life. No instance of **Wednesday** as a first name has been noted.

Turner (m) Surname, which has several possible origins, used as a first name. Regularly converted to first-name use in the 19th c. but now rare in that role.

Twila (f) H. L. Mencken had no doubt that this was a 'florid' invention, making use of a common feminine ending. Seems to have been used first by black American families in the Southern states, and in rather more general use, though never in great numbers, in the 1950s. Possibly suggested by a birth at 'twilight'. **Twyla** is also found.

Ty (m) Pet form of **Tyrone, Tyler, Tyson**, etc., used as a name in its own right since the 1970s.

Tyler (m) Occupational surname used from time to time as a first name. **Tylar** also occurs.

Tyron (m) Variant in the U.S. of **Tyrone**.

Tyrone (m) Irish county name 'Owen's country' used as a first name. The actor Tyrone Power Senior appeared in films from 1915. His son began his screen career in the 1930s, and by the late 1930s the name was in use in the U.S. Did not reach Britain until the 1940s, and was most used there in the 1960s. In the early 1980s still in quiet use, while its use in the U.S. had by that time increased, though only amongst black American parents. White American parents seem to have abandoned the name. **Tyron** occurs regularly as a variant.

Tyson (m) Surname from French *tison*, of several meanings, used from time to time as a first name.

U

Ulric(k) (m) Old English *Wulfric* 'wolf-powerful'. The name survived the Norman Conquest to give rise to surnames such as *Woolrich*, but it then seems to have disappeared. The rare use of the name in modern times is probably a borrowing from German **Ulrich**. Likewise the occasional use of the feminine form **Ulrica**, probably suggested by German **Ulrike** which is used in Germany fairly often. German scholars prefer a derivation from Old German *uodalrik* 'home-powerful'.

Ulysses (m) Latin form of Greek *Odysseus*, hero of Homer's *Odyssey*. The meaning of the name is uncertain, but 'the angry one' and 'wounded in the thigh' are amongst the suggestions. Ulysses S. Grant (1822–85) was 18th President of the U.S.A. The modern use of the name, mainly by black American families, may be with reference to him, though the name was one of the classical group bestowed in former times by slave-owners.

Una (f) Apparently an ancient Irish name of unknown meaning, though formerly associated for no good reason with Irish *uan* 'lamb' and therefore 'translated' into English as **Agnes**. The English poet Edmund Spenser seems to have heard the name while he was staying in Ireland. He naturally associated it with Latin *una* 'one' and used it with that meaning in his *Faerie Queene*. Probably also the meaning that parents in English-speaking countries have mainly had in mind when bestowing the name since the mid-19th c. The actresses Una O'Connor and Una Merkel helped to make the name known from 1930 onwards. In more recent times it has been made known by the actress Una Stubbs (1937-) of 'Till Death Do Us Part'.

Unice (f) Variant of **Eunice**.

Unique (f) The word used as a name. Two instances have been noted recently, both used to name a girl in a black American family.

Unity (f) The word used as a name. The Puritans used it for both boys and girls

in the 17th c., but in the 19th c. it was in occasional use for girls e.g. Unity Mitford. Now very rare, though a **Unita** was noted in the U.S. in 1981, as well as **Unite**, both used to name girls in black American families.

Upton (m) Common English place name and surname, used occasionally as a first name. Associated with the novelist Upton Sinclair (1878–1968). In modern times found slightly more often in the U.S. than in Britain.

Urania (f) The name of one of the Greek Muses (of Astronomy), used very rarely as a first name in English-speaking countries. Compare the occasional use of **Clio**, **Thalia**.

Urban (m) Latin *Urbanus* 'of the city, courteous'. Biblical, N.T., Romans 16:9. The name of several popes in early times. Never frequently used in English-speaking countries, though it occurred regularly throughout the 19th c. Occurs also in its English form **Urbane**, and very rarely as a feminine **Urbana(h)**.

Uriah (m) Hebrew 'my light is the Lord'. Biblical, O.T., 2 Sam 11:3, name of Bathsheba's husband. Used infrequently in the 17th and 18th cc. but very regularly throughout the 19th c. Very rarely used since the 1920s. One might have expected the name to disappear after 1850, when Dickens published *David Copperfield*. Since that time Uriah has been associated with a character in the novel, the hypocritically humble Uriah Heep. The name was sometimes recorded in the 19th c. as **Uria**, or in the Latinized form **Urias**. It was probably an attempt to create a feminine form of the name which led to the unfortunate **Urina**, used in 1843. **Urena** was also used in the 1850s.

Ursula (f) A diminutive of Latin *ursa*, feminine of *ursus* 'bear'. The name of a famous saint martyred by Attila the Hun. A decidedly popular name in England in the 17th c. and regularly used since in all English-speaking countries, though not in great numbers. One of the best-known bearers of the name in modern times is the Swiss-born actress Ursula Andress. **Ursella** and **Ersilia** have been noted as variants of the name.

V

Val (m, f) Pet form of **Valentine** as a boy's name, or **Valerie** as a girl's name. Feminine usage is more usual, though the singer Val Doonican has made it known in Britain in its male role.

Valarie (f) Fairly common variant of **Valerie**.

Valda (f) Feminine form of **Valdemar** or **Waldemar** 'famous ruler'. The name is known in Scandinavia and Yugoslavia, and is listed in the French *Dictionnaire des prénoms* (1980). Also a well-known trade name in France (throat-pastilles). Valda and **Velda** suddenly appeared in Britain in 1914, at the beginning of the First World War. It seems likely that British soldiers heard the name when they went abroad and wrote home about it. Valda is the form of the name which has survived best. Velda has been used less frequently, and seems to have become obsolete in the 1950s. Valda continues to be used regularly but infrequently in Britain. One reason for its survival may lie in its use for a comic-book heroine in the late 1970s. Both forms of the name are very rare in other English-speaking countries.

Valentia (f) Latin *valens* 'strong, healthy'. Fairly common personal name used by the early Christians, and a name the Romans gave to several places, such as Valence in France, Valencia in Spain. For a short time Valentia was also the name of one of the Roman provinces in Britain. The name is used on rare occasions, and is sometimes found as **Valencia**. The surname which derives from the name, **Valence**, has also been used as a first name.

Valentina (f) Feminine form of **Valentine**. Came into general use in the 1880s but had faded by the end of the 19th c.

Revived in the 1950s and '60s, and still being quietly used in the U.S., especially, in the early 1980s.

Valentine (m, f) Latin *Valentinus*, from *valere* 'to be strong'. Common name amongst the early Christians. The famous saint of this name was martyred in the 3rd c. His name was associated with a pagan festival in which lots were drawn for lovers, and that developed into the modern sending of Valentine cards. Used regularly if infrequently since the 16th c. in all English-speaking countries. In Britain its best-known bearer is the actor Valentine Dyall, famous during the Second World War for his radio broadcasts as 'The Man In Black'. A special flurry of interest in the name in Ireland in the 1940s and '50s. Shakespeare used the name in two of his plays. Valentine is one of *The Two Gentlemen of Verona*, also a gentleman in *Twelfth Night*.

Valeria (f) Latin form of **Valerie**, used regularly but infrequently in English-speaking countries since the 1890s

Valerie (f) Latin feminine of *Valerius*, a Roman clan name derived from *valere* 'to be strong'. Very common name amongst the early Christians judging by the frequency with which it occurs in Christian inscriptions of the Roman Empire. St Valeria was an early saint who bore the name. **Valeria** came into use in the 1890s, followed almost immediately by the French form Valerie which soon became the usual form of the name. It went on to achieve considerable popularity through the 1930s to the early 1960s, when it faded in Britain. In the U.S. it became known rather later and lasted well until the late 1960s. Variant forms of the name include **Valarie**,

Valerey, Valery (which is one of the male forms of the name in France) and **Vallerie**.

Van (m) Of several possible origins. The actor Van Heflin adapted his real name **Evan** to arrive at Van. In other cases it is a pet form of **Vance** or **Vanya**. It could be a mistaken use of the 'van' which occurs in many Dutch surnames, where the word simply means 'of' or 'from' and is not a name in its own right. Also an English surname *Van* which means that the original bearer lived near a marsh or fen. As a first name, used far more often in the U.S. than in Britain in modern times. American parents began to use the name in the early 1940s, by which time Van Heflin's screen career had begun, and Van Johnson was also to be seen regularly. By the early 1980s the name had faded in the U.S., having been most used in the 1950s.

Vance (m) Probably a use of the English surname, which indicated residence near a 'marsh' or 'fen'. Some American writers on names claim a Dutch origin for it, but Dr J. van der Schaar does not mention it in his *Woordenboek van Voornamen*. In the U.S. and Britain the name was mildly used in the 1960s.

Vanda (f) Variant of **Wanda**, which would be pronounced *Vanda* by, e.g., German-speakers. First used in the 1870s, but very infrequently until the 1930s. Since then it has been in regular use, mainly in Britain, and not in great numbers. The early use was possibly due to Sir Walter Scott's novel *The Betrothed* (1825) which has a character who bears the name. Scott would have been familiar with the name Wanda, which at that time was used more in Scotland than in any other English-speaking country.

Vanecia (f) Variant in occasional modern use of **Venetia**. **Vanetia** also occurs.

Vanessa (f) Invented by Jonathan Swift (1667–1745) with reference to Esther Vanhomrigh, the woman who fell in love with him. The story of the love-affair is told in his poem *Cadenus and Vanessa*, 'Cadenus' being an anagram of Latin *decanus* 'dean'. Vanessa seems to have remained a purely literary name until the 1920s. Increased use in the 1950s probably due to the actress Vanessa Brown (Smylla Brind), who appeared on screen from 1946. Since the later 1960s the name has more often been associated with the British actress Vanessa Redgrave. Reasonably well used throughout the 1970s in all English-speaking countries and was still well established in the early 1980s. In the U.S. it sometimes takes the form **Vanesse**. Not clear what aroused parental interest in the name in the 1920s, though a novelist might well have used the name for a character. Certainly used by Hugh Walpole for the title of his novel *Vanessa*, published in 1933.

Vanetta (f) Modern name in occasional use, no doubt influenced by the existence of both **Vanessa** (also found as **Venessa**) and **Venitia** (also found as **Vanetia**). **Vannetta** is also found, together with **Veneta, Venetta, Venita**. Other modern forms are **Vanicia, Venicia, Vanesa, Venesa**.

Vania (m, f) Variant of **Vanya** in occasional use. It has sometimes been taken to be a feminine name in English-speaking countries.

Vannetta (f) See **Vanetta**.

Vanslow (m) This name occurs from 1877 onwards, though never in great numbers. Earliest form was **Vancelo**. Vanslow later became the most common form, but **Vansalo, Vanselow** and **Vanslaw** also occur. For the moment the name defies explanation.

Vanya (m) Russian pet form of **John**, or **Ivan**, made famous by Chekhov's play *Uncle Vanya*. Used occasionally in English-speaking countries, and in the variant form of **Vania** is sometimes given to girls.

Vashti (f) Persian 'beautiful'. Biblical, O.T., Esther 1:9. In occasional use since the 1850s.

Vaughan (m) Welsh surname meaning 'little' regularly used as a first name since the 1880s in Britain, but especially in the 1950s and '60s. Associated with the English composer Ralph Vaughan Williams (1872–1958). In the U.S. the name is usually spelt **Vaughn**, and remains in steady use. The American band-leader Vaughn Monroe helped to make the name known. Vaughn has also been used occasionally in Britain since the 1940s.

Vaughn (m) See **Vaughan**.

Vear (m) Probably a variant of **Vere**. A few examples occur in the 19th c.

Veda (f) Variant of **Vida**. The Veda is any one of the four holy books of the Hindus, the word deriving from Sanskrit 'knowledge', but this is coincidental. **Veeda** also occurs.

Veina (f) See **Vina**. **Veenie** also occurs.

Velda (f) Variant of **Valda**.

Velia (f) Greek and Roman place name, also a feminine form of the Roman personal name *Velius*. Suddenly and inexplicably came into use in the late 1930s and was almost obsolete by the end of the 1940s.

Velma (f) Professor George Stewart suggests that this name was an invention, inspired by **Thelma** at the end of the 19th c. He points to the more recent **Delma** to show that the ending of the name was transferable. Actually, the oldest name of this type in use is **Selma**, and at least one example of Velma occurs in 1884, three years before Thelma was launched by the novelist Marie Corelli. (**Zelma** was also in early use as a variant of **Selma**.) Several writers link Velma to **Wilhelmina**. It is not a pet form of that name in any European language, but could have arisen in the U.S. amongst German immigrants, just as **Vilma** probably arose from **Wilma**. Velma has been used fairly regularly since the 1920s. In the U.S. in recent years it has been used by white American parents rather than black, which probably supports the Wilhelmina theory rather than the invented name.

Vena (f) Variant of **Vina**.

Venessa (f) Variant of **Vanessa** in use

since the 1940s, possibly influenced by **Venice**. **Venesa** also occurs.

Venetia (f) Latin form of the place name **Venice**. Use of Venice may have been suggested by **Florence**, which in the 17th c. was still a boy's name. Camden (1605) also suggests that it was a convenient way to hide the pagan reference in **Venus**, used at the time. The progression may therefore have been Venus – Venice – Venetia. Venetia Anastasia Stanley was a famous 17th c. beauty who married Sir Kenelm Digby, courtier and scholar, putting her notorious life behind her and becoming a model wife. In spite of this recommendation, use of the name seems to have died out almost completely by the beginning of the 18th c. Not restored until the beginning of the 19th c. when it made a special appeal to novelists in search of a name for a heroine, e.g. Benjamin Disraeli's *Venetia* (1837). The name had little popular success and has never been frequently used. Italian **Venezia** occurs very occasionally as a first name, as does French **Venise**. Many name-books continue to propound the curious theory, advanced by Charlotte Yonge, that Venetia was a translation of Welsh **Gwyneth**. This was based on a belief that Venetia was connected with the Russian form of **Benedict**, namely **Venedict** 'blessed' and was thus connected with Welsh *gwyn* which can have that meaning.

Venetta (f) See **Vanetta**. **Veneta** also occurs.

Venia (f) Variant of **Vena**, itself a form of **Vina**.

Venice (f) William Camden (1605) remarks that the name **Venus** was sometimes turned into Venice, presumably to hide the connection with the pagan goddess. Perhaps Venice, in its turn, was an acceptable Christian name because **Florence** was already in use. Venice did not survive as a normal first name, but was revived in the 19th c. significantly when Florence was beginning to become fashionable. By this time any connection with Venus was no doubt forgotten, and literary references to the name always link it to the place name. Many of the girls who were called Venice had actually been named **Venetia**. This occurs in modern times as **Venecia**. **Vennice** is also found in the U.S., where the name is used rather more often than in Britain in the early 1980s.

Venita (f) See **Vanetta**.

Venus (f) The name of an Italian goddess who came to be identified with *Aphrodite*, goddess of beauty and love. The name was in use in the 16th c., since Camden (1605) was able to describe it as 'a fit name for a good wench'. However, he added that 'for shame it is turned of some to **Venice**'. Venus was regularly in use as a slave name in the 18th c., and has mainly survived as a black American name. Found in Britain to some extent in the 19th c., but very rarely used since 1925.

Vera (f) A name common to many Slavic countries, deriving from a word meaning 'faith'. On its introduction to English-speaking countries in the 1870s it was associated with Latin *vera*, feminine of *verus* 'true'. The name was used by Ouida in her novel *Moths* (1860), but this had almost no impact on the use of the name. Began to be used regularly, however, from the 1880s, was reinforced by Marion Crawford's use of it in 1890 in his *A Cigarette-Maker's Romance*, and quickly became highly fashionable in Britain. Reached its peak in the 1920s before fading sharply. In the early 1980s is used very quietly in the U.S. and is rare in Britain. British parents no doubt associate the name with Vera Lynn, who was the 'Forces' Sweetheart' during World War Two, a singer whose voice and personality continued to be greatly admired long after the war had ended. The actress Vera Miles has also helped to spread the name.

Verdon (m) Surname indicating that the original bearer of the name came from *Verdun* in France. Occasionally used as a first name. See also **Verdun**.

Verdun (m) French place name. The defence of Verdun against the Germans in World War One (1916) was one of the longest actions in the entire war, costing countless lives. The name was first used in Britain in 1916, but it continued to be used in Britain long after the war had ended – e.g. the name was given to a British boy born in 1947.

Vere (m) French place name which became an aristocratic English surname. Used regularly as a first name from the 1850s, but rather rare since 1920. Does not seem to have reached the U.S.

Verena (f) Diminutive of Latin *vera*, feminine of *verus* 'true'. The name of a saint who is especially revered in Switzerland. Occurs sporadically in English-speaking countries. Also found as **Verina**.

Verity (f) The word used as a name. This was another of the Puritan virtue names introduced in the 16th and 17th cc. Re-introduced in the 1930s, and regularly, if quietly, used ever since. **Verita** also occurs.

Verlie (m) French place name which became an English surname, used occasionally as a first name. **Verley** also occurs.

Verna (f) Perhaps a feminine form of **Vernon**, or based on the Spanish word for 'green', or on Latin *verna* 'Spring'. In favour of the latter derivation is the fact that **Vernal** is also used as a modern first name. Vernal means 'happening in the Spring, youthful, fresh'. The Romans had the name Verna which was used for a 'house-born slave'. Just possible that the name was given by slave-owners with that meaning in mind, since it occurs in Puckett's lists of slave names; but this is more likely to be coincidental. If the name is a classical one, it is more likely to be a shortened form of **Laverna**. First occurs in Britain in the 1880s. Used very steadily until the 1960s, then faded. By the early 1980s had also faded in the U.S. The American actress Verna Felton helped spread the name in the 1950s.

Vernetta (f) Diminutive of **Verna** used
since 1940, mainly in the U.S. **Vernita**
also occurs.

Vernie (f) Probably a pet form of **Verna** or
an independent feminine form of **Vernon**. In rare use since the 1880s.

Vernon (m) French place name 'alder
tree' which became an aristocratic English surname. Used as a first name since
the beginning of the 19th c., but at its
most popular in the 1920s. In the early
1980s was being used more in the U.S.
than in Britain, and by black American
families more than whites.

Veron (f) Abbreviated form of **Verona** or
Veronica in occasional modern use.

Verona (f) German short form of **Ver-
onika** (**Veronica**) used regularly but
infrequently since the 1860s. In some
cases the name may be transferred from
the Italian city. There are also towns of
the name in the U.S.

Veronica (f) Either a Latin form of
Berenice or from Latin words meaning
'true image', as in the word 'vernicle'.
The vernicle (earlier 'veronicle') is the
cloth on which the features of Christ are
said to have been miraculously impressed when it was used to wipe his face
as he went to Calvary. The cloth is
preserved in Rome. The name of the
woman who wiped the face of Jesus was
later said to be Veronica. We have no
way of knowing whether the name Veronica already existed and was reinter-
preted as 'true image' to fit the Biblical
incident, or whether the name was given
first to the cloth, then taken to be a
personal name. The name was introduced to Scotland in the 17th c. by an
ancestor of James Boswell. Came into
general use, at first having been used
only by Roman Catholic families, in the
1850s. Mildly popular in the 1920s and
'30s, then revived again in the 1950s,
possibly due to the publicity given to the
name throughout the 1940s by Veronica Lake (Constance Ockleman). By
the early 1980s it was being rarely used
in Britain, but was surviving rather
better in the U.S., where it had reached

its peak later than in Britain. Black
American parents in particular were
remaining faithful to it, sometimes
using it in the form **Veronice** or **Vernice**.
French form **Veronique** is occasionally
found. Veronica is also a flower name.

Vesta (f) Latin, the name of the Roman
goddess of the hearth. Appeared in the
1850s in Britain. In use at roughly the
same time in the U.S. as a slave name.
Most used 1900–20 but very rarely used
since. In 1910, according to official British records, a child received the name
Vest. Vessy also occurs in 1889. Presumably these must be considered to be
pet forms of Vesta used independently.

Veta (f) Pet form in Slavic countries of
various forms of **Elizabeth**. Used on
rare occasions in English-speaking
countries.

Vian (m) Pet form of **Vivian** or **Octavian**
used independently on rare occasions.

Vicki(e) (f) Pet forms of **Victoria** in modern use. Vicki occurs since the 1930s,
perhaps inspired by the authoress Vicki
Baum, but both forms were mainly used
in the 1970s in Britain, some twenty
years earlier in the U.S. American parents have made Vicki their first choice
as to spelling, followed by Vickie, then
Vicky, Vikki etc. In Britain Vicki and
Vickie have been used as often as Vicky.

Vicky (f) Pet form of **Victoria** used independently. This form has been almost as
frequently used in Britain as **Vicki** or
Vickie, but American parents have
much preferred Vicki, then Vickie in
modern times.

Victor (m) Latin *victor* 'conqueror'. One
of the commonest names in Christian
inscriptions of the Roman Empire. The
name of many early martyrs and several
popes. Rarely used in English-speaking
countries until the 1850s. In Britain the
name was at its peak 1900–35. Popular
in the U.S. rather later, reaching its peak
in the late 1950s. The actor Victor
Mature probably had much to do with
the name's popularity in the U.S. Possible that British interest in the name
had earlier been aroused by Victor

McLaglen, star of many silent films. Another well-known bearer of the name is the pianist/comedian Victor Borge.

Victoria (f) Latin *victoria* 'victory'. The commonest name for women in Christian inscriptions of the Roman Empire. A saint of the name was martyred in the 3rd c. In Britain **Victory** was the 16th c. form of the name, Victoria itself being rarely used until the beginning of the 19th c. The accession to the English throne of Queen Victoria in 1837 naturally caused the name to come into general use but it was not intensively used during her long reign. Rather more popular around 1900, but that may have been because the male name **Victor** was by then being well used. After Queen Victoria's death in 1901 the name was little used in Britain until the 1940s, when it began to become popular. Enjoyed a period of great popularity in the 1970s. By 1980 showing clear signs of going out of fashion. In the U.S. the name was most used in the 1950s and '60s, but never as frequently as in Britain. In modern times various forms of the pet name have been well used as names in their own right. These include **Viccy**, **Vicki**, **Vickie**, **Vickki**, **Vicky**, **Vikki**.

Victorine (f) French diminutive of **Victor** in occasional use since the 1890s.

Vida (m, f) Pet form of **Davida** used independently since the 1860s. Originally used in Scotland, but steadily used elsewhere. **Veda** also occurs.

Vidette (f) Apparently a newly-formed diminutive of **Vida** in occasional modern use. The Royal Navy formerly had a ship of this name, broken up in 1946.

Vikki (f) Modern variant of **Vicki**, **Vickie** or **Vicky**, pet form of **Victoria**. In use in the U.S. since the late 1940s, and in Britain since the 1960s.

Vilma (f) Variant of **Wilma**, ultimately from **Wilhelmina**. Used infrequently since the beginning of the 20th c.

Vina (f) Pet form of **Lavina**, **Davina**, **Malvina**, **Sylvina**, etc., used as a name in its

own right since the 1840s, regularly but infrequently.

Vince (m) Pet form of **Vincent** used independently, mainly since the late 1950s. Minor spell of popularity in the early 1970s but now rarely used.

Vincent (m) Latin *Vincentius*, ultimately from *vincere* 'to conquer'. Very popular name amongst the early Christians. Borne by numerous early saints. In use in the Middle Ages and gave rise to surnames such as *Vinson*, *Vincent*. Well used in the 16th c., but rarely occurs in 18th c. records. Reappeared in the 1840s but in quiet use until the end of the 19th c. Throughout the 20th c. has been steadily used in Britain, while never being especially fashionable. In the early 1980s was being used almost exactly as in 1900, having remained remarkably consistent. In the U.S. the same pattern of usage has occurred, though by 1980 more black American families than white were making use of it. In both countries the name has always been a special favourite of Roman Catholic families. On screen the name is most associated with the actor Vincent Price, while the artist Vincent Van Gogh has made it famous in a different sphere. Feminine form **Vincentia** is occasionally found, together with **Vincetta**.

Vine (m) Occupational surname, indicating a worker in a 'vineyard', used from time to time as a first name.

Vinnie (f) Pet form of **Lavinia** used independently. Main period of use was between the 1890s and 1920. **Viney** and **Vinia** were also used to some extent.

Viola (f) Latin *viola* 'violet'. Shakespeare used the name in *Twelfth Night* to name the sister of Sebastian. Does not seem to have come into general use until the 1860s, by which time **Violet** was in use. Viola was regularly but infrequently used until the 1930s, but has been out of fashion since then.

Violet (f) The flower name used as a first name. Use of this name seems to have begun in Scotland, where probably it was due to the influence of French **Vio-lette**. In France the violet was worn by the followers of Napoleon while he was in exile to indicate their allegiance to him. By the 1830s Violet was in general use in both the U.S. and Britain, but American parents have never made the name fashionable. In Britain it became extremely popular from the end of the 19th c. until the late 1920s. Then faded and is now completely out of fashion. The early run of the name was probably begun by Lord Lytton's highly success-ful novel *The Sea-Captain* (1839) in which Violet is the heroine.

Violetta (f) The Italian diminutive of **Viola**. Used regularly in Britain, espe-cially, from the 1840s until the 1940s, then seems to have faded. Associated with Violetta Valery in *La Traviata*, Verdi's name for the Marguerite of the original story. In British politics Lady Violetta Asquith made the name well known. There has also been a song 'Hear my song, Violetta' which achieved success in modern times, but it failed to save the name.

Violette (f) French form of **Violet**, occa-sionally used in Britain at the beginning of the 20th c.

Virgil (m) English form of the Roman clan name *Vergilius*, later written as *Vir-gilius*. Made famous by the Roman poet Virgil (Publius Vergilius Maro). The 8th c. Irish saint Virgilius was probably a **Fearghal** originally. Used far more in the U.S. than in Britain, and was for-merly especially popular with black American families. They now consider the name to be out of fashion.

Virginia (f) Originally a feminine form of the Roman clan name *Verginius* (see **Virgil**). From the 4th c. the spelling became Virginia and it was assumed that the name derived from Latin *virgo* 'maiden, virgin'. Used for the American state with reference to Elizabeth I, 'the Virgin Queen'. The first girl to be born in America of English parents was named Virginia. Its long run of popular-ity in the U.S. dated from the 1870s to

the 1950s. In Britain the name was rarely used in the 19th c. but has been more common in the 20th c., with a minor peak in the 1960s. Two well-known bearers of the name are the actresses Virginia Mayo and Virginia McKenna. **Ginger** Rogers was a Vir-ginia by birth. Other pet forms of the name, which have been used as names in their own right, include **Ginny, Jinney, Jinnie, Jinny.**

Virtue (f) The ultimate 'virtue' name introduced by the Puritans in the 16th and 17th cc. Frequently used until the end of the 18th c., and remained reasonably common until the end of the 19th c. Very rarely used since the 1920s. The main survivors of this group of names introduced by the Puritans are **Charity, Constance, Faith, Felicity, Grace, Honour, Hope, Joy, Mercy, Patience, Prudence, Temperance** and **Verity.**

Vito (m) Spanish form of **Vitalis**, from Latin 'vital'. There were several early saints named Vitalis, but the name has been rare in English-speaking countries since the Middle Ages. Vito occurs in the U.S., not in Britain.

Viva (f) Latin *viva*, feminine of *vivus* 'alive, living'. In occasional use. Eve and Zoe are names with a similar meaning.

Vivia (f) Shortened form of **Vivian** in occasional modern use.

Vivian (m, f) Probably Latin *Vibianus*, a derivative from a Roman family name *Vibius*. Confusion between the b/v sounds in Mediterranean countries led to the interchange of the two letters. St Vivianus, as he is now usually known, is sometimes recorded as St Bibianus. At an early date it was assumed that Viv-ianus was from Latin *vivus* 'living, alive', and Vivian became the usual English form. In continuous if infrequent use in Britain and other English-speaking countries since the latter half of the 19th c., but has never been especially fashionable. In the U.S. this is the usual form of the name for girls, though in Britain **Vivien** or **Vivienne** is more usual.

The male name sometimes takes the surname form **Vyvyan**. **Vyvian** and **Vivyan** also occur. Benjamin Disraeli wrote a novel *Vivian Grey* in which his hero was said to be based upon himself.

Vivianne (f) Feminine form of **Vivian** in imitation of French **Vivienne**. Used mildly since the 1930s. An older literary form of **Vivien** was **Viviane**, which has also been used occasionally.

Vivien (f) Feminine form of **Vivian**. Used to some extent in the late 19th c. Lord Tennyson had published his poem *Vivien*, part of *The Idylls of the King*, by 1859, but the character of the lady who bears the name in the poem would hardly have inspired parents to name their daughters after her. The fame of the British actress Vivien Leigh (who

changed her first name's spelling from Vivian) caused the name to be more intensively used, especially after her appearance as Scarlett O'Hara in *Gone With the Wind* (1939). It was never a spectacular success, however, and by 1980 had become a rarely used name again.

Vivienne (f) French form of **Vivien**, used regularly since the beginning of the 20th c. In Britain only, this spelling became as common as **Vivien** in the 1950s, when the name was being most used.

Vyvian (m) Variant of **Vivian** in occasional use since the 1880s.

Vyvyan (m) Surname derived from **Vivian**, used as a first name infrequently since the end of the 19th c.

W

Wade (m) Surname usually derived from a place name, with the meaning 'ford, place where it was possible to wade through a stream or river'. Used occasionally as a first name in the 19th c., also in modern times. Its brevity might have helped it survive when other names of this kind faded out in the 1920s, but Margaret Mitchell, in *Gone With the Wind* (1939), gave another reason: 'In due time Charles' son was born and, because it was fashionable to name boys after their fathers' commanding officers, he was called Wade Hampton Hamilton.' No doubt some of the modern instances of the name derive in turn from the use of it in this novel.

Wainwright (m) Occupational surname, indicating someone who 'built wagons', used from time to time as a first name, especially in the 19th c.

Walburga (f) Old German 'power-protection'. The name of a well-known saint and occasionally used in her honour.

Waldo (m) German pet form of names

such as *Waldemar*, where the first element means 'rule, power'. Made famous by the writer and philosopher Ralph Waldo Emerson (1803–82). Used occasionally in English-speaking countries, especially in New England according to H. L. Mencken.

Walford (m) Surname derived from a place name meaning 'ford over a stream', used with some regularity as a first name. Most surnames of this kind, used as first names, were typical of the 19th c. Walford only began to be used in 1900 and has remained in use.

Walker (m) Occupational surname, indicating someone who walked on cloth or wool to cleanse it, used as a first name. Such usage was common in the 19th c. but faded at the beginning of the 20th c.

Wallace (m) Mainly Scottish surname, originally indicating a 'Celt, Welshman', used as a first name. In Scotland the name is associated with the patriot William Wallace (1272–1305). Came into more general use (outside Scotland) in the 1840s and was most used

1870–1925. Rarely used in modern times. In silent film days the name was associated with the actor Wallace Reid. Wallace Beery, later to become rather better known, also began his screen career before the talkies came along. **Wallis** is a variant of this name.

Waller (m) Surname of many possible origins, used from time to time as a first name.

Wallis (m, f) Variant of **Wallace**. Regularly if infrequently used as a male name during the 19th c., but made widely known as a feminine name by Wallis Warfield, who became the Duchess of Windsor in 1937. Very rarely used since then, in Britain or the U.S.

Wally (m) Pet form of **Walter**, **Wallace**, etc., used as a name in its own right, though infrequently used.

Walt (m) Pet form of **Walter**, rarely used as an independent name. The poet Walt Whitman (1819–92) was christened Walter, as was the animator Walt(er) Elias Disney (1901–66).

Walter (m) Old German 'ruling people'. Made popular by the Normans from the 11th c. onwards. Its early use gave rise to many surnames, such as *Walters*, *Watts*, *Watkins*. Shakespeare makes a famous reference to what was apparently the normal 17th c. pronunciation of Walter in *Henry VI Part Two*. When Walter Whitmore announces his name to Suffolk he is clearly supposed to say that he is 'Water' Whitmore, for Suffolk turns pale and says that a fortune-teller once predicted that he would die 'by water'. Therefore, Suffolk says, 'Thy name affrights me, in whose sound is death.' Miss Withycombe says that the form **Water** 'occurs as late as 1670', but a Water Smith was named in 1842, showing that the oral tradition lived on for a very long time. The name has been used continuously since the Middle Ages, though it was out of fashion in the 18th c. By 1850 it was fast returning to favour, and reached a peak of popularity in the 1870s. Has declined slowly since then, though still being reasonably well used in the 1930s. By the 1980s it had become a rare name in Britain, while in the U.S. it was being kept alive mainly by black American families. Well-known bearers of the name include the actors Walter Pidgeon and Walter Brennan, and Walter Cronkite the journalist. Pet form **Walt** is sometimes used independently, and surnames based on the name, such as **Watkin**, **Watson**, are also used as first names.

Walton (m) Surname derived from a common place name which can have several different origins, regularly used as a first name in the 19th c. As with many other names of this type, rarely used as a first name since the 1920s.

Wanda (f) Slavic name which is probably connected with the tribal name of the *Vandals*, a Germanic tribe known to the Anglo-Saxons as the *Wendlas*. The behaviour of the Vandals led to the modern meaning of 'vandalism'. Ouida published a novel *Wanda* in 1883 which appears to have had no effect at all on the use of the name. The American actress Wanda Hendrix clearly did have an effect, since the name came into use immediately after her screen debut in the 1940s. In the early 1980s Wanda was being quietly used, mainly by black American parents.

Wanita (f) Also **Waneta**, **Waneeta**. 20th c. phonetic forms of **Juanita**.

Ward (m) Occupational surname, indicating a 'watchman', used as a first name. In use from the 1830s, then faded completely after 1870, though only in Britain. In the U.S. the name continued to be used regularly, and since 1960 it has again been used in Britain.

Warner (m) Norman surname, possibly meaning a 'park-keeper', used from time to time as a first name. Usage more frequent in the 19th c. than in modern times.

Warren (m) Surname of more than one possible origin, also an English river name, used as a first name. In general use from the 17th c. but would probably have died out in the 1920s had it not been borne by distinguished men in both the U.S. and Britain. President Warren Gamaliel Harding (1865–1923) made the name famous in the U.S. Earlier Warren Hastings (1732–1818) had been first Governor General of India. Since the early 1960s the name has been well publicized by the actor Warren Beatty, as well as the British actor Warren Mitchell. In Britain, reasonably well used throughout the 1970s, but fading by 1980. In the U.S. it became fairly popular rather earlier and faded sooner.

Warwick (m) Place name/surname, originally indicating 'dwellings near a weir', used in Britain as a first name since the beginning of the 19th c. Also found as **Warick** and **Warrick**.

Washington (m) Place name of uncertain origin which became a surname. Later became a place name again in honour of George Washington (1732–99), first President of the U.S.A. In the U.S. Washington was formerly a common first name, abbreviated in speech to **Wash**, which was occasionally used independently. In modern times it is rarely used, though black American families occasionally restore it. As a first name it is probably best known as that of the writer Washington Irving (1783–1859).

Watkin (m) Surname based on **Wat** (**Walter**), used from time to time as a first name.

Watson (m) The surname, 'son of **Wat**' (Wat being a pet form of **Walter**), used frequently as a first name, especially in the 19th c. Used until the 1920s, but rare since.

Wayne (m) Occupational surname, originally indicating a 'maker of wagons' or a 'wagon-driver', used as a first name. Came into regular use in the U.S. in the 1930s, reaching Britain by 1940. Most used by American parents in the 1950s and '60s, but reached a peak in Britain in the early 1970s. By the early 1980s was showing clear signs of fading, especially in the U.S. Use of the name in the

first place seems to have been inspired by the actor John Wayne (Marion Michael Morrison), whose film career began in the late 1920s. **Wayn** and **Wain** are sometimes found. The actor's stage-name had been suggested by film-director Raoul Walsh, who admired a general of the American Revolution called Anthony Wayne.

Webster (m) Occupational surname, originally indicating a female 'weaver' used since the 19th c. Made well known by the singer Webster Booth; recently by TV series *Webster,* starring the young black actor Emmanuel Lewis.

Wellington (m) Surname derived from a place name, meaning uncertain but possibly 'temple in a clearing', used with some regularity as a first name in the 19th c. The surname was made famous by the Duke of Wellington (1759–1852), but respect for him was shown more readily by the use of his first name, **Arthur**.

Wells (m) Surname derived from a common place name, used occasionally as a first name, especially in the 19th c.

Wenda (f) Probably an adaptation of **Wendy**, since it seems to have been used for the first time in 1907, a few years after the production of *Peter Pan*. Used regularly but infrequently since.

Wendell (m) Surname from an Old German personal name, ultimately meaning 'one who wanders', used as a first name. Usage is infrequent in all English-speaking countries. Associated with the author Oliver Wendell Holmes (1809–94) and more recently with the actor Wendell Corey. **Wendel** also occurs, and there is a rare feminine form **Wendelle**, which may independently have been suggested by **Wendy**. **Wendle** has also been noted.

Wendi(e) (f) See **Wendy**.

Wendy (f) This name was suggested to J. M. Barrie for his *Peter Pan* (1904) by the phrase 'friendy-wendy', used to him by a child. As it happens, there were already several Germanic names in existence, such as *Wendelburg*, *Wendelgard* which might have suggested a pet name of similar form. Wendy did not come into general use until the 1920s, though some parents adapted it earlier into the more familiar feminine form **Wenda**. But it was Wendy which became more popular, reaching a considerable peak in Britain in the 1960s. Less successful in the U.S. but at its height in the mid-1970s. By the early 1980s had faded sharply on all sides. Three British actresses had helped the name along, Wendy Hiller and Wendy Barrie (Wendy Jenkins) from the 1930s onwards, Wendy Craig from the 1960s. **Wendie** was regularly used in the 1940s, while **Wendi** appeared in the 1960s.

Werner (m) Old German name of uncertain meaning, though the second element is 'army'. Occasionally used in the U.S., but very rare in Britain.

Wesley (m) English place name 'west meadow' which became a surname, borne most notably by John Wesley (1703–91) and his brother Charles Wesley (1707–88), founders of the Methodist Church. Use of Wesley as a first name began during their lifetimes, clearly in their honour. Used steadily since in all English-speaking countries. Occurs also as **Wesly**, and **Wessley** the latter indicating its correct pronunciation. In Britain, since the late 1970s, it has been popular also as **Westley**. This may be an indication that the name is now considered to be completely independent of its early religious associations.

Weston (m) Surname derived from a common place name, indicating a 'west-facing farm', used from time to time as a first name, especially in the 19th c.

Whalley (m) Place name/surname, originally indicating a wood by a hill, used as a first name in the 19th c. **Whallie** also occurred. **Walter** was in use throughout that time, but it is not clear when **Wally** became the normal pet form of that name. The latter very rarely occurs as an independent name, and is more likely to be found in the 20th c. than the 19th c.

Wharton (m) Surname derived from a place name 'farm or settlement near the shore', used from time to time as a first name, especially in the 19th c. **Warton** is also found.

Wheatley (m) Common place name 'wheat field' which became a surname, used from time to time as a first name.

Whittaker (m) Common place name 'white field' which became a surname, regularly used as a first name in the 19th c. **Whitaker** was also found.

Wilbert (m) Old English 'will-bright', a name which survived the Middle Ages only in surname form. Revived in Britain in the 1880s for a short time, but far more successfully in the U.S., mainly by black American families, in the 1940s. They continue to make regular use of the name, sometimes in the form **Wilburt**. Wilbert also occurs in Britain in modern times, mainly used by West Indian families.

Wilbur (m) Use of the surname as first name. The surname possibly derives in turn from the feminine Germanic name **Wilburg**, though there is an outside chance that it represents the personal name **Wildbore**, a nickname given to a ferocious man. In the U.S. the name is most associated with Wilbur Wright (1867–1912), one of the famous Wright brothers, the aviation pioneers. Always used more in the U.S. than in Britain since its introduction in the mid-19th c. In the early 1980s still in quiet use, especially by black American parents. **Wilber** is also found, perhaps influenced by **Wilbert**.

Wilford (m) Surname derived from a place name, meaning 'ford near the willows', used with some regularity as a first name in the 19th c., and occasionally in modern times. The name seems to have appealed to writers.

Wilfred (m) Old English 'will-peace'. The name of a 7th c. saint. Did not come into general use until the second half of the 19th c. Eric Partridge comments that Wilfred was the usual Protestant form of the name, while **Wilfrid** was a

Roman Catholic form. Sir Walter Scott used both in his novels, Wilfred in *Rob Roy* and Wilfrid in *Rokeby*, and he may well have been influential in reintroducing the name. At its peak in Britain 1900–30, but was not taken up by American parents. Well-known bearers of the name include the actors Wilfrid Brambell, known to British television viewers as Steptoe, Wilfred Hyde White and Wilfrid Lawson. Wilfred Pickles was a famous radio personality in the 1950s. Feminine form **Wilfrida** is met with on rare occasions.

Wilhelmina (f) Mainly German feminine form of **Wilhelm** (**William**), a royal name in the Netherlands. Used regularly in English-speaking countries since the end of the 18th c., and especially popular in Scotland. In modern times has tended to be replaced there by **Williamina** or by the pet form **Wilma**. **Mina** is also found. In the early 1980s Wilhelmina had clearly dropped out of fashion on all sides.

Wilhelmine (f) French form of **Wilhelmina**, used from time to time in English-speaking countries, especially in the latter part of the 19th c.

Wilkinson (m) Surname linked with **William**, used with great regularity as a first name in the 19th c. and occasionally since.

Will (m) Pet form of **William** or other names beginning with Will-, used regularly as a name in its own right from the 1850s to the 1930s. Still used in the U.S. on occasion but has become obsolete in Britain.

Willa (f) Pet form of **Wilhelmina**, occasionally used independently, e.g. Willa Cather (1876–1947), the novelist.

Willard (m) Old English personal name 'bold resolve' which became a surname. Frequency as a first name in the U.S. perhaps due to humorous TV weatherman Willard Scott.

Willey (m) Common variant of **Willie** or **Willy** in the 19th c., but now obsolete.

William (m) Old German 'will – helmet'.

Introduced to Britain by the Normans, in particular by William the Conqueror himself. Another bearer of the name, William Camden, was able to say (1605): 'This name hath been most common in England since King William the Conqueror, insomuch that upon a festival day in the court of King Henry II, when Sir William Saint-John and Sir William Fitz-Hamon had commanded that none but of the name of William should dine in the great chamber with them, they were accompanied with a hundred and twenty Williams, all knights.' From the 16th c. William gave way only to **John** in the popularity tables. In Britain parents began to turn away from the name at the beginning of the 20th c. and it began to decline steadily. This happened some twenty years later in the U.S. Had reached a very low point in Britain by 1970, but by the early 1980s there were signs of a partial recovery. In 1982 Prince Charles and the Princess of Wales named their son William. This is likely to cause many more British parents to make use of the name during the 1980s, but it has a long way to go before it returns to its former glory. In 1900, in a sample of roughly 7000 male births, 600 received the name William. In 1981, in a roughly similar sample of male births in Britain, 34 boys received the name. In a sample of just over 10,000 male births in the U.S. in 1981, 135 boys were named William. The name was being used with equal frequency by black and white parents. Another American survey made in 1940, based on 15,000 male births, showed that 635 boys were called William. One would therefore expect the use of the name to continue to rise in Britain and to fall in the U.S. especially amongst white families. Black American parents show their fondness for the name by using **Willie** in considerable numbers, as well as William itself. The case for using the name at any level was well put by the novelist Ivy Compton-Burnett, in *A House and its Head*:

'"What of William, the name of Cassie's father?" "You may have hit it, Mrs Smollett. Little William Edgeworth. By that name Baby Edgeworth may walk in our midst. And a good solid old name, too, suitable from king to peasant." "I suspect it is as king that this young man will take his place in the house," said Beatrice.' Apart from the name's royal connections, past and present, it has been borne by many famous men almost too numerous to mention. It was the name of Shakespeare and Thackeray, Blake, Wordsworth and Yeats. William Faulkner continues the association of the name with great writers. Also the name of three American Presidents, Harrison, McKinley and Taft, of William Penn and William Hogarth. In the cinema the name suggests William Holden, William Bendix, William Boyd. It gave rise to a great many surnames, many of which have frequently been used as first names, especially **Wilkinson**, **Wilson**, **Willis**. Normal feminine form of the name is **Wilhelmina**, but **Williamina** has also been used. Pet forms **Bill**, **Billie**, **Billy**, **Will**, etc., have taken on a life of their own.

Williamina (f) Feminine form of **William** used especially in Scotland from the 1840s to the 1920s as a variant of **Wilhelmina**. Now appears to be obsolete.

Willie (m) Pet form of **William** or other names beginning with Will-. Popular name with black American families in the early 1980s. In Britain was mainly used in the second half of the 19th c. and is now rare.

Willis (m) One of the many surnames linked with **William**, used regularly as a first name since the 1830s. More frequently found in the 19th c. than in the 20th c., but survived fairly well until the 1960s in Britain, longer in the U.S. Black American parents remain especially fond of the name.

Willoughby (m) Surname derived from a place name, meaning 'farm near the willows', regularly used as a first name throughout the 19th c. Still very occa-

sionally used, but rather rare since the 1920s.

Willow (f) The tree name used as a first name. Examples are found in the U.S. in the 1940s, and in Britain in the 1970s, but it remains very rare.

Willy (m) Variant of **Willie** used in the second half of the 19th c. but now very rare.

Wilma (f) Pet form of **Wilhelmina** in use since the 1880s. More popular in Scotland than elsewhere in Britain, while American families of German descent also made use of it formerly. Now out of fashion, though it was much publicised in the early 1960s by the athlete Wilma Rudolph Ward, winner of three gold medals in the 1960 Olympic Games. **Wilmer** is properly a separate name, though it sometimes occurs as a spelling variant of Wilma. **Wylma** also occurs as a variant.

Wilmer (m) Form of German **Willimar** 'will-fame'. Used more in the U.S. than in Britain, occurring also as **Wylmer**, but it does not occur frequently. Also found occasionally as a girl's name, where it is a variant of **Wilma**.

Wilmot (m) One of the many surnames linked with **William**. Used from time to time as a first name since the 1840s. Wilmott also occurs, and, most unusually, a feminine form of the name, **Wilmotina**, was used in 1862.

Wilson (m) Surname linked with **William** used as a first name with considerable frequency in the 19th c., and one of the rarer surnames which has continued to be used in that role in modern times. Apart from being a common name in all English-speaking countries it has also been the family name of an American President, Woodrow Wilson, and a British Prime Minister, Harold Wilson. Some uses of the name may have been with reference to one of these politicians.

Wilton (m) Common place name of various possible origins which became a surname, used from time to time as a first name.

Windsor (m) Common English place

name, originally indicating a 'river-bank with a winch', used to pull boats from the water. The name took on especial significance when King George V made it the surname of the British royal family during World War One. As a first name, Windsor has been in regular if infrequent use since the 1850s. In Britain it is associated with the actor Windsor Davies.

Winefred (f) Also **Winefride**. See **Winifred**.

Winfred (m) Old English 'friend-peace'. Rarely used.

Winifred (f) Welsh *Gwenfrewi* 'blessed reconciliation'. The Welsh name was Latinized as *Wenefreda*, and the English form was no doubt influenced by existing names such as *Winfrith* 'friend-peace' (occasionally in modern use as the masculine name **Winfred**). Winifred has been in regular use since the 16th c. but was at its most popular 1880–1930, though only in England, Wales and Scotland. Elsewhere the name has remained rather a rarity. British parents have used it in a number of forms, such as the common **Winefred** and **Winnifred**, and the occasional **Winefride**, **Winefriede**, **Winifreda**, **Winifrede**, **Winifrid**, **Winifride**, **Winifryde**, **Winnafred**, **Winnefred**, **Winniefred**, **Winniefrida**, **Winnifrid**, **Wynifred**. Pet forms **Winn** and **Winnie** have been used independently, and **Freda** is sometimes from Winifred. In the early 1980s little used in any English-speaking country.

Winnie (f) Pet form of **Winifred**, **Edwina**, etc., used independently. In speech it is also a pet form of **Winston** or **Windsor**. In regular use from the 1860s, reaching a minor peak around 1900. Rarely used since the 1930s, perhaps because A. A. Milne associated the name with *Winnie-the-Pooh*.

Winnifred (f) Common variant of **Winifred**.

Winsome (f) The word used as a name. Winsome is little used in everyday conversation, but it means 'attractive, pleasant, cheerful'. It tended to be used

when **Winnie** and similar names were still in use, but it was never frequent.

Winston (m) Surname derived from place name 'Wine's settlement', used as a first name. Strongly associated with the Churchill family, in modern times with Sir Winston Spencer Churchill (1874–1965). Perhaps the most surprising fact about the name is how little it has been used in modern times, given the popularity of the former British Prime Minister at the end of the Second World War. Perhaps the name was felt to be his personal property, not to be used without his express permission. Only West Indian families living in Britain have made regular use of it. In the U.S. the name is used infrequently, and black Americans are more likely to choose it than whites. **Winstone** occurs from time to time.

Winthrop (m) Surname derived from an English place name of more than one possible origin. The -throp refers to a farm or village, and the Win- can be from an Anglo-Saxon personal name meaning 'friend'. Winthrop Ames in his *What Shall We Name the Baby?* therefore chose to interpret the name as 'from the friendly village'. Used in honour of John Winthrop (1588–1649), the Puritan leader who became governor of Massachusetts. Used in the U.S. regularly, but infrequently, until modern times. Now a comic strip name.

Wisdom (m, f) Use of the word as a first name, or the surname transferred to first-name use. 'Wisdom' translates Greek **Sophia**, a name used by early Christians because of the great significance attached to wisdom in the Bible. There the reader is constantly reminded that 'wisdom is better than strength'; 'wisdom is better than weapons'; 'the price of wisdom is above rubies'; 'fools die for want of wisdom', etc. Bardsley does not seem to have found Wisdom as a Puritan name, but it was regularly in use in the 19th c. and has continued in modern times. Examples of the name occurred in

Britain, for instance, for every year between 1970–77.

Wolfgang (m) German 'wolf-strife'. In the U.S. the occasional use of this name may be directly due to German descent. In Britain the name is sometimes given in honour of Wolfgang Amadeus Mozart. 'Wolf' names are common in several European countries, but are rare in Britain and America. The surname **Woolf** has been noted as a first name, but the modern slang meaning of 'wolf', a man who is lecherously interested in women, probably makes such names difficult to use.

Woodfine (m) Place name/surname used from time to time as a first name. Similar names linking with 'wood' include **Woodfield, Woodford, Woodforde, Woodlock, Woodville, Woodrow**.

Woodrow (m) Surname derived from a place name 'row of cottages in a wood', well established as a first name in the U.S. especially since Woodrow Wilson (1856–1924) was President. In his case Woodrow was actually his middle name, Thomas being the first name which he dropped. In Britain the name is extremely rare.

Woolf (m) Surname used as a first name. Like **Wolfe**, which also occurs, it derives from 'wolf'.

Worthy (m) Surname derived from a place name, meaning 'enclosure', regularly used as a first name in the second half of the 19th c. **Worthey** was also used, but both have been rare since the beginning of the 20th c. This name is unlikely to have been a use of the word 'worthy'.

Wright (m) Occupational surname, originally meaning a 'carpenter' or 'joiner', used with some frequency as a first name thoughout the 19th c. For some reason parents no longer thought it suitable in this role after 1930, with very rare exceptions.

Wybert (m) Surname which probably meant 'battle bright' in Anglo-Saxon times, used occasionally as a first name.

Wyndham (m) Aristocratic surname derived from a place name 'Wyman's settlement', used regularly if infrequently as a first name since the 1850s, mainly in Britain. The name would probably have faded, along with other surnames turned first names, after the 1920s, had it not been for the writer Wyndham Lewis (1884–1957). Lewis, also well-known as an artist, dropped his first name Percy, preferring to be known by his middle name, Wyndham.

Wynford (m) Place name derived from the name of a stream 'white torrent'. Became a surname and has been used as a first name regularly if infrequently since 1910, mainly in Wales. **Wenford** also occurs, and is probably a variant of the same name.

Wynn (f) Welsh 'white, pure'. In very occasional use.

Wynne (m, f) English or Welsh surname, meaning either 'friend' or 'fair, white', used as a first name since the 1930s. Never an especially popular name.

X

Xanthe (f) Greek feminine of *xanthos* 'yellow', referring to fair, golden hair. The last example of the name noted in Britain in the 1950s. *Xanthos* itself was the name of Achilles' horse. No modern examples of **Xantippe** or **Xanthippe** have been found, though this occurs as a girl's name in parish registers of the 18th c. It was the name of Socrates' proverbially shrewish wife, of whom Dr Brewer tells the following anecdote: 'One day, after storming at the philosopher, she emptied a vessel of dirty water on his head, whereupon Socrates simply remarked, "Ay, ay, we always look for rain after thunder." '

Xanthippe originally meant 'yellow mare'.

Xavier (m) The name of Saint Francis Xavier (1506–52) used as a first name, mainly by Roman Catholic families. Xavier, according to Dauzat, represents a Basque place name, originally meaning 'new house'. Sometimes found in English-speaking countries as **Zavier**.

Xenia (f) Greek 'hospitable'. Rarely used in its true form; more frequent as **Zena** or **Zina**.

Y

Yale (m) Surname derived from a place name 'fertile upland', used as a first name with some regularity in the U.S., though not in Britain. Associated with Yale University, named for Elihu Yale, and with the Yale lock, invented by Linus Yale.

Yalonda (f) See **Yolande**.

Yancy (m) Surname used occasionally as a first name in the U.S., honouring William Lowndes Yancey (1814–65), a Southern political leader who strongly supported slavery.

Yasmin(e) (f) See **Jasmine**.

Yehudi (m) The Hebrew form of **Judah** 'Jew'. Made famous by the violinist Yehudi Menuhin, but very rarely used.

Yetta (f) Pet form of **Henrietta** used independently, especially at the end of the 19th c. Yette was likewise used from **Henriette**. Both forms now extremely rare.

Yiesha (f) See **Aisha**.

Yola (f) Form of **Iola** or pet form of **Yolande** used independently. Rarely used.

Yolanda (f) See **Yolande** for the derivation, but Yolanda has been the preferred form of the name in the U.S. in recent times.

Yolande (f) Modern French form of **Iolanthe**, ultimately from Greek *ion* 'violet' and *anthos* 'flower', influenced by Latin **Violante**, which is still used in Italy. Borne by a 13th c. Spanish saint as **Jolantha**, and later a royal name in Hungary. Modern Hungarian form is **Jolan**, which has caused the name to be interpreted there as if it were *jó lány*

'good girl'. In the U.S. Yolanda has been much the preferred spelling in modern times, with variants such as **Yalonda, Yolonda, Yulanda, Yulonda, Yalinda, Youlanda, Yalanda, Ylonda**. Most of these forms have been used by black American families rather than whites, and all were especially popular during the 1960s. In Britain Yolande has been in regular if infrequent use since the 1920s. Yolanda has occurred since the 1950s, while Yoland and Yollande are rarer variants. Pet form Yola has been used independently, and the French diminutive Yolette occurs.

Yolonda (f) See **Yolande**.

Yorath (m) English rendering of Welsh Iorwerth.

York (m) Place name/surname used as a first name. Rare in modern times.

Ysanne (f) A blend of **Isabel** and **Ann**, made known in Britain by Ysanne Churchman, the actress who was 'Grace' in *The Archers* in the 1950s. Occasionally used.

Young (m) Surname used as a first name. Use of the name in the latter role died out around 1920, when surname/firstnames generally went out of fashion.

Yul (m) Made known by the actor Yul Brynner, and occasionally used in modern times, especially in the U.S. Mr Brynner wrote to the authors of *What to Name Your Baby* to explain that his name was an adaptation of a Mongolian name, meaning 'beyond the horizon'. The name in Mongolian would be pronounced *Yaugh*, Mr Brynner says. **Yule** was a fairly common name in the

Middle Ages, leading to modern surnames such as *Youle*, *Yeowell*, *Yuell*. It has been replaced in modern times by **Noel**, earlier **Christmas**. The name was used for a boy born at that time of year.

Yvette (f) French feminine form of **Ivo**, but **Yvonne** has been preferred in English-speaking countries.

Yvonne (f) French feminine form of Ivon, see Ivo. Introduced to English-speaking countries at the beginning of 20th c. Made widely known in 1940s by the Canadian actress Yvonne de Carlo. Among top fifty girls' names in Britain, 1970. Less used elsewhere. Variant forms include **Yvone**, **Evon**, **Evonne**.

Z

Zacariah (m) See **Zachariah**.

Zaccheus (m) Either a form of **Zachariah** or from an Aramaic word meaning 'pure'. Biblical, N.T., Luke 19. Also found as **Zacceus**, **Zacchaeus**. Miss Withycombe says it was commonly used in the 17th c. Occurs regularly in 19th c. records, though never a popular name.

Zachariah (m) Hebrew 'Jehovah has remembered'. Biblical, O.T. and N.T. Name of a king of Israel and a prophet. In common use from the 16th to the 18th cc., then continued to be regularly used throughout the 19th c. Became rare in the 20th c. but survived as **Zachary**, probably under the influence of the actor Zachary Scott. Also found in its Latin form **Zacharias**. Variant spellings include **Zacariah**, **Zachery**, **Zackery**, **Zacarias**, **Zechariah**. See also **Zak**, which has led to **Zakaria** on occasion. In the early 1980s Zachary was mainly being used in the U.S., and by both black and white parents.

Zaida (f) Arabic 'prosperous'. Rarely used in English-speaking countries. French writers such as Molière made use of it at a time when names beginning with Z- were fashionable in romances.

Zaira (f) Also **Zaire**. See **Zara**.

Zak (m) Pet form of **Zachary**, **Zachariah** or **Isaac** (**Izaak**) used independently. Much publicized in 1965 when Ringo Starr (Richard Starkey) of The Beatles chose it for his first child. Starr was quoted at the time as saying that he was fond of Westerns, and that the name

combined a Biblical and Western flavour. The former image might have been helped by actors such as Zachary Scott. The name was used generally from 1965 until the early 1970s, but then seems to have faded.

Zana (f) This name also occurs as **Zanna**. Likely to be a pet form of **Susannah**, though Johnson and Sleigh connect it with a Persian word for 'woman'. Occurs infrequently. (The explanation given above is perhaps supported by German **Sanna**, which derives from **Rosanna**.)

Zandra (f) Pet form of **Alexandra** or a variant of **Sandra** in occasional use.

Zane (m) Surname used as a first name. The first name is mainly associated with the writer Zane Grey (1875–1939), whose great-grandfather was Ebenezer Zane, founder of Zanesville, Ohio. Zane Grey was born in that town. When he began to write, having begun his career as a dentist, his first book was *Betty Zane*, the fictionalized story of one of his ancestors. There he says that Ebenezer Zane's father was 'a Dane of aristocratic lineage'. If this is so, one would expect Zane to be a form of a Danish place name. It is commonly explained in name books as 'a form of **John**', perhaps because it has been identified with an *Italian* surname which has such an origin. Zane is in regular but infrequent use as a first name in the U.S. In Britain it has been rarely used.

Zanna (f) See **Zana**.

Zara (f) Arabic 'splendour, brightness of the east'. This explanation of the name was first given by Sophy Moody in *What is Your Name?* (1860s). Zara occurs in European literature fairly often, usually referring to an Arabian princess. This fact, together with the similarity in spelling, may be why Charlotte Yonge took it to be a form of **Sarah** or **Sara**, which means 'princess'. Congreve used the name for an African queen in his *Mourning Bride* (1697), and it was made known still further when Aaron Hill used it as the English form of *Zaïre*, Voltaire's heroine in his play of that name. Hill's translation of the play was completed in 1735. It is Congreve's Zara who is most often quoted, or rather misquoted. She says in the play:

Heav'n has no rage, like love to hatred
   turned,
Nor Hell a fury, like a woman scorn'd.

The name is mentioned in *Little Women,* by Louisa M. Alcott and occurs in *Utopia Unlimited* by Gilbert and Sullivan. Zara was almost unknown as a first name, however, until the late 1960s, when British parents suddenly discovered it. They used it fairly well throughout the 1970s, but it appeared to be fading by 1980. Princess Anne used it to name her daughter in 1981, which may cause it to be more widely used in the future. It remains almost unknown in the U.S. It is listed in Italian name dictionaries, sometimes explained as meaning 'flowery'.

Zarita (f) See **Sarita**.

Zavier (m) See **Xavier**.

Zebulun (m) Hebrew 'to exalt, honour', probably in the sense, 'Now will my husband honour me (because I have given birth to this son)'. Biblical, O.T., Jacob's tenth son by Leah, the reputed ancestor of the tribe of Israel which bore his name. Occasionally used in the 19th c. but now very rare.

Zechariah (m) Common variant of **Zachariah** in the 19th c.

Zedekiah (m) Hebrew 'God is my justice'. Biblical, O.T., the name of the last king of Judah and Jerusalem. Used from time to time in the 19th c.

Zelda (f) See **Griselda**. F. Scott Fitzgerald's wife was a Zelda.

Zelia (f) The French saint *Solenne* is also known by the name **Soline, Solina, Souline, Soulle, Zelie, Zeline**. Zelia appears to be a Latinized form of **Zelie**, which is used in modern France. The original meaning of the name was probably 'solemn'. **Zelina** has also been used in Britain, a Latinized form of **Zelene**, but neither Zelia nor Zelina occurs frequently.

Zella (f) German pet form of **Marzella** (**Marcelle**). Used only occasionally. H. L. Mencken took it to be one of the artificial names used in what he called 'the swell name zone', but it would have been a normal name to German immigrants.

Zelma (f) Pet form of **Anselma** (see **Anselm**) used independently, regularly if infrequently since the 1890s. The real first name of the actress who became Kathryn Grayson.

Zena (f) Probably a pet form of **Rosina** or a variant of **Xenia**, though a link with a Persian word meaning 'woman' is claimed by Johnson and Sleigh. Regularly used in Britain. In the U.S. **Zina** is the preferred form.

Zenobia (f) Greek 'force of Zeus'. The name of a queen of Palmyra in the 3rd c., briefly a ruler of the eastern part of the Roman Empire. Nathaniel Hawthorne made use of the name in his *Blithedale Romance* (1852), but the character portrayed was an impulsive woman who eventually drowned herself. Nevertheless, the name came into use in the latter part of the 19th c. Rarely used in modern times, though a Zenobia Smith was named in Britain in 1978 and black American families occasionally make use of it.

Zephaniah (m) Hebrew 'Jehovah protects'. Biblical, O.T., the name of several men, especially the ninth of the

Minor Prophets who gives his name to one of the O.T. books. Occurs from time to time in 19th c. records.

Zeppelina (f) A name given to one or two English girls during the First World War when Zeppelins arrived over England. The airships took their name from Count von Zeppelin, whose family name according to German scholars was of Slavic origin, but of unknown meaning.

Zeta (f) Usually a variant of Zita, the resemblance to the name of the sixth letter of the Greek alphabet being coincidental. Used from time to time in the 20th c.

Zetta (f) Pet form of Rosetta used independently, but rarely.

Zia (m) Hebrew name of a man mentioned in the O.T., 1 Chron. 5:13, in a genealogical list. Has been used as a first name in Britain since the 1960s, but is likely to be mistaken for a girl's name.

Zilah (f) see Zillah.

Zillah (f) Hebrew 'shadow'. Biblical, O.T., Gen. 4:19. Like other names of its type it was introduced in the 16th c. Used with great regularity in the 19th c. and has continued to be used, though less frequently, in modern times. **Zilla** is a frequent variant, and **Zylla** is found. **Zilah** is rare.

Zilpah (f) Arabic 'with a little nose'. Biblical, O.T., Gen 30:9, name of the wife of Jacob. Well used throughout the 18th c., but regularly used in the 19th c. In the 20th c. used very infrequently and has tended to become **Zilpha**. **Zylpha** also occurs.

Zimri (m) Hebrew 'celebrated in song'. Biblical, O.T., the name of several men, including the ill-fated king (1 Kings 16:9) whose reign lasted for seven days. Occasionally occurs in 19th c. records.

Zina (f) Variant of **Xenia**, favoured by black American families.

Zinnia (f) Name of a flower (of the aster family) used occasionally since the 1940s as a first name.

Zipporah (f) Hebrew 'bird'. Biblical,

O.T., Ex. 2:21, the name of the wife of Moses. Used with some regularity until the end of the 19th c., but extremely rare since. Also occurs in records as **Ziporah, Ziproh**. The word 'zipper', at first a trade name, was not coined until the 1920s.

Zita (f) Greek, from *zetein* 'to seek'. The name of a popular 13th c. saint, patroness of domestic servants. Used sporadically since the 1880s.

Zoë (f) Greek 'life'. The name was brought into being as a translation of Eve. St Zoë was a 3rd c. martyr, but the name was not used in English-speaking countries until the mid-19th c., when English parents began using it. By 1980 its popularity was rapidly increasing in Britain, its fashionable run having begun in the late 1960s. American parents still seemed to be unaware of the name at that time. Rarely mentioned in literature, but it occurs in a novel by F. Marion Crawford, *Arethusa*. Apart from the girl who bears the name, another character is made to say: 'My husband says that I am his Zoë, his "life", because he would surely die of starvation without me.' The unfamiliarity of the diacritic above the final 'e' in the name leads many parents to use a phonetic spelling such as **Zoey, Zoie, Zowie** or **Zoee**.

Zola (f) An Italian surname 'clod of earth' associated with the French writer Emile Zola (1840–1902). Rarely used, but made famous as a first name by the athlete Zola Budd.

Zona (f) Made well known by the novelist and poet Zona Gale (1874–1938), winner of the Pulitzer Prize in 1921. Presumably the name was originally chosen for its sound rather than its meaning of 'belt, girdle'. Also a medical term for the disease otherwise known as shingles. Mainly American, but a couple of British instances have been noted since 1910.

Zonia (f) Apparently a variant of **Sonia** or **Zona**. In occasional use since the 1930s.

299

Zorah (f) Appears to be a use of the Biblical place name as a first name. Mentioned in the O.T., Josh. 19:41. Used very occasionally in the 20th c., probably because of the character who bears the name in the Gilbert and Sullivan comic opera, *Ruddigore*, first performed in 1887. Zorah is the professional bridesmaid.

Zowie (f) Form of Zoë in use since the 1970s. Zoie also occurs. The name was also given to Zowie Bowie, son of pop star David Bowie, but this does not seem to have been imitated by other parents.

Zuba (f) See **Azubah**.

Zylla (f) See **Zillah**.

Zylpha (f) See **Zilpah**.

The top fifty first names for boys, England and Wales

1925	1950	1965	1975	1993
1 John	1 David	1 Paul	1 Stephen	1 Daniel
2 William	2 John	2 David	2 Mark	2 Matthew
3 George	3 Peter	3 Andrew	3 Paul	3 James
4 James	4 Michael	4 Stephen	4 Andrew	4 Christopher
5 Ronald	5 Alan	5 Mark	5 David	5 Thomas
6 Robert	6 Robert	6 Michael	6 Richard	6 Joshua
7 Kenneth	7 Stephen	7 Ian	7 Matthew	7 Adam
8 Frederick	8 Paul	8 Gary	8 Daniel	8 Michael
9 Thomas	9 Brian	9 Robert	9 Christopher	9 Luke
10 Albert	10 Graham	10 Richard	10 Darren	10 Andrew
11 Eric	11 Philip	11 Peter	11 Michael	11 Benjamin
12 Edward	12 Anthony	12 John	12 James	12 Samuel
13 Arthur	13 Colin	13 Anthony	13 Robert	13 Stephen
14 Charles	14 Christopher	14 Christopher	14 Simon	14 Robert
15 Leslie	15 Geoffrey	15 Darren	15 Jason	15 Jamie
16 Sidney	16 William	16 Kevin	16 Stuart	16 Aaron
17 Frank	17 James	17 Martin	17 Neil	17 Jonathan
18 Peter	18 Keith	18 Simon	18 Lee	18 Alexander
19 Dennis	Terence	19 Philip	19 Jonathan	19 Joseph
20 Joseph	20 Barry	20 Graham	20 Ian	20 Ryan
21 Alan	Malcolm	21 Colin	Nicholas	21 David
22 Stanley	Richard	22 Adrian	22 Gary	22 Liam
23 Ernest	23 Ian	23 Nigel	23 Craig	23 Jack
24 Harold	24 Derek	24 Alan	24 Martin	24 Richard
25 Norman	25 Roger	25 Neil	25 John	25 William
26 Raymond	26 Raymond	26 Shaun	26 Carl	26 Jordan
27 Leonard	27 Kenneth	27 Jonathan	27 Philip	27 Craig
28 Alfred	28 Andrew	28 Nicholas	28 Kevin	28 Mark
Harry	29 Trevor	29 Stuart	29 Benjamin	29 Nicholas
30 Donald	30 Martin	30 Timothy	30 Peter	30 Ashley
Reginald	31 Kevin	31 Wayne	31 Wayne	31 Nathan
32 Roy	32 Ronald	32 Brian	32 Adam	32 Lee
33 Derek	33 Leslie	33 James	33 Anthony	33 Oliver
34 Henry	34 Charles	34 Carl	34 Alan	34 Shaun
35 Geoffrey	George	35 Jeffrey	35 Graham	35 Scott
36 David	36 Thomas	36 Barry	36 Adrian	36 Callum
Gordon	37 Nigel	37 Dean	37 Colin	37 Lewis
Herbert	Stuart	38 Matthew	Scott	38 Paul
Walter	39 Edward	39 William	39 Timothy	39 Ben
40 Cyril	40 Gordon	40 Keith	40 Barry	40 John
41 Jack	41 Roy	41 Julian	41 William	41 Edward
42 Richard	42 Dennis	42 Trevor	42 Dean	42 Anthony
43 Douglas	43 Neil	43 Roger	Jamie	43 Jake
44 Maurice	44 Laurence	Russell	44 Nathan	44 Charles
45 Bernard	45 Clive	45 Derek	45 Justin	45 Martin
Gerald	Eric	Lee	46 Damian	46 Philip
47 Brian	47 Frederick	47 Clive	Thomas	47 Carl
48 Victor	Patrick	Jeremy	48 Joseph	48 Bradley
Wilfred	Robin	49 Patrick	49 Alexander	49 Kieran
50 Francis	50 Donald	50 Daniel	Alistair	50 Simon
	Joseph	Kenneth	Nigel	
		Raymond	Shaun	

The top fifty first names for girls, England and Wales

1925	1950	1965	1975	1993
1 Joan	1 Susan	1 Trac(e)y	1 Claire	1 Rebecca
2 Mary	2 Linda	2 Deborah	2 Sarah	2 Charlotte
3 Joyce	3 Christine	3 Julie	3 Nicola	3 Laura
4 Margaret	4 Margaret	4 Karen	4 Emma	4 Amy
5 Dorothy	5 Carol	5 Susan	5 Joanne	5 Emma
6 Doris	6 Jennifer	6 Alison	6 Helen	6 Jessica
7 Kathleen	7 Janet	7 Jacqueline	7 Rachel	7 Lauren
8 Irene	8 Patricia	8 Helen	8 Lisa	8 Sarah
9 Betty	9 Barbara	9 Amanda	9 Rebecca	9 Rachel
10 Eileen	10 Ann	10 Sharon	10 Karen	10 Catherine
11 Doreen	11 Sandra	11 Sarah	Michelle	11 Hannah
12 Lilian	12 Pamela	12 Joanne	12 Victoria	12 Katie
Vera	Pauline	13 Jane	13 Catherine	13 Emily
14 Jean	14 Jean	14 Catherine	14 Amanda	14 Sophie
15 Marjorie	15 Jacqueline	15 Angela	15 Trac(e)y	15 Victoria
16 Barbara	16 Kathleen	16 Linda	16 Samantha	16 Stacey
17 Edna	17 Sheila	17 Carol	17 Kelly	17 Natalie
18 Gladys	18 Valerie	18 Diane	18 Deborah	18 Jade
19 Audrey	19 Maureen	19 Wendy	19 Julie	19 Stephanie
20 Elsie	20 Gillian	20 Beverley	Louise	20 Lucy
21 Florence	21 Marilyn	21 Caroline	21 Sharon	21 Danielle
Hilda	Mary	22 Dawn	22 Donna	22 Kirsty
Winifred	23 Elizabeth	23 Nicola	23 Kerry	23 Samantha
24 Olive	24 Lesley	24 Michelle	24 Zoë	24 Gemma
25 Violet	25 Catherine	Sally	25 Melanie	25 Abigail
26 Elizabeth	26 Brenda	26 Claire	26 Alison	26 Chloe
27 Edith	27 Wendy	27 Sandra	27 Caroline	27 Holly
28 Ivy	28 Angela	28 Lorraine	28 Lynsey	28 Claire
29 Peggy	29 Rosemary	29 Janet	29 Jennifer	29 Hayley
Phyllis	30 Shirley	30 Gillian	30 Angela	30 Zoe
31 Evelyn	31 Diane	31 Elizabeth	31 Susan	31 Jodie
32 Iris	Joan	32 Paula	32 Hayley	32 Elizabeth
33 Annie	33 Jane	33 Donna	33 Dawn	33 Kelly
Rose	Lynne	Jennifer	Joanna	34 Kimberley
35 Beryl	35 Irene	Lesley	Lucy	35 Natasha
Lily	36 Janice	Louise	36 Natalie	36 Alexandra
Muriel	37 Elaine	37 Ann	37 Charlotte	37 Nicola
Sheila	Heather	38 Andrea	38 Andrea	38 Kerry
39 Ethel	Marion	39 Mandy	Laura	39 Chelsea
40 Alice	40 June	40 Elaine	40 Paula	40 Eleanor
41 Constance	41 Eileen	41 Denise	41 Marie	41 Jennifer
Ellen	42 Denise	42 Christine	42 Teresa	42 Leanne
43 Gwendoline	Doreen	Teresa	43 Elizabeth	43 Melissa
Patricia	Judith	44 Maria	Suzanne	44 Alice
45 Sylvia	Sylvia	Melanie	45 Kirsty	45 Louise
46 Nora	46 Helen	46 Julia	Sally	46 Harriet
Pamela	Yvonne	Lisa	Tina	47 Lisa
48 Grace	48 Hilary	48 Tina	48 Jane	48 Kayleigh
49 Jessie	49 Dorothy	49 Margaret	49 Ann(e)	49 Megan
50 Mabel	Joyce	50 Lynn	Jacqueline	50 Naomi
	Julia			
	Teresa			

The top fifty first names for boys, USA

1925	1950	1970	1993: *white*	1993: *non-white*
1 Robert	1 Robert	1 Michael	1 Michael	1 Michael
2 John	2 Michael	2 Robert	2 Christopher	2 Christopher
3 William	3 James	3 David	3 Matthew	3 Brandon
4 James	4 John	4 James	4 Joshua	4 Anthony
5 Charles	5 David	5 John	5 Andrew	5 James
6 Richard	6 William	6 Jeffrey	6 James	6 Joshua
7 George	7 Thomas	7 Steven	7 John	7 Jonathan
8 Donald	8 Richard	8 Christopher	8 Nicholas	8 Robert
9 Joseph	9 Gary	9 Brian	9 Justin	9 Eric
10 Edward	10 Charles	10 Mark	10 David	10 David
11 Thomas	11 Ronald	11 William	11 Daniel	11 Justin
12 David	12 Dennis	12 Eric	12 Ryan	12 Marcus
13 Frank	13 Steven	13 Kevin	13 Steven	13 Brian
14 Harold	14 Kenneth	14 Scott	14 Robert	14 Steven
15 Arthur	15 Joseph	15 Joseph	15 Joseph	15 Kevin
16 Jack	16 Mark	16 Daniel	16 Zachary	16 William
17 Paul	17 Daniel	17 Thomas	17 Jonathan	17 John
18 Kenneth	18 Paul	18 Anthony	18 William	18 Antonio
19 Walter	19 Donald	19 Richard	19 Kyle	19 Jeremy
20 Raymond	20 Gregory	20 Charles	20 Tyler	20 Derrick
21 Carl	21 Larry	21 Kenneth	21 Jacob	21 Joseph
22 Albert	22 Lawrence	22 Matthew	22 Brian	22 Darius
23 Henry	23 Timothy	23 Jason	23 Brandon	23 Sean
24 Harry	24 Alan	24 Paul	24 Eric	24 Darryl
25 Francis	25 Edward	25 Timothy	25 Sean	25 Charles
26 Ralph	26 Gerald	26 Sean	26 Cody	26 Corey
27 Eugene	27 Douglas	27 Gregory	27 Anthony	27 Daniel
28 Howard	28 George	28 Ronald	28 Thomas	28 Terrance
29 Lawrence	29 Frank	29 Todd	29 Kevin	29 Kenneth
30 Louis	30 Patrick	30 Edward	30 Alexander	30 Aaron
31 Alan	31 Anthony	31 Derrick	31 Jordan	31 Timothy
32 Norman	32 Philip	32 Keith	32 Timothy	32 Devin
33 Gerald	33 Raymond	33 Patrick	33 Benjamin	33 Matthew
34 Herbert	34 Bruce	34 Darryl	34 Corey	34 Nicholas
35 Fred	35 Jeffrey	35 Dennis	35 Adam	35 Andrew
36 Earl	36 Brian	36 Andrew	36 Jeffrey	36 Ryan
Philip	37 Peter	37 Donald	37 Aaron	37 Jordan
Stanley	38 Frederick	38 Gary	38 Richard	38 Travis
39 Daniel	39 Roger	39 Allen	39 Nathan	39 Jeffrey
40 Leonard	40 Carl	40 Douglas	40 Travis	40 Richard
Marvin	41 Dale	41 George	41 Charles	41 Jamal
42 Frederick	Walter	42 Marcus	42 Derek	42 Gregory
43 Anthony	43 Christopher	43 Raymond	43 Patrick	43 André
Samuel	44 Martin	44 Peter	44 Mark	44 Dominique
45 Bernard	45 Craig	45 Gerald	45 Jeremy	45 Willie
Edwin	46 Arthur	46 Frank	46 Jason	46 Thomas
47 Alfred	47 Andrew	Jonathan	47 Jesse	47 Antoine
48 Russell	48 Jerome	Lawrence	48 Samuel	48 Donte
Warren	49 Leonard	49 Aaron	49 Jared	49 Marquis
50 Ernest	50 Henry	Philip	50 Dustin	50 Mark

The top fifty first names for girls, USA

1925	1950	1970	1993: *white*	1993: *non-white*
1 Mary	1 Linda	1 Michelle	1 Brittany	1 Brittany
2 Barbara	2 Mary	2 Jennifer	2 Ashley	2 Jasmine
3 Dorothy	3 Patricia	3 Kimberly	3 Jessica	3 Ashley
4 Betty	4 Susan	4 Lisa	4 Amanda	4 Jessica
5 Ruth	5 Deborah	5 Tracy	5 Sarah	5 Tiffany
6 Margaret	6 Kathleen	6 Kelly	6 Megan	6 Courtney
7 Helen	7 Barbara	7 Nicole	7 Caitlin	7 Erica
8 Elizabeth	8 Nancy	8 Angela	8 Samantha	8 Briana
9 Jean	9 Sharon	9 Pamela	9 Stephanie	9 Crystal
10 Ann(e)	10 Karen	10 Christine	10 Katherine	10 Amber
11 Patricia	11 Carol(e)	11 Dawn	11 Emily	11 Danielle
12 Shirley	12 Sandra	12 Amy	12 Lauren	12 Sierra
13 Virgina	13 Diane	13 Deborah	13 Kayla	13 Alicia
14 Nancy	14 Catherine	14 Karen	14 Rachel	14 Michelle
15 Joan	15 Christine	15 Julie	15 Nicole	15 Christina
16 Martha	16 Cynthia	Mary	16 Jennifer	16 Kiara
17 Marion	17 Donna	17 Laura	17 Elizabeth	17 Ebony
18 Doris	18 Judith	18 Stacey	18 Chelsea	18 Stephanie
19 Frances	19 Margaret	19 Catherine	19 Courtney	19 Kanisha
Marjorie	20 Janice	20 Lori	20 Rebecca	20 Jennifer
21 Marilyn	21 Janet	21 Tammy	21 Amber	21 Alexis
22 Alice	22 Pamela	22 Elizabeth	22 Christina	22 Nicole
23 Eleanor	23 Gail	Shannon	23 Kristen	23 Bianca
Catherine	24 Cheryl	24 Stephanie	24 Heather	24 Tanisha
25 Lois	25 Suzanne	25 Kristin	25 Lindsey	25 Amanda
26 Jane	26 Marilyn	26 Heather	26 Danielle	26 Kimberly
27 Phyllis	27 Brenda	Susan	27 Melissa	27 Victoria
28 Florence	28 Beverly	28 Sandra	28 Tiffany	28 Kierra
Mildred	Carolyn	29 Denise	29 Kelsey	29 Candice
30 Carol(e)	30 Ann(e)	30 Theresa	30 Kelly	30 Kayla
31 Carolyn	31 Shirley	31 Christina	31 Michelle	31 Dominique
Marie	32 Jacqueline	Tina	32 Alyssa	32 Samantha
Norma	33 Joanne	33 Cynthia	33 Hannah	33 Whitney
34 Anna	34 Lynn(e)	Melissa	34 Allison	34 Tiara
Louise	Marcia	Patricia	35 Erica	35 Andrea
36 Beverly	36 Denise	36 Renée	36 Alicia	36 Chelsea
Janet	37 Gloria	37 Cheryl	37 Amy	37 Latoya
38 Sarah	38 Joyce	38 Sherry	38 Crystal	38 Shaniqua
39 Evelyn	39 Kathy	39 Donna	39 Jamie	39 Raven
40 Edith	40 Elizabeth	40 Erica	40 Kimberly	40 Monique
Jacqueline	41 Laura	41 Rachel	41 Laura	41 Lauren
Lorraine	42 Darlene	Sharon	42 Erin	42 Kiana
43 Grace	43 Theresa	43 Linda	43 Alexandra	43 Jalisa
44 Ethel	44 Joan	44 Barbara	44 Mary	44 Tierra
Gloria	45 Elaine	Jacqueline	45 Katie	45 Iesha
Laura	46 Michelle	Rhonda	46 Cassandra	46 Briana
47 Audrey	47 Judy	47 Andrea	47 Anna	47 Kristen
Esther	48 Diana	48 Rebecca	48 Casey	48 Natasha
Joanne	49 Frances	Wendy	49 Victoria	49 Sarah
Sally	Maureen	50 Maria	50 Taylor	50 Lakeisha
	Phyllis			
	Ruth			